Medieval Society and the Manor Court

MEDIEVAL SOCIETY AND THE MANOR COURT

edited by
ZVI RAZI
and
RICHARD SMITH

CLARENDON PRESS · OXFORD
1996

Oxford University Press, Walton Street, Oxford OX2 6DP
Oxford New York
Athens Auckland Bangkok Bombay
Calcutta Cape Town Dar es Salaam Delhi
Florence Hong Kong Istanbul Karachi
Kuala Lumpur Madras Madrid Melbourne
Mexico City Nairobi Paris Singapore
Taipei Tokyo Toronto
and associated companies in
Berlin Ibadan

Oxford is a trade mark of Oxford University Press

Published in the United States
by Oxford University Press Inc., New York

British Library Cataloguing in Publication Data
Data available

Library of Congress Cataloging in Publication Data
Medieval society and the manor court / edited by Zvi Razi and Richard
Smith.
p.   cm.
Includes bibliographical references (p.   ) and index.
1. Great Britain—History—Medieval period, 1066–1485.
2. England—Social conditions—1066–1485. 3. Community life—
England—History. 4. Manorial courts—England. 5. Peasantry—
England. 6. Feudalism—England. 7. Manors—England. 8. Law,
Medieval. I. Razi, Zvi. II. Smith, Richard Michael, 1946–
DA176.M43 1996
941—dc20 96–2644
ISBN 0–19–820190–7

1 3 5 7 9 10 8 6 4 2

Typeset by Graphicraft Typesetters Ltd., Hong Kong
Printed in Great Britain
on acid-free paper by
Bookcraft Ltd., Midsomer Norton
Nr. Bath, Avon

Acknowledgements

The editors are grateful to the following journals for permission to reprint essays that form two chapters of this book: Chapter 4 appeared in *Cambridge Law Journal*, 47 (1988), 403–27; Chapter 9 appeared as L. R. Poos and R. M. Smith, ' "Legal Windows onto Historical Populations"? Recent Research on Demography and the Manor Court in Medieval England', *Law and History Review*, 2 (1984), 128–52; Z. Razi, 'The Use of Manorial Court Rolls in Demographic Analysis: A Reconsideration', *Law and History Review*, 3 (1985), 191–200; L. R. Poos and R. M. Smith, 'Shades Still on the Window: A Reply to Zvi Razi', *Law and History Review*, 4 (1986), 409–29; Z. Razi, 'The Demographic Transparency of Manorial Court Rolls', *Law and History Review*, 5 (1987), 523–35.

The editors are deeply indebted to Humaira Ahmed who typed many of these essays and prepared a complete version of the text on disk. She also solved many of the problems of preparing a satisfactory format for the presentation of the Appendix. This book could not have appeared without her assistance which she has invariably provided with much good humour.

List of Contributors

A. D. M. BARRELL is Lecturer in Later Medieval History at The Queen's University of Belfast.

LLOYD BONFIELD is Professor of Law at Tulane University, New Orleans.

ELAINE CLARK is Professor of History at the University of Michigan-Dearborn.

JUDITH CRIPPS is City Archivist, Aberdeen.

R. R. DAVIES is Chichele Professor of Medieval History, University of Oxford at All Souls College.

RALPH EVANS was project co-ordinator of the new *History of the University of Oxford*.

PETER FRANKLIN is the author of *The Taxpayers of Medieval Gloucestershire: An Analysis of the 1327 Lay Subsidy* (1993).

H. S. A. FOX is Senior Lecturer in English Topography, University of Leicester.

PAUL D. A. HARVEY is Professor Emeritus of Medieval History at the University of Durham.

RODNEY HILTON is Professor Emeritus of Medieval Social History at the University of Birmingham.

PAUL R. HYAMS is Associate Professor of History at Cornell University.

O. J. PADEL is Lecturer in Celtic, University of Cambridge.

L. R. POOS is Professor and Chairman of the Department of History at The Catholic University of America.

ZVI RAZI is Professor of Medieval Social History at Tel Aviv University, Israel.

PHILLIPP R. SCHOFIELD is a Research Fellow at the Wellcome Unit for the History of Medicine, University of Oxford.

Ll. B. SMITH is Senior Lecturer in the Department of History and Welsh History at the University of Wales, Aberystwyth.

RICHARD M. SMITH is Director, The Cambridge Group for the History of Population and Social Structure, and Fellow of Downing College, Cambridge.

JANET WILLIAMSON was a research officer in the School of History, University of Birmingham.

Contents

List of Tables, Figures, and Maps

List of Tables

List of Figures

List of Maps

List of Abbreviations

AASRP	*Associated Architectural Societies' Reports and Papers*
AgHR	*Agricultural History Review*
AHR	*American History Review*
Annales E.S.C.	*Annales Economies, Sociétés, Civilisations*
BAR	British Archaeological Reports
BIHR	*Bulletin of the Institute of Historical Research*
CHJ	*Cambridge Historical Journal*
CLJ	*Cambridge Law Journal*
EETS	Early English Text Society
EcHR	*Economic History Review*
EHR	*English Historical Review*
EPNS	English Place-Name Society
JBS	*Journal of British Studies*
JEH	*Journal of Ecclesiastical History*
JFH	*Journal of Family History*
JLH	*Journal of Legal History*
JLS	*Journal of Legal Studies*
JMH	*Journal of Medieval History*
LHR	*Law and History Review*
P&P	*Past and Present*
TRHS	*Transactions of the Royal Historical Society*
VCH	*Victoria County History*

MAP 0.1 Principal places mentioned in the text

Introduction

The Historiography of Manorial Court Rolls

ZVI RAZI AND RICHARD M. SMITH

IN the 1960s and 1970s, historians who made an important contribution to the study of medieval English villages by quantitatively analysing manorial court rolls, claimed that this has been only a recent development. Previously, they argued, historians were interested in the manor and in the peasants' legal status, rather than in the village community and in the peasants themselves and made little use of court rolls.[1] These rather inaccurate historiographical observations have never been scrutinized. Therefore, we decided to present in the introduction to this volume a short summary of a systematic study of the historiography of court rolls, carried out by us in recent years. Our aim is not just to put the record straight, but also to show that older historical works, hardly read attentively any more, or even completely forgotten, include abundant and still useful, empirical evidence derived from the court rolls, as well as many insights into the history of medieval rural society.

We will, at first, examine the uses that antiquarians and scholars have made of court rolls from the seventeenth century to the late 1930s and then from the 1940s to the present.[2] However, since the number of studies utilizing court rolls' evidence has increased considerably in recent decades, the second part of our survey will deal less with individual studies than with historiographical trends. Furthermore, the space at our disposal does not allow us to engage in a detailed critical discussion of the methods and the findings of the historians with which we deal here. In the third part of the introduction we will briefly discuss the essays in this volume.

---

[1] J. A. Raftis, *Tenure and Mobility: Studies in the Social History of the Mediaeval English Village* (Toronto, 1964), 11–13; E. B. Dewindt, *Land and People in Holywell-cum-Needingworth: Structures of Tenure and Patterns of Social Organization in an East Midlands Village, 1252–1457* (Toronto, 1972), 1–3; E. Britton, *The Community of the Vill: A Study in the History of the Family and Village Life in Fourteenth-Century England* (Toronto, 1977), 1–4.

[2] The historiography from the 17th cent. to late 1930s was written by Zvi Razi (who wishes to thank Paul Brand, Barbara Harvey, Susan Reynolds, and Keith Wrightson for their useful comments) and from the 1940s to the present by Richard Smith.

TABLE 1:   *Statistics of publications of manorial court rolls, both extracts*
and whole series between 1840 and 1969

Period of publications	Number of publications
1840–9	1
1850–9	2
1860–9	1
1870–9	2
1880–9	14
1890–9	14
1900–9	14
1910–19	8
1920–9	12
1930–9	7
1940–9	2
1950–9	6
1960–9	1
TOTAL	84

I

From the mid-seventeenth century antiquarians and county historians
investigated the records of numerous medieval manors, but they made
little use of court rolls since they were interested in the landlords rather
than in their socially inferior tenants.[3] However, sometimes, when manorial surveys were not available, they did, as for instance, Francis Blomefield
in his study of the history of the Norfolk manor of Gissing,[4] use court
rolls in their search for information about landlords' rights and tenants'
obligations. Only in the second half of the nineteenth century, as a result

---

[3] These observations are based on an examination of a large sample of county and local
histories, written from the mid-17th to the early 19th cent.

[4] He used the Gissing court rolls from the years 1346–50, 1365–6, and 1476 to show the
considerable control exercised by the landlords over their customary tenants. F. Blomefield,
An Essay towards a Topographical History of the County of Norfolk (new edn., 11 vols.;
London, 1805–10), i., 171–2. County historians also cited from court rolls when they found
in them an unusual fact. For example, Treadway Nash included in his book an entry from
the 1274 Halesowen court rolls recording a lease by the Abbey of two local pits of sea coal
for a considerable annual rent of £26 19s. 4d. T. R. Nash, *Collection for the history of
Worcestershire* (2nd edn., 2 vols.; London, 1799), i. 508.

of the growing interest in the social and economic history of rural England, was the importance of court rolls as an historical source recognized. In 1852 George Scrope published the first local study based largely on court rolls.[5] He was also the first to print long extracts from these records which, he wrote, 'will shew the character of some of the proceedings at these courts and may serve to illustrate the manners and social conditions of the middle and humbler classes at this period'.[6] Thorold Rogers, who mainly used manorial accounts in his pioneering study of the history of agriculture and prices in England, nevertheless realized the great value of court rolls. In the first volume of his study (1866), he wrote a chapter about the medieval judicial system which was focused on the manor, rather than on the higher, courts of the land. 'The proceedings of the manor court', he argued, 'are of greater interest and throw more light on the proceedings in ordinary life and business, than those of higher powers.'[7]

The interest in manorial court rolls, however, gained momentum only in the 1880s and 1890s, when the number of publications of court rolls rose sharply as Table 1 indicates.[8] Many of those who edited court rolls for publication were local historians who were fully aware of the value of these records. Henry Chandler, for example, who edited, in 1885, the court rolls of the Norfolk manor of Great Cressingham, wrote:

For many years past, manorial rolls have been sold by the cartload and boiled down into size or gelatine yet they contain materials of priceless value to the historian, to the topographer, to the genealogist, to the student of social life and even the philologist.[9]

Moreover, the court records, according to him, 'enable us to drop down suddenly on an obscure English village five hundred years ago and almost to see with our own eyes what the inhabitants are doing'.[10] However, only with the works of three great historians, who were contemporaries, Seebohm, Vinogradoff, and Maitland, was the unique potentiality of court rolls as an historical source realized.

---

[5] G. P. Scrope, *History of the Manor and Barony of Castle Combe, in the County of Wiltshire* (London, 1852).

[6] Ibid. 159.

[7] J. E. T. Rogers, *A History of Agriculture and Prices in England*, vol. i, 1259–1400 (Oxford, 1866), 127.

[8] The data are taken from E. B. Graves (ed.), *A Bibliography of English History to 1485* (Oxford, 1985).

[9] *Five Court Rolls of Great Cressingham, 1328–1584*, ed. H. W. Chandler (London, 1885), 111.

[10] Ibid. vi .

Frederic Seebohm was the first historian to use court rolls for a macro rather than just for a micro study of medieval rural society. His investigation of the medieval manorial system in his book about the English village community (1883) started with an examination of the fourteenth-century court records of Winslow in Buckinghamshire, a manor belonging to St Albans Abbey. From these records, he obtained information about open field husbandry, the structure of customary holdings, and the villein's obligations. Although no fourteenth-century survey of Winslow had survived, Seebohm was able to determine the distribution of the tenants' land by using references in the court rolls of this manor to the holdings of the plague victims. On the assumption that the holdings which changed hands as a result of the plague provide a representative sample of the tenantry at large, he inferred that while large tenants of a virgate or half a virgate constituted only a minority among the tenants of Winslow, they held the bulk of the land in the open fields.[11] He also showed, by identifying the names of the plague victims who had served as jurymen, that the substantial tenants constituted the village élite group.[12] Subsequently, Seebohm tested the representativeness of the Winslow records by using the Hundred Rolls of 1279 and many other thirteenth- and twelfth-century manorial surveys. As the result was positive, he concluded that the agrarian system reflected in the Winslow court rolls prevailed in most parts of lowland England from the Norman Conquest to the Black Death.[13] He then investigated pre-1066 records which, according to him, showed that serfdom and the manorial system had existed in England since the Roman Conquest.

This view was successfully challenged by Paul Vinogradoff in his famous study of the development of villeinage in England, published in Russian in 1887 and in English in 1892.[14] He argued that the majority of the peasants in England were enserfed only in the second half of the twelfth century and that the thirteenth-century manorial organization, in which demesnes were largely cultivated by the labour of unfree tenants, was also a recent development.[15] Vinogradoff based his conclusions on the records of the royal courts and the legal treatises, principally those

[11] F. Seebhom, *The English Village Community* (London, 1883), 21–31.

[12] Of the 27 jurymen who died in the plague, 16 were virgate and 9 were half-virgate holders. Ibid. 29 n. 1.

[13] Ibid. 32–80.

[14] P. Vinogradoff, *Villeinage in England* (Oxford, 1892). It was based on his doctoral dissertation which was published in Russian, as *Isledovnia po social'noy istorii ve sredinie veka* [Research in the Social History of Medieval England], (St Petersburg, 1887).

[15] Vinogradoff, *Villeinage*, 218–20, 397–409.

of Glanvill and Bracton, which had been ignored by Seebohm, and to a lesser extent on manorial documents. He utilized state and private surveys, *IPM*s, cartularies, and monastic registers, court rolls, and farming and administrative manuals. He used many thirteenth- and fourteenth-century court-roll series to verify and supplement the common-law sources, as for instance, in discussing the status and privileges of the villein sokeman on the ancient demesne.[16] He also employed court-roll evidence to modify the often distorted picture of village society obtained from manorial surveys. For example, Vinogradoff showed by using such evidence that the remarkable survival of the unity of customary holdings observed in the surveys of many manors was more apparent than real.[17] 'We must remember', he wrote, 'that the artificial unity and indivisibility of the tenement may be a mere screen, behind which there exists a complex mass of rights sanctioned by morality and custom though not by law.'[18] Vinogradoff's study demonstrated the importance of using both the records of the manorial and the royal courts, and legal treatises in enabling the complexities of village society to be comprehended.

Frederic Maitland shared Vinogradoff's view of the importance of manorial court rolls as an historical source. He not only used these records in his historical studies but also edited them. In 1889 the Selden Society published his famous edition of court rolls from the period 1246–1303.[19] Two years later he and William Baildon, edited another volume for the Selden Society, which included four short treatises about manorial courts in French and Latin, written in the second half of the thirteenth and the early fourteenth centuries. In this volume Maitland also edited the court rolls of the Bishop of Ely's manor of Littleport from 1285 to 1327.[20] In the introduction to the 1889 Selden Society volume and to the Littleport court rolls, Maitland identified the earliest surviving court rolls and traced the development of the manorial courts in the second half of the thirteenth century and the early fourteenth centuries. He also provided an illuminating and still useful account of the jurisdiction, procedures, and

---

[16] He used the court rolls of Letcombe Regis (Berks.), and King's Ripton (Hunts.). Ibid. 91, 97, 105, 107, 117–18.

[17] Ibid. 246–50.

[18] Ibid. 33. Vinogradoff also argued that since the villagers often modified the inheritance rules to endow non-inheriting children, many indivisible customary holdings 'contained more than one family and perhaps more than one household'. Ibid. 247. For supportive evidence see Ch. 11 below.

[19] *Select Pleas in Manorial and Other Seignorial Courts*, ed. F. W. Maitland (Selden Soc. 2, 1889).

[20] *The Court Baron: Precedents of Pleading in Manorial and Other Local Courts*, ed. F. W. Maitland and W. P. Baildon (Selden Soc. 4, 1891).

customs practised in the manorial courts in relation to other contemporary legal institutions and laws.[21]

It is clear that Maitland edited court rolls because of their value not only for legal, but also for social and economic, history. However, unlike his contemporaries and later historians, who assumed that evidence can be easily and unproblematically obtained from court rolls, Maitland realized that these records are 'taciturn' and consequently 'they do not easily yield up their testimony, but must be examined and cross examined'.[22] Furthermore, he argued that valid historical observations can be drawn only from complete, or almost complete, series of court rolls covering a long period of time. He maintained, for instance, that such court records should be examined decade by decade and year by year, for a proper study of customary tenure, since 'only by a careful comparison of names of tenants, the amount of fines on admittance and other small details shall we obtain secure information as to the true and practical nature of tenure'.[23]

Maitland demonstrated the usefulness of this method by meticulously tracing the names of tenants mentioned in Littleport court rolls between 1307 and 1325 and by noting down all their recorded activities. He thus discovered that during this period 'a class of thriving yeomen seems to be forming itself, a manorial aristocracy, but still an aristocracy of villains'.[24] As Maitland investigated the court rolls more thoroughly and systematically than Seebohm, he was able to throw more light on the village élite. He found that the members of this group not only inherited large holdings but also accumulated much land through the market and monopolized not only the jury service, but also other village and manorial offices.[25]

Maitland used court rolls for social and economic history more comprehensively in his study of the bishop of Ely's Cambridgeshire manor of Wilburton from the thirteenth to the sixteenth century.[26] In addition to the court rolls of this manor, which run with some gaps from the reign of Edward I to that of Henry VII, he drew his evidence from two surveys from 1221 and 1277 and from manorial accounts. Maitland undertook this study because he was critical of those contemporary scholars, who attempted to write the history of the medieval manorial system, while knowing very little about the history of particular manors. The court rolls were used by him primarily to examine how the post-plague demographic

[21] *Select Pleas in Manorial Courts*, xi–lxxvii; *The Court Baron*, 107–18.
[22] *Select Pleas in Manorial Courts*, xi.   [23] Ibid.
[24] *The Court Baron*, 113.   [25] Ibid.
[26] F. W. Maitland, 'The History of a Cambridgeshire Manor', *EHR* 7 (1894), 417–39.

and economic changes affected the tenants and the manorial organization. He noted down all the entries relating to the demesne, customary holdings, incidence of servility and flight of serfs. Then, by adding this information to that of the manorial accounts, he found that the old manorial organization based on serfdom, showed a considerable resilience and collapsed only after the second decade of the fifteenth century. From that period the heavy labour services were commuted, the demesne was leased out, and few traces of personal servitude remained in Wilburton.[27]

Maitland, unlike many modern legal historians, recognized that it is necessary to investigate the customary as well as the common law in order to understand the nature and the development of the medieval legal system. Consequently in writing with Frederick Pollock the history of English law (1895), Maitland utilized manorial court evidence to elucidate such topics as tenure and status, ancient demesne, seigneurial jurisdiction, and the village community. Like Vinogradoff, he used manorial court rolls to verify and supplement the evidence provided by other manorial and state records and by the jurists.[28]

Seebohm, Vinogradoff, and Maitland showed that manorial court rolls, despite their local character, provide important evidence for the study of medieval English rural society as a whole. They investigated, through these records, the agricultural system, the seigneurial regime, the peasants' landholdings and legal status, the village community, the distribution of land and power in village society, the land market, inheritance customs and the family, and the disintegration of the manorial system based on serfdom. The contributions of Vinogradoff and Maitland were distinctive in highlighting the importance of observing medieval agrarian society through the records of both local and central legal institutions.

The early 1900s witnessed the first attempts to obtain statistical data from court rolls and even to submit these records to statistical analysis. In 1900 the American historian, William Page, traced the chronology of the commutation of labour services in England by statistically analysing the data taken from accounts and court rolls of 291 manors. These indicated that, in the post-Black Death period, labour services were commuted into money rents rapidly and extensively. Page saw in the commutation of labour services the cause of the disintegration of the manorial system based on serfdom, since the supply of labour for the demesne was the

---

[27] Ibid. 438–9.
[28] F. Pollock and F. W. Maitland, *The History of English Law before the Time of Edward I* (2 vols.; 2nd edn., with an introduction by S. F. C. Milsom, Cambridge, 1968), i. 360–432, 560–637.

raison d'être of this system.[29] A much more innovative and sophisticated use of court rolls, however, was made by another American historian, Frances Davenport.

In an article published in 1900, she showed that a good series of court rolls enables us not only to observe the decline of serfdom in late medieval England but also to find out how it came about. Davenport utilized the court rolls of the Norfolk manor of Forncett which run with few minor gaps from 1400 to 1565.[30] She noted down the names of all the villeins appearing in the court rolls during this period and linked them to families. Then she traced the history of these families through the court records, and found that 62 per cent of the bond families disappeared in the fifteenth century and the rest in the first half of the sixteenth century. The disappearance of serfdom from Forncett was due, according to her, to the withdrawal of serfs from the manor, to the lack of male heirs, and the refusal of serfs to take up their inheritance.[31] In conclusion, Davenport argued that although it was impossible to generalize from her case study, it casts serious doubts on the view that serfdom simply lapsed in the later Middle Ages and indicated that historians had underestimated the role of migration in bringing about the decline of serfdom.[32]

In addition to pioneering the use of court rolls for family reconstitution, Davenport was the first historian to submit court roll data to systematic statistical analysis. In her book about the economic history of Forncett between 1086 and 1565, she used the court records from 1400 to 1565 to observe the changes which occurred in that manor in the later Middle Ages. She noted down and tabulated all the data relating to customary land and found that the turnover of properties during the period under consideration was generally high, but that in the years 1400–12 it was especially rapid. Davenport attributed this trend to the impact, not only of high rates of mortality and emigration, but also of a buoyant inter-tenant land market.[33] She also found, by compiling a list of land transactions recorded in the court rolls, that while the annual number

---

[29] T. W. Page, *The End of Villainage in England* (New York, 1900), 45–96. For a criticism of Page's findings regarding the chronology of the labour services commutation see H. L. Gray, 'The Commutation of Villein Services in England before the Black Death', *EHR* 29 (1914), 625–58; M. M. Postan, 'The Chronology of Labour Services', in M. M. Postan (ed.), *Essays on Medieval Agriculture and General Problems of Medieval Economy* (Cambridge, 1973).

[30] F. G. Davenport, 'The Decay of Villainage in East Anglia', *TRHS* NS 14 (1900), 123–41.

[31] Ibid. 130–41.   [32] Ibid. 140.

[33] F. G. Davenport, *The Economic Development of a Norfolk Manor* (Cambridge, 1906), 79–80 and Appendix XII, lxxvi.

of land transactions between 1400 and 1565 was decreasing, the average amount of land involved was increasing.[34] Davenport showed that the active land market and the ample supply of vacant holdings enabled individual tenants to accumulate large holdings especially after 1450.[35] She also noticed that from the early fifteenth century onwards, individual tenants began to enclose their land in the common-fields and that, as a result, by the 1560s about half of Forncett's fields were enclosed.[36]

Furthermore, Davenport was also the first historian to utilize court rolls for demography. She started her enquiry with the evidence about peasants' dwellings available in the court rolls between 1400 and 1565 and the 1565 survey of the manor. This evidence indicated that of the 135 peasant houses which stood on 135 unfree tenements in the pre-plague period, only 57 (42 per cent) were occupied in 1565. She inferred from this that the population of post-plague Forncett declined sharply. To test this hypothesis, she counted the names of the people appearing in the court rolls of 1332-3 and 1460-1, and found that 250 names are noted in the former and only 126 in the latter—a decline of 49.6 per cent. Then she argued that, since the sharp fall in the number of villagers noted in the post-plague court rolls is compatible with the evidence about the considerable decline in the number of peasants' houses, it was likely that the population of Forncett in the 1460s was only half as large as it had been in the 1300s.[37]

Davenport's brilliant and innovative work was too far ahead of its time to exert any influence on contemporary historians. Only some sixty years later did historians again submit court rolls to comprehensive statistical analysis. None the less, during the first two decades of the twentieth century, historians who employed conventional methods, succeeded in further developing the research potentialities of court rolls.

In his study of *The Growth of the Manor*, Vinogradoff used court rolls more extensively than in *Villeinage in England* to obtain information about the open fields, the management of commons, the issue of by-laws, and other activities of the village community.[38] However, unlike Maitland, he interpreted these activities as a clear indication of the existence of a strong communality in medieval villages.[39]

[34] Ibid. 79 n. 2.   [35] Ibid. 80–2, 85–8.   [36] Ibid. 80–1.
[37] Ibid. 98–105 and Appendix IV.
[38] P. Vinogradoff, *The Growth of the Manor* (London, 1905), 165–89, 318–26.
[39] Maitland found plenty of evidence concerning the economic roles of the vill and its multifarious duties and obligations to the landlords and the state. Nevertheless, he claimed that this evidence did not necessarily imply that a real community existed in medieval villages, since peasant farming was strictly controlled by custom and the use of the commons

Vinogradoff had a major influence on the younger generation of agrarian historians. His students loom large among those who wrote essays on the medieval social and economic history of eighteen counties for the *VCH* volumes published between 1905 and 1912.[40] The majority of the authors utilized court rolls in addition to other manorial and state records.[41] Mary Tanner who wrote about Middlesex, for instance, was the first historian to use both manorial and royal court records to study peasant movements in medieval England. She traced through these records the struggle between the landlords of Harmondsworth and their tenants, which began in the 1230s and continued well into the fifteenth century.[42]

as well as the vill's duties and obligations were apportioned and attached to individual tenements. Pollock and Maitland, *History of English Law*, i. 563–6, 610–33. See also [his] *Domesday Book and Beyond* (Cambridge, 1887), 340–56. Vinogradoff wrote in response, 'Some sort of constant organization was needed to settle the many questions concerning the conduct of communal business in the fields, woods and waste. It does not help us much to say that things were carried out automatically, because this could only mean that they were left to take care of themselves, and surely it is to men and not to things that we have to look for the making of plans, the settlement of difficulties and enforcement of rules. Custom is a great force when it has been set going, but in order to get its motion it must start from arrangements or decisions of some kind . . . Besides, whatever the repetitions and memories of arrangements may have been, life was nevertheless a growing and ever-changing process.' Vinogradoff, *Growth of the Manor*, 115–16. See also ibid. 165–89, 313–26. As Vinogradoff's interpretation of the village community better accords with the sources than Maitland's, it has been generally adopted by medievalists. See H. M. Cam, 'The Community of the Vill', in H. M. Cam, *Law-Finders and Law-Makers in Medieval England* (London, 1962); W. O. Ault, *Open Field Husbandry and the Village Community: A Study of Agrarian By-Laws in Medieval England* (Trans. of the American Philosophical Soc, NS 55, Philadelphia, 1965); S. Reynolds, *Kingdom and Communities in Western Europe, 900–1300* (Oxford, 1984), 128–9, 140, 143–4, 148–54; C. Dyer, 'The English Medieval Village Community and its Decline', *JBS* 33 (1994), 407–29.

   [40] The counties are Bedford, Berkshire, Buckingham, Derby, Dorset, Durham, Essex, Gloucester, Lancashire, Lincoln, Middlesex, Nottingham, Oxford, Somerset, Suffolk, Sussex, Warwick, and York. Except for William Massingberd and George Unwin, all the other seventeen contributors of social and economic essays to the *VCH*, were in print for the first time. Eleven of them were Oxford graduates and another three who had no degree, undoubtedly, also studied at Oxford. Therefore, it is likely that 74 per cent of the contributors had participated in the Oxford medieval seminar run by Vinogradoff. It is interesting to note that fifteen (79%) of the *VCH* social and economic essays were written by women. The above information was drawn from R. B. Pugh, *The Victoria History of the Counties of England: General Introduction* (Oxford, 1970).

   [41] The best-documented studies are those of Berkshire, Buckinghamshire, Durham, Gloucestershire, Lincolnshire, Middlesex, and Sussex. However, Unwin's essay about Suffolk, is by far the best regional study to be found in the early *VCH* volumes, as he was the only author who took account of the agrarian as well as the urban sector and had a better understanding of demographic and economic processes. *Victoria History of the County of Suffolk*, ed. W. Page *et al.* (in progress; London, 1911 to date), i. 633–60.

   [42] *Victoria History of the County of Middlesex*, ed. W. Page *et al.* (in progress; London, 1907 to date), ii. 80–4.

Frederic Bradshaw, who based his study of rural Durham on the excellent court rolls of the bishop and prior of Durham, and other county records, produced one of the best accounts ever written about the medieval peasantry. There is hardly any topic concerning the peasants which he overlooked, from housing, diet, clothing, and health to landholdings, farming, social relations, and the seigneurial regime.[43] None the less, Bradshaw's brilliant essay has rarely been cited by historians and is almost completely forgotten. Although the use of court rolls by other *VCH* authors was less imaginative, by investigating many unpublished series they unearthed important new evidence about village society and economy. The *VCH* essays and the works of previous medieval historians were put to good use by Richard Tawney in his study of the agrarian problem of the sixteenth century published in 1912. As he assumed that the processes leading to the emergence of agrarian capitalism in early modern England had originated within the framework of the medieval manorial system, he devoted a third of his book to the study of rural society from the thirteenth to the sixteenth century.[44]

Tawney maintained that the peasant land market was a major factor in the development of English rural society from the thirteenth to the sixteenth century. He studied this market through the printed court rolls of a few Wiltshire, Hampshire, Lincolnshire, and Lancashire manors. Although he did not submit the land transactions registered in these records to a statistical analysis, and although he relied heavily on secondary sources, he succeeded in providing the first, and for many years to come the only, comprehensive analysis of the nature, course, and consequences of the peasant land market in medieval England. He also attributed the existence of a brisk inter-peasant land market in the thirteenth and in the first half of the fourteenth centuries to the growing commercialization of agriculture and the land hunger of the rapidly growing population.[45] This led to the transfer of property from the weak to the economically strong peasants, who were also better placed to compete for the land reclaimed from the waste, thus further enlarging their landed resources. The prosperous peasants financed their land dealings by marketing their surplus agricultural produce, by engaging in cottage industries, by lending money or corn at high interest to their needy neighbours and by serving in the manorial administration.[46] The polarization of village society accelerated

[43] *Victoria History of the County of Durham*, ed. W. Page *et al.* (in progress; London, 1907 to date), ii. 175–261.
[44] R. H. Tawney, *The Agrarian Problem of the Sixteenth Century* (London, 1912), 40–172.
[45] Ibid. 72–87, 93.   [46] Ibid. 79–90.

considerably as a result of the sharp population decline and the disintegration of the manorial system based on serfdom in the post-plague
period. The prosperous peasants were able to accumulate much more
land than ever before by buying land from their poorer neighbours, by
taking up vacant holdings, and by the leasing of demesnes which landlords had ceased to exploit directly. At the same time, the intensive land
market weakened the bond between family and land, as the least successful peasants were left without any land at all.[47] The growing gap between
the landholders and the other members of the village community led to
the weakening of the traditional open field agricultural system. The customary rules regulating this system constrained the substantial peasants,
who, in addition to growing corn, engaged in large-scale livestock farming, and therefore increasingly ignored these rules, as late medieval court
rolls show. They also consolidated their lands and enclosed them. Thus,
by the end of the fifteenth century, in the economically more advanced
parts of the country, village society was more polarized and less communal than in previous centuries.[48] Tawney was the first and, until very
recently, the only early modern social historian who dared to cross the
1500 border line to investigate the history of medieval England.[49] Unfortunately, his illuminating and original analysis of the medieval peasantry
failed to have an immediate effect on medievalists. Only after the Second
World War did it exert a major influence on the historiography of medieval England, and, then, through the works of Rodney Hilton and Michael
Postan.[50] Tawney's contemporary, Elizabeth Levett, for instance, who

---

[47] Ibid. 90–7, 138 n. 1.   [48] Ibid. 136–9, 159–66, 208–11.

[49] A. Macfarlane, *The Origins of English Individualism* (Oxford, 1978); R. Brenner, 'Agrarian
Class Structure and Economic Development in Pre-industrial Europe', *P&P* 70 (1976), 30–
75, reproduced in T. H. Aston and C. H. E. Philpin (eds.), *The Brenner Debate* (Cambridge,
1985), 10–63.

[50] See R. H. Hilton, *The Economic Development of Some Leicestershire Estates in the
Fourteenth and Fifteenth Centuries* (Oxford, 1947), 1–3, 94–105. Postan was Tawney's graduate
student at the London School of Economics in the 1920s. Admittedly, Postan adopted a
Chayanovian, rather than Tawney's Marxist interpretation of the land market in medieval
England. See M. M Postan, 'The Charters of the Villeins', in Postan, *Essays on Medieval
Agriculture*, 114–17. None the less, Postan must have been influenced by Tawney in constructing his famous demographic model of the long-term development of the English
medieval economy. 'In the Middle Ages', wrote Tawney, 'land was abundant and men were
scarce; the land wanted the people much more than the people wanted the land. Moreover,
with the simple methods of cultivation prevailing, the number of persons which a villein
holding could maintain was strictly limited, and the tendency to diminishing returns, with
the consequent difficulty of maintaining a growing population on the same area, must have
come into play very soon and very sharply. It is not surprising, therefore, to find at a
comparatively early date the manorial population began to overflow the boundaries of the
customary land and to occupy the waste, with the result that the area under cultivation

worked for many years on St Albans court books, showed little interest in the inter-peasant land market, although these records included abundant data relating to land transactions.

In her famous study of the economic consequences of the Black Death on the Winchester estates, Levett discovered that the plague did not cause a revolution either in agriculture or in tenure. She also thought that the virulence of the plague was considerably overestimated by historians. However, since she was unable to estimate the Black Death mortality from the heriots recorded in the Winchester account rolls, she began working on the St Albans court books.[51] In 1924 she read to the Royal Historical Society a preliminary research report. She discussed the nature and the development of St Albans manorial courts, described the making of the court books, analysed their contents and dealt briefly with the causes of the 1381 rising in St Albans in light of the court records.[52] Subsequently, Levett undertook to edit extracts from the St Albans court books for the British Academy and to accompany these with an extensive introduction. This work was well advanced at the time of her death in 1932. She had already transcribed many entries from the court books and written a draft of the introduction for each section she intended to compose. Some of these materials were edited by her students and published in 1938.[53]

The book edited from Levett's notes is rather fragmentary and most of the knowledge she gained during the long years she had been working on St Albans records was, unfortunately, buried with her. None the less, it includes her pioneering demographic study of St Albans manors during the Black Death which demonstrated that it is possible to estimate the plague mortality from manorial court rolls, the most representative source available to us.[54] Levett's book also made an important contribution to the study of the manor court as an institution and showed new ways in which

grew, in some cases, enormously.' Ibid. 88–9. This and many other passages in Tawney's book clearly show that he believed, like Postan, that the demographic increase in the pre-plague period, strongly stimulated the agrarian sector of the economy, and inevitably led to the pauperization of a large section of the peasantry.

[51] *The Black Death on the Estates of the See of Winchester* (Oxford Studies in Social and Legal History; 5, 1916). For a later attempt to use of the Winchester heriots to estimate mortality see, M. M. Postan and J. Z. Titow, 'Heriots and Prices on Winchester Manors', *EcHR* 2nd ser. 11 (1959), 392–417.

[52] A. E. Levett, 'The Courts and the Court Rolls of St Albans', *TRHS* 4th ser. 7 (1924), 52–76.

[53] Levett, *Studies in Manorial History*, ed. H. M. Cam, M. Coate, and L. S. Sutherland (Oxford, 1938).

[54] Ibid. 248–86.

court rolls can be used by social historians. Especially useful and stimulating are her notes about marriage and marriage fines and about villeins'
wills and the entries transcribed by her from the court books concerning
these matters.[55]

Levett could not estimate the rate of the Black Death mortality on four
St Albans manors although the names of the plague victims were registered in the court books, because in the absence of surveys she could not
estimate the population at risk.[56] A similar problem, however, was ingen-
iously tackled by Frances Page in her study of the estates of Crowland
Abbey (1934). The 1349 rolls of the joint court of three of the Abbey's
Cambridgeshire manors recorded the deaths of the plague victims. However there was a rental from the 1340s only for Dry Drayton and Oakington,
and not for Cottenham. None the less, by counting in the court rolls of
1346 and 1348 the names of the villagers appearing as tenants of Cottenham,
Page obtained an estimate of the landholding population in the manor on
the eve of the Black Death. She calculated that 57 per cent of the tenants
in Cottenham, 48 per cent in Dry Drayton, and 70 per cent in Oakington
lost their lives in the plague of 1349.[57]

Except for the way in which Page investigated the Black Death mortality, her method of analysing the court rolls of the Crowland Abbey
manors was rather conventional. None the less, she broke new ground in
the use of court rolls as a source for social history. Page initiated the use
of manorial court rolls for studying the welfare system in medieval villages. She was able to do this without compiling from the court rolls
detailed peasants' biographies, since unlike most contemporary manors,
in Oakington, Cottenham, and Drayton formal customs regulated not
only the property rights of widows, but also the distribution of land to
non-inheriting children and the terms of pension agreements between
retiring tenants and those who supported them.[58]

Page was also the first historian to investigate the social behaviour of
medieval peasants through court rolls. She argued that the evidence
about the peasants' interactions in the pre-plague court rolls indicate that,
although village society was not harmonious, it was none the less cohesive
and highly co-operative. However, the post-plague records revealed a

[55] Ibid. 208–47.   [56] Ibid. 284–5.

[57] F. M. Page, *The Estates of Crowland Abbey* (Cambridge, 1934), 120–1. For a more
accurate estimate of the plague mortality on these manors, see J. Ravensdale, 'Population
Changes and the Transfer of Customary Land on a Cambridgeshire Manor in the Fourteenth Century', in R. M. Smith, *Land, Kinship and Life-Cycle* (Cambridge, 1984), 197–8.

[58] Ibid. 108–12. See also, F. M. Page, 'The Customary Poor Law of Three Cambridgeshire Manors', *Cambridge Historical Journal*, 3 (1929), 225–33.

large-scale land accumulation and a growing tendency on the part of the peasants to escape from the manor, to resist seigneurial authority, and to violate communal rights and regulations. These changes suggested to her that in late medieval villages there was a transition from a co-operative to an individualistic social system.[59]

To sum up, the unique value of manorial court rolls as an historical source was first noted by English local historians in the second half of the nineteenth century. The research potentialities of these records were first realized by Seebhom, Vinogradoff, and Maitland and further developed in the first four decades of the twentieth century. Already in the late nineteenth and early twentieth centuries historians successfully obtained from the medieval court rolls abundant evidence about village society, economy, and demography by employing both qualitative and quantitative methods. Furthermore, these scholars who pioneered both the social history of rural England and the use of court rolls for historical analysis had an advantage over many of the modern social and economic historians, in two important respects: they studied village society within the framework of the power structure and legal system of medieval England, and they had a far better grasp of the limitations of court rolls as an historical source.

II

In the interval elapsing between the publication of Frances Page's research and renewed activity on the part of medievalists who were based or trained in British universities there occurred an interesting phase of research by social and economic historians using manorial court rolls which was very largely pursued in North America. Starting with the monograph published by the Harvard-based sociologist George Homans in 1941 it is possible to detect a style of research intent upon depicting the presence of a certain kind of village community in medieval England. Homans's book, and his subsequent articles in the 1950s and 1960s, were concerned with emphasizing a particular social configuration that was associated with different constellations of agrarian organization, field systems, and peasant inheritance customs.[60] He was clearly influenced by

---

[59] Page, *Estates of Crowland*, 138–55.

[60] G. C. Homans, *English Villagers in the Thirteenth Century* (Cambridge, Mass., 1941; 2nd edn., New York, 1960); some of his key ideas appeared in 'Terroirs ordonnés et camps orientés: une hypothèse sur le village anglais', *Annales d'histoire économique et sociale*, 8 (1936), 438–49; 'The Rural Sociology of Medieval England', *P&P* 4 (1953), 32–43; 'The Frisians in East Anglia', *EcHR* 2nd ser. 10 (1957–8), 189–206; 'The Explanation of English Regional Differences', *P&P* 42 (1969), 18–34.

certain sociological ideas that derived from the nineteenth-century French sociologist, Frédéric Le Play, who utilized the family as the basis for classifying society at large, and whose ideas also influenced his Harvard colleague, the anthropologist, Conrad Arensberg.[61] Le Play had emphasized, in particular, the ways in which the transfer of property between and within families sustained, or conversely, undermined their social cohesion, generational relations, and authority structures. While institutions outside the family and the village community were not ignored by Homans in his transportation of Le Play's models to late thirteenth-century England, they were given only a limited place in his treatment, to such an extent that the societies so reconstructed assumed an essentially timeless quality. In fact there is a sense in which the villagers of Homans's studies could derive from any nameless pre-industrial society. Questions to do with demography, the state of the economy, the place of lordship, serfdom, the relationship between village organization and central government, the character of customary law, and many other themes relevant to the social and economic history of the period were regarded as of limited relevance to this essentially synchronic approach, which was in no sense seen as problematic. It is noteworthy that the ideas which were beginning to emerge in the publications of M. M. Postan from the late 1930s, regarding the dynamic of the medieval economy and society were never integrated into Homans's work. This is especially significant given Homans's focus on manorial records from the late thirteenth century and the centrality of this period for the 'Postan model' of deteriorating living standards in rural communities that were seen to be occurring against a background of rising population numbers and increasing frequency of harvest failures, high food prices and land shortages.[62] Homans's methodology was essentially anecdotal in so far as he extracted cases from a great

---

[61] F. Le Play, *L'Organisation de la famille* (Paris, 1871). For a useful introduction to his influence in the social sciences, see C. B. Silver, *Frédéric Le Play: On Family, Work and Social Change* (Chicago, 1982). Although references to Le Play are limited to only three pages of *English Villagers in the Thirteenth Century*, 113, 119, and 215, they are highly significant. For instance, when writing of the stem-family organization which he believed to characterize 'champion England', Homans states: 'This traditional family organization had great virtues . . . every child knew what he had to expect and knew that if he were once given the means of making his living he was secure in holding them. Some certainty and security for the future are necessary to men if they are to be useful members of society' (214–15). See too, C. Arensberg, *The Irish Countryman* (New York, 1937); C. Arensberg and S. Kimball, *Family and Community in Ireland* (Cambridge, Mass., 1940).

[62] R. M. Smith, 'The Manorial Court and the Elderly Tenant in Late Medieval England', in M. Pelling and R. M. Smith (eds.), *Life, Death and the Elderly: Historical Perspectives* (London, 1991), 43–4.

many court roll series, all lodged in the British Library or the Public Record Record.[63] He produced an account of English society that was fundamentally static and based upon a bipartite regional division between, on the one hand, Midland or 'champion' England, where a system of primogeniture, open field agriculture, and a strong village community coincided, and on the other hand, those areas of partibility, enclosed fields, and weakly integrated village society, where it was also believed that joint-families were common. These latter characteristics, Homans supposed, were especially prevalent in the eastern and south-eastern counties of England. It is possible that one particularly strong influence impacting on Homans, apart from the earlier work of Le Play and the investigations of the Irish peasantry by Arensberg, was the Harvard historian, H. L. Gray, who earlier in the century had been interested in regional divisions in medieval England through his own research on field systems.[64] It is therefore not surprising that Homans's major influence in the wider field of historical research in the early to middle 1960s can be seen in the work of certain agricultural historians and historical geographers who investigated medieval field systems, particularly from the perspective of inheritance customs, their relationship to field morphology, and the processes of strip creation. Indeed the debate on the origins of the open fields that raged in the early 1960s certainly engaged with issues that loomed large in Homans's early work.[65] Indeed, he himself entered that debate on more than one occasion in this period, although he never returned to work on the original sources to further his claims.[66]

Another development of significance that in part arose out of Homans's work can be detected in the growing interest in the study of the peasant family. Links from Homans and Le Play to the work of historians who were making early contributions to the history of the family and household structure such as Thirsk, Hallam, and possibly Laslett, can be detected

---

[63] Of course, in focusing on such repositories, Homans was in no sense exceptional since the county records offices are very largely a post-World War II creation and their great collections of manorial documents that came from the archives of county landed families and solicitors' offices were not generally accessible to historians.

[64] H. L. Gray, *English Field Systems* (Cambridge, Mass., 1915); See too, A. R. H. Baker, 'Howard Levi Gray and *English Field Systems*: An Evaluation', *Agricultural History*, 39 (1965), 86–91.

[65] J. Thirsk, 'The Common Fields', *P&P* 29 (1964), 3–25; J. Z. Titow, 'Medieval England and the Open Field System', *P&P* 32 (1965), 86–102; J. Thirsk, 'The Origin of the Common Fields', *P&P* 33 (1966), 142–7; A. R. H. Baker, 'Open Fields and Partible Inheritance on a Kent Manor', *EcHR* 2nd ser. 17 (1964), 1–23; A. R. H. Baker and R. A. Butlin (eds.), *Studies of Field Systems in the British Isles* (Cambridge, 1973).

[66] Homans, 'Explanation of English Regional Differences'.

in the 1960s.[67] It is within this context that there appeared a highly innovative study based upon quite intensive, quantitatively pioneering use
of manorial court roll series. Ros Faith's University of Leicester doctoral
dissertation on the peasant land market in late medieval Berkshire was
heavily dependent upon the court roll as its primary source.[68] She subsequently published an important essay on the changing character of the
family land-bond over the course of the late Middle Ages that added
significantly to the understanding of the geography of medieval inheritance practices. She was critical of the static approach that had been
characteristic of Homans's work on this subject area and also significantly
revised his geographical account of medieval peasant inheritance practices.[69]

Warren Ault was another scholar whose work and influence extended
over both the pre- and post-World War II eras. In his earliest research he
had investigated seigneurial courts and jurisdictions, but it is through his
investigations of manorial by-laws and self-government, particularly in
matters to do with the rules and regulations of agrarian practice, that his
influence upon subsequent researchers was most marked.[70] Ault also concerned himself with broader issues concerning the relationship between
the manor and the vill and the manor and the parish which constitute
themes that have long remained under-researched.[71] In a similar vein,
Helen Cam's interesting writing on 'the community of the vill' published
before World War II was to prove influential.[72] Conceptually the most
notable influence stemming from the work of Homans, Ault, and Cam
came to be focused upon the Pontifical Institute of Medieval Studies in
Toronto where J. A. Raftis, who had established his reputation in the
early part of his career with an orthodox economic history of a medieval
estate, began to promote the use of court rolls by the development of an

---

[67] J. Thirsk, 'The Family', *P&P* 27 (1964), 116–22; J. Thirsk, 'Younger Sons in the
Seventeenth Century', *History*, 54 (1967), 358–77; H. E. Hallam, 'Some Thirteenth-
Century Censuses', *EcHR* 2nd ser. 36 (1957–8), 340–61; P. Laslett, and R. Wall (eds.),
Household and Family in Past Times (Cambridge, 1972), 16–21.

[68] R. J. Faith, 'The Peasant Land Market in Berkshire During the Later Middle Ages',
Ph.D. Thesis (University of Leicester, 1962).

[69] R. J. Faith, 'Peasant Families and Inheritance Customs in Medieval England', *AgHR*
14 (1966), 77–95.

[70] W. O. Ault, *Private Jurisdiction in England* (New Haven, Conn., 1923), 'By-laws of
Gleaning and the Problem of Harvest', *EcHR* 2nd ser. 14 (1961), 210–17, *Open Field
Farming in Medieval England* (London, 1972), and *Open Field Husbandry*.

[71] W. O. Ault, 'Village Assemblies in Medieval England', in *Album Helen Maud Cam*,
Studies Presented to the International Commission for the History of Representative and
Parliamentary Institutions, no. 23 (Louvain, 1960); W. O. Ault, 'Manor Court and Parish
Church in Fifteenth-Century England', *Speculum*, 42 (1967), 53–67.

[72] Cam, 'Community of the Vill'.

active graduate 'school' of court-roll based research in the late 1960s and 1970s.[73] While his interest in the nature of village society shared many similarities with the concerns of Homans, his methodology (and that of his students) was fundamentally different. Sixty years after Frances Davenport's pioneering research, Raftis and his pupils, DeWindt and Britton, established a quantitative approach to these sources which was distinguished by its attempt to utilize all the information in the court rolls relating to individuals and individual 'families'.[74] This particular approach to social history was premised on the idea that through the use of this methodology the forgotten or disregarded medieval villager could be resurrected and retrieved from the 'condecension of time' and saved from the clutches of legal and economic historians whose approaches to issues bearing upon rural economy and society were distinguished by being highly impersonal in their treatment of village populations. Unlike Homans, these users of the manorial court roll had a stronger sense of change through time and over space, stressing in particular mutations in village society in the post-Black Death period, by their adoption of an interpretation that had previously been provided by the Cambridge historian, Frances Page.[75] One highly distinctive characteristic of this school was its stress upon families, their involvement in the community, and its leadership groups or office-holders. Particular emphasis was placed by this school on their identification of a more individualistic, less communally orientated, pattern of personal behaviour among English villagers after 1349.[76] These scholars also stressed migration, particularly its supposed increase, after 1349, as a key factor undermining a sense of community that was thought to be more apparent before the demographic losses of the mid-fourteenth century.[77] They were also more concerned with demographic processes than Homans and showed some awareness of the

[73] Two key publications appearing in the early 1960s were: *Tenure and Mobility* and 'Social Structures of Five East Midland Villages', *EcHR* 2nd ser. 18 (1965), 84–99.

[74] The principal publications which were associated with this 'school' at that juncture are: J. A. Raftis, 'The Concentration of Responsibility in Five Villages', *Medieval Studies*, 28 (1966), 92–118, 'Changes in an English Village after the Black Death', *Medieval Studies* 29 (1967), 158–77, and *Warboys: Two Hundred Years in the Life of an English Medieval Village* (Toronto, 1974); A. DeWindt, 'Peasant Power Structures in Fourteenth-Century King's Ripton', *Medieval Studies*, 38 (1976), 244–67, and *Land and People*; Britton, *Community of the Vill*.

[75] Page, *Estates of Crowland*, 138–55.

[76] Raftis, 'Changes in an English Village', 164–5, *Warboys*, 219–21; DeWindt, *Land and People*, 264–74.

[77] Raftis, *Tenure and Mobility*, 129–82; DeWindt, *Land and People*, 171–205; Raftis, *Warboys*, 130–52.

new developments associated with the growing formalization of historical demography that were occurring in France and diffusing internationally under the influence of Louis Henry and the Institut National d'Études Démographiques and the Cambridge Group for the History of Population and Social Structure.[78]

Likewise, it was, perhaps, from within the intellectual concerns of an emerging historical demography that another development can be traced in the 1960s. In 1964 Sylvia Thrupp published a pioneering article on the derivation and interpretation of male replacement rates using East Anglian manorial court rolls and wills.[79] She had been somewhat influenced in the specification of her concerns by a debate about generational replacement that had involved Hallam, Russell, and Krause, and eventually attracted the attention of Peter Laslett.[80] That debate, however, was not based upon research with court rolls and it was Thrupp who first exposed the possibility of systematic use of those sources for demographic research at a time when historical demography was beginning to be associated with the techniques of family reconstitution which employed nominative linkage of entries relating to identified 'individuals' in parish registers, At the same time, Thrupp drew attention to information bearing upon female rights and access to property which the court roll was distinctive in exposing.[81]

It is possible to suggest that in the post-war generation of English research into medieval economy and society the dominance of Michael Postan must be seen as negatively influencing the use of manorial court rolls. While certainly not ignoring this source, he used them in a piecemeal and anecdotal fashion whereas the manorial account roll took pride of place among the key sources exploited.[82] In fact the attitude of his

[78] For Raftis's acknowledgement of Henry's influence, see, *Warboys*, ix; E. Britton, 'The Peasant Family in Fourteenth-Century England', *Peasant Studies*, 5 (1976), 2–7.

[79] S. L. Thrupp, 'The Problem of Replacement-Rates in Late Medieval English Population', *EcHR* 2nd ser. 18 (1965), 101–19.

[80] J. Krause, 'The Medieval Household: Large or Small?' *EcHR* 2nd ser. 9 (1957), 420–32; Hallam, 'Thirteenth-Century Censuses'; H. E. Hallam, 'Further Observations on the Spalding Serf Lists', *EcHR* 2nd ser. 16 (1963–4), 338–60; J. C. Russell, 'Demographic Limitations of Spalding Serf Lists', *EcHR* 2nd ser. 15 (1962–3), 340–61 Laslett and Wall (eds.), *Household and Family in Past Time*, 16–21.

[81] Thrupp, 'The Problem of Replacement Rates', 109–10.

[82] For instance, he certainly drew attention to their value in his classic assessment of the peasant land market in 'The Charters of the Villeins', 107–49, which initially appeared as an introduction to '*Carte Nativorum*', a *Peterborough Abbey Cartulary of the Fourteenth Century*, ed. C. N. L. Brooke and M. M. Postan (Northants Rec. Soc., 1960). In this wide-ranging essay Postan made use of a large number of published and unpublished manorial court rolls and provided the first systematic published reference to those important early manorial court rolls from Suffolk deposited in the Sir Nicholas Bacon Collection, University of Chicago Library.

principal disciple and frequent collaborator, J. Z. Titow, may be regarded as symptomatic of this apparent indifference to the records of the manorial curiae. In 1969 Titow was moved to state that

the main trouble with court rolls as a source of information is that the majority of the recorded items are, in the nature of things, accidental and unless the series is exceptionally good it is almost impossible to construct complete case histories, or to follow any case of litigation to its end. Thus the information provided seldom lends itself to statistical treatment and one has to rely on impressions when trying to decide if there were any significant changes in the course of time.[83]

Titow's somewhat sceptical remarks concerning the value of the court roll were made after the appearance of Paul Harvey's highly significant study of the Oxfordshire village of Cuxham in which he made extensive use of all classes of manorial documentation. Harvey's use of court rolls was exemplary and enabled him to produce the most comprehensive community reconstruction achieved by any scholar working on medieval English rural society on either side of the North Atlantic.[84]

One university context in Britain where the court roll was centrally integrated into the study of rural society was within the department of history at the University of Birmingham where Rodney Hilton exploited them in his classic monograph on the West Midlands in the thirteenth century.[85] At the same time he supervised a novel investigation of peasant chattels and housing by R. K. Field. In his University of Birmingham MA dissertation, Field made important new observations on central issues to do with peasant culture and material life.[86] Hilton also encouraged

---

[83] J. Z. Titow, *English Rural Society 1200–1350* (London, 1969), 31–2. Of course, court rolls were constructively employed in a number of highly influential studies both of individual estates and of individual manors. Edward Miller had made skilful use of these sources in his highly influential estate study, *The Abbey and Bishopric of Ely* (Cambridge, 1951). Elinora Carus-Wilson had displayed their value for detailed study of textile production and rural industrial workers in the manor of Castle Combe, Wiltshire in 'Evidences of Industrial Growth on Some Fifteenth-Century Manors', *EcHR* 2nd ser. 12 (1959), 190–205. Edmund King had taken Postan's analysis of villein charters and the land market considerably further by situating evidence in the *Carte Nativorum* within a larger collection of late thirteenth- and early fourteenth century manorial court rolls in his *Peterborough Abbey 1086–1310: A Study in the Land Market* (Cambridge, 1973).

[84] P. D. A. Harvey, *A Medieval Oxfordshire Village: Cuxham 1240–1400* (Oxford, 1965). Harvey subsequently produced the most scholarly and complete edition of any set of manorial records currently in print with important introductions to the history of all classes of manorial documentation. See *Manorial Records of Cuxham, Oxfordshire, c.1200–1359*, ed. P. D. A. Harvey (Oxfordshire Rec. Soc., 50 and Hist. Manuscripts Comm. JP 23, 1976).

[85] R. H. Hilton, *A Medieval Society: The West Midlands at the End of the Thirteenth Century* (London, 1966), see esp. pp. 140–66.

[86] R. K. Field, 'Worcestershire Peasant Building, Household Goods and Farming Equipment in the Later Middle Ages', *Medieval Archaeology*, 11 (1965), 105–45.

Christopher Dyer in the late 1960s and early 1970s to use court rolls in his work on various aspects of medieval economy and society.[87] Jean Birrell also undertook research in the University of Birmingham, under Hilton's supervision, and proceeded to publish a pioneering article concerning peasant craftsmen in Staffordshire that made heavy use of the Alrewas court rolls.[88]

In Cambridge, Richard Smith, working initially in historical geography, had been exposed to court rolls through the recent research of Alan Baker, who prior to moving to Cambridge in 1966, had also taught him as an undergraduate at University College London. In his University of London Ph.D., Baker had actively exploited court rolls in his investigations of Kentish medieval field systems.[89] At the same time Smith was influenced by the work of Alfred May who had undertaken an important study under Edward Miller's supervision at the University of Sheffield.[90] In the early 1970s Miller had returned to Cambridge as Master of Fitzwilliam College where Smith was eventually to become a fellow. Smith came increasingly under the sway of the family and historical demographic interests of the newly formed Cambridge Group for the History of Population and Social Structure where he eventually took an appointment in 1975, having resigned his lecturership in the Department of Geography.[91] While a graduate student within the Department of Geography in the early 1970s he had encountered Harold Fox and Bruce Campbell who were also preparing doctoral dissertations in historical geography. Fox recognized the value of manor court rolls for the study of the processes creating field morphologies in medieval England and exploited them in his important regional studies of Devon and Cornwall.[92] Campbell in the early 1970s undertook a Cambridge Ph.D. in historical geography that made heavy use of court rolls for an understanding of the

---

[87] See, in particular, C. Dyer, 'A Redistribution of Incomes in Fifteenth-Century England?', *P&P* 39 (1968), 11–33, repr in R. H. Hilton (ed.) *Peasants, Knights and Heretics: Studies in Medieval English Social History* (Cambridge, 1976), 192–215.

[88] J. R. Birrell, 'Peasant Craftsmen in the Medieval Forest', *AgHR* 17 (1969), 91–107.

[89] See references to particularly significant works by Baker in n. 65 above.

[90] A. N. May, 'An Index of Thirteenth-Century Peasant Impoverishment? Manor Court Fines', *EcHR* 2nd ser. 26 (1973), 389–401. For another innovative thesis prepared under Miller's supervision, see D. A. Crowley, 'Frankpledge and Leet Jurisdiction in Later Medieval Essex', Ph.D. Thesis (University of Sheffield, 1971).

[91] For a particularly important essay by one of its members in which the potential of manorial court rolls for demographic purposes was recognized and their further use encouraged, see R. S. Schofield, 'Historical Demography: Some Possibilities and Some Limitations', *TRHS* 5th ser. 21 (1971), 119–32, esp. 132.

[92] H. S. A. Fox, 'The Chronology of Enclosure and Economic Development in Medieval Devon', *EcHR* 2nd ser. 28 (1975), 181–202.

impact of partible inheritance and land markets on field arrangements in eastern Norfolk.[93]

All of the above-mentioned young historians and historical geographers, then working in Birmingham and Cambridge, were undoubtedly influenced by the publications of the Toronto School. Raftis's earliest major publication, based almost exclusively on court rolls—*Tenure and Mobility*—had been an extremely stimulating study, partly because it dealt intensively with certain key issues to do with family relationships and mobility, and was a distinctive advance upon the work of Homans. From the early 1970s, the Toronto School's research output became increasingly characterized by its commitment to community reconstructions. In the 1970s a string of monographs based upon detailed analysis of individual manors within the estate of the Abbots of Ramsey appeared, either directly authored by Professor Raftis or his pupils.[94] A number of doctoral theses were also completed under Professor Raftis's supervision, although not leading to published monographs.[95]

By the end of the 1970s the methodologies of this school were becoming subject to criticism both by early modernists and medievalists. Part of this criticism derived from a growing sophistication of approach to village reconstruction, as early modernists in particular, utilized a variety of sources and came to acquire a fuller sense of the biases that might follow from overdependence on one particular class of record. Some of these criticisms were more appropriately directed against those later medieval court rolls that certainly were less comprehensive in their coverage of a wide range of issues in village society than were the court rolls of the 'classic period' from *c.*1270–1380. However, a common criticism focused upon the use of court roll series for detailed community reconstruction, particularly if the principal purpose was to produce demographic and

---

[93] B. M. S. Campbell, 'Field Systems in Eastern Norfolk during the Middle Ages', Ph.D. Thesis (Cambridge University, 1975).

[94] See n. 73 above.

[95] P. M. Hogan, 'Wistow: A Social and Economic Reconstitution in the Fourteenth Century', Ph.D. Thesis (University of Toronto, 1971); A. Dewindt, 'Society and Change'. Publications emanating from these dissertations, include P. M. Hogan, 'Medieval Villainy: A Study in the Meaning and Control of Crime in an English Village', *Studies in Medieval and Renaissance History*, 17 (1981), 123–214 and A. Dewindt, 'A Peasant Land Market and its Participants: Kings's Ripton, 1280–1400', *Midland History*, 4 (1978), 142–59. For more recent studies from this school, see *The Court Rolls of Ramsey, Hepmangrove and Bury, 1268–1600*, ed. E. B. Dewindt (Toronto, 1990); S. Olson, 'Jurors of the Village Court: Local Leadership before and after the Plague in Ellington, Huntingdonshire', *JBS* 30 (1991), 237–56; S. Olson, 'Family Linkages and the Structure of the Local Élite in the Medieval and Early Modern Village', *Medieval Prosopography*, 13 (1992), 53–82.

family history, when the rolls employed were fragmented in their survival
and incomplete in their coverage of the whole community. These were
shortcomings that afflicted many of the series used from the Ramsey
estates in Huntingdonshire and Cambridgeshire by the Toronto School.[96]
Professor Judith Bennett, a pupil of Raftis, who had undertaken detailed
work on Brigstock, a Northamptonshire village, not within the Ramsey
estate, offered a distinctive methodological criticism which argued that it
was impossible with court rolls to undertake total reconstruction of village society, and that the only satisfactory research method to adopt was
to engage in detailed individual family case studies—case studies that
might be regarded as representative of various experiences within local
society. However, it was not clear from this method how representativeness was to be established without prior, large-scale reconstruction against
which to set the case studies, however detailed they might be.[97]

The only study that resulted in a village-focused monograph, and not
undertaken at the University of Toronto, was Zvi Razi's primarily demographic reconstruction of the Worcestershire manor of Halesowen.[98] It
certainly did employ methodologies that differed from those that had
been adopted by the Toronto School. It must be stressed, however, that
to focus on village- or manor-based research that relied heavily or exclusively on the manorial court roll would produce a distorted impression of
the increasing use of court rolls by medievalists in the 1970s. Two major
studies by Barbara Harvey and Christopher Dyer on the estates of Westminster Abbey and the Bishop of Worcester respectively, made heavy use
of court rolls and addressed key themes to do with the nature of lordship,
the development of customary tenure, the land market, and the changing

[96] For some of the principal criticisms see, J. S. Beckerman, 'Customary Law in English
Manorial Courts in the Thirteenth and Fourteenth Centuries', Ph.D. Thesis (University of
London, 1972), 236–41; K. Wrightson, 'Medieval Villagers in Perspective', *Peasant Studies*,
7 (1978), 203–16; Z. Razi, 'The Toronto School's Reconstitution of Medieval Peasant
Society: A Critical View', *P&P* 85 (1978), 141–57. See too, M. Pimsler, 'Solidarity in the
Medieval Village? The Evidence of Personal Pledging at Elton, Huntingdonshire', *JBS* 17
(1977), 1–11 and D. Postles, 'Personal Pledging in Manorial Courts in the Late Middle
Ages', *Bulletin of the John Rylands Library Manchester*, 75 (1993), 65–78.

[97] J. M. Bennett, 'Gender, Family and Community: A Comparative Study of the English
Peasantry, 1287–1349', Ph.D. Thesis (University of Toronto, 1981), and 'Spouses, Siblings
and Surnames: Reconstructing Families from Medieval Village Court Rolls', *JBS* 23 (1983),
26–46. For the implementation of her methodology see J. M. Bennett, 'The Tie that Binds:
Peasant Marriages and Families in Late Medieval England', *Journal of Interdisciplinary
History*, 15 (1984), 111–29.

[98] Z. Razi, *Life, Marriage and Death in a Medieval Parish: Economy, Society and Demography in Halesowen, 1270–1400* (Cambridge, 1980).

character of the peasant family.[99] In addition doctoral theses were completed using court rolls to investigate various aspects of the peasant land market in the counties of Norfolk, Bedfordshire, and Durham, which some years later were brought together with Faith's much earlier, but highly influential study of Berkshire, in an important essay collection concerned with the peasant land market under Paul Harvey's editorship.[100]

Different approaches to the land market and the peasant family were developed by Richard Smith which brought issues to do with the similarities and contrasts between medieval and early modern rural society into the centre of debate.[101] One community study that was also distinctive in covering a long period of time from the early thirteenth to the late seventeenth century, made extensive, although not exclusive use of the court roll. That study, by Cecily Howell of the Leicestershire village of Kibworth Harcourt, still stands as the one attempt to cross the early modern–medieval divide in a single, published monograph.[102]

In 1984 a set of essays by medievalists based heavily on court rolls appeared in a volume entitled, *Land, Kinship and Life-cycle* under Richard Smith's editorship. These essays were representative of themes that were proving to be increasingly interesting to social and economic historians concerning the character of the medieval peasant family, the bond between family and land, and the underlying character of the land market. These were more methodologically and theoretically preoccupied than much of the earlier research.[103] In fact a concern with methodological and

---

[99] B. F. Harvey, *Westminster Abbey and its Estates in the Middle Ages* (Oxford, 1977); C. Dyer, *Lords and Peasants in a Changing Society: The Estates of the Bishopric of Worcester, 680–1540* (Cambridge, 1980).

[100] A. C. Jones, 'The Customary Land Market in Bedfordshire in the Fifteenth Century', Ph.D. Thesis (University of Southampton, 1975); R. A. Lomas, 'Durham Cathedral Priory as a Landowner and a Landlord, 1290–1540', Ph.D. Thesis (University of Durham, 1978); J. Williamson, 'Peasant Holdings in Medieval Norfolk', Ph.D. Thesis (University of Reading, 1976); P. D. A. Harvey (ed.), *The Peasant Land Market in Medieval England* (Oxford, 1984). For a recent contribution to this subject, see M. E. Mate, 'The East Sussex Land Market and Agrarian Class Structure in the Late Middle Ages', *P&P* 139 (1993), 46–65.

[101] R. M. Smith, 'English Peasant Life Cycles and Socio-Economic Networks', Ph.D. Thesis (University of Cambridge, 1974), 'Kin and Neighbours in a Thirteenth-Century Suffolk Community', *JFH* 4 (1979), 219–56, and 'The Bastardy Prone Sub-Society: An Appendix', in P. Laslett, K. Oosterveen, and R. M. Smith (eds.), *Bastardy and its Comparative History* (London, 1980), 240–8.

[102] C. Howell, *Land, Family and Inheritance in Transition: Kibworth Harcourt 1280–1700* (Cambridge, 1983).

[103] Matters discussed by R. M. Smith, 'Some Issues Concerning Families and their Properties in England, 1250–1800', in Smith (ed.), *Land, Kinship and Life-Cycle*, 1–69.

conceptual problems in the uses to which court rolls were put has been a distinctive development during the 1980s.

One particular development may be identified as increasingly pervasive in the debate over the use of the manor court roll. Earlier studies had been decidedly neglectful of the legal and curial contexts within which the court records had been produced. One study is deserving of special attention in so far as it proved to be particularly seminal and influential. John Beckerman's University of London Ph.D. thesis on customary law, supervised by S. F. Milsom, became the foundation from which much rethinking of the strengths and weaknesses of the court roll emanated.[104] Furthermore, Beckerman's thesis, for long unpublished, set off a series of studies concerned with the manor court as an institution, the nature of customary law, its relationship to common law and the links between manor courts and higher courts in the jurisdictional hierarchy.[105] In this development we do undoubtedly observe a return to a number of the issues that preocuppied Maitland and Vinogradoff in the late nineteenth century.

In the aftermath of the successful completion of Zvi Razi's innovative demographic study of Halesowen, it was inevitable that efforts would be made to assess the extent to which such work could be replicated on other court-roll series. In 1977 Rodney Hilton secured a grant from the Social Science Research Council (now, Economic and Social Research Council) to undertake a survey of court roll series that were thought to be sufficiently complete chronologically, and jurisdictionally comprehensive of their village community, to permit demographic analysis in the manner of Razi's research on Halesowen. The results of that survey undertaken by Judith Cripps and Janet Williamson are published in this volume. It was

---

[104] J. S. Beckerman, 'Customary Law in English Manorial Courts', and a recently published article containing a summary of some of its most important findings, 'Procedural Innovation and Institutional Change in Medieval English Manorial Courts', *LHR* 10 (1992), 197–252.

[105] R. M. Smith, 'Some Thoughts on "Hereditary" and "Proprietary" Rights in Land under Custumary Law in Thirteenth- and Early Fourteenth-Century England', *LHR* 1 (1983), 95–128; Z. Razi, 'The Erosion of the Family-Land Bond in the Late Fourteenth and Fifteenth Centuries: A Methodological Note', in Smith (ed), *Land, Kinship and Life-Cycle*, 295–305; R. H. Helmholz (ed.), *Select Cases on Defamation to 1600* (Selden Soc. 101, 1985), xlviii–lxvi and 27–40; C. Dyer, 'Les Cours manoriales', *Études Rurales*, 103–4 (1986), 19–27; L. R. Poos and L. Bonfield, 'Law and Individualism in Medieval England', *Social History*, 11 (1986), 287–301; R. M. Smith, 'Women's Property Rights under Customary Law: Some Developments in the Thirteenth and Fourteenth Centuries', *TRHS* 5th ser. 36 (1986), 165–94; L. Bonfield, 'The Nature of Customary Law in the Manorial Courts of Medieval England', *Comparative Studies in Society and History*, 31 (1989), 514–34; R. M. Smith 'Coping With Uncertainty: Women's Tenure of Customary Land in England *c.*1370–1430', in J. Kermode (ed.) *Enterprise and Individuals in Fifteenth-Century England* (Gloucester, 1991), 43–67.

a noteworthy and disappointing discovery of this work that few court-roll series were as complete as the series that Razi had utilized. However, it was also clear that a great mass of material decidedly superior in its coverage of social behaviour, within individual communities than the source materials that had been used by the Toronto School primarily from manorial court records from the manors within the estates of the abbot of Ramsey, was available for future research. Such an abundance of source materials implied that historians interested in a wide array of issues relating to English medieval society could address issues to do with medieval rural and small town society that could not be tackled for most of England's European neighbours where comparable sources were noteworthy for their absence.

Throughout the 1970s and 1980s both Birmingham and Cambridge remained centres in Britain for the study of court-roll-based research and, in the latter considerable advances were made in the development of computerized approaches to the analysis of these sources that succeeded with their inputting format in retaining the integrity of the primary source. Subsequently a number of researchers have used these computer-based techniques.[106] Prior to the SSRC-funded survey conducted under his direction, Rodney Hilton had undertaken innovative work utilizing court rolls from the West Midlands which were sources that loomed large

---

[106] In the late 1970s Ros Davies and Richard Smith utilized GENDATA to provide a system of record generation and management for the analysis of manorial court rolls. For a description of the conceptual basis of GENDATA see R. S. Schofield and R. Davies, 'Towards a Flexible Data Input and Record Management System', *Historical Methods Newsletter*, 7 (1974), 115–24. GENDATA was employed by L. Poos in 'Population and Resources in Two Fourteenth-Century Essex Communities: Great Waltham and High Easter, 1327–89', Ph.D. Thesis (Cambridge, 1983). It was also this record management system that Janet Williamson and Judith Cripps adopted in their analysis of the manorial court rolls of Lakenheath and Alrewas, as part of the SSRC-funded project within the Department of History, University of Birmingham. See J. Williamson, 'On the Use of the Computer in Historical Studies: Demographic, Social and Economic History from Medieval English Manor Court Rolls', in A. Gilmour-Bryson (ed.) *Computer Applications to Historical Studies* (Kalamazoo, Mich., 1984), 51–61. For a study based on these computerized data, see J. Williamson, 'Dispute Settlement in the Manorial Court: Early Fourteenth-Century Lakenheath', *Reading Medieval Studies*, 11 (1985), 33–41. Subsequently the GENDATA-based system has been used with SAS by Jacques Beauroy in an analysis of the manorial court rolls of the Norfolk manor of Heacham as part of his forthcoming French *doctorat d'état*. In recent years the ready availability of relational data base software packages has greatly facilitated computer-based analysis of manorial court rolls. In this volume, Professor Davies and his colleagues reveal the results of their use of IDEALIST with the court rolls of Dyffryn Clwyd. Currently the relational data base, PARADOX, has been, or is being used, to analyse the court rolls of Hinderclay, Suffolk by Dr Phillipp Schofield, Wellcome Unit for the History of Medicine, Oxford, Hevingham, Norfolk by Jane Whittle, St Hugh's College, Oxford and West Hanney, Berkshire by Margaret Yates, Manchester College, Oxford.

in his Ford lectures delivered in the University of Oxford and published in 1975 as *The English Peasantry in the Later Middle Ages*. Contained within that collection was one novel study of small towns in West Midland society.[107] That subject was taken further by Hilton in the 1980s who revealed how the court rolls of small seigneurial boroughs could be profitably exploited to further our understanding of these highly distinctive urban centres.[108] Chris Dyer completed a particularly successful exercise involving the linkage of individuals, known to have been implicated in Peasants Revolt of 1381, to their activities as revealed in local manorial courts. He also published a set of studies demonstrating the great value of court rolls for the study of living standards, various aspects of peasant diet, material culture, and marketing and encouraged the integration of evidence from the court roll with archaeological data from particular excavations.[109] In this respect Birmingham set up a research agenda that was more wide-ranging than that attempted anywhere in Britain and North America. Under the influence of Rodney Hilton, students employing the court roll at the University of Birmingham did not neglect the fact that these sources were generated in tribunals in which the influence of lordship was a factor that could not be ignored. Serfdom and resistance to landlord authority was a subject that was given very serious attention. This can be seen in the work of Zvi Razi, Chris Dyer, Peter Franklin, and in doctoral theses by Helena Graham and Dong-Wook Ko who were supervised by Chris Dyer. In addition these sources were successfully exploited in other Birmingham-based research concerning medieval technological change, particularly the subjects of medieval milling and transportation.[110] An interesting debate concerning the nature of villeinage,

---

[107] R. H. Hilton, 'The Small Town as Part of Peasant Society', in his *The English Peasantry in the Later Middle Ages* (Oxford, 1975), 76–94.

[108] R. H. Hilton, 'Lords, Burgesses and Hucksters', *P&P* 97 (1983), 1–15, and 'Small Town Society in England before the Black Death', *P&P* 105 (1984), 53–78.

[109] C. Dyer, 'The Social and Economic Background of the Rural Revolt of 1381', in R. H. Hilton and T. H. Aston (eds.), *The English Rising of 1381* (Cambridge, 1984), pp. 27–33; C. Dyer, 'English Diet in the Late Middle Ages', in T. H. Aston, P. R. Coss, C. Dyer, and J. Thirsk (eds.), *Social Relations and Ideas: Essays in Honour of R. H. Hilton* (Cambridge, 1983), 191–216; C. Dyer, 'English Peasant Buildings in the Later Middle Ages', *Medieval Archaeology*, 30 (1986), 19–45; C. Dyer, 'The Rise and Fall of a Medieval Village: Little Aston (in Aston Blank), Gloucestershire', *Trans. of the Bristol and Gloucestershire Archeological Society*, 105 (1987), 165–81; N. Palmer and C. Dyer, 'An Inscribed Stone from Burton Dassett, Warwickshire', *Medieval Archaeology*, 32 (1988), 216–19; C. Dyer, *Standards of Living in the Later Middle Ages* (Cambridge, 1989).

[110] Z. Razi, 'The Struggles between the Abbots of Halesowen and their Tenants in the Thirteenth and Fourteenth Centuries', in Aston *et al.* (eds.), *Social Relations and Ideas*, 169–91; C. Dyer, 'The Rising of 1381 in Suffolk: Its Origins and Participants', *Proceedings*

focused on the determinants of the marriage fine or *merchet*, was conducted in the pages of *Past and Present* and depended very heavily, although not entirely, on evidence from court rolls. The approach of the principal participants in this debate were somewhat anecdotal in their employment of court rolls.[111] More recent studies, attempting to establish whether there was substance in the claim that liability to pay *merchet* was linked with the transfer of dowry to their daughters and therefore a charge met primarily by villein parents from within the most affluent sections of custumary, have been based upon detailed community-based and decidedly quantitative reconstructions from the records of fairly complete court-roll series or summaries.[112]

In general the work undertaken in Birmingham had been regionally focused on the Midland counties. The smaller body of research that had accrued in Cambridge had been mainly concerned with communities from the Eastern Counties. Larry Poos had completed his thesis in 1983 based on two fourteenth-century Essex manors that were studied largely from the material derived from their voluminous court roll evidence.[113]

of the Suffolk Institute of Archaeology and History 36 (1988), 274–87; P. Franklin, 'Peasant Widows' "Liberation" and Remarriage', *EcHR* 2nd ser. 39 (1986), 186–204, and 'Thornbury In the Age of the Black Death: Peasant Society, Landholding and Agriculture in Gloucestershire, 1328–52', Ph.D. Thesis (University of Birmingham, 1982); H. Graham, 'A Social and Economic Study of the Late Medieval Peasantry; Alrewas, Staffordshire, in the Fourteenth Century', Ph.D. Thesis (University of Birmingham, 1994); D.-W. Ko, 'Society and Conflict in Barnet, Hertfordshire, 1337–1450', Ph.D. Thesis (University of Birmingham, 1994); J. Langdon, *Horses, Oxen and Technological Innovation: The Use of Draught Animals in English Farming from 1066 to 1500* (Cambridge, 1986); R. Holt, *The Mills of Medieval England* (Oxford, 1988).

[111] E. Searle, 'Seignorial Control of Women's Marriage: The Antecedents and Function of Merchet in England', *P&P* 82 (1979), 3–43; P. A. Brand and P. R. Hyams, 'Seigneurial Control of Women's Marriage', *P&P* 99 (1983), 122–33; R. J. Faith, 'Seigneurial Control of Women's Marriage', *P&P* 99 (1983), 133–48; T. North, 'Legerwite in the Thirteenth and Fourteenth Centuries', *P&P* 111 (1986), 3–16.

[112] J. M. Bennett, 'Medieval Peasant Marriage: An Examination of Marriage Licence Fines in the *Liber Gersumarum*', in J. A. Raftis (ed.), *Pathways to Medieval Peasants* (Toronto, 1981), 193–246; R. M. Smith, 'Marriage Processes in the English Past', in L. Bonfield, R. M. Smith, and K. Wrightson (eds.), *The World We Have Gained: Histories of Population and Social Structure* (Oxford, 1986), 43–99, and 'Further "Models" of Medieval Marriage: Landlords, Serfs and Priests in Rural England, c.1290–1370', in C. Amado and G. Lobrichon (eds.), *Mélanges Georges Duby* (Paris, 1995), 85–99.

[113] Poos, 'Population and Resources'. It would be incorrect to create the impression that intensive use of manorial court rolls was not pursued elsewhere in Britain. Barbara Harvey supervised two important doctoral theses, both based on communities from the east of England. See C. Clark, 'Peasant Society and Land Transactions in Chesterton, Cambridgeshire, 1277–1325', D.Phil. Thesis (University of Oxford, 1983) and P. R. Schofield, 'Land, Family and Inheritance in a Later Medieval Community: Birdbrook, 1292–1412', D.Phil. Thesis (University of Oxford, 1992).

He had furthermore alighted upon a valuable set of data found in the views of frankpledge of a substantial grouping of Essex manors relating to the number of resident males aged 12 years and over, which provide unique information on population trends in that area from the late thirteenth to the early sixteenth centuries.[114] Smith continued to work on various aspects of Suffolk society as exemplified by Redgrave and Rickinghall.[115] Furthermore Campbell's earlier research on field systems and land markets using court rolls had been directed to the especially densely populated parts of north-eastern Norfolk.[116] Only Razi began to look seriously at the similarities and contrasts between the patterns, particularly relating to family patterns that were emerging from the Midlands and East Anglia, and in the process helped to clarify and reconcile some of the divergent interpretations of medieval society which had come to characterize ideas associated with Cambridge on the one hand and Birmingham on the other.[117]

In North America the 1980s saw a growing diversification of uses made of manorial court rolls by medievalists, not based or trained in the University of Toronto, who researched into English society. Judith Bennett, while initially a student trained at the University of Toronto, had developed a distinctive interest in women in medieval rural society which resulted in an innovative study of the manorial court rolls of Brigstock, Northamptonshire, thereby setting her apart from most of the members of the Raftis 'school'. Her subsequent interests in women's history have

---

[114] L. R. Poos, 'The Social Context of the Statute of Labourers Enforcement', *LHR* 1 (1983), 27–52, and *A Rural Society after the Black Death: Essex 1350–1525* (Cambridge, 1991), 91–110; see also his 'Population Turnover in Medieval Essex: The Evidence of Some Early Fourteenth-Century Tithing Lists', in Bonfield *et al.* (eds.), *The World We Have Gained*, 1–22; P. R. Schofield, 'Frankpledge Lists as Indices of Migration and Mortality: Some Evidence from Essex Lists', *Local Population Studies*, 52 (1994), 23–9. For an early study using information from tithing penny payments see K. C. Newton, 'A Source for Medieval Population Statistics', *Journal of the Society of Archivists*, 3 (1969), 543–6, and another that employs tithing payments from a Leicestershire manor, see D. Postles, 'Demographic Change in Kibworth Harcourt, Leicestershire in the Late Middle Ages', *Local Population Studies*, 48 (1992), 41–8.

[115] 'Families and their Land in an Area of Partible Inheritance: Redgrave, Suffolk 1260–1320', in Smith (ed.), *Land, Kinship and Life-Cycle*, 38–92; R. M. Smith, 'Transactional Analysis and the Measurement of Institutional Determinants of Fertility: A Comparison of Communities in Present-Day Bangladesh and pre-Industrial England', in J. C. Caldwell, J. A. Hill and V. J. Hull (eds.), *Micro-Approaches to Demographic Research* (London, 1988), 227–40.

[116] B. M. S. Campbell, 'Population Change and the Genesis of Common Fields on a Norfolk Manor', *EcHR* 2nd ser. 33 (1980), 174–92, and 'Population Pressure, Inheritance and the Land Market in a Fourteenth-Century Peasant Commmunity', in Smith (ed.), *Land, Kinship and Life-Cycle*, 87–134.

[117] Z. Razi, 'The Myth of the Immutable English Family', *P&P* 140 (1993), 3–44.

broadened, but her major research into brewing and the involvement of women in that activity, finds its roots to her initial research on evidence concerning those listed in the manor courts of Brigstock for infractions of the Assize of Ale.[118] Another North American student of the manor court who, over the 1980s, has produced a steady stream of innovative research using manorial court rolls, is Elaine Clark. She had initially completed a thesis, supervised by Professor Thrupp, at the University of Michigan on peasant indebtedness, using the manorial court rolls of the Essex manor of Writtle. Subsequently she has opened up a number of themes to do with various aspects of personal security and autonomy. Her studies of old age, orphans, guardians, and marriage have given a significant boost to another area of research which she has helped to foster.[119] Her interest in common and customary law is reflected in all of these studies and has been taken somewhat further by the doctoral research of Leon Slota which she supervised on the land market on various manors of the abbots of St Albans.[120] This research revealed important links between the royal

---

[118] J. M. Bennett, *Women in the Medieval English Countryside. Gender and Household in Brigstock Before the Plague* (Oxford, 1987), 'Widows in the Medieval Countryside', in L. Mirrer (ed.), *Upon My Husband's Death: Widows in the Literature and Histories of Medieval Europe* (Ann Arbor, 1992), 69–114, and 'The Village Ale-Wife, Women and Brewing in Fourteenth-Century England', in B. A. Hanawalt (ed.), *Women and Work in Pre-industrial Europe* (Bloomington, 1986), 20–36. For other studies of brewing based on court rolls, see Smith, 'English Peasant Life-Cycles and Socio-Economic Networks', 150–78; Smith, 'Some Issues Concerning Families', 27–32; H. Graham, '"A Woman's Work . . .": Labour and Gender in the Late Medieval Countryside', in P. J. P. Goldberg (ed.), *Woman is a Worthy Wight: Women in English Society c.1200–1500* (Gloucester, 1992), 126–48; D. Postles, 'Brewing and the Peasant Economy: Some Manors in Late Medieval Devon', *Rural History*, 3 (1992), 133–44. See too, H. M. Jewell, 'Women at the Courts of the Manor of Wakefield, 1348–50', *Northern History*, 26 (1990), 59–81.
[119] E. Clark, 'Debt Litigation in a Late Medieval English Vill', in Raftis (ed.) *Pathways to Medieval Peasants*, 247–79. Clark was not the first to exploit the rich court rolls of the manor of Writtle, see K. C. Newton, *The Manor of Writtle: The Development of a Royal Manor in Essex c.1096–c.1500* (Chichester, 1970). For Clark's other very distinctive interest concerning issues to do with personal security in the medieval countryside see the following: E. Clark, 'Some Aspects of Social Security in Medieval England', *JFH* 7 (1982), 307–20, 'The Custody of Children in English Manor Courts', *LHR* 3 (1985), 333–48, 'The Decision to Marry in Thirteenth and Early Fourteenth Century Norfolk', *Medieval Studies*, 49 (1987), 496–511, 'The Quest for Security in Medieval England', in M. M. Sheehan (ed.), *Aging and the Aged in Medieval Europe* (Toronto, 1990), 189–200, 'Mothers at Risk of Poverty in the Medieval English Countryside', in J. Henderson and R. Wall (eds.), *Poor Women and Children in the European Past* (London, 1994), 139–59, and 'Social Welfare and Mutual Aid in the Medieval Countryside', *JBS* 33 (1994), 381–406.
[120] L. A. Slota, 'The Village Land Market on the St Albans Manors of Park and Codicite: 1237–1399', Ph.D. Thesis (University of Michigan, 1984), and 'Law, Land Transfer and Lordship on the Estates of St Albans Abbey in the Thirteenth and Fourteenth Centuries', *LHR* 6 (1988), 119–38.

courts and customary procedures, as well as taking into account the influence of seigneurial authority on the procedures concerning the transfer
of property under customary tenure. During the same period Larry Poos,
having returned to an academic appointment in the USA, began to investigate a number of issues to do with customary law jointly with his
Cambridge-trained colleague, Lloyd Bonfield, who holds an appointment
in Tulane University Law School.[121] This interest should soon culminate
in the publication of a substantial volume on various aspects of family-
related issues under customary law in the Selden Society series—the first
to deal specifically with manorial court evidence since Maitland's editions
in that same series in the late nineteenth century. Poos had also, in
revising and substantially extending his Cambridge thesis, incorporated
manorial court evidence within a wider framework of source materials
and established a new style of regional study of late medieval society
which no doubt will be replicated.[122] Marjorie McIntosh's work represents another major contribution from a North American scholar, who,
while initially trained at Harvard, had established strong associations with
Cambridge as she began to develop her study of the Essex manor of
Havering.[123] This study was important because of the fact that the manor
concerned was ancient demesne. The legal processes associated with this
highly specific legal environment enabled her to pursue a number of
issues that were generally difficult to investigate in other contexts.[124] It
should be stressed that McIntosh distinguished her work by endowing it
with a more substantial concern with law and its institutions than had
characterized most previous single-manor or village studies. Following
the publication of her medieval sudy of Havering she went on to complete a second volume concerned with its early modern history which
utilized a wide range of sources from that data-rich county of Essex.[125]
More recently her research has returned to focus unambiguously on the
late medieval–early modern divide and through her use of manorial courts,
especially leet courts of the fifteenth century, she has been able to pursue

---

[121] See n. 103 above.
[122] Poos, *Rural Society*. For an earlier, important study that linked persons appearing in
the gaol delivery rolls and local manorial courts, see B. A. Hanawalt, 'Community Conflict
and Social Control: Crime and Justice in the Ramsey Abbey Villages', *Medieval Studies*, 39
(1977), 402–33.
[123] M. K. McIntosh, *Autonomy and Community: The Royal Manor of Havering, 1200–
1500* (Cambridge, 1986).
[124] M. K. McIntosh, 'The Privileged Villeins of the English Ancient Demesne', *Viator*,
7 (1976), 295–328.
[125] M. K. McIntosh, *A Community Transformed: The Manor and Liberty of Havering-atte-
Bower 1500–1620* (Cambridge, 1990).

a number of issues to do with social control, popular culture and morality, thereby questioning the assumed novelty of certain developments
occurring in the late sixteenth and early seventeenth centuries.[126]

III

The essays in this current collection, involving authors who have been
trained in Britain and North America, reflect and take further, many of
the developments identifiable in manorial court roll studies of the 1980s
and early 1990s. Razi and Smith have returned to reconsider many matters that attracted Maitland's attention regarding the origins of the court
roll and the relationship between the manor court and other legal institutions in twelfth- and thirteenth-century England. Likewise Paul Hyams
engages with similar matters in his essay written from the perspective of
a common-law historian looking into the manor court from an 'external'
vantage point, whereas Razi and Smith approach a similar set of issues
from a diametrically opposite direction. Bonfield in his short essay takes
up the same question and, in partnership with Poos, addresses similar
matters through a consideration of deathbed transfers and the nature of
the manorial court and its use, by individuals in their strategies developed
for the devolving of property. Paul Harvey's re-evaluation of the recent
historiography of the land market requires him to reflect more on these
larger issues to do with the nature of law and property that extend
beyond the inevitable focus on customary tenure provided by court rolls.
Many of the somewhat tortuous debates about technical and methodological problems surrounding the use of the manorial court for specific
study of matters, such as demography, have also been obliged to take law
and curial institutions more seriously into account than hitherto. The
debate over the use of court rolls for demographic purposes involving
Poos, Razi, and Smith in this volume exemplifies this highly complex and
dauntingly technical area of enquiry.

The remaining essays reflect the results of new work addressing large
questions. Rodney Hilton's and Richard Smith's essays on a small seigneurial borough and a seigneurial periodic market, respectively, are symptomatic of an increasing interest in commercialization and the relationship

---

[126] Most of this new work is unpublished but some of the issues are detectable in K. C.
Newton and M. K. McIntosh, 'Leet Jurisdiction in Essex Manor Courts during the Elizabethan Period', *Essex Archaeology and History*, 3rd ser. 13 (1981), 3–14; M. K. McIntosh,
'Local Responses to the Poor of Late Medieval and Tudor England', *Continuity and Change*,
3 (1988), 209–45.

between the rural and urban sectors.[127] They furthermore demonstrate
the uniqueness of English evidence and its capacity for probing into
economic and social processes that all too frequently in much continental
European medieval scholarship can rarely be addressed outside the larger
towns.

Harold Fox's essay is a pioneering investigation of labour forms and
labour usages in medieval communities. His reassessment of the *garciones*
on certain manors of the abbots of Glastonbury represents the growing
interest, among students of medieval rural society, in servants, labourers,
and their role in the wider agrarian economy, both in the pre- and post-
Black Death period. It is hard to see how such issues could be addressed
without access to the records of the manorial court, nothwithstanding the
valuable work of those historians, primarily of the later Middle Ages, who
have worked on the central government sources created as a result of the
operation of the Statute of Labourers of 1351 by royal justices. Phillipp
Schofield provides the first detailed description and systematic analysis of
the operation of a view of franklpledge and its associated tithing system
for a medieval community. This element in private jurisdiction has been
surprisingly neglected by medievalists, notwithstanding the interest,
particularly more recently, in the use of data from tithing payments for
the purposes of charting demographic change.

Both Ralph Evans's and Peter Franklin's essays represent examples
of the use of court rolls for investigating the nature of lordship, estate
administration, and the various ways in which peasants resisted such
authority. Zvi Razi's essay is an attempt to confront the issues raised by
Judith Bennett in an earlier methodological criticism of court rolls. It
represents a demonstration of the use of aggregate analysis of court roll
evidence bearing upon family arrangements and relationships. Similarly
Elaine Clark's essay demonstrates another dimension of family life and
relationships, although from the perspective of charting the drift of property outside the family for the purposes of securing both individual,
spiritual, and communal material welfare. Both the essays by Razi and
Clark make use of aggregated behaviour for the establishment of patterns
and trends that would be impossible to recreate through the use of anecdotal case studies.

[127] R. H. Britnell, *The Commercialisation of English Society 1000–1500* (Cambridge, 1993);
B. M. S. Campbell, J. A. Galloway, D. Keene, and M. Murphy, *A Medieval Capital and its
Grain Supply: Agrarian Production and Distribution in the London Region c.1300* (Hist. Geog.
Res. ser. no. 30, 1993); R. H. Britnell and B. M. S. Campbell (eds.), *A Commercialising
Economy: England 1086–c.1300* (Manchester, 1995).

Within the essays prepared for this volume and in our attempt to chart the course of court-roll based research over the last two generations, we can identify an initial phase distinguished by the work of students who, both explicitly and implicitly, criticized and, in certain surprising ways, ignored the work of an older, nineteenth- and earlier twentieth-century body of scholarship produced in England and North America, and exemplified, in particular, by the work both of Maitland and Davenport. In the 1960s and 1970s there emerged a new, and decidedly self-conscious, social history in which there was an evident desire on the part of its practitioners to investigate and to identify the individual within a village from 'the bottom upwards' through the use of nominative linkage and family reconstruction based upon the records of the manor court. However, after a period of some reflection, it can be justifiably claimed that more recent work has been distinguished by the pursuit of issues that were central to the interests of these late nineteenth- and early twentieth-century scholars who made substantial use of these sources. That the emphasis in more recent research on these sources is showing signs of moving full circle is amply demonstrated by the studies in this volume. We hope the essays in this collection may help to sustain the current momentum so that the circle is finally closed.

The Origins of the English Manorial Court Rolls as a Written Record: A Puzzle*

ZVI RAZI AND RICHARD M. SMITH

IN thirteenth-century England there was a shift from oral to written procedures in manorial courts. It appears that despite the existence of similar courts in England's continental neighbours, such a transition did not occur in them during the medieval period.[1] This is especially striking when we consider the case of French monastic landlords, such as those of Bec and Caen, whose estates contained properties located in both France and England, yet they recorded the proceedings of their English, but not their French, manorial courts. Frederick Maitland argued that the appearance of court rolls in thirteenth-century England was one of the consequences of the efforts made by contemporary landlords to improve the management of their estates. The written manor court record was intended, he wrote

to serve as a check on the manorial officers: it tells the steward and the lord of the occasional profits of the manor, the fines, amercements and perquisites which are to be collected by the bailiff or the reeve.[2]

---

* We are especially grateful to Dr Paul Brand for his extremely careful reading of an earlier version of this essay. His extensive knowledge of the legal history and the sources of the 12th–13th cents. has ensured that we have avoided many pitfalls as well as being able to clarify our argument. We must stress that the views expressed in this article are our own.

[1] Marie-Thérèse Lorcin found in the Rhône Departmental Archives a number of 14th- and 15th-cent. records of the proceedings of rural seigneurial courts from the Lyon area held by ecclesiastical bodies. It appears, however, that the French courts resemble English hundred courts rather than manorial courts. Furthermore, unlike English manorial courts, the French seigneurial courts dealt principally with petty criminal offences rather than with civil matters. See M.-T. Lorcin, 'Les Paysans et la justice dans la région Lyonnaise aux XIVᵉ et XVᵉ siècles', Le Moyen Age, 74 (1968), 269–300. We were able to locate in print only one medieval non-English document which resembles manorial court rolls. Between 1479 and 1493 the Bavarian monastery of Indersdof recorded the proceedings of its manorial court. Similar records, however, were not kept by the monastery before or after this phase. Their creation was due to the personal initiative of the *Probst*, Ulrich Prokorb who ruled with great energy and drive from 1479 to 1493, M. Toch, 'Ethics, emotion and self-interest in Rural Bavaria in the later Middle Ages', *Journal of Medieval History*, 17 (1991), 135–47. Professor Toch informed us that he has been unable to locate in German archives any other medieval manorial court rolls.

[2] *Select Pleas in Manorial Courts*, xiv.

This view on the origins of court rolls has been rejected by Paul Harvey on the grounds that these documents were not primarily a financial record since they contain far too much information that is irrelevant to account- ing procedures.[3] Indeed, it is hard to see why the full proceedings of manorial courts were written down, if landlords were only looking for a means to record the payments made in these courts. There was a simpler and a cheaper solution, namely to make a list of such payments as the bishops of Winchester did on their manorial accounts from the first decade of the thirteenth century.[4]

Unlike Maitland, both Ralph Pugh and Paul Harvey saw in the adop- tion of manorial court rolls an attempt by landlords 'to ensure that justice was done according to precedent'.[5] Although this interpretation gives a better account of the diversity and the quantity of the information found in court rolls, it does not explain the timing of their first appearance as a written record of curial procedure and decision-making. Previously, man- orial courts must have also rendered justice according to precedents by utilizing oral testimony and collective memory. It is, however, difficult to identify those developments in the thirteenth century that caused land- lords to change their minds about the method of recording and referring to precedents.

In this essay, we attempt to provide a more plausible explanation for the shift from oral to written procedures in manorial courts in England. We recognize that such an explanation needs to address the question of why such a shift did not occur in other European countries in the Middle Ages. Unfortunately, we cannot pursue this matter here since a compara- tive study of seigneurial jurisdiction would be required. We will argue that the proceedings of the manor court in England were recorded as a result of an attempt made by thirteenth-century landlords to bring their courts in line with prior developments in royal courts, as a protective measure against the growing popularity of these central courts.

This discussion begins with a review of the developments in the *docu- mentation* of English manors in general and of their courts in particular, and proceeds to investigate when and why landlords began to record the proceedings of their courts. There then follows an examination of the

[3] P. D. A. Harvey, *Manorial Records* (British Records Association, Archives and the User no. 5, London, 1984), 42.
[4] *The Pipe Roll of the Bishopric of Winchester, 1208–9*, ed. H. Hall (London, 1903); *The Pipe Roll of the Bishopric of Winchester 1210–11*, ed. N. R. Holt (Manchester, 1964).
[5] Harvey, *Manorial Records*, 42 and R. B. Pugh (ed.), *Court Rolls of the Wiltshire Lands of Adam de Stratton* (Wilts. Rec. Soc. 24, 1970), 21.

relationship between the royal and the manorial courts. A penultimate section deals with the curial clerks and the impact of manorial record-keeping on the spread of practical literacy.

I

The period between 1175 and 1240 witnessed major developments in the documentation of English manors. An archival corpus emerged and assumed forms that were retained with remarkable durability for the next two centuries or more. The precise chronology of these developments is impossible to establish since the survival pattern of the earliest dated manuscripts most certainly does not bear a very exact relationship to the dates of their origins. While absolute precision is unattainable, the volume of evidence and the pattern it assumes enables us to chart a chronology of development in which we can place considerable trust.

The proliferation of surveys between $c.1180$ and $c.1240$ has long been recognized.[6] By the second half of the thirteenth century the manorial survey had almost become a ubiquitous element in landlords' estate administration and was directed principally to providing a precise overview of manorial resources.[7] From the late 1230s the first extents survive, drawn up initially by royal officials of properties that had fallen into the hands of the Crown and distinguished by the fact that every item described had a valuation given to it. Surveys soon came to assume a common form that derived from the adherence of their makers to the formats in formularies or specimen texts which were very widely circulated.[8]

While manorial landlords were clearly concerned that a regular reckoning was made of all money received or spent, and where appropriate, all corn, livestock, and resources in hand and due to the lord, it was not until the mid-thirteenth century that it was normal to set down in writing the details of the accounts. The earliest known accounts are from the Bishopric

---

[6] For useful discussions, see *Manorial Records of Cuxham*, 72–4 and E. Miller, 'The English Economy in the Thirteenth Century: Implications of Recent Research', *P&P* 28 (1964), 23–6. For examples see *Charters and Custumals of the Abbey of Holy Trinity Caen*, ed. M. Chibnall (British Academy, Records of Social and Economic History, NS 5, London, 1982); *Two Registers Formerly Belonging to the Family of Beauchamp of Hatch*, ed. Sir H. C. Maxwell Lyte (Somerset Rec. Soc. 35, 1920), 2–10.

[7] *Manorial Records of Cuxham*, 74–6. For examples see *The Domesday of St Paul's*, ed. W. H. Hale (Camden Soc. 69, 1858); Two Registers of Beauchamp of Hatch, 10–56.

[8] R. V. Lennard, 'What is a Manorial Extent?', *EHR* 44 (1929), 256–63. Instructions for making an extent can be found in *Statutes of the Realm*, ed. A. Luders *et al.* (11 vols.; Record Comm., 1810–28), i. 242–3 and in *Legal and Manorial Formularies edited from Originals at the British Museum and the Public Record Office in Memory of J. P. Gilson* (Oxford, 1933), 25–9.

of Winchester for 1208–9.[9] Paul Harvey has identified 14 estates for which there are surviving accounts before 1250, over half of which relate to the period after 1240.[10] All but two of these earliest series come from episcopal or monastic estates. The estates concerned are in the majority of cases large and it has been suggested that they reveal an interesting tendency to swarm in a noticeably concentrated fashion within the Winchester area.[11] After 1250 the idea of account-keeping, if practice is reflected in the patterns of surviving documentation, spread rapidly, especially in the 1270s and 1280s.[12] Accounts quickly lost their strong association with larger ecclesiastical and monastic estates, since they were often produced by lay landlords or their managers with only a single manor. While spreading in such a geographically extensive fashion they swiftly came to assume an extraordinary uniformity in their physical layout, reflecting the role played by clerical staffs that were trained to adopt standard procedures, a process facilitated by the widespread circulation of specimens which were interspersed with rules and comments.[13]

The first known written records of the activities of manorial courts are found on the earliest surviving manorial accounts.[14] The enrolled accounts of the bishopric of Winchester beginning in 1209 give for each manor under the heading *Purchasia*, a detailed list of all fines and amercements imposed by the manorial court.[15] It has been suggested that the detail entered into the Winchester accounts implies the absence of court rolls in which the proceedings of manorial courts would have been recorded.[16] A well-preserved set of court books of the Hertfordshire estates of the Abbey of St Albans beginning in 1237 indirectly provide entries from the first known court records; the originals from which these copies were made in the late fourteenth century do not survive.[17] A

---

[9] See n. 3 above.

[10] See *Manorial Records of Cuxham*, 17, Harvey, *Manorial Records*, 25. Professor Harvey provided a more detailed consideration of these issues in an important paper, 'Early manorial accounts: Winchester and elsewhere', delivered at the Fourth Anglo-American Seminar on the Medieval Economy and Society, Leicester, July 1992.

[11] *Manorial Records of Cuxham*, 16–34.   [12] Ibid. 18.

[13] Ibid. 20–5.   [14] See n. 3 above.

[15] e.g. the manor court of Bitterne yielded 19 fines and amercments valued at £15 17s. 10½d. for the year 1210–11. Of these, 16 were paid by named individuals, two by named tithings and one by 5 persons so that they might be released from an obligation to perform harvest works. See the *Pipe Roll of the Bishopric of Winchester, 1210–11*, 5.

[16] W. O. Ault, 'The Earliest Rolls of Manor Courts in England', *Studia Gratiana*, 15 (1972), 511–14.

[17] Abbots Langley (Hertfordshire) Court Book, beginning in 1244 (Sidney Sussex College, Cambridge, MS ii); Barnet (Hertfordshire) Court Book beginning in 1246 (BL, Add MS 40167); Bramfield (Hertfordshire) Court Book, beginning in 1237 (HfdRO, Hertfordshire

Ramsey Abbey cartulary contains a copy of a court roll of 1239–40,[18] but the earliest surviving original court roll is for the English manors of Bec Abbey and dates from 1246.[19] This was included in the selection of manorial court rolls that Maitland edited for the Selden Society in 1888, when he noted the Bec rolls constituted 'the oldest specimen of a court roll that I have seen'.[20] Maitland's observation possesses an accuracy that remains fully intact, despite the ensuing century during which more archives in private and public hands have come to light or been better described. While there are a small number of court rolls that survive for the 1250s, from the 1260s, and especially the 1270s, a very noteworthy increase in numbers is observable. For instance, a survey undertaken by Judith Cripps and Janet Williamson of surviving court rolls that contained the proceedings of courts covering whole communities and with contents sufficiently full to enable their use for demographic reconstruction of the manors concerned, reveals that a significant increase in record-keeping may have occured in the 1260s (see Table 1.1). The court rolls preserved in the Public Record Office make their first appearance in a significant fashion a decade or so later than those in the purposefully selective survey of Cripps and Williamson (see Table 1.2). The discrepancy between these two archival samples may well reflect a more pronounced presence of manors within the administratively more innovative and responsive episcopal and monastic estates that have a prominent place in the Cripps–Williamson survey. The 1260s appear to mark a critical point of departure with further increases occurring across lay and religious estates in the 1270s. The 1270s have also been noted as years in which manorial account-keeping gained in momentum. This rise in the number of series starting in the 1270s is a striking feature of Figure 1.1 which represents an amalgamation of the evidence contained in the Cripps–

County Council Records 40702–5); Cashio (Hertfordshire) Court Book beginning in 1238 (BL, Add MS 40626); Codicote (Hertfordshire) Court Book begining in 1237 (BL, MS Stowe 849); Croxley (Hertfordshire) Court Book begining in 1257 (BL, Add MS 6057); Kingsbury (Hertfordshire) Court Book beginning in 1240 (HfdRO, Gorhambury Deeds, X.D.O; A,B, and C); Newland (Hertfordshire) Court Book beginning in 1244 (HfdRO, Hertfordshire County Council Records 65498–528); Park (Hertfordshire) Court Book beginning in 1237 (BL, Add MS 40625); Sandridge (Hertfordshire) Court Book beginning in 1237 (HfdRO, Hertfordshire County Council Records 40700–1); Winslow (Buckinghamshire) *Extracta Rotulorum* for the years 1237–46 (BL Cart. Harl. 58, F. 30).

[18] *Cartularium Monasterii de Rameseia*, ed. W. H. Hart and P. A. Lyons (3 vols.; Rolls Ser. 79a–c, 1884–93), i. 404–29.

[19] The original sources are deposited in Kings College Library, Cambridge.

[20] *Select Pleas in Manorial Courts*, 42.

TABLE 1.1. *The distribution of starting dates of manorial court rolls deposited in the PRO (List and Index of Court Rolls Preserved in the Public Record Office (London, 1894))*

Years	No. of court rolls
1250s	—
1260s	2 (2.04%)
1270s	22 (22.45%)
1280s	32 (32.65%)
1290s	42 (42.86%)
TOTAL	98 (100%)

TABLE 1.2. *The distribution of starting dates of manorial court rolls deposited in archival repositories surveyed by Judith Cripps and Janet Williamson (see Appendix)*

Years	No. of court rolls
1240s	2 (0.6%)
1250s	6 (1.8%)
1260s	31 (9.6%)
1270s	56 (17.3%)
1280s	38 (11.7%)
1290s	26 (8.0%)
TOTAL	159 (49.0%)

Williamson survey and the series of rolls preserved in the Public Record Office.[21]

In attempting to explain these trends in manorial documentation historians have placed an initial emphasis on the growth in the number of manorial surveys from the 1180s, and especially after 1200. Such a development is regarded as strongly linked with the spread of direct cultivation of manorial demesnes by landlords. The increasing demand for efficient

[21] *List and Index of Court Rolls Preserved in the Public Record Office*, pt. I (London, 1894).

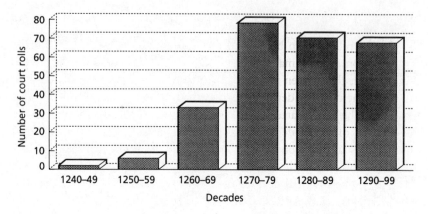

F I G. 1.1 Distribution of starting dates of manorial court roll series deposited in the PRO
and other archival repositories

management required landlords to be better informed about their local
resources; the resort to measured acres and the use of valuations in
manorial extents reflect similar influences which culminated in the appearance of treatises on estate management such as the *Rules* of Robert
Grosseteste of 1240–2 and the *Seneschaucy*.[22]

The manorial account is clearly a product of direct exploitation of
demesne farms by landlords and its appearance during the first decade of
the thirteenth century when this method of estate management was being
widely adopted is surely no coincidence. Direct management of demesne
farms had by the 1220s become widespread and continued thereafter to
be the normal mode of exploitation until the final decades of the fourteenth century when a movement towards the farming of manors got
underway.[23] It is, however, important to note that direct exploitation was
a development peculiar to England and accordingly had very real consequences for the generation of manorial surveys and accounts in a quantity
and in a form that were not replicated in continental Europe. Historians
of medieval England are consequently endowed with a corpus of archival
evidence for the investigation of farming practices, prices, rents, and
wages not generally available to students of such themes working elsewhere in Europe.

---

[22] Harvey, *Manorial Records*, 3–6, 19–24; *Walter of Henley and Other Treatises on Estate
Management and Accounting*, ed. D. Oschinsky (Oxford, 1971), 388–9, 264–5.
[23] Harvey, *Manorial Records*, 5.

II

While the relationship between direct exploitation of demesnes and the proliferation of custumals, surveys, and written accounts can be readily established, the written record of the manorial court, an equally distinctive document in a wider European setting, is less easily explained in this fashion. The last quarter of the twelfth century, while witnessing the emergence of direct demesne farming was also a phase of major legal innovations and is conventionally regarded by legal historians as the period within which the historical foundation of the common law can be located.[24] The essential development was the rise in the royal control of freemen's litigation. As R. C. Van Caenegem succinctly notes, the changes under Henry II constituted a dual phenomenon of 'centralization and specialization'.[25] The reforms meant that an enormous amount of litigation that would previously have originated in the local courts and never moved beyond that locus, now came up before a central body of royal judges. With this accumulation of business in royal hands, a division of labour ensued with itinerant justices operating on the eyres in the counties, others resided and functioned in Westminster and still others, the Bench *coram rege* travelled with the king. They came to assume a cohesiveness as they applied one common law. These increasingly pervasive

---

[24] A subject that cannot be considered without reference to Pollock and Maitland, *History of English Law*. Milsom's alternative model for the origins of the English Common Law appeared in *The Legal Framework of English Feudalism* (Cambridge, 1976). Maitland viewed writs and rules developed in the course of Henry II's reign (1154–89) in opposition to local feudal courts where lords were dominant and where actions concerning land held of them were initiated. Maitland was undoubtedly inclined to regard royal initiatives as developing in deliberate opposition to the feudal courts which were ultimately supplanted. Milsom on the other hand is not inclined to emphasize royal opposition to the feudal world and presents a complex argument in which the Crown is portrayed as wishing only to ensure that writs in such *curiae* functioned according to royal norms. Although unintentional, these actions resulted in the total diminution of the world of local feudal courts. Milsom's reinterpretation has led to a great many reflective review articles and responses. Among the most helpful are: J. Biancalana, 'For Want of Justice: Legal Reforms of Henry II', *Columbia Law Review* 88 (1988), 433–536; R. C. Palmer, 'The Feudal Framework of English Law', *Michigan Law Review*, 79 (1981), 1130–64; J. Hudson, 'Milsom's Legal Structure: Interpreting Twelfth-Century Law', *Tijdschrift voor Rechtsgeschiedenis*, 59 (1991), 47–66; P. Brand, 'The Origins of English Land Law: Milsom and After', in P. Brand, *The Making of the Common Law* (London, 1992), 203–25. The most recent and important interpretation which plays down the extent of the innovation regarding land law associated with the actions of Henry II, see J. Hudson, *Land, Law and Lordship in Anglo-Norman England* (Oxford, 1994). For a valuable and clearly presented pre-Milsom survey of the key issues, see A. Harding, *The Law Courts of Medieval England* (London, 1973), 32–85.

[25] R. C. Van Caenegem, *The Birth of the English Common Law* (2nd edn., Cambridge, 1988), 19.

royal courts were indubitably successful in attracting business. The fact that hundreds of people were prepared to pay substantial sums to have their cases heard in the royal courts suggests a very real preference for royal justice over judgements rendered by feudal or seigneurial justice.[26] It has also been effectively argued that the sheer competence of the experienced judges in the king's courts was a powerful force attracting business to them.[27] It was a justice that combined the reassurance of judicial skill with a broader social voice in so far as through the use made of juries a wider basis was given to decision-making.[28]

How could these developments impact, if at all, upon the vast bulk of the populace, if the establishment of a common law by the Angevin monarchy provided a legal machinery only for free men? By providing a forum for free tenants, as R. H. Hilton has argued, did they not lead to the abandonment of customary tenants to the jurisdiction of the manorial courts? Hilton regards it as an outcome that was consciously sought by landlords that were attempting to intensify the burdens of villeinage in the specific economic circumstances associated with direct demsene exploitation and noteworthy inflation.[29] In this interpretation we observe a monarchy portrayed as attempting to extend royal justice and jurisdiction at the expense of the baron's private courts, but at the same time compensating them by leaving villein tenants bereft of justice or at best exposed to an arbitrary justice in the manorial *curia*. Unlike Hilton, Paul Hyams in his comprehensive study of the royal courts and villeinage has identified the emergence of a common law of villeinage as a by-product, indeed an unintended accident of the reforms that had led to the creation of a common law.[30]

---

[26] Harding, *Law Courts of Medieval England*, 54–5.

[27] Van Caenegem, *Birth of the English Common Law*, xii. See too, R. V. Turner, 'The Reputation of Royal Judges under the Angevin Kings', *Albion*, 11 (1979), 316.

[28] M. T. Clanchy, *England and its Rulers* (Glasgow, 1983), 149 and 146. See too, J. P. Dawson, *A History of Lay Judges* (Cambridge, Mass., 1960), ch. 2 and Van Caenegem, *Birth of the Common Law*, xii.

[29] R. H. Hilton, 'Freedom and Villeinage in England', in R. H. Hilton (ed.), *Peasants, Knights and Heretics: Studies in Medieval English Social History* (Cambridge, 1976), 185–90 and R. H. Hilton, *The Decline of Serfdom in Medieval England* (2nd edn., London and Basingstoke, 1983), 18.

[30] P. R. Hyams, *Kings, Lords and Peasants in Medieval England: The Common Law of Villeinage in the Twelfth and Thirteenth Centuries* (Oxford, 1980), 255–65. It is important to note in relation to issues raised by Hilton and Hyams that R. C. Palmer has constructed an argument which gives legal reform a larger autonomous role in generating certain of the economic changes that are frequently regarded as responsible for direct demsene exploitation and intensified demands upon their customary tenants by landlords. See R. C. Palmer, 'The Economic and Cultural Impact of the Origins of Property 1180–1220', *LHR* 3 (1985),

Whether the crystallization of a 'common law of villeinage' was purposeful or accidental, it is clear that landlords were troubled by the possibility that their villeins might gain access to the royal courts and there is ample evidence that they were moved to insist upon the villein status of those who regarded themselves as free in the early thirteenth century through their use of the *curia regis*. There were equally assertive moves on the part of such tenants to resist what they regarded as the removal of their free status. Hyams notes the increasing precision of pleading in cases in the royal courts of the 1230s and 1240s regarding proof of villein status through their individual's kinship links, their proven liability to pay tallage and their daughter's obligation to pay *merchet*.[31] An intended consequence, therefore, of the growth in business in the king's court was the need perceived by landlords for fuller records of existing custom if potentially costly mistakes were to be avoided.[32] For to lose villeins in an era when their labour services was an important resource for the direct cultivation of their demesnes was a threat that had to be removed or minimized. The proliferation of custumals was undoubtedly another reaction to this threat.[33] However, the recording of what were regarded by royal justices as the hallmarks of villeinage need not have given rise to court rolls that contained written accounts of the activities of both villeins and freemen in forms and in contexts that would have had no bearing upon the proof of their status if such a written record had been presented in the king's court.

It is possible to give undue attention to landlord–villein relations in this matter. Since most landholders had free as well as customary tenants, the growth in business in the king's courts in the 1230s and 1240s posed another threat to them. At the same time as these courts were becoming less accessible to their customary tenants, they were increasingly attracting more of their free tenants by providing them with new and better means of resolving inter-personal and especially land disputes. While

375–96. Palmer argues that the Angevin legal reforms, by giving free tenants increased insulation from lordly control, facilitated the manipulation of land as an economic and fully alienable resource as well as its use for securing loans. The result of this growing certainty was to make land an increasingly liquid resource which had a marked inflationary effect on prices, esp. as these developments coincided with sizeable inflows of silver that were in part determined by a significant trade surplus derived from the burgeoning exportation of raw wool. Palmer's controversial views are worthy of careful consideration since they are at least consistent with the evidence that points to England's very real distinctiveness at this time both with regard to the novelty of legal reform and the severity of the inflationary trend.

[31] Hyams, *Kings, Lords and Peasants*, 266–8 and ch. 8.
[32] R. M. Smith, 'Some Thoughts', *LHR* 1 (1983), 98–102.
[33] For the 'costs', see the sums implied by Harding, *Law Courts of Medieval England*, 55.

only rich peasants could afford the expenses of pleading in the central courts, the county courts were affordable to a larger section of the free tenantry. Landlords had to find a means of limiting their resort to pleading in royal courts, otherwise their own courts would become less profitable and they might lose an important institutional context for controlling the most influential group of their tenants. Moreover, it is hard to see how landlords could have maintained the efficiency of their courts without the regular attendance and co-operation of their free tenants in manors in which such tenants constituted a majority or even a substantial minority of the tenantry. Therefore, some large ecclesiastical landlords, notably the abbeys of St Albans and Bec, must have decided to react to the growing popularity of the royal courts by making their own manorial court more attractive to freeholders.[34] To do this, they introduced to these courts some of the new procedures developed in the royal courts. One of them, introduced in the late twelfth century and rapidly became an intrinsic part of the legal system practised by the central courts, was the recording of the court proceedings.[35]

While we cannot prove that the appearance of manorial court rolls was due to the landlords' attempt to attract free tenants by providing them with better legal services, there is sufficient evidence in the earliest surviving court records to suggest that this indeed might have been the case. A preliminary analysis of a sample of such court rolls from the manors of the Abbey of Bec (1246), Alrewas in Staffordshire, (1259) and Redgrave, a manor of the abbot of Bury St Edmunds (1260) shows the relatively frequent presence in those earliest written court proceedings of freemen engaging in inter-personal plaints with parties who were by no means invariably villeins. Such plaints in relation to those directly concerned with the landlords' seigneurial interest accounted for in excess of a third of all items of court business (see Table 1.3). We also found that entries concerning inter-personal litigation were considerably longer than those directed towards the landlord's interests or claims upon his customary tenants. The prominent place of freeholders in the written proceedings of manor courts held in the 1240s and 1250s is compatible with the hypothesis their emergence as a record was the consequence of the introduction of

---

[34] The abbots of St Albans retained a long-standing dislike of their tenants using 'outside' courts. See Slota, 'Law, Land Transfer and Lordship', 119–38.

[35] The earliest surviving Plea Roll of one of the king's court comes from 1194, but there is some evidence suggesting that the recording of the proceedings of the royal courts began in fact in the 1170s. P. Brand, ' "Multis Vigillis Excogitatem et Inventam": Henry II and the Creation of the English Common Law', *Haskins Society Journal*, 2 (1990), 197–222, repr. in Brand, *Making of the Common Law*, 95. See also Harding, *Law Courts of Medieval England*, 71.

TABLE 1.3. *An analysis of the court business recorded in the rolls of the Abbey of Bec manors for the years 1246–9 and Alrewas, 1259–61*[†]

	Abbey of Bec No. of entries	No. of words	Alrewas No. of entries	No. of words
Matters concerning the lord's seigneurial interests and jurisdiction	92	1,783	104	2,875
Inter-tenant litigation and cases concerning inter-tenant trespasses and violence	30 (24.5%)	1,538 (46.3%)	65 (38.5%)	1,917 (40.0%)
TOTAL	122	3,321	169	4,792

[†] Essoins were excluded from the sample because in the Bec court rolls only a few of them were recorded.
Source: Maitland, *Select Pleas*, 6–21; W. N. Landor, 'Alrewas Court Rolls, 1259–61', *Staffordshire Historical Collection*, NS (1907), 258–93.

procedures firstly developed by the king's courts. Although the introduction
of court rolls was probably due to the landlords' attempt to attract freeholders to their courts, it is clear that once they had adopted this measure
it also enabled them to tighten their control over the customary tenants.[36]

So far, we may have explained why manorial court rolls firstly appear
in the 1230s and 1240s. However, if the surviving court records provide
a chronologically representative sample, the noteworthy 'surge' in the
number of court roll series after 1260 remains to be explained. In the
1230s, 1240s, and 1250s only a small number of large landholders took
positive action to retain their seigneurial jurisdiction over free peasants
because there were other means to do so: under Henry III's slack administration of justice freeholders were compelled by magnates to attend
their private courts, to pay high fines and amercements and even to
answer concerning their freehold without a writ.[37] If such abuses were
tolerated by the government, it is hard to believe that powerful landlords
refrained from using intimidation and coercion to force their small free
tenants to plead in their own rather than in the king's courts. However,
the freeholders who suffered from these abuses were not only peasants,
but also knights and substantial freemen who had by then considerable
political weight within the shires.[38] In order to gain the support of these
locally important people, the reforming barons took, in the Provisions of
Westminster of 1259, several measures to protect freeholders against the
enforcement of suits to private courts and against other abuses of seigneurial jurisdiction.[39] Although the earl of Gloucester and some other
powerful barons refused in the 1260s to accept the limitations on their
jurisdiction, many others did, and their number must have risen with the
re-enactment at the end of the civil war of the Provisions of Westminster
in the Statutes of Marlborough (1267).[40] Consequently during this period

---

[36] e.g. in the Bec sample inter-tenant litigation accounted for 46 per cent of the words
and only 24 per cent of the entries and at Alrewas inter-tenant litigation accounted for 38
per cent of the entries but marginally more than 40 per cent of the written text.

[37] R. F. Treharne, *The Baronial Plan of Reform, 1258–63* (Manchester, 1932; repr. 1971),
71, 134–8, 159, 166, 169–70, 176–7; D. A. Carpenter, 'King, Magnates and Society: The
Personal Rule of King Henry III, 1234–58', *Speculum*, 60 (1985), 63–6; J. R. Maddicott,
'Magna Carta and the Local Community, 1215–59', *P&P* 102 (1984), 57–9.

[38] Ibid. 55, 60–3; Carpenter, 'King, Magnates and Society', 65–6; Treharne, *Baronial
Plan of Reform*, 348–54.

[39] The issues are addressed in Articles 1, 2, 3, 5, 11, 16, 17, and 18 of the Provisions of
Westminster. See R. F. Treharne and I. J. Sanders (eds.), *Documents of the Baronial
Movement of Reform and Rebellion, 1258–67* (Oxford, 1973), 138–45.

[40] Maddicott, 'Magna Carta and the Local Community', 61; Treharne, *Baronial Plan of
Reform*, 139–40, 160–4, 364, 378–9; *Statutes of the Realm*, i. 15–25.

many more landlords than before had to attract rather than to coerce free peasants to attend and to plead in their manorial courts, which they did by 'modernizing' these courts. It is also possible that they did this in order to appease the peasants who took sides and were deeply involved in the civil war, as David Carpenter has recently shown.[41] The plausibility of this interpretation is strengthened by Alfred May's study of manorial amercements which indicates that jurisdictional amercements levied in the Winchester and Bec manorial courts declined sharply after 1259.[42] If indeed the baronial reform movement and civil war led many landlords to improve the legal services of their manorial courts by imitating the superior novel procedures of the royal courts, it explains why considerably more manorial court rolls survived from the 1260s than from previous decades.

The proliferation of the records of these courts accelerated even more in the 1270s and the 1280s. During this period strong measures were taken by Edward I to curb abuses of power by local government officials as well as by magnates and knights and to limit seigneurial jurisdiction.[43] Therefore, it must have become much more difficult for landlords to prevent their free tenants from pleading in the royal courts and they had instead to make their manorial courts more attractive. Moreover, a quantitative analysis done by Paul Brand of business in the Common Bench suggests that the royal courts became in the 1270s and 1280s considerably more successful in attracting litigants.[44] This development, it seems, provided further incentive for landlords to improve the quality of the facilities of their own manorial courts to induce their free tenants to continue using them. It is likely, therefore, that during the 1270s and 1280s the number of manor courts which were brought in line with the development of the royal courts increased considerably and so did the survival rate of court roll series (see Figure 1.1).

[41] May, 'An Index of Thirteenth-Century Peasant Impoverishment?', 399–402. For cautious comments on May's methodology, see J. B. Post, 'Manorial Amercements and Peasant Poverty', *EcHR* 2nd ser. 28 (1975), 304–11. Post's criticisms only alter the mean absolute level of the fines derived by May's methods and do not in any sense detract from his observations on the unambiguous downard trend in rates of amercement over the course of the late thirteenth century. Similar developments concerning the emergence of smaller amercements have been detected on other manors in the eastern counties of England. See Smith, 'Some Thoughts on "Hereditary" and "Proprietary" Rights', 104–5.

[42] D. A. Carpenter, 'English Peasants in Politics, 1258–1267', *P&P* 136 (1992), 3–42.

[43] J. R. Maddicot, 'Edward I and the Lessons of the Baronial Reform in Local Government, 1258–80', in P. R. Coss and D. Lloyd (eds.), *Thirteenth-Century England*, I (Woodbridge, 1985), 1–30.

[44] There was a doubling of Common Bench plea-role remembrances between 1260 and 1280 and a 78 per cent increase between 1280 and 1290. P. Brand, *The Origins of the English Legal Profession* (Oxford, 1992), 24.

III

The landlords' need to compete with the royal courts for litigants in civil matters not only had consequences for record-keeping but was similarly responsible for important changes in legal procedures in the manorial courts. The constant presence of the *curia regis* as an external reference point ensured that landlords were unable to ignore the services those 'higher' courts sought to extend to freeholders, who in principle were always at risk to drift towards them in search of the services which were most appropriate for their needs. Landlords in seeking to encourage freeholders to attend their courts were obliged to refashion them so that they came to resemble the king's courts in certain key respects. In the long term seigneurial threats or force were insufficient to engender a positive response from such free tenants. We now proceed therefore to discuss in a limited fashion, given the space at our disposal, the degree to which legal innovations in the royal courts penetrated into the courts of the manors and the results that ensued with the shift from an oral to a written law. We will also consider what the fulfilment of certain public functions by these private courts through the View of Frankpledge implied for other procedural developments.

Maitland, in his characteristically perceptive way, wrote in the introduction to edited extracts from certain early court rolls: 'We approach our rolls ... with a suspicion that the courts which they reveal will be undergoing a transformation, will be suffering the intrusion of new elements, presentments by jury and trial by jury, elements hardly compatible with their old constitution. We shall not be disappointed.'[45] Since Maitland other commentators have concluded that the lords of the halmotes borrowed freely from the procedural forms used in the king's courts, although they have not all agreed with Maitland concerning his interpretation of the consequences of these developments.[46]

On one matter, there is agreement: in the earliest records of the manorial courts it appears that the entire corpus of court suitors fulfilled the roles of 'fact-finder' and 'judgement-renderer' and the lord's steward presided over them as a moderator rather than as a judge. The plaintiff produced his 'complaint witness' whose role was to support his claim whilst the defendant brought his own oath-helpers (the number of which

---

[45] *Select Pleas in Manorial Courts*, lxviii.

[46] W. O. Ault, *Private Jurisdiction in England* (New Haven, 1923), 168–9; Dawson, *History of Lay Judges*, 201; J. S. Beckerman, 'Procedural Innovation and Institutional Change in Medieval English Manorial Courts', *LHR* 10 (1992), 197–252.

would be determined by the court) to provide support to the latter's oath of denial. By the end of the thirteenth century in all curial arenas oath-swearing or the compurgation ritual was regarded as an inferior mode of trial because of its dependence upon formalistic ceremony which lacked a concern to establish the facts of a dispute.[47]

However, it is clear that not all types of cases were tried by compurgation. Disputes involving land were settled by the sale to one or other of the disputants of the privilege of having an inquest to decide on the facts in disputes between the parties. In the early written court proceedings these inquests were generally undertaken by the full body of court suitors. None the less in the earliest surviving full set of court proceedings for the manors of the Abbey of Bec which start in 1246, references are encountered of special juries of trial (usually twelve persons) authorized to render verdicts in land disputes.[48] In the courts of St Albans' manors whose records from 1237 survive in edited form in the court books drawn up over a century later, disputes over land are shown as being investigated through inquests conducted by juries as well as by the whole halmote or vill.[49] Of course, manorial surveys of the late twelfth and early thirteenth centuries were produced using information provided by the testimony of juries drawn from a cross-section of tenants.[50] Both the trial jury in land disputes in the manorial courts, and the inquest jury of the manorial survey parallel developments in the royal courts where the inquest jury was fully instituted by the 1170s. As older modes of proof waned and the search for 'facts' became a more pervasive feature of trial procedure it was less feasible to demand a judgement of the whole court in every case, irrespective of whether it involved land or not. As juries displaced inquests by the whole court in land disputes so trial by jury, almost simultaneously, came to be employed in personal plaints.[51] Requests for trial by jury became increasingly more important and John Beckerman sees the first quarter of the fourteenth century as 'the heyday of jury trial in English manor courts'.[52] Jury trial did not, however, completely displace compurgation and some, although a distinct minority, retained it even

---

[47] Beckerman, 'Procedural Innovation and Institutional Change', 202–7.

[48] *Select Pleas in Manorial Courts*, 9, 13, 14, 15, 17, 18, 20, and 21.

[49] For example, Levett, *Studies in Manorial History*, 21, 302, 303, 307 for cases of inquest by the whole hall-moot, and 306, 321, and 326 for jury inquests.

[50] For the role played by juries in drawing up manorial surveys see R. V. Lennard, 'Early Manorial Juries', *EHR* 77 (1962), 511–18; Ault, *Private Jurisdiction*, 168–9 and *Charters and Custumals*, xlvi.

[51] Beckerman, 'Procedural Innovation and Institutional Change', 212–19.

[52] Ibid. 214.

in cases of violent and forcible trespass which were categories that a common-law judgement of 1260 had deemed to be inappropriately tried by that means.[53]

Beckerman in his important work on these developments has shown how the emergence of the trial jury coincided with, and indeed stimulated, the use of documentary proof as evidence in the establishment of 'custom'. His argument revolves around the difficulties encountered by juries in both remembering past practices and failing to have actual eye witnesses to events that were to become the subject of later dispute.[54] Beckerman's interpretation of developments is largely, although not exclusively, based on the records of the manor courts of the abbots of St Albans and the Yorkshire manor of Wakefield. Vouching the court roll, especially in land disputes, came into general use on these manors during the second half of the thirteenth century. Beckerman goes so far as to state that the court roll, especially in land disputes came into general use on these manors during the second half of the thirteenth century.[55] Beckerman's pioneering work is of very great importance in drawing attention to the manner in which the emergence of written records of court proceedings served to reduce the interpretative variance surrounding the rights of parties, whether lord or tenant.

Another innovation in the procedures of manorial courts which owes its origins to reforms made by Henry II was the use of presentment juries as a way of investigating and punishing breaches of manorial custom or infringement of seigneurial rights. According to the Assize of Clarendon of 1166 criminal offences were to be presented by sworn juries at the Sheriff's tourn. Landlords eventually saw that similar procedures were adopted on the Views of Frankpledge, privately held by seigneurial officers in conjunction with manorial courts and increasingly profitable to their lords.[56] Initially, sworn juries in manorial courts presented only offences against the King's peace. Offences against manorial customs and seigneurial rights were generally brought by manorial officers who had to support the accusation with suit and complaint witness. As this procedure was slow and inefficient, landlords subsequently adopted presentment

---

[53] T. F. T. Plucknett, *A Concise History of the Common Law* (5th edn., London, 1956), 126–7; *Select Cases of Procedure Without Writ under Henry III*, ed. H. G. Richardson and G. O. Sayles (Selden Soc. 60, 1941), 214.

[54] Beckerman, 'Procedural Innovation and Institutional Change', 219–26.

[55] Ibid. 224.

[56] Maitland had noted the link between Henry II's reforms and the adoption of presentment procedures in the Leet Courts or Views of Frankpledge in his introducton to *Select Pleas in Manorial Courts*, xxxvi.

juries to deal with such offences. Presentment reduced the likelihood of manorial officers, now no longer the originators of suits, from being subject of reprisals from their neighbours. Furthermore, the person presented by a jury almost invariably was summarily convicted.

However, the introduction of presentment juries into manorial court business to do with manorial custom and seigneurial rights lagged some way behind its application to the communal and public business of the view. An examination of pre-1300 court-keeping manuals and formularies and thirteenth-century legal text such as *Britton*, *Fleta*, and *Mirror of Justices* by Beckerman shows that presentment applied only to a very restricted range of business concerning criminal and public business of the View of Frankpledge. However a list of articles composed around 1307 contains a more extensive list of those concerned with presentment that extend well beyond criminal and public matters and the *modus tenendi curias* from the formulary book of St Albans Abbey (variously dated to 1342 by Maitland and 1382–8 by Levett) reveals an exceedingly large number of questions to which presenting juries were required to respond.[57] An investigation of Redgrave and Halesowen court rolls supports Beckerman's depiction of a sluggishly paced move towards the introduction of presentment juries to areas concerning seigneurial rights and manorial custom.[58] It is likely that this sluggish pace was due to a resistance by the peasants to the implementaton of a procedure which was largely to their disadvantage. Indeed, Beckerman documented the resistance to the introduction of presentment juries on one of the manors of St Albans Abbey and exposed the forceful way in which seigneurial authority imposed its will in this matter.[59]

The wider resort to presentment juries in manorial courts strengthened the landlords' position *vis-à-vis* their tenants and, in the long term, it led to the weakening of the civil protection afforded by these courts to the peasantry.[60] At the same time other developments in the legal instruments of these courts brought numerous benefits to tenants by providing means for recording economic transactions of indescribable variety. Furthermore, these same tenants derived very considerable security in their tenure of customary land by inheritance and transmission through

---

[57] Beckerman, 'Procedural Innovation and Institutional Change', 234–6.
[58] Smith, 'Some Thoughts', 104–5. See too, Ch. 9 below.
[59] Beckerman, 'Procedural Innovation and Institutional Change', 232–4.
[60] Beckerman shows how by 1400 many common inter-tenant offences such as assault, battery, slander, the obstruction of crops, and trespasses by animals, by being presented rather than acted upon by plaint, ceased to be remedied in manorial courts by compensation of the victim. Beckerman, 'Customary Law in English Manorial Courts', 107–10.

alienation and lease. We can observe a noteworthy trend through the late thirteenth and early fourteenth centuries towards a standardization of terms and forms in conveyancing procedures which were either responses to influences emananating from, or replications of, forms employed by the common law.[61]

These linkages were particularly apparent in the way that manorial courts reflected reforms relating to conveyancing practices under common law in Edward I's reign. The statute *Quia Emptores* in 1290 made substitution the accepted form for grant in fee simple.[62] Previously, subinfeudation had been the usual practice. One purpose of this change was the assignment of direct responsibility for rents and incidents to the new tenant and the requirement of the incoming tenant to pay an entry fine which mirrors some features of 'surrender and admittance' concerning customary land in manorial courts. Such a procedure became the principal means by which customary land was identified as being transferred in the late thirteenth- and early fourteenth-century manorial courts.[63] It constitutes a development that has been regarded as forming an element in a broader change in conveyancing practices involving both freehold and customary land in the middle of Edward I's reign. Indeed it inclines us to suppose that the direction of the causal relationship should not invariably be seen as flowing from the king's to the manorial court. For the grant of surrender and admittance in manorial courts over the decade prior to *Quia Emptores* suggests that lords were simultaneously incorporating such procedures into their private courts while encouraging statutory reform in the wider legal system.[64] Doubtlessly, *Quia Emptores*

---

[61] Smith, 'Some Thoughts', 107–12.

[62] S. F. C. Milsom, *Historical Foundations of the Common Law* (2nd edn., London, 1981), 114–15.

[63] Smith, 'Some Thoughts', 107–9; L. Slota, 'Law, Land Transfer and Lordship', 120–5.

[64] For reflections on the link between surrender and admittance in the manorial court and the common law of conveyance in the estate of the abbot of St Albans before *Quia Emptores*, see Slota, 'Law, Land Transfer and Lordship', 123. Slota notes how sensitive the abbot's administration was to the possibility that transfer of villein tenements by surrender and admittance could come dangerously close to resembling the procedure of substitution which *Quia Emptores* had made the accepted form for the transfer of free tenements. On this estate an adaptation which was an evident response to this concern emerged as land so transferred was stated to be held *ad voluntatem domini* or *in villenagio* or *per virgam* to ensure that villein grants could not be mistaken for grants of free tenure. Slota notes the links between central and seigneurial courts that followed from the fact the the seneschals who presided over the abbot's own court for his free tenants were also likely to represent the abbey in the king's courts. In observing how quickly the forms of *Quia Emptores* are reproduced in villein charters at Peterborough Abbey in the late 13th cent., Edmund King suggests that the change shows 'not so much the quickness of any "reaction" as that feudal society was a single entity' (King, *Peterborough Abbey*, 103–4).

gave this development additional momentum and presentment procedures served to embed it more deeply as a conventional and routinized practice.[65]

A particularly noteworthy instance of the incorporation of the common law of land-conveyancing into manorial courts and into the procedures relating to customary land is provided by the entail. The statute *De Donis* of 1285 protected the intention of donors from subsequent frustration. It ordained that when land was granted to a man and his wife and the heirs of their bodies, or to one person and the heirs of his or her body, the will of the donor *in forma doni* was to be observed. It is remarkable how rapidly the transfer of customary land with conditional arrangements, so highly reminiscent of those that *De Donis* was specifically designed to protect, began to be observed in manorial court proceedings of the 1280s and 1290s.[66]

It has also been noted that at approximately the same time as *De Donis*, it became a not uncommon practice among the more substantial freeholders to establish jointure arrangements.[67] When formally executed, jointures ensured that the land in question would be held in joint tenancy for their two lives by husband and wife, and by the survivor alone after the death of the other partner. Such arrangements involving customary land and married customary tenants can be found in manorial court rolls from the 1290s.[68]

Another development bearing more directly on the monitoring of female rights in customary land than jointure also has its origin in the king's court. The common law established a formal procedure to record land transfers made by husbands in the course of a marriage. A formal procedure involving the examination of the wife in the court and the levying of

---

[65] Smith, 'Some Thoughts', 109.

[66] Maitland perceptively observed an example of entail in the 1291 manorial court proceedings of Weedon Bec in Northamptonshire and remarked on its proximity to the recently enacted *De Donis*, *Select Pleas in Manorial Courts*, 40; In the manor court of Redgrave, Suffolk in 1290 three land transactions make reference to remainders for other lives in the event of the donees, dying without heirs of their body, Smith, 'Women's Property Rights', 188. In an analysis of the St Albans manor courts of Park and Codicote, 31 of 33 entails in the former and 45 of 48 in the latter manor occurred after 1285, Slota, 'Law, Land Transfer and Lordship', 125–6.

[67] It has been observed that among gentry and lawyer families that the formal execution of jointures, strictly defined as land held in joint tenancy for their two lives by husband and wife and by the survivor alone after the death of one partner, were not much older than Edward I's reign, see K. B. McFarlane, *The Nobility of Later Medieval England* (Oxford, 1973), 65.

[68] Smith, 'Women's Property Rights', 184–7, and for further developments in the late 14th and 15th cents., see Smith, 'Coping With Uncertainty', 43–67.

a fine in the event of her land being conveyanced to a third party ensured that her subsequent claims over land in her own right were barred.[69] It is noteworthy that in the earliest court roll series from the 1240s through to the 1270s land transfers are rarely recorded as being undertaken by conjugal pairs and no written record was preserved of the wife's attitude to such transactions in land to which her dower rights were attached.[70] In the last two decades of the thirteenth century manorial courts began to adopt a practice of formal examination of the wife to establish her agreement to such sales in which she and her husband had joint rights.[71]

All these developments—surrender and admittance, entails, jointures, and the formal examination of married women when they disposed of property with their spouse—reveal how intimately related were manorial and royal courts. They suggest the obvious possibility of a move towards the standardization of customary procedures concerning the tenure and transfer of land. While the variability of patterns from place to place should not be understressed or ignored, they nevertheless reveal some detectable common denominators across English manors that would have surely been less apparent if manorial custom had not come under the influence of the king's court and a written record of its proceedings not been kept.[72]

[69] Pollock and Maitland, *History of English Law*, ii. 413 and J. S. Loengard, '"Of the Gift of her Husband": English Dower and Its Consequences in the Year 1200', in J. Kirshner and S. F. Wemple (eds.), *Women of the Medieval World* (Oxford, 1985), 143–67.

[70] On the relative frequency in the earliest court roll series of disputes involving a widow's claim to dower rights in land transferred previously by the late husband to a third party see Smith, 'Women's Property Rights', 179–80. For similar features detectable in the earliest rolls of the *Curia Regis*, see the comments of G. D. Hall in his review of *Curia Regis Rolls of the Reign of Henry III, 9–10 Henry III* (London: HMSO, 1957) in *EHR* 74 (1959), 108.

[71] For the late 13th- and early 14th-cent. emergence of the formal examination of the wife in customary land transfers see Smith 'Women's Property Rights', 180–4 and for subsequent developments see Smith, 'Coping with Uncertainty', 54–60.

[72] It should not be supposed that those 'influences' that are viewed as emanating from the king's courts led to a complete uniformity in procedures in manorial courts or in the physical appearance of court rolls. One needs only minimal familiarity with these medieval sources to realize that there was very considerable variety from place to place and over time in the types of business that came before these courts and the important role left for local custom which could and certainly did assume an entirely arbitrary character. Lloyd Bonfield makes these points most forcefully in Ch. 3 of this volume, although it must be stressed that he is not concerned in that essay, which is largely concerned with responding to Paul Hyams's argument in Ch. 2, with providing answers to why these courts maintained a written record of their proceedings or why England when compared with her European neighbours appears unique in having generated a source of this character. For the variable nature of 'custom' and the possibility of its 'invention', see Smith, 'Some Thoughts', 122–8 and C. Dyer, 'Les Cours manoriales', *Études Rurales*, 103–4 (1986), 22–3. See, however, the remarks of Britnell, *The Commercialisation of English Society*, 140–4, which are consistent with the arguments of this chapter.

IV

The influences extending from the king's courts have been stressed in our preceding discussion of procedural changes within the manorial courts whose proceedings were increasingly likely to have been preserved in writing from c.1260. Of course, it was only after 1170 or 1180 that the king's government had also become more heavily dependent on documents. This dependence upon the written record had, over the ensuing century, extended down to the levels of the manor and village. Michael Clanchy has made tentative, but illuminating, estimates of the very considerable expansion of documentary production as the royal bureaucracy experienced a growth in its personnel as well as becoming more differentiated in skills and expertise.[73] Simultaneously an English legal profession emerged around the common law to be unambiguously recognizable by the second half of the thirteenth century when business at Common Bench was growing at a particularly fast pace.[74]

Clanchy regards all of these developments as stimulating a practical or utilitarian literacy, since in England even outside the ambit of royal government and the common law, there was a substantial deepening in the availability and broadening of the functional necessity of clerical skills.[75] Such skills were also spread more widely across space and constituted a feature of English society that was both a *cause* and a *consequence* of the need to produce a corpus of manorial documents that was certainly growing significantly in bulk after 1260. Our knowledge of those who made up the body of clerks who produced this documenation and of how their skills were acquired is still very limited. However, Paul Harvey in his meticulous investigation of the history of manorial accounting in the thirteenth century, particularly, his charting of what he has termed the shift from 'Phase 1' to 'Phase 2' accounting, has identified certain features of document creation that may also have applied to the production of court rolls. Harvey has shown 'Phase 1' accounts to have been associated with large estates and shared a common tendency in being produced in an enrolled form by the clerks or scribes of the estate's central administration. 'Phase 2' of account production, Harvey believes, begins after 1260

---

[73] M. T. Clanchy, *From Memory to Written Record, England 1066–1307* (2nd edn., Oxford, 1993), 57–62.

[74] Brand, *Origins of the English Legal Profession*, 50–69.

[75] Clanchy, *From Memory to Written Record*, 46–51, 247 and 286. See too, M. B. Parkes, 'The Literacy of the Laity', in D. Daiches and A. Thorlby (eds.), *The Medieval World* (London, 1973), 555–77.

or 1270 and is distinguished by its association with far greater decentralization of estate management with the local bailiff or reeve assuming sole and direct responsibility for his charge to the estate's central organization. In Phase 2 the accounts were drawn up locally by a clerk who was paid by the reeve or bailiff. Such clerks most likely hailed from a new or much enlarged class of professional writers, drafters of letters, conveyancers. The most striking evidence in favour of this view is that the accounts of different manors within the same estate were written in different hands; this was a feature which Harvey regards as indicative of the employment of *local* clerks. Notwithstanding the move to decentralization of estate administration, the accounts produced under the new management regime assumed a far more standardized appearance than those of Phase 1. This greater uniformity of appearance and content reflected influences deriving from the deliberate diffusion of ideas and methods between estates and the use of sample and model accounts.[76]

There is also sufficient evidence to suggest that the means to train jobbing clerks who might combine their scribal activities for manorial offices with miscellaneous tasks for other local clients were provided in Oxford and possibly elsewhere by such courses as *ars dictaminis*. These courses, taught on the fringes of the university, offered a combination of legal and practical education with perhaps a small amount of grammar and rhetoric. In England in the thirteenth century *dictamen* was especially noteworthy for its association with basic clerical skills such as accountancy and conveyancing, the drafting of legal documents, perhaps some French, the language used for the practice of the law.[77] As Harvey has suggested, even if a relatively small proportion of the clerks who wrote up the manorial documnents were trained in this way, through their own pupils and their pupils' pupils, they would have constituted a significant force helping to diffuse both skills and a standardized set of procedures which combined to give manorial court rolls a more structured appearance.[78]

The developments that were associated with the move away from highly centralized account-keeping, and the increasing use of literate lower-order bureaucrats who operated from bases that were firmly planted

---

[76] *Manorial Records of Cuxham*, 12–34.

[77] H. G. Richardson, 'Business Training in Medieval Oxford', *AHR* 46 (1940–1), 259–80, 'Letters of the Oxford *dictatores*', in H. E. Salter and W. A. Pantin (eds.), *Formularies which Bear on the History of Oxford c.1204–1420* (2 vols.; Oxford Hist. Soc. 4–5, 1942), i. 331–54, and 'An Oxford Teacher of the Fifteenth Century', *Bulletin of the John Rylands Library*, 23 (1939), 436–57.

[78] *Manorial Records of Cuxham*, 21.

upon the manors, also had implications for the role of the steward. It seems that manorial courts, following the resumption of direct management of demesnes in the late twelfth century, were held by stewards, who also assumed the responsibility for the whole estate, regularly touring the manors, inspecting the bailiff's and reeve's conduct of affairs. This hierarchical arrangement fell away after 1260 as an increasing proportion of stewards no longer assumed the duties of inspecting the actvities of their subordinate officers who were able to act with considerable independence. Under these conditions the duties of the steward were becoming confined to holding courts.[79] As the role of the steward became more restricted and probably more specialized, we also are able to detect changes in the character of the rolls produced in his court. The earliest court rolls occasionally reflect the additional duties of the steward when items to do with the demesne farms are included as unpredictable *addenda* or *memoranda*.[80] However, such matters not strictly related to the manorial court are lost from the rolls as the steward shifts from being an estate manager to a lawyer. To assist them in fulfilling this more specialized, legalistic role, stewards had at their disposal treatises on court-keeping or may have acquired the necessary expertise through formal tuition in legal skills, through training in the *ars dictaminis* at Oxford, or by being taught by those who had been so trained. That the *ars dictaminis* most likely taught such matters is indicated by the treatise *de placitis et curiis tenendis* written or edited by John of Oxford in the second half of the thirteenth century.[81]

In general, however, we find that the treatises on court-keeping were written in French for the stewards, whereas the rules and specimens for writing court rolls were written in Latin for the clerks. A similar linguistic distinction applied to the treatises on estate management for the bailiffs and rules and specimens for manorial accounting for the clerks.[82] The increasing professionalization of the 'lawyers' who held the courts in association with the growing resort to presentment procedures which we discussed earlier, helped to give a more regular format to court rolls which between the 1270s and the early fourteenth century grew in length. They did so, in part, because of a genuine growth in business, but also because individual entries were enlarged as clerks diligently introduced

---

[79] Ibid. 29.   [80] Ibid. 80–1.

[81] *Court Baron*, 68–78; see too, T. F. T. Plucknett, *Early English Legal Literature* (Cambridge, 1958), 88–9 and *Walter of Henley*, 29–32. Also relevant is R. Evans and R. J. Faith, 'A Formulary of About 1300', in *Bodleian Library Record*, 13 (1988–91), 324–8.

[82] *Manorial Records of Cuxham*, 81.

additional wordage through the application of set formulae for many
categories of business, particularly those to do with land transactions.[83]

In the course of the second half of the thirteenth century the increasingly decentralized estate administration had produced a more functionally differentiated manorial bureaucracy which in seeking to record its
activities made widespread use of a small army of jobbing clerks. The
latter were present in sufficient numbers, particularly through the service
they gave to manorial stewards, to have created a notable occupational
category in rural communities.[84] Many would have combined their clerical pursuits with farming or related actvities in the local rural economy,
as did a surprisingly large number of identifiable clerks appearing in the
court rolls of Halesowen in Worcestershire and Redgrave in Suffolk in
the late thirteenth and early fourteenth centuries. As such persons, who
almost certainly played an important role in English medieval rural society, have been both undervalued and under-researched by students of
that society, it is worthwhile setting out relevant evidence from sample
periods from these two detailed and nearly complete series of court rolls.

The names of fourteen people who acted as clerks and described as
'clericus' or 'le clerk' appear in the Halesowen court rolls between 1270
and 1349. Thirteen clerks can be identified as active in the Redgrave
manorial courts between 1260 and 1300. There is sufficient evidence to
positively identify only four of the fourteen from Halesowen and four
of the thirteen clerks from Redgrave.[85] Three of the identifiable clerks
in Halesowen were freeholders and one a bondman; in Redgrave two

---

[83] Harvey, *Manorial Records*, 51–3.

[84] For innovative remarks on this subject and some highly pertinent examples of individuals involved in these occupations see *Manorial Records of Cuxham*, 36–42. See too, an
endorsement of Harvey's views in Britnell, *Commercialisation of English Society*, 80–1. It
might be cautiously suggested that to focus heavily on an argument that regards the demand
for clerical skills as deriving exclusively from the needs experienced by manorial administrations is to miss other sources of demand such as that associated with the writing of
peasant charters. See the growth in the number of charters that can be dated and assigned
to the second half of the 13th cent. in the register known as the *Carte nativorum*, *Carte
Nativorum: A Peterborough Abbey Cartulary of the Fourteenth Century*, ed. C. N. L. Brooke
and M. M. Postan (Northants Rec. Soc., vol. 20, 1960), xviii.

[85] e.g. it is impossible to know if the name 'Ralph clericus' noted three times in the
Halesowen court rolls of 1270 and again in 1302 and 1305, decribes one or two persons.
Court Rolls of the Manor of Hales, 1270–1307, ed. J. Amphlett, S. G. Hamilton and R. A.
Wilson (3 vols; Worcs. Hist. Soc., 1910–33), i. 5–6, 8, 13; iii. 463, 500. Likewise in the case
of Redgrave, it is not possible to establish whether the 'Richard clericus', who appeared as
a pledge in 1273 and 1274, was the same person who appeared in 1299 and 1300 when in
both years he acted as a pledge and an essoin, and his wife was amerced for brewing against
the assize. University of Chicago Bacon MS 2, courts of 20.4.1273 and 6.3.1274; courts of
12.11.1299, 11.2.1300, 6.6.1300 and 17.10.1300.

of the four whose identity could be specified were villeins and two were free men. Others who carried the name 'clericus' deriving from a father previously described as clerk are excluded from the group of 27 individuals in this composite sample.[86]

Alexander or Tandi of Kelmestowe the clerk, a customary tenant from the township of Romsley, is mentioned for the first time in 1274.[87] However, it would seem that he had been active in Halesowen from the late 1250s.[88] Alexander's court appearances do not provide any evidence relating to his activities as a clerk, but they reveal that he was engaged in arable and pastoral farming. He was amerced a few times for having brewed against the assize of ale, was elected once as an ale taster, served once in an inquest jury and acted as pledge on four occasions.[89] He was married and had three sons and a daughter.[90]

Roger Coc the clerk (1293–1323), a middling freeholder from the township of Hill, although better documented than Alexander of Kelmestowe, leaves no evidence in the court proceedings of his clerical work.[91] Roger's court appearances suggest that although he grew corn he specialized in pastoral farming.[92] Such an emphasis on his pastoral husbandry may explain why, unlike other tenant-clerks, he was not engaged in brewing. We know that he employed hired labour since two of his maids are noted

---

[86] The fact that 3 of the 8 clerks identified in Halesowen and Redgrave court rolls were unfree casts considerable doubt on a recent claim that one of the main aims of the rebels of 1381 was to break the association of unfreedom and illiteracy. It is maintained that unfree peasants were excluded from writing, and that confirmed their unfreedom and the rightness of it (S. Justice, *Writing and Rebellion: England in 1381* (Berkeley and Los Angeles, 1994), 37). The author also makes a fantastic claim that peasants' land charters came from the royal chancery (Ibid. 36).

[87] An entry recorded in the roll of 1295 reveals that the names 'Alexander' and 'Tandi' of Kelmstoew describe the same person, *Court Rolls of the Manor of Hales*, ii. 336. In the court held in April 1274 he is noted as Alexander de Kelmestowe and in the court held in August of the same year he is called 'Alexander clericus', ibid. 50 and 57. As Clemens, Alexander's son is noted in the court rolls of June 1294 as 'nativus' it can be assumed that Alexander was of unfree status, ibid. iii. 174.

[88] His son Henry became a landholder in 1281, ibid. iii. 168. Since the minimum age for holding land in Halesowen was 20, we can assume that in 1281 Henry was at least that age and his father no younger than his early 40s.

[89] Ibid. 50, 57, 151, 159, 178, 188, 191; ii. 584–5; iii. 12, 105, 164, 168, 170, 173.

[90] Ibid. ii. 595, 599, 607; iii. 209, 212, 216.

[91] He is sometimes noted as 'Rogerus Coc clericus' but more often as 'Rogerus le Coc', ibid. ii. 249, 359, 361, 362, 364.

[92] He is noted very frequently for trespassing on the lord's and tenants' land with his animals, e.g. in 1311 he was amerced twice for trespassing on the lords land with his beasts. BRL 346233. In 1317 John Laysal was required to pay him 7*d*. for harming the cow he had leased from him and in 1319 Roger was amerced for releasing two impounded cows without permission, BRL 346236, 346237.

in 1309 and 1311.[93] Roger Coc acted fifteen times as a pledger and was elected four times as a juror.[94]

Walter Clericus of Redgrave, held at least 12 acres of customary land, that he left behind on his death which cannot be precisely dated because of a loss of certain court rolls in the late 1270s. He was survived by a widow and two sons, Robert and Walter as his heirs. We also know of a daughter, for whom he paid merchet to marry in 1275.[95] In his adult life he had steadily accumulated land through purchase of small plots. His largest individual purchase, totalling 1 acre 3 rods was made from his brother Richard Stanmer in 1269. He is distinguished by being an active pledge in the Redgrave manorial court. Beginning in 1260, he went on to act as a pledge sixteen times before 1279.[96] He received that service from others only for the fines he paid when purchasing land and never as a defendant in a plaint or as a result of being amerced in the court. Such an assymetry in pledging patterns is typical of clerks as a whole in both of these manors, but especially of those who, like Walter Clericus and Alexander of Kelmstowe, based their livelihood upon the use of their clerical skills alongside farming and the exploitation of other local resources.[97]

Augustinus Clericus left the first indication of his presence in the Redgrave manorial court in 1284 when he acted as an essoin for William le Barkere who was a plaintiff in a debt plea and unable to be in court since he was 'in the King's service'.[98] Augustinus came from the most highly privileged and wealthy villein stock in this densely settled Suffolk

[93] BRL 346353, 356357.

[94] He was elected as a juror in 1307, 1311 and 1314, *Court Rolls of the Manor of Hales*, ii. 562, BRL 346360, 346235 and 346357.

[95] University of Chicago Bacon MS 2, 4, and 6. We know that Walter Clericus made his last recorded court appearance as a pledge in a court of 16.6.1277. An entry in the court of 22.12.1279 records a grant by Walter's son Robert to his brother Thomas of the whole of his share (partible inheritance applying to customary land of which a tenant died seised) in a messuage and croft formerly held by his father (*quondam patris sui*). In 1291 the two sons and their widowed mother Basilia sold 1 acre of land that they held jointly to William Crane, court held 2.2.1279. The record of Walter's daughter's marriage fine can be found in the court of 11.7.1275. We know from a detailed survey of the manor of Redgrave that the Robert and Thomas held 12 acres of customary land, although during the 1280s we know that as individuals they had sold at least three acres of that that they had presumably inherited from their father. The 1289 extent of Redgrave exists in two copies: University of Chicago Bacon MS 805 and BL, MS Add. 14850, fos. 65–84ᵛ.

[96] Pledges were given on courts held 8.8.1261, 8.5.1262, 29.6.1262, 8.2.1263, 22.1.1265, 27.4.1266, 21.7.1267, 11.11.1273, 31.12.1273, 3.3.1276, 3.9.1276, 16.6.1277, Bacon MS 1, 2 and 3.

[97] Walter Clericus held marshland in the valley of the river Waveney that ran along the northern edge of the manor. He paid a fine for the registration of his rights in a court of 31.12.1272, Bacon MS 2.

[98] Court held on 23.1.1284, Bacon MS 4.

manor. His uncle was Adam Jop, the most overtly acquisitive individual in Redgrave, whose career can be documented in great detail from the start of the court rolls in 1260 until 1320. Adam Jop is shown on the extent of the manor in 1289 holding 39 acres of customary land and a further 9 acres of free land. In addition he held three messuages and proceeded to acquire a further 9 acres of customary land before his death. Augustinus was one of Adam's three nephews who as individuals had acquired a further 60 acres of land during the first two decades of the fourteenth century which were years of exceptional economic difficulty for smallholders—the principal sellers of land in this community. By 1320 Augustinus, his two brothers and two cousins who were sons of Adam Jop, held 11 per cent of the non-demesne land of Redgrave, although they constituted less than 1 per cent of the tenantry. For a family whose landed assets were so much larger than the average the presence in their midst of an individual with clerical skills must have been of very considerable practical benefit.[99]

The Halesowen court rolls do provide some limited information about the roles played by two other local tenants who are known to have been clerks. Thomas Clerk of Hasbury (1293–1335d.) was accused in a court held in November 1300, by Agnes Don of Hasbury of incorrectly recording what had been said in court. Her accusation was rejected and she was amerced and ordered to pay Thomas 12*d.* in damages.[100] In a court held in August 1301 Thomas took part in the formal manumission of a Halesowen bondman and most probably drew up the manumission charter.[101] Thomas was employed as a scribe not only by the lord, but also by his neighbours. In May 1308 he sued John Shirlet, a rich tenant for failing to pay him his fee.[102]

---

[99] Marginally under half the holdings in Redgrave were less than two acres in size and only 10 per cent exceeded 10 acres in area. The Jops were clearly many orders of magnitude wealthier than the average Redgrave tenant, whether villein or freeholder. For the details of landholding distributions on this manor and of the land-marketing pursuits of the Jop family see Smith, 'Families and their Land', 142–5 and 165–70.

[100] '*Agnes Dones in misericordia quia dixit quod Thomas clericus aliter inrotulavit in curia quam inrotulavit in curia . . .*' *Court Rolls of the Manor of Hales,* iii. 137. She was probably referring to a presentment which had been made by the township of Hasbury in the previous court about her and her servants, ibid. iii. 133. In 1295 a similar accusation regarding presentment was made against William the Clerk. '*Ricardus Cok vadit emenda Willelmo clerico quia dixit quod ex querela Johanis Edrich versus villatam de Rugaker non fuit per presentamentum et vadit domino misericoriam*', ibid. ii. 340.

[101] '*Memorandum quod dominus tradidit & manumissit Willelmum filium Thome de la More de communi consilio et assensu conventus Thome de Hasslbur clerico cum tota sequela sua et omnibus catallis suis in perpetuum per scriptuum sigillatum de communi sigillo capitali*', ibid. 420.

[102] BRL 346353.

It seems, however, that Thomas of Hasbury derived a significant part of his income from farming and was far from dependant upon the earnings secured through the sale of his clerical services. The court rolls clearly show that Thomas was one of the largest and most successful farmers in Halesowen during the early decades of the fourteenth century.[103] He inherited half a virgate and acquired another quarter virgate through marriage. He bought from his neighbours two meadows and another fourteen acres of arable land and a small cottage holding. In addition, he leased even more land for various terms of years and as a result by 1320 he was farming as much as 50 acres. He was also engaged in large-scale pastoral farming. He employed living-in-servants as well as casual labour during the harvest and had two cottage-tenants of his own. Thomas was also a major ale brewer and a money lender. He served twice as a juror and acted 42 times as a pledge. His family was large and at least six children survived to reach maturity.

John Clerk of Oldbury (1331–49d.)[104] was another substantial freeholder who combined his part-time occupation as a scribe for the Abbots of Halesowen and for his neighbours with farming.[105] As he died in his prime he failed to achieve the same high economic status as Thomas of Hasbury or Augustinus Clericus of Redgrave. However, the court rolls reveal that he prospered as an arable and pastoral farmer and as a commercial brewer. He was active in the inter-peasant land market, as a lessor rather than as a buyer.[106] John did not act as frequently as Thomas of Hasbury as a pledger, but he was elected considerably more times than him as a juror.[107] When John died of plague in 1349 he left an adolescent daughter and a 2-year-old son.[108]

The two freemen on the manor of Redgrave whose names suggest that they were clerks reveal rather different careers from Walter Clericus and Augustinus Clericus, customary tenants of the same manor. The pattern of their activities suggest a greater degree of concentration upon clerical

[103] Thomas described by a locative surname, or by an occupational one or by both, is noted 118 times in the court rolls between 1293 and 1335.

[104] BRL 3460264–322.

[105] At the end of the roll on which the proceedings of the court held in February 1339 are recorded, it is written that John Clerk of Oldbury was the clerk of this court, BRL 346287. In 1338 he sued John de Moulowe for failing to pay him his fee, for what we may presume were clerical services, BRL 346280.

[106] He appeared as a lessor in four land transactions recorded in 1339, 1342, 1343, and 1348.

[107] In 17 years John acted 12 times as a pledge and 18 times as a juror.

[108] Richard, John's son, entered his father's virgate tenement 'held by charter' in 1367, BRL 346347.

tasks, although the contrast may reflect the fact that they held less land than many of their customary neighbours. John Clericus is known to have held a cottage freely, but no other evidence of his landholdings is forthcoming from the proceedings of the manorial court, although he was amerced in the leet court for placing a small enclosure on one of the manor's two commons. He made frequent appearances in the manorial court between 1286 and 1301, acting as a pledge on 14 occasions and 9 times as an essoin. His wife was, however, amerced for brewing against the assize regularly in the 1290s, although on one occasion her fine was pardoned on account of her 'poverty' (*condonatur quia pauper*). An active involvement in ale-brewing was a characteristic often, although not invariably, associated with landlessness in this manor so we must assume that John's household purchased grain to undertake the income-generating activity that this by-employment enabled, indeed stimulated by the presence within the community of periodic market, whose stallholders and shop-tenants are listed in great detail on the survey of 1289.[109] John's role in servicing not only the scribal requirements of local society but also acting as a custodian of written records is particularly well illustrated by an entry in the court of 1301 relating to the death of Walter Beneit, a customary tenant of the abbot of Bury St Edmunds who also held free land. Walter died seised of 4 acres of freeland and it is noted that his ancestors had been granted that land in the time of Abbot Hugh by a charter stated to be in the custody of John Clericus. Walter Beneit's sons Robert and John came to court and paid a relief for entry into their father's freeholding and the fine was pledged by John Clericus who also pledged the fines of two other persons entering in land as purchasers in the same court session.[110] This example, along with that of Thomas of Hasbury above, should alert us to the relatively high frequency with which clerical services were extended by these individuals to the wider community and not just to the task of preparing documents for the manorial administration. Such an observation should not be interpreted as an attempt to down-play the importance of the case made and examples deployed by Paul Harvey whose reconstruction of the career of the

[109] The relevant entries in the Redgrave court rolls for John Clericus are as follows: Bacon MS 4, 5, 6, 7, 8, and 9, courts held on 12.7.1282, 25.3.1286, 9.7.1288, 27.6.1290, 18.10.1291, 27.11.1291, 13.3.1292, 11.2.1295, 8.6.1295, 20.4.1297, 11.10.1297, 24.6.1297, 9.6.1298, 3.12.1299, 11.2.1300, 6.6.1300, 20.6.1300, 20.6.1301.

[110] Bacon MS 9, court held on 20.6.1301: *Et sciendum quod quidem Abbas Hugonis nomine proxime ante Sampsonis feoffavit antecessores dicti Walteri per quaedam cartam qui est in custodia Johannis Clerici. Et dicunt quod Johannes et Robertus filii eiusdem Walteri sunt eius propinquiores heres. Et dant pro relennio dictorum iiij acras plegius Johannes Clericus.*

non-tenanted clerk, variously named Robert Molendinarius, Robert
Clericus son of Adam Molendinarius and Robert Clericus who lived in
Cuxham from 1302 to his death in the 1320s, focuses exclusively on the
services he rendered to the manorial bureaucracy.[111]

Simon Clericus, a Redgrave freeholder with 9 acres of land in 1289,
provides evidence of what may be regarded as the most specialized
'career' of a clerk on this Suffolk manor in the late thirteenth century. He
was on three occasions mentioned as 'attornatus' when working on behalf
of his clients. In one such case he was in the service of the most substantial freeholder in Redgrave, John Irelande whose landholding amounted
to nearly 30 acres and for whom he acted as legal representative in a
complex land dispute in 1291.[112] On another occasion he represented
Robert Irelande's son, John, in a land plea.[113] He was essoined on 13
occasions and a pledge on 14 occasions between 1287 and 1300.[114] None
the less, his relations with members of Redgrave society leave in the court
proceedings some evidence of discord, which reflected the extent to which
he was integrated within the local community. He was amerced for assault in 1290 and in 1293 appears to have been involved in a brawl with
two other persons including a member of the Irelande family, in which
his servant, Robert, was also implicated.[115] He acquired two cottages held
in customary tenure to add to his freehold land in the early 1290s and his
wife appears regularly on the list of persons amerced for brewing against
the assize of ale throughout the 1290s.[116] While he displays an active role
as 'legal aid' to members of Redgrave society, both freeholders and customary tenants, he is not infrequently found in court as a defendant and

---

[111] See n. 89 above.   [112] Bacon MS 6 court held on 27.11.1291.
[113] Bacon MS 7 court held on 14.10.1297. For another occasion on which Simon Clericus
acted as 'attornatus' see the proceedings of the court held on 28.10.1299, Bacon MS 8. For
additional examples of clerks acting as attorneys see Graham, 'A Social and Economic
Study of the Late Medieval Peasantry', 153, where the case of Thomas the Clerk, a free
sokeman, who acted as attorney three times and pledge on 56 occasions between 1324 and
1339 is reported, and the example of Harvey, the Clerk of Holkham, who acted on a number
of occasions as an essoin and served as attorney to Peter Ran, the chaplain of Stiffkey in
1348, *Lordship and Landscape in Norfolk, 1250–1350: The Early Records of Holkham*, ed. W.
O. Hassall and J. Beauroy (Records of Social and Economic History, New Ser., 20, Oxford,
1993), 469.
[114] The relevant entries are to be found in Bacon MS 5–8, courts held on ?.9.1287,
25.8.1289, 25.11.1289, 26.4.1290, 27.6.1290, 26.7.1290, 17.8.1290, 27.8.1291, 18.10.1291,
27.11.1291, 5.10.1292, 16.10.1292, 13.3.1292, 13.3.1292, 8.10.1292, 26.5.1293, ?.7.1293,
25.12.1295, 26.2.1296, 8.6.1296, 15.6.1296, 10.8.1297, 14.10.1298, 28.10.1299, 12.11.1299,
17.10.1300.
[115] Bacon MS 5–8, courts held on 25.8.1289, 28.6.1290, ?.7.1293, ?.7.1293.
[116] Bacon MS 6, court held on 27.6.1290 and on 26.5.1293.

he clearly had significant agricultural interests that are reflected in the amercements he paid for digging illegally in the common, for damage done in the meadowland of a neighbour, for raising a ditch and draining water without the permission of the leet court.[117] He does, notwithstanding his agrarian pursuits, convey an impression of intensive curial activity since he is noted 60 times in the surviving rolls from 1287 to 1300 (an average rate of appearance of 5 times per annum).[118]

In addition to the eight clerks whose activities we have described in some detail who evidently belonged, perhaps with a few exceptions, to the middling and upper ranks of village society, the abbots of Halesowen and Bury St Edmunds and their tenants must have used during the late thirteenth and early fourteenth centuries the services of many other peripatetic and possibly less well-off clerks. For instance, of the nine individuals carrying the name 'clericus' in Redgrave from 1260 to 1300, in addition to the four we have discussed above, all were distinguished by making appearances as pledges and/or essoins in the manor court, although they were visible for only a few instances in any one year. However, since such clerks were either non-residents in the manor or non-tenanted residents their court appearances are generally insufficient for us to gain a full understanding of their social and economic backgrounds.[119] None the less the number of such individuals active in these two manors and detectable in the court records suggest that the requirement to draw up charters and court rolls along with the legal services demanded by the peasantry, ensured that England, certainly between 1250 and 1349, contained a larger proportion of its rural population in possession of practical literary skills than was to be found in any of her European neighbours.

CONCLUSIONS

The search for the origins of manorial court rolls as a written record has revealed that these private local courts were integrated into the public court system to a far greater extent than was once supposed, although Maitland had hinted at the posssibility of some of the developments we have emphasized in the present discussion. This investigation has also

---

[117] Bacon MS 6 court held on ?.7.1293.

[118] This must represent a minimum rate of appearance as the roles for two years in the early 1290s are badly damaged and a large number of court sessions are missing.

[119] A non-resident clerk, William of Walsall, 'clericus', appeared in Halesowen manor court in December 1281 and complained that a local tenant had kept back 2s. 0d. of his fee, *Court Rolls of the Manor of Hales*, i. 176–7.

revealed that the extent of practical literacy in thirteenth- and fourteenth-
century English villages was much wider than allowed, even by historians
such as Clanchy. It appears that the success of the Angevin legal reforms
and the popularity of the royal courts forced English landlords to adopt
some of the superior procedures of these courts, including the recording
of court proceedings in order to draw their free tenants to their private
curiae. These hypotheses need to be verified by further investigations of
the development of the manor court as a legal institution and by a comparative study of seigneurial jurisdiction in medieval Europe. We sin-
cerely hope that our preliminary investigations will stimulate such research.

but special

2

What did Edwardian Villagers Understand by 'Law'?

PAUL R. HYAMS

THE sheaf of studies on and around the manorial court in this present volume sheds brilliant light on its social role and the sociological insights which its records can be made to surrender. In this expert company, I who have not previously published directly on manorial courts, may seem slightly out of place. My presence here stems from two personal concerns, one mildly critical, the other more positive.[1]

Studies on village life sometimes leave one with a feeling of unease over the insouciance with which certain students of the manor have approached their rolls. That first rule of source criticism which dictates that one must know how one's documents were produced before one uses them is often honoured most in the breach. One pulls plums off plea rolls of any kind at one's peril. Lloyd Bonfield has recently hailed the value to village historians of the on-going if often neglected 'inquest . . . into the nature of customary law'.[2] Manorial courts are as demanding of specific legal and sociological understanding as any. Each constituted in some sense its own localized legal system catering for its own clients and customers. Yet no court stood alone; in various degrees each was linked to others in its lordship or area, even within the same village. To use court rolls, one should understand first the system of law they record; and

---

[1] This paper developed out of one given in March 1985 at a Caltech–Weingart Conference in the Humanities on 'Law and Society under Edward I', under the auspices of the California Institute of Technology and the Huntington Library. Eleanor Searle and Paul Brand, in particular, know how much and in what different ways I owe to each of them and to the other participants, who included Leon Slota (below n. 44). I started at that time from the printed transcripts of Edwardian rolls from Ramsey Abbey manors and the Huntingdon eyre of 1286. I am more indebted than may appear below to the 'Toronto School' around Father Ambrose Raftis. John Beckerman, my student Michael Biggs, and David Sabean were each kind enough to read this in draft; their reactions were very helpful in my revisions. My wife, Elaine Marcotte Hyams, contributed at the proofing stage just as in the old days.

[2] L. Bonfield, 'The Nature of Customary Law in the Manorial Courts of Medieval England', *Comparative Studies in Society and History*, 31 (1989), 514–34. L. Bonfield and L. R. Poos, 'The Development of the Deathbed Transfer in Medieval English Manorial Courts' (Ch. 4 below) makes an excellent contribution to this inquest and promises a larger study of family and property in customary law in due course.

then the way this mini-system fitted into some larger, much larger, legal and cultural context. My first concern, then, was to seize in outline the context within which villagers pursuing their own relationships, activities, and transactions made use of the manorial court.

That this wider context is far more than legal needs no argument. Yet, the wider cultural context of law still receives relatively little attention in works on conventional legal history. Thus the act of assembling data about the role of the manor court offers a golden opportunity to explore the villagers' own sense of law, a topic still largely unstudied at *any* level of medieval society. The milieu of the prosperous villager is the lowest in medieval English society whose documentation enables the attempt to be made.[3] Enough extra-manorial sources exist to show the villagers' world stretching off seamlessly upwards towards gentry and even higher beings. If we grant the existence in Edwardian England of some kind of shared national legal culture that transcended the notorious jurisdictional tangles, as we probably should, an intriguing question then arises: How possible it was for prosperous villagers to participate in this legal world beyond the village. To the degree that they could so participate, the manorial court can hardly constitute for them their natural forum or enclosure. So I attempt in the last part of this paper below a preliminary sketch of this legal culture,[4] or at least of the ways in which we might and should be seeking it.

Let me present at the outset the most obvious objection to my undertaking and explain why it does not deter me. This is villeinage. The Edwardian common law quite specifically excluded from its benefits as unfree and legally rightless those whom it labelled in its records and literature 'villeins', *villani*. Those proven as such are all villagers, virtually without exception. Most of us have at some stage of our lives been taught that the majority of medieval villagers were villeins. We certainly know of estates exercising such strong, direct lordship over their tenants as to justify their classification as serfs. Many scholars have succumbed to the resulting temptation to equate these servile customary tenants with 'villeins' *ipso facto* abandoned to their lords' will by a common law that

---

[3] I am tempted by the modern analogy with Tsarist Russia (which has its critics) begun with E. A. Kosminsky, *Studies*. The term 'prosperous villager' in this paper refers almost exclusively to men. This reflects in part the difficulties of the sources and literature. Women hold few village offices and can seldom be *seen* to operate on the level that interests me here. The nature of their cultural contribution (in so far as this is a matter of gender) has hardly been broached to date.

[4] G. Duby, 'The Diffusion of Cultural Patterns in Feudal Society', *P&P* 39 (1968), 1–10 was the starting-point for many such questions.

excluded them absolutely. If we accept this, then my problems ought not to exist; villeins who may not sue in royal and other public courts are inevitably confined to the manor and slim hopes of seignorial grace.

This objection founders for two good reasons. First is the certainty that many Edwardian villagers were personally free. The seas of free status in eastern England are especially familiar to scholars, some of whom profess now to believe that villeins were already in the thirteenth century 'a clear minority'.[5] No judgement is required here on a question which is probably inappropriate for quantitative treatment. The real crux is the artificiality of villein status at common law. Its connection to the weight of real-life lordship and servility is quite distant. No villager walked round his village wearing on his sleeve a badge that proclaimed his unfreedom as a ghetto Jew did. The question of villein status only arose when some villager attempted to sue an opponent who chose to object to his capacity to sue. No litigant was forced to raise such an exception of villeinage; some who could have done so successfully did not think to do so. Nevertheless, the central point is that the royal courts came to restrict the right to plead an exception of villeinage to the plaintiff's own lord.[6]

In principle, this means that even undoubted villeins might hope to sue other commoners in courts beyond the manor without challenge or comeback. (It might on occasion suit their lord to encourage their suit.) Their aspirations could still founder on their inability to raise the necessary cash, to find the time or even to make their way to the required location. Such practical impediments common to all village would-be litigants were more decisive than any legal barriers. The effectiveness of lordly discipline is hard to assess; clearly, on numerous occasions, prosperous villagers circumvented it. The presumption that villeinage itself was much less of a bar than has been thought, serves as an invitation to historians to do what we do best and seek out villagers of unfree or uncertain status actually suing.

My focus here is what prosperous villagers did about their relationships, activities, and transactions. I shall therefore say little more about villeinage, and must accept the risk of appearing to understate the importance

---

[5] R. M. Smith, '"Modernisation" and the Corporate Village Community in England: Some Sceptical Reflections', in A. R. H. Baker and D. Gregory (eds.), *Explorations in Historical Geography: Interpretative Essays* (Cambridge, 1984), 172 citing two supporting predecessors.

[6] See Hyams, *King, Lords and Peasants*, 100–2. The main change postdates the period covered most fully in the book and coincides closely with increasingly widespread knowledge of Bractonian views as the treatise *De Legibus* became well-known.

of lordship. The manor is, of course, unequivocally an institution of lordship, and in most areas one so artificial that it rarely coincided with the village. One would think that it followed naturally that, in principle at least, the manorial court was the lord's and functioned primarily for his seignorial purposes.[7] Yet many historians experience the temptation to treat the court of the manor as if it had been a village court, or even a forum for treating the 'factual equities' of village issues.[8] Many more in practice regard the manor as 'the court of first and last resort' for most villagers most of the time.[9] Enough apparently superfluous 'village' business appears on the rolls of manorial courts for some historians to interpret what they find there as the product of village self-government.

Certainly, the manorial court was the quintessential forum in which villagers might express, to each other and especially to the lord or his representatives, their concerns about communal interests, the agricultural round, stances *vis-à-vis* outsiders and so on. Its rolls are and will remain a central source for the attempt to reconstitute the daily routine of village life. They contain much solid evidence of everyday business. Many of the entries do, indeed, document the lord's point of view, his interest in rents services and manorial discipline, but equally many display no obvious seignorial interest at all. We know from royal courts that a monarchy as keen on its own interest as the most grasping lord was nevertheless capable of administering in a relatively dispassionate manner litigation issues that did not involve it closely.[10] Historians have learned from the rolls of the thirteenth and fourteenth centuries a great deal also about the village's agricultural routine, its pattern of debt, its handling of disputes between villagers, and, in general, its methods of social discipline through such means as by-laws.[11] It is hard to read through many rolls

---

[7] Beckerman, 'Procedural Innovation and Institutional Change', 197–252. Beckerman points out to me that lords commonly sought out by presentment any tenants who had sued unnecessarily outside the manor. Cf. for references his 'The Articles of Presentment of a Court Leet and Court Baron in English, *c*.1400', *BIHR* 47 (1974), 434.

[8] The quotation is from the 'tentative hypothesis' advanced by Bonfield, 'Nature of Customary Law', see n. 2 above. I express reservations on some of his imaginative suggestions in an Appendix.

[9] The phrase is from Beckerman, 'Customary Law in English Manorial Courts', 1, 9: 'completely self-contained legal systems'. He informs me that he 'would today amend this to "largely"'. See Beckerman, 'Procedural Innovation and Institutional Change', 197–201, 250–1.

[10] R. V. Turner, *The King and His Courts: The Role of John and Henry III in the Administration of Justice, 1199–1240* (Ithaca, NY, 1968). Cf. Bonfield, 'Nature of Customary Law', 520.

[11] See e.g. works in the last generation by J. Bennett, A. R. and E. B. DeWindt, Z. Razi, and the classic work by Ault, *Open Field Husbandry and the Village Community*.

without receiving a strong impression that the manor court is *the* place for villagers to record their deals and property arrangements, especially those concerning land held of the lord. The rolls carry little sign of any anxiety that the agreements there recorded may not hold or may be defeated by events beyond the village boundaries. This is a good test of autonomy.[12]

Lords recognized their interest in the exclusion of outside jurisdictions and can be seen battling to keep their peasants' dirty washing within the manor. At stake was what they considered essential controls over land and tenants. Consider, for example, the threat that tenants would come under external domination through their acquisition of lands outside the manor. The earliest Ramsey court records of all, from a lost roll of 1239– 40, depict a special drive on one manor against tenants who had been engaging in the local land market without the abbot's license and to his potential damage.[13] Or again consider the not uncommon references to the amercement (fining) of villein tenants for 'losing the lord's chattels' by allowing themselves to be amerced elsewhere. This happened, for example, to Reginald le Wyse's wife after her 1292 ecclesiastical prosecution at the rural chapter for adultery.[14] In such ways do manorial court rolls contain a wide scattering of allusions to other courts. We should treat them almost as the Old English scholar does the Beowulf poet's casual allusions to lost tales that his audience certainly knew. Each reveals a landscape blindingly obvious to contemporary eyes but which might well be invisible to us without this spur to the imagination.[15]

Even where manor and village coincide, the village as a whole is most easily visible only when you get beyond it. Then suddenly, it is hard to concentrate on it alone; all around you is a 'fair field full of folk', with other villages, looming castles, and crowded towns, each of them housing

---

[12] P. R. Hyams, 'The Charter as a Source for Early Common Law', *JLH* 12 (1991), 173– 89, presented to a 1988 symposium at the Institute of State and Law in Moscow, is concerned with changes at an earlier period and at a higher level of society.

[13] *Cartularium Monasterii de Rameseia*, i. 411–12, 423–9. This inquiry probably started when a Ramsey tenant acknowledged holding in villeinage at a royal eyre whose judges included Abbot Rannulf himself. The record has quite a Common-Law flavour about it. A full study would further contribute to the inquiry below.

[14] *Elton Manorial Records, 1279–1351*, ed. S. C. Radcliff (Roxburghe Club, Cambridge 1946), 34. As a matter of fact, the roll does tell us who Mrs Le Wyse's lover was. He was John of Elton, the village's wealthiest and most prominent denizen. He was not amerced with her, no doubt because he was a free man.

[15] Some examples in *Select Pleas in Manorial Courts*, 93; *Elton Manorial Records*, 46, 95; *Court Rolls of the Abbey of Ramsey and of the Honor of Clare*, ed. W. O. Ault (New Haven, 1928), 18, 41–2, etc.

courts and jurisdictions of their own. As so often, we need to question the manorial court rolls most pressingly about the subjects *not* to be found there.

Patently, the manor lacked monopoly jurisdiction over its inhabitants, even in the rare cases where all its tenants were proven villeins at common law or (less rare) its lord added franchisal authority (regalian powers as if by delegation from the king) to those he enjoyed *qua* lord.[16]

Manorial authority logically ought not to extend over disputes with outsiders, those inhabitants of neighbouring villages, relations with whom were the very stuff of everyday life.[17] The court's power could not extend much beyond the authority of its lord, who could not routinely enforce his 'peace' over other lords' men or distrain beyond his fee.

Contemporaries recognized the difficulty. We can discern various ways of dealing with it. Formal solutions were possible. In one three-manor village, Walsoken, the lords held a joint leet twice a year to deal with the realities of their interdependent life there.[18] In the absence of such exceptional arrangements, what could a villager do when he felt himself entitled to justice against some outsider? The legal theory held that a villein, unable himself to sue outside, could nevertheless provide the cause of action for his lord to sue. An aggrieved villager might then plead with his lord, through the steward or whatever estate official he could reach, to take up his wrong. A fair body of material can be gathered from royal plea rolls to illustrate the proposition.[19] Manor rolls themselves record cases, particularly of border encroachments from other villages belonging to foreign lords, where the words *loquendum cum abbate* indicate the possibility of action at a higher level. It is not, however, encouraging to find these entries repeated year after year, as you do in some of the printed

---

[16] Franchisal jurisdiction at this level implies a seigneurial right to administer some at least of the Pleas of the Crown. Royal lawyers increasingly regard this as exercised by royal delegation; its real historical origins are not relevant here. Ault, *Private Jurisdiction in England* remains the only attempt at a global treatment. Helen Cam recognized the significance of franchise acquisition in many essays; see esp. her *Law-Finders and Law-Makers in Medieval England*, (London, 1962), Ch. 1.

[17] In fact, many manorial court rolls provide names of actors unknown in the home manor, presumably denizens of neighbouring manors or even near-by villages. It would be very interesting to collect such texts and study the efficacy of the justice exercised. The kind of inter-village confrontation which a single court clearly could not handle, because of inability either to compel outsiders to appear, and/or to enforce its judgements over them, is typified (from an earlier period) by the well-known violent struggle over water-meadows between the villagers of Culham and Sutton Courtenay heard Coram Rege and recorded in *Curia Regis Rolls*, vi. 390–1 (1212).

[18] Ault, *Private Jurisdiction*, 171 ff., prints a Walsoken roll of 1295.

[19] Cf. Hyams. *King, Lords and Peasants*, 18, 67.

Ramsey rolls.[20] Ordinary villagers found distant lords hard to move into action on their behalf. They had no guarantee, even if he agreed, that the benefits would descend to them. Far better for a peasant of ambition to sue for himself in some appropriate forum beyond his home manor. This, I believe, is what frequently happened.

The manor court obviously did not stand in isolation. Those who frequented it, suitors and others, were inevitably drawn into the common-law ambit in a number of different ways.

The most spectacular of these concern violence and disorder, that is they come under the head of the Pleas of the Crown. Bad blood within the village constantly threatened to provoke consequences in the wider world beyond. A concrete example can show how hard it was to conceal violence and theft from royal officialdom. Henry Godsweyn and Andrew Hermit were prominent villagers from the Ramsey manor of Elton, a few miles north-east of the Northants border in Hunts. Both figure in printed manorial court rolls. Henry, whose legal status is unknown, served in various offices and as tithing-man. His duties brought him before royal justices at the 1286 Huntingdon Eyre as well as into the manor court for successive Views of Frankpledge. The two men who stood surety for him in 1278 after a manorial amercement can themselves be seen performing similar offices at the eyre.[21] Andrew seems to have been both free and by the 1280s quite old. His household included at least one lodger, a woman called Sara Blundell who is herself not known to have been unfree.

One night in the years before 1286 four men came to Andrew's house, broke in and tied all the occupants up to facilitate their aim of burglary. Somehow in doing so, Sara Blundell was killed and the men at once fled. Local people must have performed the necessary public duties, raising and pursuing the hue and cry, since nothing was said before the justices in 1286 about any default. Certainly the other routine duties were duly performed in the usual way. The four were exacted and then outlawed in proper form at the shire. The coroner held an inquest, at which he was told that the culprits were unknown vagabonds, who left no goods to be seized for the king or a tithing to be held responsible for their crime.

---

[20] *Select Pleas in Manorial Courts*, 93; *Elton Manorial Records*, 114. These entries echo the 'loquendum cum rege' entries common on early royal plea rolls; cf. Turner, *King and His Courts*, 122 and Index s.vv. John; Henry III, 'consulted by justices'.

[21] *Select Pleas in Manorial Courts*, 91; *Elton Manorial Records*, 6; *Royal Justice and the English Countryside: the Huntingdonshire Eyre of 1286, the Ramsey Banlieu Court of 1287, and the Assizes of 1287–8*, ed. A. R. and E. B. DeWindt (2 vols.; Toronto, 1981), no. 616, ii. 563, 595. *A Descriptive Catalogue of Ancient Deeds in the Public Record Office* (6 vols.; HMSO, 1890–1915), i. 144; iii. 185, 231, 236, 239; iv. 90, 96, 125.

This was not true. One at least of the criminals was a local man. William le Talliur, an Elton villein, at some stage fled to the village church and claimed sanctuary. When the coroner arrived, he abjured the realm and the villagers, so it was alleged later, under-assessed his goods. Tongues must have been wagging; perhaps William lost his nerve. The other three involved may well also have been local. All were named in 1286. One, Richard Blackcalf, from a likely kulak family, was registered at the same eyre as outlawed for several other larcenies after he and his accomplices had again been at first concealed as vagabond strangers. Another villager, Roger Goscelin, suspected of harbouring the four killers, was cleared by a jury.[22] Andrew can hardly not have known some of his assailants. Yet for a time village solidarity had held firm against the representatives of outside justice. William's very public and well-recorded abjuration must then have forced the jurors to tell something closer to the truth at the eyre.[23]

The duties of the village and its inhabitants within the royal system of criminal justice inevitably exercised a powerful if intermittent influence on village life. Every detail of the complex and nuanced rhythm of national lawkeeping so well studied from the governmental perspective deserves equal care and imagination from the village end.[24] While the structure lasted,[25] it forced representative villagers to attend each of a whole string of secular courts throughout the months and years that separated the visitations of royal justices. The village élite thus faced a never-ending challenge on how best to keep officialdom at bay and minimize their inevitable financial obligations for murdrum fines, felons' chattels, deodands and amercements of all kinds. The full list is a long one. It was all too easy to get drawn into inquiries before the justices into any matter specified on the articles of the eyre or felt to conceal potential offences or sources of royal profit.[26] Deaths, all of which had to be reported and assigned to someone's responsibility,[27] produce some

---

[22] *The Huntingdonshire Eyre*, no. 642, ii. 560, 611, 659.   [23] Ibid. nos. 576, 582.

[24] The best guides are H. R. E. Summerson, 'The Structure of Law Enforcement in Thirteenth-Century England', *American Journal of Legal History*, 23 (1979), 313–27; *The 1235 Surrey Eyre*, ed. C. A. F. Meekings (prepared for press, D. Crook), (2 vols.; Surrey Rec. Soc. 31–2, 1979–83), esp. i. Also R. F. Hunnisett, *The Medieval Coroner* (Cambridge, 1961).

[25] Approximately to the turn of the 14th cent.; D. Crook, 'The Later Eyres', *EHR* 97 (1982), 241–68.

[26] Cf. *Huntingdonshire Eyre*, nos. 391, 791.

[27] The obligation to report deaths admitted of no exceptions. N. D. Hurnard, *The King's Pardon for Homicide Before 1307* (Oxford, 1968), Chs. 3–6 cites many examples. The accidental killer in *Huntingdonshire Eyre*, no. 349 was as so often a child.

particularly amusing situations reminiscent of the movie 'The Trouble with Harry' a few years ago. Allegations of walking corpses bring to life, as it were, the desperate efforts to escape communal liability.[28]

But royal criminal justice represented for some villagers a good deal more than liabilities to avoid. In mastery of its rules and practices lay opportunities too. Prosperous villagers dominated the major juries at the eyre and surrounding court sessions. They therefore possessed a considerable say in who was prosecuted (juries of presentment) and what happened to them (trial juries). They were most favourably placed too for screening complaints as they entered the system. They and their clients could insinuate their own grievances, true and false, and they could exclude those of their enemies.[29] No wonder that allegations of crime were a staple of defamation suits in the Church and local courts where these were actionable.[30] Everyone must have known of this. Men had to swallow it as a recognized part of the administration of justice in Edwardian England. Despite various attempts to tackle the problem from the end of the thirteenth century,[31] it is unlikely that prosperous villagers and their patrons felt any deep need to justify themselves.

Although the Pleas of the Crown seem likely to have furnished villagers with their basic education in the royal law, civil pleas affected them all too in a lesser degree. First, suits of their lord's frequently involved their interests. Villagers will have noted the result of disputes with neighbouring lords over such matters as fishing rights in a mill race.[32] They could even be named as co-defendants in actions for novel disseisin resulting from their participation in forceful assertions of rights legally belonging to their lords. Their involvement will have been deeper where their own complaints had pushed the lord into suing. But such successes were doubtless few and far between.

[28] Ibid. nos. 634, 702: cxx concern the strangled body of a Lincs. man found in Elton, Hunts. but proved to have been brought across the county border from Northants., where his widow had appealed those she held responsible in the shire court. Cf. ibid. no. 155, which may explain the deceased's presence in the area and nos 616, 702: xciv–c for another similar case again involving Elton.

[29] Largely unavailing government attempts to exclude private interests (often under the head of 'malice') were a feature of the system of public prosecutions from their inception by the Assizes of Clarendon and Northampton. See for example the 'Inquest of Sheriffs' 1170, c. vi in *Select Charters*, ed. W. Stubbs (9th edn., rev. H. W. C. Davis; Oxford, 1913), 176–7.

[30] *Select Cases on Defamation to 1600*, ed. R. H. Helmholz (Selden Soc. 101, 1985), esp. xli ff., lxxvi. Radcliff, 90 (1300) illustrates the commonest case comprising a theft allegation.

[31] A. Harding, 'The Origins of the Crime of Conspiracy', *TRHS* 5th ser. 33 (1983), 89–108.

[32] *The Huntingdonshire Eyre*, no. 137 has this situation in a case that went on to the Bench at Westminster before being settled by Fine.

More surprising to modern students are the occasions when a few villagers sued on behalf of the community or some other larger group. Their representative capacity arguably sprang from fiscal and peacekeeping duties on the vill of the kind already discussed. The requirement, that each vill must be represented at the shire and eyre by its reeve, priest, and four men, going back to the twelfth century at least, is clearly geared to ensuring that vills carried out their public responsibilities.[33] But representation apparently held for positive purposes too. We can see villagers suing and being sued in a variety of courts beyond the manor for a whole range of run-of-the-mill causes. The evidence comes from 'all over the legal landscape', Church courts as well as secular ones. The capability seems most comprehensible where villagers farmed their own manor, for they might then be said to enjoy lord-like powers. But the cases are certainly not confined to any special situations, and it is remarkable that their opponents never raised objections and exceptions either on the principle of such representation or against any of the named litigants on the ground of villeinage. We can probably assume that most of these spokesmen were prosperous villagers. Their enterprise nevertheless implies wider discussion before the initiation of proceedings. And, as with much seignorial litigation, the outcomes often affected all villagers alike.[34]

The case for a villagers' presence in Church courts is at least as strong as that for secular litigation. All kinds of suit drew in villagers to act as witnesses even where they were not themselves suing.[35] The manorial penalties for 'loss of the lord's chattels' in the Rural Chapter, mentioned above, fit the picture of villagers figuring widely in court Christian offered by the actions of Prohibition and other materials on royal plea rolls.[36] The Norwich 'Circumspecte Agatis' inquiry of 1286 contains abundant material, though admittedly centring on an area where Church courts were said to be particularly active. The lower echelons of ecclesiastical justice constituted less of a system of formal courts than a rather effective network of men possessing, as part of their ecclesiastical dignity, the

---

[33] Cf. *Leges Henrici Primi*, ed. L. J. Downer (Oxford, 1973), c.7. 7b.

[34] Cam, 'The Community of the Vill', 71–84, esp. 78 ff.; S. Yeazell, *From Medieval Group Litigation to the Modern Class Action* (New Haven and London, 1987), Ch. 2.

[35] A Huntingdonshire illustration can be found in *Select Cases from the Ecclesiastical Courts of the Province of Canterbury, c.1200–1301*, ed. N. Adams and C. Donahue jr. (Selden Soc. 95, 1981), 112–18 (1270–2). The rural chapter hearings before the Archdeacon of Huntingdon's official took parties, witnesses and others on a broad circuit of venues around Kimbolton, Hunts.

[36] See for copious earlier illustration C. T. Flower, *Introduction to the Curia Regis Rolls, 1199–1230 AD* (Selden Soc. 62, 1944), Ch. ix.

ability to summon and coerce any Christian, and every incentive to use this to attract money by imposing commutable penances. Office prosecutions even enabled the real accuser to remain anonymous,[37] so that ordinary men could, for a consideration, use their friendly local dean or his official to harass their neighbours in much the way that others used royal and local juries of presentment. That villagers with grudges got a swifter and heavier bang for their buck here than anywhere else was one important reason for the vitality of ecclesiastical justice which *Circumspecte* \ *Agatis* was framed to control and restrain.[38] One might go so far as to take all indications of success for church reform in influencing village morals and ideas towards the Christian models of marriage, wills and other proper behaviour as further evidence against the monopoly jurisdiction of the manor.

Enough has now been said to demonstrate that a proper study, proceeding from fuller use of the estate records of Ramsey or any other major religious house, would certainly identify many peasant litigants and make possible a more nuanced description of their place in this system of courts, how they made their choices, where best to sue, how to formulate their grievances most effectively. Villagers who faced such choices, as many will have done, must have felt a need for knowledge of the rules of royal law. To win cases, one required accurate translation into the forms approved by royal justices. One consequence is to raise again old questions about the work of professional lawyers and the speed and timing of their penetration into the countryside.[39]

Another response would be to swing the spotlight back onto the manorial court and the character of its justice. Common-law influence on manorial courts shines out as soon as one asks of the court rolls serious

---

[37] This is the situation that provoked the issue of royal writs of prohibition *ex relatu plurium*.

[38] P. R. Hyams, 'Deans and their Doings: the Norwich Inquiry of 1286', *Proc. of the Berkeley Congress of Medieval Canon Law, 1980* (Monumenta Iuris Canonici, Series C, Subsidia, 7, Vatican City, 1985), 619–46 should be read with D. Millon, 'Circumspecte Agatis Revisited', *LHR* 2 (1984), 105–27 and his 'Ecclesiastical Jurisdiction in Medieval England', *University of Illinois Law Review* (1984), 621–38.

[39] R. C. Palmer, 'County Year Book Reports: The Professional Lawyer in the Medieval County Court', *EHR* 91 (1976), 776–801 is a good starting-point. Paul Brand's recent book on the legal profession puts a more restrictive interpretation on professionalism and thus places penetration later. See Brand, *Origins of the English Legal Profession*, 141–2. See also Levett, *Studies in Manorial History*, 33. The Ramsey prohibition of *placitatores* (*Cartularium Monasterii de Rameseia*, i. 412, 428) may refer to strong-armed supporters not lawyers. For a manuscript, associated with the name of Robert Carpenter, worth considering in this context, see the references in *Tractatus de Legibus et Consuetudines Regni Angli qui Glanvilla vocatur*, ed. G. D. G. Hall (Edinburgh, 1965), 195–8.

questions about procedure and custom. Generalization to date is mostly based on sample manors from a few major estates, with the important early Ramsey materials kept essentially separate (alas) from the rest. There is already enough, however, to establish the degree of common-law influence on some estates and the need to look for it everywhere.

Manorial materials themselves make the basic case. There is in the first place much that looks familiar to the student of the common law on manorial court rolls, themselves often dated by the king's regnal years. The basic procedure, essoins, defaults, distraints, and so forth, is recognizably from the same world. Every time the rolls refer to livery of seisin, love-days, or the hue and cry, to name but a few, they point to institutions shaped and defined in the last resort by the common law. Notoriously too, the common law determined in principle, through its law of villeinage, the jurisdictional limits of justice for the unfree.[40] Manorial forms will perhaps strike those used to common-law records as watered down or technically imprecise. But this technicality gap demonstrably diminishes on many manors as Edward I's reign wears on.[41] It looks as if manorial courts are responding in their own way to the coercive influence of royal justice.[42] The important studies of John Beckerman, as publicized and extended more recently, notably by Richard Smith and colleagues, go beyond this to argue for a transformation of manorial justice quite largely effected within the reign of Edward I.[43] They argue that the character of proof and procedure in manorial courts moved in the late thirteenth and early fourteenth centuries much closer to that in higher courts, far beyond the archaic, popular village moot which it conceivably had once been, towards modern techniques of documentary evidence and jury trial. Their location of this transformation as effectively commencing in the years 1260 to 1280 may not find ultimate favour, because of the cautionary coincidence with the first age of full documentation from manorial court rolls. That said, one can certainly trace from the first generations of

[40] See Hyams, *King, Lords and Peasants*, esp. Ch. 13.

[41] I was struck reading *Court Rolls of the Manor of Hales*, ii, for example, by changes evident after rolls reappeared in the 1290s. Technical argument about defaults etc. is much more frequent, as are references by name to such actions as covenant and trespass.

[42] The obvious analogy for this coercive influence is the argument of Milsom, *Legal Framework of English Feudalism*. See below for one likely route. Bonfield and Poos, 'Development of the Deathbed Transfer', Ch. 4 below, show well how much more this creation of 'the missing technical tool' for free disposition was than a simple borrowing from the Common Law which excluded such transfers and had great difficulty in analysing their 'quite subtle . . . legal nature'.

[43] Beckerman's thesis is the *locus classicus*; but cf. too Slota's article referred to in the next note.

court rolls substantial change in the nature of both court procedure and important aspects of court function along lines that profoundly affected the meaning of its law for the better-off villager.

Since landholdings are so central to village order, the processing of land transactions comes first to mind. Here procedural changes argue for a close and early integration of village society into the sophisticated world of Edwardian land conveyancing, an art undergoing its own fierce development at the time. From the 1280s, in East Anglia, perhaps a little earlier in some other areas, court rolls begin to record land transfers in new ways.[44] First they specify with increasing frequency that transfers were effected by Surrender and Admission. This meant that the tenant formally surrendered his holding to the lord (through the presiding steward) 'to the use of' his intended grantee. In practice, he was requesting the lord's ratification of an agreement already made with some other villager who had doubtless already paid him for the property. Undeniably though, the formalities proclaim to their manorial audience the lord's theoretical authority and legal interests ultimately enforceable at common law. That is, title must be transferred under the lord's eye and subject to his supervision. Whether this represents village demand for registration of title or the potentially repressive character of the seignorial response here is a question partly of scholarly emphasis and partly dependent on the estates and areas studied.[45]

The connotations of servility, though undoubtedly present, are easily exaggerated. Summonses from the manorial court compel villagers to bring into court charters relating to their acquisitions of free land outside the manor, for registration on the rolls, perhaps also to be taken into the lord's 'safekeeping'. The context is coercive. But the villagers involved were not necessarily unfree by personal status. In 1290 the statute *Quia Emptores* promulgated a similar norm of grants in 'substitution' for higher tenures, causing on some estates a further refinement of the language in which transfers were recorded to distinguish manorial (and villein) substitution from freeholders' substitution.[46]

Another set of changes date from around the same time. Smith has drawn attention to an increasingly free use of the language of heritability

---

[44] Slota, 'Law, Land Transfer and Lordship', 119–38 notes that standardization on that abbey's rolls came during the third quarter of the century, too early for any causal connection with presentments, ibid. 121–3.

[45] Ibid. esp. 119, 124–5, 132 ff., working on St Albans, lays a far stronger emphasis on the protection of seignorial interest.

[46] Ibid. 123.

on East Anglian rolls and associated documents. Men make grants, for example to grantees 'sibi et heredibus suis', in blithe disregard of the Bractonian warnings that such formulaic references to the heirs of men, who as villeins could by definition have no heirs, risked their enfranchisement.[47]

These more detailed enrolments clearly reflect a seignorial interest in keeping closer records of the movement of their land and the location of their rents and rights. The timing coincides a little too nicely with other conventional evidence of intelligent extension of the exploitative devices sometimes generalized into a system of 'High Farming'. Neither practice was necessarily novel; at least one other major new conveyancing device, entails, already began to appear on St Albans rolls in the 1250s.[48] Chronology is crucial to all these arguments about the causation of change. The new detail of the rolls positively invited villagers to partake of the extraordinary power of contemporary conveyancing techniques. This, possibly as much as socio-economic forces, weaned them from charters of a character that seignorial advisers, their eyes on the common law, might deem threatening.

None of this need be by chance. Some lords went on trying to retain control over their tenantry through villeinage; but others realized that the rising volume of authorized transactions (taking over from the illegal traffic elsewhere) increased their court revenues, sometimes quite dramatically. One conscious legislative change of inheritance custom (Norfolk 1287) from impartible to partible was said to be made 'because (the lord) wants more tenants'.[49] The existence of these alternative strategies will have diminished the attractions of continued repression on the St Albans model. The retention of villagers' affection for their friendly neighbourhood manor court was very much in the lords' interest.[50]

[47] Cf. Hyams, *King, Lords and Peasants*, 44–5. Smith, 'Some Thoughts', 95–128. Bracton's treatise was probably only coming into widespread use among common lawyers at very much this time. Cf. Bracton, *De Legibus et Consuetudinibus Angliae*, ed. G. E. Woodbine, tr. S. E. Thorne (4 vols.; Cambridge, Mass., 1968–77), iii, xlviii ff.

[48] Slota, 'Law, Land Transfer and Lordship', 125–6. This is intriguingly early in the common-law history of entails. Its significance remains debatable. Slota interprets it within the overall growth in land transfers, but entails were likely to slow this down by freezing some land. This innovation looks less like a seignorial innovation than a measure forced by demands that lords could not withstand. Further research must examine the way manor courts interpreted limitations to 'X and the heirs of his/her body', which had figured in rural charters from the twelfth century, especially during the period of common-law uncertainty 1285–1312.

[49] Smith, 'Some Thoughts', 122.

[50] Slota, 'Law, Land Transfer and Lordship', 135, emphasizes the abbot of St Albans' sense of competing with outside courts for his tenant's business.

The still-burgeoning land market offered kulaks myriad opportunities for expansion. For the enterprising few, economic differentiation was more a challenge than a threat. The remodelled manorial courts became an essential premise to a higher level of entrepreneurial activity at the village level. They offered enhanced effective tenurial protection together with a greater flexibility in the marshalling of property resources. The recall and administration of oral entails and marriage settlements, though certainly possible, presents severe problems in real life without some kind of permanent record. Security of disposition almost compels written registration.[51]

Edmund King has commented on the speed with which the statute *Quia Emptores* of 1290 affected his 'villein charters' at Peterborough Abbey. His conclusion, that village property was now revealed as part of a single, seamless land market, is surely correct.[52] This must have scared some lords and their advisers. The logical conclusion of the process was the birth of Copyhold and the consequent appearance of a distinct customary terminology based on the notion of the 'copy' of the court-roll entry as the villager's title-deed, firmly outside the common law.

The earliest rolls portray the kind of court where villagers played a powerful role as suitors. They were apparently able both to influence the release of relevant information into court and make the judgements. Many cases ended in wager of law, an oath to be made by one litigant and a stated number of helpers presumably coming from the body of village suitors. Here a wide range of villagers had a role; each could choose whether to furnish or withhold his support. Litigants purchased fewer inquests than later.[53] Even the meanest suitor had some part to play; the verdict, when it came, was that of the whole *curia* or *homagium*.

To some degree this is theory, and thus artificial. In medieval society, some animals are always much more equal than others. Yet the theory could well have encouraged villagers to identify with the lord's manorial court. Significantly, however, the gradual extension of jury trial, in rough imitation of the common law, progressively squeezed out this quasi-democratic possibility. On some (not all) estates, juries came close to displacing compurgation entirely, so that phrases like 'tota curia' became

---

[51] Cf. J. Campbell, 'The Significance of the Anglo-Norman State in the Administrative History of Western Europe', in J. Campbell, *Essays in Anglo-Saxon History* (London, 1986), 171–90. On the other hand, we all know from experiences of reading fine print in a hostile environment that written records carry their own problems and generate legal business.

[52] King, *Peterborough Abbey, 1086–1310*, Ch. 6.

[53] Use of inquests was still treated as a privilege rather than a right. See Hyams, *King, Lords and Peasants*, 155.

largely empty formulations.[54] Increased power accrued to the seigneurial
steward through his control of the privilege of jury trial, and also, one
may guess, to those prosperous villagers who predominate as jurors and
also as conservers of the collective memory.

The presenting jury is the clearest case of benefit to the leading villager. Its purpose was to identify offences for prosecution, in some sense
on behalf of the community. Again the idea came from the common law,
via the Sheriff's Tourn, and its privatized equivalent, the private View of
Frankpledge. Its spread onto the different estates was uneven[55] and its
use for purely manorial (as opposed to franchisal, i.e. public) business
remained comparatively rare before the early fourteenth century. Initially
it must have seemed a very inquisitorial innovation serving the lord's
interests. Because it generated more prosecutions, fines could be lower
yet produce a greater overall revenue. Manorial officials escaped the
worst backlash of resentment; and, since presentment usually approx-
imated pretty closely to summary conviction, it reduced the fuss in court.[56]

But countervailing advantages swiftly became evident to prosperous
villagers also. As influential jurors, they could exercise real power, safe
to a fair degree even from seigneurial control. It was their investigations
between sessions that decided what information reached the next court,
what acts (and by whom) would or would not be treated as offences.
Their pre-screening of prosecutions in effect set most of the primary
standards of village behaviour.[57] Even presentment of illegal land alienations
could buttress the system of tenurial protection by proto-copyhold touched
on above.

These various changes together justify an hypothesis of a quite profound transformation of the way the manor court functioned all over
England. Further research is badly needed to elucidate the profundity of
the changes and their diffusion beyond particular regions and lordships.

---

[54] M. Toch, 'Asking the Way and Telling the Law: Speech in Medieval Germany', *JMH*
16 (1986), 667–82 makes an interesting comparison here. I owe this reference to Gadi
Algazi whose own work promises further illumination.
[55] Cf. n. 44 above for St Albans.
[56] T. A. Green, *Verdict According to Conscience: Perspectives on the English Criminal Trial
Jury, 1200–1800* (Chicago, 1985), Ch. 1. describes the analogous situation in royal courts.
[57] This must have been significant even in royal villeinage cases; see Hyams, *King, Lords
and Peasants*, 114, 212. I take my cue from Green, *Verdict According to Conscience*, Ch. 1. I
pursue some implications for the effectiveness of criminal presentment procedures and the
pleas of the crown in general in my forthcoming book, *Rancour and Reconciliation in
Medieval England*, esp. Ch. 6. We still need a study of the pros and cons of service on
manorial juries, especially presentment juries. Costs included the acquisition of new enemies.

But one already suspects that prosperous villagers felt considerably more at ease in their home courts by the end of Edward I's reign than they had been at the close of his father's. That most of the ideas that fuelled these changes patently descended from higher social levels shows the direction from which the competition to manorial courts came and argues compellingly for more, and more intense common-law influence in the manor in 1307 than there had been at Edward I's accession.

Supporting evidence for this is abundant and familiar. By the early fourteenth century, many courts allowed land pleas 'in the form of' assizes or the writ of right. Double-size juries of attaint start to review the verdicts of trial juries. Descent rules are adjusted so as to narrow the gap from common-law standards. Wives are wheeled into court to assent to their husbands' alienation of their inheritance, some of them noted as *lacrimens* at the time. An approved pattern of mesne process begins to emerge. Penetration of written documents encourages a certain refinement of decision-making.

Direct contact with royal courts was responsible for much of this. Lords deeply enmeshed in central court litigation on their own account and flush with technical advisers[58] inevitably blazed a trail that their tenants could then sometimes follow to sharp effect. The Edwardian common law was almost bound to become a standard measure of subordinate laws much as Roman law had been for the first secular lawyers to gather round the *curia regis* in force a century earlier. Once this idea gained currency, disputants would always be tempted to ape common-law forms to add verisimilitude and plausibility to otherwise bald and unconvincing narratives. Others would soon follow suit in case they were missing something.[59] Prosperous villagers themselves appeared on occasion before royal justices as litigants (as we shall see) and over their adult lives frequently served on one or other of the various kinds of royal jury. These experiences reinforced common-law models of law. Even where men were not themselves intimately familiar with royal courts and justices,

---

[58] The material assembled in S. L. Waugh, 'Tenure to Contract: Lordship and Clientage in Thirteenth-Century England', *EHR* 101 (1986), 811–39 carries very important implications for the history of seigneurial administration and exploitation in the thirteenth century and invites wide debate. For seigneurial use of legal counsel, see also J. R. Maddicott, *Law and Lordship: Royal Justices as Retainers in Thirteenth- and Fourteenth-Century England* (*P&P* Supplement 4, 1978), 10–11 and references there cited.

[59] F. L. Cheyette, 'Suum Cuique Tribuere', *French Historical Studies*, 6 (1969), 287–99 demonstrates the manner in which Roman Law first seeped into the legal vocabulary of southern France well before its ideas were properly assimilated.

they learned by contiguity with those who were. One may recall here the surely justified suspicion that manors close to privileged towns found it especially hard to hold the line against villein enfranchisement.[60]

Ancient Demesne manors will have played a special role here. The myth that Ancient Demesne privileges originated in Anglo-Saxon times raised the prestige of their practices in the eyes of their village neighbours. Even before the concept of Ancient Demesne crystallized fully, Ancient Demesne manors enjoyed a far greater degree of contact with royal justice than others. For a time in the early thirteenth century villagers of villein or doubtful status managed nevertheless to use the same standard common-law procedures for their land suits as freeholders.[61] Publicity and some-times protracted royal litigation between lords and men over status and services must have cast wide ripples over the countryside.[62]

By the early fourteenth century, it may even have seemed possible that in time the prestigious coin of royal law, in real or counterfeit form, would drive out the products of local mints. The court of the manor was undeniably within the reach of some major currents of contemporary legal change. All courtholders at whatever level were well aware of a royal determination to subordinate their jurisdictions to the common law. Con-temporaries could not afford to believe that the 1290 statute meant the end of royal efforts in this direction. The claim implied by the phrase 'common law', that the king's justice is public justice and on offer to *all* his subjects,[63] could in principle include the meanest villein, who was now, like others, 'subject' to royal taxation, as good a test as any.[64] Edward did not intend his justices to waste their time on peasant trivialities, but he probably still hoped to compel general acceptance of the important idea that all adjudicative processes in his kingdom without exception were subject to the supervision of himself and his justices.[65] If so, we need

[60] See R. H. Hilton, 'A Thirteenth-Century Poem on Disputed Villein Services', *EHR* 56 (1941), 90–7.
[61] R. S. Hoyt, *The Royal Demesne in English Constitutional History, 1066–1272* (Ithaca, NY, 1950); cf. McIntosh, 'Privileged Villeins', 295–328; also R. J. Faith, 'The "Great Rumour" of 1377 and Peasant Ideology', in R. H. Hilton and T. H. Aston (eds.), *The English Rising of 1381* (Cambridge, 1984), 48–63.
[62] Halesowen, Worcs. is an easily accessible illustration because of its records in print. See Razi, *Life, Marriage and Death*.
[63] Cf. P. Petot, 'Le droit commun en France selon les coutumiers', *Revue historique de droit français et étranger*, 4e s., 38 (1960), 412–29.
[64] See Hyams, *King, Lords and Peasants*, 152–3.
[65] I briefly suggest this way of looking at Edward's aims in Hyams, 'Deans and Their Doings', 620–1, 643–4. Contrast the received view of D. W. Sutherland, *Quo Warranto Proceedings in the Reign of Edward I, 1278–1294* (Oxford, 1963).

to ask whether there was not a real possibility in the years around 1300 that something approaching an integrated legal system administered through many different kinds of courts under the supervision of the king's common law might actually come to be in England?[66] In the nether regions of such a system, unconfined by manorial jurisdiction, prosperous villagers could operate in some comfort.

Robert Palmer's book on the shire courts openly implies something like this.[67] He argues for a major jurisdictional shift right at the beginning of Edward I's reign, stemming from the young king's 'new broom' attempts at reform on his return from the Holy Land in 1274. Alongside the other consequences of the government inquiries into local corruption (the 'Ragman Quest'), he proposes a major adjustment in the processing of personal actions at common law, most notably Trespass and Debt-Detinue. Edward's advisers had identified the administration of the shire court as one of their targets. Its justice was so tainted in royal eyes, that the king felt entitled to offer litigants something better. After an initially over-generous offer had triggered off an unexpectedly massive response, some retrenchment was required.[68] Even so, the means of challenging at Westminster judgements made in the shire and other local courts were much improved.

These reforms were certainly not intended to affect manorial jurisdiction and the process was probably longer prepared than Palmer makes it appear[69] and somewhat transitory in its effect. Their likely impact on the peasant litigant remains substantial. What Edward's ministers called (for their own purposes) a corrupt shire court had no doubt seemed to influential villagers a system they understood, could live with and manipulate to their own ends. The shire's demotion, especially in the substantial removal of its residual real property business, and its consequent reduction in standing may have had the paradoxical effect of bringing it more within the prosperous villager's grasp. There was still no great disadvantage in suing in the shire.[70] Where the central courts still loomed as a

---

[66] R. C. Palmer, *The County Courts of Medieval England, 1150–1350* (Princeton, 1982), 298, 300–1.

[67] Ibid. 169–73, 229–34, 240, 261–2.

[68] J. S. Beckerman, 'The Forty-Shilling Jurisdictional Limit in Medieval English Personal Actions', in D. Jenkins (ed.), *Legal History Studies 1972* (Cardiff, 1975), 110–17 will be known to all students of local courts.

[69] As Paul Brand pointed out to me, citing from the period before 1275 *Radulphi de Hengham summae*, ed. W. H. Dunham (Cambridge, 1932), 13 and a writ in 'Pone' form designed for pleas initiated without writ.

[70] Palmer, *County Courts*, 220 ff.

luxury, the shire and other local courts (not least the ecclesiastical ones) offered alluring opportunities of swifter and cheaper justice.

I have argued up to this point in favour of a rather broader view of the legal facilities available at least to the more prosperous villagers than has been customary. One would like to integrate this picture with the other routine experiences of village life, the struggle for sustinence in the face of poor soils, the English weather and the demands of lords and tax gatherers. What part did litigation and its surrounding decisions play in their life? How conscious were they of law as a discrete system of rules and ideas? In what ways did their life experiences inform their sense of law itself? These are not questions that have been much asked.[71] In the hope of gently goading village specialists to venture afresh into the territory of *mentalités*, I devote the rest of this paper to exploring some of the parameters within which they might be approached.

First I must briefly explain what I have in mind by a 'sense of law'. This is something both more and less than lawyers' law. It is acquired differently: The best way is actually to 'do' law yourself, as litigant, suitor, or judge. But you may also acquire it through some lesser category of experience such as court attendance or even at one or more removes. You begin to pick it up at your father's knee or by watching and listening to older people. This is perhaps the most usual method for most people. In the Edwardian village, as in many pre-modern milieus, legal consciousness is simply an aspect of general culture. You learn it the kind of way we all learn our native tongue, in contrast to the routes by which most of us today study history, law or other professional disciplines.

Legal culture gained from specialized lawyers spells trouble. To approach a lawyer is to incur liabilities from the very start. 'Chi va dall' avocato perde son ultimo ducato' is only one of a myriad proverbs that express popular fears of the professional lawyer. Worse still, what you purchase from him is a view of the world packaged and skeletized in an alien manner. Now this is undeniably some part of a man's sense of law, and the extent to which villagers now used, now feared and reviled professional lawyers is important and needs more attention. At best, though, it remains only a small part of what I have in mind.

Since the annual rhythm of court sessions in the area furnished the framework for experiencing law, it may be helpful at this point simply to

---

[71] J. A. Sharpe, 'The People and the Law', in B. Reay (ed.), *Popular Culture in Seventeenth Century England* (London and New York, 1985), 244–70, attempts something of the kind for the early modern period in instructive fashion.

list the courts and meetings as they existed in the main part of Edward I's kingdom in the first half of the reign:

The MANOR COURT often met every three weeks. So did the standard HUNDRED COURT, where long before all litigants had been told to start their suits.[72] Some free villagers may have been obliged to attend as suitors; others served as manorial representatives or (as we have seen) were there on their own business. Twice a year were held the special sessions of the SHERIFF'S TOURN (royal) or VIEW OF FRANKPLEDGE (when in private hands) to review the policing arrangements of tithing, an institution now deeply entwined into village life.

The SHIRE had a similar double aspect, once a month for normal meetings, twice a year for the 'full' ones. Villager attendance was mutatis mutandis on similar lines to the Hundred, though no doubt with a heavier emphasis on jury service.

Both the Hundred and the Shire had once been in theory public, hence in some sense royal courts. Royal courts proper were at least as important in the thirteenth century. The EYRE, which can be regarded as a royal afforcement of the shire court, is the most important for present purposes.[73] One over-riding reason why villagers could not ignore the presence of royal justices in their shire is the fact that the activities of all other courts were postponed during its sessions, on occasion for over a year. It would be no great exaggeration to say that all lesser courts were adjourned before the justices for the duration, their village participants along with them.

The central courts themselves, mainly the BENCH (COMMON PLEAS) but occasionally even THE KING'S BENCH too, also affected shire society. Increasingly more important locally were a whole group of ad hoc commissions that were to fill the gap left by the eyre's demise: ASSIZES, NISI PRIUS (to hold inquests), GAOL DELIVERY, OYER AND TERMINER etc. etc. No shire received less than one of these visitations a year and a statute of 1285 enacted that each should hold assizes three times a year. The villager could expect fairly frequent if irregular contact with royal justice through them 'in a town near you'.[74]

Some reference to the court system of the Church is needed to complete the picture. Most relevant are the judicial activities of inferior prelates, Deans, Arch-

[72] III Eg, 2; II Cn, 17; Leges Willelmi, 43 (*Die Gesetze der Angelsächen*, ed. F. Liebermann (3 vols.; Halle, 1903–16), 200–1, 320–1, 517). Cf. the suggestive comment of The Hundred Ordinance, I Eg, 1 (Liebermann, i. 192) : 'they shall assemble without fail every four weeks, and every man shall *do justice* to his fellow' (my emphasis).

[73] As will be apparent from its footnotes, this paper began life during a reading of the De Windt edition of *Huntingdon Eyre of 1286*. This was the first eyre in the shire since 1272 and, as it turned out, the last of its line.

[74] R. B. Pugh, 'Itinerant Justices in English History' (The Harte Memorial Lecture 1965, Exeter, 1967) gives a convenient summary of the various commissions. Cf. C. A. F. Meekings's comment that 'in the long history of the administration of law in the provinces through teams sent thither under commissions by the central government, the eyre occupies an early but comparatively short space', *1235 Surrey Eyre*, i, 5.

deacons and their Officials. Their RURAL CHAPTERS seem often to have met monthly on a set circuit, but also, I think, held unscheduled sessions at the parties' convenience. These petty prelates were always pretty easily available and little more than that was needed for low-level ecclesiastical justice.[75]

To this basic framework, one should add various other courts including some not easily classified, franchises, fair, and small-town courts. But all these courts, relatively formal settings for justice, are certainly only part of the story. The child too young to have business in them was already experiencing law directly through what he saw. Distraint to enforce court appearances has to have been among the commonest of sights.[76] Then there were the coroners' inquests that followed deaths and the Hue-and-Cry when a theft was detected.[77] The youngest child experienced these and began to learn what was expected of him in time for his induction into tithing at around the age of 12. Less lucky would be the child who witnessed one of those bands of strangers to whom royal jurors (themselves villagers) attributed all the unsolved crime they could.

These experiences were uneven in their effect. Some were much more positive than others. One effect of the changes that drained phrases like 'tota villata' of their content was to exclude many villagers from 'doing' some of the manorial justice their grandfathers had. Crudely put, the further from the manor justice was situated, the more negative its likely effect. This is most easily seen with royal justice, whose major characteristics will have been fines (amercements), hangings, and the browbeating of friends and acquaintances by haughty judges and uppity lawyers. All men knew that merely to draw an enemy by summons or citation into some distant court caused him anxiety and expense at relatively little cost or risk to themselves.

It would not be surprising if villagers experienced something like the clash of views of law, how it ought to be and how it actually was, that modern observers have noted in some modern communities. Members of one community in the American South apparently espouse a kind of natural law theory, which holds that Law should mean a set of rules of

---

[75] See Hyams, 'Deans and their Doings', 626 ff.

[76] Pending the appearance of Paul Brand's forthcoming Selden Society volume of *Select Cases of Replevin*, T. F. T. Plucknett, *Legislation of Edward I* (Oxford, 1949), *passim* has much to say about Distress. But the future study of the social history of distress will contain much for village historians to conjure with.

[77] P. R. Hyams, 'The Strange Case of Thomas of Elderfield', *History Today*, 36 (June 1986), 9–15 contains some vivid detail.

approved behaviour for all to follow.[78] In practice, however, they are compelled to recognize law as consisting of rules imposed from outside and above. This kind of opposition would be a natural outgrowth of the way that the common law appeared for so many as primarily the Pleas of the Crown, an external imposition ignorant of local verities and ways, to be feared or fooled. How far, one wonders, did this kind of view coexist with a feeling that this fell far short of the standard of 'real' law?

Such questions are easier to ask than to answer. Talk of approved behaviour takes one beyond litigation to the vast pyramid of dispute that often lay beneath and of which we know almost nothing. We should at least take note that even villagers had a number of alternative responses to grievance. Besides the obvious violence, which may appear dimly in case entries on the defendant's side of the score, there was also recourse to God and His saints. Recent accounts of the traffic at major shrines necessarily say little about the very kind of minor, local shrine to which villagers had freest access.[79] But certainly, holy men and hermits did not lack for village clients at some periods.[80] However, the existence of a litigation option, whether within the manor or beyond it, always affects the choice. Its mere threat can sometimes achieve the complainant's purpose, which may be something non-obvious (to punish an opponent or establish his own potency) from a wide range of possibilities.[81] Given that the litigation option always deeply affects the context for negotiation between disputing parties, it would be exciting to map the kinds of controversy that did not reach court too.[82] Though this is a pipe-dream for medieval village historians, our sources and skills license some shrewd

---

[78] C. Greenhouse, 'Interpreting America's Litigiousness', in J. Starr and J. F. Collier (eds.), *History and Power in the Study of Law: New Directions in Legal Anthropology* (Ithaca, NY, 1989), 252–73 at 265 ff, 269. We know that even justices of the US Supreme Court can recognize the attractions of Natural Law theories during their career.

[79] The identification of peasant pilgrims will not be easy. For some discussion and other relevant comments, see R. C. Finucane, *Miracles and Pilgrims: Popular Beliefs in Medieval England* (London, 1977), 142–6; B. Ward, *Miracles and the Medieval Mind: Theory, Record and Event, 1000–1215* (London, 1982), 64, 73, 80–1, 86–7, 103, 106–8.

[80] Cf. H. M. R. E. Mayr-Harting, 'Functions of a Twelfth-Century Recluse', *History*, 60 (1975), 337–52.

[81] For modern American options, see M. Galanter, 'Reading the Landscape of Disputes: What We Know and Don't Know (and Think We Know) about our Allegedly Contentious and Litigious Society', *UCLA Law Review*, 31 (1983), 4–71 at 12, 22, 26, 32; D. M. Engel, 'The Oven Bird's Song: Insiders, Outsiders and Personal Injuries in an American Community', *LHR* 18 (1984), 551–82 at 564–5.

[82] Cf. Galanter, 'Reading the Landscape of Disputes', 45, Engel, 'Oven Bird's Song', 574–7.

guesses. One notices, for example, how rarely the manorial court deals with physical injuries beyond the trivial scratches of village routine. For these, presumably, villagers must swallow hard and deal directly with their enemies or move beyond the village, even to sue for civil compensation.

Airy speculation of this kind has its contribution to make here. In my own mind, I try to organize it with the help of a small number of pertinent propositions on the villagers' sense of law.

1. The recognition that most behaviour affecting others (with public consequences, that is) must follow some approved lines, whether these are set within the village or imposed from outside. Examples are coercive sanctions for and against certain kinds of act ('crime'); and the rules that enact the proper forms without which attempts to effect property dispositions or reach certain social goals will risk failure.

2. What might be called the instrumental approach to law. This sees law as a way to pursue one's own interests. One might almost say a language with which to voice one's aspirations. It comprises both the means to harm one's enemies with impunity, one without the potential disadvantages of self-help, and the 'Bad Man's View of Law' as something to use or evade for his own ends.[83]

3. Vernacular conceptions of what is right and just, that sometimes surface through and modify formal law.[84]

4. The degree to which people in a particular environment favoured litigation over other ·responses to the perception of grievance. Viewed one way this is litigiousness.

5. Law as what royal officials (who in a sense personify it) actually *do*. These 'officials' may include the manorial lord (especially those with franchisal powers) as well as the Sheriff and other royal officials.

6. (As a last resort!) The Common Law's book rules and doctrine. For present purposes this is best seen from the angle of the consumer without a direct say in the formulation of the rules.

Each of these propositions suggests many questions that go well beyond the scope of this paper. I hope that some will find their way into the central canon of the field, for a fuller understanding of the villager's sense of law stands to teach us as much about village society as about law itself. I confine myself at this stage to a few comments on each of these.

---

[83] For the immediate inspiration here, see W. Twining and D. Miers, *How to Do Things with Rules* (2nd edn., London, 1982), esp. 67–70.

[84] The now classic illustration of this is the demonstration by T. A. Green, 'Societal Concepts of Criminal Liability for Homicide in Medieval England', *Speculum*, 47 (1972), 669–94 that jurors held and frequently implemented a view of culpable homicide quite distinct from that administered by the royal justices.

1. External sanctions are a source of both fear and attraction. In general they boosted villagers feelings of alienation from royal justice. All villagers were aware that royal law had power over life and limb, that justices hanged men.[85] But it was different when one was in the driving seat. Sanctions meant pressure that one could use by threatening to sue or to feed allegations into the system of indictments. In general, the system favoured the knowing few, including, one suspects, the villager with jury experience.

This advantage extended to the implementation of the various decisions that propertied people have to make during their life-cycle. A good test is the question of marriage. Here the Church had in the century before 1250 fashioned a legal framework for its ideal of Christian marriage. The important question of the degree to which it managed to enforce this at the village level remains much controverted.[86] The technical advances in methods of land transfer discussed earlier all required knowledge not easily acquired by mere attendance on others. This may have encouraged a degree of specialization parallelling the emergence of drafting specialists higher up society.[87] Men who do know their way around the law might thus programme their behaviour to avoid the pitfalls.

2. 'Bad men', seeking to use the courts to create the maximum trouble for their enemies at minimum risk and trouble, probably found it best to avoid direct confrontation. The presenting juries may have been their main chance. Common-law evidence for the crime of conspiracy, a novelty still in 1300, can document at a higher level some of the ways these were exploited for personal gain during the period. Those who can be seen, for example, holding the strings of power in a Yorkshire inquest into abuses held at the 1293 eyre represent the type of men whose aid village 'bad men' might seek to hire against their opponents.[88] Similarly,

---

[85] Nor did the Church disapprove. See *Thomae de Chobham Summa Confessorum*, ed. F. Broomfield (Analecta Medievalia Namurcensia, 25, Louvain and Paris, 1968), 304–6, 422–3, 432–3.

[86] For the Church's doctrine, see J. Brundage, *Law, Sex and Christian Society in Medieval Europe* (Chicago, 1987); G. Duby, *The Knight, the Lady and the Priest*, tr. B. Bray (London, 1983); R. H. Helmholz, *Marriage Litigation in Medieval England* (Cambridge, 1974). Bonfield, 'Nature of Customary Law', 532–4 has his own view on the recent debate over the nature of English peasant marriage; but note that the argument on 529 about bastardy takes no account of the developments summarized in Hyams, *King, Lords and Peasants*, 181–2.

[87] I say something about this in Hyams, 'Observations on the Charter'.

[88] PRO, Justices Itinerant 1/1095, on which cf. the remarks of *Select Cases at King's Bench in the Reign of Edward I*, ed. G. O. Sayles (3 vols.; Selden Soc. 55–58; 1936–9), iii. liv. I hope some day to publish a study of this roll.

behind a number of the ecclesiastical suits that came to the attention of
the Norwich eyre justices at the 1286 inquiry into abuses of Church
courts, there lie villagers out to cause trouble for neighbours.[89] Such
sources do more than document what may be isolated cases or the tip of
the proverbial iceberg. They document also patterns worth seeking in the
administration of presentments in the manor. Their confirmation by actual cases from the manor expands the circle of light from a few prosperous villagers onto a wider group whose route to instrumental use of the
system may perforce have had to run through more influential village
patrons. This is speculation and impure at that, but if ever verified it
would tell us something extremely important about intra-village relations.
And the village 'bad man' almost certainly did set local standards. Positing an instrumental view towards law provides a context, for example, for
the much-commented fact that most of those accused of serious crime
knew enough to flee unless they were sure of acquittal.

3. The villagers' own conceptions of equity—what was fair and just—
constitute custom in an unusual sense which coincides with no formal
sets of rules, not even the unrecorded ones of the manor court. They
would have been hard to record in any formal fashion. Yet they are real
enough, and include incorrect law, such as the notion that possession of
any charter makes a man free;[90] rules imposed upwards, by jurors on
royal justices, such as the categories of excusable homicide, already mentioned;[91] and regularities of practice, 'the way we do things here', that
might only sporadically (when something had gone amiss) reach the
courts for adjudication. These would include the inherited styles in which
men reached extra-curial settlements (arbitration) and drew up the records
of these and other dispositions.[92]

These vernacular or mistaken notions spilled into formal law most
easily through jury service. The opportunity to declare the facts of the
case, in a legal system whose distinction between fact and law was still
young, conferred a power to 'make' facts and thereby to protect justice as
it appeared to village jurors. Rates of conviction that were higher for outsiders than for village colleagues and lower still for 'A' villagers, or which
decreased in times of dearth, proclaimed this power in unmistakable

---

[89] See above n. 38.   [90] Hyams, *King, Lord and Peasants*, 44–6.
[91] Above n. 84.

[92] E. Powell, 'Arbitration and the Law in England in the Later Middle Ages', *TRHS* 5th
ser. 33 (1983), 49–67 looks mostly at a higher social level. Cf. J. W. Bennett, 'The Medieval
Loveday', *Speculum*, 33 (1958), 35–70 and M. T. Clanchy, 'Law and Love' in J. Bossy (ed.),
Disputes and Settlements: Law and Human Relations in the West (Cambridge, 1986), 49–68.

terms.[93] Watchful research will surely uncover other illustrations of the point.

Each time it does so, we shall become a little clearer in our perception of village equity, though a complete grasp of so shifting and cloudy a cluster of concepts is by its nature unattainable. The challenge here is to explore the links with the Church's teaching, as broadcast through preaching confession, diocesan statutes, and (by no means least because last) the Rural Chapter. Christian theology, with its ideal standard of a Divine law alongside corrupt human ones, justified consciences in evading or nullifying the common-law rules they disliked. Here is a little-used test for the influence of Reform in the Edwardian period.

4. The question of just how litigious modern Americans are has spawned a controversial and inconclusive literature, which may nevertheless be the best place to seek guidance on the kinds of question under examination here.[94] Litigiousness is not one of the areas where simple counting provides useful answers. Interestingly, modern studies stress the importance of very local conditions, which for the Edwardian village brings one back always to the strength and character of lordship. Beyond that, even to deduce that plaintiffs named on the rolls had a greater propensity to sue than others is dangerous. There is no way we can measure self-help or compromises reached out of court or without litigation. Recorded cases are in any court only the residue of unsettled grievances. What we might do is to begin the compilation of a working hypothesis on what kinds of dispute are most likely to reach court.

One of the legal scholars' key points concerns the availability of 'embedded forums', those resources to which one turns as a first defence against conflict. This reminds one how little we really know about the functioning of households and relations between neighbouring families. One deduction might be that the more prosperous villagers were better placed than the rest by their social network to keep their disputes out of court and the historians' eye. If so their litigiousness may be underestimated by their appearances on the rolls, a worrying thought. Some modern studies suggest that the characteristic litigants are those excluded from an established, central power group, more especially those who have least to lose in the way of established social relations. The least inhibited

---

[93] Smith, '"Modernisation" and the Corporate Medieval Community', 174–5 has these examples.

[94] I have used as guides the studies of Galanter, 'Reading the Landscape of Disputes' and Engel, 'Oven Bird's Song' and Greenhouse 'Interpreting America's Litigiousness'.

are strangers, who may even sue just in order to challenge the establishment. Such people have to hope for greater impartiality and chances for
a fair deal through the courts than if they followed the 'usual channels'.
This strikes a chord in Edwardian records,[95] and seems promising enough
to follow up in the records of courts outside the manor.

The decision to sue often turns less on knowledge of the rules expected
to be applicable in some court than on more general perceptions. People
feel differently about some kinds of cause than others. Some, for instance,
see the collection of debts as a moral duty, where personal injuries are the
victim's own problem; he should have been more careful. Medieval jurisdictional rules provide a dim echo of this by encouraging the diversion of
most cases of physical injury outside the manor thus perhaps directing
sufferers towards the holy where they swelled the vast numbers of healing
miracles in the collections.

Village historians might pursue this ideological variable more vigorously than hitherto. That abundance of money in the Edwardian countryside, with its concomitant of thinking in monetary and commercial terms,
as hammered into the recent literature by Alan Macfarlane,[96] inevitably
affected attitudes towards matters like litigation even in the absence of
'deep-pocket defendants', as lawyers call them.[97] But all individualisms
are not the same. One suggested distinction blunt enough to be service-
able to the historian sees two categories of individualism. It may be 'rights-
oriented', involving the belief that a wrong creates an almost automatic
right to compensation and redress. Or it may place so high a valuation on
'self-sufficiency and personal responsibility' that its proponents wish to
exclude public intervention in private affairs where possible.[98] Patently,
the first view encourages a higher level of litigiousness than the second.
That it also seems more characteristic of Edwardian England overall
might prompt one to ask why the virtues of self-sufficiency seem so much
less trumpeted in medieval Christianity than in some more modern varieties. In an age when serious injury in the course of everyday agricultural
duties or travel or household activity was so common, their inclusion into
litigation could have swamped the courts.[99] One might easily conclude

[95] Smith, ' "Modernisation" and the Corporate Medieval Community', 162–5, 174–5.
[96] Macfarlane, *The Origins of English Individualism*.
[97] Cf. Engel, 'Oven Bird's Song', 579 n. 21.
[98] Ibid. 558–60. Cf. Smith, ' "Modernisation" and the Corporate Medieval Community',
160–1 for criticism of Macfarlane's undifferentiated approach.
[99] One might compare findings from any roll of Crown Pleas (or the illustrations scattered through a book like N. D. Hurnard, *The King's Pardon for Homicide before A.D. 1307*
(Oxford, 1968), with Engel, 'The Oven Bird's Song', 558.

from the New Testament condemnations of discord that the Christian should give the courts a wide berth, that litigation was the vicious fruit of Greed and Envy. Yet Thomas of Chobham, to take one thirteenth-century writer widely read amongst village priests, explicitly licenses suing as a last resort in the midst of his pressing pleas for parishioners to make peace with their enemies.[100]

We can perhaps expect a diocesan official like Thomas to commend the use of the courts he ran. But what other general attitudes to courts and lawyers affected the village? The absence of Edwardian criticism of unworthy people using the system of justice contrasts with a certain evidence that there had been such feelings in the common law's early days.[101] Exceptions of villeinage in royal and (occasionally) other courts are the only hint of any widespread feeling that peasants in general ought to stick to their manorial court.[102] As for lawyers, the well-known hostility of fourteenth-century rural rebels towards them are largely explicable in terms of the jobs they performed for the lords, hence against the tenantry. Evidence on the number and professionalism of lawyers actually practising in some sense in local courts is rare. That some lords tried to ban them from their courts confirms that certain villagers found them useful, though we know little enough of the underlying reasons.[103] Access to legal advice at the expense of neighbour or lord could have been an issue. One can at present only say that the provision of legal services in the village and the significance of this for the developments described in the first part of the paper is another promising field for research.

5. The realist notion that law is what those who run the particular legal system (traffic wardens and policeman as much as judges) *do* ought to prompt village historians to juxtapose their descriptions of office-holding and jury service on the manor with the adjudicative business of the manorial court. To some extent such descriptions are, of course, presumed behind accounts of the way, for example, that some villagers dominated through their control of manorial office. I still find it hard to

---

[100] *Thomae de Chobham*, 245. I am grateful to Lauren Jared (University of California, Santa Barbara) for a sight of her draft on 'Towards a Greater Self-Sufficiency: Horizontal and Vertical Communities in the *Summae* of Peter the Chanter and Thomas of Chobham'.

[101] For Gilbert Foliot, see Hyams, *King, Lords and Peasants*, 249–50. Cf. also M. T. Clanchy, *'Moderni* in Education and Government in England', *Speculum*, 50 (1975), 671–88. Greenhouse, 'Interpreting America's Litigiousness', 266–8, reveals differential attitudes towards particular courts among her subjects.

[102] Cf. Hyams, *King, Lords and Peasants*, Ch. 12 for the fear, gathering strength in the fourteenth century, that 'villeins' were getting away with things in the courts.

[103] Above n. 39.

build up from the literature any very clear picture of these officials' overall role within the community.[104] Royal officials too played at least an occasional role in villagers' lives, as illustrated, for example, by demands for royal taxation and military service in Edward's wars.[105] Much needed in this context is some description of the routine everyday village role of the sheriff and his subordinates, hundred bailiffs, apparitors, and the like. The abundant records at national level of the hatred such men inspired highlight the desirability of weaving them into studies of village society. In the century after 1258 confrontation with royal law in the form of the demands of corrupt officials must have claims to being the villager's most formative legal experience of all.

6. Finally, law is inescapably also that system of rules and doctrine that jurists study, not least in works designed to serve manorial lords.[106] In Golden Ages, past and to be achieved, everything may be simple and comprehensible to all. But in the real life of Edwardian England, many of these rules were technical far beyond the understanding of kulaks and most of their superiors, for all 'the intense "law-mindedness"' that has been ascribed to late medieval England.[107] And I have said something already on the exceptional subjects which one came across in everyday life.

I have attempted to make here the strongest prima-facie case I can for seeing the more prosperous villagers within a legal culture that stretches far beyond the bounds of their villages. My plea entails no perverse denial that the manor, its court, and its custom in the narrow sense remain a central part of the villager's sense of law. The challenge is to place the village in its proper adjudicative context. By the time that Edward I died, it seems possible that the more substantial villagers held rather positive feelings about 'their' manorial courts. More definitely than in 1272, they could see it as *theirs*, the court that served their interests and convenience far more directly than any other. One nice indication of this is the fact that a villager could still sue there in defamation or trespass for damage to his reputation, something not (or no longer) permitted in royal courts.[108]

---

[104] Cf. the notion that amercements for trespass on the lord's demesne or for brewing against the assize amount in practice to a license fee. One may ask how such a convention developed.

[105] J. Maddicott, *The English Peasantry and the Demands of the Crown, 1294–1341* (*P&P* Supplements 1, 1975), has much to teach on the wider national setting of village life.

[106] *The Court Baron*, 1–106.

[107] E. W. Ives, *The Common Lawyers in Pre-Reformation England: Thomas Kebel, a Case Study* (Cambridge, 1983), 7.

[108] *Select Cases on Defamation*, lii–lxv; J. S. Beckerman, 'Adding Insult to *Iniuria*: Affronts to Honor and the Origins of Trespass', in M. S. Arnold, T. A. Green, S. A. Scully, and S. D. White (eds.), *On the Laws and Customs of England: Essays in Honor of S. E. Thorne* (Chapel Hill, NC, 1980), 159–81.

And of all these other courts, most villagers no doubt reserved their most negative feelings for the periodic intrusions of royal justices from the centre, commissions of assize, oyer and terminer, gaol delivery, and the rest. Just a few of the more prosperous and ambitious welcomed the chance to draw upon royal power, doubtless recognizing that enforcement of the Pleas of the Crown did something to keep violence against their goods within limits. Prosperous villagers figured among the early purchasers of commissions of oyer and terminer to 'get' their enemies.[109]

In the village as everywhere else in medieval England, the historian ignores the Crown at his peril. The successful villager absolutely had to include royal law in his calculations, and his sense of law surely stretched as far as some degree of awareness of the rarified legal culture of the Westminster pleaders and the men who compiled the Year Books. A question to be pursued on another occasion is whether this was still true in the same way in 1350 and 1400.

The vernacular sense of law is obviously much harder to get hold of than more conventional legal history, but patently interesting enough to be pursued with more rigour and through fuller data than in the present paper. Nor is there any good reason to confine such an inquiry to the level of village and countryside as I have here. Yet this further *enquête à poursuivre* promises special dividends to students of the village and peasant society at little extra cost. The names of the villagers we find in our manorial surveys and accounts and on our court rolls may find themselves in the future indexed on our computers as a matter of course. To use these lists to locate villagers' appearances in other forums is consequently much simpler now than it ever was before. We can and ought to research the patterns of villagers' exposure and recourse to law outside the village, to discover how prominently each lordship and region figures and to measure the discrepancies.[110] Local studies at the level of estate, region or village might fruitfully consider some of these questions as a matter of course. This will generate further questions on the regional patterns so important in rural sociology. Suits from eastern England are known to have figured disproportionately in the courts of the early common law.

[109] R. Kaeuper, 'Law and Order in Fourteenth-Century England: the Evidence of Special Commissions of Oyer and Terminer', *Speculum* 54 (1979), 734–84, esp. 752; and cf. his *War, Justice and Public Order*, Ch. 2.

[110] The regionalization that emerges may not fall along the same sociological lines as those propounded by Homans, *English Villagers*. My own first thoughts on this long ago are to be found in P. R. Hyams, 'The Origins of a Peasant Land Market in England', *EcHR* 2nd ser. 23 (1970), 22 and n. 5.

Did this over-representation continue in the Edwardian period?[111] And surely some lordships were more lax than others in opposing access to outside courts. What effect did the ending of the eyre system, largely ignored here, and the resulting transformation of royal justice in the countryside during the fourteenth century have on villagers and their sense of law? The dividends to be expected from bridging the current gulf that separates commendable studies of manor and village from a real understanding of the medieval peasant and his wider world are quite as substantial as those forecast from the 'Peace Dividend' and the opening up of Eastern Europe to trade.

[111] Flower, *Introduction to the Curia Regis Rolls*, 11 thought this imbalance disappeared about 1225. If it lingered, this would affect some of the arguments above, based as they are in the first instance so largely on Ramsey Abbey materials from eastern England.

Appendix 2.1

The central argument of Lloyd Bonfield's recent article on 'The Nature of Customary Law in the Manorial Courts of Medieval England' is too interesting and too acutely expressed for treatment only in a single footnote which will inevitably appear dismissive.[1] Yet the arguments for his 'tentative hypothesis' that the manor relied more on 'factual equities than substantive law' deserve an answer, if only to explain why I cannot at this stage accept them.

There is no question that manorial courts match poorly a modern model of 'principled adjudication' as he frames it. But this reads like an ideal type, whose prevalence in full at any date is open to question. Many medieval courts performed positive adjudicative functions without approximating to the Bonfield model. This rests on three 'jurisprudential assumptions' (521–3), that it (1) uses the 'principles of substantive law' to create 'rights', (2) follows a 'notion of precedent' in which the 'rules of customary law were either immutable or altered through some legally recognized manner'; and (3) accepts due process and equal protection through 'a proper application of customary law regardless of the status of the parties involved and the equities of the dispute'. By this restrictive formulation, the Edwardian common law, for all its Year-Books and its law-school rules of law, also fails the test; so too do civil-law jurisdictions as a group! Yet the common law and its French cousin each possessed a doctrine of precedent, albeit rather different from modern ones such as that administered in Anglo-American courts. The familiar formula that 'similar cases should be decided by similar reasoning' recalls a phrase 'in consimili casu' familiar to legal historians from the Statute of Westminster II 1285 and most telling in its French form: 'cas semblables' are the very heart of precedent.[2] Similarly, the common law indisputably recognized principle (3) as an ideal, but one pursued in a way that would not satisfy this formulation.[3] To require that courts ignore both the parties' status and the equities rules out systems much more recent than Edward I's Common Law! These are unrealistic tests for manorial justice.[4]

Bonfield has certainly stoked the investigative fires with good combustible

[1] *Comparative Studies in Society and History*, 31 (1989), 514–34.
[2] F. L. Cheyette, 'Custom, Case Law and Medieval "Constitutionalism": A Re-examination', *Political Science Quarterly*, 78 (1963), 362–90 makes a basic case from accessible sources. It needs restating with full reference to the whole range of available sources. For 'cas semblables', see Petot, 'Le Droit commun en France' (above n. 63), 422 ff.
[3] Similarly, not everyone will accept the demonstration (529) that manorial custom was 'malleable'. See Slota, 'Law, Land Transfer and Lordship', 132–3 and above, n. 86.
[4] Michael Biggs pointed out to me that the US courts denied right to substantive due process in one area between *Lochner v. New York*, 198 US 45 (1865) and *Nebbia v. New York*, 291 US 502 (1935).

material. (i) The explanation for the manor's inability to generate substantive law from detailed consideration of the facts of the cases that came before them is clear enough. Manorial lords never really exercised a controlling jurisdiction. From the later thirteenth century, they tended to receive their new rules from above (the common law) and they arrived more or less whole. That did not encourage legislative fertility, though Bonfield rightly points also to seignorial innovations made with little resistance from the suitors. (ii) The manor's possession of insider knowledge of people and events indeed marks it off from the common law and rendered irrelevant many of the senior system's devices largely designed to make up for the absence of precisely that kind of information. But arguably, in 1272 neither the devices nor the common law's posture of impartiality and ignorance that made them necessary were yet fully formed. (iii) That the manor fell below common-law standards of lawyerliness, while undoubtedly true, does not entail that it peddled mere informal equity. The rolls, even more laconically unhelpful than those of the very early common law, make it hard to tell what kind of jurisprudence was actually being practised. In the circumstances, one ought perhaps to remember how much sophistication of rules Milsom has wrung from their silences with Glanvill's aid. It is most unlikely that all the issues presented on manorial court rolls as factual really were factual alone. And even if they were, a succession of factual findings generates as a minimum expectations for the future that come in time to resemble strongly customary rules of the kind that Beckerman, and Maitland and others before him, thought to find there.

To probe the unique character of the manor court, Bonfield understandably directs attention towards the analogies offered by 'Alternative Dispute Resolution' models, though these may equally be relevant to the common law itself in both its early and its modern forms.[5] As he indicates, the insights thrown up by the dispute resolution industry offer some good starting-points. The key could even so turn out to relate to the ancient conundrum concerning the balance of manorial power between tenants (especially office-holders) and their lord. We need more scholars like Bonfield with his keen interest in lawyer's legal questions to consider afresh the political nature of the manor. Meanwhile, I see no reason to be deterred from seeking cultural norms on the manorial court rolls.

---

[5] D. Kairys, *The Politics of Law* (New York, 1982), 11–17 etc. floats the idea of an 'ADR' model for modern American law.

3

What Did English Villagers Mean by 'Customary Law'?

LLOYD BONFIELD

NEARLY a decade ago, I became interested in the use of manor court rolls as a vehicle for studying the intergenerational transfer of property amongst the peasantry of medieval and early modern England. As a legal historian whose research interest had hitherto been confined to the records of the royal courts and to documents of land transfer such as marriage settlements and deeds of a later period, I was astonished to find peppered amongst the litany of transfers of land an active forum for the resolution of civil disputes among those members of rural society whom we loosely heap together under the rubric of 'peasant'. Professor L. R. Poos, an historian who was using the manor court rolls in conjunction with other records to shed light upon a variety of socio-economic aspects of late medieval rural society, and I resolved to study as a team the manor court as a self-contained jurisdiction. We would focus upon the legal rules elaborated therein, the 'law' if you will, that could be gleaned from the manor courts, and that presumably had an impact upon medieval English rural society.

Such a foray into the manor courts as an institution that made and administered civil or private law in medieval England was not pathbreaking. As legal historians frequently are forced to acknowledge, F. W. Maitland was there first. A century earlier he had published a collection of *Select Pleas in Manorial and other Seignorial Courts* and likewise marvelled at the 'abundant harvest . . . that will not easily be reaped'.[1] Maitland, however, confined his 'sickle' to a modest collection of manors in East Anglia, and he was primarily interested in illustrating the variety of types of business which the courts he had selected considered.

Other historians have followed in his wake, observing the manor court primarily as a legal institution. Most notable amongst them was John Beckerman whose doctoral thesis is widely cited as the leading comprehensive study of the procedure and law of manor courts.[2] In common

---

[1] *Select Pleas in Manorial Courts*, xi.
[2] Beckerman, 'Customary Law in English Manorial Courts'.

with Maitland, Beckerman's research focused on a group of manors, but his was a larger sample.

Perhaps the most important development in the use of the records of the manor court, however, was their adoption by social historians and local historians.[3] Indeed Maitland himself recognized that editing rolls might best be left to 'one who had not only plenty of leisure, but also an intimate knowledge of and a special interest in the villages with which he would have to deal'.[4] Over the course of the past decade, medieval historians have increasingly used the manor court rolls as evidence of the social, economic, and legal condition of the English peasantry.

On the legal front, Maitland's argument that the manor courts of medieval England borrowed procedural workings from the central royal court has been extended to encompass also the assimilation of substantive principles of law. When articulated in its most extreme fashion, this argument would seem to regard the manor courts and manorial custom as no more than offshoots, and subordinate ones at that, of the royal courts. Were proponents of this position pressed to select a modern jurisdiction analogous to the medieval manor court, they would perchance select the small claims courts that have proliferated in modern America: forums with limited jurisdictional competence, employing procedures modelled upon, but not exactly parallel to, higher courts of first instance, and applying largely similar (though not in all circumstances exactly the same) principles of substantive law. While perhaps eschewing this precise metaphor, legal historians who argued first that significant borrowing of procedure occured and now also suggest the assimilation of substantive law seem rather close to such a characterization of the manor courts. Regardless of whether this comparison would be settled upon, the conclusion to be drawn from their depiction of the manor court must be that in many areas, custom as a distinct concept of jurisprudence disappeared or was very close to extinction in medieval England and more precisely, in the course of the reign of Edward I. Such a thesis, were it to be widely accepted, posits the disappearance of manorial custom nearly two centuries before litigation disappears from court rolls. Their view would have a profound effect upon characterizations of medieval society, as well as its legal order.

Our study is concerned with a more narrow series of issues, the substantive law of family and property relations in medieval English manorial

---

[3] To compile a complete bibliography of such work is one of the purposes of this volume.
[4] *Select Pleas in Manorial Courts*, xii.

courts, and has its own panoply of methodological windmills to tilt at without presuming to resolve the question of precisely how unified the legal system of England had actually become by late thirteenth century. Yet such difficult issues cannot entirely be avoided, because it is incumbent upon legal historians who seek to exploit court records to consider the structural nature of the institution that produced it. Threshold questions must be framed, and among them: what were the individual forum's jurisprudential parameters; what were the assumptions shared (or at least recognized) by its participants governing jurisdiction, process, proof, and remedy; or, in short, what was the court really like that produced the record under examination?

These queries are all the more troublesome to answer when the study is one of the manor courts of medieval England. Many factors peculiar to medieval manorial courts, not least of which is the fact that countless thousands of courts existed in the course of the Middle Ages (and they met frequently generating an enormous mass of litigation between peasants), a small percentage of which have left records that presently survive (and a still more modest number of those that can be examined by two researchers with limited life expectancy) argue for sympathy or at least critical forbearance for legal historians who endeavour to draw a survey of manorial law. The legal nature of the courts that produced what we shall call the 'customary law' of English peasantry, (and following our brief, our attention was devoted to the body of norms which directed property and family relations before the middle of the sixteenth century by which time villein tenures had been converted into 'copyhold' and villenage as a legal concept was moribund) is difficult to discern.

Moreover, the variety of functions which the jurisdiction served renders it rather unique as a court (save perhaps for parliament). A striking difference between the manor court and other medieval English jurisdictions is apparent when one observes the array of non-litigation functions which the manor court served. It is beyond question that the manor court directed the affairs of those subject to its jurisdiction to a far greater extent than a modern or contemporary court. A primary purpose of the manor court was the regulation of the community's agrarian economic order. The manor court established and enforced village by-laws that were calculated to oversee a variety of aspects of community life, and in particular, governed the use of common land and the common fields. The production of the two most important staple commodities was regulated by the assize of bread and ale. Local officials were elected, disturbances between villagers were enquired into, migration was monitored, vital events were recorded, and the lord's seigneurial dues enforced, all by the manor court. Indeed it has been argued that the written record of court meetings, the documents which we have examined, were more likely compiled to memorialize services to be performed and accounts owed to the lord, rather than to serve as a register of litigation or a compendium or digest of decisions of the court.[5]

I

Early on, then, Maitland recognized the many splendours of the manor court roll as historical evidence; it is, at the same time, a legal, social, economic, and administrative document. Court rolls can therefore be used effectively by historians of all academic persuasions. In the main, the quality of scholarship employing court rolls is admirable. But in embarking upon our research project, one that would purport to gather 'pronouncements'[6] of the law of the manor courts in the area of property and family relations by fashioning a more comprehensive sample of jurisdictions (as we were about to do), it was necessary for us to ponder what I christened elsewhere the 'jurisprudential nature' of the institution.[7] In short, it was incumbent upon me as the team 'lawyer' to ponder the important question: what is this very odd court that at times spewed forth law to resolve civil disputes (but did so very much more) really like?

In surveying the literature, I found that this question was rarely broached, and when it was, historians in the main viewed the manor court as a jurisdiction remarkably similar to a modern court. Indeed historians have regarded the manor court at times more akin to a twentieth-century jurisdiction than to the contemporary royal courts.[8] The result of my unease with this characterization led me to speculate about manorial law in particular a very imperfect article published in *Comparative Studies in Society and History*, which is discussed by Professor Hyams in his essay. To recount briefly the substance of this article, I query therein whether a variety of forces that might have been at work in the manor court and

[5] Smith, 'Some Thoughts', 98.

[6] We define 'pronouncements' of law as the articulation of substantive principles either formulated in the abstract (as statements of custom) by the jury or in the settlement or resolution of a cause before the court. Such 'pronouncements' purport (at least in our view) to have guided 'rights' in the past, and at least by implication should do so in the future. The awkwardness in formulation of what we mean by substantive pronouncements of law is in part due to the uniqueness of the legal jurisdiction. Although the manor court seems to adopt the myth that the principle itself has always existed, these pronouncements of law, phrased in terms of time-honoured principle, may well be properly regarded as 'legislation'.

[7] For an elaboration of this argument, see Bonfield, 'Nature of Customary Law', 521–3.

[8] Ibid. 523–6.

concealed in the record would allow historians to extrapolate cultural norms from the articulation of rationales for decisions in causes before the manor court. Now what does this mean? I proceeded by way of example. The Wakefield court in an inheritance dispute finds for elder son born after 'trothplight', but before marriage at the church door, and says that he shall hereafter hold the land in dispute. From that pronouncement, can we say that the peasantry of England had assimilated what legal and social historians often refer to as the 'canon law marriage formation rules' (that an exchange of words of consent to marry given in the present tense or a promise to marry in the future followed by intercourse gave rise to a valid marriage) into their psyche, and shaped the law of inheritance of customary land to conform to that principle?[9]

Whether the historian accepts the link between legal norms of the manor court and cultural norms in the fashion described above depends upon how he or she approaches the court record. More specifically, the historian's view may be directed by assumptions on how the manor court reaches decisions, particularly in controversies based upon detailed fact situations which, like the Wakefield case (and indeed most other interesting cases), probably come before the court only very infrequently, and are even more rarely resolved by explicit references to 'custom'. Three explanations (amongst others) may be offered to explain the logic of the decision-making process. First, the court may draw on pre-existing custom, rather like 'precedent'; the homage may rely upon their recollections, and/or search the rolls, for past similar cases and decisions and follow them. Second, they may create custom; the homage may select a substantive principle from a number of choices, and apply it to resolve the particular cause, because the homage believes that the appropriate rule ought to govern the issue in dispute. Finally, the court might reason more inductively, creating the rule to reach the result between parties that they may wish to see transpire. In the first and second situation, the rule resolves the controversy; in my third scenario, the controversy creates a rule.

Historians who wish to extrapolate cultural norms from the cases seem to suggest that if there is no clear custom, then the second process obtains. I still remain unprepared to make that leap, and it is perhaps because of another 'jurisdictional' dispute: perhaps it is because the lawyer approaches the record of a court with a good deal more scepticism than do most historians. Yet the boundary that separates us is far less

---

[9] R. M. Smith, 'Marriage Processes in the English Past', in L. Bonfield, R. M. Smith and K. Wrightson, *The World We Have Gained: Histories of Population and Social Structure* (Oxford, 1986), 55–69.

formidable, and not insurmountable, in that I do not wish to argue that the pronouncement of manorial court juries are of no value in understanding either the cultural values of medieval villagers, or the extent to which substantive principles of canon or common law permeated 'customary law'. Rather, I suggest that the general context of litigation in the manor court (disputes between neighbours); the occasional, but by no means incessant or even periodic reversals of position which casually seem to alter pre-existing rights or expectations (changes in custom); and the fact that each manor court operated independently of other manor courts, and again not infrequently adopted differing substantive principles, made me wary of extrapolating cultural norms from scattered pronouncements of custom.[10] To highlight this point, I posited an alternative model to the modern court (and one which I willingly concede is likewise speculative): a jurisdiction whose form is more akin to modern 'alternative dispute resolution' forum; in short a court that pondered 'factual equities' not apparent in the record, and perhaps valued fairness over the creation of a body of substantive principles of law to uniformly adjudicate disputes.[11] In short, a court that may have sometimes relied on my third scenario (the 'just' result) above to reach a decision. If I am correct in my characterization of the legal nature of the manor court (however tenuous the analogy with respect to particular modern forum), than the record, the manor court rolls, must be approached with more caution than has hitherto been the case.

That is not to say that I would suggest that the articulation of 'law' by manorial court juries is of no interest to either lawyers or historians of medieval society. Nor would I argue that there were no fixed substantive legal principles governing peasant relations recognized in the manor court. To the contrary; we were beginning an exhaustive study of manor court rolls to try to demonstrate just how interesting the 'pronouncement' of law in resolving cases could in fact be! In the article, I was suggesting that the underlying nature of the court (what makes it tick, if you will) requires us to assess the strength and the possible interplay of other factors: that some forces in addition to 'cultural norms' might have been at work in the legal order of the manor courts. Indeed few cultural norms are so fixed, or principles of law so accepted, or underlying facts of a dispute so

---

[10] Bonfield, 'Nature of Customary Law', 525–30.
[11] Ibid. 531. Of course, drawing analogies between any medieval court and a modern legal forum must always be regarded as tenuous. I trust that my initial suggestion was cloaked with sufficient tentativeness. A particular problem with respect to the manor court is the question 'alternative to what?'

clear-cut to immunize legal process from the predispositions of juries towards their own version of the just result; and we must bear in mind that manor court juries were well-acquainted with the litigants and the controversy to a degree probably unparalleled in the royal courts. At the risk of presuming to fashion responses for the other side in this debate in a teacup, I doubt many lawyers or historians would disagree with this premise; and therefore our dialogue herein is perhaps really just a matter of degree or emphasis, or perhaps even one of phraseology.

II

Thus, in some sense my argument in the *Comparative Studies* article was an apology for the enterprise which Professor Poos and I were about to undertake. A broader temporal and geographical survey of the manor courts (though by no means itself fully comprehensive) as a legal institution should be of assistance in developing an understanding of the substantive principles articulated in the court. So too our survey would test the presumption of uniformity amongst manor courts that historians were at least unconsciously positing: we would consider the regularity of application of individual rules within individual courts and amongst the myriad of jurisdictions, the appearance of rules, and the contexts in which they surfaced. Likewise, we would consider the procedures employed in manor courts to bring forth and to resolve disputes. More focus on the manor courts as a legal institution that played a primary role in mediating the civil affairs of the peasantry would allow even this sceptical lawyer (who always feels it necessary to go beyond what courts say to be quite certain what they really mean and why they mean it) to be comfortable with extrapolating cultural norms from the pronouncements of the manor court jury.

This is not the place to elaborate on our findings after three years of archival research. Rather, in this essay, I wish to address some of the issues which have been raised by those who argue for an early absorption of royal law by manor courts. In his essay in this volume, Professor Paul Hyams has stressed the point that the villeins who owed suit to the manor court were not excluded from the king's courts; that manor courts were not the only jurisdiction to which the peasantry could turn, and that therefore controlled their behaviour. His arguments have provided scholars whose research interests lie with the manor court with a salutary reminder that no legal jurisdiction operates in a vacuum, hermetically sealed from other courts or providers and/or enforcers of law. On the criminal side or perhaps more broadly phrased, the sphere of the enforcement of order, there was indeed a variety of mechanisms and institutions in the fray, many largely those of central government. Students who have mined manor court archives have often referred to the overlap. For example, Barbara Hanawalt's study of the frequency of crime in the half-century before the Black Death draws on gaol delivery records as well as manor court rolls.[12] Likewise, her study of the peasant family employs coroners' rolls.[13] As Professor Hyams notes, it is unlikely that a peasant of almost any degree of wealth or influence would have not understood, and even found himself or herself enmeshed in other aspects of medieval English legal culture besides merely the 'custom' of the manor courts.

On the civil side, however, I would argue that the intrusion of royal law and legal institutions into the peasant legal culture was less far marked than on the 'criminal'. There are two points which I wish to stress that are related to this issue. The first is that while Professor Beckerman may rightly be convicted of excessive zeal in regarding the manor court as the court of 'first and last resort'[14] (thanks largely to the efforts of Professor Hyams in illustrating the ability of villeins to sue in the royal court),[15] we would continue to consider the manor court to be the primary civil jurisdiction of the 'peasants' of Edwardian England. While litigants could and did go elsewhere for justice, the sheer volume of civil causes in the manor courts (and the relative cost-effectiveness of pursuing a cause in that court) as opposed to the number of peasant cases documented in 'royal' courts of any persuasion may, in fact, justify Professor Beckerman's hyperbole. Secondly, at the risk of falling into the well-worn academic charade of restating the other sides' position in the extreme so as to render it implausible (an abuse which Professor Hyams graciously avoids in discussing my essay), Professor Hyams suggests that the manor courts were becoming a jurisdictional arm of '. . . something approaching an integrated legal system administered through many different kinds of courts under the supervision of the King's Common Law . . .'.[16] Based upon our incursion into family and property law in the broadest range of manor courts thus far surveyed, we cannot accept that view for a number of reasons.

Let me briefly explain why a view of customary law as a clone of the

---

[12] B. A. Hanawalt, *Crime and Conflict in English Communities, 1300–1348* (Cambridge, Mass. 1979).

[13] B. A. Hanawalt, *The Ties that Bound: Peasant Families in Medieval England* (New York, 1986). On the civil side, Professor Richard Helmholz's Selden Society volume on defamation reproduces cases in manorial courts as well as a variety of local courts, as well as the royal courts. *Select Cases on Defamation.*

[14] Ch. 2 above.   [15] Hyams, *King, Lords and Peasants.*   [16] Ch. 2 above.

common law, at least with regard to substantive principles, cannot be accepted. In some sense, ours is a fundamental disagreement, because we differ upon the interpretation of the nature of the common law as it obtained in the first decade of the fourteenth century. During the Edwardian era, royal courts in my view were still largely concerned with delineating their jurisdiction and refining process; they were only beginning the task of articulating substantive principles of law.[17] Certainly, a number of substantive principles of inheritance law, for example, had been fixed. Yet in the manor court rolls we have found cases that raise issues far more complex, technical, and particular than the sample applications of pattern of descent. These cases raised questions that appear not to have been resolved in the royal courts, or at least we have not discovered discussion of them in the secondary literature.[18] In short, I would argue that in many cases which we have found in our survey there may not have been substantive common law for the manor courts to mimic had the court been so inclined.

Before returning to a discussion of our differing conceptions of medieval English law in more detail, I should like to address an interrelated issue which has a bearing on this question of adoption of royal law: the diversity of custom amongst the myriad of manor courts. In my *Comparative Studies* article, I noted the significant differences in opinion, procedure, and jurisdiction amongst the manor courts; such diversity I argued rendered it difficult to extrapolate 'national cultural norms' from a single case. The same reasoning in my view would render it unlikely that manor courts were mimicking such substantive common law as did exist. Diversity in reference to the medieval English manor courts does not extend merely to positions taken on a particular narrow issue like canons of descent. Rather it also runs to broader questions of the types of disputes that came before the individual court and the procedural means by which they were litigated and resolved. Space constraints do not permit me to articulate the reasons that may substantiate our argument (again likely one of emphasis) that well into even the fifteenth century manor courts must be regarded properly as local and largely unconnected institutions,

---

[17] Again Maitland can be cited: 'Knowledge of the procedure in the various forms of actions is the core of English medieval jurisprudence. The Year Books are largely occupied by this.' F. W. Maitland, *The Forms of Action at Common Law*, ed. A. H. Chaytor and W. T. Whittaker (Cambridge, 1971), 8. John Baker likewise stresses the tentative nature of the Year Books as accounts of substantive law well past the reign of Edward I. J. H. Baker, *An Introduction to English Legal History* (3rd edn., London, 1990), 204–6.

[18] For a full discussion of cases, see the introduction to our forthcoming Selden Society volume.

but one example may illustrate the difficulty in regarding the courts as an undifferentiated mass of similar courts.

In compiling our 'reporter' of customary law, it was incumbent upon us to explore the records of a variety of manors that were geographically diverse. It would not have been acceptable to have focused on, say, East Anglia, which has probably been over-represented in studies making use of manor court rolls, and eschewed the Midlands or the West Country. Yet since our brief was to exhume cases that articulated interesting substantive legal principles we were drawn to particular courts that seemed consistently to produce such cases. One might sift through a herd of sheep membranes in the manor of Nuneaton in Warwickshire, and uncover one case in which a dispute was resolved with reference to what one might regard as a recorded substantive legal principle. On the other hand, our attention was constantly being drawn to Great Horwood in Buckinghamshire and Hatfield Chase in Yorkshire where scarcely a year went by without some interesting case (as we had defined the term) 'emerging' from the court rolls.

Does this mean that interesting controversies were absent in Nuneaton, or was it that they were concealed (as Milsom suggests for the earlier royal courts)[19] in the general issue? Or was it due to the particular manor court's recording peculiarities? Regardless of your choice from the above menu (and my list herein is not exhaustive),[20] this aspect of diversity (and one recognized frequently by historians) within the universe of the manor courts seems to me to pose a serious dilemma for those who might consider the manor courts of the realm to be an undifferentiated mass that can be discussed as a single entity following the lead of the royal courts. Those manor courts that articulate principles of law and commit them to parchment may well be fundamentally dissimilar forums both structurally and procedurally from those which do not (or something else is afoot), and at the very least they are faced with a very different situation when a similar case comes along the next year or even a decade later. As Professor Jack Goody has noted, it is far easier to change previously accepted custom in an oral legal culture than one which articulates law in writing.[21] The more specific that elaboration of custom in writing is allowed to become, the more difficult it is to fashion change.

[19] S. F. C. Milsom, 'Law and Fact in Legal Development', *University of Toronto Law Journal*, 17 (1967), 1–19.
[20] Indeed some manor courts seem not to have entertained land pleas at all.
[21] J. Goody, *The Logic of Writing and the Organization of Society* (Cambridge, 1986), ch. 5, esp. 136–40.

The issue of diversity aside, let me briefly raise a further point to challenge the hypothesis of an integrated court system for Edwardian England governed by common-law principles. In our survey of manor court rolls, we find very little to suggest the 'shining out' of substantive principles of the developing common law in the manor courts. It is axiomatic (and annoying!) that principles of substantive law emerge only grudgingly from any of the medieval English jurisdictions. This is surely the case in most of the manor courts whose records we have examined. But those pronouncements of law which surface, and surface they do, are not necessarily (or even frequently) following the common law.

Again space constraints do not permit detailed discussion or citation of authority, but the manor courts whose rolls which we have surveyed are replete with formulations of different approaches to inheritance rights, different succession patterns, different rules relating to dower or freebench, different notions of the effects of illegitimacy on customary land, different concepts of tenure, and different spheres of jurisdiction. As such it is difficult to view these manor courts as being guided by common law.

Indeed examples can be found of the manor court noting that its decision is not consistent with the common law.[22] This evidence seems to support Professor Hyams' suggestion that the legal universe of the English villager extended beyond the boundaries of the manor. Indeed, his is a salutary reminder. Surely the manor court was not operating in an intellectual vacuum. But to note and even at times to implement similar principles in the manor court is neither to mimic nor to be controlled by the law of the royal courts. To accept the logic of such a connection would render the reverse as theoretically plausible: that the common law courts were adopting 'customary law'! Very little is known about the intellectual origins of substantive principles of either the common law or manorial law to be certain whether their development was truly intertwined or separate. Likewise, little is known about the individuals who presided over manorial courts, and the extent to which they were educated in the law. And finally we encounter very few explicit references to adoption or assimilation of common law principles within manor court rolls.

Finally it must be stressed that in the late thirteenth century, the royal courts were more concerned with jurisdiction, process, and proof than with substantive law. Our interesting cases seem to be raising and pleading complex facts requiring the articulation of arcane and substantive

---

[22] BL Add. MS 40167 fo. 31b, Barnet (Hertfordshire) court, 11 July 1306. *Et hoc habent & utuntur secundum consuetudines halimote eorundum & non secundum legem communem.*

principles in detailed responses to particular facts. Therefore, it should come as no surprise that we can find 'pronouncements' of law in the manor court for which we believe there is no common–law analogue.[23] At this juncture, therefore, we view the substantive law of the English manor court as distinct from the royal courts and worthy of study in its own right. The proponents of this 'trickle down' theory of peasant law removes from the participants in manorial court dramas considerable autonomy in decision-making; we place the burden of proof on its proponents, and regard it at present as unproved.

III

Having suggested above the reasons why we cannot at this juncture accept an argument for extensive connection between common law and the law of the manorial courts as they governed civil relations, I should be obligated to proffer a theory of our own regarding the intellectual inspiration of customary law in the medieval English manorial court. This is a challenge which I am unable to accept, at least without further consideration of the meaning of the cases which we have assembled from our survey of manor courts. My argument here must therefore be regarded as conjectural and destructive rather than constructive, rather like the *Comparative Studies* article.

Yet it is important to stress that there is much common ground in positions between those who regard manorial law to be largely similar to common law and their sceptics. In the first place, we agree that customary land was often settled by employing many of the same conveyancing forms as those used with respect to freehold land; entails, remainders (both contingent and vested), and reversions appear frequently in the court rolls, though the proper legal words of art are not always employed, and interests created are sometimes incorrectly described.[24] Second, even manors which were not ancient demesne sometimes refer to the plaintiff's claim by reference to a form of action, for example, *novel disseisin* and *mort d'ancestor* though we have seen examples where such characterization is technically incorrect.[25] Finally, it must be conceded that some of

---

[23] We have, for example, cases on guardianship which would not have found its source in common law. Moreover, some of the inheritance customs are far more complex than those which pertain to freehold.

[24] We are presently preparing an article on conveyancing of customary land that will address these issues directly.

[25] For example, CRO 619/M1, Abington (Cambridgeshire) court, 22 February 1363. In the case, one John Freborn brings an action against Robert Smith '*in natura assise nove*

the cases that articulate principles which we shall print in our volume roughly parallel the position of the common law on the same issue.

But manor courts also produced distinctive legal concepts. For example, some (though not all) manor courts countenanced a form of 'convey-- ance' of customary land that could not be accomplished with respect to freehold land, the 'deathbed transfer': to allow such transfers theories of customary tenure must have differed and therefore aspects of 'customary land law' must be regarded as different. In our study of the 'deathbed transfer', we argued that the greater flexibility accorded to customary tenure, tantamount in reality to the acceptance of the passage of land by will, was sanctioned so long as it did not clash with seigneurial pecuniary interest; so long as it was, to use contemporary tax lawyers' jargon, 'revenue neutral'.

May this notion in some sense be extended to other areas of customary law? To what extent were manorial courts free to construct their own legal principles in resolving disputes between peasants? More specifically, can we posit that with regard to disputes in legal arenas where the seigneurial interest was absent could not the rule (at least at times) be selected by the jury either by appeal to time honoured custom (either actual or bogus) or expressly by 'legislation?' And why should that rule necessarily be the same as the rule elaborated by the common law, save if the logic which produced the principle as law in the royal court was likewise applicable to the 'peasant' condition? And further, why should the rule not be altered when it is no longer appropriate in the abstract or in the particular case? The 'pronouncement' of law might be altered either explicitly or the change could be concealed by ignoring previous cases or even 'forgotten' surreptitiously in the general issue. And such pronouncements were required when the court was forced by the facts of particular disputes to go beyond previously resolved 'core' customs controlling inheritance, property or family relations.

Such speculation here must be regarded as airy. But to fashion comprehensive theories of the jurisprudential nature of a court that has for all intents and purposes closed its doors almost four centuries ago, and has left only the opaquest of records as did this institution requires some imagination. Imagination, however, must be followed by archival research. Like the hypothesis of the manor court as an Alternative Dispute

disseisine'. Inasmuch as Freborn does not allege that he was seised but that his father died siesed, *mort d'ancestor* would have been the appropriate form of action. Other plaintiffs got it right. PRO DL30. 58. 721, Barnston (Essex) court, 3 June 1449, where *mort d'ancestor* was properly brought. Neither manor was ancient demesne.

Resolution (ADR) forum, that of the manor court as a clone of the common law courts has to pass muster in light of further work. We hope that our efforts in that direction may eventually cast some light on how litigation in the manor court arose and was disposed.

4

The Development of the Deathbed Transfers in Medieval English Manor Courts

LLOYD BONFIELD AND L. R. POOS

PROPERTY owners in modern common-law jurisdictions have a wide variety of legal instruments at their disposal to effect the intergenerational transfer of wealth. Indeed the object of much reform in the area of estate transmission in the course of this century has been to reduce the formality required to execute the comprehensive succession arrangements[1] which anthropologists and historians have termed 'strategies'.[2] Yet the process of relaxation of formality has not produced a law devoid of requirement, because societal interest is thought at times to conflict with unimpinged informality of transfer.[3] For example, legislatures and courts believe that some formality protects the property owner (who at the time his act has legal effect may be dead) from those who seek to influence or subvert the succession process.[4] Moreover, because nearly all members of society partake of the process, the administrative burden on the judicial system is lessened when law provides a clear set of hurdles for a disposition to

---

[1] In the USA the National Conference of Commissioners on Uniform State Laws has drafted a series of model acts, some dealing with simplification in property transmission. The Uniform Probate Code's statement of purpose is 'to simplify and clarify the law concerning the affairs of decedents . . .' S. 1–102(b) (1). It has been adopted in fifteen states. Other Uniform Acts dealing with devolution, for example, the Uniform Testamentary Additions to Trust Act (which facilitates the creation of 'pour-over wills') has been adopted in forty-two states and the District of Columbia. In England, the Administration of Justice Act 1982 S. 17 relaxes some of the very elaborate formalities of execution required by S. 9 of the Wills Act 1837 and Wills Act Amendment Act 1852 S. 1. Moreover, S. 21 of the 1982 Act allows all evidence of the testator's intention in construing ambiguities within a will.

[2] The term 'strategy' has been widely used as a means of conceptualizing individual and group behaviour. We hear of strategies of heirship (J. Goody and G. A. Harrison, 'Strategies of Heirship', *Comparative Studies in Society and History*, 15 (1973), 3–21); fertility strategies (E. A. Wrigley, 'Fertility Strategy for the Individual and the Group' in *Historical Studies in Changing Fertility*, ed. C. Tilly (Princeton, 1978), 135–54); marriage strategies (P. Bourdieu, 'Les Strategies matrimoniales dans le système de reproduction', *Annales ESC* 27 (1972), 1105–25). See generally the articles in J. Goody, J. Thirsk, and E. P. Thompson (eds.), *Family and Inheritance: Rural Society in Western Europe, 1700–1800* (Cambridge, 1976).

[3] For a discussion, see A. Gulliver and C. Tilson, 'Classification of Gratuitous Transfers', *Yale Law Journal*, 51 (1941), 1–16.

[4] Ibid. at 9–13.

clear in order to be valid.[5] Likewise, the more detailed and tailored to these aims the requirements for validity are constructed, the less likely disputes regarding dispositions will arise.[6] Thus, in modern law, the virtue of simplification is balanced with protective concerns, creating a law of wills and trusts on the one hand sufficiently complex both to embarrass practitioners and confound students, but leaving individuals relatively free to craft estate plans consistent with their own desires.

The jurisprudential underpinnings of this modern qualified simplification of legal requirements for wealth transmission may well be the individualistic[7] perception of rights in property that obtains at common law. While the varying jurisdictions recognize different degrees of restraint on the right to construct estate plans through statutory control on freedom of disposition (for example, the prescribed share of the surviving spouse),[8] limitations in common-law systems are minimal in contrast with other legal systems;[9] near boundless discretion is reposed in common-law property-holders to dispose of wealth. While such liberty no doubt helps to explain the complexity of transmission devices that the legal profession has contrived, it likewise justifies the goal of minimal formality for those who wish to transmit their property in uncomplicated fashion. To sanction plenary powers of disposition over property while inhibiting

---

   [5] I. Eherlich and R. Posner, 'An Economic Analysis of Legal Rulemaking', *JLS* 3 (1973), 257–76, at 264 (common law rulemaking is less efficient); L. Friedman, 'The Law of the Living, the Law of the Dead: Property, Succession and Society', *Wisconsin Law Review*, 30 (1966), 340–78, at 368.
   [6] For a contrary view, see J. Langbein, 'Substantial Compliance with the Wills Act', *Harvard Law Review*, 88 (1975), 489–534, at 524.
   [7] The term 'individualistic' has a number of different definitions depending upon context. As legal historians, we wish to avoid the debate of legal theorists over the elements of a legal culture that is 'individualistic'. Nor do we wish to engage in the historical debate regarding England's different development proffered by A. Macfarlane in *Origins of English Individualism*, having engaged in dialogue elsewhere Poos and Bonfield, 'Law and Individualism in Medieval England', 287–301. Here we simply mean that a property holder deals with property free from the control of family members, and selects a pattern with a minimal interference in law.
   [8] To some extent, all American states protect the surviving spouse against disinheritance either through the 'community property' system or the 'elective share'. In England, a court can order maintenance for a surviving spouse (or other dependent relative left without 'reasonable provision'). Inheritance (Family Provision) Act 1938, S. 1; Inheritance (Family Provision) Act 1975, S. 1.
   [9] Contrast the prohibition on the disinheritance of children in Louisiana (whose private law is derived from the French civil code), La. Civil Code Article, SS. 1493, 1495, 1497, 1502–4 with the plenary power to disinherit children in the other 49 states. See C. Samuel, W. Shaw and K. Spaht, 'Successions and Donations', *Louisiana Law Review*, 45 (1985), 575; M. A. Glendon, 'Fixed Rules and Discretion in Contemporary Family Law and Succession Law', *Tulane Law Review*, 60 (1986), 1165.

its free exercise by insisting upon burdensome formality would seem inconsistent.

Such is the present, but what of the past? To what extent did the principle of freedom of disposition obtain in pre-modern England, and had the mechanical forms been developed to maximize the principle? In short, were Englishmen in the past free to effect strategies of inheritance according to particular, individual desires? Just as societal interest regulates freedom of disposition in modern society, counterposed interests may have existed in earlier times to limit the creation of inheritance strategies. For example, in a society organized along kinship lines, as some historians have perceived early Anglo-Saxon England,[10] individual freedom of disposition might clash with the interest of the family group.

In this paper, however, we wish to come forward several centuries and narrow our focus to consider the ability of the English peasantry who held customary land in the later Middle Ages to construct inheritance strategies. The juxtaposed interest which we shall consider is that of the lord. Our aim is to systematize the transmission options of customary tenants and observe the way that they were enlarged to enable them to implement more individualized and complex inheritance strategies. Ultimately we shall be speculating on the nature of the system of law implemented in manorial courts. Just as our modern system of devolution is indicative of present social organization and legal culture, an investigation of past practice should assist historians in understanding the position of customary tenants. Before embarking on our investigation of practice amongst customary tenants we wish to consider the evolution of freedom of disposition.

I

Freedom of disposition, and therefore the ability to create inheritance strategies, is a relative rather than absolute concept because, as mentioned above, some limitations will likely exist in any legal culture in accordance with other societal values. Perhaps the most straightforward way to understand its relativity is to view the more distant past and observe the earliest stages of the evolution of freedom of disposition in England.

It is generally agreed that if one delves far enough back into pre-Conquest England, an era will be reached in which land was held by families whose members possessed rights and whose heads managed the

---

[10] H. R. Loyn, *Anglo-Saxon England and the Norman Conquest* (London, 1962), 292–8, F. M. Stenton, *Anglo-Saxon England* (3rd edn. Oxford, 1971), 315–18. Pollock and Maitland, *History of English Law*, ii. 242–6.

holding in a corporate rather than individual capacity.[11] In earlier society, rights in land were acquired by birth rather than transfer. One's 'birthright' (as it is termed) was not subject to disposition *inter vivos*. Because death terminated any interest in familial property, *post-mortem* disposition was precluded. The role of the head of the family was not to construct inheritance strategies but to balance resources with family size, and to pass the patrimony to his successor in at least as good a condition as he had received it. Mechanical forms of conveyance were therefore limited to those that would effect transfers of land between family groups.

Exactly when this system of familial ownership gave way to one in which some degree of individual right was recognized is unclear. Michael Sheehan persuasively argues that the Christianization of the Anglo-Saxons was the crucial event, because it brought with it a recognition of an afterlife and a concomitant need to give alms for the benefit of the soul.[12] To do so required Germanic customs to allow individuals some right at their death over hitherto familial property. As might be expected, this shift in the conception of property gave rise to a number of mechanical forms of transfer, most notably the will.

Yet there is some evidence to suggest that the turn towards individual as opposed to familial rights went even further than the good of the soul. Maitland noted the creation and protection of 'something like the estate entail male' directing the descent of land as early as the eighth century.[13] That the descent of land could be prescribed in a particular fashion for a non-spiritual purpose suggests even deeper inroads into the concept of collective, familial ownership. With a wider recognition of individual freedom of disposition came the beginnings of the ability to construct inheritance strategies.

If the inspiration for the movement towards the recognition of some degree of individualistic rights in property was derived from Christianization, Anglo-Saxon law ultimately came to strike a balance between family and freedom. Birthright by the tenth century was transformed from a present interest attaching at birth to one more akin to a future interest, a right to a share in familial wealth at the death of the family head of household. Thus birthright was in large measure transposed into a negative right, a right not to be excluded completely from family property. Accordingly, property owners became free to dispose of a 'reasonable

---

[11] Ibid. ii. 247–53.

[12] M. M. Sheehan, *The Will in Medieval England from the Conversion of the Anglo-Saxons to the End of the Thirteenth Century* (Toronto, 1963), 5–12.

[13] Pollock and Maitland, *History of English Law*, ii. 244.

share' of their wealth.[14] Although the proportion appears never to have been quantified, a principle allowing some degree of freedom of disposition was codified in the laws of Cnut: holders of bookland who had fulfilled their 'obligations' were free to dispose of their land during their life and at death.[15]

The specific reference to bookland in Cnut's law suggests the complexity and relativity of freedom of disposition within a legal culture, because it may be limited by social class or more specifically by the nature of property to be disposed. Here a particular type of tenure held by the upper reaches of Anglo-Saxon society was in part freed of the claims of family, and the power to dispose either *inter vivos* or testamentary was countenanced. Other forms of land tenure were excluded. Indeed, Vinogradoff argued that freedom of disposition was a major distinction between bookland and the folkland held by the peasantry, suggesting that the latter never was 'sufficiently free of the claims of inheritance' to be freely transferred.[16]

Thus a divide along lines of status has been posited with respect to Anglo-Saxon law: movement from family property to individual property occurred earlier in the upper classes. Historical debate, however, is fuelled by sources, and it must be conceded that such early evidence of disposition as exists is heavily weighted towards the upper classes. Vinogradoff's view of a divide, though thinly documented, is thought by some to continue through the Conquest and on into the later Middle Ages.[17] While historians have documented a move, though admittedly not linear, towards freedom of disposition for the holders of free tenements by reference to legal texts and charters, a parallel tendency for the unfree has been denied by others.[18]

To some extent the explanation for the divide in conceptions of rights in property is viewed as self-evident. Freeholders participated in the formation of law. By statute and common law, but also through the ingenuity of the legal profession, the upper classes were able to forge a system of inheritance that suited their needs; and their goals were so diverse that a rather flexible system was created. On the other side of the divide, no such transition could take place. The unfree were, after all,

---

[14] Ibid. 249.

[15] *Die Gesetze der Angelsächsen*, i. 366–7; Sheehan, *Will in Medieval England*, 98.

[16] P. Vinogradoff, 'Folkland', *EHR* 8 (1893), 1–17.

[17] e.g. Homans, *English Villagers*.

[18] Poos and Bonfield, 'Law and Individualism', 287, 301, and esp. works cited in note 14 in response to S. White and R. Vann, 'The Invention of English Individualism: Alan Macfarlane and the Modernization of pre-Modern England', *Social History*, 8 (1983), 345.

unfree; seigneurial interest dominated, and villeins had only a very limited ability to formulate an inheritance structure responsive to their needs. Moreover, as argued above, freedom of disposition is linked to the development of conveyancing techniques to accomplish it; and the legal culture of the peasantry was insufficiently sophisticated to produce the necessary devices.

Further thought must be given to these conclusions before accepting this divide. In the first place, seigneurial interest is a complex matter and in the arena of inheritance is not always easily discernible.[19] Lords were concerned primarily with the performance of services and the payment of rent. To secure what was due may have required orderly inheritance, but individual control over the pattern of devolution would not necessarily be inconsistent with that end. With regard to the issue of whether techniques necessary for the creation of individual strategies of property devolution existed, a systematic study of the records of various jurisdictions to which villeins were subject, both manorial courts and ecclesiastical courts, must be undertaken before concluding that the peasant legal culture was insufficiently advanced to allow the execution of the more complex strategies of inheritance that were being implemented by freeholders. Just as other aspects of common-law substance and procedure were having an impact on manorial courts, a similar tendency may have been occurring in the area of inheritance.[20]

What is clear is that freedom of alienation was a necessary ingredient to accomplish inheritance strategies. A movement from a family-based system of property ownership to one in which rights in property were held by individuals, who could freely dispose of them and construct 'strategies of inheritance', had to occur. Yet transition was not without certain tension because other cultural, social and political values conflicted, and a system of 'law' existed, customs recognized in the manorial court, to regulate property transfers. In this paper, our attention will focus on the various options available to customary tenants in later medieval England to control the devolution of property and then observe the introduction of a form of transfer that enlarged the customary tenants' ability to effect inheritance strategies. By so doing, we hope to illuminate how change occurred in the manor court, and thus learn something about the nature of customary law.

---

[19] Bonfield, 'The Nature of Customary Law'.
[20] *Select Pleas in Manorial Courts*, lxvii, lxxii. Beckerman, 'Customary Law in Manorial Courts', 10–11.

II

By the fourteenth century, tenants of customary land in many English manors had a fairly broad range of options from which to choose when contemplating the transmission of that property to the next generation. Perhaps the most straightforward—and certainly the one which has traditionally claimed the most attention from both legal and social historians—is inheritance by 'the custom of the manor', whatever pattern of distribution was in force in a given manorial jurisdiction. The tenant died, in modern if perhaps anachronistic terms, 'intestate' with regard to his customary tenement. The inheritance custom of the manor in question, whether it be partible or impartible, primogeniture or ultimogeniture, then dictated the particular category of heir(s) or heiress(es) to whom the tenement would descend. This often included provision for the widow (if any), who might be entitled to enjoy a life estate in some or all of the tenement, often conditional upon her remaining unmarried.[21]

To the extent that tenants whose landholding descended in this way made a conscious choice of the 'intestate' pattern, its acceptance may have reflected a cultural norm dictating a preferred heir (as some historians have seen it, a coincidence of popular culture and customary law),[22] or might imply that the tenement that devolved in this manner was merely one part of a larger estate whose other elements (such as chattels) could be disposed of by other means such as *pre-mortem* gifts or testamentary disposition. One of the more important contributions in recent years to historians' understanding of inheritance processes in action has been an appreciation of the extent to which demographic variables affected the outcome of devolution patterns in pre-modern societies. These variables included the frequency with which men would die without surviving sons or even daughters (due to combinations of fertility and infant-survival rates), requiring the disposal of significant quantities of property outside 'normal' inheritance channels; or conversely, the frequency with which property-holders died suddenly or relatively early in life, leaving very young children and so complicating any attempts to fashion conscious devolution 'strategies'.[23]

---

[21] Homans, *English Villagers*, 109–43; Faith, 'Peasant Families', 77–95; Harvey (ed.), *Peasant Land Market*, 39–50, 91–4; C. Howell, 'Peasant Inheritance Customs in the Midlands 1280–1700', in Goody *et al.* (eds.), *Family and Inheritance*, 112–55.
[22] This approach particularly informs the views of Homans, *English Villagers* and Faith, 'Peasant Families'.
[23] Wrigley, 'Fertility Strategy', 135–54; Smith, 'Some Issues Concerning Families', 38–62.

A second alternative was for the customary tenant to make dispositions of his property _inter vivos_, through the process of surrender and admission in the manorial court. By the beginning of the fourteenth century (at the latest) in the majority of English manors observed, historians have established that permanent alienation of customary property, with a considerable degree of tenurial security, was widely sanctioned.[24]

Within the broad category of _inter vivos_ transfers a further range of options was possible. Most straightforward was simple surrender and admission, in which a grantor came into the manorial court and surrendered the property into the lord's hands in favour [_ad opus_] of the intended grantee, to whom the property was then re-granted.[25] In its simplest form this procedure transferred a present possessory interest to the grantee at the time of the transaction. In the context of intergenerational transfer a tenant might use surrender and admission to effect _pre-mortem_ endowment for a child (for example, a younger son or daughter) who would not inherit under the 'custom of the manor'.[26]

By the last decades of the thirteenth century, however, further alternatives existed in manorial courts with the recognition of grants in which donors retained life interests in the property, but limited future interests to grantees. These grants differed from the outright _inter vivos_ surrender and admission because the selected heirs' actual possession was postponed until, or conditional upon, certain future events. These grants assumed many forms. In perhaps the simplest, the tenant surrendered the property to the lord and received it back to tenant for life with remainder to a specified individual (or individuals).[27] In the context of devolution, the process would allow, say, a father to retain a life-estate in his property but to direct its descent to a particular successor. This type of transfer was a form of _post-obit_ gift recognized in Anglo-Saxon practice by the sixth century.[28] Indeed, these arrangements, rudimentary marriage or family settlements, allowed the fashioning of elaborate provisions.[29] By so disposing of one portion of his property to a younger son or daughter,

---

[24] A protracted debate has surrounded this issue. For a summary of views and a guide to the secondary literature, see Smith, 'Some Thoughts', 95–128.

[25] Ibid. 107–26; Beckerman, 'Customary Law in Manorial Courts', 138–9; Hyams, _King, Lords and Peasants_, 38–40.

[26] Documented examples of this may be found in Dyer, _Lords and Peasants_, 305–12; Razi, _Life, Marriage and Death_, 50–60.

[27] Harvey, _Westminster Abbey_, 280–3; Dyer, _Lords and Peasants_, 303; for examples of texts see Poos, 'Population and Resources', 230–3.

[28] Sheehan, _Will in Medieval England_, 24.

[29] Pollock and Maitland, _History of English Law_, i. 319–20.

but none the less allowing the remainder of his property to descend by manorial 'custom' of primogeniture, a father of even quite humble legal or social status could in effect execute an 'estate plan'.

Tenants could also employ the customary law equivalent of the entail of freehold property. An example was the situation in which father granted property to son and daughter-in-law (or daughter and son-in-law) and the heirs of their bodies, in default of whose issue the land would revert to the heirs general of the original donor. This arrangement has been observed in a number of manors within a very few years of their recognition at common law by the statute *De donis*, and the evidence so far unearthed indicates that manorial courts were prepared to respect donors' wishes in this regard.[30]

A final alternative, allowing further flexibility, was a somewhat different version of the conditional grant: the arrangement which social historians have termed the 'maintenance agreement'.[31] Tenant (presumably aged) granted the tenement to offspring (or indeed in some cases to a relative or even a person or persons entirely unrelated to him) on the condition that the latter render lodging, food, and other necessities to the donor for the duration of the donor's life. Maintenance agreements are conditional grants in that failure to perform these often quite closely specified services resulted (as can be shown in a number of cases) in the return of the property to the original donor, whereas the satisfactory performance of these duties resulted, under the terms of most of these agreements, in the grantee's assumption of unqualified tenure at the grantor's death. These grants therefore could be employed as part of an overall devolution 'strategy', though their use was aimed primarily at securing provision for the donor.

All these varieties of grants required only minor alterations in the forms of land transfer at customary law. They occurred in the manor court, and required merely the acceptance of a right to grant future interests and retain reversions. Thus they did not infringe upon the lord's curial supervision of land transfers or threaten his fiscal interest in the 'transfer fee', the entry fine, issuing from them.

But from the perspective of the holder of rights in customary land the inception of these avenues of devolution were insufficient in themselves to allow what we shall argue was a critical component of a genuine devolution 'strategy': the property-holder's ability to make comprehensive,

---

[30] Poos and Bonfield, 'Law and Individualism', 287–301; an early example of this form of transfer in a manorial court is printed in *Select Pleas in Manorial Courts*, 40.

[31] Clark, 'Some Aspects of Social Security', 307–20.

last minute arrangements at the end of his life and in full cognisance of the demographic configuration of his family as a modern testator can do when making a last will in which both real and personal property pass. To accomplish this required a further conveyancing advance, to which we shall now turn.

III

Our primary focus in this paper is to trace the development of yet another avenue of devolution at customary law, one which has thus far received scant attention from legal historians. We shall term this form the 'deathbed transfer'. It occurred when a tenant 'languishing near death' or 'on his deathbed' [_languens in extremis, in mortali lecto_] instructed a manorial officer or other person (usually in the presence of other manorial tenants or witnesses) regarding the devolution of his tenement on his death; those present then came to the next meeting of the manorial court and the tenement was transferred to the intended beneficiary by the usual process of surrender and admission. The procedure may or may not have been explicitly described in the court roll as the execution of the dying tenant's will or testament.

The present discussion is part of a larger forthcoming study of the law of family and property in English customary courts before 1600, and our cases here are drawn from a preliminary survey of 113 deathbed transfers in the court records primarily of one county, Essex. We shall cite as an example of the legal form of the 'deathbed transfer' at its simplest, the following case from the manor of Priors Hall in Birchanger in 1507:[32]

At this court it is shown by the homage that John Clerke, languishing _in extremis_, out of court, before this court, following the custom of the manor surrendered into the lord's hands by the hand of Thomas Parant, tenant, in the presence of other tenants of the lord, a customary tenement with appurtenances called Smertes, in favour of Katherine his wife for the term of her life, with remainder after

---

[32] New College, Oxford, Archives (hereafter NCO), (cited by kind permission of the Warden and Scholars) 3598, m. 7. (Priors Hall leet, 18 Dec. 1507): _Ad hanc curiam compertum est per homagium quod Johannes Clerke languens in extremis extra curiam ante istam curiam secundum consuetudines manerij sursumreddit in manum domini per manum Thome Parant tenentis in presencia aliorum tenentium domini unum tenementum custumarium cum pertinentiis vocatum Smertes ad opus Katerine uxoris eius pro termino vite sue Remanere inde post decessum ipsius Katerine Jacobo Clerke filio eorundem Johannis & Katerine uxoris eius heredibus & assignatis ipsius Jacobi Cui quidem Katerine liberata est seisina Tenendum sibi pro termino vite sue de domino ad voluntatem domini secundum consuetudines manerij . . . Remanere inde prefato Jacobo heredibus & assignatis suis prout supradictum est . . ._

Katherine's death to James Clerke son of the same John and Katherine, and James' heirs and assigns. To which Katherine seisin is delivered, to be held to her for the term of her life at the lord's will following the custom of the manor with remainder therein to the said James . . .

This procedure appears at first blush to be highly questionable at customary law, for its recognition seems tantamount to accepting a villein's right to make an oral will of customary property. Moreover, the acceptance of the transfer clashed with the lord's concern to regulate transfers of customary land within the manor court. On the first point, as Sheehan and Hyams have shown, the right of people of unfree personal status to make wills at all was a contentious issue into the fourteenth century, representing as it did an unusual trilateral conflict among ecclesiastical law (which generally urged that the right be extended to all persons), common law (which sought to safeguard lords' potential losses from recognition of this right on the part of their villeins), and customary law (which in practice appears, at least in some manors, not only to have sanctioned this right but also to have directed probate of villein wills into manorial courts).[33] Some evidence exists to suggest that the ecclesiastical position may have prevailed in some manors, because as early as the first quarter of the thirteenth century, a few manorial jurisdictions included testamentary matters as part of their regular business. Perhaps the best known of those manors are those of the abbey of St Albans, discussed at length by Levett.[34] In this instance the courts acted straightforwardly as venues of probate over unfree tenants. It is possible that the ability of villeins to prove wills in manorial courts was particularly associated with the estates of ecclesiastical lords, since (upon preliminary investigation) other known examples included the estates of the abbeys of Ramsey and Bec and the bishopric of Winchester.[35]

But these manorial courts only countenanced the right of villeins to dispose of *chattels* by will. Land raised a more difficult issue. English law was by and large inimical to testamentary transfers of land throughout the Middle Ages; it was only the special case of borough tenure that enjoyed this privilege, and even here the right was not usually recognized in a

---

[33] Sheehan, *Will in Medieval England*, 253–4; Hyams, *King, Lords and Peasants*, 69–74; H. S. Bennett, *Life on the English Manor* (Cambridge, 1937; reissued. 1971), 248–51.
[34] Levett, *Studies in Manorial History*, 208–34.
[35] Ibid. 209; Sheehan, *Will in Medieval England*, 254. A possible example of a non-ecclesiastical lordship holding this jurisdiction by the early 14th cent. is the Honour of Knaresborough; *Wills and Administrations from the Knaresborough Court Rolls*, ed. F. Collins (Surtees Soc. 104, 1900), xix.

formal manner until well into the high Middle Ages. In his treatment of the disposition of freehold property by will, Sheehan discusses at length the arguments of Glanvill, who warned against disposition of property on the donor's deathbed. Nevertheless, the effect of the common-law developments of Henry II's reign was to render any conveyance, accompanied by livery of seisin by a donor still *compos mentis*, valid.[36]

In this light the critical point about the development of the customary deathbed transfer was not so much whether manorial courts were prepared to sanction the straightforward devise of customary land by will as it was to determine how a complete transfer of present customary interests would be effected by the courts under the circumstances of a dying tenant's expressed wishes. For perhaps the more remarkable aspect of these transfers is that they reveal manorial courts prepared to accept a transfer of tenure that was initiated out of court. This point went to the heart of a manorial lord's prerogative, as an expression of financial if not of seigneurial interest, and on a number of manors to transfer customary land to another person (except for short-term leases), without physical attendance of both grantor and grantee at the manorial court and without surrender and admission through the lord's hands, was a central issue of confrontation between lord and tenant.[37] And on some manors, it would seem, circumvention of this principle never was permitted during the Middle Ages.[38] On others, it appears, under special circumstances it was permitted from as early as the beginning of the fourteenth century, and the ability to do so appears in some custumals.[39] In still other instances, it was the middle decades of the fourteenth century when such a procedure began to be permitted.

[36] Sheehan, *Will in Medieval England*, 270–4.

[37] Harvey, *Westminster Abbey*, 306–7, 309; Dyer, 'Social and Economic Background to the Rural Revolt of 1381', 27–33; Levett, *Studies in Manorial History*, 79, 138, 149–50; Slota, 'Law Land Transfer, and Lordship', 119–38.

[38] The manor of Alrewas (Staffordshire) does not appear to have adopted any variant of the deathbed transfer during the later Middle Ages. All the surviving manor court records from Alrewas between 1341 and 1470 were searched and nothing resembling a deathbed transfer as it has been described in our article has been found. Staffordshire Record Office (D(W)D/3/31–D(W)D/3/136).

[39] e.g. 'A customary of the lords Archbishops of Canterburye for the dominyon and lordship of south Mallinge in the county of Sussexe conformede in the fourth yeare of the raigne of King Edwarde the Thirde late of Ingland Kinge'. 'Also we saye that the beadle or his deputye with two of the tenants hath authoritye to take surrender of all coppyenollde within the saide beadlewicke of any tenant in extremes so that he presete it at the Nexte coorte after the death of the tenant els to stand voide' (*Customals of the Sussex Manor of the Archbishop of Canterbury*, ed. B. C. Redwood and A. E. Wilson (Sussex Rec. Soc. 57, 1958), 137).

One case from the manor of High Easter (Essex) is significant as a rare, explicit instance of the apparent initiation of such a 'custom'. In 1361, the beadle of the manor appeared in court, claiming that a tenant who was dying, but 'of sound mind' had surrendered into his hands a customary tenement, which the beadle then attempted to transfer to its intended recipient in full court:[40]

> ... And because it appears to the court's seneschal that no one holding at the lord's will can demise his lands and tenements without the lord's licence, and this in full court, the surrender is not allowed but is held for nought. And immediately the whole community of the vill of High Easter comes ... and they say that it is the custom ... from the time to which memory does not run ... that any villein of the lord and anyone holding in the lord's bondage, ill and languishing, not able to go to court ... can surrender into the hands of the reeve or beadle ... his tenements ... so that the reeve or beadle, in court, can surrender the tenement into the lord's hands in favour of the purchasers.

This claim would seem to have been patently false, because in none of the earlier surviving court records of this manor can such a transaction be found. Nevertheless, an inquest confirmed that such was the 'custom', and these transfers were thenceforth a regular (though not an especially frequent) feature of court business.

In other manors, rules were being enunciated by which the conditions rendering such transactions permissible in the eyes of the local court were specified with greater precision, reinforcing the impression that the deathbed transfer was still evolving into more regular usage in the later middle ages. At Barnston (Essex), in 1420, a customary tenant made a deathbed transfer attested by several people, none of whom apparently was a tenant of the same manor:[41]

---

[40] PRO DL30/65/817 (High Easter Court, 10 May 1361): *Ad istam curiam venit Thomas Bowyere bedellus domini cum Galfridus Pynaunt in sua magna egritudine tamen sanus mente secundum consuetudines manerij ut dicitur et reddidit tria quarteria terre customarie cum suis pertinentiis vocata Yonges boven et modo in ista plena curia venit predictus Thomas et sursumreddit in manum domini predicta tria quarteria terre . . . ad opus Johannis Poynaunt . . . et quia videtur senescallo curie quod nullus tenens ad voluntatem domini possit se dimittere de terris et tenementis . . . absque licencia domini et hoc in plena curia prefata redditio . . . non allocatur sed pro nullo tenetur . . . et statim venit communitas villate de Alta Estre et similiter communitas de Waltham et dicunt quod est consuetudo usitata in utraque villata et a tempore quo non existat memoria . . . quod quilibet nativus domini et quicumque tenens in bondagio domini eger et languens non potens ire ad curiam . . . potuit reddere in manum praepositi seu bedelli villatarum predictarum tenementa sua . . . ita quod ipse praepositus aut bedellus in curia . . . sursumredderet illud tenementum in manum domini ad opus perquisitorum . . .*

[41] PRO DL30/58/719 (Barnston Court, 10 Apr. 1420): *Tamen quia ista sursumreddicio non videtur curie esse effectionalis pro eo quod Ballivus huius manerij . . . non interfuit ad recipiendum sursumreddicionem predictam nec aliquis tenens huius manerij interfuit cum predicto Johanne*

... [but] this surrender does not seem effective to the court, because the bailiff of this manor ... was not present, nor was any tenant of this manor present ...

None the less, since the witnesses swore to the grant, the court, 'by its special grace', permitted the transfer to stand (itself testimony to a customary court's willingness to countenance the wishes of the dying tenant), though not without declaring: 'It is henceforth forbidden that any such surrender be made except in the presence of two or three tenants to attest to it.'

To permit these transfers, then, the manor court made a considerable concession, that a 'surrender' of some sort be permitted from tenant to manorial official outside the meeting of the court itself. But the legal nature of that surrender is quite subtle and one searches (almost in vain) for modern analogies. First, it should be emphasized that the surrender did not pass a right to immediate entry, because the donee had to be admitted subsequently at the next meeting of the manor court. Thus the intended recipient of the property did not gain customary law's equivalent to right or title until the land was surrendered into the lord's hands and was regranted (and an entry fine paid and fealty sworn). Nor, it seems clear, was the reeve or bailiff who received the surrender at the deathbed actually given an interest in the land. The transfer was not tantamount to a feoffment to uses in which the bailiff would take legal title subject to equitable interests in another.[42] Transfer of customary law's equivalent to title could only occur in court through a formal admittance, and the terms of the transaction suggest that all parties (including the court) seemed to concur that the official was merely the conduit or intermediary through which the presumptive interest passed from dying donor to recipient. On the other hand, it seems that the declaration had some legal effect because if the languishing donor recovered, he or she had to pay a fine to be readmitted. Such at any rate is indicated by a case from Bocking (Essex) in 1383:[43]

Cook tempore sursumreddicionis predicte ad testificandum predictam sursumreddicionem ... [but because the four witnesses] *testificaverunt per eorum sacramentum quod sursumreddicio predicti Johannis Neel est vera & fideliter facta fuit prout superius expressatur habito respectu ad testificacionem & iuramentum predictorum quatuor hominum de sua gratia speciale* [the lord] *concessit predicta mesuagium & terram. ... Memorandum tamen inhibitum est de cetero nulla talis sursumreddicio facta sit nisi in presencia duorum vel trium tenentium illud testifcantum.*

[42] See generally, A. W. B. Simpson, *An Introduction to the History of the Land Law* (Oxford, 1961), ch. 9.

[43] Cathedral Archives and Library, Canterbury, U15. 11. 3 (Bocking Court, 6 Oct 1383): *Ad hanc curiam venerunt Johannes Gray & Margeria uxor eius & dant domino de fine ad rehabendum statum in tenemento quod ipsa nuper languens sursumreddidit in manum ballivi tenendum de domino ut in pristino stato suo* ...

To this court came John Gray and Margery his wife, and they give the lord a fine to regain their status in a tenement which she, recently languishing, surrendered into the bailiff's hands, to hold from the lord as in its original state [*ut in pristino statu suo*].

The curious legal nature of the *in extremis* transfer within the framework of land transfers renders precise classification difficult. Perhaps the closest modern analogue is the gift *causa mortis*, a Roman law derivative, whereby a person on his deathbed delivers personalty to another to hold in the event of his death. Yet we should not become too preoccupied with classification. Even modern courts, when faced with irregular property transfers, are at pains to classify the interests created therein within the traditional property law structure.[44] All we can observe is what the court recognizes: it will honour tenant's out-of-court wishes, but allow tenant to revoke if tenant recovers. Nothing 'passed' from the dying tenant through the statement of intention; nothing was received by bailiff or intended beneficiary. Transfer of an interest occurred subsequently, when the property was surrendered into the lord's hands and regranted (as was the case with *inter vivos* transfer). Should tenant survive, a penalty must be paid to cancel the arrangement.

From the donor's point of view the deathbed transfer was a *pre-mortem* transfer with possession postponed until after death, and thus it allowed him to direct the descent of the tenement to a designated recipient, whether a familial 'heir', someone unrelated to the grantor, or indeed (as will be shown) to the grantor's executors for the purpose of paying off his debts, making charitable or pious donations, or the like. Where it differs from other arrangements discussed above is that it occurred when the tenant was at death's door, and out of court. From the lord's perspective, it would seem that once the principle of deathbed transfers was conceded under closely defined circumstances, an out-of-court surrender should be honoured, subsequent transfer of tenure or right was merely another (though admittedly rather special) variety of surrender and admission, and therefore valid.

For the purposes of the present discussion, the similarities between this situation and Sheehan's treatment of the devise of freehold property by will are striking. As Sheehan remarks, 'the basic and permanent cause of the prohibition of the bequest of (freehold) land is to be found in the

---

[44] An interesting American case that creates a hitherto undiscovered property interest christened a 'contingent equitable interest in remainder' is *Farkas v. Williams*, 125 N. E. 2d 600 (1955) noted in J. Dukeminier and S. M. Johanson, *Wills, Trusts and Estates* (3rd edn., London, 1984), 505, who suggest the interest ought to be called a 'Farkas'.

rules of conveyance'.[45] If a freehold tenant at death's door none the less managed to effect a conveyance of seisin valid at common law, it was effective and unchallengable. Alternatively, freehold tenants made *post obit* gifts well into the fourteenth century, but again subject to the requirement that such transfers be made under conveyance forms recognized at common law (in this case, enfeoffment of the donee followed by recovery with life interest by the donor).

Thus the customary deathbed transfer allowed the tenant greater flexibility than that permitted the freeholder. In form, it was tantamount to a bequest of land by will. Yet it is hardly likely that such was the intention of the customary court. In a technical sense, the court was merely accepting a new conveyancing technique, rather than unilaterally transforming itself into an arena of probate jurisdiction with powers concerning land greatly exceeding that permissible with freehold property until the enactment of the Statute of Wills (1540). The lord allowed the extension because the process did not enable a tenant to circumvent the manor court (which would have occurred if the procedure was a will cognizable in the church court). Transfer (and therefore payment of entry fines) occurred in the lord's court.

Nevertheless it should be re-emphasized that, on the basis of our own admittedly preliminary survey of manorial court records, different manors proceeded in different ways and with different chronologies in absorbing these transfers into their own 'customs'. For one thing, it is possible to find instances in which, at least ostensibly, manorial courts were prepared to honour the donor's 'will' or expressed wishes without any explicit use of an intermediary. Such would seem to be the implications of the cases cited by DeWindt from the Ramsey Abbey manors. As early as 1309, the court of King's Ripton (Hunts.) recorded such entries as:[46]

Roger Dyke, who is dead, bequeathed [*legavit*] to Mariota daughter of Hugh Russel one 'place' which he had purchased, containing one rod . . .

Similarly at Barnston in 1407, the court recorded the death of one Thomas Celer and noted that Alice Baker was occupying his property without the lord's license:[47]

---

[45] Sheehan, *Will in Medieval England* , 274.

[46] A. DeWindt, 'A peasant land market and its participants: King's Ripton, 1280–1400' *Midland History*, 4 (1978), 158 n. 36: *Rogerus Dyke qui mortuus est legavit Mariote filie Hugonis Russel unam placiam de perquistione suo continentem i rodam que dat domino etc. i d.* (cited from BL Add. Roll 34770).

[47] PRO D130/58/718 (Barnston Court, 30 May 1407): *Voluntas—Ec . . . quia testatum est quod ultima voluntas predicti Thome fuit quod Agnes filia predicti Thome Bastard haberet predicta terram & tenementa sibi & heredibus suis imperpetuum Ideo per considerationem domini*

And because it is attested that the last will [*ultima voluntas*] of the aforesaid Thomas was that Agnes, daughter of the said Thomas, bastard, have the said land and tenements . . . by the consideration of the lord and court the aforesaid messuage and half-virgate of land are delivered to Alice Baker, mother of the said Agnes, to keep until [Agnes's] full age . . .

That these transfers were the subject of slow evolution and a search for clearer criteria of permissibility in many places is indicated by a case from Priors Hall in Widdington (Essex) in 1417–19, where (again) it seems clear that a manorial court was prepared to accept a dying tenant's statement of intentions. In 1417 Thomas Douce died, and the jurors said that he declared, 'I will that my wife have that land to herself and her heirs.' The record betrays some uncertainty on the part of the court as to what force this expression of preference might carry: 'it is to be discussed with the lord's advice whether by such words a surrender can take effect.'[48] Nineteen months later the court granted Thomas's widow the property.[49]

It should be added here that in some manors, out-of-court surrenders were countenanced even when the grantor was not on his deathbed, and in fact in a few places the out-of-court statement of intent to transfer became, even before the end of the fourteenth century, a standard form of *inter vivos* grant.[50] Even so, the same underlying rationale appears to have existed: the grantor manifested an intention to surrender the property, that would later be accomplished in the next meeting of the manor court; and if it subsequently proved impossible to complete the transfer in the manor court the grantor would still have to reclaim his previous interest. At Takeley in 1407, the court recorded that one John Bernard had surrendered into the bailiff's hands five and a quarter acres of land

& curie predicta mesuagium & dimidia virgata terre liberantur Alicie Baker matri predicte Agnetis ad custodiendum usque ad plenam etatem . . .

[48] NCO 3620 m. 7ᵛ (Priors Hall leet, 15 Dec. 1417): *Jurati dicunt quod Thomas Douce qui de domino tenuit duas acras & j rodam terre obiit post ultimam curiam. Et predicti jurati dicunt quod predictus Thomas declaravit volo quod Agnes uxor mea habeat dictam terram sibi & heredibus suis nulla alia sursumreddicione inde facta nisi per talia verba superius declarata unde consulendum est cum consilio domini si per talia verba sursumreddicionis effectum capere poterit nec ne.*

[49] Ibid. m. 9ᵛ (Priors Hall Court, 11 July 1419): *Et habito respectu ad voluntatem predicti Thome coram predictis [three witnesses] declaratam dominus de sua gratia speciale concessit predictam terram predicte Agneti. Tenendum eidem Agneti & heredibus suis de domino ad voluntatem . . .*

[50] e.g. *Court Rolls of Tooting Bec Manor*, ed. G. L. Gomme (London, 1909), 52–3, 78–81, 100–1, 116–17, 136–9, 146–9, 150–1, 152–3, 156–7, 158–9, 162–3, 166–7, 186–7, 190–1, 196–7, 198–9, 202–3, 206–7, 214–15, 218–19. At this manor between 1394 and 1422, 'out-of-court' surrenders into the bailiff's hands (though it is never made entirely clear whether the grantor is actually on his or her 'deathbed') accounted for 21 property transfers, compared with 23 'normal' surrender-and-admission-type transfers.

in favour of Richard Payn; but Payn, for reasons unknown, subsequently refused to come into court and accept the property. Bernard then had to seek the court's permission, and pay a fine, to be readmitted to the tenement 'as in its original state' [*ut in pristino statu suo*].[51]

It would be misleading, on the basis of this cursory survey, to imply that such transfers necessarily accounted for a very large proportion of transfers of property in English manorial courts in the later Middle Ages. Only a more rigorous survey would uncover the quantitative weight of this new means of customary devolution, and even so the situation was demonstrably quite different in different manors. None the less in some circumstances the customary deathbed transfer permitted a remarkably wide range of options, in many instances of considerable complexity also, to any tenant able or willing to make use of them.

IV

The acceptance of *in extremis* transfers by a number of manor courts in the course of the fourteenth century enhanced the ability of customary tenants to fashion comprehensive estate plans for the devolution of property. Prior to its recognition a tenant had to arrange *inter vivos* transfers of land or alternatively allow succession according to the custom of the manor. Although the tenant could remain in possession until his death through the *post obit* gift, it was necessary for him to commit the succession to his customary land well in advance of his death (to be sure that his individual estate plan was implemented), relinquishing the power to revoke the arrangement. Thereafter, in manors where the deathbed transfer of land obtained, a tenant could express the course of succession of his customary land in what appeared to be his last illness; and, if he recovered, his directions could be 'revoked'. In substance, then, customary land could be willed, and the missing mechanical tool in transmitting wealth of customary landholders was forged.

Below, we shall discuss examples of the way in which medieval English peasants manipulated the various transmission devices,[52] including the

---

[51] NCO 3698 m. 5ᵛ (Takeley court, 23 Mar. 1407): *Cum alias ad curiam hic tentam die Mercurie proximo post Hokemonday anno regni regis Henrici sexti Johannes Bernard sursumreddidit in manum domini per manum Petri Bakere ballivi . . . quinque acras & unam rodam terre customarie ad opus Ricardi Payn qui quidem Ricardus licet sepius premunitus dictam terram hic in curia recipere non curavit sed in presencia . . . tenentum dictam terram recusavit & nichil inde solvere voluit. . . . Et modo ad hanc curiam venit predictus Johannes Bernard & petit se admitti ad dictam terram habendum ut in pristino statu suo. Cui quidem Johanni predicta terra concessa est Tenendum sibi & heredibus ad voluntatem domini . . . Et dat de fine ut patet . . .*

[52] Section V.

deathbed transfer, to distribute the various forms of wealth to selected heirs: in short how they framed what historians and anthropologists call 'strategies of inheritance'. Before doing so, however, we wish to sound a cautionary note regarding the concept of strategy at least as applied to customary tenants in medieval England, lest it appear that our discussion suggests that the adoption of deathbed transfers in some manors drastically altered the practice of devolution amongst the propertied peasantry. A definition first, and then a word about strategies of inheritance in the context of the medieval English peasantry are in order.

Research into inheritance practice in past societies has attempted to analyse patterns of transmission in terms of 'strategies'.[53] Although the term is rarely defined explicitly, a strategy, when applied to inheritance, consists of an intentional decision or series of decisions regarding the transmission of property undertaken by a holder (usually though not invariably the household head) pursued with varying degrees of calculation (be it conscious or subconscious) designed to achieve a particular familial reproductive goal. To cite an example of a common strategy, father in order to maintain the relative social or economic standing of the family in the community decides to pass the bulk of the patrimony to his eldest son giving his daughters and younger sons cash portions that amount to much less than a proportional share of familial wealth.

That the implementation of this strategy will result in an array of economic and demographic consequences is well recognized and has been analysed by anthropologists and historians: the daughter may migrate to towns; younger sons may not marry.[54] Yet the concept of strategy may be more a useful analytic tool for researchers to systematize inheritance patterns for the purpose of cross-cultural comparison than it is to understand the actions of property holders in the past. Anthropological theoreticians differ on the extent to which they believe strategies are the outcome of rational decision-making. Strategies, it is argued, may be unconscious and generated by a variety of implicit norms inculcated in the individual by his culture.[55] For example, fathers believe patrimonies ought to remain

---

[53] J. Goody's 'Introduction' to Goody *et al.* (eds.), *Family and Inheritance*, 1–9, provides a useful description of the application of the concept of strategy to inheritance. More detailed consideration can be found in the work of anthropologists, particularly, F. Barth, *Models of Social Organization* (London, 1966); P. Bourdieu, *Outline of a Theory of Practice* (Cambridge, 1977) and his 'Les Stratégies matrimoniales', 1105–27.

[54] Bourdieu, *Outline of a Theory*, 59–71. J. Goody, *Production and Reproduction: A Comparative Study of the Domestic Domain* (Cambridge, 1986), 86–98.

[55] Bourdieu, 'Les Stratégies matrimoniales', 1106–7; contrasted with N. Zemon Davis, 'Ghosts, Kin and Progeny: Some Features of Family Life in Early Modern France', *Daedalus*, 106 (1977), 87–114.

undivided or younger brothers accept that their eldest siblings will inherit, not through an unfettered process of deduction but because of a
general acceptance of certain cultural principles.

Perhaps the most significant assumption that underpins the theoretical
discussion of strategies of inheritance is that they are pursued with some
degree of contemplation and volition. The difficulty with the concept of
strategy as applied to an historical population like the medieval English
peasantry, in our view, is that it envisages property owners in the past in
present terms, as individuals who might sit down in a lawyer's office in,
say, their mid-sixties to carve up wealth that is in large measure surplus
to current needs. Discussion of strategies in historical populations seems
to assume that the individual has a range of devolutionary options, and
further that he is aware of the configuration of his family at his death (for
example, the number and sex of children that will survive him or whether
his wife will survive) and economic forces (for example, the value of land,
or short-term agricultural prospects) that would allow him to make an
informed decision in exercising those options to implement a goal. Finally,
the concept presumes that inheritance decisions take place in a context
that allows the actor to relate options to goals (that death is not sudden,
or that preparations occur in advance). As Natalie Zemon Davis, a staunch
advocate of systematizing behaviour into strategies, suggests, some degree
of economic and demographic certainty must prevail in a society before
decisions can be formulated.[56] Pre-modern demographic reality was such
that certainty was lacking. Indeed many fathers, at least in medieval
England, would probably have died before their children reached adulthood or even adolescence, many so young that they could not even be
certain of having a male successor who would reach maturity, and some
so suddenly in such circumstances that calculation, unless it was truly
prospective, could not occur.[57] Prospective estate planning amongst the
young and middle-aged is hardly universal even in our own highly developed legal culture; and it seems likely that the fear that 'estate planning'
might actually prompt untimely demise which Swinburne noted amongst
the 'ruder sort' in early modern England obtained two centuries earlier.[58]

Thus we wish to make clear that the individuals whose estate plan we
shall observe in the following section are likely to be atypical in that they

---

[56] Bourdieu, 'Les Stratégies matrimoniales', 92.

[57] Bonfield proposes to use the results of microsimulation exercises to calculate percentages of family needs in the medieval English peasantry who would have been able to
construct a strategy.

[58] H. Swinburne, *A Brief Treatise of Testaments and Last Wills* (London, 1590).

took fullest advantage of the mechanical tools available, and perhaps exhibit the volition requisite for the composition of a 'strategy'. What we wish to illuminate by example is the 'technical advance' that was embodied in the deathbed transfer, and to suggest that strategies of devolution can only be as complex as the mechanical forms a legal system develops. The peasants observed, unlike most of their neighbours, constructed elaborate plans for their property, and the complexity of transmission scheme and the variety of legal forms employed suggest a level of volition that is suggestive of strategy.

V

We have suggested that the primary obstacle to crafting a comprehensive 'devolution strategy' was the manorial courts' refusal to sanction wills of customary land. To a considerable degree, the acceptance of the deathbed transfer provided a remedy. But these transfers should be viewed as a single component within a broader range of options that could be used in various permutations with other forms of *inter vivos* dispositions of customary land, testamentary devolution of chattels, and even the 'intestate' inheritance by the custom of the manor for property not otherwise disposed of. Some or all of these means could even be used to achieve other ends besides those of devolving property onto chosen heirs. For example, grantors used deathbed transfers to direct some of their property to executors, under the stipulation that the property be sold for 'pious purposes', for the good of the grantor's soul. Similar directions were made for the purpose of paying off the grantor's debts.

It is only when both the 'will' (in the conventional, ecclesiastical sense), that dealt usually with only chattels (but in certain instances also with freehold property held by feoffees to use) and the records of *inter vivos* and deathbed transfers of customary land in manorial courts can be perused for the same individual that it becomes apparent how far each instrument was merely one component in the testator's overall 'estate plan'. By so doing it becomes possible to speak of a 'will' in a broader sense, as the totality of a grantor's wishes as expressed (probably orally) at the time of his death, different portions of which reached tangible form as written records in quite different contexts and dealing with different categories of property: the 'will' in the conventional sense is a venue of probate for chattels (and occasionally, under special circumstances, freehold land), the deathbed transfer in manorial court for customary property. A few examples have been chosen from our survey to illustrate the possible permutations which this range of options allowed.

1. John Artor of Great Waltham (Essex) died in 1483. His will disposed of the usual chattels, sums of money, livestock and so forth, and further expressed his intentions for several pieces of freehold property to go to his widow, with specified remainders.[59] At the same time, four different deathbed transfers in the Waltham manorial court disposed of various portions of customary land with quite complex conditions. Artor's widow received a life-interest (so long as she did not re-marry) with remainder to Artor's son John, conditional upon the latter's paying specified sums of money to four of his siblings.[60] Another transfer gave the widow a life-interest in other land, with remainder to Artor's son Richard.[61] A third customary tenement was disposed of in a similar manner, but this time with the stipulation that Richard make a payment of money to one of his sisters.[62] Finally, a fourth was surrendered without reservation to the widow and her heirs general and assigns, conditional upon her paying a sum of money to an apparently unrelated man.[63] Thus by a combination

---

[59] Essex Record Office (hereafter ERO) D/AER 1/35.

[60] ERO D/DTu M244 m. 61ᵛ (Great Waltham Court, 23 Jan. 1483): *Ad hanc curiam compertum est per homagium quod Johannis Artor senior languens in extremis extra curiam post ultimam curiam sursumreddidit in manum Thome Everard bedelli huius manerij in presencia Thome Wayte Willelmi Ram & Johannis Whitlock tenentium eiusdem manerij unum tenementum . . . ad opus Agnetis nuper uxoris prefati Johannis Artor senioris. Cui quidem Agneti nunc vidue domina Regina concessit inde seisinam Tenedum eidem Agneti & assignatis suis pro termino vite sue sub condicione quod eadem Agnes sola vivat & non maritata durante tota vita sua Tenendum de domina Regina ad voluntatem per omnia antiqua servicia Ita quod post mortem predicte Agnetis vel quando sit maritata tunc* [one or two words illegible] *tamdiu dictum tenementum cum suis pertinentiis remaneat Johanni Artor filio & heredi predicti Johannis Artor senioris Tenendum eidem Johanni Artor filio & heredibus suis Proviso quod idem Johannes Artor filius post mortem dicte Agnetis vel postquam ipsa remaritata fuerit solvat sue solvi facerti Ricardo fratri suo xl s. xl s. bone monete & Edithe sorori sue & modo uxori Willelmi Goos xl s. bone monete ac Emme sorori ipsius Edithe modo uxori Thome Knyghtbregge xx s. bone monete & Alicie sorori ipsius Emme & nunc uxori Willelmi Bygelon xx s. bone monete . . .*

[61] Ibid.: *Ad hanc curiam compertum est per homangium quod dictus Johannis Artor senior languens in extremis extra curiam post ultiman curiam sursumreddit in manum dicti Thome Everard bedelli . . . unum tenementum . . . ocatum Aleynes & unum quarterium terre de molland ac unum quarterium customarie . . . ad opus dicte Agnetis nuper uxoris . . . cui vero Agneti domina Regina concessit inde seisinam Tenendum eidem pro termino vite sue de domina ad voluntatem . . . Ita quod post mortem prefate Agnetis omnia predicta tenementa & quarteria terre . . . remaneant Ricardo Arto filio predicti Johannis Artor senioris & heredibus ipsuis Ricardi . . .*

[62] Ibid.: *Ad hanc curiam compertum est per homagium quod prefatus Johannis Artor senior languens in extremis extra curiam post ultiman curiam sursumreddidt in manum dicti Thome Everard bedelli . . . unam croftam terre vocatam Turnorscroft ad opus prefate Agnetis Cui dominia Regina concessit inde sesinam Tenendum eidem Agneti & assignatis suis pro termino vite sue de domina Regina ad voluntatem . . . Ita quod post mortem prefate Agnetis dicta crofta terre cum suis pertinentiis remaneat prefato Ricardo Artor filio dicti Johannis Artor senioris & heredibus ipsius Ricardi Proviso semper quod idem Ricardus* [one or two words illegible] *post obitum dicte Agnetis solverit seu solvi facerit prefate Edithe xiij s. iiij d. bone monete . . .*

[63] Ibid.: *Ad hanc curiam compertum est quod dictus Johannes Artor senior iacens in mortali lecto extra curiam post ulitmam curiam sursumreddidit in manus predicti Thome Everard bedelli . . .*

of 'will' (in the narrow sense) and deathbed transfer, Artor disposed of chattels, freehold and customary property, and managed to provide money portions for several non-inheriting children, while at the same time giving his widow some property absolutely, but also some more which she held on condition that she remain unmarried.

2. William Samwell of Great Totham (Essex) died in 1559. His will dictated that the house and tenement in which he had lived, 'bothe fre & copye', should go to his widow Margery for her life, with remainder to Edward his son.[64] Another son, Thomas, was to receive his house and land at Wickham (an adjacent parish) and elsewhere upon reaching the age of 14, his mother retaining it in guardianship before then. Each son also received various items of furniture and a cash portion of £10, with Margery as residuary legatee. The manorial court of Wickham in the next year recorded that Samwell, 'languishing *in extremis* and in danger of death', had surrendered into the manorial bailiff's hands a tenement, 16 acres of land and a garden, in favour of his wife Margery until his son Thomas reached the age of 14.[65] In this case, then, the 'will' (in the conventional sense) contained Samwell's expression of intentions. But in order for those intentions to be carried out at customary law, the transfer of possessory interests still needed to be implemented via the deathbed transfer with subsequent transfer in the manorial court, without which the copyhold would not have passed. Thus although at first glance the customary-court record appears to have duplicated the will's contents, it was the former which effected at customary law the dying tenant's wishes contained in the latter.

---

unum tenementum & tria quarteria terre vocata Poliarde . . . ad opus dicte Agnetis cui domina Regina concessit inde seisinam Tenendum eidem Agneti & heredibus suis de domina Regina ad voluntatem per antiqua servicia ac solvendo Willelmo Hull vj s. viij s. bone monete . . .

[64] ERO D/ABW 33/386: 'Item I gave & bequeth to Thomas my sonne my howse & lands at Wickham & also my howse & lands at Totham Hill called Gardeners otherwise Paines he for to have it at his age of xiiij yeres and his mother to have it tyll that tyme . . .'.

[65] Guildhall Library, London, 10313/216 (Wickham court, 2 May 1560): *Homagium presentat quod Willelmus Samwell qui tenuit de domino per virgam secundum consuetudines manerij sibi & heredibus suis unum tenementum et xiij acras terre adiacentes vocatum Smethestenement & unam croftam terre inclusam vocatum Crouchcroft . . . & unam gardinum vocatum Smethegarden cum quadam fabrica in eadem edificata . . . Qui quidem Willelmus Samwell obiit post ultimam curiam . . . Tamen ipse ante mortem suam languens in extremis & in periculo mortis per manum Gilberti Wodeward deputi Ballivi domini ibeidem in presencia Johannis Peachy & Ricardi Sanghall tenentium domini ad hoc iuratorum & testimonium perhibentum sursumreddidit in manum domini predicta tenementum & terram cum pertinentiis ad opus et usum sequentes videlicet ad opus Margeri uxoris sue quousque Thomas Samwell filius ipsius Willelmi pervenerit ad etatem quatuordecim annorum & post termini illius finem remanet prefato Thome Samwell & heredibus suis imperpetuum cui quidem Margerie dominus per senescallum suum concessit inde seisinam . . .*

3. Thomas Makke of Cromer (Norfolk) died in 1497. In his will, after various bequests to several churches and for masses for himself, Makke directed that his animals and grain be divided into two equal portions, one to go to his widow Cecilia and the other to his executors.[66] He also requested that the executors, Richard Makke and Robert Makke, sell his messuage in East Runton and all his lands and tenements in Runton, Cromer, and Beeston Regis, along with a cart, and use the proceeds to pay off his debts and to distribute the remainder as alms for the good of his soul.[67] Approximately one month after his will was probated, the manorial court of Beeston Regis recorded that 'Thomas Makke, languishing *in extremis*, out of court, following the custom of the manor', had surrendered about 17 acres of land in favour of Richard Makke and Robert Makke, 'executors of the said Thomas' testament, to sell and to dispose of the resulting money following the said Thomas' will'.[68] Richard and Robert were then granted seisin and swore fealty. At the next meeting of the Beeston court, in February 1498, Richard and Robert 'by virtue of the testament and last will of the same Thomas': sold the land to a certain William Miller.[69]

This case, then, is somewhat different from the previous two in that Thomas's 'strategy' in these transactions was not primarily concerned with devolving property onto relatives, either because there was none other than his widow, or because sons or other presumptive heirs had

[66] NRO reg. Multon to. 66 (will dated 19 Aug. 1497, probated 24 Oct. 1497): *Item volo quod omnes oves mee & omnes eque & equi mei & omnia grana mea pervenianta de vestura omnia terrarum mearum . . . equaliter in duas partes unde volo quod una pars remaneat Cecilie uxori mee & altera pars inde remaneat executoribus meis . . .*

[67] Ibid.: *Item volo quod executores mei vendant mesuagium meum in Runton cum omnibus terris et tenementis Runton predicta Beeston & Crowmer cum pertinentiis ac unam carectam & denarios provenientes ac omnia debita mea remaneant executoribus meis ad omnia premisa perimplenda debita mea persolvenda . . . ac . . . pro anima mea & animis omnium benefactorum meorum distribuenda & exequanda . . .*

[68] PRO DL30/102/1408 m. 12 (Beeston Regis Court, 23 Nov. 1497): *Thomas Makke languidens in extremis extra curiam secundum consuetudinem manerij sursumreddidit in manus domini per manus Johannis Wynter nativi tenentis in presencia Roberti Makke Johannis Mors similiter nativorum tenentium et aliorum de homagio . . . ad opus Ricardi Makke capellani et Roberti Makke executorum testamenti dicti Thome Makke ad vendenda et denarios inde provenientes ad disponendos secundum voluntatem ipsius Thome quibus liberata est eis seisina . . . et fecerunt domino fidelitatem . . .* These pious or charitable 'bequests' in manorial court records have been studied extensively by Elaine Clark, see below Ch. 5.

[69] PRO DL30/102/1408 m. 12^v (Beeston Regis Court, 14 Feb. 1498): *Ricardus Makke Capellanus & Robertus Makke executores testamenti Thome Makke virtute testamenti & ultime voluntatis eiusdem Thome vendunt . . . omnia terram soliatam & nativam quondam dicti Thome Makke . . . ad opus Willelmi Miller nuper de Handworth Johanne uxoris eius & Roberti filij dictorum Willelmi Miller & Johanne heredum & assignatorum eorum . . .*

already been provided for by other means. Yet, implicitly Thomas must have desired to remain in possession of his customary property to the point of his death and make a last-minute disposition in accordance with his wishes. The means afforded by Beeston's customary law to effect these aims are essentially identical to the cases of Artor and Samwell. Makke's ecclesiastical will expressed his intention, but his deathbed transfer was still necessary at customary law in order to transfer interest to Richard and Robert. The latter, as a result of Thomas's deathbed transfer, received an interest in the property whose nature is, again, somewhat ambiguous: the terminology employed in the court record to describe it 'to themselves, their heirs and assigns, in the form aforesaid'.[70] It would appear that Richard and Robert were admitted to Thomas's customary land as executors of his ecclesiastical will.[71]

VI

To sum up, we have argued that the acceptance of the deathbed transfer, when employed in tandem with other avenues of devolution, enabled the customary tenant so inclined (and demographically and economically fortunate enough) to fashion true strategies of inheritance as they have been defined by historians and anthropologists. Thus far in this paper we have considered the introduction of the deathbed transfer, conceptualized its legal nature and observed its role in the process of intergenerational transmission; in conclusion, we wish to draw some very tentative inferences about the nature of customary law based upon our inquiry into deathbed transfers.

In the first place, the customary law governing land transfers was complex. There was a fixed set of rules regarding transfer, and an alteration in conveyancing technique like the deathbed transfer had to occur within that legal context. Manor courts that accepted the deathbed transfer did not change the legal process of transfer; surrender and admittance remained the means by which rights in customary land passed. What the courts did to varying degrees was protect the desires of a customary tenant, and allow out-of-court directions to be implemented at a later date in *plena curia*. To some extent, then (and we can only speculate upon whether the introduction of deathbed transfers occurred with forethought or accidentally), the acceptance of an alteration like the deathbed transfer

---

[70] PRO DL30/102/1408 m. 12 (Beeston Regis Court, 23 Nov. 1497): *tenenda eis heredibus et assignatis eorum in forma predicta per virgam ad voluntatem domini . . .*

[71] Clark (below Ch. 5), concurs in viewing this as a conditional interest and cites cases where failure by the executors to proceed expeditiously resulted in seigneurial intervention.

was accomplished without modifying the theoretical construct of the customary law touching land transfer. That customary law at least with respect to conveyancing had an internal coherence and that a modification like the deathbed transfer occurred without violating its principles are in our view suggestive of its technical sophistication.

Second, the acceptance of the deathbed transfer sheds light upon the nature of the seigneurial relationship. The broadening of the control over devolution occasioned by the deathbed transfer was accepted by manorial lords because it did not prejudice their interests. While this point cannot be pressed too far without further corroborating research into other areas of customary law, it appears that lords were prepared to concede considerable freedom to their villeins in ordering familial and proprietary relations.

Finally, our inquiry suggests that diversity in practice characterized the customary courts in medieval England. Not all manor courts recognized the deathbed transfer. This point should sound a cautionary note to historians who wish to select a case or two from a series of court rolls and extrapolate a 'national' rule of customary law. Why the deathbed transfer was implemented in, for example, High Easter and does not appear in Alrewas is unclear. The diversity of rules suggests the need for a much broader survey of manorial court jurisdictions before principles enumerated in cases can help historians to define the social relations of the medieval England peasantry.

Our investigation, and the painstaking work of others suggests that the manor court is one worthy of study as a legal institution. Other scholars have made contributions in perceiving it as a social institution. This disciplinary coincidence should further the historian's knowledge of what customary law was, and how it affected the fortunes of those who were subject to it.

5

Charitable Bequests, Deathbed Land Sales, and the Manor Court in Later Medieval England*

ELAINE CLARK

No historian who writes about social welfare can be unmindful of the role of charity in the medieval world. Ever since William Ashley published his research on poor relief in England the view has prevailed that during the Middle Ages 'well nigh all the assistance' that was afforded the needy was in the form of almsgiving by monks, lords, merchants, and people of ample means.[1] There was no governmental system of relief, no state funding or programme for the impoverished other than the Church's directive to the faithful to assist all who were in need. Everywhere this mandate was the same. To feed the hungry, to help the sick, to console the widowed, and support the orphaned remained the duty of clergy and laity alike. What resulted was a system of voluntary relief informed by the commandments of religion and characterized by the belief that almsgiving was, for the donor, a way to salvation. Nevertheless if the problem is charity, and the setting is England, we must pose a question which Ashley did not. Was the design of social welfare during the Middle Ages solely the product of dogma and the organized Church?

Any answer obviously depends on what aspects of the problem we choose to discuss and whether we focus on rhetoric and doctrine or the complexities of actual behaviour. If we look primarily at popular behaviour, as this essay will do, we encounter a world where most people lived not in cities but in villages and small market settlements. Throughout the countryside it was never easy to exclude the needy from the business of daily life. Many villagers periodically suffered from want themselves and

---

* A briefer version of this paper was presented at the Social Science History Association meeting in St Louis, 1986. I am grateful for helpful comments from the audience and from the commentators: Dr Edwin DeWindt and Professor Michael Sheehan. For archival references to the court rolls cited in this essay, see Appendix 5.1.

[1] W. J. Ashley, *An Introduction to English Economic History and Theory* (London, 1888; reissued New York, 1966), 305–76. Also see, E. M. Leonard, *The Early History of English Poor Relief* (London, 1900; reissued 1965), 4–5; S. and B. Webb, *English Local Government: English Poor-Law History*, pt. 1: *The Old Poor Law* (1927), 1–22.

certainly appeared poor when compared to the seigneurial lords on whose estates they worked. Chroniclers and contemporary commentators often dismissed these labourers and serfs as 'simple, common folk', although such a view clearly was biased.[2] English villagers were not all alike. They understood inequality and knew how the uneven distribution of land and resources created differences in wealth. Under these circumstances people recognized that charity was hardly a simple matter. What troubled many was how the man or woman of limited means should assist the poor. When asked—'to whom shall I give my alms when I cannot help all?'—the Church counselled charity to Christians before heathens, the aged before the young, the infirm before the healthy, and kin before strangers if the needs of both seemed equal.[3] Problems of status and the causes of poverty also came into play. The faithful were advised to support neighbours and friends impoverished by misfortune rather than sin, to aid the 'righteous' imprisoned in jail, and to assist any folk of 'noble' character too ashamed to beg from door to door. Questions of how to raise money and alms concerned the clergy less, although they certainly realized, as most villagers did, that the demands of property played a necessary part in any plans for mutual support.

By the mid-fourteenth century, when plague and epidemic disease disrupted the countryside, peasants already had a long tradition of working together to mediate the effects of hardship and loss. Insofar as they had property, neighbours and kin co-operated in the sharing of resources and channelled the income derived from land towards the welfare of widows, orphans, and wards.[4] When confronted with adversity themselves, rural householders utilized the property they controlled to offset uncertainty. These villagers often became what historians have called 'natural' sellers and lessors of land, disposing of resources not simply to make a profit but to ensure subsistence and personal support.[5] This

---

[2] S. L. Thrupp, 'The Problem of Conservatism in Fifteenth-Century England,' in R. Grew and N. H. Steneck (eds.), *Society and History: Essays by Sylvia L. Thrupp* (Ann Arbor, 1977), 241.

[3] *Dives and Pauper*, ed. P. Heath Barnum, (EETS 280, 1980), 292. *Dan Michel, Ayenbite of Inwyt or Remorse of Conscience (in the Kentish Dialect, 1340 AD)*, ed. R. Morris (EETS 23, 1866), 192–5. *Jacob's Well: An English Treatise on the Cleansing of Man's Conscience*, ed. Arthur Brandeis (EETS 115, 1900), 310. *Walter of Henley's Husbandry*, ed. E. Lamond (Royal Hist. Soc., 1890), 5–7. For further discussion, from the perspective of canon law, see B. Tierney, 'The Decretists and the "Deserving Poor"', *Comparative Studies in Society and History*, 1 (1959), 360–73.

[4] Clark, 'Some Aspects of Social Security', 307–20; Clark, 'The Custody of Children', 333–48; E. Clark, 'Social Welfare and Mutual Aid in the Medieval Countryside', *JBS* 33 (1994), 381–406.

[5] M. M. Postan, 'The Charters of the Villeins', in his *Essays on Medieval Agriculture and General Problems of the Medieval Economy* (Cambridge, 1973), 115–17.

support afforded care and sustenance to the old, companionship to the widowed, and solace to the dying. In fact the dying, much like the living, were 'natural' sellers of land. As such, the mortally ill secured the funds that enabled them to have an enduring and highly valued role in the distribution of alms to the poor. This may be illustrated, in a specific way, by questioning the terms and conditions of the transactions arranged by the dying and the buyers of their land. How were prices set? Who distributed the alms of the dead? Did sales of land and charitable bequests conflict with the inheritance claims of family and kin? Or was there, instead, a sense of solidarity and shared resources between the living and the dead in common cause with the poor?

I

By way of introduction we may recall that the exchange of land in English villages was never simply a matter of leases and sales. It was a question of people and of their individual needs and priorities whenever the allocation of land was at issue. Professor Levett made this point, half a century ago, when she called attention to the testamentary disposition of villein land in the medieval countryside.[6] On the manors of the abbots of St Albans Levett found that peasants initially made deathbed sales and transfers of land to request masses and prayers for the souls of the dead. From this it was a simple step for the dying to make bequests to benefit the living by settling property on spouses, children, and kin. By the later fourteenth century property settlements, although still informed by duty to family, were sufficiently complex to govern the distribution and use of land long after the testator's death. These testamentary gifts and sales of land came under the jurisdiction of manor courts. With the cellarer's guidance, courts enforced the probate of villein wills and informed the Abbot of all land transactions made by peasants near death.

The St Albans evidence, spanning the generations after the Black Death, is remarkably detailed but not unique. From the Ramsey Abbey manor of King's Ripton, Dr Anne DeWindt cited documents that closely paralleled the St Albans material in content and format.[7] Since her work on this Huntingdonshire manor appeared in 1978, more evidence has been accumulating on charitable bequests and sales of land in extremis.[8]

---

[6] Levett, *Studies in Manorial History*, 208–23. For further comment on villein wills, see C. Howell, 'Peasant Inheritance Customs', 120–1.

[7] A. DeWindt, 'A Peasant Land Market and its Participants: King's Ripton, 1280–1400', *Midland History*, 4 (1978), 142–58.

[8] Hanawalt, *The Ties That Bound*, 239–42. For a detailed discussion of the legal dimensions of these bequests, see Bonfield and Poos, 'The Development of the Deathbed Transfer', Ch. 4 above.

This evidence is not difficult to describe. The records of the deBohun family, the Earls Warenne, Barking Abbey and Norwich Cathedral Priory, to name but a few, all show that in East Anglian villages, as elsewhere, manor courts steadily gained experience during the later fourteenth century in administering the bequests of the dead. By mid-fifteenth century in the Essex villages of Wethersfield and Ingatestone, court officials had facilitated the transfer of 290 acres of customary land to meet the pious provisions of the mortally ill. At Winslow in Buckinghamshire, between 1433 and 1460, courts oversaw the reallocation of 153 acres to benefit the dead. On 15 Norfolk manors, during the same span of years, peasants near death asked manorial officials to implement the transfer of 579 acres of bond land for charitable and pious purposes.[9] These bequests and sales *in extremis* all played a part, as Dr DeWindt has suggested, in rural land markets.

Throughout the countryside the sale of customary land had a well-known, albeit legally mandated, protocol. Sellers surrendered land into the hands of the lord who then granted the land to buyers, formally admitting them to its use in return for payment of an entry fine. Failure to follow this procedure resulted in penalties of varied severity. Bailiffs summoned delinquent sellers and buyers into court and exacted fines or seized their land, attaching crops until they were redeemed by cash. At issue was the right of the lord to approve all the tenants of his land. Seigneurial interests remained in effect whether land was acquired by purchase, gift, or rights of inheritance. Even if land were transferred by will, executors had to inform the lord and purchase his consent.[10] No one, neither the dying nor their kin, lawfully arranged the sale of land without seigneurial license.[11] Nor did the jurors of a manor court escape account-ability if they failed to report the men and women holding land from the lord on the day they died.

It was hardly surprising, then, to see manorial officials at the bedside of the dying. At the lord's request small groups of jurors, along with the bailiff or reeve, visited the mortally ill and oversaw the disposition of villein land. Officials always questioned the dying for if a man were of unsound mind, his last wishes had no force.[12] Officials also wanted to

---

[9] Courts of Antingham, Beeston, Bexwell, Bressingham, Gymingham, Hindolveston, Horsham St Faith, Heacham, Hevyngham, Little Fransham, Newton, Northwold, Wells, West Lexham, Wymondham.

[10] Levett, *Studies in Manorial History*, 220–1.

[11] Court of Gymingham: 13 Dec. 1411: *Generalis inquisitio presentat quod Thomas Thurkild, languens in extremis, reddit per manus Willelmi West in presencia Rogeri Rug et aliorum tenentum domini ij acras de selond et j acram terre ad vendendas sine licencia. Ideo preceptum est seisire.*

[12] Court of Winslow 6 May 1435.

know whether a woman near death had been coerced into settling property on her spouse. To learn if provisions were 'freely made', jurors called on the steward to question the woman alone.[13] Manorial officials again visited the sick whenever a doubt arose as to the severity of an illness. Should a villager become well enough to go to market or attend the parish church, the lord's court had the right to declare any property settlements, made under the pretext of fatal illness, null and void.[14] Still it was more often the case that a bailiff visited the mortally ill. They simply asked his help to settle their estates according to the custom of the manor. The public way of dying tended to formalize the request, since its realization depended on the very officials gathered around a peasant's deathbed: the bailiff, the jurors, and, when needed, the steward, the lord, and the clerk of his court.[15]

With witnesses such as these, the dying had the opportunity to voice whatever plans they had for the use of their land. Although in theory the land belonged to the lord and reverted to him at death, no lord remained unsympathetic to his tenants' last requests. As long as the dying adhered to customary procedures, the lord allowed them the freedom to sell and transfer land as they wished. Hence the man who was burdened with debts honoured his obligations at death by selling land to settle overdue accounts.[16] In a similar way the villager with few resources other than land arranged its sale to enable executors to implement his will.[17] Other men sold land to finance annuities for wives enfeebled by age, while a younger man wanted his children to have a lump sum of cash if their mother remarried.[18] In any case the freedom to sell land at death was hardly an unimportant gain. It enabled the dying to plan how best to meet familial needs and still obligate the living to honour the memory of the dead. This the dying did whenever they stipulated that the proceeds of a sale must also benefit their souls.

Charitable bequests frequently mirrored religious concerns by bringing into focus the question of what lay in store for the dying. No villager wanted to die unprepared. To die without warning, the faithful feared,

[13] Court of Sustead 6 Dec. 1419; Hindolveston 12 July 1421.

[14] Levett, *Studies in Manorial History*, 222.

[15] e.g. Court of Newton 8 Jul. 1377; Wymondham 29 Sep. 1378; Hindolveston 22 Feb. 1388; Sedgeford 12 Mar. 1428; Wells 6 Oct. 1426 and 6 Aug. 1433; Hindolveston 20 Oct. 1438; Horsham St Faith 18 Oct. 1442; Sustead 29 Sep. 1448.

[16] Court of Gymingham 6 Apr. 1382; Winslow 25 July 1460.

[17] Court of Ingatestone 18 Oct. 1451; Castleacre Priory (date faded) 1474.

[18] Court of Great Waltham 22 Feb. 1429; Westwood 3 Apr. 1433; Hindolveston 1 Nov. 1443.

was to die unconfessed, and for such a person there was no sure and certain hope for the future.[19] In the view of the Church salvation required more than a fleeting sense of having 'lived amiss'. Remorse and expiation had to accompany the confession of wrong. Parish priests visited the dying not only to pray but also to inquire: 'Are you sorry for your sins; do you desire to make amends?'[20] Penance through alms, the clergy said, elicited mercy and enhanced the welfare of the dead. Should the faithful fail to intercede on their behalf, the souls of the departed lingered long in purgatory. To counter this fear, villagers instructed executors to dispose of estates in such a way as to generate funds for 'pious and charitable uses'. At the same time neighbours and kin as well as the clergy expected the dying to settle property on surviving children and spouses. For all concerned there was, then, the problem of finding a balance between the allocation of limited resources and the disparate needs of the living and the dead. As a result charitable bequests came to incorporate rules of tenure and contract in order to accommodate the requests of the dying to the long term interests of families and heirs. Given the complexity of this accommodation, land was transferred and sold in a variety of ways.

The simplest transactions involved no overt family ties. The dying surrendered land into the hands of the bailiff to the use of the lord and asked that he sell it, then distribute the proceeds in alms for the sake of the souls of the dead.[21] This the lord did with the help of the bailiff, the reeve, or a committee composed of the chief steward, the chamberlain, and the understeward. When they offered the land for sale, they came into court and, like auctioneers, demanded the best price.[22] The land in question ranged from little garden plots to holdings of twenty acres and more. The tenants of this land had neither spouses nor children able to honour deathbed requests. Consequently the lord became an executor of last resort. At his disposal were the resources and personnel to enforce the lawful sale of land in any village. If, as occasionally happened, buyers defaulted on payment, the lord had the right to eject them, resell the

[19] W. S. Holdsworth, A *History of English Law* (3rd edn.; 12 vols.; London, 1922–38), iii. 535. P. Ariès, *The Hour of Our Death*, tr. H. Weaver (New York, 1981), 10–13.

[20] *John Myrc's Instructions for Parish Priests*, ed. E. Peacock (EETS 32, 1868), 69–70; these queries are included in the 'Seven questions to be asked of a dying man', 69–71. For further discussion of how to enhance the welfare of the dead through charity, see *Dan Michael, Ayenbite of Inwyt*, 197; *Vices and Virtues being A Soul's Confessions of its Sins, with Reason's Description of the Virtues*, ed. F. Holthausen (EETS 89, 1967), 36–8.

[21] Court of Beeston, 24 Feb. 1427; Winslow, 13 June 1451; Ingatestone 6 Nov. 1461. Also see Levett, *Studies in Manorial History*, 219.

[22] Court of Ingatestone 25 March 1416; 10 Nov. 1420. See Appendix 5.2 for data on prices.

land, and disburse the sale-price in keeping with the wishes of the deceased.[23] Knowing this, the widowed and the childless depended on the sanction of lordship, rather than the good intentions of friends, to facilitate the sale of land at death.

A different set of circumstances and concerns characterized deathbed bequests that called for the immediate sale of land by family and kin. This was a task that usually fell to bereaved husbands and wives. Even though they had the option of buying the property themselves, many did not. Instead they sold the land to neighbours, then appeared with them in court to testify to the transaction.[24] From their testimony we learn that the dying had wanted money channelled towards charitable works but not at the expense of the well-being of heirs. Often times the property for sale was only a small portion of the deceased's total holdings. In 1447 a butcher in Wethersfield (Essex) died in possession of five acres of land, eight of pasture, an enclosure, and a shop; he bequeathed everything to his widow and son, instructing them to sell the shop and distribute the money in alms to the needy.[25] His bequest was the norm. Although the dying wanted property sold for the sake of their souls, a sense of duty to the living tempered the transactions. As a rule husbands and fathers asked that only two to three acres of land, or less, be sold immediately upon their death.

This sense of obligation to the living influenced deathbed bequests based on the delayed sale of land. The bequests involved property settlements dictated by the dying, then implemented by estate administrators. Their witness and involvement enabled customary tenants to settle land on heirs and still ensure prayers and alms for the souls of the dead. What the dying did was to ask manorial officers to defer the sale of land until spouses or kin had died. Hence a man near death provided for his widow by surrendering land to her use on the condition that when she died this land would be sold for the salvation of his soul.[26] In much the same way a peasant woman settled what little property she had on her husband, arranging for its sale only after the man had died.[27] Mothers did the same for daughters, fathers for sons, sons for fathers, and brothers for each other.[28]

---

[23] Court of Beeston, 24 Feb. 1427; Winslow, 13 June 1451.
[24] e.g. Court of Gimingham, 7 July 1387; 25 Nov. 1387; 28 Oct. 1400.
[25] Court of Wethersfield, 8 Dec. 1447.
[26] Court of Gymingham, 22 Feb. 1384; South Elmham, 1 May 1419; Westwood, 12 Mar. 1428; Wells, 6 Aug. 1433.
[27] Court of Barnet, 12 Apr. 1456.
[28] Court of Worlingworth, 25 July 1409; Gymingham, 23 Apr. 1403 and 1 Aug. 1410; Brancaster, 29 June 1414.

All expected the steward or the bailiff to make sure that land eventually was sold according to the terms 'wished, mandated, and set forth' in the original bequest. To these wishes the lord and his officials regularly acquiesced. As a result the living had full use of the resources of the dead, albeit on the understanding that within a generation or less the lord and his court would intervene and supervise the sale of land to benefit the souls of the deceased.

There were finally property settlements that postponed the sale of land indefinitely. Such were the bequests of peasants intent on keeping land in family hands. To this end the dying arranged for a holding to descend from one generation to the next and only to be sold for pious uses if heirs died without children of their own. Thus in 1421 Thomas Groom, the tenant of a messuage and eight acres of land in South Elmham (Suffolk), surrendered this holding to the bailiff, asking him to supervise its future use.[29] Groom wanted his widow to have his land until her death, whence it was to descend to John their son. Should he die childless, the land went to Roger, his brother, from whom it reverted to Cristina, a sister, and then to the bailiff for him to sell if both brother and sister died without lawfully procreated heirs. In this way the dying provided for the continuity of the family estate by acknowledging the claims of the yet to be born. Even so, the force of deathbed provisions over time required the support of the lord and his court. Together they reminded heirs seeking admittance to a patrimony that land must be held in accord with the wishes of the dead.[30]

By now it should be clear that the dying were not without choices when settling estates. To be sure the sale of land remained subject to practical limitations imposed by the demands of lordship and the subsistence needs of family and kin. Yet the mortally ill still had the option of disposing of property to meet personal needs. Consequently when pious villagers requested the sale of land, they also asked administrators to raise and distribute money for the faithful departed, including parents, spouses, and friends. Moreover, the dying often explained how the money generated by the sale of land was to be channelled into alms and 'good works' to benefit the poor. At Ingatestone (Essex) in 1446 a village glass-maker expressed the wish to aid those of his neighbours in greatest need of his charity.[31] In 1472 at Isleworth (Middlesex) a cultivator with forty-five acres of land remembered all the poor and indigent requiring his help.[32]

---

[29] Court of South Elmham, 25 Jan. 1421.   [30] Court of Ingatestone, 25 Mar. 1469.
[31] Court of Ingatestone, 18 Oct. 1446.   [32] Court of Isleworth, 23 Apr. 1472.

Even peasants with much smaller holdings asked visitors crowded around a deathbed to give alms to the poor and bread to the needy.[33] This is not to say that the dying cared little about masses and prayers for the dead. Many peasants clearly did.[34] None the less the sale of land by the mortally ill reflected an equal, if not greater, interest in directing money towards neighbours in need.

II

In English villages, as elsewhere, the ecclesiastical view prevailed that the poor were powerful advocates on behalf of the dead.[35] Abbots, bishops, and monks all taught that 'charity ransomed sin' and enabled the dying to secure the good will of the poor.[36] When Bishop Brinton of Rochester preached in the 1370s, he reminded the faithful of Augustine's contention that God obliged the pauper to pray for the almsgiver; and if this obligation went unfulfilled, the alm itself became a prayer.[37] Even critics of the riches of merchants and lords allowed that charity accompanied by sorrow secured peace for the dying and rest for the dead.[38] Everywhere preachers emphasized the redemptive merit of almsdeeds and promoted a sense of how the exercises of salvation required co-operation and mutual aid. Yet the confidence which the Church reposed in charitable works heightened popular fears of sudden death.[39] Through prayer and fasts the faithful sought deliverance from an untimely demise, while anxious parishioners wanted the assurance of knowing that no matter the 'hour or manner of death', they had already secured alms to propitiate God's wrath. Even when mortality posed no immediate threat, the cautious

---

[33] Court of Barnet, 12 Apr. 1456 and 8 Jul. 1459.

[34] Court of Newton, 8 Jul. 1377; Sedgeford, 12 Mar. 1428; Westwood, 29 Sep. 1436; Ingatestone, 20 Nov. 1455 and 8 Dec. 1466; Castleacre Priory, 15 Apr. 1468. Villagers also relied on parish guilds to pray for the dead. See, Hanawalt, *Ties That Bound*, 262; H. F. Westlake, *The Parish Guilds of Medieval England* (London, 1919). McIntosh, 'Local Responses', 209–45, notes on 215 that fraternities provided alms to impoverished members and occasionally to non-members. For bequests to fraternities, see Court of Wymondham, 13 Jan. 1425; Court of Barnet, 8 July 1459 at which it was reported that William Nicol, *in extremis*, arranged for a tenement and garden to be sold 'with all haste' after his death and the money given to the fraternity of the Holy Trinity for the sake of his soul.

[35] *Jacob's Well*, 121.

[36] Ibid. 122; *Dives and Pauper*, ii. 177, 284; *Middle English Sermons.*, ed. W. O. Ross (EETS 209, 1940), 151–2.

[37] *The Sermons of Thomas Brinton, Bishop of Rochester (1373–89)*, ed. Sister Mary Aquinas Devlin (Camden Soc., v. 85 London, 1954), 194: *In tamtum quod statim cum acceperit elemosinam a diuite obligatur pro eo orare, quod si non facit, ipsa elomosina satis orat. . . .*'

[38] *Langland, William Piers the Plowman*, ed. Revd. W. W. Skeat (Oxford, 1886; reissued 1954), 229 (C. Passus X, ll. 36–40).

[39] *Dives and Pauper*, i. 172–3.

planned requiem masses and solicited alms from family and friends. In villages this behaviour usually characterized ageing peasants who sold land in return for income maintenance while they lived and alms after they died.[40] In 1392 a widow at Walsham le Willows (Suffolk) obtained such support from a neighbour, then elicited his promise to lead a cow before her bier on the day she was buried.[41] Apparently the animal was to be her 'corpse present' to the village church.[42]

Poorer villagers had less opportunity for generosity to the Church. In fact the disabilities of old age occasionally forced peasant householders to difficult choices. In 1425 a widower at Winslow (Buckinghamshire), after selling his messuage and shop to a married couple, requested shelter, food, clothing, and his caretakers' assurance that should he fall ill, they would expend on his health the 40s. he otherwise wanted them to distribute in alms for his soul.[43] While not all villagers were as hard-pressed, many understood the risk involved in linking almsdeeds to the sale of land during retirement or at death. The threat of insecurity made men and women circumspect. Prolonged sickness clearly frightened the old. The welfare of surviving kin worried the terminally ill. They in particular had to balance the needs of the soul against the subsistence needs of children and heirs. Under these circumstances parents near death arranged for adult children to enter land and hold it in perpetuity, provided they honoured the deceased with alms and charitable works.[44] Equally practical arrangements were made on behalf of children orphaned underage. Philip Barneby of Barnet (Hertfordshire), when dying in 1439, entrusted the care of his motherless daughter to two of his neighbours, also granting them custody of a grove of trees; in return, Philip said, they must gather underbrush and wood, sell what they could, and while supporting his child, distribute alms to the poor.[45]

Husbands and wives, too, carefully utilized scarce resources to afford one another a measure of security at death. In 1383 Joan Baker of Wethersfield, (Essex) arranged with Geoffrey Baker, her terminally ill spouse, to farm his croft of one and a half acres for twenty years, then sell the land at its 'best price' and distribute the money in alms on his

---

[40] Clark, 'Some Aspects of Social Security', 312 n. 7.

[41] Court of Walsham le Willows, 7 July 1392.

[42] For discussion of 'corpse-present', see J. Brand, *Observances on Popular Antiquities* (London, 1877), 448.

[43] Court of Winslow, 25 July 1425.

[44] Court of Hindolveston, 22 Feb. 1388; Bressingham, 2 June 1398; Barnet, 24 May 1408; Wethersfield, 12 Mar. 1480.

[45] Court of Barnet, 6 Oct. 1439.

behalf.[46] In 1434 Edmund Creik of Wymondham (Norfolk), in a final bequest and disposition of eight acres of land, surrendered all to Letitia, his wife, enabling her to raise the 26s. 8d. she had agreed to disburse in charitable works after his death.[47] Not that it was only widows who distributed alms for the dead. John King of Winslow (Buckinghamshire) accompanied his wife, Alice King, to court in 1455 to enrol the agreement they had made to raise 40s. to insure the safety of her soul.[48] As arranged, John surrendered a messuage and its yard into the hands of the lord who regranted the property to the couple on the understanding that when Alice died, William immediately would give her assigns 40s. for alms or risk the distraint and sale of his moveable goods. Property agreements between husbands and wives were not unusual, although men generally dictated the terms governing the transfer of land at death. These terms often subjected the tenure of holdings to recall so that if widows remarried, the land in question reverted to executors or to the lord.[49] They arranged its sale and, in doing so, affirmed the administrative burden imposed on courts by the charitable bequests of the dead.

The implementation of these bequests had a cumulative effect on manor courts. The land in question was considerable; the terms governing its redistribution were complex (see Table 5.1). Much depended on the conditions prescribed by the dying and whether the sale of land was immediate upon the death of the donor, delayed one generation, or indefinitely deferred. As a result courts had to devise procedures and keep records that were sufficiently detailed to remind the living of the obligations they bore to the dead. At Ingatestone (Essex) the lady of the manor urged her steward to question all villagers about the sale and use of land lest she appear remiss in supervising pious bequests. Her concern had noticeable results if no heirs survived to dispense alms for the deceased. When this happened in 1459, the lady summoned two of her tenants into court, admitted them to three acres of land, then ordered the men, as the executors of Roger Turnour, to sell the land for the sake of his soul.[50] Twenty-two years had passed since Turnour's death in 1437 when he had surrendered the three acres to his widow for life and thence to John their son.[51] John died childless in 1459 and his mother lived but another year. Soon thereafter Turnour's long-standing bequest was honoured as his

---

[46] Court of Wethersfield, 6 Jan. 1383.   [47] Court of Wymondham, 18 Oct. 1434.
[48] Court of Winslow, 25 May 1455.
[49] Court of Harlow Bury, 12 Mar. 1402; Worlingworth, 25 Mar. 1409; Hindolveston, 1 Nov. 1443; Barnet, 12 Apr. 1456.
[50] Court of Ingatestone, 14 Sep. 1459.   [51] Court of Ingatestone, 12 Mar. 1437.

TABLE 5.1. *Deathbed sales of land and charitable bequests, 1378–1461*

Court	Years	Sale at donor's death		Sale delayed a generation or less		Sale deferred indefinitely	
		No. of cases	Total acres	No. of cases	Total acres	No. of cases	Total acres
Wymondham	1378–1437	14	73	3	11.5	2	34
Hindolveston	1380–1461	4	40.5	6	34	5	53
Gymingham	1382–1440	15	15	8	23	17	106
Wethersfield	1383–1447	3	5	10	44	1	3
Ingatestone	1416–1450	7	69.5	5	57	2	38
Winslow	1433–1460	7	95.5	5	15.5	3	32
TOTAL		50	298.5	37	185	30	266

Source: see Appendix 5.1.

executors distributed alms, at the lady's bequest, to villagers in 'greatest' need of charitable help.

The watchfulness of the lady in this case was not an isolated incident.[52] The time and energy that manorial administrators invested in handling bequests reflected a widespread concern not merely to supervise almsgiving but to regulate the sale of land whenever it was linked to the redistribution of resources by the mortally ill. Regulation prevented secrecy and warned the community of 'false executors who would make themselves rich with dead men's goods'.[53] Fraud, deception, and negligence troubled any court and gave pause to officials entrusted by the dying with the administration of estates. Expectations of fair play required public censure of executors guilty of 'keeping all to themselves'.[54] They betrayed the trust of the dead and wronged the living by denying alms to 'poor folk without the power to help themselves'.[55] Throughout the countryside dishonest executors risked prosecution and the reproach of secular lords as well as of the Church.[56] The misuse of estates for personal gain was never sanctioned. To squander the alms of the dead was a 'great folly and also a sin'.[57] It bespoke trickery along with malice and warranted accusations of deception and fraud in manorial courts. Such was the charge brought against John Byrchhach of Ingatestone (Essex) in 1416, when the court learned that a certain John Resoun had implored his executors, of whom Byrchhach was one, to sell fifteen acres of land for the souls of the faithful departed.[58] Instead Byrchhach 'fraudulently' exploited the estate, hiding its 'profit' from all concerned. When questioned, he misled officials and 'secretly' agreed to a price of 5 li. although the husband of Resoun's widow had bid 10 li. for the land. In court the steward asked all present if any villager wished to pay more. None did, and in 1420 the sale was completed for 10 li. under the supervision of the lady and her council.

---

[52] For similar cases, see Court of Ingatestone, 12 Jun. 1435; 18 Oct. 1451; 25 Mar. 1469. Also see Court of Hindolveston, 22 Feb. 1388.

[53] *Dives and Pauper*, i. 214.   [54] Ibid.   [55] Ibid.

[56] For ecclesiastical censure, see visitation records of parishes in Norwich and its suburbs, *Acta et Comperti Rotuli anno* 1417: *Johannes Scut executor testamenti Johannis Hering de Brakendel, defuncti, impedivit voluntatem dicti defuncti eo quod j tenementum in Brakendel et j vaccam non vendidit et disposuit pro anima dicti defuncti.* For censure of negligent executors by manorial officials, see Court of Gymingham 9 Feb. 1439; Hevyngham 1 Aug. 1422; Wymondham 3 May 1436: John Olwytinge, *in extremis*, arranged for Richard Knyght to sell 3 acres and 3 rods for the sake of John's soul. The court noted: *Ricardus executionem ultime voluntatis predicte omnino tardavit. Ideo preceptum est seisire* etc. Richard subsequently surrendered the land into the hands of the lord who regranted it to Richard to sell for the sake of the souls of the dead.

[57] *Dives and Pauper*, i. 214. *John Myrc's Instructions*, 37.

[58] Court of Ingatestone, 25 Mar. 1416 and 10 Nov. 1420.

The effort to guarantee deathbed sales, rendering them immune from future disruptions, involved peasants and lords in a common endeavour. Together they expected manor courts to affirm the bequests of the deceased by keeping the memory of their transactions alive. Although the Church taught the faithful never to forget the dead, villagers feared the consequences of relying solely on the piety of heirs.[59] After all, the temporal dimensions of charitable bequests often delayed the sale of land until the death of the donor's children or spouse. When arranging bequests the dying rarely, if ever, knew who actually would buy their land. The mortally ill handled this uncertainty as best they could, invoking God's wrath against any intermediary daring to undermine a bequest.[60]

The sanction of lordship was no less a threat since property settlements appeared more secure if they included the lord as an interested party ready to defend the interests of the dead. Realizing as much, Geoffrey Fuller of Runton Hayes (Norfolk) arranged in 1383 for a fellow villager to have a parcel of land, along with a cottage, if he paid Fuller's executors 32s. within two years of his demise; otherwise, Fuller said, the tenement would revert to the lord for him to sell for the souls of the deceased.[61] Of course the proper administration of charitable bequests always required the lord's consent. Only his approval assured dependent tenants that the decisions of the dying had validity and force at law.

III

Admittedly, this is a formal view of deathbed bequests. Even though they involved the law in many ways, they were not simply a procedural matter; nor were these settlements utilized by peasants alone. In England merchants and nobles had long included the reallocation and sale of land in pious bequests that benefited monasteries and religious houses as well as needy folk.[62] Peasants learned of this benevolence when the executors of

[59] *John Myrc's Instructions*, 49: 'Hast thou passed by a churchyard and neglected to pray for the dead?'

[60] Court of Barnet, 6 May 1424; Ingatestone, 18 Oct. 1451; Stowe Bardolf, 25 Mar. 1459.

[61] Court of Runton Hayes, 14 Feb. 1383.

[62] For examples of deathbed bequests and sales of land by merchants, freeholders, and gentry, see A *Calendar of the Register of Henry Wakefield, Bishop of Worcester, 1375–95*, ed. W. P. Marett (Worcs. Hist. Soc., 1972) 25–7. *Testamenta Vetusta*, ed. N. H. Nicholas (2 vols.; London, 1826), i. 244, 336–7. *The Register of Henry Chichele Archbishop of Canterbury, 1414–43*, ed. E. F. Jacob (Canterbury and York Soc., 1945), 405, 408–11, 413–14, 418. *The Cartulary of the Monastery of St Frideswide at Oxford*, ed. S. R. Wigram (2 vols.; Oxford Hist. Soc., 1895–6) i. nos. 149, 404. For further discussion, see C. Burgess, '"By Quick and by Dead": Wills and Pious Provision in Late Medieval Bristol', *EHR* 305 (1987), 837–58. Note in particular his argument that 'wills convey altogether too meager an impression of

the wealthy travelled the countryside to distribute alms and ask prayers for the dead.[63] Impoverished tenants thus noted the passing of manorial lords, and in rural parishes joined their funeral processions, the poor carrying torches and clad in black or white.[64] Lords and ladies absorbed the cost of this array and arranged for bread and oftentimes meals to be served mourners and neighbours. The indigent counted upon these doles, and everywhere begged 'candles, clothes, meat, and drink' at the funerals of the great.[65] What lords and ladies wanted in return was remembrance after death, and this they solicited not only through alms but also by carefully planned bequests. Such bequests rarely mentioned rural beggars by name but spoke instead of 'agricultural labourers', of 'servile tenants' and 'householders' living in want.[66] The help they received took the familiar form of small gifts in cash, bedding, clothing, or the pardon of manorial dues.

This charity comprised a work of salvation, yet the alms of the dead were also something more. The bequests of peasants and lords together supported a programme of casual relief that belied any notion that people in villages cared little about the effects of charity on the poor. The bequests of the dying never disparaged the needy by picturing them as all alike, as all inarticulate, unambitious, and shiftless. Nor did the dying claim that every beggar merited support.[67] Instead charitable bequests offset stereotypical views of beggars and paupers by acknowledging the diversity of the poor and the complexity of the problems they faced. Always at issue were the hardships experienced by needy peasants whether young or old, married or single, healthy or lame and disabled. What plagued them all was not easily overcome; none had the material resources

post obit provision' (856). In other words, Burgess shows that wills alone do not fully document the charitable donations of the faithful.

[63] S. L. Thrupp, *The Merchant Class of Medieval London* (Ann Arbor, 1948; reissued 1962), 208–9, 228, discusses London merchants bequeathing money to the poor of the village where they had been born. For the bequests of manorial lords to their own tenants and to the rural poor, see *The Fifty Earliest English Wills in the Court of Probate, London*, ed. F. J. Furnivall (EETS 78, 1882) 26–8, 49–53, 70–1. *Testamenta Vetusta*, 352–4. *Register of Henry Chichele*, ii. 14, 18, 33, 141–2, 187, 452, 599–600, 611. *Testamenta Eboracensia*, ed. J. Raine (Surtees Soc., 30, 1885), 4, 111, 219; 55, 47.

[64] *Testamenta Vetusta*, 81, 109, 118, 145, 181, 183–4, 193–4, 212, 236. *Register of Henry Chichele*, ii. 7, 91, 141, 600. *Fifty Earliest English Wills*, 26–8, 130.

[65] *Dives and Pauper*, i. 216.

[66] *Testamenta Vetusta*, 354; *Testamenta Eboracensia*, 30, no. 222; 55, no. 5; *Register of Henry Chichele*, ii. 18, 68, 141, 152, 177.

[67] *Testamenta Eboracensia*, 32 no. 3: Nicholas Strelley, knight, in 1430 bequeathed 100s. to be distributed among the poor of ten villages, but not to any paupers who frequented taverns or illicitly played with dice.

to handle adversity alone. Under these circumstances benefactors helped
bedridden villagers unable to work, agricultural labourers struggling to
support growing families, and impoverished girls without the dowries
they needed to marry.[68] And this was not all. The dying bequeathed
'milch cows', ewes, even oxen to insolvent householders, and set aside
small sums of cash for rural workers too impoverished to own 'beasts and
plows'.[69] By no measure were these workers and farmers irresponsible
misfits. They knew only too well how bad luck could ruin painstakingly
constructed household economies. Rural benefactors understood this as
well and aided the unfortunate with alms to alleviate losses occasioned by
sudden illness, physical injury, diseased livestock, or the damage that
stray animals did to much-needed crops.[70]

It was of course easy enough for the nobility and the gentry to be in
favour of charity. An identical commitment was in practice more demanding and difficult for peasants near death. Not all villagers enjoyed
the 'excesses' of wealth which the clergy taught properly belonged to the
poor.[71] Yet the basic faith of villagers fostered a sense of co-operation and
obligation whereby a concern for family predisposed the dying to respond
creatively to the needs of the poor. Indeed we will misunderstand the
nature of charitable bequests if we fail to recall how peasant householders
first arranged for the welfare of kin. Rather than disinherit spouses and
children, the dying settled what little property they had on them so that
when kinsfolk no longer had need of this land it could be sold for the sake
of the poor. Deathbed bequests were, then, unmistakably complex. At
one level they affirmed the importance of achieving the maximum use of
limited resources. At another they reflected a concern for the bereaved
and an abiding empathy for neighbours in need. In either case the bequests disclose how inextricably linked the demands of charity, property,
and family life were in village society.

For this reason the distinction usually drawn between 'private charity'
and 'public welfare' blurs if applied to deathbed bequests.[72] Although
the bequests remained privately funded, most were administered by

[68] *Register of Henry Chichele*, ii. 52–3, 607. *Testamenta-Vetusta*, 345; *Testamenta Eboracensia*,
30 no. 189.
[69] *Testamenta Vetusta*, 226; *Testamenta Eboracensia*, 30 no. 132, *Register of Henry Chichele*,
ii. 536, 607.
[70] *Register of Henry Chichele*, ii. 52–3, 140–1, 179, 569.
[71] M. Mollat, *The Poor in the Middle Ages: An Essay in Social History*, tr. A. Goldhammer
(New Haven, 1986), 130–4.
[72] McIntosh, 'Local Responses', 212–13.

stewards, bailiffs, and reeves.[73] Through them the last wishes of the dying became a permanent part of the official records belonging to manorial lords. No matter how long villagers had been dead, the lord's court honoured their memory by enjoining the living to perform 'good works' on behalf of the deceased. In doing so the court became an advocate for the dead, serving as an intermediary between ancestors and heirs as well as between departed donors and the recipients of their charity. Even though this charity had a marked religious dimension, the court and not the Church supervised the property settlements of the dead. The clergy, it is true, worked tirelessly to encourage the exercises of salvation, yet it was through the concerted activity of peasants and courts that the ideals upheld by preachers and monks more often found practical application. What this reflected was an institutional and communal response to the faithful's quest for salvation. What resulted was the gradual secularization of poor relief as manor courts continued to address their services and administrative skills to the welfare of the community of both the living and the dead.

[73] For further discussion, see Bennett, *Life on the English Manor*, 251; Dyer, *Standards of Living*, 256.

Appendix 5.1
Sources

The court rolls used in this essay are for the most part on deposit in English record offices and have not been edited. For cases involving the sale of land at death, see:

British Library: Barnet Add. MS 40167. Cashio Add. MS 40626.

Cambridge University Library: Winslow MS Dd 7 22.

Essex Record Office: Great Waltham D/DT u 24 1–2. Harlow Bury D/DEs M2. Ingatestone D/DP M32–57. Wethersfield D/DFy M5–10.

Greater London Record Office: Harrow ACC 76/24/17. Iselworth ACC 1379/10.

Holkham Hall: Castleacre Priory Bundle 5 no. 41. Wells Bundle 4 no. 57. West Lexham Bundle 2 no. 3. The Holkham material is on microfilm at the University of Michigan, Harlan Hatcher Graduate Library.

Norfolk Record Office: Antingham 6020. Beeston 10267. Bexwell 3850. Brancaster 6329. Bressingham R 192 B-D. Gymingham 5741–5791. Heacham DC 1. Hevyngham 14472. Hindolveston 4821–4822, 4871–4875. Horsham St Faith 19509. Little Fransham 13097. Newton 5074. Northwold 18630. Runton Hayes WKC 2/167. Sedgeford 5290. Stowe Bardolf Hare 3267. Sustead WKC 2/176–177. Wymondham 8861, 8785, 10103a, 11286, 18500, 18502. Deathbed sales are also noted in wills. See, for example, Dean and Chapter Muniments: 1416–1437; *Acta et comperta* Rolls: DCN 67. See, too, registered copies of wills proved in the court of the Dean and Chapter of Norwich; Register, I, 1444–1455: DCN 69.

Suffolk Record Office: South Elmham HA 12/C2/23–25. Walsham le Willows HA 504/1/3. Westwood HA 30/369/390. Worlingworth S 1/2/1.10.

Appendix 5.2
Prices

Very little evidence survives to indicate the money actually paid for land sold at the request of peasants near death. The few cases where clerks of the court recorded payments are noted in Table 5.2. When arranging sales the mortally ill rarely specified prices or set payment schedules. Peasants simply asked executors and manorial officials to sell land at the 'best price' they could. On occasion the dying did arrange for children and heirs to purchase land at a favourable price. The case of Hugo Thomeys of Hindolveston (Norfolk) provides an example. At the court of 22 February 1388, jurors reported that Hugo Thomeys, *languens in extremis*, arranged for his widow, Matilda, to hold 2½ ac. of bond land for life. When she died the bailiff or cellarer must sell the land to raise alms; but if Robert, the son and heir of Hugo, wished to purchase the land, he should be afforded preference (*ita quod si Robertus, filius et heres dicti Hugonis, dictam terram emere voluerit quod habeat dictam terram pre omnibus ut vendita potuerit vel ad minus pretium*). Subsequently, at the court of 7 July 1390, the jurors reported that Matilda Thomeys had died, whereupon the cellarer sold the aforesaid land to Hugo. For a related case, see Levett, *Studies*, 219. Also, Norfolk Record Office DCN 67/la: will of James Rode of Sedgeford (1417). He arranges for his widow to hold his tenement for life; at her death their executors must sell the tenement to raise alms. If, however, any one of his sons wished to purchase the tenement: *habeat pre omnibus aliis hominibus ad valorem melioris pretij xl s.*

TABLE 5.2.   *Charitable bequests and land prices, 1387–1460*

Years	Place	Property	Sale Price		
			li.	s.	d.
1387	Gymingham	5 ac. 1 cottage	3	15	0
1420	Ingatestone	15 ac.	10	0	0
1420	S. Elmham	14 ac.	6	13	4
1427	Beeston	1½ ac. 1 messuage	1	0	0
1433	Westwood	1 messuage	5	8	4
1435	Winslow	1 cottage	5	0	0
1436	Winslow	2 cottages	11	0	0
1437	Winslow	6 ac. 1 messuage	2	10	0
1460	Winslow	15 ac. 1 messuage	10	13	4

6

Politics in Manorial Court Rolls:
The Tactics, Social Composition, and
Aims of a pre-1381 Peasant Movement

PETER FRANKLIN

THE study of popular political movements in medieval England has been overshadowed ever since its inception by the spectacular events of the great rising of 1381. It is now some 40 years since R. H. Hilton emphasized the importance of earlier struggles at village level, but, although much has been done to put English movements into a European context and a much longer chronological framework, accounts of those local movements remain rare and brief.[1] Medieval society was founded upon an economic exploitation of the peasantry which could hardly have been more direct and peasant opposition to this was endemic, but attention has remained concentrated on the minority of campaigns which became more historically visible because they led to actions in the royal courts. Many movements are only known from royal court records, and informative recent studies of peasant ideology and claims to ancient demesne status still rely heavily upon these.[2] But it is the records of manorial courts which should offer the most valuable insights into the grassroots politics of peasant opposition to feudalism. Manorial court rolls have great strengths, notably in their evidence for the socio-economic conditions which gave rise to peasant movements, the economic, social, and legal status of those who took part, and the detailed local events of the time. Their shortcomings are, however, certainly serious. As records made for

[1] R. H. Hilton, 'Peasant Movements in England before 1381', *EcHR* 2nd ser. 2 (1949), 117–36, and *Bond Men Made Free: Medieval Peasant Movements and the English Rising of 1381* (London, 1973); M. Mollat and P. Wolff, *Ongles bleus Jacques et Ciompi. Les révolutions populaires en Europe aux XIVᵉ et XVᵉ Siècles* (Paris, 1970). Published accounts of particular pre-1381 movements will be found in R. J. Faith, 'The Class Struggle in Fourteenth-Century England', in R. Samuel (ed.), *People's History and Socialist Theory* (London, 1981), 50–60, and 'The "Great Rumour" of 1377', 43–73; Razi, 'Struggles', 151–67; J. H. Tillotson, 'Peasant Unrest in the England of Richard II: Some Evidence from Royal Records', *Historical Studies*, 16 (1974–5), 1–16; D. G. Watts, 'Peasant Discontent on the Manors of Titchfield Abbey, 1245–1405', *Proc. of the Hampshire Field Club and Arch. Soc.*, 39 (1983), 121–35.
[2] Faith, 'The "Great Rumour" of 1377'; M. A. Barg, 'The Villeins of the "Ancient Demesne"', in L. de Rosa (ed.), *Studi in memoria di Federigo Melis* (5 vols.; Rome, 1978), i. 213–37; Hilton, *Bond Men*, 88.

the lords involved in these conflicts they can misrepresent or fail to record significant events. Their terse records pose important problems of interpretation, and their concentration on the affairs of direct tenants who were mostly adult males raises difficult questions about support in the wider community. Yet comparatively little use has been made of them for this purpose, and, in particular, most of the 'medieval village studies' which have placed so much emphasis on these documents have paid little attention to local politics because of their authors' failure to recognize the significance of lord–peasants conflict.[3] Z. Razi's paper on the struggle between the abbots of Halesowen, Worcestershire, and their peasants is the exception which has shown some of the ways in which manorial court rolls can be used to reconstruct important aspects of a movement which was already known from cases in the royal courts.[4] He pursued a chronological treatment which placed most emphasis on individual cases and incidents. Another work of his has also linked this aspect of peasant politics to the debate on the social cohesion of the medieval village, the strength of the rural community, by interpreting that struggle as a cause which bound together rich, middle, and poor peasants, freemen, and villeins, in the fight against their lords.[5]

The present paper takes on a more quantitative approach to the manorial court roll evidence for peasant discontent on another large West Midlands estate, the earl of Gloucester's manor of Thornbury in Gloucestershire. It focuses, in particular, on the forms of protest used, the means of seigneurial oppression, the social composition of the movement and the aims of those who took part, four themes which demonstrate the strengths and limitations of court-roll evidence and some of the problems of interpretation which it poses. At each stage, it tries to relate conditions and events in this part of Gloucestershire to what is known of other popular movements which took place before 1381. The period under discussion has been limited to the first half of the reign of Edward III in order to draw attention to a neglected phase of popular discontent and to produce manageable numbers of cases for statistical analysis.

Thornbury Manor stood beside the Severn estuary about 12 miles north of Bristol, and the peasant movement which was active there is of interest for several reasons. Although relations between lord and peasants

---

[3] DeWindt, *Land and People*; Raftis, *Warboys*; Britton, *Community of the Vill*; Razi, *Life, Marriage and Death*; Hogan, 'Wistow'.

[4] Razi, 'Struggles', *passim*.

[5] Z. Razi, 'Family, Land and the Village Community in Later Medieval England', *P&P* 93 (1981), 15, 31, 35.

are known to have been bad in Thornbury at the start of the sixteenth century,[6] this part of the country is not well known for peasant discontent and seems from published accounts to have had little or no involvement in the 1381 rising.[7] The local movement is only known from local records and is not known to have given rise to any case in the royal courts. Whether it had direct links with other campaigns remains difficult to say, but it must be seen as a part of national discontent, for political activity there reached its peaks at the beginning and end of the 1330s, the very times when a national peasant rising was feared.[8] Its history therefore raises questions about what lay behind the wider unrest and why no national rising took place. The discontent of those years has been seen as a reaction to heavy taxation and purveyance and is said to have been ended by government conciliation.[9] But conditions and events on this estate provide little support for the interpretation of opposition as a straightforward reaction to distress and show how one lord used oppressive measures against his peasants.

With Thornbury town—which they had made a borough in the mid-thirteenth century—Thornbury Manor had formed one of the richest possessions of the Clare earls of Gloucester.[10] For most of the period 1328–52 its lord was Hugh Audley II, the younger son of a family of Staffordshire and Oxfordshire gentry who had come to prominence as a favourite of Edward II in the years after Gaveston's death. After the extinction of the Clares' male line in 1314, he was allowed to marry

---

[6] *The Itinerary of John Leland In or About the Years 1535–1543*, ed. L. Toulmin Smith (5 vols.; new edn., London, 1964), v. 100. For the career of Edward Stafford, duke of Buckingham, then Thornbury's lord, see B. J. Harris, 'Landlords and Tenants in England in the Later Middle Ages: The Buckingham Estates', *P&P* 43 (1963), 146–50, and B. J. Harris, 'Edward Stafford, Third Duke of Buckingham', Ph.D. Thesis (Harvard University, 1967).

[7] Dyer, *Lords and Peasants*, 275. There was at least one report of secret assemblies in Gloucestershire in the 1370s: J. Smyth, *The Berkeley Manuscripts: The Lives of the Berkeleys*, ed. Sir J. Maclean (3 vols.; Bristol and Gloucs. Archaeol. Soc., 1883–5), ii. 24. Popular attacks were made on a new deer park at Stoke Giffard *c.*1397 and there was a serious dispute between the abbot of Gloucester and some of his tenants in 1412: ibid. i. 259; Hilton, *The English Peasantry*, 62–3. All Thornbury manorial court rolls for 1380/1 are lost.

[8] The exact date at which the late 1330s discontent came to a head is open to dispute. Henry Knighton pointed to the year 1338, but the London chronicler suggested 1340. H. Knighton, *Chronicon Henrici Knighton*, ed. J. R. Lumby (2 vols.; Rolls Ser. 92*a–b*, 1889–95), ii. 3; *Chroniques de London*, ed. G. J. Aungier (Camden Soc. 28, 1844), 83. Discontent in Thornbury reached a peak late in 1339, but all court rolls for 1339/40 and 1340/1 are lost. Local conditions were much calmer in 1341/2. For surviving court rolls, see n.13 below.

[9] Maddicott, 'The English Peasantry', 23–4, 51–67.

[10] M. Altschul, *A Baronial Family in Medieval England: The Clares, 1217–1314* (Baltimore, Md., 1965), 300–1; H. P. R. Finberg (ed.), *Gloucestershire Studies* (Leicester, 1957), 66.

Gaveston's widow Margaret Clare and take up one-third of her family's estates.[11] He was created earl of Gloucester in 1337. Thornbury was his most valuable possession, but he spent more time at his residences in Tonbridge, Kent, and Thaxted, Essex. When he died in 1347, he was succeeded by his son-in-law Ralph Stafford, from whom most lords of the manor traced their descent until the twentieth century.[12] Audley and his successors proved to be excellent makers and preservers of records. No local documents survive from the time of the Clares, but some 216 manorial court rolls survived from the years 1328–52, of which twelve are combined manorial court and leet sessions and six are rolls of separate leets. The first court roll dates from 18 October 1328, and sessions were held at irregular intervals until the autumn of 1333 when they began to be held every three or four weeks. Rolls covering some five years and nine months are missing from this period of nearly 24 years, the largest gap being of just over two years.[13] Coverage of the year of the Black Death appears to be complete, and this study ends at the first post-plague break in the series, after 11 June 1352. The quality of the rolls is very good and they show many signs of the business efficiency commonly associated with Audley's successors, the Stafford family of 'grinding landlords'.[14] For example, Audley's men collected heriots from villeins who were not direct tenants and sometimes tried to take them from freemen who did not owe them, followed up numerous reports of illegal subletting, and extracted merchet on an unusually wide basis.[15] Their determination to pursue and exploit seigneurial rights is the best guarantee of the quality of these records and was the chief motive for their preservation in later centuries. Nor have manorial court rolls survived alone, for the Stafford Family Collections also contain records from this period of the courts of

---

[11] The other shares went to Hugh Despenser and Roger Damory, the husbands of Margaret's two full sisters. Neither of these men survived the troubles of Edward II's reign.

[12] V. Gibbs *et al.* (eds.), *The Complete Peerage of England* (12 vols., in 13; London, 1910–59), i. 346–7; J. Wedgwood, 'The Inquests on the Staffordshire Estates of the Audleys, 1273, 1276, 1283, 1299, 1308' (Staffs. Rec. Soc. NS 11, 1908), 233–70; J. R. Maddicott, *Thomas of Lancaster, 1307–22: A Study in the Reign of Edward II* (Oxford, 1970), 192–5; K. B. McFarlane, *The Nobility of Later Medieval England* (Oxford, 1973), 201–3.

[13] StRO D641/1/4C/1(i) 1328–33, /1(ii) 1333–6, /1(iii) 1337–9, /2 1341–52. All sessions have been dated by day, month and year *anno domini*. To avoid superfluous footnotes, references are not repeated below for individual sessions. Leets were held only once per year, in the spring.

[14] McFarlane, *Nobility*, 223–7; C. Rawcliffe, *The Staffords, Earls of Stafford and Dukes of Buckingham, 1394–1521* (Cambridge, 1978), esp. 59–61; C. Ross, *Richard III* (London, 1981), 116.

[15] It is difficult to provide adequate references for these activities in a footnote, but a full account will be given in the long-term study of Thornbury which I hope to publish shortly.

Thornbury Borough and the Honour of Gloucester (which also sat at Thornbury) and a valuable series of manorial account rolls.[16] Two surveys ordered by Audley are lost, but extents of the manor survive in *inquisitiones post mortem* and in the so-called 'Contrariants' Survey' of 1322.[17] These other sources help to put the court rolls' evidence into context and reveal some of its problems and shortcomings.

The course of the local movement appears to be particularly well-documented in the court rolls. To take a well-known form of protest as an example, there were 759 cases of labour services not done or badly done in this short period, compared with 256 in 29 years on the abbot of Ramsey's manor of Broughton, Huntingdonshire, and 271 in nearly 50 years on the same abbot's neighbouring manor of Holywell-cum-Needingworth.[18] These are the largest samples found in published works— R. Faith's valuable account of a movement on the abbot of St Albans' manor of Park, near St Albans town, appears to be based upon very limited numbers of cases.[19] The greater volume of evidence from Thornbury can also be put to fuller use, because deaths recorded in the court rolls can be used to provide individual identification. This makes it possible to produce firm statements about real people's involvement in local politics and not just about masses of names.[20] No fewer than 372 people can be identified in this way, and the records of villein tenants' deaths are particularly valuable because the sizes of the tenements they held directly of the lord of the manor were recorded. This enabled them to be assigned to the different economic groups within the peasantry. Many deaths of villeins who owned land but did *not* hold land directly of the lord were also noted, but this did not extend coverage to the whole population as many deaths of women and under-age villeins of both sexes still went unrecorded. Free peasants' deaths were heavily under-recorded, but every

[16] Eighty borough court rolls (StRO D641/1/4E/1, /2, and D641/1/4C/1(i) where four sessions are bound in with the earliest manorial court rolls), 114 honour of Gloucester court of fees rolls (StRO D641/1/4F/3, /4) and 16 manorial account rolls (StRO D641/1/2/116–17, /119–32) survive from before 1352.

[17] *Abstract of Inquisitiones post mortem for Gloucestershire, 1236–1358*, ed. S. J. Madge and E. A. Fry (pts. iv–v, British Rec. Soc. 30, 40 1903–10), iv, 182, v, 85–8. The two unprinted extents of 1307 and 1322 are deposited in PRO C134/42 and C135/87.

[18] Britton, *Community of the Vill*, 170 table 51 (1288–1340), 275–7; Dewindt, *Land and People*, 269 table v, 164–5.

[19] Faith, 'Class Struggle', 52.

[20] Razi, 'The Toronto School's Reconstitution', 141–57. But the short period under study and high plague casualties of 1348/9 make family reconstitution impracticable, see E. A. Wrigley, 'Family Reconstitution', in E. A. Wrigley (ed.), *An Introduction to English Historical Demography* (London, 1966), 102.

source agrees that they formed only a small part of the population. It is on the basis of this large body of information, much of it relating to identified people who can be firmly placed within economic groups, that I will attempt to offer a more comprehensive analysis of a local peasant movement than has been available before.

The Clares and their immediate successors held the whole of the old parish of Thornbury, which covered about 10,670 acres.[21] Only about 6,000 acres of this had been reclaimed for agriculture by the early fourteenth century. Earl Gilbert Clare IV had created two deer parks, *c*.1281, which fieldwork suggests covered more than 1200 acres,[22] but most of the unrecorded land comprised the great Oldbury Marsh which was flooded from the Severn to power tidal corn mills and was probably the breeding ground for mosquitoes which spread malaria in dry seasons.[23] There are many signs of a relatively low long-term population and at this time there were probably not many more than 600 adults in the manor, with another 500 or more in the borough.[24] There is no evidence from this estate to support Sir Michael Postan's influential thesis of a grand 'neo-Malthusian', or 'neo-Ricardian', crisis in the period before the Black Death.[25] For example, the evidence of heriots, which Postan used to such telling effect,[26] reveals that many Thornbury peasants of different economic groups enjoyed a relative prosperity at that time. The estate's economy was heavily geared towards the production of corn, which was shipped down the Severn. Fishing and the processing of corn and rural products were part-time occupations for some peasants. Some processing was also undertaken

[21] S. Rudder, *A New History of Gloucestershire* (Cirencester, 1779), 749. *Victoria County History of Gloucestershire*, ed. W. Page *et al.* (in progress, 1907–present), ii. 185. The old parish was divided in 1864 to form the present parishes of Oldbury-on-Severn, Thornbury and Falfield.

[22] P. Franklin, 'Thornbury Woodlands and Deer Parks, I. The Earls of Gloucester's Deer Parks', *Trans. Bristol and Gloucs. Arch. Soc.*, 107 (1989), 149–63; References to Eastwood Park in 1199 and 1200 in A. H. Smith, *The Place-Names of Gloucestershire. Part III. The Lower Severn Valley, The Forest of Dean* (EPNS 60, Cambridge, 1964), 6, are inaccurate.

[23] P. Franklin, 'Malaria in Medieval Gloucestershire: An Essay in Epidemiology', *Trans. of the Bristol and Glouc. Arch. Soc.*, 101 (1983), 111–22; Rudder, *New History*, 749–50, 755.

[24] Franklin, 'Malaria', 120; Hilton, 'Lords, Burgesses and Hucksters', 13.

[25] M. M. Postan, 'Medieval Agrarian Society in its Prime: England', in M. M. Postan (ed.), *The Cambridge Economic History of Europe, I. The Agrarian Life of the Middle Ages* (2nd edn., Cambridge, 1966), 548–632, *The Medieval Economy and Society: An Economic History of Britain in the Middle Ages* (London, 1972), and with J. Hatcher, 'Population and Class Relations in Feudal Society', in T. H. Aston and C. H. E. Philpin (eds.), *The Brenner Debate: Agrarian Class Structure and Economic Development in Pre-Industrial Europe* (Cambridge, 1985), 64–78.

[26] M. M. Postan and J. Z. Titow, 'Heriots and Prices on Winchester Manors', *EcHR* 2nd ser. II (1959), 392–417.

in the borough, which had had a valuable market since at least 1086. The familiar tripartite division of the peasantry into rich, middle, and poor groups based upon holding sizes can be applied to this rural society in a very straightforward way. I have followed Sir Michael Postan in interpreting tenants of more than a quarter virgate but less than a full virgate as middle peasants who took little part in market production and worked their holding mainly or entirely with family labour. Those who held full virgates, which in Thornbury contained about 38 acres, are seen as rich peasants with holdings so large that their families could not usually have worked them unaided, nor have directly consumed so much produce. They are seen as regular market producers and employers of wage labour. Poor peasants with a quarter virgate or less are seen as having too little land to support their families in classical peasant fashion, and as having to perform agricultural work for wages or craftwork in order to survive.[27] The heriots collected from all three groups suggest that they enjoyed a considerable relative prosperity in the 20 years before the plague. No fewer than 17 per cent of poor, 88 per cent of middle, and 96 per cent of rich Thornbury peasants had livestock when they died. All were better equipped with animals than people on any other estate for which such evidence has been published. The reasons for this are obscure and cannot be properly explored here. Little of the evidence from other estates has been broken down by economic groups, and it is not yet possible to analyse the parts played by, for example, the growth of the poor group and differences in retirement customs.

The manorial court rolls themselves provide the best evidence for a reconstruction of landholding on the estate.[28] Local landholding was complicated by the existence of three distinct villein tenures called customary land ('terra operabilis' or 'werklond'), gavel land ('terra gabulis' or 'gavellond'), and forland ('forlond'). The tenants of customary land owed most of their rent in the form of labour services which were due at all times of the year and which were heavy—about 25*s.* per year from each virgate and 14*s.* from each half virgate—though not unusually so for this

---

[27] Postan, 'Medieval Agrarian Society', 617–28. It should be noted that some scholars include virgaters to produce a much larger 'middling range of tenantry' than this definition allows for: Kosminsky, *Studies*, 198, 222; E. Miller and J. Hatcher, *Medieval England—Rural Society and Economic Change, 1086–1348* (London, 1978), 144–5.

[28] No extent provides a survey which is both comprehensive and sufficiently detailed. An unpublished reconstruction based upon the 1322 Extent fails to allow for the way in which many holdings were divided at that date. S. L. Waugh, 'The Confiscated Lands of the "Contrariants" in Gloucestershire and Herefordshire in 1322: An Economic and Social Study', Ph.D. Thesis (University of London, 1975), 222–3.

part of the country. Local conditions did, however, vary a great deal. The bishop of Worcester's tenants at Henbury, 10 miles to the south, owed heavy services, but villein holdings at Ham, just north of Thornbury, were being turned into free ones by a Berkeley lord who saw his interest in increased money rents, and all labour services at Tockington, just south of Thornbury, were being commuted by that manor's gentry lord.[29] A very few references to customary land as 'the new tenure' identify its burdens as impositions made to provide free labour for the demesne in the 'high farming' era. The money rents it owed varied widely, some virgaters and half-virgaters owing about 10s. per year while several paid nothing at all.[30] Tenants of gavel land, the most important Thornbury villein tenure, did only a few services at corn harvest and wheat-sowing and owed most of their rent in the form of money. The actual sums were never set out in detail, but an extent shows that gavel land commonly paid about 6d. money rent per acre per year, which would be 19s. from each virgate.[31] Forland was made up of parcels of reclaimed marsh. It resembled gavel land so strongly that scribes sometimes confused the two, but it is not clear whether it owed labour services.[32] Many villeins, not just the rich, had put together multiple holdings and some held land by all three villein tenures. Several had parcels of demesne land, much of which had been leased out since 1328,[33] but few had any free land. Villein landholding thus had many complications, and the compositions of holdings and their rents in money and labour services varied greatly within each of the three economic groups.

The court rolls from the plague year can be used to produce a list of 100 villein tenants, all identified by records of death, with the amount of land which each held on the eve of the plague. This survey of direct landholding reveals that 35 per cent were rich peasants, 33 per cent middle peasants and 32 per cent poor peasants. The overall result closely matches E. A. Kosminsky's for villein landholding on large estates in the 1279 Hundred Rolls;[34] but there was also a very wide local range of

---

[29] Henbury virgaters owed corvee worth between 20s. 0½d. and 23s. 3½d. per year and half-virgaters between 7s. and 11s. 7¾d.: Dyer, *Lords and Peasants*, 101 table 9. For Ham, see B. R. Harvey, 'The Berkeleys of Berkeley 1281–1417: A Study in the Lesser Peerage of Late Medieval England', Ph.D. Thesis (University of St Andrews, 1988), 86–137. Half-virgaters at Tockington, held by the Pointz family, owed services worth 10s. 8½d. per year, which were commuted at some date between 1308 and 1345: *IPMs for Gloucestershire*, v. 98–100, 123–4, 308–9.

[30] PRO Ancient Extents E142/24 (1322 Extent).   [31] Ibid.

[32] e.g. Court Rolls, 23 May 1350, 7 Dec. 1350 (Mildemay holding).

[33] The largest grants were made in Dec. 1334: StRO D641/1/2/123.

[34] Kosminsky, *Studies*, 223 table 11.

holding sizes, from less than one acre to about 80 and 100 acres. The wide range was also characteristic of local free landholding, but the basic structure of this land became very different. Thornbury's lords were anxious to preserve villein middle holdings, but free middle holdings were open to the economic pressures of the process of differentiation and most had been engrossed by the rich or broken up as their tenants fell into poverty. The development of substantial numbers of very large holdings suggests that the social cohesion of the community was coming under some strain. The peasant community of Halesowen, an estate of similar size and population density, depended upon mutual co-operation both within the family and between neighbours. Inheritance was by male primogeniture, but the local practice of constantly redistributing land among non-inheriting siblings put a check on the process of differentiation and prevented the growth of very large holdings and a large poor group. The Halesowen rich also exercised self-restraint in their behaviour in order to win the good will and co-operation of other peasants because they still needed to be part of a strong community.[35] Life in Thornbury was very different. Thornbury peasants had taken to primogeniture with a vengeance, and it was unusual for any non-inheriting child to receive family land.[36] The holdings of both free and villein rich peasants were expanding, largely through the engrossing of other people's family holdings, and very little land was redistributed. The social effects of this were of great importance. The richest freemen began to form their own sub-manors, when land market conditions were propitious, and to push towards lesser gentry status. The local market in small parcels of land had a chequered history in which times of relative freedom alternated with periods of considerable restriction. Its complicated workings involved all the peasant groups and some non-peasants, but its main overall effect was to enable rich free peasants to transfer small parcels to the poor, some of whom could not get direct tenancies as the engrossment of holdings proceeded. Some of the poor were installed as tenants in the sub-manors where they would presumably act as their landlords' wage labourers. This development had not taken place on the scale noted at Havering, Essex,[37] but the holding of exclusive subtenancies which are not accounted for in the earlier survey of direct landholding probably did make poor peasants the

[35] Razi, 'Family, Land and the Village Community', *passim*.
[36] A few cases which show the remains of earlier practices of partible inheritance and ultimogeniture will be explored in my Thornbury book.
[37] M. K. McIntosh, 'Land, Tenure and Population in the Royal Manor of Havering, Essex, 1251–1352/3', *EcHR* 2nd ser. 33 (1980), 17–31.

most numerous economic group. Unfree status prevented most villeins from following this path of development, and they had to make do with the community influence, manorial offices and seats on manor-court juries which are well known from other estates. Although there is the usual lack of direct evidence for disputes between employers and workers, there is little doubt that the employment of wage labour—the basic feature of primitive rural capitalism[38]—was widespread and was increasing as the rich tenements continued to expand. Thus the local rich were taking over more land, and becoming the landlords and employers of some of their poorer neighbours. How much 'self-restraint' they showed towards other peasants cannot be properly discussed here, but the widening economic divisions in Thornbury would seem to have posed a grave threat to the social cohesion of a community which sorely needed to maintain a united front.

The first half of the fourteenth century was a period of aggressive lordship on this estate, with the Clares and their successors trying to increase feudal rent and draw more of their tenants into villeinage. Detailed extents show how they had imposed extra burdens on customary land in the years before 1328.[39] Earl Gilbert Clare V, lord of the manor from 1307 to 1314, imposed new services on customary virgaters and half-virgaters. Virgaters' services were lightened by 1322 but then increased again, with the result that they owed about the same value of services in 1328 as in 1307. Half-virgaters' burdens were, however, increased by more than one-eighth during that 21-year period and they got no remission.[40] It is not clear whether the obligations of other tenures were also increased. R. H. Hilton has publicized the case of a Worcestershire man who drowned himself in the Severn in 1293 rather than take up villein land of the earl of Gloucester and run the risk of becoming the earl's villein.[41] Some Thornbury free families were in danger of losing their status as the lord's men tried to raise heriots—which they saw as a clear mark of villeinage—after their members' deaths, and the few

[38] V. I. Lenin, *The Development of Capitalism in Russia* (2nd edn., Moscow, 1964), 71–191.

[39] *IPMs for Gloucestershire*, v, 85–8; PRO C134/42; PRO Ancient Extents E142/24. Note that 40 Harvest works worth 1½d. each were omitted from the 1322 record of customary virgaters' obligations by mistake, for their value is included there.

[40] Customary virgaters' services were valued at 24s. 11½d. in 1307, 27s. 7½d. in 1314, 24s. 7d. in 1322, and c.25s. in the 1327/8 account roll. Account roll totals vary a little from year to year because works due on feast days were remitted. Customary half-virgaters' services were increased from 12s. 5¾d. in 1307 to 13s. 9¾d. in 1314, 14s. 1¾d. in 1322, and 14s. 2d. in the 1327/8 account roll. PRO C134/42, E142/24; StRO D641/1/2/116.

[41] Hilton, 'Peasant Movements', 135.

immigrants who settled in the manor ran the risk of being treated as villeins.[42]

The stage was set for a fierce struggle between lords and peasants, but the times at which the campaign reached its peaks were those at which national opposition to the government was at its height. This is of interest because economic distress did not, at first, play a significant part in Thornbury. Local people's relative prosperity gave them protection against government demands, and signs of the distress which taxation and purveyance are said to have caused in the early 1330s are not easy to find. In later years the situation was different for there was real distress, though its extent is difficult to assess. Significant numbers of ruinous holdings were first reported after the onset of heavy taxation in 1336 and were followed by unusual signs of hardship such as the theft of food.[43] Family holdings began to be given up for want, including one held by a known moneylender whose problems may indicate a wide circle of distress.[44] Some peasants had evidently been drawn to sell livestock and other possessions as the political song 'Against the King's Taxes'—which is believed to date from this period—complained.[45] The best possessions which two middle peasants had left for heriot were an axe and 2*s*. cash; two poor peasants' were a worn-out pan and a hood worth 1*d*. each.[46] Nor were the middle and poor groups the only ones affected, for the widespread collapse in corn prices caused by government monetary policy led to the breaking of rich peasants' contracts with Bristol corn merchants.[47] Low corn prices may have brought relief to the poor, but middle peasants must have had to sell more produce and may have gone hungry.

The court rolls have little obvious evidence of opposition to government policy,[48] but recent links between Thornbury's lords and the crown

---

[42] It was the opinion of the court that no free tenant owed heriot, court roll 9 Aug. 1336. The loss of free status is hard to prove, but the surnames Hathewy and Monseye were used only by free tenants in pre-1328 extents and only by villeins and alleged villeins in the surviving court rolls. The immigrants Adam Baldok and John Shog were never called villeins, but heriot was raised after their deaths, court rolls 24 Nov. 1348, 5 Jan. 1349.

[43] Court Rolls, 2 Sept. 1338, 16 Sept. 1339.

[44] Walter in the Field surrendered half a virgate, 6 Nov. 1337, and died holding his remaining half virgate, 2 Apr. 1338.

[45] *Anglo-Norman Political Songs*, ed. I. S. T. Aspin (Oxford, 1953), 109.

[46] Court Rolls, 2 Sept. 1338, 16 Sept. 1339.

[47] StRO D641/1/2/125 reveals that demesne corn prices fell by 25–50 per cent in 1338/9 reaching levels almost as low as those reported in Knighton, *Chronicon*, ii. 8.

[48] A known supporter of the movement objected to the lay subsidy when the heaviest period of taxation began, court roll 28 May 1336 (Fortheye). The men of one tithing quarrelled for four months over the expense of supplying a horse for the war effort, court rolls 6 Nov. 1337, 27 Nov. 1337, 18 Dec. 1337, 8 Jan. 1338, 29 Jan. 1338, 19 Feb. 1338, 12

were so close that the peasants may not have made a clear distinction between opposing the lord and opposing the government. Joan of Acre had been lady of the manor until her death in 1307. The last Clare lord was Edward I's grandson. Audley had probably risen to favour through a homosexual relationship with Edward II, and his wife was Edward III's first cousin. The bailiff who was in overall charge of the estate in the late 1330s had sat in some of the parliaments which granted the lay subsidies of this period.[49] These records may thus relate more directly to national discontent than would at first appear.

This rather lengthy introduction has been necessary in order to show the distinctive features of Thornbury's development. Some aspects of this may appear unusual, but I would contend that they will seem much less so when medievalists take a more critical approach to the Postan thesis. Rural society in this part of Gloucestershire had much in common with that in other parts of lowland England, and the peasants' struggle had many features known from other pre-1381 movements, including the refusal to do labour services.[50] Students of modern peasantries have seen a dichotomy in peasant political order between rebellion, which is rare, highly organized and open, and passive resistance, which is very common and involves many acts carried out in secret.[51] The refusal to do labour services is of particular interest because it was an intermediate kind of protest. It was common enough to be recognized as part of the ubiquitous language of peasant protest under feudal conditions.[52] It involved a considerable degree of organization and was a form of open defiance which challenged the lord's rights, but stopped far short of rebellion.

Mar. 1338. Two collectors of the wool tax imposed 24 July 1338 appeared before the manor court in an attempt to track down a recalcitrant payer, Knighton, *Chronicon*, ii. 4. court roll 12 Nov. 1338.

[49] This man, William Tytherington, came from the neighbouring parish of Tytherington, and much of his career can be reconstructed from N. Saul, *Knights and Esquires: The Gloucestershire Gentry in the Fourteenth Century* (Oxford, 1981), 87, 121, 143. He had been the Sheriff of Gloucester's itinerant bailiff, MP for Gloucester borough in 1330 and for the county in 1332 and 1336, and coroner. After serving Audley, he became steward of the Llanthony Priory estates. Saul does not mention his appointment to a commission of oyer and terminer with the Earl of Devon to try Devonshire men charged with taking away beasts impounded by Audley's officers in 1341: *Cal. Pat. Rolls 1340–3*, 365, 439–40. Was this part of another peasant movement?

[50] Levett, *Studies in Manorial History*, 203; Hilton, 'Peasant Movements', 127; Faith, 'The "Great Rumour" of 1377', 66–7.

[51] J. C. Scott, 'Everyday Forms of Peasant Resistance', *Journal of Peasant Studies*, 13 (1985–6), 5–35; J. C. Scott, *Weapons of the Weak. Everyday Forms of Peasant Resistance* (New Haven and London, 1985).

[52] Hilton, *Bond Men*, 88; he notes that their origins can be traced back to the Early Middle Ages, ibid. 65.

The first significant gap in the Thornbury court rolls series extends from 7 August 1330 to 1 October 1331, and it is clear from the latter roll that there had been a major change in the life of the estate, for the first refusals to do labour services now appeared and so many tenants were involved that it is possible to speak of a 'mass movement'. Audley's economy was heavily dependent upon the nine different kinds of services, totalling more than 12,000 individual one-day and half-day works, with which the tenants of his villein land were burdened. These provided much of the labour for his demesne and nearly all that needed to repair the pales of his deer parks, while the sale of commuted services itself produced a substantial income. The refusal to do services was both an immediate challenge to his right to extract unpaid labour and a means of disrupting his economy.

It is convenient to refer to this kind of action as a labour service 'strike'. R. Faith has questioned the term,[53] and care is certainly needed when borrowing terms from the world of capitalist industry, but it is a useful shorthand. The Thornbury records make it clear that peasants did not usually 'down tools' and leave work, but that their offence lay in not coming to work after they had been summoned. More than 70 per cent of cases explicitly record that offenders 'did not come' to do a particular task or to perform unspecified services.[54] The word 'strike' also suggests the collective action which R. H. Hilton rightly stressed as an important part of this form of protest.[55] Those who had committed the same offence paid separate amercements, but their names were often grouped together in the rolls. It is probably safe to accept that these were groups who had acted together to refuse particular services on particular days rather than just lists of names made for scribal convenience.[56] In one roll, for example, 62 villeins who had not come to reaping were amerced in batches of 15, 13, 10, 9, 8, 6, and 1, which probably represent the groups who refused to work on particular days.[57] The numbers doing services each day must have varied greatly according to the season, weather, and state

[53] Faith, 'The "Great Rumour" of 1377', 52.

[54] That is, 513 out of 719 cases. The same phrase was used in Ramsey Abbey court rolls: Dewindt, *Land and People*, 270 n. 102.

[55] Hilton, 'Peasant Movements', 127.

[56] In only six cases do names appear twice within one group. Three of these probably reflect the use of the same name by different people and one may be a scribal error, for an attempt has been made to alter the roll. The other two cases occur in the list of 127 offenders in the 11 Oct. 1347 court roll. That entry is worded in an unusual way and may not concern a single group acting together on one day.

[57] Court Roll, 8 Sept. 1332.

of agricultural operations. The manorial account rolls never went into these minutiae of detail, but a list of tenants who were actually doing services on a particular day has survived from 9 December 1335. Many suitors were absent from that day's manor court, and seven of them were forgiven because they were doing corvée. Group action appears to have played a most important part in labour-service refusals at Thornbury, for more than 90 per cent of the offences were committed by members of groups which ranged in size from two people to 127. Groups of less than 20 were by far the most common.[58] Besides reflecting the small numbers summoned to work on particular days, this tendency to act in small groups may also reflect the dispersed pattern of settlement in this part of England where most people lived in hamlets rather than in villages. Groups which appeared in the court rolls in other contexts were usually small in size.

But in dealing with any aspect of labour service refusals it must be noted that the ordinary amercements imposed need not necessarily refer to single one-day or half-day works. It would seem unrealistic to have punished refusals of many services by the standard amercements of 3*d*. each. Some longer refusals were noted and heavier penalties imposed, but this was not done in a regular fashion. Thus one rich peasant was amerced 3*s*. when he would not come to unspecified services on three days, but only 3*d*. for not coming to plough on a further five days.[59] But it does seem that short strikes were involved rather than the complete suspension of services.

It has never been established whether labour services done badly were a form of protest, as R. H. Hilton suggested in 1949, or were inherent within the corvée system, as R. Faith believes.[60] The timing of such cases at Thornbury suggests that they were a form of protest, for they were not scattered throughout the rolls. Most occurred during the 'mass movement' of the early 1330s and the greatest number were reported at the same court as the largest number of refusals at that time (see Table 6.1).[61] Some cases show clear protest action, such as those in which substantial tenants withdrew their servants from works 'before the ninth hour' or would not let them stay long enough to eat lunch.[62] These are the clearest

[58] Little comparative evidence is available because labour service refusals are usually given in annual totals, but see Hilton, 'Peasant Movements', 127.

[59] Court Roll, 9 Feb. 1333 (Wilkins).

[60] Hilton, 'Peasant Movements', 127; Faith, 'The "Great Rumour" of 1377', 67.

[61] Court Roll, 8 Sept. 1332. It records 64 services not done and 13 done badly.

[62] Ibid. Cf. the Houghton, Ramsey Abbey, tenants who 'went away' from uncompleted services after 'dinner', Hilton, 'Peasant Movements', 127.

TABLE 6.1. *Labour service-offences at Thornbury, 1328–52*

Year	Cases of services not done	Cases of services done badly	Total offences	Mean offences	
				per court	per month
1328/9	0	0	0	0	0
1329/30*	0	0	0	0	0
1330/1	—	—	—	—	—
1331/2	191	15	206	29.4	17.2
1332/3*	93	13	106	35.3	14.7
1333/4*	†50	†12	†62	†5.6	†5.6
1334/5	†50	†0	†50	†3.1	†4.2
1335/6	7	0	7	0.6	0.6
1336/7	—	—	—	—	—
1337/8	24	0	24	1.4	0.5
1338/9	48	0	48	3.4	4.0
1339/40	—	—	—	—	—
1341/2	7	0	7	0.6	0.6
1342/3	—	—	—	—	—
1343/4	50	0	50	4.2	4.2
1344/5	0	0	0	0	0
1345/6	7	0	7	0.5	0.6
1346/7	1	0	1	0.1	0.1
1347/8	†137	0	†137	†12.5	†11.4
1348/9	17	0	17	1.4	1.4
1349/50	20	0	20	2.2	1.7
1350/1	15	0	15	1.1	1.3
1351/2	2	0	2	0.2	0.2
TOTALS	†719	†40	†759	†3.5	†3.5

Notes: — = All court rolls lost   * = Court rolls' series incomplete
† = Numbers of offences incomplete as not all names given

local examples of striking by walking off a job. In several other cases, peasants were said to have worked 'badly and falsely'.[63] The composition of those amerced for bad work supports this interpretation, for no fewer than 14 of the 18 identified men who did (or whose servants did) tasks badly refused to do services at some time. Nearly 40 per cent of all cases of bad work only involved single peasants, so they seem to have been a more individual form of protest, intermediate between well-organized labour service refusals and loosely organized or uncoordinated forms of passive resistance. These characteristics would support this interpretation. Some instances of bad work might have gone undetected and so have satisfied the desire to protest while saving the cost of an amercement. But others, such as coming to work without tools,[64] were clearly detectable. Most cases did still involve group action, though no group comprised more than eight people.

Arguments that labour-service offences were without political significance are hard to accept in the face of the evidence for 759 recorded during this period at Thornbury[65]—a total which is incomplete because peasant officials sometimes refused to summon tenants to work or to say who had been summoned. The reader should not be misled by the fact that 'refusal' to do services is actually mentioned at only a few court sessions.[66] Their connections with other events of political significance and the evidence of organization show that much more was involved than 'the disposition or inclination of the individual to work'[67] or any form of *de facto* commutation undertaken on peasant initiative,[68] and only a few reflect tenants' difficulties in performing services. The case of a widow tenant who could only send a 'feeble servant' to ploughing and who later remarried suggests that such problems were unusual, for the phrasing of the court roll entry was unusual and, in practice, very few offences can be linked with tenants' difficulties.[69] There were few signs of economic distress when offences were at their peak in the early 1330s, but significant numbers of them when offences were much less common at the end of that decade. I hope that enough has been said in another paper to put an end to the myth of weak and incapable women tenants who could not

---

[63] Court Rolls, 9 Feb. 1333 (5 times), 18 May 1333.

[64] Court Rolls, 8 Sept. 1332, 18 May 1333.

[65] The figure of 759 excludes a few similarly-worded offences committed by people who were probably demesne *famuli*.

[66] Court Rolls, 9 July 1334, 10 Sept. 1334 (three cases), 18 Feb. 1342 (two cases), 19 Aug. 1344 (fifty cases), 9 Jan. 1346, 20 Feb. 1346 (three cases), 25 Apr. 1346.

[67] Dewindt, *Land and People*, 89.   [68] Britton, *Community of the Vill*, 170.

[69] Franklin, 'Peasant Widows', 194.

TABLE 6.2. *Group involvement in labour-service offences at Thornbury, 1328–52*

Group sizes	Services not done				Services done badly			
	Numbers of groups		Cases in each group size		Numbers of groups		Cases in each group size	
	n	%	n	%	n	%	n	%
1	70	52.6	70	9.7	15	75.0	15	37.5
2–4	26	19.5	75	10.4	1	5.0	2	5.0
5–9	20	15.0	136	18.9	4	20.0	23	57.5
10–19	10	7.5	132	18.4	—	—	—	—
20–49	5	3.8	129	17.9	—	—	—	—
50+	2	1.5	177	24.6	—	—	—	—
TOTALS	133	100	719	100	20	100	40	100

fulfil obligations, so that their involvement in this form of protest can be seen in its true light.[70] Opposition to *corvée* was obviously a form of political action, but it did not take the form here of an all-out strike. The complete suspension of services which is known from some estates was an escalation in the direction of open rebellion, and one which might bring strong reprisals from the lord. Only a couple of ruined tenants are known to have completely stopped their services at Thornbury. The 759 labour-service offences must be seen in the context of the more than 12,000 services local tenants owed each year. Though many of these were not required to be performed, and though each amercement may represent more than one service not done or done badly, the maximum number of 206 offences in a single year can only represent a tiny proportion of the services which were demanded. Labour-service offences here never approached an all-out strike, but should rather be seen as a kind of economic guerilla warfare.

These offences were the movement's major weapons in the early 1330s, but when protest activity revived again at the end of that decade it took a very different form. The list of charges brought against the lord's bailiff, who was in overall charge of the estate, in 1339 is perhaps the only form of local political protest which is instantly recognizable as such. This is another practice known from other estates, and it invites comparison with the Bocking Hall petition by which the tenants of one of Christ Church, Canterbury's Essex manors had presented their grievances to their lord not many years earlier.[71] If a written petition had been sent to Audley it has not survived, but he was said to have been given news while in Wales of seven charges against his bailiff which were referred to as 'articles'. Communications of this kind may have been encouraged by lords anxious to keep an eye on what their officers did on far-flung estates. The Bocking Hall petition with its complaints about a steward's misdeeds seems to have been well received in Canterbury, though it is not possible to say how far the peasants' grievances were redressed.[72] K. B. McFarlane drew attention to the Stafford family's practice of encouraging tenants to report officers' misdeeds in the later fourteenth century,[73]

---

[70] Ibid. *passim.*

[71] J. F. Nichols, 'An Early Fourteenth Century Petition from the Tenants of Bocking to their Manorial Lord', *EcHR* 1st ser. 2 (1929–30), 300–7: this probably dates from the first quarter of the 14th cent. and is not later than 1331. For a much later attempt to remove an unpopular seigneurial officer in Gloucestershire by similar means, see D. Rollison, 'Property, Ideology and Popular Culture in a Gloucestershire Village 1660–1740', *P&P* 93 (1981), 70–97.

[72] Nichols, 'Petition', 302, 305–7.   [73] McFarlane, *Nobility*, 220.

and this may be one of a number of their practices which was inherited along with Audley's estates. Audley's men used Thornbury manor court juries to check the accuracy of items in the account rolls,[74] and six peasants were later appointed as manorial surveyors to oversee important aspects of the estate's working and report directly to the chief steward, over the bailiff's head.[75]

Audley's response to the complaints was to send his chief steward, who convened a special session of the manor court 18 September 1339, two days after its regular sitting. The roll of this court provides the only surviving record of the charges. Seven articles are listed at the head of the roll, and then a jury was empanelled which presented a further eight, making fifteen in all. There is no close parallel to the contents of the Bocking Hall petition. The Essex peasants objected mainly to novel ways the steward had found for extracting money from them in the manor court and appealed to common law, statute law, the custom of the manor, and Magna Carta.[76] The Thornbury articles make no such appeals, but concentrate on a list of thefts and frauds which had damaged the lord's interests. Of the fifteen articles, six allege that the bailiff had stolen Audley's wool, timber, and oats; one claims that he had used corvée to work his own land; three or four claim that he was responsible for Audley's horses being severely overworked, and one blames the burning down of the cowshed on a man he had appointed. The articles were framed to appeal directly to Audley's self interest and contain no reference to what I will later argue was the movement's major aim. Eleven or twelve articles claimed that the bailiff's actions had caused the lord loss and only three claimed that the peasants had been oppressed. Except for the claims that a named peasant had been cheated of money, the charges of oppression were placed at the end of the two lists (that is, as articles seven and fifteen) as though they were matters of only secondary consequence. Though the bailiff was the person called to account, the articles—and especially the later ones in each list—build up a picture of his wife, sons, and servants also helping themselves to the lord's property while the manor suffered through the negligence and dishonesty of those who worked under him.

[74] StRO D641/1/2/123. /124 (account rolls 1334/5, 1336/7).

[75] Court Roll, 30 Sept. 1344. Most of the surveyors previously noted on late medieval estates were officers responsible for groups of manors, but C. Howell found peasant surveyors at Kibworth Harcourt, Leicestershire. *Ministers' Accounts of the Warwickshire Estates of the Duke of Clarence 1479–80*, R. H. Hilton (Dugdale Soc. 21, 1952), xxiv; Dyer, *Lords and Peasants*, 155, 385; Howell, *Land, Family and Inheritance*, 31, 55.

[76] Nichols, 'Petition', 300–1.

The labour service offences and the fifteen articles were the forms of protest which made the greatest mark on the records, which appear to have been the most important and which are readily recognizable as forms of political protest. They took place against a background of other activities which were prejudicial to the lord's authority and economy but which cannot be linked to the organized movement. Both English and European popular movements challenged lords' rights to restrict access to natural resources.[77] Local people attacked Sir Maurice Berkeley's new park at Stoke Gifford, six miles south of Thornbury, in Richard II's reign, and the duke of Buckingham's seizure of land to make a new park in Thornbury in the sixteenth century is known to have caused much ill feeling.[78] There were recurrent problems with the largest Thornbury park before the Black Death, but the small numbers of people known to have been involved and the general timing of incidents suggests that they were not part of the organized peasant movement. Local poachers were boldest in the late 1320s—before a single strike had taken place—when two groups made up of local burgesses, free and unfree peasants, and the occasional outsider went hunting there in broad daylight.[79] A small and well-organized gang stole timber from the same park, and a group of fifteen people put their beasts into it and claimed common pasture rights. The last group made their claim in the spring of 1339 when the movement was showing signs of revival, but they were defeated at the very court at which some results of the movement's chief success were recorded.[80] Extents of the manor suggest that there was a long-running dispute over pasture in the parks, of which this was only one phase.[81]

Peasants on some estates attacked manor houses and tried to destroy manorial records.[82] The earliest phase of the Thornbury campaign saw two occasions when groups of peasants were amerced for default of suit of court, and it seemed at first that these might have been organized boycotts which challenged the lord's rights to private jurisdiction just as the strikes challenged his right to free labour. But later cases, and comparison with an incident at Bocking Hall, suggest that they are more probably the results of an oppressive measure which will be described below. It may be that some of the individual defaults and some of the

---

[77] Hilton, *Bond Men*, 70–2, 110–11; Faith, 'The "Great Rumour" of 1377', 63, 65, 67; Faith, 'Class Struggle', 53; J. A. Raftis noted many woodland offences at Warboys, *Warboys*, 217.
[78] *Berkeley Manuscripts*, i. 259; *Itinerary of John Leland*, v. 100–1.
[79] Court Roll, 27 Jan. 1329.
[80] Court Roll, 7 Oct. 1343; Franklin, 'Thornbury Woodlands'.   [81] Ibid.
[82] Hilton, 'Peasant Movements', 128; Faith, 'The "Great Rumour" of 1377', 67.

increasing numbers of withdrawals of suit contained an element of boy-
cott, but this cannot be proved. There are a few indications of attempts
to disrupt the court by brawling and talking while it sat, and (once) by
tearing up a list of offenders.[83] Such individual actions may well have
included a significant political content, but it is hard to link them to an
organized movement. It is partly for this reason, and partly because of the
very large amount of evidence involved, that I have not made an analysis
of all thefts and trespasses. It is worth noting as a comment on changing
forms of rural protest that there is no clear Thornbury evidence for a
money rent strike,[84] and little to suggest the incendiarism or animal-
maiming known from modern protests.[85]

Why did the peasants' tactics change within our period? The answer
lies in the success which the lord had had in frustrating labour service
strikes by attacking the organization of the movement, and in the growth
of opposition to the bailiff's oppressive measures. Struggles over the right
to appoint local officials are known to have been important in many French,
Italian, and western German communities where peasants fought successfully to replace seigneurial nominees with their own men, and much
has been read into the failure of eastern German peasants to displace their
lords' men.[86] Little attention has been given to the role of such struggles
in English peasant movements,[87] but events at Thornbury show that they
could be vital to the organization of peasant protest. The need for these
movements to have good organization, especially in order to collect funds
and have lawyers to plead in the royal courts, has been frequently pointed
out.[88] The Thornbury movement made extensive use in the manorial
organization of peasant officials. The beadle could play an obvious role in
promoting or hindering labour-service offences, and it is clearly recorded
that one beadle did not summon all the tenants to do reaping services

[83] Court Rolls, 8 Aug. 1329, 18 Feb. 1332, 22 Apr. 1342, 10 Oct. 1351.

[84] Dyer, 'Redistribution of Incomes', 11–33; Howell, *Land, Family*, 50; Tillotson, 'Peasant Unrest', 5.

[85] E. Hobsbawm and G. Rude, *Captain Swing* (Harmondsworth, 1973); J. E. Archer, '"A
Fiendish Outrage"? A Study of Animal Maiming in East Anglia: 1830–70', *AgHR* 33
(1985), 147–57.

[86] Hilton, *Bond Men*, 76–8; Brenner, 'Agrarian Class Structure', 40–6.

[87] A few published references suggest that they were not unusual. For a dispute over
choosing a reeve at Halesowen, see Razi, 'Family Land and the Village Community', 15.
For an outsider installed as reeve at Holywell-cum-Needingworth, see Dewindt, *Land and
People*, 224 n. 148 (this man's family can be traced in Britton, *Community of the Vill*, 195–
6, 223).

[88] Hilton, *Bond Men*, 88–9; Hilton, 'Thirteenth-Century Poem', 92; Razi, 'Family Land
and the Village Community', 16; Faith, 'The "Great Rumour" of 1377', 44, 62.

and that another refused to say whom he had or had not summoned to works.[89] The tithingman has remained a neglected figure in recent studies and it has long been accepted that his importance was declining at this time.[90] Hampshire tithingmen, however, played a part in resistance to the abbot of Titchfield and it has been suggested that the 1370s' idea of getting exemplifications from Domesday Book in support of peasant claims may have spread through tithingmen meeting at hundred courts.[91] Thornbury tithingmen evidently played important parts in the local movement, partly because their duties included helping the beadle summon people to labour services.[92]

The importance of such offices to the movement made them contentious. Numbers of beadles and tithingmen not only left office in mid-term but paid money to do so.[93] There is, of course, an old argument that many kinds of medieval official or representative were unwilling to serve in posts which brought them much trouble and little direct reward.[94] W. A. Morris noted the amercements of tithingmen who would not serve and some fifteenth-century payments to be quit of the office,[95] but almost every Thornbury official who left office in mid-term during this period had been involved in the movement while many of their replacements had not. Some ex-officials were actually said to have been removed. To give only one example, John Pleystud was a poor peasant who refused to do labour services on twelve separate occasions.[96] He was also amerced 2s. for 'contempt' to the bailiff. He was chosen to be a tithingman at the court at which his fifth labour service offence was reported and took part

[89] Court Rolls, 30 Jan. 1335, 14 Feb. 1348. Both these beadles took part in labour-service offences themselves, one during his period of office: court rolls 18 Feb. 1332, 8 Sept. 1332, 25 Feb. 1339, 11 Oct. 1347 (Robert Andrew I); Court Roll, 11 Oct. 1347 (twice, Walter Sanford).

[90] W. A. Morris, *The Frankpledge System* (New York, 1910), 103–10; Britton, *Community*, 98–9; Dewindt, *Land and People*, 211 n. 128, 214.

[91] Watts, 'Peasant Discontent', 125, 128; Tillotson, 'Peasant Unrest', 3–4.

[92] Court Roll, 8 Sept. 1332 records that the Oldbury tithingman had failed to summon 'operarios' to reaping. Labour terminology here was as vague as elsewhere, but as Audley employed no wage labourers in fieldwork this must refer to summoning to labour services. This is a vital detail in the operation of the corvée system on so large an estate.

[93] Court Rolls, 4 Nov. 1334 (Gregory), 16 Dec. 1334 (King), 22 Apr. 1335 (Andrew).

[94] N. Denholm-Young, *The Country Gentry in the Fourteenth Century with Special Reference to the Heraldic Rolls of Arms* (Oxford, 1969), 48–52, 60.

[95] Morris, *Frankpledge System*, 110; *Pleas of the Crown for the County of Gloucester before the Justices Itinerant*, ed. F. W. Maitland (London, 1884), 57, cites the case of a Gloucestershire tithingman who claimed he could not do his duties because he had taken the cross, c.1221.

[96] Court Rolls, 1 Oct. 1331, 13 July 1332, 8 Sept. 1332 (twice), 9 Oct. 1333, 6 Nov. 1333, 12 Feb. 1334, 21 May 1334, 29 June 1336, 26 July 1339, 11 Oct. 1347, 10 Aug. 1348.

in more strikes within the following months. He was removed from office after twice breaking the lord's pinfold to retrieve his beasts, but was chosen for the post again three months later.[97]

These struggles raise an important point about the coverage of the court rolls. The disputes over tithingmen's posts seem well recorded, but, as on many other estates, the names of most officials appear in manorial court rolls only rarely and it is the account rolls which provide the fullest lists of office holders.[98] Turning to the most important office, it is known from the court rolls (and from them only) that Audley made an unsuccessful attempt during the mass movement to replace the peasant leader and reeve William Cole II by a man who was in the service of the Berkeley family.[99] The 9 October 1333 roll records Cole's later removal from office, but those of 13 October 1334, 4 November 1334, and 30 January 1335 make no mention of the rapid changes of the following years which ended when Cole came back to office again. The dates of the latter three changes are given in the 1334/5 account roll[100] and they are the dates of courts, but the rolls of those courts contain no references to them.[101] The surviving account rolls show that he served at least eight terms as reeve and one as granger during this period,[102] but only two terms as reeve are known from the court rolls.[103] Nor is this the end of their shortcomings. From the year of the Black Death onwards the court rolls began to record the names of those chosen as reeves and beadles.[104] Whereas each post had formerly been held by only one man at a time, two or three reeves and two or three beadles were now appointed each year. The account rolls, however, single out only one of the court-roll reeves to bear that title and name beadles who were not amongst those chosen in

---

[97] Court Rolls, 9 Apr. 1332 (contempt), 9 Oct. 1333 (chosen tithingman), 29 June 1336 (removed), 20 Sept. 1336 (chosen tithingman again).

[98] e.g. Dewindt, *Land and People*, 224; Britton, *Community of the Vill*, 5.

[99] This man, Robert Wilkins I, was a rich Thornbury villein. He had probably served as reeve of the little sub-manor of Mars in Thornbury parish which Maurice Berkeley III had gained by marriage to Gilbert Clare V's half sister Isabel. Court Rolls, 1 Oct. 1331, 12 Dec. 1331, 18 Feb. 1332, 11 May 1349; *The Berkeley Manuscripts*, i. 244–5.

[100] StRO D641/1/2/123.

[101] Yet it is not clear exactly when offices changed hands. The head of the 1333/4 account roll agrees with the court roll that Cole held office until 9 Oct., but a membrane attached to the roll suggests he kept his post until 1 Nov. StRO D641/1/2/122.

[102] Account Rolls 1329/30, 1330/1, 1331/2, 1332/3, 1333/4 (part), 1334/5 (part), 1338/9, 1344/5, StRO D641/1/2/117, /119–23, /125, /129, show his service as reeve, 1339/40, StRO D641/1/2/126, as granger. The 1327/8 account roll shows him serving as granger in the year before the court rolls series begins, StRO D641/1/2/116.

[103] Court Rolls, 8 Sept. 1332, 9 Oct. 1333.

[104] Court Rolls, 20 Oct. 1348, 28 Sept. 1349, 20 Sept. 1350, 19 Sept. 1351.

court. The account-roll beadles had taken no known part in the movement and there is little doubt that they were Stafford's nominees. One
beadle chosen in court, and who was taking part in strikes at the time, was
given his title in a later court roll[105] and it remains uncertain whether
lords' and peasants' nominees were sharing these offices or disputing
them. The court rolls made no reference to the struggle over the post of
granger, and only the account rolls reveal that this office was taken out of
peasant hands when the movement suffered serious defeats and again in
the mid-1340s.[106]

Men as powerful as Audley and Stafford would have been able to
counter peasant protest with many special acts of oppression, but it is no
straightforward task to trace these in the court rolls. Indeed, as records
made by the lords' men they do not hesitate to misrepresent their relationships with the peasants. For example, they claim that the homage
gave Audley large sums of money 'of their free will' and that he had
nothing to do with his bailiff's oppressions.[107] Readers need not strain
their credulity to believe statements which are at odds with the mass of
other evidence on which this paper relies. The whole court apparatus for
controlling the peasantry and extracting payments from them was oppressive, but the real problem is that special acts of oppression are not
well recorded in its rolls or in any other local documents. The court was
an obvious instrument for browbeating and punishing discontented peasants, but only limited use was made of it for these purposes. The most
obvious tactic would have been to impose heavy amercements. This is
known from other estates,[108] but most individual acts of protest at
Thornbury were punished by standard amercements of 3*d*. or 6*d*. Very
heavy ones were rarely used, and the best examples come from 1339
when a threatened revival of strike action was stopped by imposing
amercements of between 12*d*. and 5*s*. for each offence, and when the
jurors who brought the articles were given a collective amercement of
£20.[109]

---

[105] Court Roll, 30 Mar. 1350 (Fowler).

[106] In 1333/4 and 1334/5 the bailiff took charge of the lord's corn, but some duties were
still performed by peasants. Outsiders were appointed as grangers in 1339/40 and 1344/5.
The first was displaced by William Cole II, but was back in office in 1340/1: StRO D641/
1/2/122, /123, /126, /127, /129.

[107] Court Rolls, 14 Sept. 1333, 7 Oct. 1343. See also account roll 1339/40, to which a
statement has been added that the outsider who served as granger that year was appointed
by the bailiff and not by Audley, his chief steward or his auditor of accounts: StRO D641/
1/2/126.

[108] Nichols, 'Petition', 303, 306.   [109] Court Rolls, 25 Feb. 1339, 18 Sept. 1339.

Some enigmatic amercements of groups of peasants for default of suit of court should probably be seen as the results of oppressive unrecorded changes in the rules on court attendance. The first such cases suggest that suitors had not been given proper notice of its sittings, with the result that increasing numbers were absent.[110] Those who were doing labour services when the court sat were forgiven, but at least 120 amercements were collected from the other absentees (see Table 6.3). Similar tactics were said to have been used by a steward who began court sessions at Bocking Hall at a very early hour and amerced those not present.[111] Defaults at a later court appear to mark the extension of payments to withdraw suit, which had mostly been made by local gentry, as a means of squeezing more money from the peasants.[112] Villein tenants made only two payments to withdraw suit before that session, but no fewer than 247 afterwards.

Large single sums of money were extracted from the peasants in order to defray the costs of Audley's expenses in the wars against the Scots and French, to marry his daughter[113] and—on one occasion—to pay for transporting victuals to his Cotswold estate of Fairford. The largest total raised in one year was £23 6s. 8d. in 1332/3, most of which came from the manor court jurors when the first phase of the movement was defeated.[114] This sum was more than three times what the whole peasant body had been assessed to pay to the 1327 Lay Subsidy.[115] The largest sum, a tallage of £20, was demanded in the late 1330s,[116] and was accompanied by a range of oppressive measures including the payments to withdraw suit, the seizure of demesne parcels, and the placing of the land market under strict regulation. All of these measures were designed to hit local people at the time of their greatest economic difficulties. But it is a

[110] Court Rolls, 21 May 1332, 13 July 1332, 9 Dec. 1335.
[111] Nichols, 'Petition', 304–5, 307.
[112] Gentry paid 2s. per year to do this. In the early part of the period it was so unusual for a peasant to withdraw suit that no standard rate had been set, and a rich peasant was charged 12d. 'and no more because (he is) old and sick', court roll 9 Feb. 1333. Peasants later paid only 3d. or 6d.
[113] The £10 aid to marry his daughter was raised in 1332/3, though her marriage to Ralph Stafford did not take place until the latter had abducted her from Audley's house at Thaxted in 1336. StRO D641/1/2/121; *Cal. of Patent Rolls, 1334–8*, 298.
[114] Court Roll, 14 Sept. 1333 (£13 6s. 8d.).
[115] *Gloucestershire Subsidy Roll, 1 Edward III. A.D. 1327*, ed. Sir T. Phillipps (Middle Hill Press, n.d.), 44–5, sections 'Hope et Bokoure' to 'Sibelond et Hobelond' inclusive. The total from the estate was £8. 4s. 1d., £7 10s. 10d. of which was due from peasants. The total due from the estate was raised in 1334 to £10. 11s. 0d.: *The Lay Subsidy of 1334*, ed. R. E. Glasscock (London, 1975), 101, sections 'Hope & Bokevor' to 'Sibelond & Oldeiond' inclusive.
[116] Court Roll, 22 July 1338.

TABLE 6.3. *Manorial court sessions and non-attendance at Thornbury,*
1328–52

Year	Surviving court rolls	Defaults of suit	Withdrawals of suit by villeins
1328/9	7	1	0
1329/30	**5	9	0
1330/1	—	—	—
1331/2	7	63	0
1332/3	**3	1	1
1333/4	*11	4	0
1334/5	16	6	0
1335/6	12	76	1
1336/7	—	—	—
1337/8	17	27	12
1338/9	14	14	12
1339/40	—	—	—
1340/1	—	—	—
1341/2	11	12	19
1342/3	—	—	—
1343/4	12	5	20
1344/5	15	2	31
1345/6	15	5	36
1346/7	15	5	32
1347/8	11	19	45
1348/9	12	4	2
1349/50	9	0	6
1350/1	14	1	15
1351/2	10	1	17
TOTAL	216	255	249

Notes: — = All court rolls lost
* = One court roll known to be lost
** = Two court rolls known to be lost

tribute to the strength of peasant opposition that, during the whole of this period, Audley and Stafford could do very little to increase corvée obligations or money rents. Indeed, the tenants of customary virgates and half-virgates were able to secure small reductions in the numbers of services they owed at corn harvest, and the ending of the practice of carrying over some unused works from one year to the next which had led to the build-up of a large 'debt' of services.[117] The lords were only able to impose increases on the demesne parcels which had been leased.[118]

But the imposition of amercements and forced payments does not explain how the lord was able to make jurors change their minds, force officials from their posts and defeat the movement's widely-supported first phase. A formal account of its *second* defeat, that of 1339, is given in the roll of the special court. The bailiff refused to answer the articles on the grounds that he was a free man and the jurors who accused him were merely villeins. A new jury of free peasants, burgesses, and villeins then declared the charges false and the protest collapsed. But how had the seven villeins who sat on both juries been induced to change their opinions? Instances will be given later of cases which went against Audley's interests in the manor court but were brought back until the jurors were ready to produce verdicts favourable to him. In the absence of other evidence, there must be a strong suspicion that jurors, officials, and peasants who took prominent parts in the movement were subjected to intimidation. Quite a list could be drawn up of the ecclesiastical lords of the late thirteenth or early fourteenth centuries who are known to have imprisoned discontented peasants or had their leaders beaten up. The principal Halesowen leader was assaulted so severely that he died.[119] The Stafford family imprisoned tenants on other estates and were unwilling to

---

[117] These successes were won in 1339/40. Lower numbers of Harvest works demanded reduced customary half-virgaters' annual burdens by 1.875d. Virgaters' savings are unclear because of the feast days allowed to them. Only Harvest works had been carried over from year to year, the numbers owed growing from 108 in 1327/8 to 1296 in 1338/9. (The annual total due before 1339/40 was 1667.) Lower numbers of Harvest ploughings were entered in the 1339/40 roll, but struck through there. These would have reduced customary virgaters' burdens by 1½d. and half-virgaters' by 2¼d. StRO D641/1/2/116, /125, /126.

[118] Court Rolls, 2 Apr. 1338, 7 Oct. 1343. Stafford increased many of these money rents by one-half or one-third in the first year of his lordship, 1347/8, but they were cut back to their old levels between 1349/50 and 1353/4. StRO D641/1/2/130, /132, /133.

[119] Such a list would include the abbots of Halesowen, Bec, Waltham and Abingdon, the Prior of Christ Church, Canterbury and the Prior of Ely. Razi, 'Struggles', 162–3; M. Morgan, *The English Lands of the Abbey of Bec* (Oxford, 1946), 107; Hilton, 'Freedom and Villeinage', 17; Tillotson, 'Peasant Unrest', 12–13; Nichols, 'Petition'. 300 n. 1; R. B. Pugh, *Imprisonment in Medieval England* (Cambridge, 1968), 54. Lawyers generally agreed that lords could put their villeins in the stocks, but whether they had the right to imprison them was open to debate: Pugh, *Imprisonment*, 52–5.

let them go. They had a prison in Thornbury in the fifteenth century, but there is no trace of one in pre-1352 records, nor—perhaps surprisingly— of any defences which would have protected the *curia* from angry peasants. Although Audley figures little in most general accounts of this time, he had an established military reputation. He had played a major part in the defeat of Llewellyn Bren's rebellion in Glamorganshire, and he paid a personal visit to Thornbury in March 1333 before going north to fight the Scots.[120] It is dangerous to conclude, as some authors have done, that there were no violent incidents or threats of coercion simply because none can be clearly recognized.[121] The threat of seigneurial violence is a recurring theme in the best studies of conflict between lords and peasants.[122]

If such things happened in Thornbury, they might have left traces in the rolls of courts held in 1333, the year when the mass movement ended with the curtailment of the large numbers of strikes. The 9 cases of bloodshed and 11 raisings of the hue recorded at that year's court leet can be compared with annual means of 7.4 and 15.4 respectively, suggesting that this was not a violent time.[123] Most of the victims of bloodshed had played no part in the movement and none can be recognized as a leader. This does, however, beg the question—if Audley's men had begun to assault peasants, would the tithingmen have dared to report it? But if Audley had begun to hang peasants there should be a good chance of tracing their deaths in the rolls. Only two villein men's and three villein women's deaths were recorded in the year following Michaelmas 1332, as against annual means of 6.8 and 3.2 respectively.[124] The loss of two court rolls may have made these figures incomplete, but there is nothing to suggest a high mortality from any cause.[125] But the death of a poor

---

[120] I. S. Leadam, 'The Last Days of Bondage in England', *Law Quarterly Review*, 9 (1893), 364 n. 1. A. D. K. Hawkyard, 'Thornbury Castle', *Trans. Bristol & Gloucs. Arch. Soc.* 95 (1977), 52 n. 17. The building of the castle did not begin until 1511. The abbot of Halesowen obtained permission to fortify parts of his abbey: Razi, 'Struggles', 160. J. B. Smith, 'The Rebellion of Llewellyn Bren', in T. B. Pugh (ed.), *Glamorgan County History III. The Middle Ages* (Cardiff, 1971), 72–86. StRO D641/1/2/121 records his expenses of 29s. 8d. and £40 in Thornbury before moving to Thaxted and Newcastle-upon-Tyne.

[121] Britton, *Community*, 170–1.

[122] Hilton, 'Freedom and Villeinage'; Razi, 'Struggles'.

[123] Means were calculated from the 14 surviving pre-plague leet rolls, court rolls 24 May 1329, 14 May 1330, 21 May 1332, 18 May 1333, 22 Apr. 1335, 20 Apr. 1336, 23 Apr. 1338, 15 Apr. 1339, 22 Apr. 1342, 24 Apr. 1344, 30 Mar. 1345, 25 Apr. 1346, 12 Apr. 1347, 19 May 1348.

[124] Means were calculated from the 167 surviving pre-plague court rolls, including rolls of combined sessions and separate leets.

[125] Numbers of recorded deaths rose quite dramatically after Michaelmas 1333 because of the malarial epidemic which chiefly affected the west of the parish: Franklin, 'Malaria', 114, fig. 1.

peasant called Agnes Kenting, whose holding escheated because of 'felony', 18 May 1333, is suspicious. No details of her offence are known, but the record does suggest that she had been executed—perhaps at the time of Audley's visit—and it is interesting that she was the only one of that year's dead who had been heavily involved in the mass movement.[126] Does this incident provide the key to how peasant movements could be defeated, their leaders forced out of office or jurors made to change their verdicts? The court rolls simply do not tell us.

Whatever the means used, the peasant movement was dealt a severe blow in 1333 and it was never again able to mount a sustained campaign of strike action on the early model. The disputes over offices seem to have hamstrung it. Indeed, at the risk of oversimplifying complicated events, it may be said that the Thornbury Peasant Movement could only take effective action when a small number of men were in office and that their influence could often be negated by the power of other officials who look very like seigneurial nominees. The leaders of more widely based popular movements might be drawn from the ranks of the gentry, townsmen (including lawyers) or clergy,[127] but the leaders of peasant protests which drew little support from other social classes have usually been seen as rich peasants.[128] The principal leader might well be the reeve, whose office was often monopolized by the local rich.[129] This is easy to accept as rich peasants suffered the most from the restrictions of feudalism, while possessing economic and social power which brought them political influence in their communities. No one has stressed their power more strongly than Z. Razi, who found that the Romsley rebellion in Halesowen was led by a tiny group from the wealthiest local families.[130] But the Thornbury evidence reveals that the officials involved in that movement's leadership came from much more varied backgrounds. The principal leader, William Cole II, sounds very like the men with whom historians are familiar. He was not only a rich peasant, but one of the richest in the parish.[131]

---

[126] She was amerced for refusal to do services 13 July 1332, 8 Sept. 1332, 18 May 1333.
[127] Hilton, *Bond Men*, 124, 207–13.
[128] e.g. Razi, 'Struggles', 161–2, 165. For parallels in continental western Europe, see Hilton, *Bond Men*, 84, 115; G. Fourquin, *The Anatomy of Popular Rebellion in the Middle Ages*, trans. A. Chesters (Amsterdam, 1978), 56, 71.
[129] Hilton, 'Thirteenth-Century Poem', 92.
[130] Razi, *Life, Marriage and Death*, 76–83, but see his 'Family, Land and the Village Community' for their relations with other groups; Razi, 'Struggles', 165.
[131] The early part of his personal file is complicated by a few court roll entries relating to William Cole I, an unfree middle peasant whose death was recorded 18 Feb. 1332, and William Cole III, a knight who bought 20 acres of arable and woodland in the neighbouring parish of Tytherington, 1 Oct. 1331. The latter makes no appearance in Saul, *Knights and Esquires*.

He held about 82 acres and his tax assessment of 3s. 1d. in the 1327 Lay Subsidy Roll was the fifth highest owed by any local peasant.[132] Besides serving as reeve and granger, he was a frequent manor court juror and acted as an affeeror.[133] But not all followed this pattern. Two senior posts were held by a middle peasant, and the tithingmen who played an important part in the movement's organization were a mixture of middle and poor group members. But this picture of the leaders as peasant officials may be incomplete because only villein men held such posts. The involvement of freemen is unlikely, in view of what is said below, but villein women may have taken a part. It would be interesting to have any other source which gave the lord's view of who the 'ringleaders' were, in the way that the poem about the Stoughton peasant movement in Leicestershire appears to. One of the Romsley leaders was a woman and the two women mentioned in the Stoughton poem must have played important parts to have merited inclusion there.[134]

Besides providing leaders, rich peasants have been seen as a major group in the rank and file of medieval movements. This has strengthened the case of historians who have been concerned to establish that these were not just reactions to dire poverty, but often took place in relatively well-off areas.[135] J. R. Maddicott's interpretation of 1330s discontent in terms of distress fits better with the Postan thesis than with most modern work on the economic background to peasant protest.[136] R. H. Hilton's 1949 paper drew attention to the different economic groups' motives for opposing their lords, recognizing that poor and middle peasants fought against exactions which threatened their living standards whilst rich peasants struggled to defeat seigneurial controls on their road to economic expansion.[137] But medievalists have given little attention to the contributions of middle and poor peasants, although studies which show these groups taking important parts in modern movements provide food for

---

[132] *Gloucestershire Subsidy Roll, 1327*, 45.

[133] He served as a juror at the courts of 24 May 1329, 21 May 1334, 13 Oct. 1334, 30 Jan. 1335, 16 Oct. 1337, 6 Nov. 1337, 27 Nov. 1337, 18 Dec. 1337, 8 Jan. 1338, 19 Feb. 1338, 12 Mar. 1338, 4 June 1338, 12 Aug. 1338, 2 Sept. 1338, 18 Sept. 1339, 17 June 1342, 9 Feb. 1344, 15 Jan. 1347, 12 Apr. 1347, 3 May 1347, 19 May 1348, 3 Feb. 1349. Affeerors' names were not usually recorded, but Cole filled this office at the courts of 24 May 1329, 14 Nov. 1329, 29 Mar. 1348.

[134] Hilton, 'Thirteenth-Century Poem', 92; Razi, 'Struggles', 166.

[135] Hilton, 'Peasant Movements', esp. 130–1; Hilton, *Bond Men*, 116–17; Faith, 'Class Struggle', 52; Fourquin, *Anatomy*, 56, 60; A. DeWindt, 'Peasant Power Structures in Fourteenth-Century King's Ripton, 1280–1400', *Mediaeval Studies*, 38 (1976), 236–67.

[136] Maddicott, 'English Peasantry', *passim*.

[137] Hilton, 'Peasant Movements', 122.

thought.[138] As it is generally agreed that the rich group are the best represented in medieval sources—and certainly in manorial court rolls[139]—particular care must be taken not to underrate other groups' involvement in politics.

The presence of middle and poor peasant leaders suggested that the Thornbury movement had substantial support from below the rich group. As the commission of labour service offences was such an important form of protest in this and other movements, it was decided to use the large sample of identified people who refused to do services or did them badly as a basis for analysing the social composition of the movement. This produces the largest samples to work with, but it obviously concentrates attention on the tenants of villein land, most of whom were adult male villeins, and away from other family members, women, exclusive sub-tenants, landless peasants, freemen and any non-peasants who may have played a part. The following survey's concentration upon villeins is, however, not misleading, for a careful search revealed very few actions by free peasants or burgesses which could be interpreted as support for the movement. Indeed, the jury which inflicted a major defeat on it by dismissing the 1339 articles included a majority of wealthy free peasants and burgesses. Organized opposition to the lord only developed in the borough *after* the Black Death.[140] But the other problems of coverage remain.

A total of 138 identified villein men and women took part in labour-service offences, of whom 127 were direct tenants of the lord. Fifty-three of these were rich peasants (38 per cent), 41 middle peasants (30 per cent), 25 poor peasants (18 per cent) and 8 (6 per cent) could not be placed.[141] The remaining 11 (8 per cent) were a mixture of exclusive subtenants and landless members of tenant families. As poor peasants were the most numerous group in the manor, these figures suggest that the rich were much more likely to be involved in such protests than they were. Rich peasants were also the most heavily involved, in the sense that those who committed labour-service offences committed more than other peasants—a mean of 4.1 offences each, as against 2.9 for each middle peasant and 2.4 for each poor one. It thus appears that both the likelihood

---

[138] H. A. Landsberger, 'Peasant Unrest: Themes and Variations' in H. A. Landsberger (ed.), *Rural Protest: Peasant Movements and Social Change* (London, 1974), esp. 14–15, 26; E. R. Wolf, *Peasant Wars of the Twentieth Century* (London, 1973), esp. 291–2.

[139] See Ch. 9 below.   [140] Hilton, 'Lords, Burgesses and Hucksters', 14.

[141] Some of the eight moved between economic groups and some names were shared by members of different groups.

and the strength of involvement were greatest amongst the rich group and declined with holding size.

The chief objections to this argument are that the rich may have been more likely to commit these offences and to have committed them more frequently because they owed more services. Their strong presence among the offenders and high numbers of offences may simply reflect their greater opportunities. The major reason why other groups were less likely to take part in labour-service offences was that they had smaller opportunities to do so, and they may well have been more strongly involved than the rich in that they made more use of the opportunities to protest which they did have.

Most of the tenants who committed these offences were men. Women's involvement in politics is one of the many aspects of their lives which has received little attention from historians, despite the evidence mentioned earlier that they sometimes played leading roles. Women commonly formed about one in seven or one in eight of tenants, most of those being widows who could take advantage of manorial custom to secure an independent position. Widows formed about 14 per cent, or a little more, of villein tenants at Thornbury[142] and they took a full part in supporting the movement. They made up 16.5 per cent of those who committed labour-service offences. The samples available for an attempt to measure 'strength of involvement' are very small,[143] but the results do suggest that women were as strongly involved as men.[144] The small groups of peasants who seem to have acted together to refuse services often included at least one woman.[145] The participation of these widows probably continued support for the movement which had begun as wives, but wives' activities are much less well recorded.[146]

Besides the tenants who were amerced for these offences, there was a group of 11 identified villeins who did not hold land of Audley but who had been summoned to do services on behalf of relatives or employers. Their presence is important because it shows that support for the campaign

---

[142] Franklin, 'Peasant Widows', 188–9.   [143] Twelve women in all.

[144] Comparisons could be made for middle and poor peasants with customary land, for all groups with gavel land and for rich peasants who held both customary and gavel land. Women's scores for labour service offences per 100 works owed were higher than men's in three of these six cases and lower in three. The reservations about the numbers of works actually called upon to be performed still apply.

[145] e.g. this was true of the six groups of 6–15 people amerced for not coming to reaping, Court Roll, 8 Sept. 1332.

[146] Franklin, 'Peasant Widows', 195–6. Married women's refusals to do services at Broughton are known because they held land independently of their husbands: Britton, *Community of the Vill*, 22–4.

was not confined to direct tenants, but extended to some of their children, grandchildren and employees. Again, some of those involved were women. The involvement of members of younger generations must have contributed to the establishment of a tradition of resistance like that which R. Faith found in St Albans town,[147] for there is good evidence at Thornbury of supporters' descendants and successors—including sons, grandsons, and widows' second husbands—taking up the fight.[148]

It is clear that substantial numbers of middle and poor peasants were involved as well as the rich. It may well be that middle and poor tenants played a more active part than the rich who figure more prominently in the records. Women tenants were as much involved as men and support came from family members who did not hold land. In short, the villein community was able to work together despite the very real and growing differences between the rich, middle, and poor groups, but the villeins remained unable to win for their cause the support of their free peasant neighbours or of the burgesses in Thornbury town.

What were they trying to achieve? The wide range of historians who see the interests of lords and peasants as being in opposition seek the basic cause of peasant discontent in the lords' expropriation of peasants' surplus and restrictions upon their economic activities. The underlying aims of peasant movements were to reduce the amount of the surplus taken and to remove such restrictions. The local nature of medieval life and fragmentation of the countryside into manors encouraged a tendency to limited, localized, aims, but R. H. Hilton has argued persuasively that the desire for personal freedom was continuously present.[149] Personal freedom would provide much better protection for peasants' surplus than manorial custom, especially when the latter was open to attack from powerful noblemen, and would have strengthened the development of pioneering agrarian capitalism of which some elements were already present before the Black Death.

The aims of the Thornbury Peasant Movement can be inferred from the social composition of its supporters and the detailed events of the period, most of which are known from the court rolls. It is probably safe to include among its more limited aims the dismissal of the unpopular bailiff, the regranting of demesne parcels which had been seized, the

---

[147] Faith drew attention to the role of old people in passing on stories of liberties and privileges: 'The "Great Rumour" of 1377', 64. The discontented Stoughton peasants included one '*Rusticus antiquus Rogerus*', Hilton, 'Thirteenth-Century Poem', 95.

[148] Cf. Faith, 'Class Struggle', 52, 57; Faith, 'The "Great Rumour" of 1377', 66–7.

[149] Hilton, 'Peasant Movements'; Hilton, *Bond Men*, esp. 72; Razi, 'Struggles'.

appointment of peasants as manorial surveyors and the deregulation of the land market. These were all things which were accomplished when movement leaders were in power.[150]

The manorial court rolls of the thirteenth and fourteenth centuries reveal a rural society seething with discontent, and the frequency with which evidence of lord–peasants conflict is found in them provides strong support for those who see class struggle as the driving force of history. Labour-service offences occur in 16 of the 19 years' Thornbury court rolls used in this study and in 28 of 34 years' Holywell-cum-Needingworth rolls,[151] and they are supplemented by records of other kinds of offence which reflect peasant resistance of varying degrees of organization and overtones. Hundreds of cases were recorded, involving large numbers of protesters. Not only do manorial court rolls provide so much evidence for these movements but they provide the *only* surviving evidence for most of them, those which did not come to the attention of the royal courts or of monkish writers. There is no substitute for their evidence, because without it these movements would be forgotten.

The Thornbury Peasant Movement, which is unknown from any royal court record or chronicle, was in many ways typical of such movements, and the exploration of some of its aspects has brought out both the strengths and weaknesses of the court rolls' record of local politics. Labour-service offences are revealed as a form of well-organized group protest which—even when large numbers were committed—worked by disrupting the lord's economy in a kind of economic guerilla warfare. Yet the exact meanings of most of the records of such individual offences remain open to question. The court rolls' record of the economic, social and legal status of protesters has emerged as one of their greatest strengths. They reveal that the leadership and organization were not entirely dominated by the 'village rich', and that this group's appearance as the strongest supporters of local movements is probably an illusion based upon their greater opportunities to refuse labour services. All three economic groups had vital interests to defend and they were still able to unite as a community, despite the ever-widening gaps between them and the absence of the land redistribution which Razi believed was important to

---

[150] The first two aims were achieved towards the end of 1342/3 (that year's court rolls are lost, but some results of the changes appear in that for 7 Oct. 1343) when a movement leader called Robert Andrew I was beadle. The second two were achieved at the 30 Sept. 1344 court when Cole was again serving as reeve.

[151] Dewindt, *Land and People*, 164–5, 269 table v. Rolls survive from 13 years later than the period 1288–1403 covered by that Table, but no details are given of further offences.

village solidarity.[152] But the strength of involvement of the different groups has proved hard to measure, though it remains much easier to discuss these smaller tenants' contributions to local politics than those of their relatives and neighbours who made much less mark in the rolls because they were not the lord's direct tenants. The aims for which peasants united have had to be reconstructed from the social composition of the protesters and from the detailed record of local events which is another great strength of manorial documents. Local events show clearly how the conditions of English villeinage were the products of the continual struggle between lords and peasants. The court rolls themselves were a weapon in this struggle and were preserved, in part, for use in future rounds of the conflict. Hence their direct statements about the relationship between lords and peasants are chiefly of value for studies of seigneurial attitudes and propaganda.

Most of this new evidence came from the court rolls, but if there is no *substitute* for court-roll evidence there is every reason to add to it at each opportunity. This is particularly true because of its limitations as a source for the changes in feudal rent and in office holders which underlie the courses of peasant movements. Much of the fundamental economic battle can be traced through manorial account rolls and extents. The account rolls' evidence for the progress of the struggle over offices is also of great value, for a movement's ability to pursue certain forms of protest clearly depended upon having its men in power and lack of evidence for protest does not necessarily mean that there was no discontent. No combination of written sources will provide a truly comprehensive view of a movement undertaken by illiterate peasants, but the use of additional material produces a much fuller picture of a movement's history and enables a much more valuable appraisal of its successes and failures to be made. The combination of documents shows how well it defended peasant interests against powerful and grasping lords, preventing increases in feudal rent and winning victories on secondary issues. These were no mean achievements.

The historian who works painstakingly on a single estate must always question the extent to which his findings can be applied to other historical communities. J. R. Maddicott's interpretation of this period's national discontent as a straightforward reaction to economic distress relies heavily upon the accounts of the commentators who criticized government policy at that time.[153] If Thornbury's experience was at all typical, then

---

[152] Razi, 'Family Land and the Village Community', 9–10.
[153] Maddicott, 'English Peasantry', *passim*.

much of this must be challenged. Risings which never happen have only a limited appeal, and little is known about the national discontent of the 1330s and early 1340s. The printed evidence for trouble in the early 1330s relies heavily on messages sent to the king by concerned clergymen.[154] The Calendars of Patent and Close Rolls have more information on the later troubles, but mention only a dozen specific instances of disturbances or refusals to pay. These provide only three lists of protesters and some isolated names—44 names in all—and the social composition of these has never been analysed.[155] The records of the Thornbury Peasant Movement make a substantial addition to the evidence for this discontent, and provide the first detailed picture of events at local level. The scope of the present argument must be restricted because information from other estates is to date so limited and because Thornbury's economic conditions were so different from the generally-accepted view of pre-plague England, but some useful points can be made.

It must first be recognized that 1330s discontent rested upon a basis of the ubiquitous nationwide local struggles between lords and peasants which show up so well in manorial court rolls. Peasant discontent was ever present, and its increase by heavy taxation and purveyance does not mean that these were its only, or its chief, causes. But it is the particular difficulties faced by the Thornbury movement which suggest why no effective national popular movement like that of 1381 emerged in the earlier period. Though rich, middle, and poor peasants could work together, villeins got little support from their neighbours. This seems to have been a widespread problem, and if the campaign for freedom was particularly active at this time it may have driven a wedge between villeins and freemen, and between peasants and burgesses.[156] In 1381, it was possible to make the abolition of serfdom a leading popular demand,

---

[154] *De Speculo Regis Edwardi Tertii*, ed. J. Moisant (Paris, 1891); L. E. Boyle, 'The *Oculus Sacerdotis* and Some Other Works of William of Pagula', *TRHS* 5th ser. 5 (1955), 81–110; W. A. Pantin, 'The Letters of John Mason: A Fourteenth-Century Formulary from St Augustine's, Canterbury', in T. A. Sandquist and M. R. Powicke (eds.), *Essays in Medieval History presented to Bertie Wilkinson* (Toronto, 1969), 204–6.

[155] *Cal. Pat. Rolls 1338–40*, 76 (two cases, one of them doubtful), 187–8, 273; *Cal. Pat. Rolls 1342–3*, 103–4, 324–5 (two cases); *Cal. Close Rolls 1339–41*, 495, 536, 546, 625–6 (two cases), 647, 652.

[156] Z. Razi only mentions freemen taking part in the Halesowen movement in 1380, and the Romsley village rebellion was the work of villeins: 'Family, Land and the Village Community', 35; 'Struggles', 165–6. They do not appear to have found support in Halesowen borough, nor are the Stoughton villeins known to have found any in Leicester, which lay only two or three miles from the vill: Hilton, 'Thirteenth-Century Poem', *passim*. There was co-operation at St Albans, but its lords had refused the town burghal status and townspeople and peasants overlapped: Faith, 'The "Great Rumour" of 1377', 63–8.

but in the 1330s it threatened real privileges, especially those of rich free peasants who were anxious to turn their holdings into little manors. This campaign seems to have been locked into a round of well-established forms of protest which depended on having its leaders in office. Powerful lords must have been well used to dealing with these, though they could not prevent determined campaigns from winning limited successes. The local nature of the ubiquitous struggles over feudal rent may also have made it difficult for peasants on different estates to combine, whilst peasants used to these struggles against their own lords may have found it hard to oppose a government which was represented directly by only a couple of chief tax collectors in each county.[157] For this reason it would be of interest to know if there was more discontent on the estates of lords who had close royal connections and whose officers had sat in parliament than on others. The abbot of Ramsey's estates of Broughton and Holywell-cum-Needingworth were quiet at this time.[158] But how could these limited local actions have influenced the government?

What was needed to turn the separate local campaigns into an effective national movement was a single overwhelming grievance which affected both villeins and freemen, burgesses and peasants of all economic groups. The taxation and purveyance of the 1330s and early 1340s and the oppressions of government agents were never quite severe enough. The violent incidents to which they gave rise—at Fordwich, Kent, *c.*1332, at Clarborough, Nottinghamshire, in 1340, and at Thornham, Norfolk, in 1341[159]—were sparks which could not ignite a fire like that begun at Brentwood 40 years later. Discontent is the common experience of peasantries, but armed risings are rare. The immediate reason why there was not even an abortive rising at this time was probably, as J. R. Maddicott says, simply that the peasants were not pushed to the brink. It was still possible for them to employ passive resistance against taxmen and purveyors,[160] and the old weapons of collective action against their own lords. They were not forced to escalate their struggle, and the tension was gradually defused after government exactions were reduced.

---

[157] Maddicott, 'English Peasantry', 66.

[158] I mention these because tables of labour-service offences have been published. Broughton court rolls survive from eight years in the period 1330–40, Holywell ones only from 1332 and 1339. The former had only its mean number of offences, the latter very few indeed. Britton, *Community of the Vill*, 170 Table 51; Dewindt, *Land and People*, 269 table v.

[159] Pantin, 'Letters', *Cal. Pat. Rolls 1340–3*, 103–4, 324–5.

[160] Maddicott, 'English Peasantry', 65–6.

7

Merton College's Control of its Tenants at Thorncroft 1270–1349

RALPH EVANS

MANORIAL documents have long provided the basis for the analysis of domanial economy, and in recent years more than ever they have been used to study peasant communities.[1] The nature of the relationship between the lord of a manor and his tenants remains, however, a difficult and in some ways an elusive subject. Its importance to both sides was great. Rent received from tenants—broadly defined to include more than fixed annual payments in money—could be vital even to a lord engaged in extensive demesne cultivation, and its true economic significance is commonly underestimated. Conversely of course tenants were deprived of a proportion of their resources—a proportion which varied enormously between tenants. Furthermore unfree tenants in particular were subject to the lord's control in a range of matters, some of them as fundamental as marriage or the buying and leasing of land. These seigneurial rights may or may not have become essentially financial in nature, but they gave a lord at least the opportunity of intervention in the life of peasant households. It is a valuable historical exercise to assess these liabilities in particular cases. An overlapping but somewhat different task is to consider the variable factors. Was manorial custom unchanging or could it be altered by pressure from one side or the other? How did the particular character of each manor or lord condition the way in which rights were

[1] The present study is based on a longer, unpublished paper on 'Merton College and its Tenants at Thorncroft and Cuxham c.1270–c.1350', completed in 1979. This in turn had its origins in a more general investigation of Merton's estates by various researchers working under the direction of the late Trevor Aston; the results of much of this work were published in T. H. Aston, 'The External Administration and Resources of Merton College to circa 1348' in J. I. Catto and T. A. R. Evans (eds.), The Early Oxford Schools (History of the University of Oxford, i, Oxford, 1984). I am indebted to the Warden and Fellows of Merton College, Oxford for allowing me to use their archives, and to Dr J. R. L. Highfield, formerly librarian, and especially to Mr J. B. Burgass, formerly assistant librarian and now librarian, for their great helpfulness in making the documents available to me. I am grateful to the late Trevor Aston for introducing me to the archives of Merton and to Dr John Blair, Dr Rosamond Faith, Professor Rodney Hilton, Professor Zvi Razi, and Dr Richard Smith for their helpful comments.

exercised? What was the scope for a lord to pursue a positive policy either across a whole estate or within a single manor?

The manorial court was at the centre of the relationship between lord and tenant, and its proceedings provide the principal means of monitoring that relationship. Furthermore the value of the court's records can be augmented significantly when they are used in conjunction with manorial surveys and accounts. The court was in large measure the guardian of the lord's rights and interests, but it could provide too a means of resisting his claims. The court might also function as a communal assembly which dealt with matters in which the lord was simply one suitor among many, or in which he had no interest at all. These different, sometimes contradictory roles of the court cannot always be disentangled. A crucial aspect of a lord's dealings with his tenants, but one which remains very obscure, is the mechanism by which the lord's rights were enforced. It was one thing to issue orders in the manorial court but quite another to make them effective, especially in a manor with a distant lord and dispersed tenements. The activities of the men whose duty it was to implement judgements made in court, especially those officers of lesser standing than the manorial reeve or his equivalent, are not always clearly documented, but they were essential to the maintenance of the lord's authority over his tenants.

The significance and operation of the manorial court were treated extensively in the classic works of Maitland, Vinogradoff, Bennett, and Homans, and its procedures have been examined more recently by Beckerman. Often however these questions, especially those regarding the mechanism by which a lord's instructions were given effect at the lowest level, receive only slight attention in works whose main concern is with estate history on the one hand or with the reconstruction of individual communities on the other. More detailed studies of particular manors are necessary for a fuller understanding of the impact of seigneurial power on peasant society.

MERTON COLLEGE

Merton College, Oxford, held an estate of middling size formed in the later thirteenth century of manors in several parts of England (mainly the south-east and midlands) which had been held previously by a variety of lords. The college's first statutes were issued in 1264; by 1274, when it received its definitive statutes, it held ten manors and several appropriated churches, besides various other miscellaneous properties.[2] For the estate as a whole the survival of administrative documents is patchy before the late 1270s. The tenurial structures of the manors with which Walter of Merton endowed his college were already well established, but the college proved capable of pursuing policies which could significantly adjust the balance between free land, unfree land, and demesne on some of its manors.[3] Furthermore, although the rent that could be extracted from individual free and unfree holdings on any manor had been largely defined before the college gained possession, the precise ways in which it exercised its rights were not entirely predetermined. The question must be posed whether the college's character as a body of university clerks influenced its behaviour as a landlord.

THE MANOR OF THORNCROFT

In 1266 Merton College received the manor of Thorncroft, which was situated in the parish of Leatherhead in Surrey, alongside the River Mole where it flowed northwards out of the north downs.[4] By the later thirteenth century the parish contained extensive and long-established enclosures as well as a single common field to the south-east of the town; the pattern of dispersed homesteads and closes was probably older than that of consolidated settlements and common field. The small town which

---

[2] For the endowment of Merton College see *The Early Rolls of Merton College, Oxford*, ed. J. R. L. Highfield (Oxford Hist. Soc. NS 18, 1964), introduction, 40–9; T. H. Aston and R. J. Faith, 'The Endowments of the University and Colleges to *circa* 1348' in Catto and Evans, *Early Oxford Schools*, 295–9. On the college's statutes see *Early Rolls of Merton*, app. I. The statutes of 1264 and 1274 are reproduced in facsimile and edited from Merton College Records (hereafter MCR) 194 and 232 in *Merton Muniments*, ed. P. S. Allen and H. W. Garrod (Oxford Hist. Soc. 76, 1928), 15–17 and 21–6; those of 1270 (MCR 231) are edited in *Early Rolls of Merton*, 378–91. There is an English translation of the statutes of 1274 in G. C. Brodrick, *Memorials of Merton College* (Oxford Hist. Soc. 4, 1885), 317–40.

[3] See Harvey, *Cuxham* (London, 1965), 120–3; and R. H. Hilton, 'Kibworth Harcourt: A Merton College Manor in the Thirteenth and Fourteenth Centuries' in W. G. Hoskins (ed.), *Studies in Leicestershire Agrarian History* (Leics. Arch. Soc., 1949), esp. 24–6.

[4] Medieval Leatherhead has been studied in great detail by Dr John Blair. The brief description in this and the following paragraph is based on: 'The Early Manorial Records of Leatherhead', ed. W. J. Blair, 5 pts. in *Proc. Leatherhead and District Local Hist. Soc.* iii (1967–76), 218–45, 268–97, 329–46, and iv (1976–86), 12–8; W. J. Blair, 'A Military Holding in Twelfth Century Leatherhead', ibid. iv. 3–12; W. J. Blair, *Discovering Early Leatherhead* (Leatherhead and District Local Hist. Soc. occasional paper 1, 1975); and his chapters on 'The Early Middle Ages, *c*.600–1250' and 'The Late Middle Ages 1250–1558', in E. Vardey (ed.), *History of Leatherhead: A Town at the Crossroads* (Leatherhead and District Local History Soc., 1988), 27–39, 41–67. In addition much of the discussion of patterns of settlement and landholding in W. J. Blair, *Early Medieval Surrey: Landholding, Church and Settlement before 1300* (Stroud, 1991) relates to Leatherhead.

developed at a crossroads in the centre of the parish may be of later origin
than the two main manors of the parish. There was pasture on the edge
of the downs to the south, and rough pasture in the north. The manor of
Thorncroft had land in the common field, on the downs and in closes in
various parts of the parish, and demesne meadow by the Mole. Much of
the demesne lay in consolidated blocks. There were also outlying tenements at Mickleham, slightly higher up the Mole valley, and at Newdigate,
in the weald some ten miles south of Leatherhead. The manorial buildings were located on the west bank of the Mole, across the river and a
short distance from the town. There may perhaps have been a settlement
dependent on the manor of Thorncroft on the east bank near the church
of Leatherhead, absorbed by the later growth of the town.

Thorncroft was the largest but not the only manor in the parish. The
manor of (Great) Pachesham, the successor to a pre-conquest royal vill,
lay mainly in the north-west of the parish where it had its own small
settlement, but it included land in other parts too. In the Domesday Book
the entire parish was divided between the manors of Thorncroft and
Pachesham, both then in private hands. It is possible that the town of
Leatherhead, sited on the boundary between the two manors, was in
some sense a creation of the post-conquest lords of Pachesham. Most of
the tenements in the town pertained to Pachesham rather than Thorncroft,
and it was to the lord of Pachesham that Leatherhead's weekly market
and annual fair were granted in 1248. Between 1286 and 1343 the lords
of Pachesham were royal administrators, probably non-resident much of
the time. In the north of the parish there was also a small manor known
as Little Pachesham (and later as Randalls) which was greatly augmented
around 1170 by a grant of lands from the manor of Thorncroft, both in
the common field and in closes in the south of the parish. Each manor
had its separate commons. By the 1220s the family which held Little
Pachesham had adopted the surname 'of Leatherhead'; it had the largest
estate of those who were normally resident in the parish in the thirteenth
and fourteenth centuries. Other families of substantial freeholders in this
period—such as the Aperdeles, Punshursts, Brademeres, Broks, and
Pynchouns—probably took their names from the discrete farmsteads on
which they lived, and commonly had tenurial links with more than one
manor.

Thorncroft was clearly more extensive than either Pachesham manor.
Its demesne arable consisted of several large blocks of enclosures and
perhaps 300 acres in the common field. In addition to outlying holdings
in Mickleham and Newdigate tenants of Thorncroft held various closes

east of the common field of Leatherhead and up to 200 acres in the common field itself.[5] The manor's eight principal unfree tenements were a yardlander, six half-yardlanders, and a quarter-yardlander. The extent of the unfree half-yardlands, when recorded, as for example at the court of 28 March 1349, was either 8 or 10 acres; the quarter-yardland was described once as 3 acres and 1 rood and once as 4 acres. There were also seven unfree smallholdings, each with an acre of land. In 1279 there were approximately twenty free holdings, most consisting of half a yardland or of one or even two complete yardlands, but by 1357 these had fragmented into a multiplicity of smaller holdings.[6]

It might be expected in view of the juxtaposition of the lands of the three manors that some free tenants would have held land of more than one manor, and that in general the affairs of the tenants would frequently transcend manorial boundaries. This expectation is confirmed by the surviving rentals and records of the courts of the manors, even though very few fourteenth-century court rolls survive from either Pachesham manor.[7] Thus a man who appears in the court rolls of Thorncroft as the tenant of a small plot may in fact hold a large tenement of another manor. And it is possible—as with all court rolls—than occasionally a man may

[5] Blair, 'Late Middle Ages', 45–7. The estimate of 200 acres is a maximum based on a notional half-yardland of 13 acres. In fact unfree half-yardlands contained only 8 or 10 acres, and free half-yardlands of similar sizes are to be found in, for example, the rental of 1333. Within a few years of his death the free tenement of Walter of Hambledon was variously described in the accounts for 1319–20 and 1320–1 (MCR 5750, 5710) and the courts of 4 Nov. 1316, 22 Feb. 1319, and 3 May 1323 as: 10 acres; 3 crofts; 3 crofts with a curtilage and barn; a half-yardland; a messuage and yardland. On the nature and variable size of free yardlands see Blair, *Early Medieval Surrey*, 46–7, 71–4; the manor's single unfree yardland is mapped ibid. 47.

[6] Details of rentals and surveys of Thorncroft compiled between about 1279 and 1357 are given in Appendix 7.2. Proceedings of the court are here cited by the date of the court in modern style; their archival location is given in Appendix 7.1. The number and date of courts may often be checked against details given in the manorial accounts. The manorial accounts of Thorncroft (together with views of account etc.) up to July 1349 are to be found in MCR 5688–5728, 5735–59, and 5790. There are accounts for every year between 1278–9 and 1289–90 inclusive and all but six years between 1308–9 and 1348–9 inclusive, besides several years outside these main sequences.

[7] All known medieval rentals and proceedings of the courts of the Pachesham manors have been printed. The proceedings of a court of Pachesham in 1319 is edited by J. H. Harvey as 'The Earliest Surviving Court Roll of the Manor of Pachenesham', in *Proc. Leatherhead and District Local History Soc.* ii (1957–66), 170–6; courts of 29 July and 21 Oct. 1322, 7 May, 22 June, 20 Sept., and 13 Dec. 1323, 23 Apr. 1324, and 22 June 1472 are printed in 'The Early Manorial Records of Leatherhead', iv. 12–18. Courts of Little Pachesham of 30 July 1328, 31 Jan. 1331, 13 Dec. 1333, 2 July, and 23 Nov. 1336 and 30 June 1338 are ibid. iii. 276–89. Rentals or surveys of Pachesham of 1343, *c.*1380 (part), 1414, 1418, 1474/5, and 1509 are ibid. iii, 290–7, 329–46; rentals of Little Pachesham of *c.*1300, *c.*1327, *c.*1330, and 1383 are ibid. iii. 218–43, 268–75.

be mentioned who holds land in another place altogether. A lord like the prior of Reigate may cause no confusion, but lesser gentry or substantial peasants from adjoining areas may not be readily identifiable. Such a man was Richard ate Legh of Headley, south-east of Leatherhead, who inherited a small estate in Headley, Walton-on-the-Hill, and Epsom; between the early 1290s and 1335 he added to this at least 70 acres of arable to form a compact unit in adjoining parts of the parishes of Leatherhead, Ashtead, and Headley.[8]

The proceedings of the manorial court of Thorncroft survive in a more or less complete series from 1279 to 1343, though none is extant between 1343 and 1349. Typically a court was held two or three times in a year, but the number could rise to eight and there was no court at all in several years.[9] The primary purpose of the court, to judge by its written proceedings, was to protect the lord's interests. The presentation of trespasses on the demesne, for example, is a very common item of business. As the manor's free holdings became increasingly fragmented, recording new tenants and bringing them to recognize their—often very slight— obligations to the lord became a major preoccupation. Registering changes in the tenancy of unfree holdings was also an important matter; so too, if more fitfully, was the supervision of short-term leases undertaken by unfree tenants. And of course the enforcement of the various obligations of unfree tenure, including the maintenance of holdings and the performance of labour-rent, came within the court's purview. Occasionally the court was called on to determine a point of manorial custom. It was sometimes used to investigate the conduct of the manorial reeve, but it was asked to consider the management of the demesne rather less frequently than was the court of the college's manor of Cuxham in Oxfordshire; this was perhaps because the demesne and the unfree holdings of Thorncroft were rather more dispersed than those of Cuxham.[10] The selection and supervision of manorial officers is also recorded in a rather unsystematic manner. Litigation between the court's suitors other than the lord was less common at Thorncroft than in some manors. And when the proceedings record matters relating only to tenants, for example an inquiry made at a tenant's request or pleas of contract or debt, they tend

---

[8] On the Legh estate see Blair, 'Late Middle Ages', 50–1, 55; Blair, *Early Medieval Surrey*, 82–3.

[9] See Appendix 7.1.

[10] The records of the manorial court of Cuxham 1279–1358 are printed in *Manorial Records of Cuxham*. On the demesne of Cuxham and its management see Harvey, *Cuxham*, 32–86.

to provide regrettably little detail. The extant records of the courts of Pachesham and Little Pachesham suggest that their business was similar to that of Thorncroft. None of the manorial courts in this divided parish enacted agricultural by-laws. The court of Thorncroft did not have the devolved public jurisdiction associated with the view of frankpledge; it was, in lawyer's jargon, a court baron but not a court leet. It therefore did not present minor criminal offences nor maintain the assizes of bread and ale.

At Thorncroft as elsewhere the lord's rights reflected the strength of his coercive power relative to the tenants' capacity for resistance; to say that they would vary with changes in that relationship is not to deny that they could develop an inertial force of their own. The very mechanism by which the college enforced its claims against its tenants reflected this balance—or imbalance—of forces. The college employed a chain of officers to implement its commands but at the lower end of the official hierarchy, which has a surprisingly shadowy existence in our sources, it was of course dependent on men who were themselves tenants. More significantly these officers acted within the framework provided by the manorial court. Thus the manorial court was central to the college's control of its tenants and its records are the principal source in which its policy towards them may be discerned. For there is little doubt that the college's officers had considerable initiative and authority in the conduct of the court. But at the same time the suitors to the court collectively had functions and rights which could not easily be by-passed or overthrown. Even for the discovery and declaration of its rights the college was dependent on the formal knowledge of the court.[11] The records of the court do not generally reveal where the initiative for particular decisions or actions lay and they doubtless conceal a good deal of discussion, manoeuvre and pressure; but none the less they give a real insight into the role of the college in the lives of its tenants.

THE WARDEN AND FELLOWS OF MERTON COLLEGE

Merton College was a corporate landlord governed by written statutes— statutes composed, moreover, in the great age of the direct exploitation of estates. The statutes of 1274 placed the warden (*custos*) of the college at

---

[11] On the college's surveys of its manors and the role of the tenants in their composition see Aston, 'Merton', 313–21, based on my 'Surveys of the Manors of Merton College before 1400' (typescript 1976), esp. 16–21.

the head both of its resident scholars and of the officers charged with the administration of its affairs, whether internal or external. In reality as in the statutes the warden was deeply involved in the management of the college's estates and required a considerable degree of technical exper- tise.[12] Long-serving wardens like Peter of Abingdon (1264–86), John of Wantage (fellow 1291–9, warden 1299–1328), and Robert of Tring (fel- low 1313–28, warden 1328–51) must have acquired a detailed knowledge of a wide range of agricultural and tenurial matters.[13] One of the warden's main duties was to visit the college's manors each year to assess the har- vest. It was this statutory annual visitation, often supplemented by further visits in the course of the year, which provided a constant framework for the personal transaction of business between the warden and the college's tenants. This recurring if sporadic personal contact between the warden and even the lowliest tenants at Thorncroft is a marked characteristic of the college's relationship with the peasant community, and it derived from the college's institutional nature. While it is easy to see that the lord of a single manor might have preserved close personal links with his tenants, it is difficult to imagine that the heads of many lay or even ecclesiastical estates of a size comparable to that of Merton College would have exercised a similarly close personal supervision of their tenants over several generations.

There can be no doubt that the warden was present in person at some sessions of the court. On 3 February 1289 for example it was recorded that 'Luke Tailor came to this court and did fealty before the warden for the tenement which he claims to hold of the said warden'. At this same court a widow was granted entry into her husband's tenement 'by the warden's special grace' pending an investigation by the steward of its correct reversion. The warden certainly visited the manor on occasions other than meetings of the court, and some references in the court's proceedings to business conducted by him probably relate to such visits. Decisions reached in these circumstances are not normally registered in the records of the court, which may thus understate the personal element in the relationship between the college and its tenants.

Even when he was present in person in his own court the warden was

---

[12] Statutes of 1274, esp. lines 17–18, 52–65, 74–6, 94–5, *Merton Muniments*, 22, 23–4, 25, 26. On the role of the warden see too J. R. L. Highfield, 'The Early Colleges' in Catto and Evans, *The Early Oxford Schools*, 231, 255; Aston, 'Merton', 331–3.

[13] Cf. A. B. Emden, *A Biographical Register of the University of Oxford to A.D. 1500* (3 vols.; Oxford, 1957–9) i. 4, iii. 1908, 1978–9; on Abingdon see also Highfield in *Early Rolls of Merton*, 1, 61, 70.

far from omnicompetent. A dispute concerning succession to a free tenement was held over to another day because not enough freemen were in
attendance.[14] Conversely, however, the warden is most frequently mentioned when cases respecting free tenants were reserved for his next
visit—not necessarily at a session of the court. The men in question were
often among the college's most substantial tenants and the warden may
have considered it prudent to deal with them personally. Indeed it is very
plausible that a large proportion of the cases in which matters concerning
free tenants were referred to the warden in person arose when free tenants exercised a right of appeal directly to the lord in person.

This personal exercise of lordship was not confined to the college's
more substantial free tenants, nor indeed were the unfree entirely excluded. For example, while the steward was empowered to admit new
tenants to their holdings on behalf of the college, it was only natural for
the warden to do so when he happened to be present in court and on
occasion he personally admitted men even to very modest tenements.
Thus at the court of 28 October 1318 Robert Crynewyne was admitted
to an unfree tenement of a messuage and an acre of land and Richard
Wylekins to a curtilage in the presence of Warden John of Wantage. The
personal element was most persistent in regard to the act of homage, and
tenants were sometimes admitted by the steward while their homage was
reserved for the warden in person. It is difficult however to determine
whether or not homage could be received only by the warden in person.

The warden's activities in the court were not simply formal, as may be
seen in some of the examples already cited. Presumably the cases reserved
for him, which were probably dealt with out of court more often than not,
involved him in real negotiations with his tenants, some of them very
humble. And from time to time—admittedly very infrequently—a particularly difficult case seems to have called for his special authority. In
1296 the warden was called upon to untangle a mess of his own creation.
At the court of 12 November 1294 the villein half-yardland formerly held
by William Neel had been granted on an eight-year lease to Roger
Shoterich, but less than two years later, on 21 March 1296, William's son
Henry came to court and claimed his father's holding. This was evidently
too much for the court, which declared that because this tenement had
been granted to Shoterich by the warden the matter should be reserved
until the warden was present.

Little is known of the social origins of the early fellows of Merton

----

[14] See p. 233 below.

College, but it is very possible that few came from families which exercised manorial lordship in their own right. Although they represented a well-endowed corporation the warden and fellows may not have been as far removed socially from their tenants as many lords who held estates of comparable size. In the period before 1350 the fellows certainly played an important part in the administration of its estates and often visited its manors, including Thorncroft, but they were more likely to supervise agricultural operations or scrutinize accounts than to deal with the tenants.[15] Manorial courts were sometimes held by a fellow of the college, but this seems to have been all but unknown at Thorncroft.[16] It is not always possible to know the activities of fellows recorded as visiting the manor, but apart from a visit by Simon of Iffley in 1336 there is no explicit record of a fellow holding the court of Thorncroft or intervening in its proceedings.

THE STEWARD

If the early wardens of the college certainly took an active part in the management of its properties, they were none the less dependent on professional estate officers, notably their estate stewards—the *yconomi* of the statutes, though the word normally used in the college's documents is *senescallus* rather than the classical *oeconomus* (*economus*, *yconomus*). This dependence was probably increased about 1297, when the single steward responsible for all the college's properties in southern England was replaced by several stewards, each responsible for a group of manors and therefore presumably having a closer grasp of the particular conditions of their more limited area of responsibility.[17] The complexity of the administrative structure and the names given to offices within it could vary between estates of differing type and size. A steward of a lay magnate like Isabella de Fortibus, countess of Devon and Aumale, or Roger Bigod, earl of Norfolk, would be a much grander personage than any of Merton's stewards, both in the responsibilities he bore and in his own social standing. On their estates an officer comparable to one of Merton's local stewards, having oversight of relatively few manors, would be termed not

---

[15] Cf. Aston, 'Merton', esp. 333–5, 342–5.
[16] For example the court of the college's manor at Barkby in Leicestershire was held by Richard of Hagbourne in 1311 and 1314–15, by Richard of Medmenham in 1346–7 and by Medmenham and John of Reynham (subsequently chancellor of the university) in 1347–8. MCR 6568, 6502, 6523, 6524. Cf. Emden, *Biographical Register* ii. 847, 1255, iii. 1570–1.
[17] See Aston, 'Merton', 326–31. John de Brok served briefly as a local steward at Thorncroft as early as 1285: cf. pp. 224–5, 253 below.

a steward but a bailiff.[18] The steward of Merton's lands in Surrey cannot be shown to have taken the close and regular interest in husbandry urged by such contemporary manuals of estate-management as *Seneschaucy* and *Fleta*, but his work is broadly recognizable in their other recommendations.[19] It is likely that from the college's earliest years the warden was frequently—perhaps usually—accompanied by the steward on his visits to the estates. It would be as unreasonable to doubt the steward's part in the framing of policy as to deny the warden's role in its implementation.

The steward normally presided over meetings of the manorial court. The very first record of a court at Thorncroft which survives is headed 'the court of Thorncroft [on 1 May 1279], Richard of St John steward'. The steward is not named in the heading of any other court, and it is in fact the manorial accounts of Thorncroft which confirm that the court was held by the steward, for almost every account before 1350 gives the expenses incurred by the steward in holding the court.

While the warden dealt with a certain amount of business out of court, it is clear that in court the college's chief representative and the most active protector of its rights was the steward. It is not to be expected that the records of the manorial court would identify every order made by the steward and every action initiated by him—his role was too central to the court's routine for that. But the few instances in which the steward is explicitly mentioned none the less give some impression of his activities in court.

Some of these merely show, quite unsurprisingly, that although he normally depended on the judgement of the court as to matters of fact the steward had certain discretionary powers as president of the court. Thus amercements might be pardoned by the steward, as in the court of 26 April 1294. It is likely that the assessment of amercements was carried out not by the steward but by special affeerors, although the existence of these officers is recorded in the proceedings only of 8 May and 8 November 1337, two men being named at each court. None the less at the court of 26 April 1294 an amercement was set after an appeal not to the steward, as might perhaps have been expected, but to the court itself

---

[18] N. Denholm-Young, *Seignorial Administration in England* (Oxford, 1937), 32–53, 66–85. The college's statutes use the word *yconomi* to cover a range of officers which might embrace manorial officers as well as stewards. They refer at one point to *yconomi seu ballivi, quocumque nomine censeantur*: statutes of 1274, lines 17–18, *Merton Muniments*, 22.

[19] *Walter of Henley and other Treatises on Estate Management and Accounting*, ed. D. Oschinsky (Oxford, 1971), 264–9; *Fleta*, ed. H. G. Richardson and G. O. Sayles (3 vols., Selden Soc. 72, 89, 99, 1955–84), ii. 241–3; cf. P. D. A. Harvey, 'Agricultural Treatises and Manorial Accounting in Medieval England', *AgHR* 20 (1972), 178–90.

(*petierunt taxationem curie*). The routine duties of the steward also included the granting to parties in dispute leave to reach a settlement (*licencia concordandi*) as in a court held in 1309 or 1310.

The court of 27 November 1333 witnessed an exceptionally interesting episode which demonstrated that the close local knowledge of the steward and his authority as the lord's representative were sufficient to overturn the judgement of a formal inquisition by the court's suitors. An inquisition declared that William ate Bergh, a free smallholder, had taken into his own cultivation a small portion of the lord's land. But the jurors were ordered to go back to the land in question in the presence of the steward and bailiff, and when they did so they found that he had appropriated much more of the lord's land, and for more than three years. It is a fair guess that the steward's immediate informant was the bailiff and it is hard to believe that information which was accessible to the manorial officers would have eluded the jurors. More likely the jurors were prepared to shield their fellows but failed in this particular case.

The steward had authority to admit men to tenements whether on short-term leases or a more permanent footing, and probably did so at all courts unless the warden happened to be present in person. It is clear that the steward had authority to take villein tenements in hand for default. It was reported on 14 April 1306 that 'William Meydestane, the lord's bondman, has not performed the service due from his holding and it is therefore decided (*consideratum*) by the steward that the said land should be taken into the lord's hand'. No doubt it was only the explicit mention of the steward that was unusual, for it was surely the steward who directed all the many inquiries into tenants' title to their land which form perhaps the single largest class of business recorded in the proceedings of the court. Like the warden the steward dealt with some business out of court. At the court of 27 June 1302 Richard ate Chert was required to answer why he had not brought Richard ate Haselette to court to show title to his tenement as Chert had undertaken at the previous court of 20 March. Chert replied that after that court the steward, Robert of Walton, had permitted Haselette to show his muniments out of court, and that the steward had inspected them in the cemetery of Leatherhead.

Another of the steward's functions, and one that was absolutely crucial to the efficient administration of the college's estates, was the supervision of the manorial officers. To a large extent this supervision concerned agricultural matters but the records of the court also say something about the dealings of the college's most lowly representatives with its tenants. Furthermore, even the investigation of agricultural matters can sometimes throw light on the relationship between the manorial officers and the tenants.

THE REEVE OF THE MANOR

By far the most important of these officers and the one whose activities are most fully recorded was of course the manorial accountant, the man who was directly responsible to the college for the profits of the manor. Until 1349 the college's manor of Cuxham in Oxfordshire was normally in the care of a reeve (*prepositus*) and the two men who successively held this office between 1288 and 1349 were both drawn from the very top stratum of the manor's unfree tenants.[20] The substantial hereditary holdings of these men must have assured them of a relatively strong position in relation both to the college and to their poorer neighbours. The pattern of recruitment at Thorncroft however was significantly different. Reeves of the type familiar at Cuxham were not unknown at Thorncroft. Gilbert Broun, who was reeve of Thorncroft at his death in 1272, was probably a member of the villein family of that name which held a yardland around 1279 and long afterwards.[21] At the court of 2 August 1322 Simon Broun, who had been admitted to an unfree half-yardland in 1319, was chosen (*electus*) for the office of reeve and took the oath; he was to remain in office at the lord's will, and the whole villein homage stood surety for him, 'as is proper'. The formal wording tells us little about the way in which the choice was made. In the event Broun remained in office for one year only.

But Thorncroft was also entrusted to officers who were not the tenants of substantial customary holdings; these men were termed, apparently indifferently, either serjeant (*serviens*) or bailiff (*ballivus*). The reeve Gilbert Broun was followed in successive years by Henry Cook, Robert Gardener and Robert of Stanton, each of whom was described as serjeant.[22] Despite the differences in their status, by this date the duties of a bailiff or serjeant were essentially the same as those of a reeve. Vinogradoff's view that 'in every single manor we find two persons of authority', namely the bailiff and the reeve, representing respectively the lord and the village community, derived more from thirteenth-century handbooks of estate management—notably *Seneschaucy* and *Fleta*—than from actual accounts. These manuals described a system which may once have been normal but had become exceptional by the last quarter of the thirteenth century, and in this respect they were probably somewhat out of date even as they

[20] Harvey, *Cuxham*, 63–74 and 133.
[21] MCR 5688 (account 1271–2); cf. the rentals listed in Appendix 7.2.
[22] MCR 5635 (1272–5).

were written. More familiar in surviving manorial accounts is the arrangement envisaged by the anonymous late thirteenth-century *Husbandry*
possibly associated with Ramsey Abbey: 'manors which are supervised by
bailiffs, and where they have no reeve besides the bailiff'. On Merton's
manors—as was usual by the later thirteenth century—the manorial bailiff or serjeant was an alternative to a reeve, not his resident supervisor.[23]

Already in Robert of Stanton's term of office as serjeant some rent was
being received and cash paid to the warden by Simon of Burford, whose
name appears again and again in the records of the next fifty years or
so and who for much of that time must have seemed, to the tenants of
Thorncroft at least, the principal representative of Merton College. Burford
is a local placename and Simon was probably a local man. By about 1279
at the latest he held a villein half-yardland in the manor of Thorncroft,
though he was not himself of villein status, as the manorial court confirmed after his death in 1323.[24] He was reeve by 1278–9 (possibly by
1275–6) and although he was replaced by a serjeant between 1282 and
1286 he was reinstated as reeve in 1286–7. From 1291–2 he was normally
described as lessee (*firmarius*) though he was occasionally styled reeve or
serjeant and there was presumably considerable continuity in the real
nature of his position. He probably retained responsibility for the manor
until October 1308.[25] Soon after leaving office Simon of Burford became
a pensioner of the college, perhaps in recognition of the continued usefulness of his unrivalled knowledge of the manor, its fields, and its tenants.
Between 1310–11 and 1320–1 he received gifts of grain and payments
in cash of up to 13s. which were sometimes described as wages (*vadia*).
From 1315–16 some 5 acres of his land were sown and harvested along
with the demesne barley, and he received in return a corrody of four
quarters and about 2 bushels of barley each year, this being roughly two
thirds of the produce of his land in these years.[26]

[23] Vinogradoff, *Villainage*, 317–18; *Walter of Henley*, 104–5, 200–1, 268–81, 290–1, 442–
3; *Fleta*, ii. 244–51; *Manorial Records of Cuxham*, 33–4; Harvey, *Manorial Records*, 5–6;
Denholm-Young, *Seignorial Administration*, 32–4. W. Cunningham in *Walter of Henley's
Husbandry*, ed. E. Lamond (London, 1890), pp. xii–xiii.

[24] J. E. B. Gover, A. Mawer, F. M. Stenton, and A. Bonner, *The Place-Names of Surrey*
(EPNS 11, Cambridge, 1934), 81; MCR 4122, 5786ᵛ and 5777c (*c.*1279); court of 24 Nov. 1323.

[25] MCR 5690 (1278–9), 5692, 5737, 5693 (1281–2), 5738 and 5694–7 (1282–6), 5698 and
5739 (1286–7), 5699–5701, 5790 (1291–4), 5702, 5704–5, 5741, 5740, 5706 (Oct. 1308–July
1309); *Early Rolls of Merton*, 274. There is some uncertainty about the dating of the
accounts between 1301 and 1308. A lease of Thorncroft to Simon of Burford for three years
from 24 June 1303 is printed from MCR 632 in 'Medieval Deeds of the Leatherhead
District', ed. W. J. Blair, 8 pts in *Proc. Leatherhead and District Local History Soc.*, iv (1976–
86), 30–8, 58–62, 86–96, 118–25, 150–7, 170–81, 203–19, 268–74.

[26] MCR 5744 (1310–11), 5707–8, 5743, 5709, 5745 (1314–15), 5746–50, 5710 (1320–1).

The long career of Simon of Burford as reeve and lessee of Thorncroft illustrates the ways in which the college tried to control its manorial officers and its tenants. Simon was made responsible for the tenants in part by the simple expedient of obliging him to act as surety for men who were defaulting in their obligations to the college; the frequency with which he did so, especially in difficult cases, distinguishes him from the tenants of other similar holdings. It was clearly the reeve, bailiff, or lessee who bore the main responsibility of enforcing the court's decisions. His duties evidently included the issuing of summonses and the taking of sureties. He was amerced on 19 January 1294 when Maud *Rubea* claimed that she had not been summoned and on 9 November 1290 because he had not taken a surety from Robert Deghe to prosecute his suit against William Shepherd. A more burdensome task still was the levying of distraints, on which the court's authority was largely dependent. Failure to levy a distraint ordered by the court was usually followed by the amercement of the officer at fault and renewal of the order to distrain; this was a particularly vulnerable point in the chain of the lord's authority, where theory had to be translated into practice, and the steward or other superior officers of the college could not afford to neglect lapses in the implementation of distraints. A slightly different procedure was adopted at the sessions of 14 September and 3 November 1307 when Burford was instructed to implement two renewed orders to distrain under the penalty of two shillings; it appears that the distraints were levied and that Burford therefore escaped these relatively heavy penalties. It seems that in some instances Burford tried unsuccessfully to distrain, but in others it is clear that he made no attempt to do so. On 2 October 1293 he was amerced because he had failed to distrain on the holding of William Wilkelot although he could have done so. Such failures to distrain may have been due to favour on the reeve's part but they may also have been caused by fear. It is of course very difficult to determine whether or how the reeve used his position to shield his associates from the sanctions of the manorial court.

Likewise the court's proceedings say little about the passive and active resistance which its officers must have encountered, though occasionally some evidence comes to light. Thus it was reported to the court of 3 February 1288 that Walter Gedding had refused to surrender a horse in distraint (*denegavit distrinctionem*) and two of his men (*manupasti*) had ambushed the reeve (*fecerunt forestallum Symoni preposito*). As early as 7 November 1283 it had been reported that Gedding had taken a lease of 10 acres without licence, and by 9 February 1290 he had been distrained by no less than fifty sheep in order that he should answer to the lord in a plea of trespass, but Nicholas Broun (a junior manorial officer) had released this distraint, contrary to the reeve's prohibition, and was amerced accordingly. On 13 July 1291 it was ordered that Gedding was to be distrained (by a *superstogium nigrum*) in respect of an entry-fine, and on 8 November 1292 an inquisition found that he held 13 acres on lease but deferred its findings as to his other holdings, if any, to a later date; meanwhile of course he was to be distrained, if anything of his could be found on the lord's fee. On 12 November 1294 Simon of Burford acknowledged that he had again fallen foul of the formidable Walter: he had taken a horse as a distraint on Gedding's tenement but had returned it to him on the strength of his own surety and had failed to bring Walter to court. It is clear that a relatively powerful and wealthy man who held land outside the manor was successfully intimidating the men responsible for enforcing the college's authority.[27]

But if the college relied on its reeve to control its tenants it also had recourse to its tenants as a check on the activities of the reeve. The method employed might be a formal inquisition in the manorial court as to the reeve's conduct. Such an inquisition reported on 31 October 1289 that Simon of Burford had discharged his office well and faithfully in every particular, and added that anyone who had said otherwise to the steward or warden had acted out of malice. Whether the jurors had been influenced—by fear or favour—to conceal shortcomings or even malpractice on Simon's part, it is likely that this judgement was taken into consideration when the manor was granted to him on lease in 1291. The college continued to consult the court about Burford's activities when he had assumed the role of lessee. An inquisition of 7 May 1297 found that all the arable, whether under winter or spring corn, had been properly sown with good seed.

Another aspect of the reeve's affairs which might call for attention was his custody of the lord's land in regard to tenurial rather than agricultural matters. Although it was the steward who was empowered to grant land on lease it was the reeve or bailiff who was the more immediate and

---

[27] On 22 June 1295 an inquisition declared that Gedding held 15½ arable acres for 6s. rent and suit of court. This was probably the land in Polesden Lacey (two miles west of Mickleham) which in 1322 passed from Maud Gedding to John Ellerker, as recorded at the courts of June–Nov. 1322. According to an inquisition of 28 Oct. 1311, he had held the manor of Leigh, some seven miles south of Leatherhead, jointly with his wife Maud, besides a moiety of the manor of Bramley, about twelve miles to the south-west: *Calendar of Inquisitions Post Mortem and other Analogous Documents Preserved in the Public Record Office* (1904–), v. 192–3. He was sheriff of Surrey and Sussex in 1303 and 1307: D. Burns, *The Sheriffs of Surrey* (Chichester, 1992), 53.

effective guardian of manorial land. The proceedings of the court of 27 October 1306 show that on occasion the college detected irregularities in this sphere but at the same time they suggest that detection could be long delayed and perhaps completely evaded. For at this court it was revealed that Simon of Burford had occupied some of the lord's land without authority for no less than ten years. Not only had Simon used his position to augment his own land, he had also demised villein land and leased small parcels of the demesne, apparently without informing his superiors and sometimes taking the profits for himself. It may have been the discovery that Gilbert Glovere, who was listed as one of the college's free tenants in the rental of 1319/20, had been admitted to villein land, as reported to this same court, that provoked a formal inquisition into the cultivation of the manor's villein land by men other than its customary tenants. On 26 January 1307 all the tenants were amerced for concealing that William ate Capele had cultivated an acre of the land of John Akenoc (an unfree half-yardlander) without permission from the steward or bailiff. There is a suggestion that the steward had been informed of this arrangement by Gilbert Glovere, whose own illicit lease had been detected in the previous year. It appears that once discovered most of the unauthorized leases were not cancelled but regularized for a small fee.

It is not possible to know exactly how well Simon of Burford served Merton College, still less to discover how much he profited from his official position. It can hardly be doubted that he managed to pull the wool over the eyes of his superiors on many occasions, to the benefit of himself and quite probably to that of his fellow tenants, and practices which escaped the scrutiny of these officers will thus go unrecorded in the sources; but the court's proceedings show that the college was able to detect many kinds of misconduct on the part of even so experienced and knowledgeable a reeve as Burford. And his financial responsibility also appears to have been discharged satisfactorily, for while his final account opened with arrears of seven pounds, his closing liability was only 16*s.* 2¼*d.*, some of which may have been allowed at his petition.[28] At the court of 10 October 1308 Simon was pardoned an amercement because he was poor (*pauper*). He may well have been suffering from a temporary lack of liquidity if his arrears had been paid in cash rather than written off by the college, but it is hard to credit that poverty would normally have been his lot while he was reeve and lessee of Thorncroft. Unfortunately the sources

<hr>

[28] MCR 5740.

reveal almost nothing about Burford's economic position in those years. He held a customary half yardland, the annual money-rent of which amounted to 18*d*. but was remitted while he was reeve (as presumably was the labour-rent). He also held the smallholding known as Ringestane for an annual money-rent of 2*s*. 4*d*. which was not, however, similarly remitted. Burford had his own barn (*grangia*) which in 1319–20 was leased to another tenant for two shillings.[29] It is conceivable that his free personal status and background may have made him a more difficult and independent subordinate than a man of unfree birth would have been. While the extent to which Burford took advantage of his position to exploit or to conspire with his fellow tenants and the degree of his success in lining his own pockets at the college's expense remain matters for guesswork, the provision that the college made for him in his retirement is sufficient testimony to its belief that Simon's service had been satisfactory.

THE BAILIFF OR SERJEANT OF THE MANOR

Once Simon of Burford had been relieved of the administration of Thorncroft the college turned away from the practice of entrusting the manor to one of the more substantial customary tenants serving as reeve. Of the nine men known to have accounted for Thorncroft between Burford's retirement and the Black Death only Simon Broun, a villein half-yardlander, served as reeve (1322–3) rather than bailiff or serjeant. Six or seven may have come from outside the manor. The short tenure of office of most of Burford's successors is also notable. The longest-serving of the nine was William Blakeloke, an unfree cottager who was bailiff probably from 1329 to 1332 and again from February 1339 until his death early in 1349. While it is conceivable that the college had difficulty in finding a customary tenant competent to assume the post of reeve, it is more likely that these appointments represent a genuine change of policy.

Broun and Blakeloke were tenants, and William le Lepere (bailiff 1332–6) was quite probably a local man.[30] It is perhaps precisely because the other bailiffs were outsiders that little is known of their status and origins. Their names suggest that Ralph of Kibworth had been recruited from the college's manor of Kibworth Harcourt in Leicestershire, and that John of Elham was a native of Elham in Kent, the church of which had been appropriated to Merton College, just as John of Cheddington, serjeant of

[29] MCR 5750.
[30] For earlier Leperes see 'Medieval Deeds of Leatherhead', iv. 95, nos. 93 (MCR 643), 96 (MCR 916). According to the rental of Thorncroft of 1333 William le Lepere held only a rood of free land.

Leatherhead 1282–6, had presumably come from Cheddington in Buckinghamshire, where the college had a manor.[31] Whatever their place of origin it was relatively common for bailiffs to move from one of the college's properties to another.[32] It is to be presumed that the bailiffs drawn from outside the manor were more or less professional administrators and that they were of free status. The college was unable to encumber each incoming bailiff with the arrears, often quite substantial, accumulated by his predecessor, though it could pursue him for his own arrears when he had left office.[33] The purely administrative character of the links between the peasant community and the bailiffs assigned to the manor by the college is emphasized by the lack of reference in the court rolls to any of them before his appointment as bailiff and the appearance of only one of the seven men in question after his term in office. They were thus very much the college's men and free of local loyalties and interests.

Richard Wylekins, the one member of this group who certainly remained at Thorncroft when he had left office, is especially interesting in that he settled on the manor even though he was able to acquire no more than a few small parcels of land. Wylekins rendered his final account for the manor in July 1311 but at the court of 27 June 1314 it was found that John Akenoc had leased two half-acres of land to him for a term of three years without licence; on 19 January 1317 Wylekins did fealty for a certain plot (*pecia*) of land which he had apparently acquired from a free tenant of the college; on 28 October 1318 he received a curtilage from the warden in person to hold at the lord's will for an annual rent of two shillings; by 1319/20 he was leasing half an acre and two curtilages for 2s. 6d. Wylekins's settlement at Thorncroft went beyond the acquisition of

[31] Harvey, *Cuxham*, 65 notes that one villein of Cuxham is known to have served as reeve of Cheddington and another as reeve of Holywell, the college's manor just outside Oxford itself.

[32] Simon of Burford served as reeve of Malden (Surrey) for a few months in 1299 (MCR 4641–2); William Blakeloke accounted for both Thorncroft and Farleigh (Surrey) for part of 1330 (MCR 5753) as did William le Lepere for the year 1332–3 (MCR 5716, 4837); William ate Doune, bailiff of Thorncroft in 1349–50, had already accounted for Farleigh in 1345–6 and 1347–8 (MCR 4846, 4848). William le Lepere accounted for Elham (Kent) from 1325 to 1331 (MCR 5280–5). Malden is some 7 miles north of Leatherhead as the crow flies and Farleigh is about 13 miles west, but Elham is much further afield, near Folkestone.

[33] Arrears of earlier bailiffs were received in 1326–7 and 1339–40: MCR 3656, 5720. On a lord's recourse against a defaulting bailiff, especially by action of account under the statute of Marlborough (1267) and the second statute of Westminster (1285) see Denholm-Young, *Seignorial Administration*, 151–61; T. F. T. Plucknett, *Statutes and their Interpretation in the First Half of the Fourteenth Century* (Cambridge, 1922), 84–5; T. F. T. Plucknett, *The Mediaeval Bailiff* (London, 1954), 25–30.

land, for he married the daughter of Ralph Smerehele, one of the college's free tenants. The date of the marriage is not recorded but by 10 March 1321 Smerehele had transferred a free tenement to Wylekins and on 2 April 1330 a messuage and half an acre reverted to Wylekins and his wife after his father-in-law's death. By 1333, when a new rental of Thorncroft was made, Richard Wylekins had been on the manor for 24 years and yet his recognized tenements were merely a messuage and three parcels of land amounting to 3½ acres; he also held at least one small plot of another manor in Leatherhead, for by about 1327 he held half an acre of the manor of Little Pachesham.[34] It is impossible to determine whether or not the college's other professional bailiffs were men of similarly slender resources, though it may be noted that on 17 October 1326 John the bailiff (John of Tackele) was twice amerced for trespasses committed by his animals. William le Lepere, who died in office in 1336, was a man of some substance despite his negligible recorded landholding in Thorncroft, for in 1336–7 the college received forty ewes by his bequest and 6s. 8d. from his executors in place of a bed.

The bailiffs (or serjeants) who followed Simon of Burford at Thorncroft appear to have been disciplined in much the same way as Burford had as reeve and lessee. All except William le Lepere (1332–6) and John of Elham (?1336–9) were amerced for failing to distrain. Like Burford these later bailiffs encountered repeated difficulties in levying certain distraints, and it was still the steward who directed and disciplined the bailiff. At the same time, of course, the steward was ready to reinforce the authority of his bailiff whenever necessary. Thus on 10 March 1321, when Reginald ate Grene was bailiff, a tenant who had removed two horses (probably taken in distraint) from the lord's park at Thorncroft 'against the will of the bailiff and without consulting anyone' was obliged to pay a fine of twenty shillings. To challenge the authority of the bailiff was to question that of the lord. The working relationship between steward and bailiff is well expressed in an entry in the proceedings of the court of 29 December 1320 concerning a 6-year lease of land, when Roger Deghe 'made an agreement with John of Aperdele, the steward, and Reginald his bailiff to take all that land'.

The change to the appointment of professional bailiffs instead of traditional reeves avoided the risks of employing a man who might use his authority (and perhaps the college's live and deadstock) to the benefit of his personal holding or in the interests of his neighbours. Conversely, however, a free bailiff with no tenurial association with the manor was,

---

[34] 'The Early Manorial Records of Leatherhead', iii. 228–9, 234–7, 280–1, 286–7.

to a far greater degree than the unfree tenant of a substantial customary holding, likely to abscond when he ran into difficulties or accumulated alarming arrears. And it is not impossible that several bailiffs of Thorncroft departed in such circumstances. Similarly, although a reeve was not directly dependent on the lord for his status and livelihood in the way that a professional bailiff was, his villein tenure and the accessibility of his land and possessions gave the lord a ready means of exerting pressure should he fail in his duty.

By choosing as bailiff William Blakeloke, the hereditary and unfree tenant of a cottage and an acre of land, the college may have been trying to find a satisfactory compromise between a reeve and a free bailiff brought in from outside the manor.[35] Blakeloke may have been the officer in charge of Thorncroft between July 1329 and July 1331, though the only account that survives from this period is his interim account for both Thorncroft and Farleigh for part of 1330 which does not state his office.[36] The court's records (notably 30 November 1331) reveal that his title was bailiff. He returned to office in February 1339 and continued as bailiff or serjeant until his death some time before 3 April 1349, when he was succeeded for the remainder of the accounting year 1348–9 by his son, also named William. The proceedings of the courts between July 1343 and February 1348 are not extant, but there is enough in the courts of 1329–32 and 1339–43 to show that while Blakeloke's duties were essentially the same as those of his predecessors as reeve and bailiff, his position as a customary tenant laid him open to characteristic temptations and at the same time gave the college specific means of redress.

William Blakeloke succeeded his father John at the court of 14 April 1306, and he must have been of mature years when he first assumed office in 1329 or thereabouts, but his social and economic status within the community would not have been comparable to that of villein half-yardlanders. On 2 April 1330 Blakeloke was amerced for concealing for a long time that one of his fellow cottagers had encroached on the lord's land. Blakeloke also used his position to favour his own family, for on 21 December he was amerced 12*d*. because he, his wife, and children had gathered the lord's corn. In the case of a smallholder like Blakeloke with a family to feed, such an offence may have been born not of greed but of

[35] For his holding see the rentals of 1319/20, 1320/1, and 1333; the annual rent was 2*s.* and some labour-services, and he was classed with the (unfree) *coterelli*. By 1320 he held on lease for 2*s.* 2*d.* a further acre behind his curtilage: MCR 5777d (rental 1319/20), 5750 (account for 1319–20).

[36] MCR 5753.

necessity. In the time of Reginald ate Grene, a free bailiff, the whole homage of the villeins had been charged on 6 August 1319 with raising for the bailiff 7s. 7¼d. arrears of rent from a villein tenement then in the lord's hand (*ista pecunia levatur citra proximam curiam ad opus Reginaldi ballivi*). There was no need to observe this nice distinction between the accountability of the customary tenants as a group and that of the bailiff when the bailiff was himself unfree. Thus at the court of 30 November 1331 all the customary tenants undertook (*manuceperunt*) to satisfy the lord in respect of 50s. in arrears from the time when William Blakeloke had been bailiff; if William defaulted the money would be levied from the goods of the tenants. This remedy would hardly have been available when a free bailiff defaulted and it may well have been considerations of this kind that persuaded the college to reinstate Blakeloke as bailiff in 1339.

JUNIOR MANORIAL OFFICERS

Examination of the career of William Blakeloke leads to investigation of an extremely important but poorly documented sector of the college's administrative machinery, one that might be termed the infrastructure of junior manorial officers. For between his replacement as bailiff by William le Lepere about 1332 and his reappointment in 1339 Blakeloke served as beadle (*bedellus*) and in that office played a central part in the college's relations with its tenants. On 11 November 1334 Blakeloke, explicitly described as beadle, was amerced because he had declined to distrain on a tenant. In this case as in others the duties of the beadle coincided to a large extent with those of the bailiff. And it is hardly to be expected that the bailiff would have been able to cope with all the business arising from the proceedings of the court in addition to his agricultural responsibilities without the assistance of deputies. Beadles and other manorial officers of lesser rank, together with the reeve or bailiff himself, were charged with bringing the lord's authority to bear on its tenants. They were acting on behalf of a distant lord against men who were not only their neighbours but also, within wide but real divisions, members of the same social class.

The great obstacle to the analysis of the activities of the junior manorial officers is that the sources take their existence and their functions so much for granted. They are not neglected by the manuals of estate management, but as ever these works cannot be assumed to mirror actual practice in every case.[37] At any time it must have been well known who

---

[37] See for example *Walter of Henley*, 280–1; *Fleta*, ii. 258–9. Cf. Denholm-Young, *Seignorial Administration*, 34; Homans, *English Villagers*, 290–7; Bennett, *Life on the English Manor*, 178–82.

held which office, and as a consequence men are often designated by their office without their name or by name but not office. It is impossible to know, for example, whether or not there might be more than one beadle at any time or whether, in many instances, a man is acting in an official capacity or merely on an *ad hoc* basis. Nor should it be assumed that the same functions were exercised consistently by men with the same title. It is apparent that beadles often remained in office for several years and that the same man might occupy the position more than once. Henry Akenoc was described as beadle at the court of 1 June 1312; although Roger Newenham was appointed to the same office on 20 January 1316 Henry Akenoc was again designated beadle on 10 March 1321 and 2 August 1322. Similarly the election of junior officers is recorded occasionally but by no means systematically. Thus at the court of 22 June 1295 Nicholas Broun and John Akenoc were chosen by the whole court to collect the year's rent and to answer for it, but no more is heard of this office. In fact it seems that Broun had been performing this duty in conjunction with Simon of Burford as early as 1285–6, while John of Cheddington had been serjeant. Money-rent for Michaelmas term 1311 and payments in place of the tenants' work at harvest were collected by Henry Akenoc, presumably as part of his duties as beadle.[38] At the court of 20 January 1316 the customary tenants chose Roger Newenham for the office of beadle and he took the oath (*elegerunt Rogerum de Nywenham ad officium beddelli & est juratus*). Other men undoubtedly served as beadle in the period 1279–1349 but no other election to the office is recorded in the numerous extant court rolls. The fact that junior officers were formally nominated by the tenants is interesting whether or not the lord had a say in their appointment. It would be hard, however, to establish that these officers were essentially chosen by and for the community. The court's records are themselves concerned almost exclusively with the interests of the lord and business transacted between tenants figures in them hardly at all. The manorial officers are accordingly represented primarily as the lord's agents; the courts of 10 March 1321 and 1 August 1330 for example considered the conduct of 'the lord's beadle'.

The beadle was especially active in the routine but none the less vital matter of the levying of distraints, though it is of course his failure in this respect which is generally recorded. The probable intimidation of Nicholas Broun by Walter Gedding, a powerful outsider, has already been mentioned.[39] Similar factors may have been at work in a case described on 10

---

[38] MCR 5697 (1285–6), 5707 (1311).   [39] See pp. 213–14 above.

March 1321. Henry Akenoc, the lord's beadle, had been ordered to distrain William Ewell, a free tenant, in respect of suit of court. Henry had duly taken a horse in distraint but was in mercy because he had then released it without the bailiff's permission. That this amercement was pardoned by the steward would be consistent with a background of intimidation rather than collusion. This was not only the lowest but also the weakest link in the chain of seigneurial authority. A graphic description of the difficulties which might be encountered by junior manorial officers when they attempted to implement the decisions of the court is to be found in the proceedings of the court of 15 November 1302. John of Burford claimed that 'when he came to Bronesdone as the lord's bailiff to take a distraint from Richard Hammond, the said Richard came and took stones and attacked the said John and inflicted other outrages on him and drove off that distraint of 20 sheep'.

Although Burford is termed bailiff it is almost certain that he was not the manorial accountant at this time but was in fact the beadle. Indeed the word *ballivus* was used rather loosely for a range of manorial officers and the word *ballivi* was sometimes applied to the manorial functionaries as a group. Thus in 1287–8 an officer who was said not to have summoned a tenant to court was designated both bailiff and serjeant; he must have been a beadle, for Simon of Burford was reeve of Thorncroft at that time. Like the reeve or bailiff the beadle received orders from the steward. On 14 November 1335 it was found that William Blakeloke, probably then beadle, had failed to obey the steward's instruction to guard the corn in Candeleslond. It is possible that the duties which elsewhere were entrusted to a hayward (*messor*) may at Thorncroft more often have fallen to the beadle or perhaps the reeve. It was reported to the courts of 21 December 1331 and 22 July 1332 that the *messor* had impounded animals found in the lord's pasture; they were in due course delivered to their owners by the steward. These specific references to the office of hayward are however exceptional. On 1 August 1330 Robert Crynewyne, beadle, was pardoned for falsely stating that one man was the surety of another— an item which throws a little light on the role of the beadle in the routine procedures of the court. In February 1331 Crynewyne was pardoned an amercement 'because he was in the steward's service'. He may well have accompanied the steward to assist him in the transaction of his business outside the manor, but it is quite feasible that the beadle was thought simply by virtue of his office to have been in the steward's service. In short it seems probable that while the reeve or bailiff who accounted for the manor was responsible for implementing the court's directives, he was in practice assisted by subordinate officers whose appointment, status, and activities are not generally recorded in the court's proceedings.

The holding of a minor manorial office was certainly made less burdensome than it might have been by the frequent pardoning of the amercements which were almost inevitably incurred by these officers (on the whole amercements were not often pardoned at Thorncroft). But unlike the reeve, who received a regular allowance of grain, the more junior manorial officers do not seem to have received a regular stipend, nor was their rent remitted. However, the manorial accounts record occasional payments of cash or grain to customary tenants, and these are almost invariably to men known to have held some manorial office. For example Robert Crynewyne received a bushel of wheat by order of the warden in 1311–12, 1312–13, 1313–14, and 1314–15; in 1312–13 Henry Akenoc received a quarter of barley and in 1323–4 a gift of 12*d.* from the warden; in 1334–5 one bushel of wheat was given by order of the warden to William Blakeloke, who was probably serving as beadle at that date, and another bushel to his sub-bailiff, who was not named. So strong is the correlation that it is tempting to think that such a payment is of itself evidence of official service.

It would have been a quite unremarkable situation had the manorial offices been monopolized by the handful of families which constituted the upper stratum of the unfree tenantry, that is those which held whole or half-yardlands. And indeed Nicholas Broun, who seems to have acted as beadle or sub-bailiff in 1290 and who was elected collector of rents in 1295, was the tenant of the manor's only unfree tenement which consisted of a full yardland; and Roger Newenham, whom the customary tenants selected to be beadle in 1316, was an unfree half-yardlander. But John Akenoc, who was also chosen to collect rent in 1295, his name having been added to Broun's, only entered the unfree half-yardland previously held by John Eme after 1297; and Henry Akenoc, who was beadle in 1312 and 1321, was an unfree cottager. The officer named Gilbert who discharged the functions of a beadle in 1288–9 almost certainly was not a half-yardlander but was quite probably the Gilbert le Ferun recorded as holding a messuage and an acre of land around 1279. William Blakeloke, successively bailiff, beadle, and then bailiff again, was a hereditary unfree cottager. Two further men who served as beadle were granted unfree tenements temporarily in the college's hand. John of Burford, who was beadle by 1302, had taken a half-yardland at will in 1289 and in 1302 leased two half-acres from the half-yardland of Adam Meydestane for a term of four years; between 10 October 1308 and

7 October 1310, when it was claimed by Adam's son William, the entire Meydestane holding was held by a John of Burford, probably the beadle's son. At the court of 28 October 1318 the unfree smallholding once held by William le Grey and then by his widow Gillian la Grey, then in lord's hand, was regranted by the warden in person to Robert Crynewyne.[40] Crynewyne was certainly acting as beadle in 1330 and 1331 and held the cottage in 1333, but may not have been alive on 14 November 1335 when John the son of William le Grey successfully claimed it by hereditary right. It is striking that these manorial officers held land not by hereditary right but at the lord's will. Crynewyne in particular must have been very much the warden's man and even more dependent on the lord than the free bailiffs employed by the college in this period.

OTHER TENANTS IN THE COLLEGE'S SERVICE

The college called upon the assistance of its tenants in matters other than those arising from the proceedings of the manorial court, and in these instances the tenant did not necessarily hold any formal manorial office. Some of the manor's free tenants, for example John of Leatherhead, lord of the adjacent manor of Little Pachesham, were important local personages to whom it was prudent to make gifts from time to time, whether for help in particular matters or for their general goodwill. Tenants might be engaged to supervise agricultural operations, as in 1322–3 when Roger of Aperdele, a free tenant, answered for the grain threshed by piecework and for the sowing of 85 acres with wheat.[41] On occasion the college's officers received assistance from a free tenant in respect of legal or official business, as in 1292–3 when Adam of Aperdele went to London with Simon of Burford, the lessee of the manor, and Peter the vicar, apparently to secure the return of a royal writ from the under-sheriff of Surrey. As the free tenant of a yardland Aperdele may well have had experience of official affairs on his own account. Sometimes the local royal officers whom the college sought to influence were themselves free tenants of Thorncroft. Thus a schedule of expenses for 1291–2 names Walter le Hore, a free tenant of Thorncroft, as collector of the king's fifteenth.[42] The college might well seek to recruit men of this kind into its more permanent service. The John de Brok whose expenses in holding the

---

[40] See pp. 241–2 below.
[41] MCR 5751; for his tenure see the court of 10 Mar. 1321 and the rental of 1333.
[42] MCR 5790 (1291–4), 5752 (1328–9); for Aperdele's holding c.1279 see MCR 5786ᵛ and 5777c.

court of Thorncroft are recorded in the account of 1284–5, where he is described as steward, presumably belonged to the substantial local family of that name. It is probable that he then held only an acre of meadow of the manor of Thorncroft, but on 27 October 1288 he became at least the nominal tenant of one of its villein half-yardlands; in addition to the customary rents he was responsible for the celebration in Leatherhead each year of a mass for the soul of Walter of Merton.[43]

Especially instructive is the career of John of Aperdele, the son and heir of Adam of Aperdele. By February 1293 Adam was dead and his 16-year-old son John was in the custody of John ate Legh; John came of age in February 1298.[44] It seems that John of Aperdele's management of his own affairs was from the outset very vigorous. By 17 January 1303—and probably several years previously—he had purchased a tenement to add to his inheritance and by 11 July 1317 he had leased villein land without permission; and the rental of 1333 testifies to the determination with which he continued to add parcels of free land to his patrimony. At an early date he was also active as a royal officer, for in the accounting year 1308–9 the serjeant of Thorncroft gave four bushels of wheat to John of Aperdele, the king's bailiff. Aperdele probably occupied this post as early as 1299–1300 when money was paid to William ate Brokhole and John of Aperdele on the instructions of the warden; William had been under-sheriff of Surrey in 1292–3, when John's father Adam had had dealings with him on the college's behalf. The college was able to take advantage of the official standing of its tenant, for in 1312–13 John of Aperdele and others gave advice on how to avoid having the manor's corn taken for the king's use. By 28 October 1318 Aperdele had been taken fully into the college's service as steward of its lands in Surrey. He was soon putting his knowledge of the royal administration to good account: in 1318–19 he went to Westminster to obtain from the royal exchequer a writ of respite in the payment of the twentieth and sixteenth from Farleigh and Malden.[45] John of Aperdele continued in the office of steward until his death, which was reported to the court of 15 June 1336; his experience in the royal

---

[43] MCR 5696 (1284–5); see too 5697 (1285–6). The Robert de Broc who held an acre of meadow of the college *c.*1279 was dead by 7 Nov. 1283. On the Hores and Broks see Blair, 'Early Middle Ages', 36–7. Merton sometimes recruited stewards for other parts of its estate from among its tenants: Aston, 'Merton', 327–8.

[44] See MCR 630, bond of 11 Feb. 1293; at the court of 7 May 1297 it was declared that John son of Adam of Aperdele would be of age, that is twenty-one years old, at the following Candlemas.

[45] MCR 5790 (1291–4), 5702 (1299–1300), 5706 (1308–9), 5743 (1312–13), 5749 (1318–19).

service allied to his local knowledge must have made him an extremely valuable servant of the college. And there is every likelihood that his links with the college were reinforced by the presence of his son at Oxford as one of the young scholars lodged in the town (*scolares in villa degentes*) by Merton College. There was a scholar *in villa* named John of Aperdele in 1314 and 1315 who was quite probably identical with the John son and heir of John of Aperdele who was said at the court of 15 June 1336 to have inherited and then sold his father's lands; at the court of 8 May 1337 he was referred to as John of Aperdele *capellanus*.[46] Thus John of Aperdele's successful career as a landowner and estate-administrator launched his son into a very different life which severed the association with the land John had inherited from his own father.

THE EFFECTIVENESS OF MANORIAL JURISDICTION

The role of the court as an instrument of seigneurial control was especially prominent at Thorncroft, where the manor did not coincide with a unit of settlement and the volume of business transacted between tenants was insignificant by comparison with that which touched the interests of the lord. The use of the manorial court imposed certain constraints on the lord's power but at the same time it probably rendered it more acceptable. While there is no doubt that the officers of the court were essentially the lord's men, and were sometimes so described, their authority may have had a wider endorsement. The court's proceedings do not reveal much about the composition of juries, and what they do say does not fall into a clear pattern. An exceptional entry relating to the session of 2 October 1293 names five jurors who were to inquire into several unspecified articles; four were certainly tenants of customary land and the fifth was soon to become a customary tenant if he was not one already. Inquisitions by the whole court were also common. On 13 January 1294 an *inquisitio per totam curiam* delivered judgement concerning

---

[46] Emden, *Biographical Register*, i. 39, citing MCR 3640–3; Emden suggests he may perhaps have been the John of Aperdele presented to the rectory of Little Laver, Essex, in 1319. Emden also notes (citing MCR 3656, 3664–6, 3668–9, 3671) that there was a scholar *in villa* named John of Aperdele between 1327 and 1337. In a bursar's account for 1330–1 (MCR 3665) he is said to be a relative of John of Aperdele, the college's steward in Surrey; another scholar in this category in the same account is the son of Robert of Gaddesby, the college's steward in Leicestershire. The proceedings of the court of Thorncroft of 2 Aug. 1322 refer to land formerly held by John of Aperdele *clericus*, whose identity is unclear. On the Aperdeles see too Blair, 'Late Middle Ages', 51–2, 54, 55.

a marriage beyond the lord's fee and a villein's unauthorized residence beyond the manor. On 14 March 1332 a jury of the whole court deliberated on the transfer of land between two free tenants. But juries consisting entirely of customary tenants are also common, and there is no doubt that on occasion they determined cases which affected free tenants. Thus on 8 November 1339 the customary tenants presented that Thomas Pynchoun had encroached on the lord's demesne and that John le Heyward had ploughed up a path between his land and that of John le Grey. Pynchoun and Heyward were free tenants, though Grey was not.

It is more or less impossible to know the degree of efficiency with which offences were detected and brought to court. In this regard the lord was dependent both on his officers and on the generality of suitors to his court. Instances have already been cited in which the steward discovered irregularities in the conduct of the manorial bailiff and concealment of offences (or at the least culpable negligence) on the part of jurors.[47] But the significance of cases such as these may be either that these practices were common and normally passed undetected or, alternatively, that their discovery was almost certain even though it might be long delayed. One aspect of the court's business which suggests a reasonable level of conscientious vigilance, if not necessarily total detection, is the amercement of men with animals known to have trespassed on the lord's land. The number of these amercements varies considerably from court to court—as no doubt did the number of trespasses—but the frequency with which these offences came into court implies an active guardianship of the lord's interests. In general, however, it is possible to consider only the court's action in respect of those matters which were brought before it.

A reading of the court rolls of Thorncroft gives the impression that the court's authority was accepted by its suitors and that claims by the college which were authorized by the court were not often resisted by the tenants. Perhaps this was merely because the tenants themselves played such an important and relatively independent role in the workings of the court that none but the college's more moderate demands would pass the court's scrutiny and meet with its co-operation. Whatever the reasons, neither the court's proceedings nor the manorial accounts hint that fines or amercements remained unpaid. Of course there were difficulties in compelling people to come to court to justify their actions, to show their charters, to pay arrears of rent—or simply to attend the court. The

---

[47] See pp. 210, 215 above.

problems of taking effective distraints have already been illustrated.[48] It was quite normal for orders to distrain to be repeated at many successive courts without the respondent's appearing in court, sometimes defaulting for several years. Robert Toune for example, against whom distraint was ordered at the court of 9 January 1328, did not appear in court until 29 November 1329, having failed to appear at either of the two intervening courts. This kind of judicial delay was characteristic of medieval England and reveals nothing about the courts of Merton College in particular. What is more significant is that while justice at Thorncroft was not especially swift it was none the less surprisingly sure. Long lists of defaulters are found in many courts and instructions to distrain against them were renewed at court after court, but these were by no means empty formalities. The nature of the distraints taken are, more often than not, undisclosed. But on occasion quite substantial distraints are recorded; quite frequently initial distraints which had been ineffective were augmented. A good example is the dispute concerning John of Aperdele and Adam Crol which arose at an unknown date before the court of 25 April 1301, when it was said that Aperdele had been distrained by the seizure of a horse and that more was to be taken. By the court of 29 November 1301 a horse and six bullocks had been taken from Aperdele, and a heifer and a calf from Crol; it was ordered that more was to be taken from each. This instruction had to be repeated at the court of 3 February 1302, and by 20 March 1302 Crol had been deprived of nine sheep in addition to his heifer and calf; this distraint was to be augmented yet again, and by 27 June 1302 a cow and two bullocks (the heifer and calf having aged significantly in the interval) and eight sheep belonging to Crol were in custody, besides Aperdele's horse and six bullocks. The dispute was duly settled at the court of 17 January 1303. Few tenants could have lightly disregarded the loss of such valuable animals for extended periods.

JURISDICTION OVER FREE TENANTS

A very large proportion of the proceedings of the court of Thorncroft in the period 1279–1349 records the efforts of the college to bring its free tenants to court in order to record and regularize the terms of their tenure.[49] The volume and the complexity of this type of business derived from the rapid and often extreme fragmentation of the manor's free tenements.[50] Indeed it seems that the frequency with which the court was

---

[48] See pp. 213–14, 221–2 above.
[49] This question is examined in greater detail in my 'Surveys', 33–5.
[50] See too Blair, *Early Medieval Surrey*, 77–83.

convened was in some years greatly increased to cope with the flood of inquiries concerning the occupation of free tenements. It was unusual for the court to meet more than four times in the year; it sat five times in 1306, 1307, and 1308. But it assembled seven times in 1323, eight in 1331, and five in 1332, dates which coincide with two distinct climaxes in the campaign to register the manor's free tenants. These investigations bore fruit in the lengthy and detailed rental of 1333. Although this was not the end of proceedings of this kind it is notable that the court sat three times in 1333, twice in 1334 and 1335, three times in 1336, twice in 1337, and only once in 1339, 1340, 1341, 1342, and 1343. The motivation behind this activity was presumably jurisdictional and administrative rather than financial. The rents in question were usually very small or even nominal and the college did not receive much by way of fines or amercements when tenants were formally recognized. The court was concerned to define how free tenements had been divided, how the old rent was to be apportioned between the new tenants, and who was to perform suit of court.

The numerous and frequently repeated orders to distrain which were engendered by this policy were, however, accompanied by the appearance in court of many free tenants whose tenure was duly determined. At the court of 17 March 1323, for example, the tenancy of the free half-yardland held by William Shepherd about 1279 was greatly clarified. Joan of Brademere did fealty for an acre of this land which she was holding at an annual rent of 4*d*. William the son of Richard Tannere did fealty for 2½ acres of the same land which he held in fee simple in accordance with a charter of his father, and his portion of the rent was set at 10*d*. yearly. Four further men had their rents fixed for portions of the tenement once held by William Shepherd and one of them, Thomas ate Novene, was made responsible for suit of court on behalf of all. It was then established that the king also paid 6*d*. each year for 3 acres of the same holding. Thomas ate Novene also did fealty for a parcel of land formerly held by Giles ate Boxe, a contemporary of William Shepherd.

A quite spectacular example of non-appearance which none the less demonstrates the great perseverance of the manorial administration concerns William Husee, lord of the manor of Norbury in Mickleham, who was in dispute with the college as early as 1313–14. By 28 October 1318 several directives to distrain Husee had been issued in order that he might show by what right he had occupied a parcel of land in the area known as Coledoune. The tenurial status of this land was clearly defined in the rental of 1333 which said that Husee held 4 acres at Coledoune which he had bought from Gilbert le Hore, 'who is the mesne tenant by military service between him and the lord'. None the less it was not until 8 May 1337 that Husee and his wife Isabel came to court and it was formally recorded that Walter son of Gilbert le Hore was to render to the college all services due from the land they held. Thus a series of orders to distrain Husee which spanned twenty years or more was finally ended. Since the rent of the whole yardland of which this land was a fragment was only a pound of cummin and the real tenurial situation was perfectly clear from 1333 at the latest, the rationale behind these innumerable orders to distrain must surely have lain in a sense of jurisdictional tidiness and not in any more immediately material consideration.

It was of course more difficult to bring effective pressure to bear on some tenants than others. It was reported to the court of 26 May 1323 that a directive to distrain either Elias Follere or Joan his wife to show by what right they occupied a shop (*shopa*) had remained ineffective because the bailiff had been able to find nothing he could take. At the same court there were contrary difficulties in distraining a man who was at the opposite end of the social spectrum, for two cows had already been taken from John Ellerker but more was to be sought. That Ellerker was a man to reckon with is confirmed by the proceedings of the court of 8 January 1325 which note that John ate Purie of Polesden, the reeve of John Ellerker at nearby Polesden Lacey paid a fine of two shillings in respect of suit of court which had been in arrears for more than two years and for the return of a horse taken as a distraint for the same; he also paid a shilling for respite of the payment of seven shillings in relief. Purie paid a further shilling on 31 March 1326 and at the court of 17 October 1326 Margaret of Gatwick was received as life tenant of the land in question and as the person responsible for its rent and services.[51] Other cases too were settled when the college accepted a subtenant who was to discharge the tenant's responsibilities towards the college. The opposite solution was adopted in the case of Edmund of St Clement, the parson of Mickleham, who by 10 March 1321 had been distrained by the taking of a horse in order that he might do fealty and homage. On 24 March 1322 St Clement appeared in court and stated that the only land he held in the college's fee was the half-acre he held freely at the will of Gilbert Toune and it was declared that for the college's purposes Toune was the tenant.

[51] Cf. n. 27 above. A king's clerk named John Ellerker was royal chamberlain of north Wales 1338–40 and 1341–3; John Pirie, king's clerk, held the same office 1343–5. T. F. Tout, *Chapters in the Administrative History of Medieval England* (6 vols.; Manchester, 1920–33) vi. 62.

Nor were the frequent directives to distrain those more distant and influential ecclesiastics, the priors of Reigate and Merton, merely empty words. It was reported to the court of 19 January 1317 that a certain Piers Auffray had come to reclaim a plough-horse (*affer*) taken in distraint from the prior of Merton (very probably from his local subtenant). And the prior of Reigate came in person to the court of 13 November 1296 to show by charter that he did not owe suit of court.

Occasionally defaulters had to pay amercements which were by no means nominal. Repeated attempts to distrain Roger of Stratton in respect of suit of court and rent due from his free tenement called Blakelond led to his appearance in court on 31 October 1319, when he was amerced 40*d.* for his many defaults. On 10 March 1321 Maud la Gavelere did fealty for part of the land once held by Giles ate Boxe and was amerced fifteen shillings for her many defaults. Nine years previously, on 1 June 1312, an inquisition had found that Gilbert Glovere and John le Gavelere were withholding the suit to the court of Thorncroft due from a house and 2 acres in the common field, which Giles ate Boxe had performed in his time. If John and his successor Maud had continued to default in this duty until 1321 this might well explain the weight of the amercement.

It remains true, however, that cases in which the court's authority was defied are very rare. Defiance should be distinguished from mere tardiness in coming to court. Refusal to accept the established procedures of the court and unwillingness to comply with its duly declared judgements should also be seen as distinct from infringements of the lord's rights and property, which were common. Walter Nighenight, the unfree holder of a quarter-yardland, showed scant respect for the college in an incident described at the court of 26 January 1307, for he had driven the lord's wethers out of the lord's pasture where they should have been grazing and replaced them with his own sheep. But even cases like this were fundamentally different from those in which men refused to accept the discipline of the manorial court, which was intended to protect the interests not only of the lord but also of the generality of tenants. Refusal to participate in the routine workings of the court is found in the proceedings of the session of 21 December 1331. All the bondmen were charged to determine whether or not a certain tenement was burdened with suit of court, but William Follere refused to take part (*contempsit adire*) and William Glovere joined the inquisition without having taken the oath and refused to do so (*contempsit iurare*). Amercements of 6*d.* were imposed on the cottager Follere and 12*d.* on the half-yardlander Glovere.

A case in which tenants went beyond the normal conventions was reported to the court of 10 March 1321. Roger of Aperdele had been distrained for suit of court by the taking of two horses but together with Nicholas the son of Richard Tannere he had retaken his horses from the lord's park. Tannere was said to have acted against the bailiff's wishes and without taking anyone's advice (*deliberatio*) and he may perhaps have been responsible for the impounded animals. For this offence against the lord (*transgressio illata domino*) he was fined twenty shillings, a crushing imposition on a smallholder.[52] The mere fact that he owned two horses shows that Roger of Aperdele was a man of far from slender means, but according to the rental of 1333 he held only a small parcel of land of the college, and it is difficult to establish his relationship, or perhaps identity with the Roger of Aperdele listed as holding not only this land but also more than two full yardlands of free land in the rental of 1357. Aperdele did fealty for his land but otherwise remained unrepentant (*tamen sanare defaltas non concessit*). There is no indication as to how further pressure was brought to bear, but the court's authority was swiftly reasserted and at the court of 31 March 1321 he placed himself in the warden's mercy in respect of his arrears and his breaking into the park and found four sureties that he would pay a fine which would be determined by the warden at his next visit. In the event the fine was set at no less than one hundred shillings. Both the extraordinary severity of the fine and the personal involvement of the warden reflect the seriousness with which this offence was viewed.

The proceedings against Aperdele conformed to a pattern common in more routine cases in that distraints were used to bring respondents to court while sureties (*plegii*) were used to ensure that any consequent amercement or fine was paid. Sureties were used to constrain both free and unfree tenants, though where an unfree tenant was concerned it was possible to make the whole body of customary tenants stand surety. Thus at the court of 14 September 1307 all the customary tenants were in mercy because they had collectively stood surety that Thomas Knotte, the temporary tenant of a customary holding, would make amends for all defaults outstanding from his predecessor's tenure of the holding. But sureties might also be used to bring men to court, even if they were

---

[52] Nicholas was the son but not the heir of Richard Tannere, who held both unfree and free tenements. William the son of Richard Tannere received 2½ acres of free land from his father by charter before 17 Mar. 1323 and inherited his unfree smallholding on 31 Mar. 1326. Nicholas held 2 acres of free land in 1333. By about 1300 Richard Tannere had bought 3 acres in the manor of Little Pachesham: 'The Early Manorial Records of Leatherhead', iii. 228–9.

wealthy non-residents like John Ellerker: on 24 November 1323 two free tenants were each amerced 6*d.* for failing to produce Ellerker in court.[53] Distraints and sureties could be used in conjunction, as in Ellerker's case, or alternately, when the sequence could become quite intricate. On 8 January 1325 one of Richard le Goldsmyth's sureties was amerced for failing to bring him to court to show title to his land and for failing to ensure the due return of a horse taken in distraint; Richard's second surety was not present at this court so he in turn was distrained to give satisfaction at the next court (he duly did so and that distraint was released). The proceedings of the manorial court of Thorncroft give the impression that the combination of sureties and distraint brought about a very effective—though not instantaneous—enforcement of the court's decisions. There seems to have been no need for external sanctions.

The lord's rights over free tenements were of course most apparent when succession to a tenement was in doubt or when the heir was a minor. Thus it was declared at the court of 3 February 1289 that Alice the wife of Robert ate Gosebrugge was to be admitted to her husband's tenement pending a decision by the steward as to who should rightfully inherit it, and that this concession had been granted 'by the warden's special grace'. Alice was formally admitted on 13 July 1291. Even in these circumstances it appears that the lord was dependent on the judgement of the other free tenants, and at the session of 3 February 1289 another dispute over succession to a free tenement was adjourned because insufficient free suitors were present (*quia curia non fuit plena nec sufficiens de liberis hominibus*). The heirs to this tenement were declared at the court of 30 June 1289 and the statement that the late tenant had held land from another lord besides the college seems to have prompted the steward to assert the primacy of the college's rights by claiming the *maritagium* of the new tenant, who he alleged was under age. In the case of small free tenements in particular it may not have been easy for the lord to know that an heir was under age. At the court of 27 November 1324 it emerged that John son of John Scot of Cuddington had held an acre while he was under age 'secretly and without the knowledge of the lord's bailiffs'.

In more normal circumstances the college had little control over the land held by its free tenants beyond the right to insist that all new tenants should be formally recognized—and of course that the appropriate rents should be paid. These rents could be far from nominal. About 1279

---

[53] See p. 230 above.

typical rents for the larger free tenements were 3*s*., 5*s*., and 6*s*. per yard-land (a few paid less but one as much as 8*s*.). By comparison a typical unfree half-yardlander paid 1*s*. 6*d*. or 1*s*. 8*d*. in money, though this was much less than the value of his labour-rent; the money-rents for unfree small-holdings of a messuage and acre of land were exceptionally high at 1*s*., 16*d*., or 2*s*., and they too bore a significant rent in labour.[54] For a free smallholder like Thomas Aldwyne, who held 2 acres of land around 1279, an annual rent of a shilling could have been a severe burden. And the obligation to attend the college's court, which was so zealously enforced, may have seemed unduly onerous to men to whom it had so little to offer. On occasion the court addressed itself to disputes between tenants, as on 19 January 1294 when Nicholas of Aperdele paid 6*d*. in order that the boundaries between his land and that of Richard Tannere should be measured and made known, but by far the greater part of the court's work was directed towards the safeguarding of the college's interests. And although the amercements imposed by the court were on the whole moderate, rarely exceeding 6*d*., they must have seemed substantial enough to most free smallholders, for whom they may often have formed a significant proportion of their real rent. On 5 June 1283 William Shepherd, listed as the free tenant of half a yardland about 1279, was in mercy for having concealed the sale of several portions of his land. His amercements were pardoned on account of his poverty, but he was subjected to a fine of 3*s*., of which 2*s*. 6*d*. was respited on the condition of his good behaviour. Here was a free tenant whose freedom had worn very thin indeed. An early attempt to extend the college's control of the manor's free land was successfully opposed by the free tenants. It was presented at the court of 22 April 1284 that Luke Tailor had cut down fourteen trees, evidently on his own tenement, 'against the prohibition of the lord's bailiffs'. Tailor, the free tenant of only 2 or possibly 3 acres, was however supported by his fellows who declared that he was not bound to answer for his free holding in the manorial court.

There are statements in a few courts which suggest that the college was scrutinizing the tenure of free land at Thorncroft in relation to the statute *Quia emptores* of 1290, which restricted the subinfeudation of land held

---

[54] The rentals do not value labour-services, but payments in place of their performance are often recorded in the accounts. Payments of at least 4*s*. 4*d*. would have been required for the remission of all the labour-services of a customary half-yardland in any year; the corresponding figure for unfree cottagers may have been about 1*s*. See e.g. MCR 5742, 5744, 5716, 5718. Where measured portions of free land are assigned exact rents in the rental of 1333 the rate is generally in the range 2*d*.–4*d*. per acre, and sometimes it falls still lower.

in fee simple. The statute was not retrospective and did not apply to subinfeudations effected before St Andrew's day 1290.[55] The earliest example is in the proceedings of the court of 24 April 1296, when it was ordered that the tenement of Ralph Shepherd was to be taken into the lord's hand 'until he should show how he bought it against the statute'. A more explicit statement survives from the court held on 14 April 1306: 'Richard ate Haselette was attached to come to show how he had entered the lord's fee . . . and came and showed his charter, and it was made before the statute, and it is allowed him.' Similarly at the session of 7 July 1311 Ralph Smerehele showed that he had been enfeoffed 'before the statute'. If this interpretation of these entries is correct, then this was another area in which the college had need of officers with a good and up-to-date knowledge of the law.

JURISDICTION OVER UNFREE TENANTS

It is the college's treatment of its unfree tenants, where of course its options were far wider, that reveals most about its conduct as a landlord and its impact on the local community. Around 1279 almost half of the college's tenants at Thorncroft were unfree, but between them these customary tenants occupied only a fifth or thereabouts of the manor's tenanted land.[56] None the less the money-rent paid by customary tenants amounted to nearly half that paid by free tenants. Although the exact figures for the years around 1279 are uncertain the balance was probably much the same as in the rental of 1320 or 1321 which sets the total of free rent at 63s. 11d. and of unfree money-rent at 30s.; these figures had hardly changed by 1357. If the value of labour-rent is also taken into account it becomes clear that there was little difference between the totals of free and unfree rent; in the years between 1310 and 1321, for example, twenty-nine shillings or so were received from customary tenants in lieu of harvest works alone. While these totals of rent were largely fixed by custom and did not alter significantly in the period 1279–1349, the contrast between the distribution of free and unfree land and rent changed notably in these years.

Throughout this period the customary tenements fell into two blocks:

---

[55] Plucknett, *Legislation of Edward I*, 102–8.
[56] Various factors make it impossible to give exact figures for tenants, land, or rent in the years around 1279. In particular, size of tenement is given only in MCR 5786[v], rent in MCR 5777c and status in MCR 4122. However, these complementary and nearly contemporary documents do not list exactly the same tenants (nor even the same number of tenants). In some instances it is also difficult to distinguish later additions to the original lists.

one of eight substantial virgated holdings (one full yardland, six half-
yardlands and one quarter-yardland) and the other containing seven one-
acre cottage holdings.[57] In the earlier years these cannot have seemed very
substantial by comparison with the manor's free tenements. In the scutage
list which probably dates from 1279 there are ten free tenements of one,
one and a half, or two yardlands in extent. There are also six free half-
yardlanders in the list, but few free smallholders. The fact that the prior
of Merton owed no rent for his two yardlands beyond the payment of
scutage and the tenant of a yardland and a half paid only a pound of
cummin annually helps to explain the disproportionate division of rent
between free and unfree tenants.[58] Here (as elsewhere) the distinction
between free and unfree smallholders may not have been especially sharp
in some regards, and the *kalendarium* of tenants compiled about 1279
includes seven unfree cottagers not with the *nativi* but with the *liberi
tenentes*.[59] This distinction between a relatively compact group of large
free tenements and a similar number of customary holdings which were,
on the whole, far more modest in size, was largely obscured by the
fragmentation of free tenements which characterized the late thirteenth
and early fourteenth centuries—and was under way even before 1279.[60]
By 1333 the twenty or so free tenants recorded around 1279 had been
succeeded by more than fifty new tenants, besides an uncertain number
of recognized subtenants. Only four of these free tenants of 1333 held a
full yardland or more, and less than half a dozen held half-yardlands. By
this date the vast majority of the manor's free tenants—whatever they
may have held of other lords—occupied only small shares of the college's

[57] In addition two unfree cottages which appear in the *kalendarium* of c.1279 were said to
be in the lord's hand by the rentals of 1319–21, 1333, and 1357. Although the tenants of
both these cottages are named in the *kalendarium* only one occurs in the scutage list and
neither in the near-contemporary rental. One was probably in hand as early as 1281–2 and
in the years 1283–6 its rent was allowed under the head *expense famulorum*, which may hint
at the real function of both cottages.

[58] The slightly different figures for virgated holdings c.1279 given by Blair, *Early Medieval Surrey*, 79 exclude holdings in Mickleham and Newdigate. In the later thirteenth
century the price of a pound of cummin might have ranged between 2*d.* and 10*d.* See
M. W. Labarge, *A Baronial Household of the Thirteenth Century* (London, 1965, repr.
Brighton, 1980), 93.

[59] The unfree cottagers were included with the customary tenants in the rentals of 1319/
20 and 1320/1, and in 1333 they followed the *nativi* in their own category of *coterelli*; their
unfree status is confirmed in the court's proceedings.

[60] Blair, pointing out that the scutage list of 1279 ignores free subtenants, notes the
mention of subtenants on a free half-yardland in a deed perhaps dating from about 1250–
60. Blair, *Early Medieval Surrey*, 80 and 'Medieval Deeds of the Leatherhead District', iv.
95, no. 93 (MCR 643).

land at Thorncroft, almost invariably less than 10 acres each and more typically 3 acres or less. As a consequence of this rapid disintegration of free tenements and of the long-term indivisibility of customary holdings, the eight unfree virgated tenements of Thorncroft must soon have appeared as the solid core of the manor's tenanted land. This development, coupled with the importance of the customary tenants in the running of the manorial court, both as a body and in the discharge of particular functions, underlines the significance of the college's close control of its unfree tenants—a significance which was not entirely dependent on the numerical strength of this group.

Within the unchanging framework of the fifteen unfree tenements the customary tenants formed a stable hereditary group. It seems that normally a tenement would descend from a deceased tenant to his wife if she survived him, and from her, according to circumstance, to their youngest son, their daughter, or to the widow's new husband. Under the practice of ultimogeniture or 'borough English', which was usual in Surrey, it was particularly likely that the heir would be under the age of majority, that is twenty-one; the precise rights of the widow relative to the inheriting son, however, are not absolutely clear.[61] In the natural course of events tenements fell vacant through lack of heirs, and only four of the customary tenants of 1357 can be identified as the patrilineal successors of the tenants who had occupied their land around 1279, though the total rises to six if direct matrilineal succession is included. Interruptions to the hereditary descent of tenements were no more frequent in the years around the plague of 1348–9 than, for example, in the 1280s. Thus eleven of the fifteen customary tenants in the rental of 1357 were either identical with tenants of 1333 or bore the same family names as their predecessors of 1333, and a twelfth held by reason of his marriage in 1340 to the daughter of one of the tenants of 1333.

It is on the occasions when customary land did not descend by the normal course of inheritance that the relative strengths of custom and seigneurial rights are revealed. The widow's right to a life-tenancy in her husband's holding was well established and was perhaps a natural concomitant of ultimogeniture. The lord's principal interest in the marriage of unfree widows or heiresses lay in the chance that they might take their customary tenement into the hands of a free man. The lord's rights were

[61] Compare the descent of the yardland of Nicholas Broun recorded in the proceedings of 4 Nov. 1316 and 9 Apr. 1331 with that of the quarter-yardland of William of Clandon registered on 3 Mar. 1294 and 9 Nov. 1305. For the prevalence of borough English in Surrey see Blair, *Early Medieval Surrey*, 85.

also diminished, if only slightly, when an unfree woman who was not likely to inherit any of his land married a free man. Before 7 February 1285 John Newenham obtained the warden's permission to marry Maud Est, who inherited an unfree half-yardland from her mother; none the less on 3 February 1288 Maud's mother was amerced 2s. for the unlicensed marriage of her daughter Alice. In the only other clear instance of a woman who was not a tenant requiring the lord's permission to marry the offence consisted in her failure to obtain the lord's licence to marry beyond the lord's fee.[62] There is no clear statement of custom in this matter, and perhaps in normal circumstances members of unfree families who were not themselves tenants or heiresses were not obliged to pay for permission to marry. But the threat to the lord's interests when a woman who held customary land was allowed to marry a free man are well illustrated by John Newenham's entry into the unfree half-yardland of Maud Est.

John Newenham paid an entry-fine for 3½ acres of free land on 14 September 1282, but his son had apparently disposed of this land before the compilation of the rental of 1319/20. On 14 April 1306 it was presented that John Newenham had illicitly exchanged half an acre of his free land for a more valuable half-acre of unfree land. The college's officers showed even greater alertness in detecting that John's son and heir Roger had transferred goods from his unfree to his free tenement, as reported to the court of 1 August 1307. In addition to the land he held of Merton College John Newenham held land in Mickleham of the manor of Little Pachesham from which he received rents of 6s. 4d. around 1300.[63] Roger and his son and heir, a second John Newenham, seem to have retained a very independent attitude and were for many years the college's most troublesome customary tenants at Thorncroft. On 1 April 1310 it was found that Roger was not residing on his customary land, which was to be taken into the lord's hand, and on 27 June 1314 he found sureties that he would promptly repair 'all the buildings which he holds in villeinage in Mickleham'. Again in 1331–2 it was found that Roger was not residing on his customary land and a penalty of half a mark was imposed for his persistent failure to repair buildings. Roger was succeeded in 1332 by his younger son John, who finally carried out the required repairs in 1337. Nor were non-residence and neglect of their

---

[62] Court of 19 Jan. 1294, Edith, daughter of Gilbert of Burford.

[63] 'The Early Manorial Records of Leatherhead', iii. 226–7 (he also held half an acre of meadow in Leatherhead). See also W. J. Blair, 'A Medieval Grave-Slab in Great Bookham Churchyard', *Proc. Leatherhead and District Local Hist. Soc.*, iii (1967–76), 141–3.

tenement the full extent of the Newenhams' insubordination. In ironic contrast with his election as beadle at the court of 20 January 1316, Roger Newenham was a leading defaulter in the performance of labour-services, having an especial distaste for harrowing and weeding the lord's land. The college's officers persevered in their efforts to discipline these unruly tenants and were eventually successful in each dispute, but it is difficult to escape the conclusion that these problems would hardly have arisen had the college not allowed a free tenant to enter a customary holding.

It must be conceded, however, that the college can have had little room for manoeuvre in these situations. Customary tenements inevitably descended to women from time to time and it was not to be expected that they would always find husbands within the small group of unfree families. In a few other cases therefore, and despite its difficulties with the Newenhams, the college allowed free men to enter customary holdings by marriage. William Glovere, for example, a free tenant, married Maud Akenoc, the widow of an unfree half-yardlander, without the lord's permission in or before 1325 but was accepted as joint tenant in 1326. Glovere's interest was subject to the rights of Maud's son John, who did not in fact claim his father's land after the death of his mother in 1336. Glovere died in 1348 or 1349 in occupation both of the Akenoc holding and his own acre of free land; by 1357 the customary land was again in the hands of a villein, William Neel. The same is true of the half-yardland which Walter Spray had entered in 1334 by marriage to the widow of William Boxere (ate Boxe). Spray too died in 1348 or 1349, and by 1357 the land he had held was occupied by Robert Boxere, presumably the heir of William ate Boxe.[64]

The succession of Robert Boxere satisfied both the lord's desire to keep unfree land in the hands of unfree men and the customary preference for succession by inheritance, but there were a few occasions on which the lord's interests conflicted with the principle of descent by inheritance. These suggest that while the college could temporarily divert the course of succession by inheritance it could not obstruct it indefinitely. On 12 November 1294 the tenement in Leatherhead once held by William Neel was granted by the warden for a term of eight years to Roger Shoterich, but on 21 March 1296 Henry Neel came to court and claimed his father's tenement; this difficult matter was reserved for the warden, as it had been he who had admitted Shoterich. On 13 November 1296 an inquisition of

[64] See proceedings of 17 Apr. 1325, 31 Mar. 1326, 25 Apr. 1334, 15 June 1336, 8 May 1337, and 28 Mar. 1348 and rental of 1357.

all the customary tenants declared that Henry was his father's heir in a messuage and half a yardland. But if the court could decide who was the rightful heir to a holding, only the lord could admit him to his inheritance, and the case was again held over until the arrival of the warden. The matter was still unresolved on 7 May 1297 and the record of its final outcome is lost, though Henry Neel was certainly in occupation by 1319/ 20. His right to succeed was not in question and it appears that the warden was using his authority to impede the due procedure of customary inheritance.

The college intervened more drastically in the descent of the unfree half-yardland which Adam Meydestane had held around 1279. Before his death about 1305 Adam's holding had perhaps begun to disintegrate as a unit of cultivation, for on 20 March 1302 John of Burford paid 3*d.* to lease two half-acres from Adam for four years. It is not clear when Adam died but it seems to have been his son William rather than his widow who briefly took nominal possession of his tenement. It was reported to the court held on 17 May 1305 that several named persons—including Ralph *clericus ecclesie* and Alice the widow of Adam Meydestane—had taken small parcels of the land which William had held (*que fuit Willelmi de Meydestane*) and it was ordered that these should be resumed into the lord's hand. At this and the next court on 8 July 1305 new leases of these or similar plots were granted, Alice again being one of the lessees. By 14 April 1306 the college had to accept that William Meydestane had entirely abandoned his holding, which was formally taken in hand; if he were to come and give satisfaction as to arrears of rents, however, it was to be returned to him. Meanwhile the college was not inclined to let such an asset stand idle. At the court of 11 July 1306 the tenement was valued and Thomas Knotte paid 12*d.* to be allowed to occupy it until Michaelmas 1307, but he proved unsatisfactory and on 14 September 1307 all the customary tenants were amerced as his sureties for all arrears. The tenement remained in hand until 10 October 1308, when Richard Broun, probably a non-tenant member of an unfree family, paid 12*d.* not to take it at the lord's will, but it was taken, and on the customary terms, by John of Burford—probably the son of the man of that name who had previously leased small parcels of it but was dead by this date. Hereditary right was not extinguished even when a tenant abandoned his holding leaving arrears of rent, for it was declared that any heir who came to claim this tenement would have to pay compensation (*custagium*) to Burford.

This deference to due inheritance was no empty formula, and on 7 October 1310 William Meydestane came to court and claimed his father's tenement; it is likely that he gained possession very soon after his appearance in court. The college's attitude to him may have been influenced by the behaviour of John of Burford, whose unlicensed sale of trees (especially elms) from the holding had been reported at the court of 1 April 1310. It may have been as an attempt to help and encourage William in his tenancy that the college lent him four bushels of oats in the accounting year 1310–11; it even appears that by 1 June 1312 he was filling some minor manorial position.[65] But William was soon in dispute both with the college and with his neighbours, notably Simon of Burford. There is also an echo of the earlier disintegration of the tenement in sharecropping leases of two half-acres of William's land which were authorized at the court of 19 January 1317. Whatever the exact circumstances, William Meydestane was formally deprived of his tenement on 22 February 1319, when it was declared that he had not paid his rent for more than a year and that he was not capable (*potens*) of maintaining the holding. All the unfree tenants were required to choose a capable landless bondman to replace him and duly nominated Simon Broun. Even now hereditary right could not be disregarded, but anyone who claimed the tenement as the heir of William Meydestane would have to satisfy Simon Broun in respect not only of his entry-fine of ten shillings but also of his expenses in restoring the tenement and of William's arrears, assessed at 7s. 7¼d. It is not possible to say with certainty whether Meydestane was forcibly ejected from his land or whether he had already abandoned it. The college's attempt to extract his arrears from the body of customary tenants, as ordered at the court of 6 August 1319, proved abortive.

The tenure of this particular customary half-yardland has been examined at some length because it reveals a great deal about the balance between seigneurial power and customs of inheritance at Thorncroft. The lord was entitled to insist on an adequate tenant on each of his customary tenements, but an unsatisfactory tenant might only be ejected after persistent defaults, and even then his heirs could not be thus disinherited. A similar case suggests that the hereditary rights of unfree cottagers were equally strong. Around 1279 Robert le Grey had held an unfree smallholding consisting of a messuage and an acre of land; on the death of William le Grey in 1316 these passed to William's widow Gillian. It was reported to the court of 11 July 1317 that she had demised (*tradidit*) the acre to various men without permission, and that it had been sown with barley; the tenement she had held (*tenuit*) was to be taken into the

---

[65] He was found responsible for the loss of a hen he had impounded.

lord's hand on account of its deterioration by her (*pro vasto & distrucione*). At the court of 28 October 1318 the tenement was granted by the warden in person to Robert Crynewyne, who was to become—or perhaps already was—a useful servant of the college. Crynewyne paid an entry-fine of 3*s.* and was to hold his tenement on the customary unfree terms; the whole homage stood surety for the restoration of the tenement to a good condition. Crynewyne was still in occupation when the rentals of 1319–21 and 1333 were compiled, but hereditary right again proved very resilient, for at the court held on 14 November 1335, eighteen years after the tenement had been taken into the lord's hand, John the son and heir of William le Grey asked to be admitted to the cottage and acre of land his father had held; an inquisition found that he was the rightful heir and of age and he was formally admitted at the following court on 30 January 1336.[66]

It is possible that the normal procedure for finding a new tenant for a vacant customary tenement was selection by the whole body of the customary tenants, as when Simon Broun was chosen to replace William Meydestane. The records do not of course reveal much about the actual mechanism by which the prospective tenant was selected. If agreement in advance between lord and tenant may usually be assumed, the consent of the nominee was not essential. When Richard Broun refused to take the vacant Meydestane holding in 1308 it was not recorded whether his name had been put forward by the lord or by the tenants. Whatever the exact procedure—and it would not often have been needed—it appears that the men chosen were generally members of the more substantial unfree families, and that by this means the upper crust of the customary tenantry strengthened its own position. The best-endowed unfree family at Thorncroft was that of Nicholas Broun, father and son, who held the manor's only full customary yardland throughout the period from about 1279 to 1357. The Richard Broun who refused the Meydestane half-yardland in 1308 was probably an elder son of Nicholas Broun. Presumably another member of this family was Simon Broun, who took this same half-yardland in 1319 and who held it in 1319–21 and 1333, as did a second Simon Broun in 1357. It is noteworthy that although the villein homage had been charged in 1319 to select a suitable landless bondman (*nativus non habens terram*) Simon Broun was not entirely without land for on 4 November 1316 he had done fealty for '3 acres of land that he holds in Stonycroft', perhaps the 3 acres of free land against his name in the

---

[66] On Crynewyne see also pp. 222–4 above. At Cuxham by contrast cottages were normally held for terms of lives: Harvey, *Cuxham*, 124–5.

rental of 1333. On 2 August 1322 Simon Broun was chosen to be reeve, all the bondmen being his sureties; once again the way in which the choice was made is not revealed by the formula in the court's proceedings.

The Broun family also had designs upon the customary land held by Simon of Burford. At the court of 22 November 1322, shortly before Burford's death, Simon Broun paid the large fine of two marks for entry into the unfree smallholding known as Ringestane, consisting of a messuage and acre of land, which Simon of Burford was surrendering to the lord. Broun undertook not only to maintain this holding in a better condition than previously but also to build a new house to replace the old one. Perhaps only a villein whose family already had substantial resources would have been in a position to take a holding on these terms. Simon Broun was in this way making provision for his daughter Joan, who was brought to the court held on 3 May 1323 to receive seisin. It was explained that Simon had bought (*adquisivit*) the holding for Joan but that it would remain in his keeping under villein wardenship (*nomine custodie native*). When Simon of Burford's death was reported to the court of 24 November 1323 it was found that neither Burford nor any of his kin who might otherwise inherit his customary land was a villein of the college and it was ordered that a more suitable (*melior et potentior*) landless villein should be chosen. Richard son of Nicholas Broun was nominated, the whole homage standing surety for his maintenance of the holding in good order and his payment of 10*s.* as relief. Once again the heavy cost of entering this holding must have severely restricted the number of men with any real hope of securing the tenancy. Richard Broun was still the tenant in 1357; by that date Joan the daughter of Simon Broun had been succeeded as the tenant of Ringestane by Edith Broun, though the relationship between the two is not known.[67] There is thus a very striking contrast between the list of unfree tenants around 1279, when Nicholas Broun held the only yardland, and that of 1357, when his son Nicholas Broun held that yardland, Simon Broun held a half-yardland, Richard Broun occupied another half-yardland, and Edith Broun was the tenant of an unfree smallholding. Similarly by 1357 not only had the customary half-yardland held by William Neel around 1279 passed from Henry Neel to Richard Neel, but a further unfree half-yardland was in the hands of another

---

[67] Simon Broun perhaps outlived his daughter, for when his death was reported to the court of 28 Mar. 1349 it was said that he held two holdings *in bondagio*: a messuage and 8 acres (that is his half-yardland) and a messuage and an acre. He was immediately succeeded in the latter by his wife, whose name is illegible, but may of course be identical with the Edith Broun of 1357.

William Neel. No doubt the college preferred to see its customary holdings concentrated in the hands of a few unfree families than allow them
to pass to free men.

The few landless villeins who managed to raise sufficient funds to
acquire vacant customary tenements were a lucky minority in what must
have been a large body of non-tenant villeins. It is most probable that the
fundamental cause of the extreme fragmentation of free tenements within
the manor was a real increase in population, and it is difficult to imagine
that the unfree population remained stable while the number of freemen
was rapidly increasing. The effect of a rise in the number of villeins
would not be a formal division of customary holdings but an increase in
the number of non-inheriting children and perhaps also a greater frequency of short-term or unofficial transfers of land. So long as the capacity of the nominal tenements to pay their full rents was not impaired, this
development did not conflict with the lord's interests and might even
reinforce them. Non-tenant villeins appear in the documents only rarely,
however, and it is difficult to assess their relationship to the households
and holdings of the nominal tenants.

What is certain is that non-tenant villeins were to be found at Thorncroft
and that the college insisted that they were subject to the personal incidents and obligations of villeinage. Their existence might only be noted
when they left the manor without permission. An early example is that of
Henry Eme, presumably a kinsman of the unfree half-yardlander John
Eme, who was reported on 19 January 1294 to have left the manor in
contempt of the lord and to be in the service of Lady Mary of Barnes;
the sureties for his amercement were John Eme and Nicholas Broun. It
was an obvious tactic for the college to attempt to exert control over a
departed villein by making a kinsman responsible for his conduct. On 25
April 1301 John Neel, who was presumably related to the unfree half-
yardlander Henry Neel but who never himself appears as a tenant, was to
pay an amercement of 3d. for his unlicensed departure and annual chevage
of 2d. Whether or not he paid these sums, it was ordered on 18 March
1308 that he should be distrained in respect of his absence from the
manor. None the less in the accounting year 1309–10 he received a loan
of 6 bushels of oats, which he repaid to the college in the following year.
Despite his apparent lack of any tenurial standing he was placed in mercy
on 8 November 1313 for failure to attend the manorial court; in addition
he was to be distrained for his chevage. The lord's loss was the greater
when a villein moved away from the manor permanently and took his
possessions with him. Thus on 25 January 1308 John Broun, doubtless a

kinsman of the yardlander Simon Broun, was amerced because without permission 'he had married beyond the lord's fee and resided (*abitavit*) there with the lord's goods'. It was less likely that an unfree tenant would leave the manor, but even this was not unknown, and it was reported on 3 February 1302 that William ate Broge had departed from his villein holding with his goods (*elongavit se & bona sua*); he was of course ordered to return. There seems to have been a more concerted effort to regulate the unauthorized absence of villeins in 1308, when John Broun, Richard Broun, and probably John Neel were to be distrained because they had left the lord's land. Richard Broun duly came to the court of 10 October 1308 and paid 12*d.* rather than take a vacant tenement, but nothing more is heard of the distraints of John Broun and John Neel. Indeed the appearance in court of Richard Broun may have been an isolated success in this context, for despite the evident concern of the college's officers over the illicit absence of its villeins from the manor, the manorial accounts suggest that no money was actually received under the name of chevage.

All that has been said so far about the college's dealings with its unfree tenants at Thorncroft testifies to its detailed supervision of the tenure and condition of customary land and to its careful enforcement of the personal obligations of the unfree. While it is very doubtful the college had much success in imposing its control on those members of unfree families who physically left the manor, those who remained seem to have been very firmly subjected to its authority. The range of difficulties the college might encounter in respect of its customary tenants, and the measures it was prepared to adopt in response to them are well illustrated by the case-histories of the Newenham and Meydestane tenements.[68] In view of the college's active regulation of these two holdings, the extreme rarity of similar interventions in the internal affairs of other tenements surely indicates the satisfactory maintenance of most customary tenements. On the few occasions when action of this sort was required, the procedure was rigorous. For example it was reported on 11 June 1281 that Adam Goldweg, an unfree cottager, had failed to repair his house as he had been directed; Simon of Burford (the reeve), William Neel (a half-yardlander), and Nicholas Broun (the yardlander) were named as sureties to guarantee that he would do so by Lammas, and this impressive combination was evidently sufficient, for no more is heard of the matter. Slightly more elaborate provisions might be necessary to bring comparable pressure to bear on a half-yardlander. On 20 October 1328 it was reported that

---

[68] See pp. 238–9 (Newenham) and 240–1 (Meydestane) above.

Richard Broun, the recently installed tenant of Simon of Burford's half-yardland, had failed to restore, or perhaps to build, a house on his tenement: the whole homage not only guaranteed his completion of this work but also undertook to supervise its progress day by day. The college had taken a different tack in 1322 or 1323 when it paid half a mark to Maud Akenoc, the tenant of a half-yardland, for the repair of her buildings.[69] A restriction on the sale of livestock by unfree tenants is known only through a single case in the proceedings of 25 January 1308, when Nicholas Broun was amerced for the unlicensed sale of a colt. The sale of horses was not of course an option which was open to many men—Broun's animal was priced at ten shillings—and the absence of further examples may be of economic rather than administrative significance.

RESISTANCE TO THE COLLEGE'S DEMANDS

How successful were the tenants in resisting the demands of their lord? This final and fundamental question about the college's relations with its unfree tenants at Thorncroft is largely unanswerable. It has already been argued that as the college's rights over its tenants were enforced primarily by the manorial court there were real constraints on the exercise of seigneurial power. Furthermore a tenant's most prudent approach to his lord's demands was not open defiance but circumvention without detection, and defaults which escaped the lord's officers do not appear in the documentation. The nature of the offences which were detected at Thorncroft strongly suggests that the college's manorial administration there was as alert and efficient as could reasonably have been expected, but doubtless there was a significant degree of evasion which cannot now be gauged.

Refusal to pay rent is clearly of central importance in this context, but even this cannot easily be measured. Although unpaid money-rent might be included in an undifferentiated total of a manorial accountant's debt to his lord, the accounts of Thorncroft do not suggest that there were substantial arrears of rent. It is unlikely that the holding back of rent would have left no trace in so full and informative a series of court rolls as that relating to Thorncroft before 1350. And indeed the proceedings of the court of Thorncroft contain numerous references to the non-payment of free rents. These defaults are open to different interpretations: some may represent real attempts to evade payment, but many may have arisen in the genuine confusion (on the part both of lord and tenant) surrounding

---

[69] MCR 5751, view of account 1322–3. On Maud Akenoc see too p. 239 above.

the apportionment of the rent of fragmented tenements.[70] By contrast the absence of all record of any action against customary tenants whose money-rent was unpaid—with the exception of William Meydestane, who defaulted entirely and seems to have abandoned his holding—is a relatively sure sign that unfree tenants did not withhold their customary money-rents or their lease-rents in money.

Labour-rent was another matter. While rent in labour was a lesser economic imposition than rent in money, since most peasants were short of money not labour, it was probably labour-rent which provoked the greater resentment. And if the retention of money-rent could only be concealed from the auditors by extreme ingenuity, they were almost entirely dependent on the reeve's own accounting for labour-rent. If the reeve failed to notice—or wilfully concealed—the fact that a tenant had not performed a particular service, there was little chance that his superiors would uncover the default. The sources do not describe the mechanism by which labour-services were enforced and supervised at Thorncroft, but if, as in other matters, the reeve's authority was sometimes delegated the opportunities for evasion would have increased.

Labour-rent at Thorncroft was defined in the rental of 1333. Although there was no week-work the services with which the principal customary holdings were burdened covered a wide range of agricultural operations and also the washing and shearing of sheep and the roofing of the lord's buildings. The services of the cottagers were more restricted, consisting mainly of harvest-works, with the addition of a little weeding and hay-making. The manorial accounts show that particular services might be remitted for a cash payment in any year. From 1310 until some time between 1328 and 1332 most or all harvest-works were 'sold' in this way—and the real cost of the harvest increased dramatically.[71] Otherwise most labour-services were actually performed in the years before 1350. It is therefore remarkable that although the court's proceedings survive from sixty or so years, the number of defaults in labour-services which they record is only about thirty, and nine of these relate to the Newenham family. There is no clear chronological pattern, except that very few cases were reported between 1279 and 1306, for most of which time the manor was in the charge of Simon of Burford, but the distribution between the various types of service seems to be more than random. No default in ploughing or digging (*fodiendum in curtilag'*) is recorded, nor in threshing,

---

[70] See pp. 228–31 above.
[71] The accounts for the years between 1328–9 and 1332–3 are not extant.

carrying straw from the barn, or making stacks; and but for the Newenhams
there would have been no reported absence from haymaking (twice) or
weeding (several times). Only once (on 2 July 1309) was a man amerced
for failing to come to shear the lord's sheep. It is especially striking that
only two refusals of harvest-works are recorded, at the courts of 14 September 1307 and 27 November 1333.

It is notable that the obligations entailing the carting of dung, the
collection of straw, helping with the roofing of manorial buildings, and
general carrying seem to have provoked more resistance than the much
more onerous harvest-works. Even here the total number of amercements
for non-performance is tiny, and the overall impression conveyed by the
extant sources suggests an astounding level of manorial discipline. But
the nature of some of the cases strongly implies that there was positive
resistance to these more marginal services, and that some defaults arose
from more than casual non-attendance. Indeed it is so implausible that
even casual non-attendance would have produced no more than one
default every two years that the rigour with which attendance was enforced must be called into question. Perhaps a considerable degree of
discretion, not to say laxity, in the supervision of labour-services by the
reeve or bailiff was expected and accepted. The manorial accounts do not
contain separate accounts of works, which would have been a sign of a
more thoroughgoing scrutiny of labour-rent by the college's auditors.[72]

Since cases of non-attendance are so rare, those which involve several
tenants strongly imply a collective decision. On 28 October 1325, for
example, the three half-yardlanders Simon Broun, Henry Neel, and
Margery the widow of John Akenoc were each amerced 1*d.* for not carting dung when summoned. The only other known offence of this kind
was reported to the court of 27 November 1333, when Roger Broun was
amerced 6*d.* for failing to provide a man to load the dungcart. On 15
October 1327 Henry Neel, William Glovere, and Simon Broun, all half-
yardlanders, were each amerced 3*d.* for not coming as summoned to
harrow when the wheat was sown; and on 8 May 1337 Walter Spray, John
Newenham, and Simon Broun were amerced for not coming as summoned

---

[72] The auditors were by no means entirely uninformed, for under 'sale of works' the
accountant specified which works were sold and he often added that the remainder had been
performed (typically *nichil quia fecerunt opera*). And he accounted in detail for food and
drink consumed by customary workers, sometimes giving the number engaged in each
operation, as for example in 1282–3, 1309–10, 1310–11 (MCR 5694 and 5738, 5742, 5744).
In 1335–6 (MCR 5755) it was noted that a free boonwork of 78 men and women had reaped
36 acres; in 1327–8 (MCR 5715) the auditors calculated the cost per acre of customary
ploughing and noted *deficit i acra anno isto*.

to harrow the lord's land. John Newenham and his father Roger also failed to harrow in 1309, 1331, and 1336.

Opposition to the obligation to assist in the roofing of the buildings of the *curia* was taken a stage further. On 13 November 1296 John Eme was amerced 3*d*. for not going to the roofing of the barn but he denied that he had failed to perform other work as summoned, and this claim was put to an inquiry. Evidently judgement went against him, for on 16 January 1297 he was amerced 3*d*. for not coming to work as summoned. His separate pleading as regards roofing service becomes more intelligible in the light of an entry in the proceedings of a much later court. On 27 November 1324 all the customary tenants were amerced because they had not come as summoned to help in the roofing of the buildings. The amercement was set at two shillings or more (the pence are illegible). In cases such as this, where the whole body of customary tenants was united, it must have been especially difficult for the lord to secure a heavy amercement. Indeed the generally low level of amercement imposed on tenants who did not perform labour-services (normally less than 6*d*. and often as low as 1*d*. or 2*d*.) may well reflect not the indifference of the lord but the support of their fellows. Despite the collective refusal of 1324 the obligation to help with roofing was clearly applied to the tenant of each unfree yardland or half-yardland in the rental of 1333.[73] But resistance continued, and on 1 July 1342 Walter Spray and William Neel were each amerced 1*d*. because 'they did not come to help the roofer (*tector*) for half a day'. A different collective refusal was recorded at the court of 8 November 1313, when all the customary tenants were amerced 12*d*. for refusing to gather straw. In this case the tenants appear to have been denying the obligation itself (*dedicunt opera eorum & negant de stipull' coll'*). Despite the amercement of five tenants on 4 November 1316 for not performing this service, it was duly enshrined in the rental of 1333 (*debet invenire i hominem ad colligendum stipulas*).

In these instances it is difficult to know whether the tenants were disputing the legitimacy of an existing practice or resisting the imposition of a new service, for no extant survey of Thorncroft defines labour-rent at an earlier date than 1333. It is possible that services like roofing and the gathering of straw were as firmly grounded in custom as other works, but were unpopular for reasons now unknown. The collection of straw, for instance, must have been backbreaking work and followed closely upon

---

[73] MCR 5779d (*debet invenire i hominem ad deserviendum tectori quandocumque necesse fuerit ad tegendum domos*).

the intense activity of the harvest itself. The obligations to load and cart dung and to harrow posed special problems for the tenants—and were especially beneficial to the lord—in that the tenants were expected to bring their own horses and carts; they were expected to participate in the carting of dung and in the spring harrowing for as long as was necessary to complete the task. Alternatively these may have been new obligations imposed on its tenants by the college which in 1333 were given the same status as more ancient customs. That not all the unfree tenants accepted the labour-rent set out in this survey compiled around Lammas 1333 is shown by the proceedings of the following court, held on 27 November 1333. According to the survey William Follere was an unfree cottager whose annual rent included 2_s_. in money and the provision of one man to reap for three days, being fed by the lord; in addition he was to send a man to a harvest boonwork (_libera precaria_) also at the lord's food. But at the session of 27 November William was amerced 2_s_. because he refused to send a man to the boonwork. The wording suggest that he denied the obligation itself (_dedicit servicium suum faciendum_) and contrasts with the next amercement in these proceedings, that of Roger Broun for failing to send a man to load dung (_pro defectu unius hominis_). Notwithstanding this refusal the obligation was also ascribed to Follere in the survey of 1357; and indeed the definition of labour-rent in 1357 follows that of 1333 almost word for word as regards every unfree tenement.

There is however some evidence that the unfree tenants of Thorncroft successfully resisted the imposition of one particular form of labour-rent, namely _averagium_ (carrying service). This obligation was important on the college's other manors in Surrey, Farleigh, and Malden; at Farleigh it was the subject of a dispute between the tenants and the steward which was finally resolved in the college's favour between 1280 and 1290. _Averagium_ was long-distance carrying, usually but not necessarily by horse, as is made clear in the surveys of Malden and Farleigh.[74] The usefulness of _averagia_ at Malden and Farleigh may have tempted the college to attempt to introduce them at Thorncroft. John Akenoc was amerced on 26 January 1307 and Henry Neel, another customary half-yardlander, on 14 September 1307, apparently for waylaying the bearer of a summons to perform carrying service (_subsedit summonitionem pro averagio faciendo_). Despite these two amercements no more is heard of _averagium_

---

[74] The survey of Malden probably of 1279/80 has _averabit semel in quolibet termino anni infra comitatem sine cibo & extra ad cibum_; the surveys of Farleigh of 1279/80 and 1289/90 both have _averabit infra comitatem & extra ad cibum dominorum_. MCR 4782 (Malden), 4889, 4890 (Farleigh). The dispute is described by Evans, 'Surveys', 19.

at Thorncroft and it is not mentioned at all in the surveys of 1333 and 1357. As with the generality of the college's rights over its tenants at Thorncroft, the level of labour-rent was largely determined by customs which had been defined (if not written down) before the acquisition of the manor by the founder. The balance between lord and tenant may not have changed sufficiently in the period between 1279 and 1349 to effect more than an extremely marginal adjustment to the level of labour-rent. The manorial documentation may not of course tell the whole story, but so far as can be seen the college's position was strong enough for it to impose its wishes on almost every occasion when labour-services were disputed. But, if the evidence concerning *averagium* has been interpreted correctly, peasant resistance was not so weak that the college could successfully exact whatever service it cared to claim.

CONCLUSION

As a lord Merton College had much in common with other ecclesiastical corporations, but it also had a particular character as a body of university clerks governed by statutes. The warden and fellows, who probably numbered between thirty and sixty in this period, constituted both a corporate lord and a large pool of literate administrators. Their responsibility for their estates involved even the most notable scholars among them—not always very willingly—in the detailed supervision of the running of their manors.[75] It is likely that particular fellows took a special interest in manors in the regions from which they themselves came, as in the case of Richard of Worplesdon, who visited Thorncroft often in the years before his election as warden in 1286, or William of Chelsham, who was a frequent visitor in the 1280s. But it was the warden himself who had the most regular contact with tenants, dealing in person not only with important free tenants but also with unfree smallholders and junior manorial functionaries.

The warden worked closely with his steward, a professional administrator who was often a more or less local man. The steward presided over the manorial court and in general was the guardian of the college's rights and interests. He compiled rentals, helped in the drafting of the manorial account, and supervised the manorial officers. The steward was not however

---

[75] On the number of fellows see T. A. R. Evans, 'The Number, Origins and Careers of Scholars' in J. I. Catto and T. A. R. Evans (eds.), *Late Medieval Oxford* (History of the University of Oxford, ii, Oxford, 1992), 492–3. For the reluctance of fellows to act as auditors of manorial accounts see the record of college meetings 1338–9 printed from MCR 4249 in *Merton Muniments*, 33–5.

a resident officer, and the day-to-day running of the manor, especially as an agricultural enterprise but also as a tenurial unit, was in the hands of the manorial accountant, whether reeve, lessee, or bailiff. The supervision of this man by his superiors was crucial to the college's control of its manor. Although the nature of their work was the same, there were characteristic advantages and disadvantages in the employment of an unfree reeve or a free bailiff, and Merton tried both at Thorncroft; the appointment of an unfree smallholder as bailiff was probably a compromise intended to make use of the best of both systems. If the reeve or bailiff was most obviously responsible for the management of the demesne he also played an important part as an officer of the manorial court. It was often the manorial accountant who served summonses, collected fines and amercements, or stood surety. He might be assisted in any of his functions by subordinates whose exact role is hard to discern. They might sometimes have acted on an informal and *ad hoc* basis, but they could occupy a recognized office, that of beadle for example, over several years. No doubt there was considerable fluidity in the division of responsibility as in the terminology. These junior manorial officers were sometimes the unfree tenants of whole or half-yardlands, but more typically they were unfree smallholders or the lessees of small plots. Indeed it is likely that minor officers were sometimes installed in small tenements in return for their service; like the free bailiffs under whom they served they seem to have been very much the warden's men. They may have received remuneration in the form of grain, and in addition they were likely to receive loans of grain. Despite their lowly status these men were responsible for the actual enforcement of the college's rights against its tenants, often men who were their social and economic superiors and were capable of giving them a very rough ride. They therefore needed the support of the steward and warden, who in turn depended on them for reliable information as well as the implementation of their instructions. The effectiveness of the college's jurisdiction depended on quality of the co-operation of its central and regional officers with its resident representatives.

Thorncroft was only the largest of three manors in Leatherhead, and it is likely that most of its free tenants—and a few of its unfree—held land of other lords in or beyond the parish. Furthermore some of the manor's free land lay in detached portions, and the tenants of these more distant holdings, Walter Gedding for example, could pose special difficulties. Much of the manorial court's work lay in tracing and registering changes in the tenure of large free holdings which had dissolved into small fragments. Despite the obstacles in its way the college was remarkably successful in obliging free tenants to come to its court to justify their tenure of small parcels of its land and to recognize their obligations as its tenants. But the college's relationship with its free tenants could be intricate and subtle. Sometimes they appeared as important neighbours whose goodwill was to be cultivated, or assistance sought, whether in their own right or as the local agents of other lords, including the king; they might even, like John of Aperdele, be taken into the college's permanent service. And like Aperdele they in turn might entrust the education of their children to the college. It is possible for example that John, Nicholas, Robert, and William Husee, recorded as scholars between 1328 and 1350, were related to the somewhat troublesome free tenant William Husee; or that Nicholas of Hambledon, a fellow of the college by 1277, was a member of the family of that name which held half a yardland of the manor of Thorncroft. When, at Easter 1287, Nicholas of Hambledon and John de Brok appeared on behalf of the college before the itinerant justices at High Wycombe they may in some sense have been neighbours in Leatherhead.[76]

The inherent conflict of interest between lord and tenant is of course much more evident in respect of unfree tenants. At Thorncroft the unfree tenants were less numerous and held less land than the free tenants but they were of great importance to the college, not least because of their value to the manorial economy. It was the college's policy to enforce in full the rights over its unfree tenants which it had received with the manor. This extended to the non-tenant members of villein families, and the lord's hold only loosened when villeins physically left the manor. When a tenant defaulted in his obligations the college could apply the usual range of sanctions, up to the formal resumption of the tenement into the lord's hand. No tenant, however, can be shown to have been physically evicted, and it is likely that a holding was only at the lord's disposal when the tenant abandoned it or died without an heir. Hereditary right to unfree land, whether in half-yardlands or smallholdings, was scrupulously preserved by the court; the lord might introduce a temporary tenant to a vacant holding for quite a long term, but the ultimate right of an heir would be upheld by the court. In the period between 1279 and 1349 a small group of villein families seems actually to have tightened its grip on the manor's unfree land. This was probably in harmony with the interests of the lord, who had experienced problems when unfree holdings had been held by free men. The college allowed its unfree tenants to

[76] Emden, *Biographical Register*, ii. 861 (Hambledon), 990 (Husee); *Early Rolls of Merton*, 213 (1287); cf. pp. 224–5 and 229–30 above.

sublet their land, so long as it was able to register and tax these transactions and provided that the ability of the tenant to meet his obligations
to the college was not impaired. There is no evidence of what might be
termed benevolent paternalism in the college's conduct, and its approach
to such matters as the remission of amercements or loans of grain appears
to have been pragmatic rather than charitable. In short its policy was
rigorously to exploit the obligations of its unfree tenants, so as to preserve
the structure of unfree holdings and its own rights and to draw a financial
profit from them.

In its dealings with both free and unfree the manorial court of Thorncroft
consistently secured eventual compliance. The use of amercement, fine,
surety, and distraint could be slow and cumbersome, but it proved very
effective. Perhaps the court was seen to be more than the instrument of
the lord. The role of the suitors as the repository of custom, jurors, and
assessors must have placed some check on the steward's ability to settle
every matter as the lord would have wished. The evidence concerning the
tenants' resistance to the claims of the college is particularly problemati-
cal. At Thorncroft as elsewhere the nature of the manorial documentation
tends to obscure subtle shifts in the balance between lord and tenant. It
has been suggested here that the manorial court dealt not with the routine
discipline of tenants performing labour-services but only with serious or
concerted challenges to the system. Conflict over a few specific services
continued intermittently over many years. For the most part the disputes
were finally settled in the college's favour, but carrying services, an obligation which the college had managed to impose on its other manors in
Surrey, was successfully resisted by the tenants of Thorncroft.

Appendix 7.1
Manorial Courts of Thorncroft 1279–1349

Calendar date	MCR	Mem.	Calendar date	MCR	Mem.
1 May 1279	5786^r		12 Nov	5781	15a
19 Nov	5781	1	4 Feb 1295	5781	15b
1 May 1280	5781	1	22 June	5781	15a
4 Dec	5781	1	24 Apr 1296	5781	16
11 June 1281	5781	2	21 Mar	5781	17
23 Nov	5781	2	3 July	5781	16
14 Sept 1282	5782^r		13 Nov	5781	16
5 June 1283	5781	3	16 Jan 1297	5781	18
7 Nov	5781	4	7 May	5781	18
22 Apr 1284	5781	4^v	25 Apr 1301	5781	19
7 Feb 1285	5732^r		26 Oct	5781	19
15 May	5732^r		29 Nov	5783^r	
31 Oct 1287	5781	5	3 Feb 1302	5783^r	
3 Feb 1288	5781	5^v	20 Mar	5783^v	
22 May	5781	6	27 June	5781	19^v
27 Oct	5781	7	15 Nov	5781	20
3 Feb 1289	5781	7^{r-v}	17 Jan 1303	5781	20
7 May	5781	8	20 May	5781	20
30 June	5781	8^v	17 May 1305	5787[1]	1b
31 Oct	5781	9	8 July	5787	1b^{r-v}
9 Feb 1290	5781	9^v	9 Nov	5781	21
9 Nov	5781	10	26 Jan 1306	5781	21^{r-v}
7 Feb 1291	5781	10	14 Apr	5781	22
11 Apr	5781	10	11 July	5781	22^{r-v}
13 July [1291]	5781	11	27 Oct	5781	23
6 July 1292	5781	12	15 Dec	5781	23
8 Nov	5781	12	26 Jan 1307	5781	23^v
2 Oct 1293	5781	13	26 June	5781	23^v
19 Jan 1294	5781	13^v	1 Aug	5781	24
3 Mar	5781	14	14 Sept	5781	24
26 Apr	5781	14	3 Nov	5781	24^v

[1] Numbers are not marked on the membranes of bundle 5787. The numbers used here are reckoned from the back of the bundle towards the front; a and b designate membranes stitched foot to head to form a single folio; mem. 19 is loose.

Calendar date	MCR	Mem.	Calendar date	MCR	Mem.
25 Jan 1308	5781	24^v	9 Feb 1321	5787	6^v
18 Mar	5784	1	10 Mar	5787	7
5 July	5784	1	31 Mar	5787	7^v
11 Oct	5784	2	24 Nov	5787	7^v
5 Nov	5784	2^{r-v}	24 Mar 1322	5787	8
27 Feb 1309	5784	2^v	c.29 June [1322]	5787	8
15 July	5784	3	2 Aug	5787	8^v
unknown date	5784	3^v	20 Sept	5787	8^v
1 Apr 1310	5784	4	22 Nov	5785^v	
2 July	5784	4^v	22 Nov^3	5787	9
7 Oct	5784	4^v	17 Mar 1323	5787	9^v
21 Oct	5784	4^v	3 May	5787	10
25 Feb 1311	5785^r		26 May	5787	10
7 July	5785^r		16 June	5787	10^{r-v}
29 Oct	5784	5	7 July [1323]	5787	10^v
28 Feb 1312	5784	5^{r-v}	1 Aug	5787	11
1 June	5784	5^v	24 Nov	5787	11
28 Nov	5784	6	27 Nov 1324	5787	11^v
8 Nov 1313	5784	7	8 Jan 1325	5787	12
26 Feb 1314	5784	7	17 Apr	5787	12^{r-v}
27 June	5784	7^v	28 Oct	5787	12^v–13
25 July	lost^2		31 Mar 1326	5787	13^{r-v}
5 Dec	lost		17 Oct	5787	13^v
8 July 1315	lost		15 Oct 1327	5787	15
6 Nov	5787	1a	9 Jan 1328	5787	15
20 Jan 1316	5787	1a	20 Oct	5787	15^v
4 Nov	5787	1a^v	15 July 1329	5787	15^v
19 Jan 1317	5784	8	29 Nov	5787	16
11 July	5787	4	2 April 1330	5787	16^{r-v}
28 Oct 1318	5787	2	1 Aug	5787	16^v
22 Feb 1319	5787	2^v	30 Sept	5787	17
16 June	5787	3	12 Feb 1331	5787	17^{r-v}
6 Aug	5787	3^{r-v}	5 Mar	5787	17^v
31 Oct	5787	5	9 Apr	5787	17^v
16 June 1320	5787	5^{r-v}	25 May	5787	17^v–1b^v
7 July	5787	4^v	15 June	5787	1b^v
29 Dec	5787	6	1 Aug	5787	14

^{2} The proceedings of three courts mentioned in the account for 1314–15 (MCR 5745) have not been located.

^{3} A few items in the proceedings of this court on MCR 5785^v are omitted from the copy on 5787, mem. 9.

Calendar date	MCR	Mem.	Calendar date	MCR	Mem.
30 Nov	5787	14	28 Oct	5789	7
21 Dec	5787	14^{r–v}	8 May 1337	5789	7^v
22 Feb 1332	5787	14^v	8 Nov	5789	1^{r–v}
14 Mar	5788^r		*19 Oct 1338*	*lost*[5]	
4 Apr	5788^r		8 Nov 1339	5789	2
22 July	5788^r		11 July 1340	5789	2
29 Oct	5788^v		15 May 1341	5789	3
16 Mar 1333	5788^v		1 July 1342	5789	4
3 July	5787	18	7 July 1343	5789	4^v
27 Nov	5787	18^{r–v}	*25 Nov*	*lost*[6]	
25 Apr 1334	5787	18^v	*8 July 1345*	*lost*	
11 Nov	5789[4]	5^v	*12 Nov*	*lost*	
9 Jan 1335	5789	5	*30 June 1346*	*lost*	
14 Nov	5789	6	*20 Oct*	*lost*	
30 Jan 1336	5789	6	11 Feb 1348	5787	19
15 June	5789	6^v	28 Mar 1349	5787	19^{r–v}
			2 Nov	5791[7]	

[4] Numbers are not marked on the membranes of this bundle; the numbers used here are reckoned from the back of the bundle towards the front.

[5] This court is mentioned in the account for July 1338–February 1339 (MCR 5719) but its proceedings have not been located.

[6] The proceedings of five courts recorded in the accounts from 1343–4 to 1346–7 (MCR 5758, 5724–6) have not been located. The accounts record no court in the calendar year 1344.

[7] Numbers are not marked on the membranes of this bundle; the numbers used here are reckoned from the back of the bundle towards the front.

Appendix 7.2
Rentals and Surveys of Thorncroft to 1357

MCR	date	description
5777c	c.1279	undated rental, probably somewhat earlier than May 1279; gives tenants' money-rents but not their holdings; free tenants not distinguished from unfree
5786ᵛ	c.1 May 1279	undated scutage list on back of court proceedings of 1 May 1279; probably compiled on or close to that date; gives tenants' holdings but not rent; free tenants not distinguished from unfree
4122	c.1279	undated *kalendarium* of tenants owing suit of court on all the college's manors; Thorncroft section probably compiled late in 1279 or soon afterwards; some later additions; gives names but not holdings or rent; divided between *liberi tenentes* and *nativi*
5777d	1319/20	undated rental giving holdings and money-rents of free tenants and *custumarii* (including cottagers); also list of leases (headed *firma*) which matches manorial account for 1319–20; the same account records the cost of parchment for making a rental (MCR 5750, *minute expense*)
	c.1320/1	undated rental giving money-rents but not holdings of free and customary tenants (*liberi tenentes* and *custumarii/nativi*); probably compiled in or around 1320–1
	1323/4	*Firma blad' anno xvii apud Thorncroft*; lists 16 men with their annual lease-rents in barley; compiled 17 Edward III (July 1323–4)
5779a	c.1 August 1333	'Rental of Thorncroft made on Wednesday on the feast of St Peter in chains 7 Edward III in the time of John of Aperdele, then steward'; 1 August 1333 was a Sunday, so presumably Wednesday before or after was intended, 28 July or

MCR	date	description
		4 August 1333;[1] this copy gives the holdings and rents of *liberi tenentes* and the rent in money and kind of the *nativi tenentes* (including cottagers)
5779d	*c.*1 August 1333	same rental as 5779a, with minor variations; heading gives 7 Edward III but omits exact date; this copy gives in addition the labour-rent of the *nativi* and *coterelli*; MCR 5779a and 5779d are both extensively annotated with the names of later tenants, though these additions are not always the same in each copy
5802	*c.*1 August 1333	*lost*[2]
4783	June 1357	rental of Malden, Chessington, Thorncroft, and Farleigh dated June 1357; the rental of Thorncroft on the recto gives the holdings, rents, and predecessors of free tenants, the holdings and rent in money, kind, and labour of *nativi* (divided between *semivirgatarii* and *cotarii*) and leases (*firme*) for more than one year of vacant tenements and parcels of demesne; all copies of this rental are more or less heavily annotated
5779b	June 1357	undated copy of rental of Thorncroft in MCR 4783
5778[r]	June 1357	undated copy of same rental;[3] only first two villein tenements are listed
5791	June 1357	tied to this bundle of court rolls (1349–61) is an undated version of the same rental

[1] MCR 4893 is a rental of Farleigh made on 1 August 1333 by John of Aperdele, steward. The account of Thorncroft for 1333–4 (July–July) records the expenses of the steward *pro rentale faciendo cum clerico suo* and a gift by order of the warden of 4 bushels of wheat to the clerk *pro rentalibus de Farnlegh & de manerio faciendis* (MCR 5717).

[2] This copy is listed in W. H. Stevenson's calendar of the archives, where it is dated as 1 August 1333, but it was missing by 1972.

[3] A heading like that of MCR 5779a has been inserted above the original heading of this copy, mistakenly assigning it to 1333.

8

The Dyffryn Clwyd Court Roll Project, 1340–1352 and 1389–1399: A Methodology and Some Preliminary Findings*

A. D. M. BARRELL, R. R. DAVIES, O. J. PADEL, AND Ll. B. SMITH

THE HISTORICAL BACKGROUND

THE lordship of Dyffryn Clwyd or Ruthin was one of the forty or so Marcher lordships of Wales in the later Middle Ages. In order for us to understand the challenges and opportunities which its court rolls present to the historian, some of the distinctive features of Marcher lordships of Wales must briefly be explained.[1] These lordships by c.1300 were ranged in an arc from Denbigh in the north, along the eastern borderland of Wales and then in a great swathe along the southern half of the country from Newport in the east to Pembroke in the west. In total surface area they accounted for well over half of Wales; the rest of the country was composed of the five Principality shires of the north and west (Anglesey, Caernarfonshire, Merionethshire, Cardiganshire, and Carmarthenshire), and the shire of Flint, which was administered as part of the county palatine of Chester. The Marcher lordships may be defined historically, and rather loosely, as those areas of Wales which had been brought under English aristocratic control in the two centuries or so from c.1070 to 1282, mainly by the individual initiative of English aristocratic warriors and their warbands, aided by royal support and munificence. Some of them, such as Glamorgan and Pembroke, had been centuries in the making; others, such as Denbigh and Bromfield and Yale, had been created almost overnight, being bestowed on English noblemen by Edward I after

* The support of the Economic and Social Research Council (ESRC) is gratefully acknowledged. The work was funded by ESRC award number R000232548.

The Dyffryn Clwyd court rolls are in the Public Record Office (PRO), Special Collections (SC) 2/215/64–2/226/16. Those calendared in the course of this project were SC 2/217/6–2/218/3 (12 rolls, covering the years 1340–52), and SC 2/220/7–2/221/1 (7 rolls, covering the years 1389–99). References in this chapter to these rolls will be to the database record, namely roll number (1–12 and B–H respectively) followed by record number.

[1] For a general introduction see R. R. Davies, *Lordship and Society in the March of Wales, 1282–1400* (Oxford, 1978).

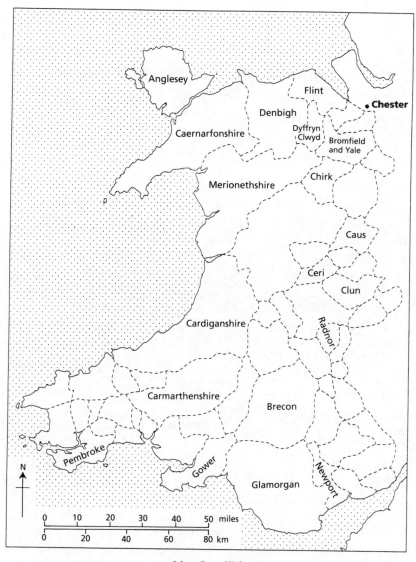

MAP 8.1 Wales

the final Welsh wars of 1277 and 1282–3. Dyffryn Clwyd belonged to this latter category; it was composed of land conquered by Edward I in the closing months of 1282.

Whether Marcher lordships were old or new, they shared by the fourteenth century certain distinctive characteristics. First, they were large territorial units by English standards. Some, such as Glamorgan or Brecon,

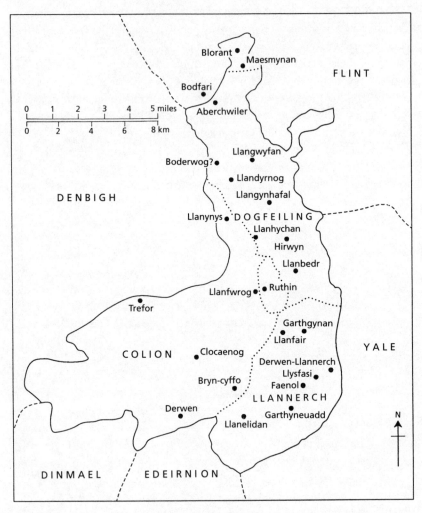

MAP 8.2   Dyffryn Clwyd

were equivalent to a small English county, and indeed in both these cases
were to form the greater part of those shires after the Union legislation of
1536–43. Others were very much smaller, but even so were much larger
than even the largest English manor, being nearer in surface area to some
of the greater English ecclesiastical franchises, such as the banlieu of Bury
St Edmunds or the liberty of St Etheldreda of Ely. Dyffryn Clwyd was
one of these smaller Marcher lordships. Even so, it covered three Welsh
commotes (Welsh *cymydau*) or hundreds, and contained within its ambit

a borough (Ruthin), several seigneurial manors (such as Maesmynan and Llysfasi) and a number of forests and parks. Its total surface area comprised approximately ninety square miles. Its court rolls thereby dealt with the judicial and disciplinary control of a much larger area and a far greater population than is usually the case with English manorial court rolls.

Marcher lordships were distinguished from English manors in other ways than by their size. They were, it is true, held feudally of the king of England; their lords were among his tenants in chief. Recently-created lordships were held by specific feudal service: thus Reginald de Grey held Dyffryn Clwyd by the service of three knights' fees. The lordships were thereby amenable to the king's feudal control (including custody and wardship), and ultimately to escheat and forfeiture. But in almost every other respect a Marcher lordship lay outside the normal governmental, fiscal and judicial machinery of the English state.[2] Its officers were exclusively answerable to its lord; no royal officers had jurisdiction in the lordship; no royal writ could be served there. No royal taxes were raised in a Marcher lordship (other than on one exceptional occasion, in 1292); no representatives of the lordship's community attended parliament. All land within the lordship, other than episcopal and monastic land, was held of the lord. The lordship was to all intents and purposes virtually an autonomous legal and jurisdictional unit. It was, to borrow some contemporary phrases, 'a royal lordship' 'with royal liberty'; its lord was 'the soveraigne governor' of his lordship, exercising 'royal jurisdiction' within it.[3] This meant that its courts had complete judicial authority over its inhabitants in secular matters (with the exception of cases of treason against the king and of advowson); there was no appeal judicially beyond its borders other than to the lord's council and to the lord himself; there was no jurisdiction in error by the royal courts over its affairs. This virtual jurisdictional autonomy meant that the court rolls of a Marcher lordship, such as those of Dyffryn Clwyd, cover a much wider range of judicial and quasi-judicial matters than those of any seigneurial or manorial court in England. Their nearest analogues would be the judicial records of the palatinates of Chester, Lancaster, and Durham; but in legal theory even the courts of these palatinates had a lesser jurisdictional range than those of a Marcher lordship. It is in a Marcher lordship and through its court records that one can glimpse most clearly what unfettered 'private' secular jurisdiction could achieve in the British Isles.

---

[2] Ibid. esp. ch. 10.
[3] For these phrases, see ibid. 217, 222, and the sources cited there.

There is a further distinctiveness about Marcher lordships which we need to bear in mind as we seek to analyse their court rolls, namely the *Marcher* character of their societies. All Marcher lordships were, to very varying degrees, frontier societies in which two (or more) peoples, cultures, laws, customs, languages, and social and economic formations met, confronted each other, and intermingled. This essential social duality was reflected in a whole host of ways—in separate Welshries and Englishries (formally or otherwise), separate Welsh and English courts and local officials, different rents, renders, and inheritance practices, separate and/or mixed juries, and so forth. Compared with some of the older Marcher lordships such as Glamorgan, Brecon, or Pembroke, the frontier character of society in Dyffryn Clwyd was less dominant. It was a recently-acquired lordship, and its English settler population was relatively small and localized. But the rental of the lordship in 1324 and the court rolls nevertheless reflect its Marcher character.[4]

Dyffryn Clwyd—a Welsh *cantref* composed of three commotes—was granted by charter on 23 October 1282[5] to Reginald de Grey, a member of an important English baronial family which owned extensive estates in midland and southern England. The descent of the lordship was diverted in 1319 to a cadet, and more richly endowed, branch of the family, henceforth known as the Greys of Ruthin. It had one outstanding record to its credit: between 1282 (the date of the acquisition of Dyffryn Clwyd) and 1523 there was not a single minority in the history of the family; eight adult barons succeeded each other in turn, a quite exceptional feat for such a family.

Dyffryn Clwyd was not, by Marcher standards, a very rich lordship: its annual yield of about £500 was half, or less, of that of lordships such as Brecon, Denbigh, or Glamorgan.[6] Nevertheless, Dyffryn Clwyd was, and was to remain, the single most valuable part of the Grey estates. It was, again by Marcher standards, a relatively small lordship in surface area; but this was more than amply compensated by its compactness and fertility.

---

[4] For explorations of the themes in this paragraph see R. I. Jack, 'Welsh and English in the Medieval Lordship of Ruthin', *Trans. Denbs. Hist. Soc.* 18 (1969), 23–49; and Davies, *Lordship and Society*, ch. 14.

[5] *Calendar of Charter Rolls 1257–1300* (6 vols.; 1903–27), ii, 262; *Calendar of Chancery Rolls Various 1277–1326* (1912), 243.

[6] Davies, *Lordship and Society*, 196–8. For a general introduction to the history and estates of the Grey family, see *The Grey of Ruthin Valor. The Valor of the English Lands of Edmund Grey, Earl of Kent, drawn up from the Ministers' Accounts of 1467–8*, ed. R. I. Jack (Sydney, 1965); R. I. Jack, 'Entail and Descent: the Hastings Inheritance, 1370–1436', *Bulletin of the Institute of Historical Research*, 38 (1965), 1–19.

At its centre lay Ruthin, a settlement of considerable significance under the Welsh princes; after the Conquest it became the seat of the Greys' castle, the site of a small but thriving market town, home to a collegiate church, and the governmental centre of the lordship.[7] Around it lay, and lies, some of the best agricultural land in north Wales. The area was probably already densely settled by Welsh standards; the number of vills mentioned in the records of the Great Courts—about sixty—suggests as much. In the wake of the Conquest English settlers, in not inconsiderable numbers in contemporary terms, moved into the town and its hinterland, establishing holdings large and small in the area.

Court rolls are one of the premier sources for an understanding of Marcher lordship and society. Since the March of Wales stood outside the normal ambit of English government and jurisdiction, its historian will find very little for his or her purposes in the central records of the English kingdom, other than in a limited degree during periods of custody or forfeiture. Instead, reliance has to be placed on the records of the Marcher lords themselves, supplemented mainly by scattered collections of deeds and vernacular poetry. Of the seigneurial records, the financial accounts submitted annually by a variety of local officers are the most common, and are invaluable in calculating the nature of seigneurial exactions and revenue. But court rolls are in many respects more rewarding. They show lordship in action, in detail—in disciplinary as well as in juridical terms. They also bring the historian much nearer than do the accounts to the character of Marcher society (albeit once more as viewed through seigneurial eyes). They are replete not only with evidence of lordship in action, but with insight into the social and economic life of the Marcher peasantry, its land transactions and inheritance patterns, its civil and criminal litigation, and an almost limitless agenda of other matters which, often tangentially and obliquely, figure in the court cases. Any picture of Marcher society and the changes within it in the later Middle Ages must rely very considerably—and arguably more so than in England—on the evidence of the court rolls.

But here one immediately confronts a problem. Seigneurial archives have survived very patchily for England for the later Middle Ages; the same is even more true of the March of Wales. This is particularly so of court rolls. There are virtually no surviving court rolls for great and old Marcher lordships such as Glamorgan, Brecon, Gower, or Pembroke; the

---

[7] R. I. Jack, 'Ruthin', in R. A. Griffiths (ed.), *Boroughs of Mediaeval Wales* (Cardiff, 1978), 244–61.

best that often survived are excerpts or exemplifications of individual court entries, or an occasional transcript by a zealous antiquary.[8] For other parts of the March, such as Radnor, a few stray and generally uninformative court rolls are extant; the same is true of Chirk and of Caus, in Shropshire.[9] The Fitzalan lordship of Clun has an exceptional dossier of thirty-two court rolls for the period 1328–99;[10] they provide invaluable insight into the social structure and customs of a truly frontier, upland lordship in the March. But it is for Dyffryn Clwyd alone of Marcher lordships that there survives what would be regarded, even by some of the best standards of English manorial court records, as a quite exceptionally rich series of court rolls.

The Dyffryn Clwyd court rolls first saw the light of archival day in 1854 when they were discovered in a loft above the Town Hall at Ruthin, 'in which the street lamps in summer, and various kinds of lumber were kept'.[11] They were transferred to the Public Record Office in London in 1859–60. In number and chronological range—there are 187 individual rolls, covering the period 1294 to 1654, with much the largest hiatus being the rolls for the reigns of James I and Charles I—they are unique for Wales. Though the format of the rolls varies from period to period (some being arranged by year, others by the unit of jurisdiction), the scale of information which they contain may be indicated by the fact that on average in the fourteenth century they contain about 1,500–2,000 entries per annum. They record the activities of a great range of courts—those of Ruthin town, of each of the three commotes of the lordship (Colion, Dogfeiling and Llannerch), of associated units (Aberchwiler, and Trefor and Clocaenog), of the Great Courts of Ruthin town and Dyffryn Clwyd, and, more irregularly, of some other courts, such as those of Ruthin fair. They also often contain a roll of fines levied, and sometimes other items such as separate lists of reliefs and entry payments, separate sets of forest and park pleas, pleas of the crown (*placita corone*), and gaol delivery and coroners' rolls. The town and commotal courts met every three or four

---

[8] Many of these excerpts and exemplifications are published in *Cartae et alia munimenta quae ad Dominium de Glamorgancia pertinent*, ed. G. T. Clark (6 vols.; Cardiff, 1910); and *Calendar of the Public Records Relating to Pembrokeshire*, ed. H. Owen (3 vols.; Cymmrodorion Record Ser., 1911–18).

[9] The court rolls for Radnor are in PRO, SC 2/227/40–57. Those for Chirk are in the National Library of Wales (NLW), Chirk Castle Collection. Those for Caus are in NLW, Peniarth MS 280, fo. 69; Staffordshire Record Office, D641/1/4T/1; and at Longleat.

[10] Salop RO, 552/1–34.

[11] The story is told by R. A. Roberts in 'The Public Records Relating to Wales', *Y Cymmrodor*, 10 (1889), 157–206, esp. 167–8.

weeks; the Great Courts twice a year. This means that, on occasion, as many as 136 court sessions were held in the lordship in a year, and their proceedings recorded in the court rolls.[12] Even making allowances for the lacunae in the series and for the illegibility or incompleteness of several extant rolls, the amount of material which they contain is, for the historian, both exhilarating and daunting. Unfortunately it is not matched by other comparable evidence for the lordship: there are no receivers' or local bailiffs' accounts, no registers of letters or petitions, no ecclesiastical records, no subsidy rolls, and no fourteenth-century wills. For the fourteenth century the court rolls can be supplemented, in documentary terms, only by a valuable if rather skeletal rental of 1324, a stray receiver-general's account for the Grey estates, and various small collections of family deeds.[13] It is, therefore, overwhelmingly from the court rolls themselves that the history of lordship and society in Dyffryn Clwyd has to be written.

Invaluable as are the Dyffryn Clwyd court rolls, one needs to recognize at the outset their character and, thereby, their limitations. Like all such rolls they are, of course, the documents of lordship; they only allow us a glimpse of the social fabric of the district in so far as the jurisdictional and financial powers of the lord impinged upon it. In appearance, form, and language their contents differ very little in most respects from contemporary English seigneurial court rolls, although they do not contain views of frankpledge or lists of those received into tithing groups, neither of which practices prevailed in Wales. They were doubtless compiled according to the guidelines of English formularies. Though Welsh terminology, customs, and procedures do figure recurrently in them, especially in the records of the commotal courts, the light that is shed on native Welsh practices and society is oblique. This shortcoming is further compounded by the important role of extra-curial arbitration and by the activities of the Welsh judge (Welsh *ynad*; Latin *iudex, iudicator*), neither of which figures, other than vestigially and tangentially, in the court rolls.[14]

---

[12] Jack, 'Welsh and English', 27. There was also a court on the demesne land at Maesmynan: see e.g. 1/674; 4/939.

[13] The rental of 1324 was published by R. I. Jack in *Trans. Denbs. Hist. Soc.* 17 (1968), 7–53; the receiver-general's account for 1393–4 is in NLW, Badminton Collection, 1559. Among collections of deeds which include material relating to Dyffryn Clwyd are NLW, Roger Lloyd Collection, and Trovarth and Coed Coch Deeds; and Clwyd Record Office, Wynnstay Collection.

[14] See respectively L. B. Smith, 'Disputes and Settlements in Medieval Wales: the Role of Arbitration', *EHR* 106 (1991), 835–60; and R. R. Davies, 'The Administration of Law in Medieval Wales: the Role of the *Ynad Cwmwd* (*Judex Patrie*)', in T. M. Charles-Edwards, M. E. Owen, and D. B. Walters (eds.), *Lawyers and Laymen* (Cardiff, 1986), 258–73.

METHODOLOGY OF THE CURRENT PROJECT

The court rolls of Dyffryn Clwyd have not received as much attention as they deserve from historians. The first five extant rolls, from the reign of Edward I, were published as long ago as 1893 by R. A. Roberts;[15] they have the interest of being the earliest rolls, and of dealing with a formative period in the early history of the lordship, but in every other respect they are more brief and far less revealing than their successors. Local historians of Denbighshire and general social historians of late medieval Wales have made very considerable use of illustrative material from the rolls. But court rolls are not the most approachable or immediately rewarding of late medieval documents; account rolls are more amenable to analysis, and they more readily reveal their riches, even though these are more limited. Furthermore, the sheer bulk of the Dyffryn Clwyd rolls rules out the feasibility of any extensive edition of them, while the mass of information which they contain will daunt even the most strong-willed historian. It was in an attempt to overcome these hurdles, at least for a segment of these rich rolls, that the Dyffryn Clwyd court rolls project, funded by the ESRC, was launched.

The initial project began in January 1991, and has concentrated on two periods in the fourteenth century for which the court rolls are especially full and well preserved, namely 1340–52 and 1389–99. These are also periods of considerable historical importance, for the first straddles the initial outbreak of the Black Death, which struck Dyffryn Clwyd in the early summer of 1349, and the second covers the decade immediately before the outbreak of the great rebellion of Owain Glyn Dŵr, which began in September 1400 with an attack on Ruthin and other English boroughs in north-east Wales. Although for some purposes a longer continuous period might have been desirable, the sheer size of the rolls did not permit a full-scale, comprehensive study of the material over several generations to be undertaken within the time-scale of the initial project. In such circumstances, it was decided to choose two separate periods of years which could then be compared and contrasted.

Because the intention of the project has been to present the material from the court rolls in machine-readable form in a manner which would allow its exploitation in a wide variety of subject areas, it was necessary to use a computer package which would allow maximum flexibility both in

---

[15] *The Court Rolls of the Lordship of Ruthin or Dyffryn-Clwyd of the Reign of King Edward the First,* ed. R. A. Roberts (Cymmrodorion Rec. Ser., 1893).

the input of the material and in its eventual use. This meant using a free-text system rather than a relational database such as those used in the past for the systematic analysis of medieval English manorial records.[16] Relational databases are best suited to research which from the outset has clearly defined and limited goals, towards which the structure of the computer records can be directed. Such an approach inevitably leads to the need to classify the material in categories, which may not be clearly distinguishable in every instance, thus possibly compromising the subtleties of the original source. Even if all the information in the original is transferred to the computer record, it is necessary to transform it to fit the structure of the database, and some features of it may then not be amenable to analysis. Since the Dyffryn Clwyd court rolls offer so many different possibilities for scholarly study, it was felt that the advantages of a free-text calendar of each entry, in a form immediately comprehensible to every researcher, and preserving the integrity of the manuscript source, would outweigh the loss of structure and potential for large-scale mathematical or statistical analysis which a relational database with a specific goal might have provided.

It was decided that a program called *Idealist*, produced by Blackwell Scientific Publications Ltd., would provide the level of flexibility required to computerize the Dyffryn Clwyd rolls in free-text form. *Idealist* allows records and fields within them to be of variable size, and permits different record types to be included within the same file. It is a straightforward database to operate, which increases its potential use by researchers unfamiliar with the techniques of computer-based historical analysis. Although this looseness of structure makes it difficult to employ *Idealist* for certain large and complex enquiries such as a study of the size of the population of the lordship or the personal interactions of members of society, from the standpoint of keeping open as many options as possible *Idealist* has proved to be admirable.

Each court roll has been made a separate file within the database, and each entry within the roll a separate record, although a certain amount of flexibility has had to be exercised. Large blocks of text which deal with a number of separate items of business, such as presentments of felonies and trespasses in the Great Courts, are more manageable as a number of separate records; but it has been more convenient to deal with lists of

---

[16] See Poos, 'Population and Resources', 298–308; Williamson, 'One Use of the Computer in Historical Studies', 51–61.

those amerced for breaking the assizes of meat, bread, or ale by using a single record to cover all those presented for breach of each assize.

The record structure is very simple, with the following fields being used:

reference — the manuscript class reference and membrane number
number — the unique number of the record within the file
court
date
persons — a list of the individuals named in the entry
text — the calendar of the entry, with the persons in the preceding field identified by the letter p and a number, e.g. p*1*, p*2* etc., together with any necessary editorial comments
extra — for the addition of interpretative phrases (see below)

It can, therefore, be seen that the only alteration to the structure of the original court roll entry has been to extract the names of persons mentioned in it. This was desirable because it aids the compilation of lists of surnames which have been made for each roll, assists in the study of individual persons, and provides the option of exporting the names alone to another package for alphabetical sorting or other analysis such as the frequency of occurrence of individual Christian names and surnames within the rolls.

Apart from a few appended petitions and letters in Norman French, the court rolls are written almost exclusively in Latin; only occasionally do English or Welsh vernacular words appear, usually for domestic or agricultural utensils, types of animal or tree, or as technical terms of law or procedure for which no Latin equivalent was available. The machine-readable calendar is, however, in English, because it is intended that the database should be exploitable by as many users as possible, including those who have not had the opportunity to become proficient in medieval Latin. To have preserved the full Latin text would, moreover, have been unacceptably laborious, because of the high level of abbreviation used by the scribes and the amount of damage incurred by parts of some membranes. In addition, many Latin words are spelt in a variety of ways by different scribes, and these idiosyncrasies would have had to have been faithfully reproduced, creating difficulties for the effective searching of the database. For these reasons English has been used; and although there has been no attempt to provide a literal translation of the original Latin, the calendar is intended to be very full and to preserve, as far as possible, the integrity of the manuscript in all its subtlety.

A list of standardized translations has been prepared, to assist both in the calendaring process and in future use of the database. Consistency in the treatment of words and phrases is obviously essential, and it is hoped that the list of standard forms will enable researchers to reconstitute the original Latin as much as possible. It also provides something of a dictionary of at least the more distinctive words and phrases found in the Dyffryn Clwyd rolls. Where a Latin word is used in an unusual context, or where the normal translation is unsuitable, the original Latin term has been included in the text of the record, as it has with many rare or potentially ambiguous words, with the aim of obviating as far as possible the need for the user to check the original rolls. Some technical terms have been left in Welsh or Latin, although in a standardized spelling: examples are terms of Welsh law such as *amobr*, *galanas*, *tremyg*, and *brwydr gyfaddef*, words connected with Welsh land transactions such as *ebediw*, *gobrestyn*, and *prid*, and some Latin procedural terms such as *vi et armis* and *vis et iniuria* which are misleading if translated literally into modern English. Also, because of the large number of words used for sheep, pigs, cattle, horses, and deer of different sizes and conditions, and the uncertainty of their translation, the Latin, or the vernacular where it is used, has been retained in these cases.

Personal names have been treated in accordance with the accepted practice of modernizing the Christian names, which are mainly drawn from a limited stock of standard names, and which are usually abbreviated in the document; the surnames, of whatever type, have been retained as they appear in the source. In printing or indexing any medieval source, let alone computerizing it, the variety of spellings of personal names is a major problem; here it is compounded by the presence of the Welsh language in addition to those which were in use in England at the period. The problems which this raises are considered below. Place-names, too, have been treated in the usual way, the spelling being given exactly as it appears in the source, except in the case of a few major and frequently-occurring names, such as the neighbouring town and lordship of Denbigh, the town of Chester, and a few others. Here the computer's requirements do not cause so much trouble, since the source itself is orientated much more towards people, and mentions of places are rarer; in addition, place-names usually consist of a single word, and variations of spelling can more easily be managed than in the multiple-word phrases which constitute personal names.

The great advantage of transforming a large and sometimes virtually impenetrable medieval source into a computer database is that it enables historians to interrogate the material in a wide range of ways in order to pursue lines of investigation which would have been hopelessly time-consuming by traditional methods. *Idealist* enables us to search the free text for particular words or groups of words, for instance proper names, types of property or legal terms. If desired, an index of all words in the file can be displayed and perused. There are also facilities to broaden a search so that records relating to a variety of persons or topics can be examined together, to narrow a search by isolating those records within a hit list which contain a further word or group of words, to exclude from consideration records containing a particular word or words, or to search only a specified field. There is the normal 'wildcard' facility, whereby an asterisk can be used to cover any subsequent characters: for instance, a search on 'blood*' would rapidly produce a hit list of all records within the file which contain a word commencing with those five letters, such as 'blood', 'bloodshed' and 'blood-letting'. The complete text of each record is displayed on screen, with the search term or terms highlighted.

Such simple searches are effective in those cases where the source uses a distinctive word which has been translated in a standardized way on being entered in the database. But not all lines of enquiry can be centred on a single word or phrase or even on a small group of words or phrases, and it is here that *Idealist*'s synonym facility has proved invaluable.

The synonym facility allows a number of words to be grouped together under one keyword, preferably a word not occurring elsewhere in the database, and thus facilitates searches under generic categories simply by typing the keyword. Some of the categories are straightforward:

foodstuffs=ale apple/apples bacon* bread butter cheese* dairy dough egg eggs fish flesh flour foods ham hams honey meat* mutton nut nuts onion* pork salt wine*

metals=bronze copper gold golden iron lead metal silver sterling

On occasions the number of words assigned to a single keyword can be very large:

feminae=administratrix amica amicae bondwoman braciatri* concubine* dau daus daughter* executrix famula famulae ferch forestallatr* girl* gossip kins-woman lady maid* meretrix mother mulier* nurse* nutrix perturbatri* prostitute* qfu regratri* relict scold* shrew* sis sister* tensatrix vagatrix ventilatrix widow widows wife wives woman women agnes alice almarie amelina amy anabil angharad beatrice cecily christine dyddgu edith efa eleanor elen elizabeth emma erddylad felicia generys godyth gwenhwyfar gwenllian gwerful gwladus gwledyr hawis hulyn hunydd ionet isabel

isoud iwerydd joan juliana katherine letitia lleucu llinno lucy mabel
mabot madrun mali malkin margaret margery marion mary mateny
maud morfudd myfanwy nest nestik olive petronilla quenhild rose susan
sybil tandreg tangwystl tibot anot bleder della dilet dillen dollen dyllan
dyllen dylen eniana hoen iony kymmen meriavon merriavon morwel
olyth tanne tege tegew toge

Here we have included all women's Christian names occurring in the
database, and also all nouns referring to women in our material, such as
'mother', 'wife', and 'prostitute'. A person studying women in fourteenth-century Dyffryn Clwyd would, therefore, merely have to search
on the word 'feminae' in order to obtain a hit list of all records within the
file which refer to women.

The synonym facility also allows the grouping of words for topics
where the limits of the subject matter are less clearly defined:

economic=alestake* borrow* buy* bought champart counted exchange* fair*
       farm* forestall* hire hires hired hiring lease* lend* lent loan* market*
       money prestium profit* regrat* retail* sale sell* sold stall stalls trade*
       trading trainter transfer* traunter* traynter usur*

violence=affray* arson* asphyx* assault* attack* battery beat* blood bloodshed
       blow crush* drag drags dragged dragging eject* fight* fought fist gladebat
       goad* gyfaddef hamesucken homicide* hurt hurts hurting kill kills
       killed killing maim* maltreat* mutilate* ransom* ravish* rescue* savag*
       seduc* shoot* shot smash* snatch* strik* struck tear* tore threat* vi
       violate* violently wound*

The choice of words entered into these categories might not be suitable
for every researcher working in these fields, but the synonym list can
easily be amended in line with individual requirements in order to achieve
maximum speed and effectiveness in searching. The synonym facility is,
therefore, an excellent tool for research into a variety of topics and at a
variety of levels of intensity. It also offers at least a partial solution to
some of the problems raised by variant spellings and forms of surnames
and place-names.

These searching mechanisms are extremely valuable; they offer the
possibility of using the source for many distinct or overlapping lines of
enquiry. However, not all topics readily lend themselves to investigation
by searching free text. Some procedural matters are hard to study because
there is no distinct word or phrase on which a search can be made.
Although there is a synonym for Welsh law:

Welsh law=amobr* brawd cyfraith galanas gyfaddef iudex iudices iudicator prid
    prid-* pridator* rhaith sub-amobr* tremyg

some of the evidence for the continuing use of Welsh legal practices has
to be inferred, using the historian's judgement. An even greater difficulty is
encountered when studying the impact of the Black Death within Dyffryn
Clwyd. The plague is specifically referred to only rarely, and it is impossible to search the database in ways which would pluck out either records
referring to individuals who perished in the plague or those hinting at
economic dislocation, desertion of holdings, land returning to pasture, or
peasants holding more land than formerly.

In other areas a search of sorts is possible, for example:

landtransactions=charter deliberata demise* demising ebediw* enfeoff* entry
    exchange* fealty gobrestyn hereditar* heriot* homage* inherit-
    ance mortuary opus prid prid-* pridator* quousque relief relin-
    quish* surrender* tradit*

but the hit list obtained is not wholly satisfactory. Although the search is
a valuable first stage in studying the succession and transfer of land, the
topic requires more sophisticated treatment than the language used in the
manuscript and thus in the database permits. Succession to Welsh land
differed from that to English land because Welsh inheritances were partible, and the number of heirs and their relationship to the deceased are
important issues for study. But because the court rolls do not always
make a distinction between Welsh and English land, at least not in a
specific, and therefore searchable, manner, the hit list obtained under the
keyword 'landtransactions' has still to be sorted by hand, a process which
is long and laborious.

Even where the synonym list works well in itself, the sheer number of
records provided and their heterogeneous nature can be intimidating.
Even with searches refined, it can be difficult to extract from the database
such records as would provide material for a particular paragraph or
section of a chapter or article, at least without taking ample notes from
relevant records. It is here that the extra field at the foot of each record
can be utilized in order to add subjective and interpretative phrases which
complement the essential objectivity of the synonym list. Without alter-
ing the calendar in any way, the material can be refined in accordance
with the needs of a particular enquiry. By extending this principle, it
would be possible to mark records as being relevant to the study of, say,
the Black Death or the hidden aspects of Welsh law, and thereby ask
fresh questions of the material.

CURRENT INVESTIGATIONS

As of January 1993, research on the court rolls using the database is still at an early stage, but work has been undertaken in a number of areas, using simple searches and the synonym facility. Within the current constraints of time-scale and technology, it is difficult to reconstruct to any extent the complex web of the personal relationships of the individuals in the lordship, but it has been possible to study the activities of certain groups in society and to compile a number of biographies of individuals and family groups. By traditional methods such exercises would have been unacceptably time-consuming; now, with the material in machine-readable form, the enquiry is relatively swift and straightforward, and even limited enquiries of this sort can shed much light on life in Dyffryn Clwyd. The examples which follow illustrate some of what can be achieved by using the database in its current form.

Names and naming-patterns

Much of the value of these rolls, as with many medieval court rolls, lies in the quantity and variety of individuals mentioned in them, from all ranks of society. The most interesting work to be done on the material will therefore probably be related to the people involved—studies of the networks of relationships within the communities, of the demography of the lordship, and the like. Indeed, almost all aspects to be studied involve individual people, which means that they need to be identified. This brings with it attendant problems, which have been extensively aired in print as regards English court rolls, and which are here compounded by the additional complication of the Welsh language and its particular naming-practices.[17]

Many Welsh men and women at this period were identified by means of the father's Christian name (and perhaps those of the grandfather, great-grandfather, or even further back, depending on circumstances or the need for an unambiguous description), and with no accompanying epithet or other descriptive term. Thus typical Welsh names might be *Ieuan ap Dafydd ap Einion*, 'Ieuan son of Dafydd son of Einion', or *Angharad ferch Gruffydd ap Maredudd*, 'Angharad daughter of Gruffydd son of Maredudd'. Since all the Christian names in such phrases are standardized within the computerized calendar, following the practice outlined above, such individuals will be spelt in the same way whenever

---

[17] e.g. Razi, *Life, Marriage and Death*, 11–24.

they occur in the database, and are thus easy to search for. However, Welsh, like English, also used a variety of descriptive or occupational surnames to identify individuals, and these bring with them the same range of problems as in comparable English records.

At the simplest level, a single surname may be spelt in a wide variety of different ways, such that there is sometimes difficulty in knowing whether one, two, or more distinct surnames are intended. The more serious problem, as in England, consists in the fact that two individuals may have shared the same name, and that a single individual may have had two or more quite different names, being identified by more than one method—say, by occupation, habitation, and descent. Thus there were two people active in the town of Ruthin in 1345–6, both called Nicholas Stalworthmon; one was a nephew of the other.[18] Similarly, there are at least seven, and probably up to sixteen, people called Iorwerth ap Dafydd ('Iorwerth son of Dafydd') mentioned in the roll containing the proceedings of the town court for the years 1390–9. The minimum number is obtained by the certainty that 'Iorwerth ap Dafydd ap Gronw' must be different from 'Iorwerth ap Dafydd ap Rhirid', and likewise from 'Iorwerth ap Dafydd ap Ithel', 'ap William', and so on; and the maximum number by assuming that additional individuals were intended when an identifying epithet was used, such as 'Iorwerth ap Dafydd Loyt' ('the grey'), 'Iorwerth ap Dafydd Penbras' ('bighead'), 'Iorwerth ap Dafydd ap William capellanus' ('the chaplain'), 'Iorwerth ap Dafydd ap William senior', and so on. Fortunately it is only rarely that anyone is referred to simply as 'Iorwerth ap Dafydd'.

Conversely, it can also be shown that Thomas *Don* was the same person as Thomas son of Roger *del Wych*,[19] and that Alice 'daughter of Adam' was also referred to as Alice 'wife of Madog ap Ieuan'.[20] One individual active in the 1340s is usually referred to as Bleddyn *ap Drew* (probably an inherited surname of some kind), but occasionally as Bleddyn *ap Cynwrig* (a patronymic) and Bleddyn *Gam* 'the crooked' (a descriptive epithet). The extra complication provided by the presence of the Welsh language is illustrated by the fact that a surname, usually an occupational one, may occur in two or more languages; one such example is seen in the three names *Kegyth* (Welsh 'cigydd'), *Flesshewer* (English) and *carnifex* (Latin), all meaning 'butcher', and all able to be used for a single individual. The variable factors may be combined; there was a man, prominent in Ruthin town in the 1390s, who was usually known as Thomas Stalworthmon or Thomas le Stalworthmon. He was involved in the butch-

---

[18] 6/64, 1544, 1655.   [19] 6/686, 711.   [20] 6/855, 879.

ering trade, and consequently was sometimes referred to as Thomas Stalworthmon *Flesshewer* or Thomas Stalworthmon *carnifex*; but sometimes simply as Thomas *le Flesshewer* or Thomas *carnifex*. (He was probably English, and has not been found with the equivalent Welsh epithet of *Kegyth*.) Several devices can be used for dealing with these problems relating to individuals, and other solutions are envisaged. In every roll calendared, the variations in spelling of the surnames have been extracted and listed. By this means one can readily select all occurrences of a particular surname, and then select those referring to a given individual. In dealing with such variations of language and terminology, as well as for the inevitable variations in spelling, the 'synonym' facility of *Idealist*, discussed above, can be a useful tool. However, the more serious problems of identification which arise from these variations cannot readily be tackled by a computer, though it can assist the historian in making his judgement.

As a result of these difficulties in identifying individuals, it is hard at present to make even an approximate guess as to the number of separate persons mentioned in the material. All that can be said is that there are upwards of 400 different surnames occurring in the court proceedings of a given year. Using that figure as a rough guide, one can take into account the many Welsh people who are not given a surname of any kind, but are identified genealogically, as outlined above; and reckon also the many instances of surnames shared by more than one individual, whether through kinship or not; then it is clear that the total number of individuals mentioned in one year must be much greater than 400, certainly of the order of at least 1,000, and perhaps around 2,000 in total, though it could be higher. The number of occasions on which a particular individual is mentioned, in a given year, may vary from 1 (or indeed none) to 30 or more, perhaps in a variety of different guises.

Despite all the problems in identifying and searching for individuals, the database can, even in its present form, present material in such a way as to illuminate our knowledge of the society. As is made clear above, this was a Marcher society, where English settlers mixed with the native Welsh population. People's names are themselves some guide as to what form that mingling took, and a study of them can go some way towards answering the question of how far the English immigrant population was assimilated into Welsh society. Certain prominent families are discernible, often with surnames denoting a place of origin in England, such as Thelwall (Cheshire); Aspull, Lytham, Pemberton, Ramsbottom, and Pleasington (Lancashire); Hagley and Cleobury (Shropshire); and Helpston and Spratton (Northamptonshire). Others had surnames of Norman-

French origin, such as Dawnay and le Marreys. The members of these families can be traced from their appearance, often early in the fourteenth century, through the course of that century. Their surnames were therefore functioning as hereditary surnames throughout that period, at an earlier date than has hitherto been generally recognized in Wales.

However, there is also a change discernible in such families during the period. In the middle of the century, the members bore Christian names mainly drawn from the same limited stock as was in widespread use in England at the same period (those Christian names being, in turn, mostly ones which had been introduced there in the wake of the Norman conquest in 1066)—names such as Alan, Brian, Henry, Hugh, John, Robert, Richard, Stephen, and William. The Welsh population, by contrast, used throughout the century a much wider range of Christian names, mostly drawn from the ancient Celtic stock of names which can be seen to have been in use in the country at an earlier date. The English families mentioned above can be seen, in several cases, to adopt some of these distinctive Welsh names during the course of the century; thus, in the 1340s, we find people such as Hugh and Richard le Mon, Almary and James le Marreys, Alan and Nicholas de Cowhop, and Henry and Adam de Hagley; they were succeeded, in the 1390s, by Iorwerth le Mon, Llywelyn le Marreys, Meilyr de Cowhop, and Ieuan de Hagley. Not only that, but the likely route of adoption can be traced, for in the middle of the century male members of such families can be seen to have had wives who bore distinctively Welsh Christian names, such as 'Angharad who was wife of John de Routhull', 'Gwenllian who was wife of John de Bradshagh', and 'Lleucu wife of Roger son of Almary Watkin'. It seems that many of the first or second generation of English settlers married Welsh women, and that their children were then often called by Welsh names as a result. The likelihood must be that these children were also Welsh-speaking from their mothers' influence (though they were no doubt English-speaking as well); the families were becoming assimilated. By contrast, a few such families continued to show 'English' Christian names at the end of the fourteenth century, and never a Welsh one; in the 1390s, we find Martin de Thelwall, and Alan and Ralph de Asphull, two prominent English families which had been in the area since the 1340s or earlier; these were presumably families which had resisted integration.

Seigneurial Administration and Economy

The seigneurial administration of the lordship involved a considerable number of individuals, partly because the separate Welsh and English communities were served by different sets of officials. Court rolls, far more than financial accounts, allow us to witness the range of activities in which the lord's officers were engaged. Below the chief officers, such as steward, receiver, escheator, coroner, and master forester, most of whom were English, there was a substantial body of bailiffs, rhingylliaid, local foresters, and parkers. There were officials to collect Welsh dues such as the virginity payment or *amobr*, bailiffs in charge of demesne lands at Maesmynan and Llysfasi, and men responsible for the lord's animals, as well as those within Ruthin town elected annually to control the assizes of meat and ale. The jurisdiction of most officials was limited by geography or by the legal status of those within their constituency, but the customary payments to which they were entitled, and the potential to exert pressure on the local community, meant that substantial sums were often paid for the farm of offices. Some, such as that of rhingyll of a particular commote, were normally held for a fixed term, often a year; others were held for life and were heritable, such as the post of Welsh judge (*ynad*) and probably some of the offices of parker. The very substantial body of evidence relating to lordship officials and their activities, licit or illicit, is readily accessible in the database, and offers a uniquely detailed insight into the administrative affairs of a Marcher lordship over an extended period.

The study of office-holders as individuals is complicated by the problems of personal identification, and can be undertaken more effectively with data from a longer period. Research has therefore concentrated on investigation of the duties pertaining to particular offices, and of the nature and number of the presentments and attachments made in the regular courts.

Several officials were engaged in caring for the lord's animals, and for receiving beasts which accrued to the lord after the death of a tenant or through forfeiture. There were also regular reports detailing animals which had died, from which can be detected both changes in administrative practice and the withdrawal of the lord's interest in farming some types of stock.

In the early 1340s, the designation of the person making the presentment of murrains is rarely given in the rolls, but such evidence as there is indicates that it was the responsibility of the official in charge of the animals in question, for example the stockman, the horse-herd, or one of the lord's shepherds. But the court rolls for June 1348 record the election of pairs of coroners (*coronatores*) to present murrains in Clocaenog, at Llysfasi, at Maesmynan and Blorant, and within the jurisdiction of Ruthin.

These were the demesne pasture lands of the lordship. Although the coroners appear to have held office only for a restricted period, the sudden record in the rolls of their election probably indicates that the office was newly established; certainly thereafter the scribe normally states that reports for these places had been made by the coroners. Between the Black Death and the 1390s the lord entirely abandoned his direct interest in the farming of sheep and pigs, although his stocks of cattle and horses continued, and this had an effect on how the administration dealt with the question of reporting deaths. The last mention of the coroners (now described as *cadaveratores*) in this context is in August 1391,[21] after which responsibility for detailing dead beasts returned to the ambit of the stockman. The great majority of his presentments in the 1390s (53 out of 61) relate to the lord's animals within the jurisdiction of Ruthin, an indication that seigneurial involvement in pastoral farming had contracted geographically as well as in its scope, and that the work of reporting murrains was now insufficiently frequent or important to justify the continued appointment of officials specifically for it.

These reports also contain a wealth of detail about farming practice. In the middle of the century the dates of lambing and shearing of sheep can be approximately ascertained, and one can trace the regular movements of stock around the lordship in the course of the farming year. It is likely that such details, when studied, will also help to elucidate the local usage of the numerous different words which referred to particular types of animal, such as (for sheep) *ovis, bidens, multo, agnus, agnellus, gercia, hogaster, hogettus, hogerellus, hurtardus*, and English 'theave'. The differences in age and sex between these various types should be, to some extent, deducible from a comparison of their occurrences within the rolls, with dates, and in the context of the other words and their usages.

In similar fashion, the large number of attachments by seigneurial officials permits examination of which species of tree were growing in the woodlands within the lordship. By far the commonest tree named as being felled was oak, with 367 mentions in the two periods studied; next comes birch (220 mentions in the two periods, although in some of these the word may be acting as a place-name); then thorn-trees (99 mentions, including 'whitethorn' and 'hawthorn'), hazel (95), and alder (88). Ash is surprisingly rare (19 occurrences); and willow, apple, and gorse have each only a handful of mentions. The notable omissions are elm and rowan,

---

[21] D/452. On 6 Nov. 1397 a butcher was amerced for selling meat of 'cadaveratores animalium infirmorum' (D/5377), but this is the only later mention of these officials in the court rolls used for the present study.

while the absence of beech confirms other evidence that this tree was then unknown in north Wales.[22] Bullace and walnut each occur once, as cultivated trees. Taking evidence such as this in conjunction with references to physical features such as pasture-lands, meadows, and watercourses, it should be possible to piece together the fourteenth-century topography of the lordship, and thereby to understand more fully the working of the local economy.

The Clergy

Ecclesiastically, the greater part of the lordship comprised the rural deanery of Dyffryn Clwyd, an outlying part of the bishopric of Bangor. Although the parochial arrangements are complex and to some extent fluid in the fourteenth century, and the existence of portionary churches makes it difficult even to assess the number of established permanent benefices at any one time, it is clear that in the 1390s at least fifteen clerks[23] would have been required to fill such benefices, quite apart from any chaplains or curates who might have been needed; if anything, there were more portions in some of the churches earlier in the century. Dyffryn Clwyd therefore had a sizeable clerical population compared with most English manors, and the court rolls afford us a glimpse into its nature and into its activities where these touched the secular sphere. Because there are virtually no extant bishops' registers for Wales before 1397, and very little survives of other ecclesiastical sources, one of the few ways in which the medieval Welsh Church can be studied is through court rolls. From them, we inevitably see clerical life from a lay perspective, and in places the terminology of the rolls is imprecise, but the Dyffryn Clwyd rolls none the less provide the best available opportunity to study the lives of the clergy of north Wales in the late Middle Ages.

The majority of the clergy have Welsh names, and many were probably born within the lordship. The parish churches of Dyffryn Clwyd were not especially valuable and seem to have held little attraction for churchmen from England, at least in the period before the Black Death. Even in the 1390s, when a number of men of English origin did hold

---

[22] W. Linnard, *'ffawydd* fel elfen mewn enwau lleoedd', *Bulletin of the Board of Celtic Studies (BBCS)*, 28 (1978–80), 83–6; and 'Beech and the Lawbooks', ibid. 605–7.

[23] i.e. Llanfair, two portions of Llanelidan, Llanfwrog, Llanbedr, Llangynhafal, Llanhychan, Llangwyfan, Llandyrnog, Bodfari (outside the deanery, but the parish included Aberchwiler), two portions of Llanynys, Derwen, Clocaenog, and the prior of the collegiate church of Ruthin. In the 1340s there was also a vicarage of Llanfwrog, which may or may not have been perpetually endowed (4/1200; 7/736, 737), and there were probably more than two portions in Llanynys.

churches within the deanery, many of these, such as Thomas de Thelwall, parson of Llangynhafal, and Robert de Backern, parson of Llandyrnog, were members of long-established settler families. Among the Welsh clergy, a very few were university graduates such as John ap Dafydd, rector of Llanfair before the Black Death, and Ithel ap Robert, one of the portioners in Llanynys, who was abortively elected bishop of Bangor in 1357 and in due course moved on to the archdeaconry of St Asaph.[24] But most of the clerics in Dyffryn Clwyd seem to have had horizons no wider than the boundaries of their lordship. They were presumably of only rudimentary education, and some of them no doubt became clerics in much the same spirit as their neighbours became bakers or shoemakers.

Even if the clerical estate differed little from the rest of society in its origins or aspirations, it none the less provides a sample group of individuals through whom the potential of the database can be investigated. Considering the relative affluence of some of them, churchmen were the victims of theft surprisingly rarely. They were more commonly the victims of violence, although by no means on a scale to indicate any significant degree of anti-clericalism. Few suffered as badly as Einion, rector of Llanhychan, who in 1345 was beaten so severely with a staff that he was on the point of death;[25] and some were certainly not averse to using force themselves, such as Hywel Goch capellanus, who was involved in a number of rumbling feuds in the 1340s. Some clerks were involved in the local land market, making use of the income they received from tithes. Others were frequently involved in legal processes such as bailing and pledging; and although these activities cannot be placed in a meaningful context until a fuller study is undertaken of a much wider cross-section of Dyffryn Clwyd society, some churchmen can already be attributed to a detectable group of semi-professional practitioners. Clerics like Ieuan Offeiriad ap Dafydd ap Cynwrig in the 1390s enjoyed being involved in legal business, and carved out a niche for themselves offering their expertise and reputation to a number of individuals across local society, most of whom were unlikely ever to have the opportunity to reciprocate in kind.

---

[24] *Calendar of Entries in the Papal Registers Relating to Great Britain and Ireland: Petitions to the Pope*, ed. W. H. Bliss (1896), i. 300–1; *Calendar of Entries in the Papal Registers Relating to Great Britain and Ireland: Papal Letters*, ed. W. H. Bliss *et al.* (18 vols.; 1893–1995), iv. 328; J. Le Neve, *Fasti Ecclesiae Anglicanae 1300–1541* (revised edn., comp. H. P. F. King, J. M. Horn, and B. Jones (12 vols.; 1962–7), xi. 43.

[25] 5/1344.

Kin Groups

Studies of personal interactions and an evaluation of the strength or weakness of kinship bonds (in so far as they may be reconstructed from the records of secular courts alone) are best conducted on the foundation of family reconstitutions based on material deriving from a longer time span than is at present available in the database, and of the compilation of a large number of detailed individual biographies. Even so, some headway can be made by using the database in its current form. Kin groups can be identified from the material already processed, a court profile of their members constructed, and the nature and context of their interactions noted. Because Welsh land was partible among male heirs and was heritable, in the absence of lineal descendants, by collateral heirs up to and including the third degree of consanguinity (i.e. second cousins) a partial reconstruction of a descent group can be attempted. Descents through the female line cannot be uncovered in this way and only by accident (for instance, the survival of a marriage contract or of disputes concerning the payment of *amobr*) can marriages and therefore affinal relationships be identified. In order to test the challenges and opportunities offered by the source material, two Welsh families, many of whose male members can be identified, have been chosen as case studies.

The male descendants of Einion ap Madog in the commote of Dogfeiling are a particularly interesting group for study and, at the same time, illustrate the problem of accurate identification inherent in the naming practices of the period. In the case of one member of this particular family, Iorwerth ap Gronw ap Einion is also identified as Iorwerth Hen (= senior) ap Gronw, as Iorwerth Hen, as Iorwerth ap Gronw senior, and as Iorwerth Hen ap Gronw ap Einion. On 2 July 1343 a group of seven co-heirs named as Iorwerth Hen, Cadwgan Goch, Dafydd Llwyd, Meilyr ap Gronw, Bleddyn Goch, Iorwerth Goch, and Gronw ap Einion ap Gronw succeeded to the lands of Dafydd ap Einion ap Madog.[26] Identification of these individuals is aided by a further entry of 23 September 1349, which records the succession to the lands of Dafydd ap Bleddyn Goch. These heirs are named as Iorwerth Hen, Cadwgan Goch ap Gronw ap Einion, Iorwerth Goch ap Gronw ap Einion, Gruffydd ap Dafydd Llwyd, Gronw ap Meilyr, Gronw ap Einion ap Gronw, and Iorwerth ap Dafydd Llwyd.[27] The rental of 1324 shows that Dafydd ap Einion, described as parson of the church of Llandyrnog, held land in the commote

---

[26] 3/742.   [27] 9/1331.

of Dogfeiling; a Gronw ap Einion is also recorded as holding land in the same commote. A reference in 1334 shows that Gronw and Dafydd with a third brother, Ieuan, described as an idiot from birth (*fatuus naturalis*) had already partitioned their father's lands between them.[28] Ieuan's share subsequently fell to his brothers, although Gronw alone answered for the ebediw and gobrestyn due upon them. In 1332 Dafydd ap Einion, parson of Llandyrnog, surrendered his English lands to the use of (*ad opus*) his nephews, retaining for himself a life interest in the land.[29] In the transaction the nephews are named as Dafydd ap Gronw, Meilyr ap Gronw, Iorwerth ap Gronw senior, Cadwgan ap Gronw, Bleddyn ap Gronw, and Iorwerth ap Gronw junior. A seventh brother, Einion, is named in the rental, although not in the surrender. The rental moreover shows that six of the brothers were already holding equal shares of land in Hirwyn and Boderwog while their father was alive, and between 1334 and 1340, to judge from the lack of later references to their father Gronw, they probably inherited their father's lands. In 1343, as seen, the lands of their uncle, Dafydd, were partitioned between six of the brothers and a nephew of theirs, as representative of the seventh brother, Einion. The death of one of the brothers, Bleddyn Goch, hanged for felony in Staffordshire by 1347, saw his lands devolve upon his son, Dafydd. The death of Dafydd without direct heirs by September 1349 saw his lands shared between three of his uncles and four of his cousins.

A reconstruction based on these entries produces a genealogical table (Fig. 8.1), and the information provided allows us to test not only the nature of the fraternal bond and that between father and son, but also that of uncle and nephew and of cousinhood. In this case, the genealogical links could be extended further by recourse to material drawn from the following decades so that more distant kinship links could be traced. Little evidence of the exploitation and organization of the family patrimony is forthcoming from the court rolls, but what there is strongly suggests that the co-heirs held their land in severalty in close geographical proximity. For instance, mention is made of the partition of the lands and tenements of Dafydd ap Einion between the co-heirs[30] and individual heirs disposed of portions of their lands to third parties without reference to their co-heirs.[31] Residential or tenurial propinquity is suggested by the pleas of breach of a cross, suggesting boundary disputes, which occasionally emerge in the court record.[32] The family's status in the commote is

---

[28] SC 2/216/14, m.14d.   [29] SC 2/216/12, m.22d.
[30] 3/761.   [31] e.g. 10/874, 875.   [32] 1/772; 4/288.

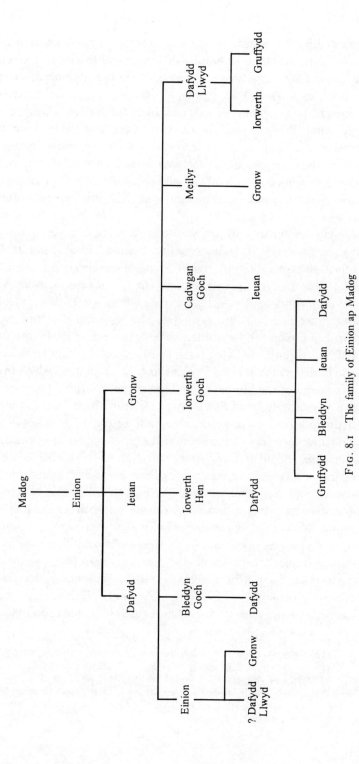

FIG. 8.1 The family of Einion ap Madog

suggested by the regular presence of several members on inquisitions[33] and by the possible identification of one, Iorwerth Goch ap Gronw, as rhingyll of Dogfeiling for a brief period.[34] On the other hand, a disparity of social, and possibly of economic, status is suggested by the more prominent public profile of Iorwerth Hen and Iorwerth Goch, as compared with Cadwgan Goch or Dafydd Llwyd ap Gronw. Whereas the former two appear acting independently and frequently in the court sessions, the latter two appear more rarely and are more often to be found acting in conjunction with other members of their kin. The age structure of the group may also be a relevant issue, but little can be ventured on that score.

Despite the apparent disparity of status between members of the group, however, the extent of family cohesion is a most notable feature. There are forty-three occasions in the period 1340–52 when two or more members of this kin group act together. On two occasions, when various members functioned as co-heirs, common interests were clearly involved.[35] Three other occasions are related to the inheritance of the estate of Dafydd ap Einion.[36] Four occasions involve several of the brothers acting together as plaintiffs or defendants, jointly accused of causing destruction to the lord's grain;[37] seeking licences to concord in pleas which involved four or more of the brothers;[38] and, most spectacularly, when six of the group were accused, and found guilty of, provoking Lleucu, daughter of Dafydd ap Einion, to prosecute an appeal for the death of her brother.[39] In only four instances do members of the group appear on opposing sides in litigation, and all save one were settled out of court. Pleas of debt and breaking of a cross were resolved by licence to concord, and the fourth instance[40] may well have involved the formal registration of a covenant rather than recording a dispute. Although members of the group were individually involved in violent action or took part together in incidents involving violence,[41] there are no instances of violent behaviour directed towards members of the kin group. The absence of public ventilation of intra-familial disputes may well suggest that informal and extra-curial means were deployed to resolve tensions. There is, indeed, at least one instance from an earlier period when a case of wounding and bloodshed

---

[33] 9/89; 11/1235; 12/151.   [34] 1/708; 2/926.   [35] 3/742; 9/1331.
[36] 3/752, 787; 11/579.   [37] 2/996, 1009, 1018, 1039.
[38] 4/243; 11/561.   [39] 6/1213; cf. 5/1345, 1608, 1627.   [40] 3/761.
[41] e.g. Dafydd Llwyd ap Einion ap Gronw was arraigned for an attack on the house of William de Clebury (2/1036); Iorwerth Goch ap Gronw ap Einion struck Einion ap Moelgrwn with a sword (2/122); Iorwerth Goch ap Gronw ap Einion and Dafydd ap Iorwerth Hen were indicted for hamesucken (11/1309).

involving one of the brothers was resolved outside the court and without the lord's licence by a group which included the perpetrator's uncle and two of his brothers.[42] In all other cases, kin interaction takes the form of pledging for other members of the group (seventeen instances), or where two or more are involved together in pledging for a third party (nine instances). In some of these latter cases, the third party may, of course, have been a now unidentifiable kinsman. A study of the group in action shows not only the solidarity of the fraternal bond but also the strength of the links between nephews and cousins. It also suggests that within this family, at least, the integrity of the inheriting group was sustained after the succession to land and its immediate attendant formalities had been completed.

Viewed as a group, therefore, the cohesion displayed by the sons and grandsons of Gronw ap Einion ap Madog seems quite remarkable. When, however, the individuals of whom the group was composed are viewed separately, the image of a closely knit group is somewhat modified. Indeed, the diversity within the group deserves to be noted. A study of the pledging relationships undertaken serves both to highlight the variety and, at the same time, to confirm that for some members the social horizons were those determined by the bonds of kinship. Although pledging in the lordship of Dyffryn Clwyd could be a function of office, it could also reflect a personal commitment and suggest a particular relationship between the participants. In the case of the family studied, a marked contrast can be detected between Iorwerth Hen and Iorwerth Goch, on the one hand, and the remaining family members on the other. As we have noted above, the curial profile of both these members was far weightier than that of their co-heirs. In both these cases, too, the sphere of activity is less circumscribed than is the case with other members of the kin group, and their involvement outside the commote, especially in the proceedings of the court of Ruthin town, is noteworthy. Equally worthy of note is their involvement in pledging commitments beyond that of their immediate circle of kinsmen. Iorwerth Goch, for instance, stood pledge for individuals outside the group in about fourteen cases, in ten of which no other member of his family circle was involved. By contrast, six out of the seven pledging commitments of Cadwgan Goch involved members of his kin group and the seventh commitment was entered into in conjunction with one of his brothers. Even so, and despite the existence within this family of individuals whose interests encompassed a fairly

---

[42] SC 2/216/10, mm. 14d, 15.

broad range of contacts, the descendants of Gronw ap Einion ap Madog represent a group, and perhaps a social stratum, for which the ties of kinship remained a primary social bond.

The second family, that of the descendants of Madog ap Ednyfed, presents points both of similarity and of contrast with that of Gronw ap Einion. Like the descendants of Gronw ap Einion, those of Madog ap Ednyfed, a Llannerch family, also figured as co-inheritors on more than one occasion during the period 1340–52. In August 1349 the lands of Gruffydd ap Madog ap Ednyfed (described as *persona ecclesiasticus*) devolved upon his brother, Dafydd, upon Llywelyn and Dafydd, his nephews and sons of his brother Ieuan Fychan (whose death is recorded in August 1349), and upon a third nephew, the son of a third brother, Madog Fychan.[43] At the end of the year the death of William, a brother of Gruffydd and Dafydd, prompted the sharing of his lands between his brother, Dafydd, and two nephews, Llywelyn ap Ieuan Fychan and Dafydd ap Madog, identified as the son of Madog Fychan (who died before July 1349).[44] Ieuan, Dafydd, and Gruffydd are mentioned in an entry for February 1346 which reveals that they, with others, had yielded lands to form the lord's park of Bryn-cyffo and had been compensated with land from Garthyneuadd forest.[45] The fourth brother, William, did not share in the partition of Gruffydd's lands in August 1349, although his own were shared between his brothers and two of his nephews at his death in the following December.[46]

This particular family, however, contrasts with that of Gronw ap Einion in that its members fulfilled several official functions within the lordship. Gruffydd ap Madog ap Ednyfed was himself rhaglaw of Dyffryn Clwyd;[47] his brother Madog figured as farmer of amobr or as amobrwr in 1347 and 1349;[48] Dafydd ap Madog ap Ednyfed was rhingyll of Llannerch[49] and farmer of two of the lordship's mills; while in the next generation, Dafydd ap Madog Fychan functioned as amobrwr between 1350 and 1352.[50] A further contrast is the fact that in no instance do members of this family stand together as plaintiffs or defendants in the courts of the lordship. Indeed, the very small number of instances when they were parties to any litigation at all is very striking. The connection of this family with the courts of Dyffryn Clwyd was overwhelmingly as pledges, a fact of further contrast with the Gronw ap Einion group. Whereas, in the case of the previous family, mutual pledging was a prominent feature of their participation

[43] 9/945.   [44] 10/1038; 9/912, 947.   [45] 6/1503.   [46] 10/1038.
[47] 10/1150.   [48] 7/844; 9/221, 1761.   [49] 4/209; 7/767; 10/1094.
[50] 10/1107, 1465; 11/596, 637, 1057; 12/644, 691, 704.

in court business, and they frequently acted with each other in that capacity, the pledging commitments of the family of Madog ap Ednyfed were entered into as individuals and very predominantly with people outside their immediate circle of relatives. *Extranei* (people from outside the lordship) figured amongst those for whom pledging was done, and in one interesting case, a rare example of two members of this family standing together as pledges, the undertaking was made on behalf of a bondman of the township of Garthyneuadd, where the family lands lay.[51] However, where co-pledgers are noted, they were drawn in most instances not from among family members but from the ranks of fellow officials.[52] Familial cohesion comes to the fore on rare occasions, when, for instance, sureties were required for the execution of the offices held.[53] But despite the joint inheritance of land, the clearest impression of this family is that the strongest identity lay with other members of the lordship's administration rather than with kinsmen by blood. If kinship was an important organizing principle in the history of this family, it was displayed in ways other than those which may be uncovered from the court records.

Land Succession and Transfer

Two issues on which the court rolls, in common with manorial court rolls in England, can be expected to shed considerable light are succession to tenements on the death of a tenant, and the transfer of land as formally sanctioned through and by the courts. In Dyffryn Clwyd there is an extra dimension of interest to both topics, in that it was an area in which English and Welsh land tenures, services, inheritance practices, and land-transfer procedures co-existed and influenced each other. One has to recognize, of course, that the silences and omissions of the rolls in this, as in so many other respects, can prove tantalizing and distorting. On the question of inheritance, for example, one needs constantly to remember that in the case of both free and unfree tenements the lord's interest extended no further than those holdings held directly of him; what was doubtless a very considerable number of sub-tenancies—let alone exchanges, leases, and mortgages—lies entirely outside the range of our records. Even in the case of holdings held directly of the lord, our records doubtless fall very far short of the complete: the court rolls themselves refer to the negligence and embezzlement of officials in concealing debts and succession dues.[54] Likewise any attempt to gauge the nature and the

---

[51] 3/913.   [52] e.g. 6/1475, 1971; 11/903, 935.
[53] 7/844.   [54] E/1786–90.

extent of the land market is considerably frustrated by the fact that until 1346–7 there was clearly no systematic practice of recording land transfers by the Welsh device of *prid*, a renewable four-year mortgage,[55] and also by the fact that in the case of *ad opus* land transfers it is often difficult to distinguish between intra-familial arrangements, especially *ante-mortem* enfeoffments,[56] or between arrangements made at or after marriage,[57] and what may be considered to be genuine sales of tenancies.

While fully acknowledging all such limitations within our records, and more than usually mindful, thereby, of the fragility of any conclusions we can draw, the Dyffryn Clwyd court rolls nevertheless provide us with much the best, and indeed in many respects the only, sustained source for studying succession to and transfer of land in a Welsh Marcher lordship in the fourteenth century.[58] While some preliminary forays into this activity have already been published,[59] the availability of a fully machine-readable text of the rolls for 1340–52 and 1389–99 and the convenience of the synonym facility can bring greater definitiveness and exhaustiveness to the analysis.

The commote chosen for initial analysis was that of Llannerch, to the south-east of Ruthin. The data on succession to land at death are summarized in Table 8.1. In the figures for the years 1340–8 attention may be drawn in particular to the impact of the Welsh custom of partibility among male heirs in the agnatic line, fifteen inheritances being divided among forty-four co-heirs. Richer Welsh families—such as those of the forebears of Owain Glyn Dŵr, or of the Griffith family of Penrhyn—may have already taken advantage of the practice of entailing their lands to

---

[55] L. B. Smith, 'The Gage and the Land Market in Late Medieval Wales', *EcHR* 2nd ser. 29 (1976), 537–50, especially 544–5 for the statute of 1345 on *prid* in Dyffryn Clwyd and its significance; and 'Tir Prid: Deeds of Gage of Land in Late-Medieval Wales', *BBCS* 27 (1976–8), 263–77. Eight cases of *prid* licences are recorded in the courts of Colion for 1345–6; but the earliest such licence in Llannerch, as opposed to cases arising indirectly from *prid* transactions, is in the court of 26 July 1347 (7/925).

[56] For an example, see 2/759, where Walter de Blakeney transfers 13 acres in Faenol to his (younger) son Almary, the remainder of his lands passing on his death in the following year to his (elder) son, Philip (3/921).

[57] See, for example, the lands bestowed by Hugh Stalworthmon on his son, Nicholas, and daughter-in-law, Margery de Lytham (6/1544; 7/809).

[58] A supplementary source for such a study is the collections of estate deeds, such as the magnificent series of deeds for north-east Wales in the Mostyn Collection, University College of North Wales, Bangor; see A. D. Carr, 'The Making of the Mostyns: The Genesis of a Landed Family', *Transactions of the Honourable Society of Cymmrodorion* (1979), 137–57. These, however, are almost invariably the archives of the estate-building activities by one, or more than one, family, and they cannot provide an overview of succession to, and transfer of, land in a particular district.

[59] Davies, *Lordship and Society*, esp. 406–7, 412, 426, 430.

TABLE 8.1. *Succession to land on death in Llannerch, 1340–8 and 1389–99*

	1340–8	1389–99
A. **Number and categories of tenants**		
1. Total number of tenants' deaths recorded	54	32
2. Of whom:		
(*a*) Women	3	4
(*b*) Lord's bond tenants	10	3
(*c*) Advowry tenants*	3	2
B. **Tenurial status of lands†**		
1. Free Welsh tenure	10	7
2. Free Welsh tenure and land *ad acras*	10	1
3. Welsh customary tenure	12	3
4. English tenure	16	19
C. **Succession**		
1. Welsh tenure, free and unfree		
(*a*) Multiple male succession		
(and total number of heirs)	15 (44)	3 (6)
(*b*) Single male succession	12	6
2. English tenure		
(*a*) Single succession, male or female	13	16
(*b*) Multiple succession by/through females	—	3
(*c*) Tenants succeeding by/through females	1	12

* For definition of advowry tenants, see Davies, *Lordship and Society*, 138–9.
† Where the tenurial status of land is not specifically stated, it has been deduced from the following pattern of succession dues:
  (i) *Ebediw* and *gobrestyn* (i.e. Welsh heriot and investiture fee) of 10s. (normally son or sons) or 20s. (more distant male relatives) signifies free Welsh hereditary tenure;
  (ii) *Ebediw* and *gobrestyn* 7s. 6d. (on one occasion 5s.) signifies Welsh customary tenure. This was also the *ebediw* sometimes charged for advowry tenants, but the latter have invariably been identified by their designation of personal status;
  (iii) Heriot and/or relief (the latter normally charged as equivalent to one year's rent) signifies English tenure. The terms 'relief' and 'entry' often seem to be used interchangeably.

their heirs by English law only, thereby preserving the integrity of the inheritance, yet among the free and unfree Welsh tenants of Dyffryn Clwyd partibility was still the norm. Or at least that was so for hereditary lands, for the other striking figure in the columns for 1340–8 is that showing that half of the free Welsh tenants (*uchelwyr*) whose deaths are recorded also held land *ad acras*, that is land for which rent was paid by the acre (as opposed to a contribution to communal renders) and for which succession was determined by English customs, that is by monogeniture other than for female heirs. In other words, while the main features of land inheritance in Dyffryn Clwyd in the 1340s were still very considerably shaped by native Welsh practices and by the contrast between them and the customs of the English settler families, the interaction between the two, and more especially the impact of English custom, is also clearly detectable.

This impression seems reinforced by the evidence on land transfers *inter vivos* during the same period. Since the evidence for licensed *prid* transactions is very defective for the period 1340–8 for Llannerch,[60] our main information comes from *ad opus* transactions, that is to say the surrender of land by the holder in court to the use (*ad opus*) of another. We may assume that such *ad opus* transactions relate to land held by English tenure and/or by English tenants, to escheated or waste land, etc. This would seem to be confirmed by the evidence: forty-six *ad opus* transfers are recorded in the court rolls for Llannerch in 1340–8, and in most cases one or both parties have English names. But, perhaps even more significant, in eleven cases both parties bear indisputably Welsh names (though that does not necessarily mean that they were holding land by Welsh tenure), and in a further eight cases at least one of the parties was Welsh. The Welsh tenantry of Dyffryn Clwyd was becoming conversant with English practices of land conveyance. Individual cases may help to pinpoint the kinds of opportunity and occasions for the growing familiarity with English practice. When William le Mon, a member of a settler family, proposed to marry Lleucu, daughter of William Howell, he arranged to settle a messuage and eight acres of land on her.[61] Even more interesting is the way that one of the most prominent Welsh clerics of Dyffryn Clwyd, Master John ap Dafydd, rector of Llanfair, bought extensive lands through *ad opus* arrangements, and equally disposed

---

[60] Only four cases are apparently recorded: 7/925; 8/1272, 1321, 1491.
[61] 2/647.

of them in the same fashion.[62] Master John had inherited a considerable Welsh estate, which was to pass eventually to four of his male co-heirs as stipulated by Welsh law,[63] and he also secured land by *prid*;[64] but he was equally conversant with English methods of land conveyance. The Englishness of those methods was more formally placarded when it became more common, from August 1346—quite probably in the wake of the seigneurial ordinance of 1345[65]—to add the phrase 'to their English heirs and assigns' in such transfer deeds.[66]

It is not easy to compare the situation in Llannerch in the 1390s with that in the 1340s; but some tentative suggestions may again be warranted by the data on succession to land on death and transfer of land *inter vivos*. The context appears to be that of a society where the population had fallen sharply, much land was vacant, and the lord was waging a constant struggle to retain his authority over his tenants, especially his bond tenants. It is indicative of the malaise that seventeen parcels of land were declared as being in the escheator's hand, eleven of them because of the poverty of the tenant, and another five through lack of heirs or claimants;[67] and that in cases where escheated land was leased the rent was frequently lower than previously.[68] The figures on succession to land on death are revealing when compared with those for the 1340s: the proportion of free land held by English tenure had increased markedly (19 : 8 compared with 16 : 20), the number of multiple successions to Welsh tenements had declined sharply (from fifteen to three), while succession to and by females, both of them practices normally precluded for Welsh tenements in north-east Wales, was high (12). The movement towards English tenure, detected in the 1340s, seems to be confirmed, but had not yet swept Welsh practices and customs before it. In the thirty-four *ad opus* transactions, six were specifically said to be 'to X and his English heirs and assigns', and in seven of the fourteen cases of the leasing of escheated land or vacant land, it was again specified that the lease was on 'free English terms', even though in one instance[69] the land had previously been held by free Welsh services. Yet Welsh land was still conveyed by *prid* (eleven cases recorded), and in at least two instances even vacant land was to be held by free Welsh services.[70]

It would be dangerous and premature to draw conclusions from what

---

[62] 4/87, 196; 5/913.　　[63] 9/944.　　[64] 9/884.　　[65] See above, n. 55.
[66] On seven occasions in Llannerch in the period Aug. 1346 to Sept. 1348.
[67] E/1, 19, 21, 22, 31, 33, 35, 44, etc.　　[68] E/406, 1352, 1394, 2142, 2379, 2658.
[69] E/272.　　[70] E/1352, 2658.

is, geographically and chronologically, a relatively small sample of evidence. Hopefully the exercise can be extended over a larger chronological time-span, although even then some of the difficulties and intractabilities posed by the evidence will remain. However, the Dyffryn Clwyd rolls remain one of the most valuable sources for studying the changes in land tenure and land practice in Wales in the era between the Edwardian Conquest and the Act of Union.

Credit and Debt

Small-scale borrowing and indebtedness in a rural society are issues which figure prominently in the court rolls. However, the information they provide is, as so often, tantalizingly brief—rarely mentioning the occasion and context of the loan and often referring the issue to an out-of-court settlement. Attempts to characterize the nature, extent, and occasions of rural indebtedness on the basis of the court-roll evidence have so far proved to be rather unrewarding; more immediately suggestive have been biographical studies of individual lenders.

Two such examples may be briefly cited from the evidence of the 1340s. One is that of Ieuan Kery, quite possibly a migrant from the mid-Wales district of Ceri, who had settled in Dyffryn Clwyd by the 1330s,[71] living in a house in the Welsh street of Ruthin to which he added an upper storey *(solarium).*[72] His career bears all the hallmarks of that of a small-town burgess: brewing ale; selling cattle, horses, and oxen; and owning his own pigs and sheep.[73] More interesting is the use he made of money at his disposal. The sums he lent were tiny—such as 3*d.*, 12*d.*, and 20*d.*—but they served to lubricate the market in commodities and land in the Ruthin district. He certainly meant to make a profit for himself. On two occasions he was charged with usury: once, for lending corn at a usurious rate for which he was fined the substantial sum of 13*s.* 4*d.* (an episode which suggests that either he was a surplus producer or, more likely, a corn merchant exploiting the market); and on another occasion lending the not inconsiderable sum, by the standards of Ruthin loans, of 6*s.* 9*d.*, charging interest on it at 6*d.* per week.[74] If the charge is true it is an extraordinary rate of interest; but it also confirms that loans were often contracted on a very short-term basis. Ieuan, not surprisingly, was active in the property market both in Ruthin town and in the surrounding

[71] SC 2/216/14, m.19d.   [72] 2/111, 1414, 1740; 4/467.
[73] 3/346, 362; 5/494, 495; 6/695; 7/995; 8/818; 10/112, 430.
[74] 5/1638; 3/1482.

countryside, especially in the vill of Garthgynan. His purchases, like his loans, were generally small—fractions of burgages and some 22 acres of land over the decade 1341–51.[75] But he was well placed to take advantage of the opportunities in the land market opened up by the great mortality of 1349—paying 40s. to acquire four acres in *prid*, and seizing on the misfortunes of a tenant overcome 'by poverty and pestilence' to secure, jointly, 18 acres in Derwen-Llannerch and Garthgynan.[76]

Men with cash or goods to spare had opportunities in abundance in 1349. Such was one of Ieuan Kery's fellow entrepreneurs in these years, Ieuan ap Einion Chwith. Unlike Ieuan Kery, he was a modest Welsh peasant rather than a townsman, in fact a customary tenant of the bond settlements of Trefor and Clocaenog, and one who jibbed at the constraints of bond tenure.[77] Interestingly, most of his loans were in animals, especially oxen, rather than in cash, and they were repaid in cereals.[78] Ieuan presumably had more oxen than his neighbours and was able to hire (*locare*) them out, especially at the height of the season, often to desperately poor neighbours. But in what was already a partly monetized society, wealth in stock could be accompanied by, or converted into, wealth in cash. So much is suggested by an incident in which 100s. silver was stolen from his house in 1350, for which two of the offenders were fined 100s. and 13s. 4d. respectively for redeeming their lives when convicted.[79] The evidence on the careers of Ieuan ap Einion Chwith and Ieuan Kery is fragmentary and often tantalizingly unspecific, but at present it appears that it is through such miniature biographies—made possible by the computerization of the court rolls—that we can begin to uncover some of the network of loans, usury, and indebtedness in a medieval Welsh rural community.

FUTURE PLANS

That such a range of topics can be profitably studied using the present database is a clear indication of its value and versatility. However, any enquiry which requires identification of more than a few individual people is liable to be long and frustrating. Furthermore, as mentioned

---

[75] 1/974, 1189; 3/1090; 7/993; 12/976.

[76] SC 2/218/4, mm. 14, 15.   [77] 9/246; 10/1551; 12/319.

[78] 10/1509, 1525, 1530; 12/282, 293. An Einion Chwith, who may have been Ieuan's father, was involved in similar activities in Clocaenog, and a man of the same name acted also in Dogfeiling and Aberchwiler (1/551, 578; 9/1262).

[79] 10/51, 52, 62, 1545, 1550, 1562, 1566, 1646; 11/1195.

above, *Idealist* is not designed for sorting and condensing a substantial quantity of material and making it available in statistical terms. Because all research options on the material have been kept open, by creating what is virtually a straightforward calendar, there is the concomitant disadvantage that the material remains in almost its raw form for purposes of computerized analysis.

These problems of identification of individuals and dealing with the quantity of material would best be tackled by having another, separate, database for the same material. However, this would be a relational database (for which, therefore, *Idealist* would not be used), and would consist of a catalogue of people. It would be much more akin to the databases employed, some years ago, for analysing some English manorial court rolls for demographic purposes; but it would have the greater flexibility of being able to refer to the full calendared text within *Idealist*, and therefore would not need to distort or over-summarize the complex and variable material of the rolls in order to make it fit the requirements of a database which had been structured with particular lines of investigation in mind.

A system of this kind should enable one to carry out complex studies, such as the demography of the lordship (so far as the material allows), or the pledging system and how it fitted, if at all, into the networks of relationships, whether of kinship or of other sorts, within the different communities. The problem of the identity, or not, of two individuals with the same name, or similar names, would still be left to the historian's judgement, of course; and the existing, much fuller, calendar-style database would still be essential for a full understanding of any particular entry. But it seems likely that an analytical tool such as this will be the way to make best use of the calendar, which itself is the necessary first step in computerizing these rolls.

In her study of women in the manor of Wakefield in the mid-fourteenth century, Helen Jewell concluded by stressing the need for further analyses of similar material, using

a data set from an archivally suitable series of records, from a statistically satisfactory size of unit, in a part of the country not previously the focus for this kind of treatment, and . . . from an estate not controlled by the Church.[80]

The Dyffryn Clwyd records fit this description exactly; our hope is to realize their potential by producing a machine-readable corpus of

---

[80] H. M. Jewell, 'Women at the Courts of the Manor of Wakefield, 1348–1350', *Northern History*, 26 (1990), 81.

information which can be exploited in a variety of ways in order to give more texture to our understanding of medieval Marcher society.[81]

[81] Since this chapter was written, the ESRC has funded a second project on the Dyffryn Clwyd court rolls (award number R000234070), during the course of which all the courts of the commote of Llannerch and all the Great Courts, rolls of fines, and other records of criminal jurisdiction between 1294 and 1422 have been calendared. The planned relational database of people did not prove feasible because of the difficulties in identifying individuals, but a number of articles have emanated from the project: A. D. M. Barrell and M. H. Brown, 'A Settler Community in Post-Conquest Rural Wales: The English of Dyffryn Clwyd, 1294–1399', *Welsh History Review (WHR)*, 17 (1995), 332–55; A. D. M. Barrell and R. R. Davies, 'Land, Lineage and Revolt in North-East Wales, 1243–1441: A Case Study', *Cambrian Medieval Celtic Studies*, 29 (1995), 27–51; M. H. Brown, 'Kinship, Land and Law in Fourteenth-Century Wales: The Kindred of Iorwerth ap Cadwgan', *WHR* 17 (1995), 493–519; A. D. M. Barrell, 'The Clergy of a Medieval Marcher Lordship: The Evidence of the Dyffryn Clwyd Court Rolls', *Trans. Denbs. Hist. Soc.* 44 (1995), 5–23; O. J. Padel, 'Locational Surnames in Fourteenth-Century Denbighshire', *Names, Places and People. An Onomastic Miscellany in Memory of John McNed Dodgson*, ed. A. R. Rumble and A. D. Mills (forthcoming, Stamford, 1966); O. J. Padel, 'Names in -*Kin* in Medieval Wales', *Names, Time and Place. Essays Presented to Richard McKinley*, ed. D. Postles and D. Hooke (forthcoming, 1996).

9

The Population History of Medieval English Villages: A Debate on the Use of Manor Court Records

L. R. POOS, ZVI RAZI, AND RICHARD M. SMITH

I. 'LEGAL WINDOWS ONTO HISTORICAL POPULATIONS'? RECENT RESEARCH ON DEMOGRAPHY AND THE MANOR COURT IN MEDIEVAL ENGLAND

(L. R. POOS AND RICHARD M. SMITH)

THE strategic role played by population movement, and its interaction with agrarian environment, in current theories of medieval economic development stands in sharp contrast to the relatively sparse direct evidence that can be marshalled to elucidate demographic change in medieval England. Indeed, work done to date has relied largely upon indirect indicators such as rents, prices, and wages or landscape changes associated with processes of reclamation, colonization, settlement re-siting, shrinkage, and desertion.[1]

In recent years medievalists have resorted increasingly to the localized village or manorial case-study as a framework for investigating English economy and society. This research focuses upon a wide variety of problems, many of which are superficially tangential to, but ultimately connected with, demographic issues. Examples include evolution in land tenure, relationships between villagers and manorial lords and between different strata within village society, and kinship and household formation. The records of English manorial courts of the thirteenth and fourteenth centuries provide the basis for most research. Recourse to this uniquely detailed source material, though hardly unprecedented,[2] has

---

[1] A summary of the types of arguments usually marshalled in this context can be found in J. Hatcher, *Plague, Population and the English Economy, 1348–1530* (London, 1977). The most recent summary of the landscape archaeologist's perspective is C. Taylor, *Village and Farmstead* (London, 1983).

[2] One of the earliest exercises in local manorial history by a legal historian, and still one of the better of this genre, was first published in 1894: Maitland, 'History of a Cambridgeshire Manor', 417–39.

recently been aimed at more rigorous 'reconstitution' of rural populations from nominative information of villagers' activities in manorial-court proceedings. In this respect, intensified scrutiny of manor-court records resembles techniques of nominal linkage of persons recorded in parish registers, employed by historical demographers for the centuries after 1538.

Yet considerable discussion concerning methodological issues has ensued, raising fundamental problems regarding the use of legal records for social and demographic inference. The debate centres upon the issue of how fully, and with what biases, these records (and the legal and administrative processes which generated them) expose to the historian's gaze the lives of the entire community under scrutiny. Variations in the quality and quantity of source material from different communities hinder development of any methodology capable of producing data to be used truly comparatively. Differences in format and informativeness of court records, in the frequency of court meetings, and in completeness of document survival render it difficult to establish a common approach.

To date, the largest number of printed pages dealing with the subject has come from Professor J. A. Raftis and his students, working exclusively with court records of the manors of Ramsey Abbey on the Cambridgeshire/Huntingdonshire fen edge.[3] The analysis employed attempts to reconstitute village society by indexing all court appearances of each named individual in a particular manor's records over a number of decades, reconstructing family links among villagers from genealogical information provided by the court rolls, and then categorizing families into status groupings and observing the differential behavioural patterns exhibited by these 'classes'.

Considerable criticism has been levelled at the methodologies employed by the 'Toronto School'. In view of the extreme incompleteness of records surviving from these particular manors, identification of individuals is complicated. Surnames rather than explicit genealogical connections apparently were used extensively in reconstructing familial links. Status groupings have been assigned to families on the basis of a variety of impressionistic criteria seldom fully articulated. 'Upper' status is equated with family members' tenure of administrative positions, for example, as manorial jurors, reeves, or constables. Once made, these classifications remain attached to families over long periods with little allowance for mobility within and between generations.[4]

---

[3] e.g. Raftis, 'Social Structures in Five East Midland Villages', 83–100; Raftis, *Tenure and Mobility*; Raftis, *Warboys*; Dewindt, *Land and People*; Britton, *Community of the Vill.*

[4] For a thoughtful, level-headed review of these difficulties, see Wrightson, 'Medieval Villagers', 203–17.

Particularly severe criticism of these historians' work has been made by
Zvi Razi, who has recently published the first ostensibly demographic
study based exclusively on manor-court records, from the manor of
Halesowen in Worcestershire.[5] Razi is particularly critical of the lack of
precise criteria by which individuals are identified from recorded names
in the 'Toronto School's' work and asserts that 'Professor Raftis has . . .
made "demographic" observations on names rather than persons.'[6] In his
study, Razi develops methodological refinements which certainly render
individuals' identification from the court records' nominal information
more systematic.[7] But his case for the feasibility of demographic analysis
from manorial-court rolls rests ultimately upon his explicit presumption
that, with some allowance for under-representation of some lower-status
groups such as women, landless villagers, and servants, essentially all
village residents may be traced from young adulthood to death or emigration from their appearances in manorial-court proceedings. Therefore,
counting individuals appearing in court transactions over specific periods
can provide the basis for calculating aggregate resident population trends,
the most basic demographic inference of Razi's study.

Our aim in this article is to address the presumption that the scope of
manorial courts' jurisdiction over medieval village society was so comprehensive that counts of individuals appearing in court transactions over
periods may be treated as if they constituted periodically constructed
'census-like enumerations'. We shall then look specifically at attempts to
study life expectancy and nuptiality, using information generated by court-
roll transactions such as tenant obituaries and merchets. Attention throughout will be focused upon the parallel problems of defining the limitations
of information which these tribunals' records yield for broader social
issues, and of interpreting this information in a broader demographic
context than has been attempted in most of this work to date.

We may begin by asking why the group of individuals recorded in
transactions of manorial court sessions may be regarded as a reasonably
full representation of that manor's resident population, or at least its adult
male population.[8] Razi, dealing with a series of court records that are
especially voluminous (as this manor incorporated twelve townships surrounding a small urban community), argued that

---

[5] Razi, 'The Toronto School's Reconstitution', 141–57; Razi, *Life, Marriage and Death.*
[6] Ibid. 12.   [7] Ibid. 12–23.
[8] This discussion will presume that village and manor were coterminous (i.e., that there
was reasonable congruity between the manor as tenurial and administrative unit and village
as physical community), and that both leet and regular manor court records have survived,
for any community under study; in practice, of course, this is often not the case and
introduces further complications.

manorial courts dealt with land conveyances and transactions; disputes about inheritance, roads and boundaries; trespasses against the lord and neighbours; debts; breach of agreement; quarrels between neighbours, failures to render services, rents and other exactions; disturbances of the public order; infringements of village by-laws and the assize of ale and bread; and the election of jurymen, reeves and other village officials. In addition, the court recorded deaths, marriages and pregnancies out of wedlock of bondwomen; entries into tithing groups; and departures of villeins from the manor with and without permission. The range of these activities is so wide that it is hard to conceive how a villager could have avoided appearing before the court from time to time.[9]

Razi is therefore content to treat the quinquennial counts of individuals appearing in the Halesowen courts over a period of more than a century as an unproblematic index of aggregate resident population trends.

But at least three major factors can be shown to have affected the volume and composition of personal appearances in manorial court records. Changes in administrative or litigational procedures in manorial courts during the thirteenth and fourteenth centuries influenced the frequency and nature of different categories of court transactions; economic or even ecological events, in origin totally unrelated to the courts' proceedings, nevertheless were reflected in the pattern of recorded court transactions; and finally, villagers in different social or economic strata exhibited significant differences in patterns of recorded court appearances. Each of these factors poses particular implications for the cross-section of village society which the court records reveal.

Two examples of procedural changes affecting the volume of business recorded in manorial courts are particularly relevant in this context. First, the nature of a court transaction may itself affect the number of persons recorded as participants; thus, the number of persons appearing in interpersonal suits, where one or two pledges for both plaintiff and defendant were listed in addition to the parties in the case, would be larger than in cases of tenants' offences against their manorial lord (such as trespasses on demesne property or failure to perform servile obligations). Second, changes in procedures initiating suits also affected the number of individuals recorded in typical cases; for example, if personally initiated pleas were increasingly replaced with presentment by jury, thereby reducing the practice of personal pledging, frequencies of individuals' appearances would be substantially affected.

Indeed there is ample evidence that notable transformations in manorial court procedures were taking place along these lines over much of

---

[9] Razi, *Life, Marriage and Death*, 2–3.

England in the later thirteenth and early fourteenth centuries.[10] For example, the early rolls of the abbot of Bury St Edmunds' manor of Rickinghall in Suffolk (where records survive from 1259) show no signs of presentment juries as a means of introducing business into court until the 1270s. By the 1280s, in contrast, presentment became the principal means by which infringements of the lord's rights were brought into court. Associated with this procedural change was a general increase in quantity of court business, as reflected in numbers and values of fines and amercements levied. At Rickinghall, the annual average number of amercements rose from 66 in the 1260s to 158 during the decade 1310–19, although total revenue from these penalties increased only marginally. Amercements related to enforcement of seigneurial rights, property and tenurial services, and exercise of franchisal jurisdictions such as Assize of Ale infractions were conspicuous among transactions increasing in frequency between 1285 and 1310, and these in particular were products of presentment procedures.

More germane to the present argument, however, is the fact that this increase in court business led to the involvement of more people in the courts' recorded activities. When numbers of persons amerced per annum are tabulated for every fifth year from 1260 to 1315, the last three sample years (1305, 1310, and 1315) produce an average of 102 persons amerced per annum, nearly one-third higher than the previous highest figure in the sample (70 persons per annum, for the years 1275, 1280, and 1285). Under the reasoning employed in Razi's study, this might be taken as evidence of growing resident population within the geographical area of the Rickinghall court jurisdiction. But internal evidence of another variety of court-roll information implies the opposite; in this case, transformations in court procedure merely widened the range of individuals directly involved in court transactions.[11] (See Table 9.1.)

Another obvious factor affecting the index of court appearances arose in periods of economic dislocation, generating a significant increase in persons circulating through court. Table 9.2 summarizes quinquennial

---

[10] For a specific study, see Smith, 'Some Thoughts'; for more highly suggestive preliminary findings, Beckerman, 'Customary Law in Manorial Courts'.

[11] The inference of declining resident population at Redgrave was made on the basis of observing that approximately 30 per cent of customary tenants died with no surviving male or female offspring, whereas in a stationary population one would expect this in no more than 20 per cent of parents' deaths. For more on this point, see E. A. Wrigley, 'Fertility Strategy for the Individual and the Group', in C. Tilly (ed.), *Historical Studies in Changing Fertility* (Princeton, 1978), 133–54; Smith, 'Some Issues Concerning Families', 38–62.

TABLE 9.1. *Court sessions, income, amercements, and amerced, Rickinghall, 1260–1319*

	1260–9	1260	1265	1270–9	1270	1275	1280–9	1280	1285	1290–9*	1290	1295	1300–9	1300	1305	1310–19	1310	1315
Average extant courts p.a.	7.6			7.5			6.1			3.9			4.9			5.0		
Extant court session		7	7		7	8		7	7		5	3		4	4		6	4
Amercements p.a. (excluding land fines)	66.1			59.9			82.8			66.7			124.9			158.6		
Amercements (excluding land fines)		70	67		110	83		70	131		98	63		72	130		145	182
Total no. of persons amerced		49	60		77	67		56	87		65	50		48	84		106	115
Court income (s.) p.a. (excluding land fines)	105.2			70.5			60.5			39.2			72.2			105.9		

* A decade of severe documentary loss and damage.

Source: Based on British Library Add. ch. 63589–63419.

TABLE 9.2. *Participants in the market in customary land, Redgrave, 1260–1319*

Years	Male	Index[†]	Female	Index[†]	Total	Index[†]
1260–4	92	100	13	100	105	100
1265–9	95	103	11	84	106	101
1270–4	177	192	53	408	230	219
1275–9	135	146	42	323	177	168
1280–4	231	251	58	446	289	275
1285–9	167	181	46	354	213	203
1290–4	201	218	51	392	252	240
1295–9	265	288	58	446	323	308
1300–4	177	192	38	292	215	205
1305–9	181	196	34	261	215	205
1310–14	264	287	48	369	312	297
1315–19	261	284	102	784	363	346

[†] 100 = 1260–4.

averages of numbers of persons appearing in court as vendors or purchasers of customary land between 1260 and 1319 at Redgrave (Suffolk), another Bury manor. Although participants in the customary land market were progressively more numerous over this period, the pattern was heavily influenced in the short term by economic circumstances.[12] Periods of harvest difficulties in the early 1270s, early 1280s, mid- to late 1290s, and the decade 1310–19 coincided with sharp increases in numbers of persons appearing in land-market transactions. The striking increase in female participants in the land market during these crisis years is also notable. Women sold land inherited in the absence of direct male heirs, while during the general agrarian crisis of 1315–17 some wealthier families became the beneficiaries of dowries or premarriage gifts. Again, as at Rickinghall, at Redgrave it is likely that a declining resident population formed the background against which growing numbers of individuals appeared in court in this context.[13]

These examples imply that the 'court-participation index' may in fact tend to be highest at times of abrupt depopulation. As tenements are

---

[12] For a detailed study of land transfers in Redgrave, see Smith, 'Families and their Land', 148–86.

[13] Smith, 'Some Issues Concerning Families', 49–54.

vacated and heirs appear (and often dispose of their inheritances soon afterward), more people may appear in court proceedings although resident population is reduced. This may account for Razi's derivation of the highest quinquennial total of males appearing in court during 1311–15, including difficult harvest years and their aftermath, and the second-highest during 1345–9 that includes the high mortality of the Black Death.[14] This point raises the broader issue of isolating factors tending to involve a greater proportion of any resident population in legal proceedings under certain contexts than others.

Both factors influencing court participation considered so far have involved simple changes of numbers over time. But certain aspects of the structure of local populations themselves interacted with these factors in quite complex ways. Economic and social stratification within village society led different groups to be represented to different degrees in court procedures. Razi acknowledged that 'poor' peasants appeared in the Halesowen manor courts less frequently than the 'rich', yet asserted that this under-representation does not totally exclude the former from adequate observation.[15] But this bald assertion is impossible to substantiate empirically without independent evidence and may lead one to overestimate the perspective upon rural populations which manor-court proceedings provide. Large numbers of people may be overlooked—undertenants, labourers, and servants, smallholders or the totally landless, as well as a majority of women—who appear in the court records sporadically (leading Raftis, for example, to regard these as 'transients' or 'marginals')[16] or even not at all, but who may in fact have been continually resident but simply had no reason to become involved in the court's business.

Ancillary material confirms this under-representation. Manorial rentals, listings of all tenants holding land in a given manor at the time of compilation, when used in conjunction with contemporary court records for the same manor yield a measure of the under-representation of some elements of medieval local society.[17] Table 9.3 presents frequency of appearance by individuals in court records between 1327 and 1349 by quantity of land held in 1328 for the manors of Great Waltham and High Easter in Essex.

Persons possessing only a cottage or messuage appeared in court-roll transactions roughly half as frequently as arable land holders with five acres or less; the latter in turn appeared roughly one-third to one-half as

---

[14] Razi, *Life, Marriage and Death*, 25.   [15] Ibid. 3.
[16] Raftis, 'Social Structures in Five East Midland Villages', 90–3.
[17] Poos, 'Population and Resources', 95–7.

TABLE 9.3. *Frequency of court-roll appearances by amount of land held in 1328, Waltham and Easter, 1327–49*

Size of tenancy	Mean no. of appearances	Standard deviation	N	No. never appearing	Per cent never appearing
Cottage or messuage only	2.8	4.7	49	20	40.8
0–5 acres	5.7	9.2	169	51	30.2
5–10 acres	7.7	10.2	75	19	25.3
15–20	8.6	12.8	22	1	4.5
20–25	20.6	20.8	8	0	0.0
30–35	15.3	17.4	4	0	0.0
35–40	22.8	18.7	6	0	0.0
40+	12.1	16.8	9	4	44.4

frequently as half or full virgators. Even more strikingly, two-fifths of the cottagers never appeared in the court records. Yet in 1328 more than half of all manorial tenants in these manors were smallholders possessing less than five acres. This underscores the serious limitations of court-roll evidence for this stratum of rural society.

An analogous pattern emerges from the manor of Redgrave. Table 9.4 compares persons listed in a 1289 rental with contemporary court appearances. Tenants listed in the rental were divided into groups according to size of tenement: over ten acres, 5–9¾ acres, 2½–4¾ acres and under 2½ acres.[18] From each of these groups, a sample of 28 individuals was randomly drawn, and their appearances in court in interpersonal transactions (both litigious and contractual) over the decade centring on 1289 are tabulated by tenement size. This sample excludes landless persons and those holding residential property but no arable land, and therefore is not directly comparable to the Waltham and Easter data. Nevertheless, frequencies of appearance in this category were almost five times greater for the 'upper' group than for the 'lowest'.

[18] For a fuller account, see Smith, 'Kin and Neighbours', 219–56, and R. M. Smith, 'Explaining Network Structure: An Exchange-Theoretical Approach to Some Thirteenth-Century English Evidence' (unpublished paper presented at the Social Science History Association's Annual Conference at Bloomington, Ind., Nov. 1982).

TABLE 9.4.   *Inter-personal contact frequencies of a stratified sample of Redgrave tenants, 1283–1292 (N = 112)*

	Total observed contacts	$\bar{X}^\dagger$
Upper Quartile	1,777	63.5
Middle Upper Quartile	1,038	38.7
Middle Lower Quartile	583	20.8
Lowest Quartile	379	13.5

† Mean appearances per person.

Manorial rentals are not entirely satisfactory as independent means of assessing the representativeness of persons appearing in manorial courts, however, because rentals furnish a list only of those holding land within the manor and are far from being enumerations of all residents within the locality in question. For the latter, the most appropriate medieval English documentation available is the later fourteenth-century poll-tax listings. These listings survive in large numbers from collections of 1379 and 1381. In theory they list all lay residents of each township aged 15 years and older, although in practice both of these collections experienced demonstrably significant levels of evasion.[19] Nevertheless, although it is likely that considerable numbers of persons resident in a given township may have escaped taxation, those listed may be taken as a minimum sample of those actually present.

When the 1381 listings of Great Waltham and High Easter are compared with the later fourteenth-century court rolls some startling differences emerge.[20] Of the 467 persons appearing with fully legible names in the 1381 listings for the two townships, only 276 (59.1 per cent) ever appeared in the court records of the period. Both sex and marital status were associated with likelihood of appearing in court. Of 157 married couples listed among 1381 taxpayers, the husbands also appeared in recorded court-roll transactions in 138 (87.9 per cent) instances; but their wives' representation was much worse, appearing in court in only 66 (42.0 per cent) instances. Of 94 single male taxpayers, 50 (53.2 per cent)

[19] For a general account of the poll-tax evidence, see M. W. Beresford, *Poll Taxes and Lay Subsidies* (Canterbury, 1963).
[20] Poos, 'Population and Resources', 97–100. The survival of these rolls is roughly as complete as those of Halesowen at the same period.

never appeared in court, and the corresponding figure for single females was 38 of 59 (64.4 per cent). To some extent, this is perhaps understandable: many of these unmarried taxpayers were probably adolescents, and commenced independent activities and thus appeared in the court records only some years after the tax collection, and, perhaps, in another locality, while young single female taxpayers may be impossible to trace if they subsequently married. But these figures once again emphasize how limited historians' scrutiny of village society is when only manor-court records are available as source material.[21] With very few exceptions, the intensive case studies of medieval village society which have been done to date are based exclusively on court evidence. The differences in appearance frequencies also suggest that there may have been a large degree of overlap between the 'singles' and the lower economic or status groups, themselves underrepresented in court transactions. The significance of this important point on the connection between economic and marital status will be considered further when discussion turns to manorial court evidence relating to marriage.

If, therefore, periodic indices of manor-court participants provide a slender basis for estimating aggregate local population change, direct evidence bearing on this problem is restricted to data such as series of tithing-penny payments.[22] But other types of information internal to manorial court proceedings which do pertain to ostensibly demographic processes might conceivably illuminate other aspects of medieval rural populations. One such test is the calculation of 'replacement rates' attempted by J. C. Russell for tenants-in-chief of the Crown from *Inquisitions Post Mortem* data,[23] by R. S. Gottfried from fifteenth-century wills,[24]

---

[21] One recent attempt to assess the importance of relative degrees of under-representation in the court-roll evidence, though still using only evidence internal to the court rolls themselves, may be noted here. Judith Bennett, using a categorization of individuals appearing in manor courts from communities with different economic contexts, found that persons associated with 'families' who participated in the villages' official hierarchy ('Rank A'), were between two and four times more likely to appear in recorded court transactions than those who were not so connected ('Rank C'). Average appearances per male were, in Brigstock (Northants), 30.0 (Rank A), and 7.9 (Rank C), between 1287 and 1348, in Iver (Bucks), 14.7 and 6.1 (1287–1349); in Houghton-cum-Wyton (Hunts), 7.8 and 3.3 (1288–1349). Bennett, 'Gender, Family and Community', 194, 276, 33–1.

[22] These data yield annual totals of resident adolescent and adult males. For a detailed analysis of tithingpenny payments as a source for demographic analysis for seven mid-Essex manors, see Poos, 'Population and Resources', 63–94.

[23] J. C. Russell, *British Medieval Population* (Albuquerque, 1948), 92–117; cf. T. H. Hollingsworth, *Historical Demography* (London, 1969), 375–88.

[24] R. S. Gottfried, *Epidemic Disease in Fifteenth-Century England* (Leicester, 1978), 187–203.

and by S. L. Thrupp for rural populations from manor-court records.[25] Razi has followed Thrupp's example for his study of Halesowen families.

Applied to manor-court evidence, this procedure consists of calculating the average number of sons identifiable in court records living at their father's death, by tracing all of each deceased tenant's sons through their various appearances in court.[26] With the exception of the decade of agrarian crisis during 1310–19,[27] the average ratio of sons to fathers derived by this procedure from the Halesowen evidence exceeded unity for the entire period from 1270 to 1349. Razi therefore observed that the replacement rates imply, as had the Halesowen court-participation index, that local population continued to expand to the eve of the Black Death: 'Halesowen families in the pre-plague period were able not only to replace themselves from generation to generation but also to produce a surplus of offspring to maintain population growth.'[28]

This procedure is more problematic in dealing with manors such as Halesowen where primogeniture was the custom of inheritance than in regions of partible inheritance, because there may well be under-recording of sons other than the single designated heir. As John Hatcher noted: 'To believe that all or even most of the extra sons ineligible to inherit will be able to be traced in other proceedings of the court is surely to be unrealistically optimistic.'[29] As we have seen, degrees of under-representation in the court records varied significantly among different economic strata, and this pattern also extended to the representation of offspring of villagers at different levels of local society.

Indeed, Razi recognizes this problem, and he notes that observable mean numbers of offspring per family were higher for 'rich' than 'poor' peasants, yet he posits inequities in living standards and thus in infant and child mortality as a major explanation for this differential.[30] However, he attempts to adjust calculated replacement rates, consistently lower for poorer than richer village families, by inflating data for the former accordingly.[31]

Apart from procedural difficulties, though, there has been a consistent lack of demographic awareness in the assumptions of historians who have attempted to calculate replacement rates from medieval data. Gottfried, for example, claims that replacement ratios represent an 'as yet not fully developed concept'.[32] To illustrate this point, the theoretical straightforward

---

[25] Thrupp, 'The Problem of Replacement-Rates', 101–19.
[26] Razi, *Life, Marriage and Death*, 32–4.   [27] Ibid. 33.   [28] Ibid.
[29] Hatcher, *Plague, Population and the English Economy*, 28.
[30] Razi, *Life, Marriage and Death*, 83–9.   [31] Ibid. 33–4.
[32] Gottfried, *Epidemic Disease*, 187.

case may be taken of exactly one son living at the father's death: in this case, the generations will replace each other only if (on average) the son himself is at that point at the age when (again on average) his own son would be born. In more formal demographers' terms, expectation of life at mean age of paternity must be equal to mean age at paternity. If, however, the father's life expectancy is shorter, his son will be 'too young' at father's death (relative to generational length) and a replacement rate of greater than unity is necessary to achieve a stationary population. Conversely, if the father's life expectancy is greater than his mean age at paternity, a stationary population can result with a replacement rate of less than unity. Even if replacement rates can be reliably calculated, therefore, one must possess data on adult life expectancy and mean age at paternity to draw meaningful demographic inferences. None of these measures can be derived from manor-court data (or other medieval sources), and has certainly not been accounted for in Razi's work.

One of the more straightforward measures of a demographic nature which manor-court evidence might be expected to provide does relate to life expectancy. It is certainly possible to calculate, from reasonably voluminous series of court records, average interval between an individual tenant's first appearance in the manorial records and his death (when the court recorded the admission of his heir to his tenement), for large numbers of people. Making valid demographic inferences from this data, of course, depends upon knowing the average age at first appearance in the court records, and upon this average being consistent over time and over a broad spectrum of the manorial population. Razi's method here is to presume that mean age at first recorded court appearance is 20 years. His rationale stems from the stipulation, under Halesowen manorial custom, of 20 years as the minimum age for landholding, and from this he argued that this was the average age of entry into property tenure.[33]

There seems little *prima facie* reason to make this equation. Moreover, it is uncertain what criteria have been adopted for defining at what point in a given individual's career 'landholding' begins. Razi does mention certain events that he regards as confirmation of tenant status. He argues that a man may be regarded as having entered into property-holding within two or three years of his first appearance in one of the following contexts: being amerced for default of court suit (since attending manorial court was a tenurial obligation); acting as personal pledge; being elected to manorial or administrative office;[34] appearing as victim of trespasses

---

[33] Razi, *Life, Marriage and Death*, 43.   [34] Ibid. 35–6, n. 30.

committed by others on one's own land.[35] Unfortunately the Halesowen data are not presented in such a way as to indicate which categories of 'first appearance' were most frequently employed in inferring entry into property, and only the latter of these 'indicators' can be regarded as firm evidence that an individual so identified was definitely a manorial tenant. Even so, a person could hold land for some time before amercement for default of court suit or before appearing as trespass victim.

Moreover, even if these procedural difficulties are ignored, and calculated mean intervals from first recorded appearance in court transactions to recorded death may be equated with life expectancy at a certain fixed age such as 20 years, these figures must still be related to a definable 'population at risk' before meaningful comparative conclusions can be drawn. Notices of tenant deaths in the manorial court records do not constitute a representative record of all adult deaths in a community. Manorial court proceedings contain references to tenants' deaths as information incidental to formal transmissions of property rights and/or payment of death duties and fines for entry into property by the deceased's heirs. Because manor-court records rarely survive for even short periods without gaps, some deaths escape; these deaths also pertain primarily to mature males, and pre-mortem sales or other transfers tantamount to pre-mortem bequests could obviate the need for an obituary entry in the court record.[36]

An analogous methodological problem arises with family reconstitution employing parish registers of the early modern period. Historical demographers calculate adult mortality based upon a sample of married persons whose ages at marriage can be determined because their baptisms are entered in the register.[37] This constitutes a base 'population at risk', consisting of persons of determinable age and demonstrably in residence over the defined period of analysis until death. Mean life-expectancies can therefore be derived.[38] Even for many persons with a sample of this sort, of course, death entries in the register will be unavailable. Many

---

[35] e.g. Dyer, *Lords and Peasants*, 229–30.

[36] Poos, 'Population and Resources', 135.

[37] These rules for calculation of mortality after families in a parish have been reconstituted were defined by E. Gautier and L. Henry, *La population du Crulai* (Paris, 1956), ch. 8 and were implemented with minor modifications by E. A. Wrigley, 'Mortality in Pre-Industrial England: The Example of Colyton, Devon, over Three Centuries', in D. V. Glass and R. Revelle (eds.), *Population and Social Change* (London, 1972), 243–74.

[38] A precise set of criteria are defined for determining what constitutes continuing residence: continuing to baptize or bury children up to age fifteen, or death of spouse, or remarriage, for example.

persons died outside their 'home' parish or 'outside the record' for other reasons; assumptions must be made to estimate measures for survivors at given ages which can then be related to the base population. It might in theory be feasible to develop criteria by which, from a reasonably full set of court records, continuing residence can be inferred for cohorts of 'first appearers', but it is unlikely that attempts to specify and control for all parameters will succeed.

Finally, these methodological difficulties are mirrored by the demographic implausibility of life expectancies derived by Razi's procedure. His estimates of life expectancy at entry into property-holding were based upon 196 'well-documented tenants' whose deaths were recorded in the Halesowen courts between 1300 and 1348. These yield a mean interval of 30.2 years. The figure must be adjusted, however, because 'poor' tenants in this sample exhibited a mean 'life expectancy' of only 20.8 years, and cottagers a figure as low as 10.0 years. An adjusted figure which takes into account further 'hypothetical' poor tenants is given as 25.3 years.[39] Razi does not consider the probability that his shorter mean for 'poor' villagers is due to first acquisition of land at a later age. No discussion is offered in the Halesowen study of evidence for status-specific differentials in life expectancy calculated for other pre-industrial populations, which would question such wide hypothesized differences.[40]

If, however, this estimate of life expectancy of between 25 and 28 years is presumed as equivalent to the values to be found in the d_x column of the Princeton Model West Life Tables, this would correspond roughly to these tables' mortality levels one to three, or an expectation of life at birth of between 18 and 22.8 years.[41] This would in turn mean that these

[39] Razi, *Life, Marriage and Death*, 43–5.

[40] The difficulties surrounding the allocation of a plausible distribution of ages of entry into property complicated the interpretations of adult mortality on manors of the bishopric of Winchester which were studied by Postan and Titow, 'Heriots and Prices'. For studies of social and economic-status-specific differentials in life expectancies for historical populations see, for example, A. Perrenoud, 'L'Inégalité sociale devant la mort à Geneve au XVIIème siècle', *Population*, numéro-special (1975), 221–43, and B. Derouet, 'Une démographic sociale differentielle', *Annales E.S.C.*, 35 (1980), 3–41.

[41] A. J. Coale and P. Demeny, *Regional Model Life Tables and Stable Populations* (2nd edn., New York, 1983), 42–3. Relating e_{20} to e_0 in this way involves assuming that the relationship between adult mortality and mortality in younger age groups was similar to that embodied in the Princeton Model West tables. For a discussion of this point, see R. S. Schofield and E. A. Wrigley, 'Infant and Child Mortality in the Late Tudor and Early Stuart Period', in C. Webster (ed.), *Health, Medicine and Mortality, in Tudor and Stuart England* (Cambridge, 1979), 61–95; in a medieval context, G. Ohlin, 'No Safety in Numbers: Some Pitfalls of Historical Statistics', in R. C. Floud (ed.), *Essays in Quantitative Economic History* (Oxford, 1974), 65–6.

estimates of e_{20} for early fourteenth-century Halesowen are perhaps eight to ten years lower than comparable values calculated for rural parishes of late-Elizabethan England, an era when real wages were plummeting.[42] Yet under Razi's reckoning the Halesowen population grew at an annual rate of 0.47 per cent for almost 70 years. To produce this level of growth with such heavy mortality requires gross reproduction levels considerably in excess of those most recently estimated for sixteenth- and seventeenth-century England, implying a nuptiality and fertility regime wholly unlike that of the later period.[43] In short, Razi's evidence, if accepted, would point unequivocally to the presence in Halesowen of a 'high-pressure' demographic system in which high mortality was counterbalanced by high fertility and to a pattern of early and near-universal marriage for Halesowen females.

As historical demographers studying early modern Europe employ increasingly sophisticated techniques of analysis, appreciation has grown of the pivotal role which fertility, heavily influenced by nuptiality patterns, plays in determining overall population growth. In describing the varieties of experience in various European regions at different periods, the term 'European marriage pattern' is used to specify a regime in which mean marriage ages are relatively high and a relatively large number of people never marry. This is generally associated with a fairly 'low-pressure' demographic situation, low fertility being coupled with low mortality. England can be shown to have possessed one variant of this pattern from as early as the mid-sixteenth century.[44]

By contrast, if Razi's data are accepted, in order to maintain the levels of population growth calculated for the pre-Black Death period and to counteract severe mortality levels implied, the population of Halesowen would need to have enjoyed a gross reproduction rate between one and a

[42] E. A. Wrigley and R. S. Schofield, *The Population History, of England, 1541–1871: A Reconstruction* (London, 1981), 230–1.
[43] See the discussion of implications of different mortality and fertility combinations in ibid. 236–48.
[44] See, among a huge body of literature, M. Anderson, *Approaches to the History of the Western Family* (London, 1981); P. Laslett, 'Characteristics of the Western Family Considered over Time', in P. Laslett, *Family Life and Illicit Love in Earlier Generations* (Cambridge, 1977), 12–49; Wrigley and Schofield, *Population History of England*, 402–83. The concept of the European marriage pattern was first articulated in a seminal paper by J. Hajnal, 'European Marriage Patterns in Perspective', in D. V. Glass and D. E. C. Eversley, *Population in History: Essays in Historical Demography* (London, 1965), 101–43. Hajnal observed (ibid. 117–19) that the 14th-cent. English poll-tax listings point to a 'non-European' marriage pattern among the rural English medieval population. More recent work, however, has altered this impression from the poll-tax evidence: cf. Poos, 'Population and Resources', 140–58.

half and two times higher than those typical of early modern England.[45] Razi in fact argues that Halesowen peasants practised a definitively 'non-European' marriage pattern, and employs three major lines of argument to support this empirically. These are: (1) that despite a practice of impartible inheritance in this manor, in many cases more than one son from a given family managed to acquire land and so to establish a household; (2) that patterns of merchet payments recorded in the court records support a low estimate of marriage age; and (3) that high levels of extra-marital pregnancy apparently prevalent among Halesowen women imply a 'high-pressure' fertility pattern associated with loose or casual popular conceptions of marriage institutions.

A. Inheritance

The pioneering work of G. C. Homans on the court rolls of champion England of the thirteenth century still stands as the fullest published account of marriage practices among medieval customary tenants.[46] Homans posits restricted prospects of marriage for men other than the designated heir due to impartible inheritance. This custom limited their access to land and, therefore, the means for establishing independent households, and often condemned them to lifetime celibacy as dependants upon siblings' tenements.

More recent projections by demographers indicate that in stationary populations with combinations of mortality and fertility levels typical of pre-industrial Europe roughly 40 per cent of all men died without any sons to succeed them. In a medieval context opportunities were thereby created for 'surplus' sons of some families to acquire land from others, by market transactions or marriage to heiresses.[47] Therefore, from a young man's viewpoint, it was not necessarily the death or retirement of his own father that determined access to property and thus the economic wherewithal to marry, but in addition any heirless man's death or retirement, or indeed sale or lease, within the community could make available a 'niche' to be 'colonized'.

---

[45] Gross reproduction rates of 3.1 to 4.1 would be needed to sustain intrinsic growth rates of close to 0.5 per cent per annum in the absence of considerable net immigration: Coale and Demeny, *Regional Model Life Tables*, 42–3. In contrast, gross reproduction rates in England during the 16th and 17th cent. were most typically in the range of 2.0 to 2.3: Wrigley and Schofield, *Population History of England*, 528–9.

[46] Homans, *English Villagers*, 133–76.

[47] See Wrigley, 'Fertility Strategy', and Smith, 'Some Issues Concerning Families'. Cf. R. S. Schofield, 'The Relationship Between Demographic Structure and Environment in Pre-industrial Western Europe', in W. Conze (ed.), *Sozialgeschichte der Familie in der Neuzeit Europas* (Stuttgart, 1976), 147–60.

In fact, both Razi and Edward Britton have been highly critical of Homans's arguments concerning the failure of men other than designated heirs to enter into matrimony because of restricted access to land. Indeed, they establish empirically that non-inheriting sons in the thirteenth and fourteenth centuries did acquire property by alternative means. Britton, considering a community where as at Halesowen inheritance practice was impartible, found that 23 per cent of resident families between 1288 and 1340 had more than one son who managed to acquire property, and concluded that Homans had grossly underestimated the non-inheriting son's prospects. He wrote: 'unless one is to conclude that there was an *incredible* [our emphasis] number of heiresses in Broughton during the period it would be difficult to explain the high degree of success of non-inheriting sons in acquiring land.'[48]

Razi, using much fuller manorial court records than those at Britton's disposal, arrived at essentially similar conclusions for Halesowen during the same period. By 'reconstituting' 788 Halesowen families between 1270 and 1348, he establishes that 590 had at least one son observable in the court records;[49] of these 590 families 290 leave evidence of two or more sons, and in 140 cases two or more siblings are observed holding land simultaneously.[50] The success of 'surplus' sons in gaining access to land led Razi to claim that 'Halesowen villagers were prepared to face economic hardships and destitution rather than to remain bachelors and spinsters.'[51] Yet Razi's own data imply that more than one-third of the male tenants of Halesowen died without direct male heirs.[52] In neither Halesowen nor Broughton, then, were the proportions of 'surplus-son tenants' any higher than would be commensurate with a situation where surplus sons from some families occupied tenements vacated by others, under heirship-failure rates compatible with pre-industrial demographic structures. This evidence, therefore, does not

---

[48] E. Britton, 'The Peasant Family in Fourteenth-Century England', *Peasant Studies*, 5 (1976), 27.

[49] Razi, *Life, Marriage and Death*, 55.   [50] Ibid. 55–6.   [51] Ibid. 57.

[52] Razi's raw data indicate that approximately 75 per cent of families in observation had at least one son (ibid. 55). Yet this sample of 'observable' sons includes those as young as 12 years (the age at swearing into tithing), and we should make some adjustment for deaths of sons between that age and fathers' deaths. Of course, we have no data on paternal deaths in the necessary form: but if we employ the adult mortality level that Razi calculated (though problematic), the 590 families with one or more sons aged 12 and older would probably be diminished to about 5–13 with one or more sons aged 20 and older, or 65 per cent. This calculation is based upon deaths occurring from exact ages 10–20 years as a percentage of survivors to exact age 10 in Model West life table, mortality levels 1–3: Coale and Demeny, *Regional Model Life Tables*, 42.

substantiate Razi's argument for a 'non-European' marriage regime in medieval Halesowen.

B. *Merchet*

Razi also analyses merchets, payments recorded in the court rolls to secure permission for villein women to marry, to estimate generational length. In large part this method again rests upon the assumption that males entered into property at or very close to the age of twenty years. His procedure uses what he calls 'three-generation families.[53] When B son of A first appears in the court record as a 'landholder', Razi argues, it can be assumed that B was roughly 20 years old; if C son of B (or D daughter of B) then appears in the record roughly twenty years later, it can be assumed that B married and bore C (or D) at about the age of 20.

According to Razi this evidence suggests the non-European character of medieval Halesowen marriage, but it depends largely upon the assumption about the synchroneity of legal age of majority and initial property acquisition. However, in fifty-nine cases in the sample of 'three-generation families' a link can be made with daughters, whose merchet payment was recorded an average of 18–22 years after their fathers' first appearance as 'landholders'.[54] In fact, these villein marriages represent only 29 per cent of the recorded merchet payments entered during 1293–1348, and this relatively low proportion raises questions regarding the representativeness of both merchet-payers whose marriages can be linked with their fathers' previous land acquisitions and of merchet-payers as a whole.

This issue is currently a subject of considerable debate. Opinions differ on whether the liability to pay merchet stemmed fundamentally from personal 'condition', or whether it was primarily linked with seigneurial jurisdiction over the transfer of customary property at marriage, the status of which the lord would have obvious interest in policing.[55] If the latter theory is more likely, then evidence relating to merchets recorded in manorial courts may not be a dispassionate index of marriage incidence, age, or even endowment practice across a broad spectrum of manorial servile populations. In fact, the evidence from Halesowen and from a

---

[53] Razi, *Life, Marriage and Death*, 63.   [54] Ibid.

[55] For this debate, see J. Scammell, 'Freedom and Marriage in Medieval England', *EcHR* 2nd ser. 27 (1974), 523–37; E. Searle, 'Freedom and Marriage in Medieval England: An Alternative Hypothesis', *EcHR* 2nd ser. 29 (1976), 482–6; J. Scammell, 'Wife-Rents and Merchet', *EcHR* 2nd ser. 29 (1976), 487–90; Searle, 'Seigneurial Control of Women's Marriage', 3–43; Brand and Hyams, 'Seigneurial Control of Women's Marriage', 122–33; Faith, 'Seigneurial Control of Women's Marriage', 133–48; Searle, 'Seigneurial Control of Women's Marriage: A Rejoinder', 148–61.

number of other contemporary communities suggests that servile marriages recorded in manorial courts represent only a fraction of the marriages which must have taken place among customary tenants under the most latitudinarian presumptions, and that women who did pay merchet were drawn disproportionately from the upper levels of village society.

Servile marriages are recorded in manorial court proceedings either directly, through licences for permission to marry, or else through fines paid by or on behalf of women who had married without seigneurial permission. For Halesowen, Razi's figures for marriage incidence drawn from both record categories and corrected for missing documents can be related to a base population of customary tenants liable to pay merchet; the crude marriage rates thereby obtained are revealingly low, rarely higher than six per 1,000 per annum.[56] In late sixteenth- and early seventeenth-century England, when population growth rates were of the order of 0.5 to 0.75 per cent per annum, crude marriage rates were generally in the range of 9–15 per 1,000.[57] For a demographic growth rate of similar dimensions, as claimed by Razi for late thirteenth- and early fourteenth-century Halesowen, recorded merchets can represent at most about half

[56] The estimated crude marriage rates have been obtained from Razi's measures of population totals based on quinquennial totals of resident males over 12 years of age appearing in the court proceedings (Razi, *Life, Marriage and Death*, 25), doubling them and adding a further 33 per cent to account for women and all persons under the age of 12. But, because merchet was a liability only of customary tenants, we have used Razi's estimate of the proportion of entire population represented by customary tenants, that is, two-thirds of overall population (ibid. 10). (As it is likely that customary tenants—as opposed to free tenants—were disproportionately more fully represented among those appearing in manorial courts, the resulting calculation of crude marriage rates are, if anything, an overestimate.) Setting recorded servile marriages corrected for incomplete document survival (ibid. 48), against these estimates of servile population yields the following crude marriage rates by quinquennium:

Quinquennia	Total population	Servile population	Crude marriage rates p.a. for servile population
1293–5	1157	763	6.9
1301–5	1216	802	5.4
1311–15	1290	851	6.2
1321–5	1095	723	3.9
1331–5	1152	760	4.3
1345–9	1250	825	7.7

[57] Wrigley and Schofield, *Population History of England*, 531–5. Like most crude demographic measures, this rate is not absolutely satisfactory when used comparatively in this manner, as it takes no account of factors such as proportions of population at marriageable ages, customs pertaining to remarriage, and so on.

of the servile marriages which would have taken place even under a 'European' marriage pattern.

Likewise, this under-representation of servile marriages is demonstrated for a number of other contemporary manors. Data for 107 servile marriages recorded at the manors of Great Waltham and High Easter during the period 1327–89 produced crude servile marriage rates little higher than five per 1,000 per annum.[58] Similarly, the court records of the manor of Redgrave between 1260 and 1319 include notices of 262 servile marriages; when these marriages are related to a base population derived from a rental of 1289, they represent only one-third to one-half the number of marriages if crude marriage rates were similar there to early modern English levels.[59] Finally, the records for five manors belonging to Spalding Priory between 1252 and 1300 yield crude marriage rates ranging from 1.7 to 2.5 per 1,000 per annum, or a global average of 2.1; again, an implausibly low figure.[60] If merchets recorded in manor-court rolls represent only a fraction of the servile marriages actually occurring, the bias that leads to under-representation is clear only in relation to the economic circumstances of the families whose daughters did pay merchet. In Waltham and Easter, figures can be produced for acreages of tenements held by parents of forty-four women whose merchets were recorded in

---

[58] Poos, 'Population and Resources', 159–84. The procedure employed in this case was slightly different from that for the Halesowen data. Observed events (recorded servile marriages in surviving court records), have been set against a time at risk (the interval of time elapsed between the court session at which the marriage was recorded and the next previous court session, as it is envisioned that a precontractual exchange of vows, regarded by canon law and perhaps also popular opinion as the initiation of a valid marriage, preceded licensing in the manorial court and solemnization in *facie ecclesie*). This gives quinquennial figures for annual rates of recorded servile marriages. Quinquennial resident population totals have been calculated from tithingpenny figures for resident males aged 12 and older; servile populations have been estimated as two-thirds of total populations, because this is roughly the ratio of tenancies recorded in 1328 as having at least some customary land or molland to all tenancies.

[59] At Redgrave, 326 tenants held customary land in 1289 (Redgrave rental, University of Chicago Library, Bacon MS 805). It is unlikely that these tenancies related to a base unfree population of less than 1,000 persons, then, and one would expect between 400 and 900 marriages over this period if crude marriage rates were similar to early modern levels. Marriages recorded in Redgrave court rolls, University of Chicago, Joseph Regenstein Library, Bacon MSS, 1–15.

[60] The evidence for this comes from the Myntling Register: Spalding Gentlemen's Society Library, Spalding, Lincolnshire. It is possible to relate the merchets paid by bond women in these five manors (440 in total during 1252–1300), to estimates of the bond population of the individual manors for points in the late 13th cent. For these estimates, see Hallam, 'Some Thirteenth-Century Censuses', 340–61. This results in crude annual marriage rates per thousand of 2.1 (Pinchbeck), 2.3 (Spalding), 2.5 (Weston), 1.7 (Moulton), and 2.2 (Sutton), or a 'global' mean annual rate of 2.1 per 1,000.

the court records during 1327–48, by combining these families' entries in rentals compiled in 1328 with subsequent land transfers and obituaries in the court records. The mean acreage held by these families was nearly double the mean tenancy size recorded in 1328.[61] These families were not drawn exclusively from the ranks of the very largest tenants; thirteen (34.2 per cent) apparently possessed less than ten acres of land at their daughters' marriage. But since 63.2 per cent of all tenancies recorded in 1328 were in this size category, the bias toward larger tenants is unmistakable.

An analysis of merchet-paying families at Redgrave produces a similar profile. The 1289 rental listed 326 tenancies involving customary properties, and the families associated with 164 (50.3 per cent) of these tenancies can be linked with 219 of the females who paid licences to marry during the sixty years centring on the rental's composition date. The 164 tenancies produced over 84 per cent of the recorded merchets, and also accounted for 81 per cent of the customary land within the manor. Quite evidently, marriage fines were paid disproportionately by the middling and wealthier villeins and only relatively rarely by smallholders and cottagers. For instance, only 11.1 per cent of the marriage fines were paid by individuals whose families possessed tenements of less than two acres at or close to time of marriage, whereas customary tenancies of that size constitute almost 44 per cent of the total. Conversely, over 25 per cent of the marriages recorded were associated with the small number of families (8.4 per cent) holding properties of more than ten acres.[62] Our analysis of merchet, then, suggests that the marriages recorded in manor-court proceedings are drawn from a relatively small group of higher status members of villein society. Any assessment of the demographic significance of merchet evidence must be set within this perspective, as must any observations bearing upon other aspects of medieval rural populations' marriage practices such as family property-endowment arrangements.[63]

---

[61] As closely as can be reconstructed at the time of merchet payment, 15.8 acres was the mean acreage held. Poos, 'Population and Resources', 159–84.

[62] For a detailed discussion of the social distribution of land in late 13th cent. Redgrave, see Smith, 'Families and Their Land'.

[63] Part of the recent debate between Eleanor Searle and Rosamund Faith on the function of merchet in the 13th and 14th cents. centred around whether the obligation was primarily a function of tenurial status or an issue of personal unfreedom. It would obviously be unrealistic to insist too strongly upon either aspect of the custom, as clearly both considerations were present, and a noteworthy minority of participants in recorded servile marriages (substantial, for example, at Waltham and Easter), failed to appear in any tenurial contexts in the surviving records. But the quantities of properties involved in marriages whose participants did appear as tenants were considerable. In Redgrave, 75 (28 per cent), of the servile

C. *Leyrwite*

To substantiate further his position on the existence of a non-European marriage pattern in medieval Halesowen, Razi utilizes evidence of leyrwite paid by servile women.[64] Razi employs a particular definition of leyrwite leading Rodney Hilton to state that 'in Halesowen from 1270 to 1348 the manor court rolls leave evidence of 117 leyrwite payments and 220 merchets and show how widespread and lacking in social stigma pregnancy out of wedlock could be.[65] Hilton relies upon Razi's explicit presumption that leyrwite payments by villein women represent extramarital pregnancy rather than simply extramarital fornication. It is unclear whether Razi is justified in his interpretation of leyrwite, but along with Hilton he is inclined to view matrimony as a rather informal institution, entered or violated lightly, in the popular culture of rural society in the late thirteenth and early fourteenth centuries.[66]

Razi notes that on some manors, specifically certain of those of Ramsey Abbey, women paid leyrwite when discovered to have fornicated and childwite when they actually bore a child out of wedlock. In Halesowen, only leyrwite was levied. Entries of this kind usually took the form *A filia B in misericordia pro leyrwite*; more rarely, the form was *A filia B deflorata est ideo leyrwite*; very infrequently, the entry was further embellished to read *A filia B deflorata est impregnata ideo in misericordia*.[67] This terminological elaboration leads Razi to believe that in all or most of the cases, leyrwite implied an actual extramarital conception and birth. Furthermore, he argues that it is difficult to see how it could have proven that a

marriages can be directly associated with gifts of land to the bride at her marriage. In Waltham and Easter, approximately one-fifth of the recorded marriages were associated with property transfers to the bride in the decades before the Black Death. Of course, court-roll evidence is likely to be generally less forthcoming in the matter of marriage endowments made in moveable goods rather than land. Furthermore, in Redgrave there is suggestive evidence that the licenses were themselves not unconnected with either the property-holding status of their parents or the size of dowry they obtained. Of the girls who cannot be shown to have a connection with a landholding family (30 cases), 80 per cent paid licence fees under 1*s*. Only 32 (30.3 per cent), of the 139 girls whose fathers' landholdings can be documented at the time of their marriages paid licence fees of 1*s*. or less. Of the girls receiving dowries (33 cases), of over half an acre of land, 73 per cent paid licence fees over 2*s*., whereas only 42 per cent of those with dowries smaller than this (42 cases), paid fees over 2*s*.

[64] Razi, *Life, Marriage and Death*, 64–71.
[65] Hilton, 'Freedom and Villeinage', 191.
[66] They believe this interpretation to be justified by the evidence concerning disputed marriage contracts in the surviving records of medieval English ecclesiastical courts. See e.g. M. M. Sheehan, 'The Formation and Stability of Marriage in Fourteenth-Century England', *Medieval Studies*, 33 (1971), 228–63 and Helmholz, *Marriage Litigation*.
[67] Razi, *Life, Marriage and Death*, 64.

woman had fornicated without the visible evidence of pregnancy. This is certainly questionable logic, in view of comparable situations revealed by fifteenth-, sixteenth-, or seventeenth-century archdeaconary court books. For instance, in the Norwich archdeaconary during the sixteenth century, only approximately one-third of all sexual delicts recorded in the commissary's court records came to the knowledge of the court because a woman had actually become pregnant.[68] In the village community, one might speculate that such tangible evidence would have been even less necessary to have secured a presentment of sexual misconduct.

We have already suggested that the evidence relating to merchet greatly underestimates the likely incidence of marriage; this, combined with the exaggerated impression of extramarital pregnancy obtained under Razi's assumptions, leads to a highly inflated measure of illegitimacy (as expressed in terms of ratios of extramarital pregnancies to recorded marriages). Furthermore, it is not certain that this evidence indicates a loose attachment to marriage.[69] Whatever interpretation is placed upon leyrwite, it is possible that it relates primarily to the actions of girls located predominantly in the lower echelons of Halesowen tenantry.[70] There might also be some tendency on the part of presentment juries to have been more zealous in exposing and punishing the actions of girls of lesser status levels than in the ranks of the tenantry from which they themselves came. None the less, as a measure of social conformity, leyrwite may be more broadly inclusive, and the 'population at risk' may have been considerably larger than the segment of the tenantry which paid marriage fines or merchets.

In the Suffolk manor of Redgrave, a servile woman paid childwite *quia peperit extra matermonium*, and this explicit reference to extramarital childbearing among daughters of customary tenants might be expected to

---

[68] R. H. Houlbrooke, *Church Courts and the People During the English Reformation, 1520–70* (Oxford, 1979), 76. For rather higher numbers of pregnancies relative to 'incontinents' and adulterers that did not involve pregnancies, see K. Wrightson and D. Levine, *Poverty and Piety in an English Village: Terling, 1525–1700* (London, 1979), 125–7. However, in the presentments in an archdeaconry of Colchester act book for the period 1600–42 relating to the Essex parish of Kelvedon, cases concerning fornication and adultery were much more frequent than bastard births and extramarital pregnancies: J. A. Sharpe, 'Crime and Delinquency in an Essex Parish, 1600–40', in J. S. Cockburn (ed.), *Crime in England, 1550–1800* (London, 1977), 109.

[69] This issue is considered in more detail in R. M. Smith, 'Illegitimacy, Customary and Common Law and Ecclesiastical Definitions of Marriage: Some Late-Thirteenth and Early-Fourteenth-Century English Evidence' (a paper presented to the Cambridge Historical Society at Girton College, Cambridge, 3 May 1983).

[70] Razi, *Life, Marriage and Death*, 64.

render a more reliable measure of actual illegitimacy than that provided by simple, unembellished references to leyrwite such as the Halesowen court records give. Yet these fines should not be related as a simple ratio to recorded servile marriages, as if the two measures were comparable to the records of marriages and bastard births in an early modern parish register.[71] We have already suggested that the 263 marriages recorded in the extant Redgrave court rolls between 1260 and 1319 relate disproportionately to the daughters of tenants with landed property above average size. Childwite, however, perhaps like leyrwite, appears to have been paid by a wider social and economic spectrum of the servile population. For instance, only 12.6 per cent of the 163 marriages recorded in Redgrave court proceedings between 1260 and 1319 related to customary families who did not also appear definitively as landholders (either through a record in the 1289 rental or as payers of heriot in the court rolls). Twenty-one (27 per cent) of the seventy-eight childwite payments recorded over the same period were made by women whose families left no evidence of customary land tenure. This strongly suggests that, as merchet-payers were disproportionately drawn from the upper social and economic strata of village society, so childwite-payers are disproportionately drawn from the lower strata. It is apparent, therefore, that the two 'populations at risk', on the one hand likely to pay childwite and on the other to pay merchet, were far from identical, and it would seem highly questionable to relate the one to the other in order to estimate simple illegitimacy levels in this particular manor.[72]

It should also be noted here that one need not, as Razi has done, infer that relatively high levels of illegitimacy are a benchmark of an early-marrying, non-European marriage regime. An inverse relationship between high illegitimacy rates and high marriage ages was certainly characteristic of the English throughout the parish-register era, when the evidence points unambiguously to a particular variant of the European marriage pattern being present.[73] In a broader comparative context, illegitimacy is often

---

[71] As e.g. could be done with the evidence in Laslett, *Family Life and Illicit Love*, 116–17. In a sample of 24 parishes the decadal ratios of recorded marriages to illegitimacies varied between 5.7 and 8.2 from 1580 to 1640. The ratio implied by the Redgrave evidence during 1260–1319 is 3.4.

[72] This unfortunate error was made in Smith, 'English Peasant Life Cycles', 456–7. These results were cited with approval by Razi, *Life, Marriage and Death*, 70, as evidence of high levels of illegitimacy in communities other than Halesowen.

[73] See the remarks of E. A. Wrigley, 'Marriage, Fertility and Population Growth in Eighteenth-Century England', in R. B. Outhwaite (ed.), *Marriage and Society: Studies in the Social History of Marriage* (London, 1981), 155–63.

low in societies where female marriage is early and marriage is universal, insofar as such societies tend to have well-developed codes of honour and shame, under which female virginity constitutes a *sine qua non* for a woman's marriage.[74]

If the tone of this essay appears negative, this should not be interpreted to mean that we see no prospect for a developing field of English medieval historical demography that incorporates the voluminous, uniquely produced, and well-preserved proceedings of the manorial court. In some respects, over-optimistic use of these sources stems from risks taken in pioneering and innovative investigations by researchers not adequately versed in technical skills, which are a necessary prerequisite for reliable demographic inference. We are currently in the trial and error phase of English medieval demography.

We would not advocate a return to the anecdotal use of court-roll material that characterized Homans's work, or an attempt to write the social history of medieval English villagers with an undue concentration on the better-documented, higher-status individuals among customary tenants as one recent worker in the field has suggested.[75] On the contrary, we believe it is vital that, as in parish-register analysis, full cognizance be taken of the 'unreconstitutable majority', and methods of analysis be formulated accordingly.

But the present state of research underlines the extent to which current secondary literature in the field has failed to integrate different categories of source material. At the outset of this discussion, it was suggested that this was a potentially serious shortcoming of any attempt to reconstruct resident populations of English communities in the Middle Ages from the proceedings of legal tribunals which were themselves developing institutions in the century after 1250. With almost no exceptions, the authors of the studies of Halesowen and Ramsey Abbey manors have failed to incorporate earlier fourteenth-century lay subsidy returns or later fourteenth-century polltax listings to confirm their premise (explicit or implicit) that court-roll evidence provides an adequate means of observing medieval rural populations over a broad social and economic spectrum; while for both Halesowen and the Ramsey estates there survive

---

[74] See the remarks in R. M. Smith, 'Some Reflections on the Evidence for the Origins of the "European Marriage Pattern" in England', in C. Harris (ed.), *The Sociology of the Family: New Directions for Britain, Sociological Review*, monograph 28 (1979), 96 and A. Macfarlane, 'Modes of Reproduction', in G. Hawthorn (ed.), *Population and Development: High and Low Fertility in Poorer Countries* (London, 1979), 112–13.

[75] This latter view seems to be an unnecessary cry of despair in Bennett, 'Spouses, Siblings and Surnames', 45–6.

no manorial rentals which might allow a systematic assessment of the representativeness of those villagers whose presence is most loudly proclaimed in manorial court evidence. The paucity of attempts at integrated approaches of this sort may be partly due to the dearth of communities for which suitable combinations of source material survive. Yet in future studies of this sort, the range of available documentation must be considered as important a factor in determining the subject locality for case studies as the quality of any particular category of source material, although we are in no doubt that for many purposes the manorial court records will still generate the largest body of data.[76]

II. THE USE OF MANORIAL COURT ROLLS IN DEMOGRAPHIC ANALYSIS: A RECONSIDERATION (ZVI RAZI)

Larry Poos and Richard Smith have strongly criticized the uses made of manorial court rolls for demographic analysis. They have argued that the data obtained from the court records are inadequate in measuring the demographic trend and in making observations about replacement rates. expectation of life, marriage, and illegitimacy. It seems to me, however, that although their criticism is partly justified, on the whole it is unduly negative. First, the claim that the demographic trend cannot be measured from court rolls will be examined; and thereafter the other issues raised by Poos and Smith will be discussed.

Poos and Smith have argued that the court rolls are unrepresentative since a significant number of villagers, especially smallholders and cottagers, never appear in them. They have also maintained that population changes obtained from the court rolls might have occurred not as a result of demographic changes but from changes in administrative or litigational procedures or in the economic and ecological situation.[77] If they are right, it is impossible to use court-roll data to estimate the demographic trend. However, it can be shown that their arguments are inconclusive.

Poos and Smith have based their claim for the unrepresentativeness of the court rolls on the known fact that cottagers and smallholders appear less frequently in the records than better-off tenants.[78] But villagers who

---

[76] See L. R. Poos, 'Peasant "Biographies" From Medieval England', in N. Bulst and J. P. Genet (eds.), *Medieval Prosopography: Proceedings of the Bielefeld Conference*, Dec. 1982 (Kalamazoo, 1986), pp. 201–14, influenced greatly by ground rules for work in later centuries presented by K. Wrightson, 'Villages, Villagers and Village Studies', *Historical Journal* 18 (1975), 632–39.

[77] Above, pp. 298–324.   [78] Above, pp. 306–8.

appear only a few times in the records can be counted as much as those who appear many times during the term of their residence. One can only prove that the court rolls are unrepresentative by showing that many resident villagers do not appear in them at all. By using the rental of High Easter and Great Waltham, the court rolls from 1327 to 1349 and the polltax listings of 1381, it has been argued that the court rolls are unrepresentative. But the procedures adopted for these tests gravely underestimate the representativeness of the court rolls. If one looks first at the figures in Table 9.3, one can see that among the 416 tenants recorded in the rental, 306 (73.5 per cent) are also recorded in the court rolls. This is in fact a large sample as the court records of only one year before 1328 are available. In order to identify in the court rolls the tenants appearing in the rental, it is necessary to take not only the court rolls after the date of the rental but the court records of at least ten to fifteen years before this date as well. Smallholders and cottagers who appear only a few times in the court records might have appeared in the court rolls before 1328, then were registered in the rental of 1328, but died or emigrated before appearing again in the manor court. Therefore, one finds that 40.8 per cent of the cottagers and 30.2 per cent of the smallholders are not noted in the court rolls between 1327 and 1348.

Table 9.3 also underestimates the representativeness of the court rolls because of the inclusion of women. The fact that Poos noted the number of tenants who appear both in the rental and the court rolls irrespective of sex, simply distorts the results. The question which we debate is to what extent males are well represented in the court rolls, because the demographic observations criticized by Poos and Smith have been made from data about males and not females, who were so poorly represented in the records. Therefore, they should have counted only the male tenants who are noted in both sources. Unfortunately, I have not been able to inspect the rental. It is reasonable to assume, however, that it includes, as in many other contemporary rentals, around 16 per cent female tenants. The majority of these women probably did not appear in the court rolls and thus inflated the percentage of those never appearing in Table 9.3. If among the 16 per cent female tenants in the rental 10 per cent are not recorded in the court rolls, the percentage of males identified in both records rises to 81.8. If between ten to fifteen years of court rolls before 1328 would have been used, it is reasonable to assume that at least another forty tenants could have been noted. In this case the percentage of tenants noted in both sources rises to 89.8 per cent. This figure gives a more accurate estimate of the representativeness of males in the court

rolls than the figure of 73.5 per cent found by Poos and Smith. The way
in which their figures are misleading can be seen even more clearly when
the 1381 polltax listing is examined. Again, the percentage of those who
appear in the 1381 polltax listing but not in the late fourteenth-century
court records has been inflated by including women. Among the 467
persons appearing in the 1381 polltax listing only 276 (59.1 per cent) ever
appear in the court records.[79] But if the appearance of only males is
counted, the percentage rises to 70.9 per cent.[80] Moreover, while 87.9 per
cent of the married male taxpayers were also noted in the court record,
among the single men only 48.8 per cent appear in the records. Poos and
Smith themselves admit that this last figure is an underestimate because
many among the taxpayers were probably adolescents who started independent activities only a few years after the collection, and perhaps in
another locality, and thus could not appear before the manor court. But
this is not all. Among the 191 taxpayers who never appeared in the court
records, eighteen (8.4 per cent) were listed as servants without a surname
and therefore cannot be traced in the court records even if they appear in
their own right.[81] Moreover, a number of taxpayers do not appear in the
court rolls simply because they lived outside the jurisdiction of Waltham
manor court.[82] If one subtracts from the total number of male taxpayers
in the sample those who cannot be identified in the court records—
servants, adolescents who emigrated, and males who lived outside the
jurisdiction of the court—the percentage of males noted in both sources
rises from 70.9 per cent to 89.8 per cent.[83]

To sum up, Poos's and Smith's claim that the adult male population of
a village is not well represented in the court rolls has not been substantiated. Moreover, the evidence adduced from the rental and tax listings of
Waltham and Easter to show that the court rolls are unrepresentative in
fact suggests that the opposite is true. We may now examine their assertion that changes in the number of people obtained from the court rolls
can be caused not only by demographic changes but also by changes in

[79] Above, p. 307.
[80] Ibid. Among the 251 males in the poll-tax listing 178 were also noted in the court rolls.
(Above, p. 307.)
[81] Poos, 'Population and Resources', 98.   [82] Ibid.
[83] I have assumed that the sex ratio among the servants (18), and the Little Waltham
taxpayers who do not appear in the court rolls (68), is the same as found for all the
taxpayers. This gives a figure of 9.6 and 36.5 males respectively. I have also assumed that
half of the male taxpayers from Little Waltham (18.2), lived outside the jurisdiction of the
court and that half (25), of the single male taxpayers who do not appear in the court rolls
emigrated. If I am close to the mark, the percentage of the taxpayers noted also in the court
rolls is 89.8 per cent.

administrative or litigational procedures or in the economic and ecological situation.

It is true that in many places in the late thirteenth century presentment juries as a means of initiating business before the court were introduced into the manor court and that the quantity of court business increased, while in the second half of the fourteenth century the quantity of court business declined as personally initiated pleas tended to be replaced with presentments by jury.[84] But these changes are easily observed in the court records and consequently can be taken into consideration. For example, the volume of court business in Rickinghall manor court increased in the 1270s (Table 9.1). Therefore, the court records before this date should be excluded. But the court rolls from the 1270s onwards can be taken into consideration when the number of people appearing in the records is counted. Indeed, it has been found that the number of villagers rises from 77 in 1270 to 115 in 1315. As no change occurred in the administration of the court or in its litigational procedures between 1270 and 1315 there is no reason to suspect that the rise in the number of people observed in the court rolls during these years was caused by reasons other than demographic ones. Poos and Smith, however, claimed that there is internal evidence of another variety of court roll information that implies that the population of Rickinghall was declining rather than growing during the period 1270–1315, as court appearances seem to indicate. It has been observed that approximately 30 per cent of customary tenants died with no surviving male or female offspring whereas in a stationary population one would expect this in no more than 20 per cent of parents' deaths.[85] This internal evidence, however, is rather problematic. In very few cases it is stated in court rolls that a tenant died childless. In most cases it is only inferred when nobody came forward to claim the holding of a dead tenant. But this does not necessarily mean that this tenant died childless. The children who might have survived him did not come to court to claim their inheritance either because they emigrated or because they could not afford to pay the entry fine. In many places in England in the late thirteenth and early fourteenth century, the entry fines were customary and consequently low. But in Rickinghall as in some other places during this period. entry fines reflected real land values and were consequently very high.[86] Therefore, the fact that 30 per cent of the holdings of dead tenants in Rickinghall were not taken by their offspring can well

---

[84] Beckerman, 'Customary Law in Manorial Courts', 63–111.
[85] Above, p. 304.   [86] Titow, *English Rural Society*, 73–8.

show, not as Poos and Smith assume, that the population declined, but that as land values rose many young villagers were pushed out of landholding by a high level of entry fines. Since the claim that the rise of people noted in Rickinghall court rolls was a result of transformations in court procedure has not been substantiated, let us examine the Halesowen court rolls.

In Halesowen the court rolls survive from 1270 onward, but by this date presentment juries, as a means of initiating business into the court, had already been adopted and no other change in the procedure and litigation practices of the court can be observed until the 1340s. By that time pledges were required in fewer cases and this trend continued after the plague. Again and again in the late 1380s personally initiated pleas tended to be replaced with presentment by jury. The number of males noted in the court records rose from 1270 to 1315, then declined by 15 per cent as a result of the 'Great Famine'. In the 1330s and the 1340s the number of males rose until the eve of the 'Black Death' in 1349.[87] The only time during this long period in which there was change in litigation procedure is the 1340s. If Poos and Smith are right, the fact that fewer pledges were required in the 1340s should have depressed the number of males noted in the records, but in fact the opposite occurred. Similarly the decline of villagers noted in the post-plague court records began long before the change in the litigational procedures was introduced in the late 1380s.[88] Consequently it is hard to see how we can explain changes in the number of villagers noted in Halesowen court records by claiming that they were caused by changes in litigational procedures rather than by demographic changes. However, we still have to examine Poos's and Smith's claim that the number of people observed in the court rolls could be affected by economic crises or plagues rather than by demographic changes. In such periods they assert there is a marked increase in persons circulating through the courts.

In order to test the validity of this claim, I checked the court rolls of Halesowen during plague years and during years of economic dislocation in which the harvests failed, and there was a sharp rise in the number of land transactions. If Poos and Smith are right, one would expect to find that a significant number of males appeared in the courts records only during these years, which artificially raised the size of the population. But if a large majority of the males noted in these years appear also in other years and therefore would have come into observation and would have

---

[87] Razi, *Life, Marriage and Death*, 31.   [88] Ibid. 117.

been counted even if these crises never occurred, they will be proven wrong.

Table 9.5 shows that although crisis years probably generated more activity in Halesowen manor court the vast majority of the males who appeared in the court also appeared either before or after these years. The number of males who surfaced in the records only during the crises is too small to explain the fluctuations in the number of males obtained from the court rolls.

The arguments and evidence produced by Poos and Smith do not justify a final verdict that a demographic trend cannot be estimated reliably from court roll data. Obviously more tests are necessary in order to determine finally the validity of the court rolls as a source for estimating population movements. The evidence from Waltham, Easter, and Halesowen, however, makes one quite optimistic.

In the second part of their article Poos and Smith criticize other demographic observations made from court rolls. They have rightly pointed out the uncritical way in which replacement rates obtained from the court rolls were used. They have also convincingly shown that in order to translate replacement rates into demographic measure it would be necessary to possess data which is unavailable to us.[89]

They have also cast doubt on the adult male expectation of life calculated by me from Halesowen court rolls. They have raised objections to the methods used to calculate life expectancy and to their demographic consequences. First, they have criticized my assumption that on the first recorded appearance of a tenant he was about 20. The reason for assuming this is not merely the fact that in Halesowen the minimum legal age for holding land was 20. It has been found that young villagers did not wait for their parents' death in order to obtain land and become landholders.[90] Therefore, it has been assumed that since young villagers were anxious to become independent and since they did not have to wait for their parents' death, they became landholders as close as possible to the age of 20, which was the minimum age for holding land. This hypothesis seems to me as plausible as many other hypotheses made by historical demographers. I also fail to see any reason to doubt, as Poos and Smith do, that a villager amerced for default of suit of court, which was a tenurial obligation, was a tenant, and the same is true about the other criteria I chose to identify tenants. As cottagers are under-represented in the sample of tenants whose deaths are recorded in the court rolls, a

[89] See above, p. 310.   [90] Razi, *Life, Marriage and Death*, 50–60.

TABLE 9.5. *Males noted in Halesowen court rolls during years of dislocation and plague and the years preceding or following crisis years*

Years	No. of court sessions	No. of dead males	No. of land transactions	Total no. of males noted in these years	No. of males noted also before or after these years	No. of males noted only in these years
1310–12	43	32	38	469	456	13 (2.7%)
1316–18	36	43	47	481	459	22 (4.5%)
1349	13	81	—	221	213	8 (3.6%)
1361–3	30	15	—	215	210	5 (2.3%)

number of hypothetical poor villagers whose expectation of life at 20 has been estimated to be between 10 and 20.8 years.[91] Poos and Smith, however, argue that this is an over estimate of the status-specific differentials since it is incompatible with figures estimated for other pre-industrial populations.[92] But why should one assume that the demographic conditions which prevailed in England in the late thirteenth and early fourteenth centuries were the same as in early modern Europe? Moreover, since the expectation of life of smallholders in the sample is 20.8 years it is reasonable to assume that this is the age of the hypothetical cottagers. The estimated life expectancy is 28, still too low for Poos and Smith. Their objection to this is that I did not consider the possibility, which they think to be very likely, that this shorter mean for 'poor' villagers could be due, rather, to a later age at which these persons first acquired land. The period for which life expectancy has been estimated, however, was a period in which the villagers of Halesowen suffered from several subsistence crises, and poor villagers faired more heavily than their wealthier neighbours.[93] As many smallholders and cottagers died in their prime, their surviving sons could take their holding at the same age as the sons of richer tenants. It is also probable that because of high infant and child mortality among smallholders, in many cases the age differences between these villagers and their sons was such that even if they survived the crises their heirs were quite young when they eventually died.

It would seem that Poos and Smith object to my life expectancy estimate not so much because it is crude but because it implies that a 'high pressure' demographic system prevailed in pre-plague Halesowen. This system is quite different from the system that has been recently estimated for sixteenth- and seventeenth-century England. Admittedly the estimation of life expectancy from Halesowen court rolls is crude. But to reject it altogether and the possibility that life expectancy from other good series of court rolls can be measured, just because it is or will be incompatible with the preconceived ideas of Poos and Smith seems to be rather dubious to me. No one has yet shown that the demographic system of thirteenth- and fourteenth-century England was similar to that which prevailed in the sixteenth and seventeenth centuries. Smith's work on the 1377 polltax returns from Rutland, which suggests a European marriage pattern, is rather problematic, because of a high degree of evasion and because the sex ratio is not known.[94] But even if he is right and if during

---

[91] Ibid. 43–4.   [92] See above, pp. 311–12.
[93] Razi, *Life, Marriage and Death*, 34–41.
[94] R. M. Smith, 'Hypothèses sur la nuptialité en Angleterre aux XIIIe–XIVe Siècles', *Annales: ESC* 38 (1983), 107–36.

the last quarter of the fourteenth century a European marriage pattern was practised in England, it does not follow that a 'low pressure' demographic system prevailed there from 1270 to 1349, the period for which my life expectancy estimate has been criticized.

The rest of Poos's and Smith's article is devoted to challenges to other observations made from Halesowen court rolls, which suggest that the villagers practised a non-European marriage pattern. One of the reasons that this hypothesis has been made is that despite the fact that impartible inheritance custom was practised in Halesowen, second and third sons were able to acquire land and establish families. This was done to such an extent that it gives the impression that Halesowen villagers were prepared to face economic hardships rather than to remain bachelors and spinsters.[95] A situation in which the rate of family formation exceeds the supply of adequate holdings is bound to produce a 'high pressure' demographic system. Poos and Smith, however, by reducing my estimate of the percentage of families with sons argue that 35 per cent of the tenants died without direct male heirs, the surplus sons from some families occupied holdings vacated by others. This, they say, is compatible with a 'low pressure' demographic system.[96] But the reduction in the number of fathers who died with sons, from 75 to 65 per cent of the sample is unjustified. It is based on the tacit assumption that the proportion of those aged twelve to twenty in the sample is similar to that which prevails in a normal population.[97]

Although young villagers below the age of 20 were sometimes noted in the court records, they constituted a very small minority. The vast majority of young villagers noted in the records were those who were already twenty and involved in landholding. Younger villagers who lived at home and were legally under the responsibility of their fathers had fewer reasons to appear before the court. Therefore, although the sample of 590 families with at least one son should be reduced to account for deaths between the ages of twelve and twenty, it should be reduced by much less than 10 per cent. If only 27 per cent of the fathers in Halesowen died without direct male heirs, it would be hard to see how the surplus sons could have found adequate holdings to occupy, especially since heiresses were often unavailable to them. In Halesowen and probably in other places, heiresses were often married to heirs. Between 1270 and 1349 the Halesowen population was rising and consequently the number of tenants who died childless or with daughters only was falling. The anxiety of second

[95] Razi, *Life, Marriage and Death*, 50–60.   [96] See above, n. 52.   [97] Ibid.

and third sons to acquire land and to start a family in the face of a diminishing supply of holdings can be explained only if we assume that in this society all the young villagers were expected to marry and to marry young.

I have also assumed a non-European marriage regime in Halesowen on the basis of leyrwite payments and an estimate of the age of marriage by using three-generation families.[98] Poos and Smith are right to point out that leyrwite payment does not necessarily mean that a woman was pregnant and gave birth out of wedlock. They are also right to assert that I was mistaken to argue that a high level of illegitimacy implies a non-European marriage pattern. However, as far as the estimate of the marriage age of women is concerned, I disagree with them. It has been found that among the women who paid a marriage fine 29 per cent did so between 18 and 22 years after the first appearance of their fathers as tenants, and therefore it has been estimated that they married between the ages of 18 and 22.[99] Poos and Smith, however, point out that even if this estimate is true, it only means that a small minority of the girls in the village married young.[100] But this is not so. The method used picks out only first- or second-born daughters. If a girl who was born five years after the first appearance of her father as a tenant in the records married at the age of 20, she nevertheless appears as a merchet payer only 25 years after father's appearance. Such cases are not included in my sample. The 29 per cent of the women whose marriage at about 20 is recorded in the court rolls probably constituted all or almost all the first- or second-born daughters who married in Halesowen during the period under study. Consequently, one can use this finding as an indication for an early age of marriage for women. Poos and Smith have shown that merchets underrepresent the marriage rate in the village and that these fines are heavily distributed among the upper levels of village society.[101] Nevertheless, if my estimate is accurate it is important to know that non-European marriage patterns prevailed among rich and middling villagers who in most villages constituted between 40 and 60 per cent of the population. As far as smallholders are concerned there is no reason to believe that they practised a much later marriage than their better-off neighbours. As the expectation of life of poor peasants was lower than that of the richer ones and as more of their children died, those who survived probably did not have to wait very long after the age of 20 to obtain their smallholdings and cottages and to marry.

---

[98] Razi, *Life, Marriage and Death*, 50–60.   [99] Ibid. 60–71.
[100] See above, pp. 321–2.   [101] See above, p. 318.

Undoubtedly Poos and Smith have pointed out some of the limitations in the use of court rolls for demographic analysis. However, they fail to show that these records are unrepresentative as far as males are concerned or that it is impossible to estimate reliably from them the demographic trend. Although they have shown that certain demographic observations made from Halesowen court rolls are mistaken, others, like the estimate of life expectancy, the settlement pattern of young villagers, and the estimated age of marriage for women, stand their criticism. It is obvious that more studies need to be conducted before we will know if a low or a high pressure demographic regime prevailed in medieval England. In the meantime, I see no justification to adopt, as Poos and Smith do, the demographic model described for sixteenth- and seventeenth-century England as a yardstick to examine the validity of the observations made from medieval records. Those which are compatible with the model are to be accepted while those which are not, like the observations made from Halesowen court rolls, are to be rejected. Poos and Smith, like Alan Macfarlane before them, wish us to believe that the society, economy, and demography of rural England from the thirteenth to the seventeenth century was more or less static.[102] They have rightly recommended that historical demographers of medieval England be versed in the techniques of modern demography, but it is no less important to have good historical sense.

Manorial court rolls are a unique and an excellent source for the study of rural society, economy, and demography. There is more potential for research here than allowed by Poos and Smith or by Judith Bennett in her recent article.[103] This, however, will be proven beyond doubt only when more studies of good series of court rolls and other documents such as rentals, manorial accounts, and tax listings are conducted.

III. 'SHADES STILL ON THE WINDOW': A RIPOSTE (L. R. POOS AND R. M. SMITH)

English manorial court documentation, in many respects unique among European countries for its information pertaining to the bulk of rural dwellers in the Middle Ages, has long provided the most voluminous evidence for studying many aspects of medieval society. We have no doubt that it will continue to do so; yet, as the metaphorical title of our earlier discussion was intended to convey, the 'window' through which we may view this society has finite dimensions. It was our intention to suggest

---

[102] Macfarlane, *Origins of English Individualism.*
[103] Bennett, 'Spouses, Siblings and Surnames', 26–46.

some ways in which these dimensions can be more clearly understood. At its most basic level, then, our concern was with one of the most fundamental questions of legal as well as social history: the relationship between the scope of a legal arena's purview and the society in which that arena operated. Our focus was, however, squarely upon Zvi Razi's attempts at demographic inference from the Halesowen court material because he has made the boldest claims to date for the ability of manorial courts' recorded transactions to reflect the whole of their communities' populations and activities.

In his reply Razi accepts a number of our arguments concerning the shortcomings of the court rolls for demographic analysis. More generally he agrees with us that in future studies of medieval communities manorial court records should be buttressed with evidence drawn from other classes of documentation, and that such work must proceed with reference to established mathematical and empirical demographic principles. The major part of his discussion consists of meeting specific methodological and interpretational points which we raised in connection with Razi's own work and with our uses of records from other contemporary manors as illustrations of our arguments. Therefore most of our rejoinder will be taken up with answering the particular charges that he has raised.

Most crucial to Razi's general argument for the uses of manorial court records in demographic inference is his notion that the group of persons appearing in these courts' proceedings over each successive 5-year interval embraces essentially all residents of the manor or village in question, or at least most adult males resident in the community during that quinquennium. In our original essay we suggested that this was not the case for manors for which we compared court appearances of persons with tenant or resident lists derived from other local records such as rentals or taxation returns. As Halesowen apparently possesses no such ancillary records,[104] Razi is unable to address these points directly in his own research; instead he has simply asserted that because the nature of manorial court business was so diverse and all-encompassing, every adult male resident must have appeared in court every few years. Therefore in his reply he can meet our objections only by criticizing our use of our own data, especially those drawn from the contiguous manors of Great Waltham and High Easter in Essex. His criticisms not only reveal that he has consistently failed to grasp the implications of our essay, but also can be dealt with quite briefly.

---

[104] In fact, Halesowen possesses a fragmentary poll-tax return, not cited by Razi, which unfortunately appears not to be susceptible of conclusive analysis: PRO E179/166/24.

We observed that, when all individuals listed as holding land at Waltham and Easter in rentals compiled in 1328 were traced through their appearances in the court records of the same manors down to the Black Death of 1349, mean numbers of court appearances and proportions of tenants never appearing in court varied greatly among those possessing different-sized tenements (Table 9.2). Razi has raised two major objections to this point. First, he correctly notes that some tenants listed in 1328 may have appeared in court in the decade or two before then, but died or emigrated soon thereafter and avoided subsequent court appearances. Thus our estimate of those never appearing in court may be misleadingly high. Our procedure here was unavoidable, simply because the court records for these manors have not survived from the decade or so prior to 1327. Second, Razi points out that because women tended to appear in court less frequently than men, combining male and female tenants results in an overly pessimistic assessment of the court records' representativeness. To this end he engages in some quite arbitrary manipulation of our published data from Waltham and Easter.[105] In Table 9.6 these data are recalculated to distinguish between male and female tenants.[106] Women holding land in their own right (the great majority of whom appear, from internal court evidence, to have been unmarried at the time of the rentals' compilation) comprised 23.1 per cent of all tenancies at these manors in 1328.[107] As the table confirms, female tenants were indeed less likely than males to appear at all in court, and to be recorded less frequently in court proceedings if they did appear. But the disparity is rather smaller than Razi implies, perhaps because as tenants in their own right these women were themselves more likely to be involved in court business than female residents of these communities in general. The table indicates that the relative under-representation of female tenants stemmed from their greater tendency to be smallholders as well from their sex *per se*.[108] Nevertheless,

---

[105] Above, pp. 325–6.

[106] It will be noted that the total number of tenants tabulated here is slightly smaller than in our original tabulation (Table 9.3). This is because the rentals record a small number of joint tenancies (husband and wife, parent and child, or siblings). In our original tabulation these were included, and court appearances of all the joint tenants of each tenement were averaged to provide a single figure for that tenement. Because for present purposes we want to isolate the differences between male and female tenants' appearance patterns, only males and females holding land alone are tabulated. The table given here also aggregates all tenements into three size-categories.

[107] Poos, 'Population and Resources', 214–16.

[108] Razi (above p. 325) presumes, quite arbitrarily, that 'it is reasonable to assume' women constituted about 16 per cent of all tenants (a figure apparently culled from Titow's calculations from rentals of several ecclesiastical estates in southern England: Titow, *English*

TABLE 9.6. *Frequency of court-roll appearances by amount of land held in 1328, Waltham and Easter, 1327–49*

Size of tenement	Men					Women				
	Mean no. of appearances	Standard deviation	N	No. never appearing	% never appearing	Mean no. of appearances	Standard deviation	N	No. never appearing	% never appearing
Cottage or messuage only or 0–10 acres	6.3	9.8	214	59	27.6	1.5	4.0	69	31	44.9
>10–25 acres	12.2	15.4	69	10	14.5	2.2	4.5	23	6	26.1
>25 acres	17.8	15.6	25	3	12.0	7.0	11.4	4	1	25.0

even when the data are rearranged in this manner nearly one-quarter of all male tenants still fail to appear in the court records.

But the fundamental article of faith in Razi's own argument is not that all male residents *ever* appear in court, but that they appear regularly enough that counting men recorded in court transactions in each five-year period is tantamount to constructing a 'census-like enumeration' of the adult resident male population.[109] Our original essay admittedly addressed the former point without dwelling upon the latter, but Razi appears oblivious to the distinction. In order to demonstrate how crucial the distinction is, the Waltham and Easter data have been restructured to show cumulative appearance rates in the two decades after the 1328 rentals, and these are illustrated in Figures 9.1 and 9.2. These figures graph the percentages of known tenants in 1328 who have appeared in court proceedings in each successive quinquennium. Thus 37.8 per cent of all male smallholders recorded in the 1328 rentals had also appeared at least once in court transactions by the end of 1330; 12.2 per cent more had appeared at least once by the end of 1335 and so on.[110] For larger tenants the cumulative appearance rates were higher at each interval, and for females they were lower than for males for each tenement size-category. The point here is not so much the absolute frequencies but the general point that, even if most tenants eventually turn up in recorded court transactions at least once, it is quite unrealistic to equate all persons appearing in court in any one quinquennium with all tenants present in the community during the time in question.

Razi is reluctant to draw a distinction between those 'at risk to appear' at any one court or in any one year and the number of individuals appearing at least once over a specified (or extended) period of time. Thus Razi found that a very high proportion of those who appear in the years of epidemic outbreaks (1349 and 1361–3) and harvest failures (1310–12 and 1316–18) appear 'before or after these years' (Table 9.5). However, any quinquennial aggregation of court participants containing one or more such years would be likely to register larger totals than quinquennia lacking such aberrant years. It would help in the clarification of this fundamental issue if Razi could have presented, for those appearing in each

Rural Society, 87), and asserts that 'the majority of these women probably did not appear in the court rolls'.

[109] Razi, *Life, Marriage and Death*, 24–6.

[110] These figures therefore do not show what proportion of 1328 tenants appeared in any particular quinquennium, but rather are intended to convey how much time must elapse before a given proportion of tenants have been observed at all in the court records.

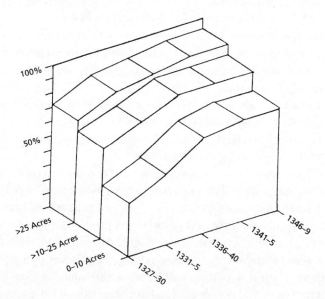

FIG. 9.1 Cumulative court appearances, 1327–49, of males holding land in 1328, Waltham and Easter

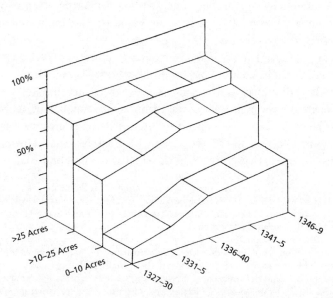

FIG. 9.2 Cumulative court appearances, 1327–49, of females holding land in 1328, Waltham and Easter

quinquennium, the frequency distributions of their previous and subsequent appearances. We suspect that quinquennia experiencing 'abnormal' conditions would show a higher proportion of 'infrequent' participants in court proceedings than others (i.e. such quinquennia would be likely to record a distribution of individual appearance frequencies markedly skewed to the left of the mean).

Furthermore, while our general point was to emphasize the need for cross-checking manorial court material with ancillary sources such as rentals in order to provide at least a rough measure of systematic biases in the court records, the cross-checking must be limited by the nature of the ancillary documentation at our disposal. In this case we have identified manorial tenants, rather than all adult residents within these communities. The indeterminately sized group of subtenants, landless, and servants is perforce excluded. Razi himself elsewhere acknowledges the presence at Halesowen of such individuals in substantial numbers, although it is unclear whether he has attempted any systematic assessment of their relative proportions.[111] Yet it is a commonplace among students of medieval English village society that people of this description appear only sporadically (if at all) in court proceedings.[112] By Razi's own reckoning it would appear that the omission of such persons from our court-appearance patterns would more than compensate for the absence of court records prior to 1327.[113] Again, by not heeding our own explicit recognition of what is being compared with what, he has failed to grasp the implications of this cross-checking exercise.

Much the same is true for Razi's treatment of our comparison between known residents listed as taxpayers in the 1381 poll-tax returns and their court-roll appearances. As we noted, substantial numbers of taxpayers failed ever to appear in the courts' transactions, amounting to 29.1 per cent of all males (12.1 per cent of married male taxpayers, 53.2 per cent of single male taxpayers).[114] We agree with Razi, as we acknowledged in our original essay, that certain factors (such as emigration by adolescents,

---

[111] e.g. Razi, 'Family, Land and the Village Community', 31: Before the Black Death, Razi estimates at least 43 per cent of the 'families' identified in the court records had at least one servant 'for some time'. Razi, *Life, Marriage and Death*, 78–80: subtenants of 'rich' tenants are noted but their relative proportions are impossible to assess from Razi's published work.

[112] Cf. Britton, *Community of the Vill*, 92, 135–7; Hilton, *English Peasantry*, 30–1.

[113] That is, if one took Razi's estimate of the dimensions of servanthood as applicable to Waltham and Easter (see n. 111) and if most of these servants never appeared in court, this would result in a degree of residents' omission from the court records several times greater than the arbitrary figure he ascribes to the 'loss' of tenants resulting from the absence of pre-1327 court records.

[114] Above, p. 307.

difficulties in identifying servants, and geographical factors of court jurisdiction) could conspire to prevent court appearance by some of these persons. But we also noted that, while tax returns in theory deal with residents rather than tenants, they (especially in the case of the 1381 returns) seriously under-enumerate total populations of communities. Indeed, by referring to the returns of the same townships for the 1377 tax (in which collection evasion was of smaller dimensions), the later listings are deficient by a factor of at least one-third of the total population of resident adolescents and adults.[115] Moreover, it is clear from the Essex returns, as well as from those of other counties, that these deficiencies in the later polltax collections systematically excluded lower economic, social, and occupational groups.[116] Thus, as was the case with our exercise involving the rentals, our cross-checking must be understood to be limited to court appearance patterns by higher-status individuals: that is, those most likely to appear in court in the first place. Finally, Razi has again failed to appreciate that these figures deal only with those who *ever* appear in court, and so hardly support his notion of the 'census-like' quality of quinquennial cohorts of court-transaction participants.

In turning to Razi's reaction to our position that developments in manorial court procedure may have influenced the court-appearance patterns of individual manorial residents independently of local demographic trends, we find that he shares our caution regarding the emergence in the later thirteenth century of manorial presentment juries and their potential effects on individual court-participation, but he suggests that 'these changes are easily observed in the court records and can consequently be taken into consideration'.[117] We do not share his confidence and our initial doubts are confirmed by his cavalier reassessment of our evidence as well as certain problems surrounding his own interpretation of procedures in the late thirteenth- and early fourteenth-century manorial courts of Halesowen.

Razi assumes, without warrant, that presentment as a means of introducing business into the courts of Redgrave and Rickinghall was fully implemented by 1270. Only presentments for infringements 'of the lord's right' were established by this date. Furthermore, we referred to this business as 'increasing in frequency between 1285 and 1310'.[118] Presentment spread

---

[115] Poos, 'Population and Resources', 139–43.

[116] Ibid. 149–50; Hilton, *English Peasantry*, 30–3; R. H. Hilton, 'Some Social and Economic Evidence in Late Medieval English Tax Returns', in S. Herbst, (ed.), *Spoleczenstwo gospodarka kultura: Studia ofiarowane Marianowi Malowistowi* (Warsaw, 1974), 120–1.

[117] Above, p. 327.   [118] Above, p. 302.

relatively slowly to other matters of curial concern and 'it was not until the end of the second decade of the fourteenth century' that in 'a typical manorial court the vast majority of court business originated through presentment by jury of twelve persons'.[119] How then could Razi conclude that 'no change occurred in the administration of the court or its litigational procedures' when referring to the Rickinghall courts from 1270 to 1315?[120]

Razi fails to view the arrival of presentment procedures at Halesowen as gradual. He argues that 'presentment juries as a mean of initiating business into the court were already operating when the court roll series begins and no other change in the procedure and litigation practices of the court can be observed until the 1340s'.[121] A perusal of the published proceedings of the manorial courts of Halesowen between 1270 and 1307 leads to different conclusions.[122] Presentment is evident in the rolls of 1270 but Razi fails to mention that it was reserved solely for 'criminal' business and in practice closely mirrors that of the earliest surviving roll (1260) for Redgrave, a neighbouring manor of Rickinghhall. In neither community was presentment used to initiate business in other areas in the early 1270s. In the presentments of the juries of the various settlements (referred to frequently as the *villata*) that fell under the jurisdiction of the Halesowen court, we can observe a preoccupation with criminal matters: the raising of the hue and cry, digging up highways, infractions of the assize of ale, assaults, and burglaries.[123] In the Halesowen court of September 30th, 1276 there is a suggestion of a jury presentment concerning an interpersonal dispute. and indeed of a marriage undertaken without seigneurial license.[124] But it is not until 1307, the last year of the published Halesowen records, that we see signs of presentments in cases of a 'non-criminal' kind; we find court proceedings liberally sprinkled with

---

[119] Smith, 'Some Thoughts', 105 and above, n. 46.   [120] Above, p. 327.
[121] Ibid.   [122] *Court Rolls of the Manor of Hales.*
[123] For instance, at the court of 13.2.1270 presentments were made by the aletasters of those breaking the assize of ale; the court of 17.2.1270 also contains presentments by the aletasters; the court of 30.4.1270 contained presentments from jurors of the various vills that made up the manor but they concerned the following matters—wrongfully raising ditches and hedges and making encroachments illegally on the king's highway and the presentment of an individual who no longer had rights of residence on the manor. *Court Rolls of the Manor of Hales*, i. 4–17. A very similar list of matters is handled in the once-yearly leet court at Redgrave in 1260 concerning infractions of the ale assize, petty thefts, diversion of water, and destruction of property boundaries: Court of 3.5.1260 (University of Chicago Library, Bacon MS 1).
[124] *Item dicunt jurati quod Willelmus de Tenhal verberavit Robertum Scout inde consideratum est quod distringatur ad veniendum ad proximam curiam. Item dicunt jurati quod Agnes le Teyng est maritata sine licentia domini unde consideratum est quod distringatur. Court Rolls of the Manor of Hales*, iii. 36.

presentments for damage to the abbot's properties and for default of court (a tenurial liability) that quite clearly brought many names into the documents.[125]

Razi's interpretation should not be challenged solely on the basis of a partial knowledge of the Halesowen sources. Yet his argument suggests that he is not aware of the developments of the manorial court as an institution and is not sensitive to the implications of this evolution to his thesis. That he fails to indicate that presentment in the first 30 years of the Halesowen record was almost wholly associated with criminal matters and not with other (especially seigneurial) concerns over which the court had jurisdiction demonstrates his insensitivity.

Unconvinced by our worries concerning the possible impact of changes in curial procedures on the appearance patterns of manorial tenants and their families, Razi furthermore doubts whether our attempts to use heirship patterns would provide a reliable indicator of demographic trends. We argued that, since 30 per cent or more of male tenants were not succeeded by their sons in Rickinghall, this suggested either stationary or declining tenant numbers. Participation indices employed by Razi would, if accepted without regard to the increasing resort to presentment and the growth of individual appearances during years of severe economic reversals, point to overall demographic growth. Razi's argument depends upon what he believes to have been the failure of the court rolls to provide an accurate account of whether the direct heirs were personally present at the hallmote sessions so that they might succeed to the patrimonial holding after their father's death. Correctly, Razi notes that court rolls do not provide specific evidence to indicate that 'a tenant died childless' for in most cases that state of affairs can only be inferred 'when nobody came forward to claim the holding of a dead tenant'.[126] The accuracy of the

---

[125] At the Halesowen Great Court of 26.4.1307 we find for instance the following presentments: Oldebure (Oldbury) presents that *Willelmus Bonde (jd). Johannes Bonde, Thomas Symond (eger), Margeria Textrix (egra), Johannes le Webbe (vacat), Willelmus atte Mulne (vacat) faciunt defaltas. Ideo in misericordia.* This is the first court session in the published Halesowen court rolls at which default of court was the object of jury presentment, *Court Rolls of the Manor of Hales*, ii. 563. For examples of presentment of individuals trespassing on or damaging seigneurial property: *Oldebure (Oldbury) presentat quod liberi Walteri de Oldebure ceperunt de busce domini ad molendinum de Oldebure.* Court of 17.5.1307, ibid. 566. At the court of 4.10.1307 the jurors *dicunt quod Alicia le Kyng cepit garbas de domini. . . . Item Thomas Bonde cepit garbas de tasso domini ad voluntatem suam* (ibid. 578).
[126] Above, p. 327. It would, however, be to distort the character of curial procedures involving the transfer of holdings to rightful heirs if we were to assume that arrangements for establishing their claims and indeed their actual existence were highly variable and arbitrary. The usual form of obituary entry in the Rickinghall court proceedings took this

heirship evidence can only be tested, as has been done with the Rickinghall evidence, by searching for other entries in the curial record that might shed light on the presence of sons who failed to claim their rightful inheritance. Razi does not argue, as do others, that lords purposefully perverted the inheritance process by refusing legitimate heirs access to their rightful properties, but he does claim that in Rickinghall as 'in some other places during this period' the lord of the manor set entry fines paid

sequence: the tenant's death was announced, the heir or heirs claimed the inheritance and his, her, or their claims were investigated and verified by an inquisition jury. For example, *Petrus Bannelone qui tenuit de domino j messagium et sex acras terre et medietatem unius messuagii obiit post ultimam curiam. Et super hoc veniunt Ricardus et Henricus fratres predicti Petri et petunt ad predicta tenementa tamquam heredes propinquiores admitti. Et quia per inquisitionem factam compertum est quod predicti Ricardus et Henricus propinquiores heredes admittuntur etc. Et dant domino de fine pro herieto (3s. 4d.) Plegii Radulfus Celastr' et Walterus Payn.* Rickinghall court 3.7.1307 (BL Add. 63419). Efforts also seem to have been made to note those rightful heirs who failed to appear in court. See e.g. a case when only one of two brothers came to take the land of their deceased father: *Rogerus Lully villanus domini obiit post ultimam curiam qui tenuit de domino die quo obiit unum messuagium et tres acras et tres rodas de villenagio domini. Et venit Ricardus filius suus et unus heres et petit admitti ad medietatem tenementi. Et predictus Ricardus dat domino pro medietate heryetti. Plegii Radulphus Silvestr' et Johannes Dulet. Et preceptum est seysire medietatem tenementi in manu domini quousque Rogerus Lully veniet.* Rickinghall Court 5.4.13 15 (BL Add. 63426). Furthermore care was taken through custodianship agreements to preserve the inheritances of under-age heirs. Typical of such arrangements was that involving William the under-age son of Thomas Bercer whose heriot for 3 acres and 3 rods of Osbert Fitte's tenement was paid but *dictus Willelmus minor etate est ideo traditur matri sue ad custodiendum etc plegii Rogerus Lune et Thomas Brunning.* Rickinghall court 6.6.1300 (BL Add. 63412). However, at the court of the previous September (23.9.1299), Thomas Bercer's death had unearthed a number of earlier actions that had eluded the court's notice. For instance, Osbert Fitte had died some years earlier and *post cuius mortem Agnes et Beatrix filie eiusdem intraverunt eo quod alius heres non se optulit pro herede . . . tenuerunt per xij annos elapsos de quibus vendiderunt Thoma dicto capellano de Fynyngham* (i.e. Thomas Bercer) *iij acras iij rodas de quibus in curia j acram et dimidiam et residuum extra curiam et inde obiit seysitus.* Thomas' death is announced at this court as was the fact that he had a son William *etatis ij anni qui nondum fecit herietum pro eodem tenemento etc. Ideo terra capiatur etc.* It is noteworthy that at this point John, the son and heir of Osbert Fitte, appeared ready to retrieve what remained of his 'inheritance' (4 acres and 1 rod) which his sisters had not sold. To enter it he paid a fine of 4s. For a fuller discussion of custody arrangements in customary courts see Clark, 'The Custody of Children', 333–48.

Further evidence of a concern to ensure adherence to correct procedures is shown in an interesting case concerning the inheritance rights of an unborn child. John Chapman's death was announced at the Rickinghall court of 14.11.1310. He died holding a messuage and 26 acres of customary land and *quia uxor dicti Johannis pregnans est ut dicitur. Ideo dicta terra capiatur et retineatur in manu domini quousque sciantur.* We can only assume that the child died at or very close to birth as at the next court (16.12.1310) John Chapman's nephews paid the heriot to take their uncle's land (BL Add. 63423). For further comments on curial procedures involving the identification and inheritances of heirs see e.g. C. Dyer, 'Changes in the Link Between Families and Land in the West Midlands in the Fourteenth and Fifteenth Centuries' in Smith (ed.), *Land Kinship and Life-Cycle,* 306–7; and Beckerman, 'Customary Law in English Manorial-Courts', 164–71.

by heirs at levels which reflected real land values' and which were 'consequently very high'.[127]

Admittedly, customary fines were low in Halesowen: on the death of a tenant his or her best beast was taken as heriot and an entry fine of 13*s.* 4*d.* (the equivalent of two years' money rent) for a full virgate (25–30 acres) was paid by the heir to gain access to the inheritance.[128] Such entry fines were certainly low compared with the notoriously high charges of £10 and more per virgate on certain of the bishop of Winchester's manors. The latter were however atypical, for entry fines, usually in the range of 13*s.* 4*d.* to £2 per virgate, are reported from manors on important medieval estates such as those of Westminster and Peterborough Abbeys and the bishops of Worcester. It is certainly possible that Halesowen customs may have given heirs an additional incentive to claim their inheritances since it appears that they paid less than non-relatives on taking up a new holding.[129]

This incentive for heirs to claim their inheritances, which Razi suggests makes the Halesowen evidence a more accurate record than that relating to many medieval manors, requires careful appraisal. Again, Razi's assumptions concerning conditions on the manors of the abbot of Bury St Edmunds do not stand up well to more detailed investigation. Firstly, unlike the practice at Halesowen, it was not the case that heirs on these

[127] For an example of such doubts as to the reliability of court proceedings in inheritance cases, see Searle, 'Seigneurial Control of Women's Marriage', 35. See however the comments of Smith. 'Some Thoughts', 112–14.

[128] Razi, *Life, Marriage and Death*, 9.

[129] This was a practice that was found on the manors of the Abbots of Bury and has also been encountered elsewhere. Titow, *English Rural Society*, 75–6; Harvey, *Westminster Abbey*, 223–5; King, *Peterborough Abbey*, 182–8: Dyer, *Lords and Peasants*, 156. For comments on the two-tier system of Halesowen entry fines by which heirs paid much less than unrelated persons on taking up a new holding see Dyer, 'Changes in the Link', 306. In Rickinghall entry fines by persons who took on holdings that escheated to the manorial lord for want of heirs were far higher than the cash heriots paid by blood relatives. For instance, the small-holder Gilbert Godchold died in 1316 and no heir came to claim the land he held. Indeed a marginal note laconically stating him to be a 'pauper' alongside this obituary entry is a very poignant indication of the fact that this year was one of great suffering in the manor on account of the deficient harvest. In a court session four weeks later the lord granted his solitary rod of land to Walter Bron who paid an entry fine of 3*s.* (equivalent to an entry fine of 12*s.* per acre and two to three times the average level of cash heriots that kin would have paid). Affines such as sons-in-law and nephews of the wife were, in Rickinghall, charged entry fines along with heriot to secure their inheritance rights. For instance, in addition to a horse as best beast the husbands of Richard Gilbert's three daughters each paid 3*s.* 4*d. ut possunt admitti ad dictam hereditatem similiter cum uxoribus suis eo quod extranei.* Rickinghall Court 20.0.1311, (BL Add. 63423). Adam Othyn, the nephew of Alice the widow of William le Sawyere paid an entry fine of £5 as well as an ox as heriot worth 15*s.* to secure his aunt's 42-acre holding in Rickinghall in July 1310. (BL Add. 63423).

Suffolk manors gained access to holdings whose capital was depleted both
by the removal of the best beast and the payment of an entry fine. The
heir's payment of the heriot, whether in the form of the holding's best
beast (when available) or as a cash sum, secured the right to inherit the
actual inheritance itself. Money heriots were certainly variable in amount,
levied at rates that ranged from 4s. to 4d. per acre (see Table 9.7). The
most expensive cash heriots (accounting for approximately 20 per cent
of the non-animal heriots between 1295 and 1319) were levied at rates
of between 2s. and 4s. per acre, higher *pro rata* than the entry fines for
Halesowen, but certainly not unduly high when compared with levels
found on many contemporary estates. Furthermore, total charges were
not necessarily more onerous than the fines levied at the death of Halesowen
tenants where both heriots and entry fines were taken by the landlord.
Taxes or levies on the transfer of customary land at Rickinghall were, if
anything, likely to have been higher on *inter-vivos* land transactions where
license fees of between 2s. and 4s. (see Table 9.8) an acre were incurred
by those who sold or bought customary property. Furthermore, the early
decades of the fourteenth century saw a succession of years where the
charges, on average, were generally closer to 4s. per acre rather than the
lower levels that prevailed earlier.[130] It is not at all clear how such charges
on the transfer of land by living persons would alter the willingness of
heirs to enter their inheritances which were not subject to unduly heavy
charges when compared with the experience of the Halesowen and indeed
many other contemporary manorial tenantries. Razi's argument proceeds,
it would appear, from the assumption that customary land had little value
over and above the seigneurial burden that went with it. To determine
whether this position is correct would require attention to the value of
customary land as a productive agricultural asset, and would require us to
provide evidence on the per acre price paid by purchasers of such land in
relation to the customary payments made by heirs or vendors to the
manorial lord.[131] Stray entries in the evidence of the Rickinghall manorial
courts suggests that customary land in the early fourteenth century fetched
prices varying from 24s. to 44s. per acre, and as such represented an asset
that possessed a 'real value' greatly in excess of 'customary charges' whether
placed upon inheritances at 2s. per acre or on *inter-vivos* transactions at

---

[130] A similar level and pattern of changes in license fees for *inter-vivos* land transfers
during these years is to be found in the adjacent manor Redgrave. See Smith, 'Some
Thoughts', 117.

[131] See the argument of J. Hatcher, 'English Serfdom and Villeinage: Towards a Reassessment', *P&P* 90 (1981), 21.

TABLE 9.7. *License fees paid by sellers of customary land (pence per rod)*
Rickinghall, 1295–1319

Years	Courts (Nos)	Transfers (area given)	Average fee	Standard deviation	Transfers (area not given)	Total transfers
1295	3	40	8.2	2.8	13	53
1296	3	18	8.6	8.6	4	22
1297	4	39	5.5	2.7	6	45
1298	3	24	6.4	2.9	8	32
1299	6	31	6.5	2.7	9	40
1300	5	17	6.1	2.9	8	25
1301	3	13	6.3	3.3	6	19
1302	1	7	10.9	4.4	2	9
1303	3	11	6.1	3.4	0	11
1304	4	13	13.5	10.9	9	22
1305	5	17	7.7	3.4	5	22
1306	6	56	9.1	4.9	12	68
1307	4	18	9.0	3.9	6	24
1308	6	21	12.5	5.5	8	29
1309	7	49	10.1	3.5	7	56
1310	6	39	12.5	4.4	6	45
1311	5	20	13.2	9.4	16	36
1312	1	8	14.0	4.4	2	10
1313	4	32	12.4	4.5	88	40
1314	4	30	11.5	2.3	8	38
1315	4	26	13.4	7.3	14	40
1316	6	64	12.2	4.2	34	98
1317	5	46	12.1	4.1	18	64
1318	4	35	11.6	2.3	11	46
1319	5	25	11.5	2.2	4	29

TABLE 9.8.   *The value of cash heriots in pence per rod,*
Rickinghall, 1295–1319

Pence	Number
1	6[a]
1–1.9	14
2–2.9	6
3–3.9	10
4–4.9	4
5–5.9	3
6–6.9	2
7+	15[b]

Notes: [a] 2 heriots were not taken on account of the
deceased person's poverty.
[b] In 10 cases the heriots were paid for holdings containing
non-residential property and other buildings.

4*s.* per acre.[132] Thus, there would be little reason to expect heirs to have
declined the opportunity of taking on customary land available to them
through inheritance on either of these Suffolk manors in the late thirteenth and early fourteenth centuries.[133]

Furthermore, it is not at all clear in Razi's argument why, if sons or
daughters were reluctant to enter their parents' lands, other relatives
should have been prepared to pay the heriots to secure these inheritances.

[132] For instance, at the Rickinghall court of 29.12.1300, the abbot sold customary land to
his tenants that had escheated to him at the following prices: half an acre for 15*s.*, 1½ rods
for 13*s.* 4*d.*, and ½ rod for 3*s.* (BL Add. 63413). In a debt case in the court of 27.9.1308
Adzurus del Hok complained that Reginald le Newman had purchased 3 rods from him and
owed him 33*s.* 4*d.* which he had agreed to pay him in two terms. (BL Add. 63420). For
similar estimates of the value of customary land to customary tenants in Redgrave, see
Smith, 'Some Thoughts', 118. For intertenant payments concerning customary land, admittedly from the later rather than the early fourteenth century, see Dyer, 'Social and
Economic Background', 22.

[133] There is only one known case of an inheritance not being taken up by sons on the
neighbouring manor of Redgrave and this occurs in the immediate aftermath of the period
of severe dearth extending from 1315 to 1317 when only Gilbert the eldest of the seven sons
of John Lord entered into the sibling group's rightful inheritance of 1½ acres of customary
land. This, however, may have involved a previous intra-familial agreement that has left no
entry in the records. Land transactions between siblings after their joint-inheritance were
very common on this manor: see Smith, 'Families and Their Land', 145.

In Rickinghall between 1295 and 1319, although almost 32 per cent of males whose holdings were liable to pay heriots were not succeeded by their children, only a little over 4 per cent of this group's properties escheated to the lord (abbot) for want of any heirs whatsoever;[134] brothers (very frequently), sisters and, much more infrequently, nephews and nieces seemed anxious enough to enter these properties. This suggests a demand for 'family' land that is confirmed by the relatively common occurrences of intrafamilial litigation surrounding competing claims to property that took place following a death.[135] Likewise, in the neighbouring manor of Redgrave, in only 49 per cent of 172 deaths recorded in the manorial court proceedings between 1295 and 1319 did sons inherit from their father, whereas in almost 41 per cent of instances other close kin (for the most part brothers) inherited through the payment of heriot. Only in 9 per cent of cases did Redgrave properties escheat to the abbot through want of heirs; and the majority of these instances were located in the period of high mortality associated with the years of dearth from 1315 to 1317.[136]

Although wary of appearing to repeat our original arguments, we feel obliged to return to Razi's reactions to our comments on his attempt to reconstruct the demography of marriage practices from the proceedings of Halesowen's manorial courts. First to be treated will be his inferences concerning the land acquisition patterns of male siblings as indications of their early marriage. Originally we considered Razi's evidence on families shown to have sons above the age of 12 and manipulated them in such a way as to estimate those who would have survived to twenty (the legal age of majority at Halesowen).[137]

Razi correctly questions our decision to treat all sons identified in the court records as if they had made their first appearances at exact age

---

[134] Most of these cases were concentrated in the years of severe economic difficulties associated with the harvest failures between 1315 and 1317 and were certainly not characteristic of the greater part of the period extending from 1295 to 1319. Some indication of the effects of this enhanced mortality between 1315 and 1317, which may have been a factor at least temporarily contributing to heirship failure, especially among close kin, can be seen from the following case concerning (perhaps characteristically) a Rickinghall smallholder; the death of Richard le Barker, who held a cottage and one rod of land, was announced at the court of Aug. 1316 and his son and heir Adam was admitted to the land with no heriot taken, since a marginal note of 'pauper' is suggestive of the family's predicament. In the next court on 30 Sept. we find the sad announcement of Adam's death when his two nephews Simon and John le Breton inherited the miniscule property by paying a cash heriot of 2s.

[135] See, for instance, the cases in Smith 'Some Thoughts', 113–14, and Smith, 'Families and Their Land', 190–3.

[136] Ibid. 184–5.   [137] Above, n. 52.

twelve in so far as he had written originally that it was possible to reconstitute 590 families from the Halesowen court rolls between 1270 and 1349 who had sons above the age of twelve.[138] Of course, court-roll evidence is incapable of providing a measurable age distribution for such sons. None the less we cannot assume that they all survived to their father's death and hence were available to inherit. We accept, however, that our reduction of their number by applying the mortality rates consistent with the debatable estimates provided by Razi's methodology would result in too severe a culling of their numbers before age 20.[139] All, it would seem, that we can do is to note the figures that Razi provides suggesting that of the 788 families in the total set of those reconstituted from the court rolls from 1270 to 1348, 140 can be shown to have had two or more sons married and holding land at the same time. This represents approximately 18 per cent of all families identifiable from the Halesowen records. Although we do not know from Razi's data whether these sons had acquired their land before or after their father's death, our original point still stands because in a stationary population at least 20 per cent of men would have died childless and a further 20 per cent with daughters only surviving.[140] Indeed, even if we make the rather unrealistic assumption that all heirs married heiresses there would still have been opportunities for the 'surplus' sons to secure holdings either through inheritance in the kin network or by purchase. Even after a more restrained reading of this evidence than we undertook previously, we would strenuously deny Razi's right to draw conclusions about the motivation behind the behaviour he believes to have underpinned the statistic's that he has produced. The statistical evidence provides no basis for observing in Halesowen an '*anxiety* [our emphasis] of second and third sons to acquire land . . . to start a family' or for claiming that the villagers 'were *expected* [our emphasis] to marry and to marry young'. In fact the evidence is still consistent with a rate of occupancy of vacant holdings or fragments of holdings by younger sons that heirship failure alone would have facilitated.[141]

In his reply Razi continues to treat his technique of establishing the

---

[138] Razi, *Life, Marriage and Death*, 55.

[139] This recension of our earlier assumptions concerning the age patterns of sons at and after their first court appearance applies equally to Smith, 'Some Issues Concerning Families', 48, although we believe that the original conclusions still stand.

[140] Smith, ibid. at 43–55, extending Wrigley, 'Fertility Strategy', 235–54.

[141] For some comments on the great difficulties confronting historical studies of the family that attempt to infer emotional attitudes or ideals from structures or actions see Smith, 'Families and Their Property', 58–9.

ages of individuals, whether through their supposed age on appearing in court for the first time or when shown to have entered into land, as unproblematic. He refers us to the examples of his 'method' that he presented in his original study. It is worth considering these case studies in more detail, constituting as they do six two- or three-generational families that contain examples of how the age of at least one of the parties at his or her marriage has been calculated.[142] These six 'families' leave direct or, at best, circumstantial indications of eight marriages. In only three of these marriages can the ages of the bride or groom be established with any certainty, and in each of these cases there exists a previous entry in the court proceedings concerning either the bride or groom's custody under the care of their mother on account of their minority which necessarily involved a specification of their age at their father's death (and most likely an earlier than average age of inheritance). In the other five 'marriages' assumptions concerning the marital status of the individual initiating the 'genealogy' on his initial appearance in the court proceedings pre-determined the allocations of ages to members of subsequent generations. For example, Razi writes

Philip son of Thomas II Lynacre . . . a half yardlander from Hunnington is noted in the court rolls for the first time as landholder in 1297. In 1316 he was amerced because Juliana his daughter married without permission. Juliana's age was then between nineteen and twenty-two.[143]

Lynacre's status as a landholder in 1297 is established by Razi through his presence on a list of tenants who did not pay a sum of money levied on the community.[144] Lynacre's actual entry into land has not been established but it is assumed in this approach that his liability to be fined on account of his tenure of land began from the time that such a fine was levied. This circular reasoning surely cannot be acceptable as an analytical procedure, nor can his assumption that Lynacre's own marriage commenced close in time to that court in 1297 at which he was fined. When we observe Lynacre amerced in 1316 for failure to pay his daughter's merchet, we therefore see no means by which Razi is justified in assuming that she married between the ages of 19 and 22.

Based both on the low number of marriages as represented by the infrequent payments of merchet in relation to the actual size of the customary population of Halesowen and on a wider treatment of the socially limited liability of villein females to pay the fine on other estates in late

---

[142] Razi, *Life, Marriage and Death*, 61–3.   [143] Ibid. 62.
[144] *Court Rolls of the Manor of Hales*, i. 367.

thirteenth- and early fourteenth-century England, we argued that female marriage ages allocated to such brides were hardly likely to be fully representative of a stratified tenantry.[145] Razi counteracts this position by arguing that his method deals only with 'first- or second-born daughters' and that the 59 female marriages identified through their associated merchet payments 'constituted all or almost all the first- or second-born daughters who married in Halesowen during the period of this study'.[146] But Razi must appreciate that manorial court rolls do not provide evidence on either births in particular, or the birth-order of individuals, except in the relatively rare cases of disputed claims to inheritances that might hinge on the accurate identification of who was the eldest son.[147] Indeed, such cases only infrequently relate to daughters who because of the absence of sons inherited partibly. There is in fact more than a hint of circularity in Razi's argument when he excludes from his marriage-age calculations girls whose marriages are recorded 23 or more years after their father's first appearance as tenants on the grounds that they might be second- or third-born children.[148] The dice would seem to be heavily loaded in favour of deriving a mean age of first marriage close to 20 if only those marriages of females who can be identified as having married within 23 years of their father's own assumed marriage are considered. Furthermore, Razi's demographic logic appears faulty if he believes that the fifty-nine girls whose marriages have been so calculated constitute all the first- and second-born daughters of all rich and middling Halesowen tenants (the latter constituting *c.*60 per cent of the total) who married in Halesowen. As we argued in our original essay, the Halesowen customary tenantry and their families, estimated by Razi at close to 800 persons, should have generated between 1270 and 1348 at least 800 to 900 marriages and of

---

[145] Further work on the social characteristics of marriage-fine payers among the tenants of the extensive estates of the bishops of Winchester in Somerset, Hampshire, Buckinghamshire, Wiltshire, and Oxfordshire is reported in Smith, 'Further "Models" of Medieval Marriage', 85–99.

[146] Above, p. 333.

[147] Information on individual ages in manorial court proceedings, especially where custodianship arrangements were being registered, was not particularly rare although most such cases do seem to have been found in years of severe demographic disturbance when parents were the victims of 'premature' deaths. Sometimes distinctive features of the local inheritance custom made such entries more frequent such as on the abbot of St Albans's manor of Winslow in Buckinghamshire where ultimogeniture regularly produced situations in which the rightful heir was under age on the death of the father. See Cambridge University Library MS D.D.7.22, Winslow Court Book. See also Clark, 'The Custody of Children', 335, where almost 40% of the 459 custodies in that study come from the years 1348–50 when plague was rampant in the population.

[148] Razi, *Life, Marriage and Death*, 61.

these 350 to 500 should have been attributable to the rich and middling tenants.[149] Only unrealistically high combinations of completed family sizes and extremely severe infant and child mortality rates (far higher than those computed by Razi) could sustain an interpretation that proposed that from 10–20 per cent of these marriages (i.e. fifty-nine) involved all first- and second-born daughters who survived to celebrate their marriages.

Finally, we strenuously object to Razi's gross distortion of a major portion of our analysis. In criticizing our citation, for comparative purposes, of data drawn from the much-better-documented demographic history of early-modern England and continental Europe, he charges that we arbitrarily presume the medieval demographic regime to have been identical to that observed for the parish-register era after 1538. Therefore, he claims, we cast out from the court-roll evidence all that which is 'incompatible with the preconceived ideas of Poos and Smith'.[150] Of course, we do no such thing. What we have suggested, among other things, is that the various components of Razi's court-roll-derived population model comprise a whole which can scarcely be demographically possible under any conceivable set of assumptions. Thus he calculates that Halesowen residents in the early fourteenth century enjoyed population growth rates roughly comparable (as we pointed out) to those of late sixteenth-century England, despite much more severe mortality (under his calculation), by means of marriage rates which (again, under his calculations) were ostensibly much lower than those of the parish-register era.[151] If we have used 'early-modern data as a yardstick' (as Razi puts it) it is only to show that something is seriously awry, either in the tale the court rolls tell or in Razi's calculation from them.

We have returned at many points in this response, as we did in our original paper, to consider one of Razi's own 'preconceptions', i.e. the notion that when a man first appeared as a tenant in manorial court proceedings, he may be presumed to have been 20 years old. This then allows expectation of life at age 20 to be calculated when the tenant's subsequent death notice has been located.[152] 'This hypothesis seems to [Razi] as plausible as many other hypotheses made by historical demographers.'[153] He bases his procedure on his postulation of the eagerness and anxiety, on the part of medieval villagers, to acquire land and to marry as early in life as the legal age of majority (20 at Halesowen) would

[149] Ibid. 10. [150] Above, p. 331. [151] Above, pp. 316–21.
[152] Razi, *Life, Marriage and Death*, 43–5. [153] Above, p. 329.

allow. His reasoning appears to be that young men are eager to enter landholding at 20; therefore when they first appear as tenants they are 20: and the fact that they are 20 when they enter landholding proves that they are eager to acquire land as young as possible. We observed that his calculated life-expectancies derived in this way show discrepancies among different size categories of tenancies out of all order of magnitude in comparison with differentials observed in any other historical European rural and urban populations (observed, incidentally, for populations more diverse economically and socially than Halesowen's 'peasants'). It is simply untrue that we claimed medieval Halesowen's demography was necessarily identical to any early-modern European patterns. We merely suggested that it is surely more plausible, in light of this comparative observation, to envisage smaller-scale tenants as entering landholding at a later age, thereby experiencing shorter intervals between property acquisition and death rather than lower e_{20}s.[154] But this will not fit Razi's own preconception, and therefore he rejects it outright (indeed, it is impossible to prove the point one way or another from court-roll evidence). We are obviously labouring under different concepts of 'good historical sense' here.

In sum, closer reflection upon the points Razi has raised reinforces our original arguments for the limitations of manorial court material by itself to permit anything like total reconstruction of the communities from which it is derived. We would reiterate that we do not wish, by so arguing, to denigrate the value of this evidence for the social history of the medieval village. Rather, it is our very conviction of this evidence's worth that leads us to attempt some preliminary assessments of its inherent shortcomings as well as its strengths, and to demonstrate the possibility of addressing these problems through integrated approaches to community study. Indeed, the local study based upon the nominal linkage of various kinds of documentary evidence will remain the most important source for progress in the interpretation both of those communities and, importantly, the institutions generating those sources. In fact, we would in no way wish to disagree with the sentiments expressed in the last sentence of Razi's rejoinder. Historical demography is always at its most revealing and most exciting when pursued at the level of the family and the individual. It is only at this level that we are able to identify how human behaviour gave rise to demographic processes and how in turn those

---

[154] Above, p. 312.

processes affected the individual concerned. We can conclude this discussion by choosing the words, highly pertinent to this debate, although written in a quite different context, of a critic of many of the pioneer community case studies produced in the early days of more formal demographic analysis of colonial America:

These projects . . . are extremely time consuming and often tedious. In these studies, however, all three parts of the historical demographer's ideal are relevant informed speculation and models for explanation, a knowledge of demographic methods and comparative findings, and hard work in the sources.[155]

IV. THE DEMOGRAPHIC TRANSPARENCY OF MANORIAL COURT ROLLS (Z. RAZI)

All historical sources reflect reality in a partial and distorted way. The past, therefore, can be understood only when the limitations of particular sources are recognized and the methods employed in making historical observations, as well as the observations themselves, are constantly tested and refined. Poos and Smith, in an earlier part of this discussion, undertook such a task when they thoroughly examined my use of manorial court rolls' data for demographic analysis of a medieval English parish.

In my reply to Poos and Smith, I accepted a number of their arguments concerning the limitations of manorial court records and the validity of some of my demographic inferences. They, in turn, reacted to my refusal to accept all their arguments and suggested that I had failed to grasp the implications of their essay and even to understand the development of the manorial court as an institution. They also stated that my objections to their arguments only reinforced their original view that court rolls can be used demographically for very limited purposes if at all. Although I have read Poos and Smith's response to my discussion of their critical reaction to my work with the utmost care, making a special effort to get their meaning right this time, it has failed to convince me that their criticism of the court records as a source for demography and of some of my inferences is justified.

In their second essay Poos and Smith maintain their objection to my use of Halesowen court rolls in estimating demographic trends on the ground that villagers are badly represented in the court rolls. In order to show this they used the court rolls of the manors of Waltham and Easter in

---

[155] D. Scott Smith, 'Estimates of Early American Demographers: Two Steps Forward, One Step Back, What Steps in the Future', *Historical Methods*, 12 (1979), 34.

Essex. However, despite the fact that these particular records underestimate the representativeness of males in court rolls, as they themselves acknowledged,[156] 77 per cent of the male tenants and 71 of the male taxpayers appear also in the court rolls. Realizing that these figures do not support their original claim about the under-representativeness of villagers in court rolls, Poos and Smith raised a new argument in their rejoinder. They argued that although most of the male tenants do turn up sooner or later in the manor court during the term of their residence, my method of estimating population movements from court rolls is inadequate. The reason for this, according to them, is that the enumeration of the Halesowen males appearing in the court rolls over 5-year periods in each decade, does not include all the tenants who resided in the manor during these periods.[157]

Poos's and Smith's new argument is clearly based on a misunderstanding of my demographic analysis of Halesowen. I never wrote nor tacitly assumed that the 5-yearly enumerations of males noted in Halesowen court rolls include all the resident males. I only assumed that these enumerations include a fair sample of them. This is the assumption, and not the one Poos and Smith wrongly attribute to me, which underlies the estimate of the population trend from Halesowen court rolls between 1270 and 1400. Admittedly, in the absence of rentals and tax lists for Halesowen, this assumption has not been tested. However, the graph of cumulative court appearances of the 1328 Easter and Waltham tenants in the court rolls between 1327 and 1349, presented by Poos and Smith in their rejoinder, is not helpful in testing the quality of the Halesowen samples (Figures 9.1 and 9.2). In order to do this one needs to know how many of the 1328 tenants appeared in each of the 5-yearly court rolls and not their cumulative appearance rates.

Fortunately, in their rejoinder, Poos and Smith provide data about the court appearances of the 1328 Easter and Waltham tenants in the records between 1327 and 1330 (Table 9.6). From these I constructed Table 9.9 which shows that 37.3 per cent of the Essex tenants listed in the rentals of 1328 appeared also in the court rolls of 1327–30. This figure underestimates the quality of the Halesowen samples taken from the records of five years while the sample from the records of Essex manors is obtained only from the rolls of four years. If the court records of 1326 were available, the sample might have been larger by 20 per cent. Therefore, it is likely that in any 5-yearly court records of Waltham and Easter one can

---

[156] Above, pp. 341–2.   [157] Above, p. 342.

TABLE 9.9.   *The appearances of the 1328 male tenants of Waltham and Easter in the court rolls of 1327–49 and 1327–30*

Size of tenement	Men recorded in the rentals of 1328	Tenants noted in the court rolls of 1327–49	Male tenants noted in the court rolls of 1327–49 and of 1327–30 only
>25 acres	25	22 (88%)	16 (72%)
<10–25 acres	69	59 (75.5%)	40 (68%)
0–10 acres	214	155 (72.5%)	59 (38%)
TOTAL	308 (100%)	236 (76.6%)	115 (37.3%)

find the names of between 37.3 and 44.8 per cent of the male tenants. This sample is smaller than the assumed Halesowen sample, but still it is a sizeable one. The real problem is not its size but rather the fact that it is biased; whereas in 1328, 69.5 per cent of the male tenants were small-holders, in the sample obtained from the court rolls they constitute only 51.3 per cent, an underestimation by 26 per cent. Therefore, if the demo-graphic trend was estimated from the court rolls of Waltham and Easter with the same method used for Halesowen, it would be quite inaccurate. As smallholders appeared considerably less frequently in the court records than middling and large holders and as such a high proportion of the tenants in the Essex manors were smallholders, periods of economic and mortality crises which brought more people into the court than more settled times artificially enlarge, as Poos and Smith maintain, the sample obtained from the court rolls during such periods.

However, the fact that the court rolls of Waltham and Easter do not generate reliable data to estimate population trends, does not justify Poos's and Smith's claim that it is also true about the court rolls of Halesowen or other medieval manors. This is so because it can be shown that the quality of the court rolls of Halesowen far exceeds that of the court records of the two Essex manors.

Poos's and Smith's comparison between the rentals and court rolls of Waltham and Easter shows clearly that the chances of a tenant to appear in the court records of few years, directly depended on the frequency of his court appearances. While the majority of the large and middling 1328 tenants who attended the court frequently appeared in the court rolls

TABLE 9.10. *The frequency of male tenants' appearances in Halesowen and Waltham and Easter court rolls between 1327–49*

Size of Holding (in acres)	Halesowen court rolls, 1327–49		Waltham & Easter court rolls, 1327–49	
	No. of tenants	Mean no. of court appearances	No. of tenants	Mean no. of court appearances
Large holders (a.30+ & 25+)	25	60.1	23	15.6
Middling holders (a.15 & 10–25)	25	37.8	59	15.4
Smallholders (a.0–7.5 & 0–10)	25	20.3	155	6.3
TOTAL	75	39.4	237	8.9

between 1327 and 1330, only the minority of the smallholders who attended the court far less frequently did so (Table 9.6).

Hence, in order to validly apply the results from the test performed on the court rolls of the Essex manors to the court records of Halesowen, it is necessary to ascertain that the frequency of the appearances of male tenants in both records is the same. In order to calculate the mean court appearances of Halesowen landholders according to their economic status, I took the court rolls of 1327–30 and identified in them the names of 201 male tenants. I used the data available in the files of these tenants to divide them into three groups: large tenants holding about 30 acres and more; middling tenants holding about 15 acres; and smallholders holding around 7.5 acres and less. From each of these groups a sample of 25 tenants was randomly drawn and their appearances in the court rolls between 1327 and 1349 are tabulated according to their economic status. The results are presented in Table 9.10, which includes also the frequency of court appearances of Waltham and Easter tenants.

Table 9.10 demonstrates that on average tenants who resided in Halesowen between 1327 and 1349 appear in the court rolls 4.4 times more often than tenants resident in the Essex manors during the same period and Halesowen smallholders appear 3.2 times more frequently than Waltham and Easter smallholders. The high frequency of court-rolls appearances of Halesowen tenants is by no means unique, as a similar frequency was estimated from the late thirteenth-century Redgrave court rolls.[158]

The consequences of the considerable difference in the frequency of court appearances between the Essex and the Halesowen records are quite clear. First, the fact that tenants are badly represented in the low-quality Waltham and Easter court rolls, does not mean, as Poos and Smith claim, that the samples of males obtained from the high-quality Halesowen court records are also unrepresentative. Second, the test performed on the records of the two Essex manors, not only fails to invalidate the assumption that the villagers are well represented in Halesowen court rolls, but also strengthens the plausibility of this assumption. If in the court rolls of Waltham and Easter between 1327 and 1330, 37 per cent of the tenants are presented, the Halesowen samples taken from 5-yearly runs of court rolls, probably include more than 75 per cent of the local tenants, since on average they appeared in the court 4.4 times more often than the Essex tenants. Obviously, this estimate is quite crude. Nevertheless, Poos's and Smith's comparison between the rentals and court rolls of Waltham and Easter suggests that in every 5-yearly run of much better quality court rolls most of the tenants are presented. As the majority of the adult males in Halesowen, like in many other west Midlands manors, were tenants, it is highly likely that the movements of the local population were estimated from large and representative samples.

Poos's and Smith's second objection to the use of court rolls for estimating population movements is that the fluctuations in the number of people noted in the court rolls might be a result of changes in the procedures and practices of the manor court rather than of changes in the size of the resident population. In their rejoinder they reacted rather angrily to my dismissal of this claim.[159] However, the new evidence and arguments presented by them fail once again to justify their criticism of the court-

---

[158] See Table 9.3 above. It is difficult, without conducting further research, to discover why the frequency of court appearances of Redgrave and Halesowen villagers was much higher than that of Waltham and Easter tenants. However, a tentative answer can be offered. The monastic landlords of Redgrave and Halesowen exercised their seigneurial jurisdiction more thoroughly and more fully than the landlords of the two Essex manors. Moreover, in Redgrave and Halesowen the percentage of unfree tenants, who had to attend the court more frequently than free tenants, was much higher than in Waltham and Easter.

[159] Above, pp. 342–5.

rolls' demographic data. In order to show this I will examine first their treatment of Redgrave and then the Halesowen court rolls.

Poos's and Smith's claim that Redgrave court rolls between 1260 and 1310 provide evidence which indicates that changes in the number of villagers noted in the court rolls were caused by alterations in the court procedures and not by changes in the population size, is based on the interpretation of the fact that 30 per cent of the tenants during this period were not succeeded by their children. They seem to believe that all these tenants died childless and therefore regard it as a firm indication for a declining population. I rejected this interpretation on the grounds that it is possible that deceased Redgrave tenants were not succeeded by their children not because the latter died but because they could not pay the seigneurial charges on the holdings. Poos's and Smith's response was to claim that seigneurial charges on vacant holdings in Redgrave were not higher than in other contemporary manors. Therefore, they argue it is difficult to explain why heirs, if they were still alive, declined the opportunity of taking on customary land available to them and why when they did not, other relatives did. I find this interpretation rather hard to accept. Most of the tenants who were not succeeded by their children were smallholders whose economic situation deteriorated during the period 1260–1310. Therefore, one cannot rule out the possibility that while the children of such tenants declined their inheritance because they could not afford paying even moderate seigneurial charges, their relatives who were better off paid these charges and took the holdings. In any case, even if Poos and Smith are right and it is unlikely that heirs in Redgrave gave up their inheritance while still alive, one cannot possibly assume that all those who were not succeeded by their offspring died childless. An unknown number of these deceased tenants must have had children who survived them, but because they had previously emigrated, they did not return to Redgrave to claim their inheritance. Therefore, Poos and Smith cannot use Wrigley's models of the percentages of childless deceased people in different demographic conditions, to claim that the population of Redgrave declined between 1260 and 1310.[160] It seems to me that the fact that 30 per cent of the tenants in Redgrave were not succeeded by their children during this period is perfectly compatible with the hypothesis that the rise in the number of villagers appearing in the court rolls of the Suffolk manor indicates that the resident population of the manor was growing. In Redgrave, as in many other contemporary manors, the

---

[160] Wrigley, 'Fertility Strategy', 133–54.

rapidly rising population must have pushed land and food prices up, salaries down, and growing numbers of poor peasants out of landholding altogether.

In their rejoinder, Poos and Smith refused to accept my observation that alterations in the procedures of Halesowen manor court did not pose insurmountable obstacles to the use of its records for estimating population movements. They searched the published Halesowen court rolls to prove that I was wrong. They maintained that although there were presentment juries already in the courts of 1270, only in 1307 did these juries start to present non-criminal cases and many villagers were amerced for default of court. As a consequence, they argued, the court records from 1307 onwards, which include more names than in the records from 1270s, cause an overestimate of the population of the manor in the early fourteenth century.

Poos and Smith, however, were too hasty in their dismissal of my observations about Halesowen manorial court. In fact, as I will presently show, there are plenty of presentments for 'non-criminal' offences as well as for default of court in Halesowen court rolls before 1307. Poos and Smith failed to find them, simply because they looked for them in the wrong place. They noticed in the court records of 1307 that such presentments are concentrated in entries in which the jurymen of each of the twelve townships of the manor reported offences committed by their members. Hence, they looked for such presentments in similar entries in previous court records. This was an error because in addition to the jurymen of the townships, there was another jury for the whole manor whose twelve members also represented cases in the court. Moreover, as a result of a change in the recording practices of the court, which occurred in the beginning of the fourteenth century, various jury presentments which are recorded in a concentrated manner in 1307 appear in previous court records everywhere in an unorderly manner. Furthermore, some of the presentments are recorded in such a way that it is quite difficult to identify them as such just by reading quickly through the court rolls.[161] All these become clear only when one proceeds very slowly and reads very carefully all the entries recorded in the court rolls and

---

[161] An example of a 'non-criminal' presentment which cannot possibly be identified as such unless one reads all the court records, can be found in the court rolls of late October 1281. Walter Archer brought an action against four villagers because they wrongly presented him in the court held in August for putting his beasts upon the common pasture of Romsley. These four villagers were not merely neighbours but the jurymen of the township of Romsley. This fact can be discovered only by a careful reading of all the court records. See *Court Rolls of the Manor of Hales*, ii. 162.

TABLE 9.11. *'Non-Criminal' presentments recorded in Halesowen court rolls of 1280 and 1307*

Types of offences	1280	1307
Essoins (apologies for absence)	[254]	[54]
Default of court	37	56
Trespasses against the lord	44	65
Failure to keep open-field discipline	15	2
Marriage without permission	2	—
Cohabitation without marriage	—	3
Fornication	8	4
Failure to perform services	2	2
Leaving the manor without permission	3	2
Grinding corn not in the lord's mills	11	—
Gleaning	—	2
Selling animals outside the manor without the lord's permission	1	—
Trespasses against neighbours	1	—
TOTAL	124	136

then tabulates all the various cases appearing in them. In Table 9.11 'non-criminal' presentments recorded in the court rolls of 1280 and 1307 are compared.[162]

Table 9.11 demonstrates that Poos's and Smith's claim that present-ment in the first thirty years of Halesowen records was almost wholly associated with criminal matters and not with other (especially seigneu-rial) concerns over which the court had jurisdiction, is wrong. They were right, however, in observing that in the first court records less people are noted for default of court than in the court rolls from the 1290s onwards. But that does not mean that this change necessarily causes an overestima-tion of the population of Halesowen in the late thirteenth and the begin-ning of the fourteenth centuries. This is due to the fact that when the number of people amerced for default of court rose, the number of

---

[162] For the year 1307 the full records of 15 court sessions survived, 14 were published and the record of the last court held in December remained unpublished. I tabulated the data available in this court record as well. I chose the year 1280 for comparison, because for this year all the records of 16 court sessions survived. See ibid. at 121–60, 555–93, and iii. 60–76.

essoins, apologies for not attending the court, fell considerably as one can see in Table 9.11. In the records of 1280, on average, 15.9 essoins are recorded for each court session, in the rolls of 1307 the average falls to 3.4. The essoins more than compensate for the small number of the defaults of court in the early courts; in a case of default only one name is noted while in a case of essoin at least two and sometimes four names are recorded. This procedural change which occurred in Halesowen in the 1290s,[163] caused a considerable fall in the number of people whose names are recorded in cases of failure to attend the court in the late 1290s and the early 1300s. If Poos and Smith are right this change should have reduced the overall number of males obtained from these court records, but exactly the opposite has been found.[164] Although Poos and Smith failed to substantiate their claim that changes in the practices and procedures of Halesowen manor court distorted the population trend estimated from its records, they might be right in other cases. However, better evidence than that which they produced in their two essays is needed before their claim can be accepted.

In their rejoinder Poos and Smith brought new arguments against my observations about the settlement and marriage patterns of young villagers in Halesowen. They argued that since only 18 per cent of the families reconstituted from Halesowen court rolls between 1270 and 1349, had more than one son to be settled in the village and since in a stationary population 20 per cent of the landholders die childless, there was a sufficient supply of holdings for the surplus sons. Therefore, they maintained, the fact that many second and third sons settled in Halesowen, where impartible inheritance custom was practised, does not justify my assertion that young villagers were quite anxious to settle down and to marry as soon as possible after reaching the age of 20.

Poos and Smith, however, overlooked some data presented in my book. It is, indeed, true that 140 (18 per cent) of the families identified in the pre-plague Halesowen court rolls had more than one son who settled in

---

[163] This change is related to the long struggle between the Abbots of Halesowen and their customary tenants. During the 1270s and the 1280s, when both sides tried to resolve the conflict by legal as well as by violent means, the seigneurial regime in Halesowen was especially harsh. One of the measures taken by the abbots against the tenants was to compel them to attend personally each court session. As a result, in the rolls of each session during this period, a large number of essoins were recorded. In the 1290s, when the customary tenants gave up their demand for a status of privileged tenants of the ancient demesne, the Abbots on their part relaxed various seigneurial exactions. Consequently, instead of personally attending each court, those tenants who had no legal business in the court, were allowed to pay a fine of 2*d*. See also Razi, 'Struggles', 169–91.

[164] Razi, *Life, Marriage and Death*, 25.

the manor. But these families had altogether 355 sons.[165] Therefore, even if the population of Halesowen was stationary, the death of 158 (20 per cent) childless tenants would still leave 57 sons unprovided for. In order to supply land to all the surplus sons during this period, 215 tenants who constituted 27 per cent of the tenants, should have died childless. This, however, could not possibly have happened because when a population is growing, as did the population of Halesowen in the pre-plague period, the percentage of the childless tenants is less than twenty. Thus, Poos and Smith are mistaken in thinking that the 'natural' supply of holdings could have provided sufficient land for all the young peasants who married in pre-plague Halesowen. A situation in which the rate of family formation far exceeds the supply of adequate holdings remains an enigma unless one assumes that the peasants were so anxious to marry that they were willing to risk their economic future. It is also plausible to assume that as the desire to marry was stronger than the fear from economic distress, young villagers in Halesowen did not wait long after arriving at the age of 20, in which they were allowed legally to hold land, to marry and start a family. In order to test this hypothesis I searched for more direct evidence to estimate the age of marriage and found that males and females in pre-plague Halesowen probably married at about the age of 20.[166]

In their first essay, Poos and Smith rejected my estimate of the age of marriage in Halesowen on the grounds that it was estimated from a small and unrepresentative sample. In my reply, however, I demonstrated that this criticism is unjustified.[167] Therefore, in their rejoinder, Poos and Smith attempted to show that my method for estimating age of marriage from genealogical data extracted from the court rolls is based on implausible assumptions and circular reasoning.[168] The method they discuss, however, hardly resembles the method I actually used and consequently it is not surprising that they found so many faults with it. Therefore, to argue about such a distorted version of my method would be a mere waste of time. Instead, I will present more fully than in my book, the method used to estimate age of marriage with all the underlying observations, inferences, and assumptions.

In order to arrive at an estimated age of marriage from genealogies obtained from Halesowen court rolls, the following observations, inferences, and assumptions were used:

---

[165] Ibid. 55.   [166] Ibid. 60–4.   [167] Above, pp. 316–23, 333–4.
[168] Above, pp. 352–4.

A. (observation) Landholders appear in Halesowen court rolls at least once in three years.

B. (observation) Legal age for holding land was 20.

C. (inference from A) When a son of a resident villager[169] appears for the first time as a landholder he must have acquired his holding sometime during the three years which preceded this date, otherwise he would have appeared in the records as landholder before this date.

D. (inference from B) As the legal age for holding land was 20 when a son of a resident villager appears in the records for the first time as a landholder he was at least 20 years old.

E. (assumption) Peasants in the thirteenth and fourteenth centuries did not marry before acquiring land.

If one accepts these assumptions and inferences, the use of my method is quite straightforward. Let us choose as an example the case of Philip son of Thomas II of Lynacre, which Poos and Smith found so hard to swallow. Philip appears as landholder for the first time in the court records of 1297. In the records of 1316 he is noted for paying a fine because his daughter Juliana married without the lord's permission. From these one can infer (C) that Philip acquired his holding between 1295 and 1297, but not before, otherwise he would have appeared as landholder before 1297. As he had no land before 1295, he could have legitimately fathered Juliana only after 1295 (E). Hence, when Juliana married in 1316 she must have been at most between the age of 19 and 21.

The same method was applied also to estimate the age of marriage of males. As an example we can choose the following three generations of the Green family from Ridgeacre. The first date which accompanies each name indicates the first appearance of the villager as landholder, the second, the time of death.

William I 1293–1320
William II 1313–1349
William III 1333–1349

This genealogy suggests that William II was between the age of 20 and 23 when he acquired a holding and married. The time of his land acquisition is inferred through his father (C) and that of his marriage through his son (D and E).

---

[169] One can use the method for estimating age of marriage from court rolls only on second-generation children of local villagers. If an immigrant appears in the court rolls as a landholder, it does not mean that he never held land before.

This genealogical method for estimating age of marriage can be employed only when brides and bridegrooms were first-born children.[170] If, for example, a villager is noted for the first time in 1280, as a tenant and his daughter for paying marriage fines in 1309, it does not necessarily mean that she was married between the age of 29 and 31. She might have been the fourth-born child of this villager, in which case she was married probably between the age of 19 and 21. Therefore, I estimated the age of marriage only of those women whose marriage fine was recorded less than twenty years after the first appearance of their fathers as landholders and found 59 such women in the court rolls between 1270 and 1349. I also assumed that the women whose marriage can be estimated by the genealogical method, constitute all or almost all of the first daughters who married in Halesowen in the pre-plague period.

This assumption, however, is regarded by Poos and Smith as unfounded. They estimate all the marriages of Halesowen women from well-off and middling families, who usually paid marriage fines. This shows that the 59 women whose age of marriage was estimated constitute only between 10 and 20 per cent of all the women who married during the pre-plague period. Therefore, they argued, the assumption that these marriages constitute all the possible marriages of the first daughters is implausible.[171] However, Poos's and Smith's method for testing the representativeness of my sample is inadequate. The estimate of the age of marriage was based on marriage fines. Therefore, one should relate the number of Halesowen women whose marriage was estimated to the number of women who paid marriage fines, rather than to total number of women who married in the pre-plague period, as Poos and Smith did. As the marriage of 202 women is recorded in the pre-plague Halesowen court rolls the percentage of women whose marriage was estimated is 29 per cent. In the harsh demographic conditions which existed in Halesowen in the pre-plague period, it is hard to believe that many more than 29 per cent of the women who married were first-born children.

There is no reason to assume that the age of marriage of women who were second- or third-born was different from that of first-born ones. Therefore, since all or almost all of the first-born daughters among the 202 women whose marriage is recorded, married about the age of 20, it is

---

[170] Earlier in this debate, I wrote that the genealogical method for estimating age of marriage picks up second- as well as first-born daughters. This was a mistake, since by including in the sample only daughters who paid marriage fines less than twenty years after the first appearance of their fathers as tenants, I excluded second-born daughters.

[171] Above, pp. 353–4.

reasonable to assume that all these women also married at that age. It was estimated that in Halesowen during the period under discussion, there were between 350 and 500 marriages of daughters of middling and well-off villagers.[172] Therefore, as the age of women was estimated from a large sample, it is probable that all the daughters of rich and middling Halesowen villagers married about the age of twenty. Unfortunately, it is difficult to estimate the age of marriage of the daughters of smallholders, who constitute 43 per cent of the tenants, because they rarely paid marriage fines. However, there is evidence in the court rolls which suggests that some of them had to postpone their marriages, but probably they did not marry later than the daughters of better off tenants.[173]

In my book I wrote the following about the estimated age of marriage, 'this obviously does not constitute an adequate calculation of mean age at first marriage but it suggests that it is plausible to assume that males and females in the pre-plague period married at an early rather than a late age'.[174] It seems to me that there is nothing in Poos's and Smith's essays which justifies any change at all in this citation. The true nature of the marriage pattern in medieval England will not be decided on methodological battle-fields but on good evidence which can only be found in hard empirical work on court rolls and other medieval records.

In summing up their second essay Poos and Smith wrote that they strongly disagree with the view that manorial court rolls by themselves permit a total demographic reconstruction of the communities from which it derived. I fully agree with them. The debate between us, however, is not about total reconstruction at all, but about the extent to which court rolls can be used for demographic analysis. My study of Halesowen convinced me that a good series of court rolls permits partial but still wide-ranging demographic inquiry. Poos and Smith, however, believe that although court rolls are essential for the study of the demography of medieval England, by themselves these records permit only quite limited demographic analysis. In fact, in view of their highly negative assessment of a good series of court rolls like that of Halesowen, it is hard to see what demographic use at all can be found for these records.

Poos and Smith demonstrated in their first essay that certain inferences drawn from Halesowen court rolls are faulty. However, they failed to substantiate their case against the use of these records for wide-ranging demographic analysis. Obviously, such an analysis cannot be as comprehensive

---

[172] Above, p. 354.　　　[173] Razi, *Life, Marriage and Death*, 64–71.　　　[174] Ibid. 63.

as that which can be done with more modern records like parish registers. Moreover, the range and quality of the demographic data available in court rolls allow us to make only weak observations which are no more than numerical hypotheses. I agree with Poos and Smith that court rolls, like all historical sources, are not transparent windows into the past. Nevertheless, I do believe, that despite the shades which the nature and quality of the court-rolls data cast over the window, we can still observe quite a lot. There are demographically better-quality sources than court rolls, like the inquisitions *post mortem* and other ecclesiastical and state records from which a lot more can still be learned about the population of medieval England.[175] But there are few if any medieval sources which are socially and geographically as representative as manorial court rolls. Therefore, I hope that future studies of these unique English records will prove that Poos's and Smith's pessimism as to their demographic use is unjustified.

---

[175] See e.g. J. Hatcher, 'Mortality in the Fifteenth Century: Some New Evidence', *EcHR* 2nd ser. 39 (1986), 19–38.

10

Interfamilial Ties and Relationships in the Medieval Village: A Quantitative Approach Employing Manor-Court Rolls

ZVI RAZI

MANORIAL court rolls recorded many intrafamilial interactions, from land transactions and disputes to pledging, debts, trespasses, and assaults, and therefore make it possible to investigate the structure and functions of the peasant family and its role in village society. Moreover, the genealogical evidence obtained from the court rolls enables us to observe the family, not only as a co-resident unit, but also as a group of relatives living in the same parish or village. The court rolls, however, pose, by their very nature, many obstacles to a comprehensive and balanced study of the family. First, women and their activities are considerably under-represented in these records, and children hardly appear in them at all. Second, the fluidity of surnames, especially in the pre-plague period, and the difficulty of tracing affinal ties in the court rolls, cause a massive underestimate of kin ties.[1] A good series of court rolls, which provided sufficient data for an extensive family reconstitution, enable us to correct this to some extent. None the less, even in such a case it is impossible to identify all the relatives of the villagers appearing in the records. Third, although the court rolls registered a variety of kin interactions, most acts of co-operation and support between them were never recorded, as well as their personal and recreational contacts. Therefore, it is often very difficult to interpret recorded kin contacts, especially as the court rolls usually provide only a few details about them. The interactions between Walter le Archer and Hawisia, his mother-in-law, are a case in point. Walter was presented in the Halesowen manor court in 1271 and 1276 for assaulting his mother-in-law.[2] As these were the only recorded contacts between them we might assume that their relations were rather weak and negative. However, in 1271 the court's clerk recorded more information than was usual in assault cases. It appears that Walter assaulted his mother-in-law because she did not allow him to enter her house 'as he

---

[1] Razi, 'Erosion of the Family-Land Bond', 295–305.
[2] *Court Rolls of the Manor of Hales*, i. 312, iii. 32.

was accustomed', to participate in an ale party she threw for her daughters and sons-in-law.[3] This suggests that although Walter and Hawisia had only two negative recorded interactions, the ties between them had been close and positive. Fourth, the court rolls recorded the actions of the villagers, but seldom the circumstances which led to these actions and very rarely the motives behind them. These obstacles rather limit the scope of a kinship study based on court rolls data. Nevertheless, as these data can be often quantified it is possible to investigate the structure and some of the functions of the peasant family, and to observe changes over time. However, to do this, it is necessary to obtain good quality reconstitution and detailed court cases, which allow us to interpret and not merely to enumerate them. The court rolls of the West Midlands manor of Halesowen between 1270 and 1400 meet these requirements. Therefore we will use these records to estimate the range of effective kin in the village, to investigate how extended kin groups were formed, to study their role and to analyse the relationships between parents and children and between siblings.

I

Data from the Halesowen court rolls suggest that the majority of households in the medieval period contained only nuclear families, even though households with extended families, both horizontally and vertically, were also quite common. For example, Thomas de Notwyck, a smallholder from the township of Hunnington, was summoned by the court in 1295, to answer for his mother who was living in his home under his responsibility.[4] In 1342 Juliana, the daughter of Henry Symon of Oldbury, transferred her half virgate holding to her uncle, William Symon, who undertook to support her 'at his table'.[5] Roger Sweyn, a half-yardlander from Oldbury, agreed in 1339 to provide Agnes, his sister-in-law, with a chamber, and to maintain her for the rest of her life in return for her share in her late father's holding.[6] Such co-resident extended families constitute 16 per cent of the 1041 families reconstituted from the court rolls between 1270 and 1400.[7] Although conjugal family households predominated in medieval Halesowen, as in early modern rural parishes, effective kinship ties were far from being confined to the members of the nuclear family. In order to estimate the range of these ties, various regular kin interactions, recorded in the court rolls between 1270 and 1400, were noted and

---

[3] Ibid. iii. 32.   [4] Ibid. i. 339.
[5] Birmingham Reference Library (hereafter BRL), 346301.
[6] BRL 346289.   [7] Razi, *Life, Marriage and Death*, 83.

classified according to the familial relations of the villagers involved. Pledging is by far the most common recorded interaction. However, in the post-plague period, Halesowen manor court limited the range of cases for which a personal pledge was required, and thus the rolls of 1350–1400 recorded far fewer pledges than those of 1270–1349.[8] To avoid a bias, the sample of kin contacts include only the pledges demanded by the court in both periods, namely when suitors transferred or obtained land, undertook to behave properly, to perform services and to pay amends, debts, amercements, fines, rents and other seigneurial dues. In the fifteenth century, however, pledges almost completely disappeared from the court records, and therefore the sample includes only the intrafamilial interactions recorded between 1270 and 1400, as presented in Table 10.1a.

Interactions between distant kin are under-represented in Table 10.1a, as court rolls obviously make it easier to trace close kinship. The fact, therefore, that they still compose 45.76 per cent of the intrafamilial interactions in this table suggests that effective kin ties in medieval Halesowen extended beyond the conjugal family, even though they did not extend very far. Cousins constitute the largest kin group for any one individual, yet interactions between cousins amount to only 6.4 per cent of all observed intrafamilial contacts.[9] We must attribute this figure to the lower frequency of interaction between cousins, since the difficulty of identifying distant kin in the court rolls would not be an adequate explanation. The very fact, however, that effective kin groups in Halesowen did extend beyond the conjugal family had, as I will show later, significant social and economic consequences.

The frequency of intrafamilial interaction was determined not only by degrees of kinship, but also by the villagers' economic position. Table 10.1b clearly shows that, on average, a large tenant interacted with kin almost twice as often as a middling tenant, six times as often as a smallholder and 12 times as often as a cottager. One could attribute the low frequency of intrafamilial contacts of land-deficient tenants to the very low frequency of their court appearances. Yet, such a claim could not account for the difference in kin contacts between large and middling landholders, who are well represented in the court rolls.[10] Besides, there

[8] Razi, 'Family, Land and the Village Community', 28. For a discussion of the institution of the personal pledge in the manor court, see Raftis, *Tenure and Mobility*, 101–2; Beckerman, 'Customary Law in Manorial Courts', 238–41.

[9] For the appearance of cousins in the court rolls of another medieval manor, see Smith, 'Kin and Neighbours', 254.

[10] See Table 10.1a.

TABLE 10.1a. *Intrafamilial interactions recorded in Halesowen court rolls, 1270–1400*

Family relationships	Pledgings	Land transactions	Trespasses	Broken agreements	Concords	Hue & cry	Assaults	Debts	False claims	Hospitality	Pledges for good behaviour	Merchets	Lerwytes	Custody	Maintenance agreements	Total	%
Wife/husband	33	22	9	—	—	69	51	1	—	—	—	—	—	—	—	185	2.98
Father/son	469	72	48	15	—	15	5	5	3	9	4	—	—	—	18	663	10.69
Father/daughter	35	41	7	—	—	3	3	3	—	5	8	43	0	—	2	148	2.39
Stepfather/ stepchildren	19	9	10	—	—	9	6	—	—	3	—	—	—	7	2	65	1.05
Mother/son	64	41	141	47	21	71	22	33	34	8	—	—	—	50	31	563	9.08
Mother/daughter	3	19	19	3	—	22	11	—	16	16	—	8	16	12	7	152	2.45
Stepmother/ stepchildren	—	4	30	—	—	—	8	—	—	—	—	—	—	—	—	42	0.68
Grandfather/ grandchildren	26	7	—	—	—	—	—	—	—	—	—	—	—	5	4	42	0.68
Grandmother/ grandchildren	9	16	—	—	—	—	—	—	—	—	—	—	—	—	4	29	0.47
Brothers	387	50	122	59	38	69	73	37	32	15	8	—	—	—	14	904	14.58
Brother/sister	141	41	51	18	7	75	62	—	—	8	5	12	7	—	20	447	7.21
Sisters	—	28	31	7	3	26	11	—	—	9	—	—	—	—	8	123	1.98
Sub-total	1,186	350	468	149	69	359	252	79	85	73	25	63	23	74	108	3,363	54.24

Relationship																Total	%
Uncle/nephew	157	11	41	11	5	12	7	—	—	6	3	—	—	15	2	270	4.36
Uncle/niece	66	7	9	1	—	—	3	—	4	5	5	—	—	7	5	112	1.81
Aunt/nephew	18	5	12	—	3	—	13	—	—	—	—	—	—	—	1	51	0.82
Aunt/niece	—	8	—	—	—	—	6	—	6	3	—	—	—	—	13	18	0.29
Father-in-law/son-in-law	186	32	59	24	25	22	13	7	—	2	—	—	—	2	13	391	6.31
Father-in-law/daughter-in-law	7	—	23	—	—	7	6	—	—	—	—	—	—	2	—	45	0.73
Mother-in-law/son-in-law	40	15	76	37	31	17	23	12	12	—	—	—	—	—	15	278	4.48
Mother-in-law/daughter-in-law	2	—	41	—	—	41	38	—	5	3	—	—	—	—	2	132	2.13
Brothers-in-law	179	13	50	19	25	28	40	17	7	3	—	—	—	6	4	391	6.31
Brother-in-law/sister-in-law	77	20	6	7	2	40	52	2	8	1	—	—	—	—	15	230	3.71
Sisters-in-law	5	5	49	—	—	22	38	—	8	3	—	—	—	—	3	133	2.14
Cousins	194	21	41	9	17	29	41	15	12	5	3	—	—	—	7	394	6.35
Unidentified relatives	199	17	46	11	15	21	25	10	13	24	5	—	—	6	—	392	6.32
Sub-total	1,130	154	453	119	123	239	305	63	75	55	16	—	—	38	67	2,837	45.76
TOTAL	2,316	504	921	268	192	598	557	142	160	128	41	63	23	112	175	6,200	100.00

TABLE 10.1*b*.   *Intrafamilial interactions of 215 Halesowen tenants noted in the court rolls between 1315 and 1317, which are recorded in the court rolls between 1270 and 1348*

Size of holding	No. of tenants	No. of interactions	Mean no. of interactions
Largeholders (about a virgate and more)	47 (21.9%)	564 (45.3%)	12.0
Middling holders (about half a virgate)	75 (34.9%)	528 (42.3%)	7.0
Smallholders (about quarter of a virgate)	43 (20.0%)	95 (7.9%)	2.2
Cottagers (0–2 acres)	50 (23.2%)	60 (5.0%)	1.2
TOTAL	215 (100%)	1,247 (100%)	5.8

is evidence showing a similar strong correlation between the peasants' economic status and the number of their kin in the village.

As Table 10.1*c* shows, 28 per cent of the smallholders and 60 per cent of the cottagers had no observed relatives in the village, and only 22 per cent of the tenants in these two groups had two relatives or more. In contrast to their poorer neighbours, all the large and middling landholders had relatives in Halesowen and 88 per cent of them had two or more. The number of relatives of land deficient tenants is undoubtedly somewhat underrated because of the low frequency of their court appearances. But in pre-plague Halesowen, as in probably many other contemporary manors, such tenants must have had far fewer kin than the larger landholders: many of the former, unlike their better-off neighbours, never survived more than one generation since their children died or emigrated, and their holdings were acquired by others.[11]

In conclusion, both the villagers' number of kin in the village and their intrafamilial contacts were largely determined by their economic status. None the less, kin ties were important to rich and poor peasants alike. To

[11] Razi, 'Family, Land and the Village Community', 4–5; Razi, *Life, Marriage and Death*, 94–9.

TABLE 10.1c. *Local relatives of the 1315–17 Halesowen tenants living outside their households (Halesowen court rolls, 1270–1348)*

Size of holding	No. of tenants	Number of relatives					
		0	1	2	3	4	5+
Largeholders (about a virgate and more)	47	—	—	8	10	13	16
Middling holders (about half a virgate)	75	—	14	18	18	13	12
Smallholders (about a quarter of a virgate)	43	12	15	7	4	5	—
Cottagers (0–2 acres)	50	30	15	4	1	—	—
TOTAL	215	42	44	37	33	31	28

show this we have first to investigate how the networks of kin in the village were formed and maintained during the period 1270–1400.

II

In pre-plague Halesowen, as in many other contemporary villages, the bond between family and land was strong, as the bulk of the tenants' land was transmitted through inheritance and marriage rather than through the land market or the landlord.[12] This bond affected both the settlement patterns of young villagers and the spatial location of the kin groups, and promoted a high degree of co-operation and cohesion among its members.

In Halesowen as in many other manors, children who reached maturity in their parents' lifetime often did not have to wait for their decease in order to settle in the village.[13] Some acquired land through marriage while others obtained it from relatives or the land market. In 1275, for example, a rich tenant, John Deepslough, married his eldest son off to his

---

[12] Razi, 'Family, Land and the Village Community', 4–7; Faith, 'Peasant Families', 86–8; Harvey, *Westminster Abbey*, 318–19; Howell, 'Peasant Inheritance Customs', 122–39. See also her book, *Land Family and Inheritance*, 237–45; D. Roden, 'Inheritance Customs and Succession to Land in the Chiltern Hills in the Thirteenth and Fourteenth Centuries', *JBS* 7 (1967), 1–12.

[13] Razi, *Life, Marriage and Death*, 50–60; Miller and Hatcher, *Medieval England*, 136–7.

ward, the daughter of his deceased neighbour Thomas Sibile, a yardlander, although both were minors.[14] In 1334 Richard Squire, a half-yardlander from Romsley, endowed his eldest son John with a messuage and a plot of land which constituted a part of his late maternal grandfather's holding.[15] Thomas Lovecok, a half-yardlander from Hasbury, provided his eldest son John in 1342 with 'a plot to build upon' and nine selions of land in the three common fields which he had acquired from another tenant in 1333.[16]

However, as land was scarce in the pre-plague period, many tenants settled their eldest children on the family holding or on land adjacent to it. Alan Tadenhurst, for example, in 1281 gave his heir Richard, 'a croft and a small piece of new land outside the door of the house'.[17] In 1302 Thomas Symon conveyed to his heir Thomas 'all his new land held in severalty', adjacent to the family holding, 'to build upon'.[18] Fathers sometimes shared the holding equally with their married children, and the formal division of the holding often coincided with the tenant's retirement.[19] When the tenant retired he and his wife usually moved to the cottage and the heir or heiress took up the main house. In 1322, for example, William Osborn, a half-yardlander from Warley, granted to Alice, his daughter and heiress, and to her husband William Hunt, who had lived on the holding since 1313, the whole of it with 'the principal house, the barn and the garden. His son-in-law undertook to provide him and his wife with a cottage, a cow and sufficient sustenance, as long as he lives'.[20] However, a widower tenant often remained in the main house and was provided with a small room by the heir or heiress who moved in.[21] These and many other recorded intrafamilial land transactions, as well as frequent references in the court rolls to the suitors' locations in the village, reveal that numerous holdings of about 6 acres and more, were occupied by more than one household.

It also appears that the occupation of tenements by more than one conjugal family was not merely a temporary phase in the life-cycle of tenants' families, but rather a permanent phenomenon. On many holdings the two households of the older and younger generation did not

---

[14] *Court Rolls of the Manor of Hales*, ii. 330.
[15] BRL 346805. [16] BRL 346301.
[17] *Court Rolls of the Manor of Hales*, i. 177. [18] Ibid. ii. 452, 533.
[19] For examples from other contemporary villages, see Homans, *English Villagers*, 146–9; Raftis, *Tenure and Mobility*, 64–8.
[20] BRL 346242, 346234.
[21] Such an arrangement, for example, was made between Roger le Per, a middling tenant and his son Thomas when the former retired in 1333. BRL 346263.

merge when the tenant died, as widows, who were entitled to keep for life
a third of the holding, often remarried in the pre-plague period and
remained on the family farm.[22] Furthermore, in Halesowen, as in many
other villages in which impartible inheritance was practised, tenants used
patrimonial land when purchased land was not available, to endow non-
inheriting children and other relatives.[23] Thus, on many holdings and the
land adjacent to them, the main house was surrounded by cottages occupied by single as well as married relations of the tenant. For example,
during the years 1295–1305, the ancestral yardland holding of the Alwerds
in Ridgeacre was occupied by Hugo Alwerd and his family, who held the
bulk of the land; by his eldest brother William who renounced his right
to inherit the holding in return for a cottage and maintenance for life;[24] by
his mother, Agnes, and her second husband, William; by his younger
brothers, Thomas and Philip, and their families, and by his sister, Lucy,
and her daughter, who all held smallholdings adjacent to the family
tenement. All in all, the Alwerds yardland holding was occupied by five
households. In the 1330s the half-yardland holding of the Geffrey family
in Oldbury was occupied by Richard the heir and his family, by his
mother Juliana who remarried, by his brother Thomas and his family and
by his cousin Felicity Geffrey, whom he provided in 1331 with a cottage
near his house and who probably subsequently married.[25] In the 1320s,
the quarter-yardland holding of the 'Kelmstowe' family in Romsley supported three families: Thomas the heir, his brother John and his mother
Felicity who remarried. Although many quarter-yardland holdings supported more than one family, few supported more than two. Unlike
quarter-yardland farms, cottage holdings were seldom occupied by more
than one family, and those which were, often belonged to artisans. Between 1309 and 1316, for example, the cottage holding of the 'Collins' in
Hawne was occupied by the tenant Thomas Collins and his wife and by

---

[22] Razi, *Life, Marriage and Death*, 67–8; Franklin, 'Peasant Widows', 186–204; J. Z.
Titow, 'Some Differences between Manors and their Effects on the Condition of the
Peasant in the Thirteenth Century', *AgHR* 10 (1962), 1–13; Ravensdale, 'Population Changes
and the Transfer of Customary Land', 197–225; On women's rights in land, see Homans,
English Villagers, 177–90; Smith, 'Women's Property Rights', 165–94.

[23] Razi, *Life, Marriage and Death*, 55–64; Britton, *Community of the Vill*, 60–4; Franklin,
'Peasant Widows', 200–1; J. Williamson, 'Norfolk: Thirteenth Century', in Harvey (ed.),
Peasant Land Market, 92–4; Miller and Hatcher, *Medieval England*, 136–9; Hanawalt, *Ties
that Bound*, 75–6; Roden, 'Inheritance Customs and Succession', 5–7. On the use of the
inter-tenant land market to endow non-inheriting children with land and daughters with
dowries, see Williamson, 'Norfolk', 94–5; Razi, *Life, Marriage and Death*, 94–8; King,
Peterborough Abbey, 123–4.

[24] *Court Rolls of the Manor of Hales*, 317.   [25] BRL 346242.

his daughter Christiana and her husband who shared the cottage with them. Both Thomas and his son-in-law were fullers.[26]

Obviously, as the population of Halesowen was growing in the pre-plague period and land was in short supply, it was impossible to provide land for all the children who reached maturity.[27] There is ample evidence in the Halesowen court rolls, as in the records of many other contemporary manors, that sons and more often daughters of tenants, especially of land deficient tenants, left the village.[28] Yet, as land was scarce in other villages too, many of them preferred to remain in Halesowen, where familial ties gave them a better chance of gaining access to land. And although the plot of land which non-inheriting children eventually obtained was often quite small, it none the less enabled them to settle in the manor and raise their own families. This settlement pattern created a large number of kin groups composed of several conjugal families whose members resided in separate but often closely situated households. Thus land shortage in pre-plague Halesowen exerted a centripetal force on many peasant families, as more and more of their members settled on and around the ancestral holding. At the same time, it also exerted centrifugal force on land deficient families, as more and more of their children had to emigrate. Therefore, while the majority of the families were spatially extended about a fifth were both residentially and spatially nuclear (see Table 10.1c).

The abundance of land available to the peasants in Halesowen, during the period 1350–1400, as a result of the sharp decrease in the population size, greatly relieved the pressure on their patrimonies.[29] Their adult children and other kin no longer clustered on and around their ancestral holdings, but settled on vacant holdings in their native townships or in other settlements on the manor. For example, when Thomas the eldest son of Adam le Hurne, a smallholder from Hasbury, reached maturity in 1362, he did not settle on his father's holding, but leased from the abbot a vacant small-holding and the mill of Hasbury for a term of ten years. In 1368 he gave up his lease in Hasbury and moved with his wife Agnes to

---

[26] BRL 350353.   [27] Razi, Life, Marriage and Death, 27–32.
[28] Ibid. 30–1; Raftis, Tenure and Mobility, 130–52; Dewindt, Land and People, 176–7; Britton, Community of the Vill, 146–50; Miller and Hatcher, Medieval England, 43–4. A list of the servile tenants of the manor of Weston (Lincs.) taken in 1268–9, shows that while 53.5 per cent of the adult daughters of local tenants left the village, only 38.2 per cent of the sons did so. Hallam, 'Some Thirteenth-Century Censuses', 355–7. On the manors of Ramsey Abbey, probably as much as a third of the young women moved away in order to get married. Bennett, 'Medieval Peasant Marriage', 219–21.
[29] Razi, Life, Marriage and Death, 99–109.

Romsley, where she had inherited a ten acre holding from her uncle William Bate.[30] When Adam le Hurne died in 1367, the family quarter-yardland in Hasbury was taken not by Thomas the eldest son, but by his younger brother John.[31] John Perkins (1361–91d.), a yardlander from Ridgeacre, endowed his eldest son Simon in 1384 with a half-yardland in Warley which his wife Alice had inherited from her father Richard Osberon. In 1386 he granted to his second son Richard, the Thomkins' half-yardland holding in Oldbury, which he had acquired from his brother Thomas Perkins in 1370.[32] As family members ceased to crowd on and around the ancestral holding, many cottages which had been occupied continuously in the past, remained vacant and became dilapidated. In 1369 for example, Philip Hipkins, a yardlander from Lapal, was ordered, under penalty of half a mark to repair a dilapidated house on his messuage.[33] In late fourteenth- and fifteenth-century Halesowen, as on other contemporary manors, such court orders increased considerably although the tenants often ignored them.[34]

The centrifugal force exerted on peasant families by the abundance of land after the Black Death in 1349, did not stop at the borders of the manor. While many children of Halesowen tenants left home to occupy vacant holdings on the manor, others left and settled in neighbouring parishes, probably on land vacated by their kin. Unlike the previous period, many of the peasants who left Halesowen after the Black Death came from middling and well-to-do families. In the 1350s, John Green the son of one of the largest landholders in the manor emigrated to the nearby manor of Northfield, as did, in 1377, William the son of William Hill, another substantial tenant.[35] The emigration of young villagers and the heavy mortality caused by the outbreaks of the plague between 1349 and 1375, greatly increased the number of deceased Halesowen tenants who had no children to succeed them on the manor. In the pre-plague period 13 per cent of the tenants, whose obituaries were recorded in the court rolls, had no children to succeed them, but the percentage rose to 39 in the period 1350–1400.[36] None the less, the survival rate of tenant

---

[30] BRL 346343–71.   [31] BRL 346814.

[32] BRL 346363–6, 346349.   [33] BRL 346349.

[34] Similar court orders can be found in the court rolls of many other contemporary manors. See, for example, Dyer, *Lords and Peasants*, 241–2; Jones, 'Bedfordshire: Fifteenth Century', in Harvey (ed.), *Peasant Land Market*, 185–6; Harvey, *Westminster Abbey*, 273–4; Dewindt, *Land and People*, 135–6.

[35] BRL 346338, 346355.

[36] In the court rolls between 1270 and 1348, the death of 320 tenants was recorded, 278 (86.9 per cent) of them had children on the manor who succeeded them. However, among

families in the second half of the fourteenth century remained quite high, since 60 per cent of the tenants in Halesowen at the end of the fourteenth century were descendants of tenants who had resided on the manor in the beginning of the century.[37] This was a result of the extent and nature of immigration to the manor during the years 1350–95, when the population influx to Halesowen increased and many of the newcomers were related to deceased local tenants whose holdings they inherited or acquired through marriage.[38] Thus, despite the high rates of mortality and emigration, many Halesowen tenant families were saved from extinction during this period by relatives who moved to the manor. It would seem that family land was much sought after by immigrants because it was cheaper, provided them with a better title and enabled them to be absorbed more easily into the village community.[39] Moreover by taking over such land, newcomers also gained relatives who could assist them and co-operate with them.

As many old Halesowen landed families survived to the end of the fourteenth century, the kin density in the manor remained fairly high. We can see from Table 10.2, that of the 142 tenants identified in the court rolls from 1397 to 1399, 76.8 per cent were related to each other. Our statistics show that the percentage of landholders related by blood and marriage falls only slightly from 80.5 in 1315 to 76.8 in 1397–9. However, the sample of tenants obtained from the court rolls of 1397–9 overestimates the kin density on the manor, because most of the kinless tenants

the 129 tenants whose deaths were recorded between 1350 and 1400, only 79 (61.1 per cent) had children who succeeded them. Hilton estimated that, in the post-plague West Midland villages, between a third and a half of the holdings were not kept in the family after the death of the head of the household. Hilton, *English Peasantry*, 41. On the Norfolk manor of Coltishal, 61.4 per cent of deceased tenants had children to succeed them between 1351 and 1400, a percentage almost identical to that in Halesowen. However, in the pre-plague period it was lower—79.8. See, B. M. S. Campbell, 'Population Pressure', 93.

[37] In the court rolls 1397–9, 142 tenants are noted, 85 (59.8 per cent) of them descended from the 45 tenants identified in the court records of 1315–17.

[38] Razi, *Life, Marriage and Death*, 117–21. When I analysed the court rolls between 1351 and 1395, I found that 42 of the 226 immigrants who settled in Halesowen were the descendants of villagers who had previously emigrated from the manor (ibid. 121). Additional genealogical evidence obtained from the 15th-cent. court rolls, reveals that another 46 of the immigrants who settled in Halesowen in the period had a blood relationship to local families. All in all, 88 (39.8 per cent) of the immigrants to Halesowen during this period were the descendants of local peasants.

[39] Ibid. 120–4, and Razi, 'Family, Land and the Village Community', 25–6. On various Westminster manors in the post-plague period, tenants were required to pay higher entry fines for holdings to which they had no inheritance right. See Harvey, *Westminster Abbey*, 225, 302–4.

TABLE 10.2. *Kinship links between tenants identified in Halesowen court rolls, 1270–1400*

Years	1315–17	1397–9
Number of Tenants	215	142
Related to others	173 (80.5%)	109 (76.8%)
Unrelated to others	42 (19.5%)	33 (23.2%)

were smallholders and these are under-represented in the sample.[40] Such tenants constitute 24.6 per cent of the sample, while the percentage of land deficient families reconstituted from the court rolls between 1350 and 1400 is 35.[41] If we had a more representative sample, the percentage of kinless tenants would have risen from 23.2 to 30.3.[42] It is likely, therefore, that the percentage of tenants with kin in Halesowen fell from 80.5 in 1315–17 to 69.7 in the years 1397–9. Moreover, the average size of the kin group on the manor was also reduced during the second half of the fourteenth century. Whereas the percentage of tenants with only one relative in 1315–17 was 20.5, in 1397–9 it rose to 32.3.

Although the kin density in Halesowen somewhat decreased in the second half of the fourteenth century, the bond between family and land was maintained. This can be learned from the land transactions recorded in the court rolls of 1351–1400, which show that the bulk of the tenants' land on the manor continued to be distributed through the family.[43]

III

It is likely that the strength of the family–land bond in Halesowen, which created a high kin density, also promoted a high degree of kin co-operation and cohesion. This hypothesis can be tested by analysing acts of pledging which involve a personal commitment and also an element of risk. The

[40] Among the 33 kinless tenants identified in the court rolls 1397–9, one (3 per cent) was a large tenant, six (18.2 per cent) were middling and 26 (78.8 per cent) were smallholders.

[41] Razi, *Life, Marriage and Death*, 147. A similar reduction in the population of smallholders has been observed by Hilton in other West Midland manors. See, Hilton, *English Peasantry*, 39–40.

[42] In order to correct the bias in our sample, I constructed a hypothetical sample in which smallholders constitute 35 per cent. Then I estimated the number of kinless tenants according to their proportion in each group of tenants in the observed sample. As a result the percentage of kinless tenants rises to 30.3.

[43] Razi, 'Family, Land and the Village Community', 16–20.

TABLE 10.3.   *Acts of pledging which involve a personal commitment and an*
element of risk, performed by the 1315–17 tenants. (Halesowen court rolls,
1270–1400)

Size of holding	No. of tenants	No. of pledges	No. of intrafamilial pledges	Percentage of intrafamilial pledges
Largeholders	47 (21.9%)	997 (69.5%)	194 (41.2%)	19.5
Middling holders	75 (34.9%)	323 (22.5%)	211 (44.8%)	65.3
Smallholders	43 (20.0%)	69 (4.8%)	41 (8.7%)	59.4
Cottagers	50 (23.2%)	46 (3.2%)	25 (5.3%)	54.3
TOTAL	215 (100%)	1,435 (100%)	471 (100%)	33.8

215 tenants noted in the court rolls between 1315 and 1317 were involved, during the term of their residence in the manor, in 1475 such
acts. Of these 33.3 per cent were intrafamilial.[44] Yet this figure conceals
the true role of kin in pledging because of the considerable involvement
of largeholders in this court-related activity.[45] We can see in Table 10.3
that such tenants were involved in 67.6 per cent of all the pledges but of
these, only 19.1 per cent were with kin. In contrast to largeholders, the
percentage of kin pledges of middling, small, and cottage tenants, who
were involved to a much lesser extent in pledging, was 65.3, 59.4, and
54.3 respectively.[46] The fact that largeholders were far less involved in

[44] The incidence of kin-pledging was estimated only from the court rolls of two other
manors. From 1288 to 1339, the percentage of such pledges estimated from the court rolls
of Holywell-cum-Needingworth is 23, and from those of Redgrave, between 1259 and 1297,
the percentage is 10.7. See Dewindt, *Land and People*, 246, and Smith, 'Kin and Neighbours', 224. The lower estimate of intrafamilial pledges obtained from Holywell court rolls
is undoubtedly due to the fact that Halesowen court rolls which survived in abundance
provide much better genealogical data than the fragmentary court records of the Huntingdonshire manor. Such an explanation, however, cannot account for the differences in the
percentage of kin pledges estimated from Redgrave and Halesowen court rolls, since the
records of the two manors are of a similar quality.

[45] In Holywell-cum-Needingworth and Redgrave, as in Halesowen, large tenants played
an overwhelming role in pledging. Dewindt, *Land and People*, 247 and Smith, 'Kin and
Neighbours', 226.

[46] While large and middling tenants and to a lesser extent smallholders both received and
gave surety in the manor court, cottagers very rarely acted as pledges for other villagers. In
Redgrave, largeholders were involved ten times less frequently than smaller tenants in
pledging with kin. Smith, 'Kin and Neighbours', 226.

intrafamilial pledging than smaller tenants does not necessarily imply that they were less kin-oriented. As a result of their economic position in the village, such tenants were involved in litigation and other court business, both as suitors and as court and village officials, far more frequently than other tenants.[47] Their contacts involved so many villagers, that their own relatives could not possibly have formed but a small minority. In any case, when a pledge involving an element of risk was required by the court, the less well-off tenants, constituting 78 per cent of the landholders, supported and relied on their kin more often than on villagers unrelated to them.

In addition to pledges, the court rolls provide further evidence about the supportive roll of kin, namely in cases concerning the elderly and the poor. Pension contracts recorded in the court rolls and breaches of such agreements give us some insight into the treatment of the elderly in medieval villages.[48] Recently Macfarlane has argued that the infrequency of retirement contracts recorded in court rolls indicate that medieval villagers did not rely on their children for support in old age, and rather leased, mortgaged, or sold land to secure their future.[49] However, although elderly tenants sometimes leased and alienated land, there is no evidence that this was common practice. Furthermore, the fact that retirement contracts were infrequently recorded in court rolls, can be explained by an altogether different hypothesis, namely that since medieval villagers were usually well provided for by their children in old age, retiring tenants only seldom required formal maintenance contracts. This hypothesis offers a better explanation for the behaviour of elderly tenants in Halesowen, and probably also in other pre-plague manors. Henry Halen, for example, a customary middling tenant, was brought to the court in 1346, two years before his death, 'ill and almost blind', to surrender half of his holding to his eldest son William, which he did unconditionally. The behaviour of Henry and 32 other tenants who also retired between 1270 and 1348, without any maintenance contract with their

---

[47] Razi, *Life, Marriage and Death*, 76–8; Dewindt, *Land and People*, 206–41; Britton, *Community of the Vill*, 94–102; Dewindt, 'Peasant Structures', 244–61.

[48] Homans, *English Villagers*, 152–7; Raftis, *Tenure and Mobility*, 42–8, 71–4; Hilton, *English Peasantry*, 29–30; Razi, 'Family, Land and the Village Community', 7–8; Clark, 'Some Aspects of Social Security', 307–20; Hanawalt, *Ties that Bound*, 229–40.

[49] Macfarlane, *Marriage and Love*, 115–16. While in this book Macfarlane infers that children in medieval villages did not provide for their elderly parents from the fact that retirement contracts were rarely recorded in court rolls, in a previous book he made the same inference from the fact that such contracts were recorded in court rolls: see Macfarlane, *Origins of English Individualism*, 141–4. For a criticism of his argument, see Razi, 'Family, Land and the Village Community', 7–8.

successors, does not make sense unless we assume that it was the norm for children to support their parents in old age.[50] Children sometimes shared the responsibility of maintaining their elderly parents, as in the cases of the brothers John and Philip de Pitway in the 1340s,[51] and of William Smith of Oldbury who, in 1281, granted his sister Lucy a croft to enable her to maintain their mother.[52] Some children obviously deviated from this norm, and retiring tenants who suspected that their offspring might not honour the moral obligation to provide for them, made the transfer of the holding conditional.[53] Other retiring tenants secured a legally binding maintenance contract. A number of such contracts were apparently preceded by informal agreements which turned sour, as did the long and elaborate contract between Thomas Bird and his widowed mother, recorded in 1281.[54]

The manor court also recorded maintenance agreements between childless retiring tenants and those who took over their holdings. Adam Green for example, a quarter-yardlander from Romsley who retired in 1318 when his wife died, surrendered his holding to his nephew Thomas Curtis. However, since Thomas was only a minor, the land was taken over by his father Robert, who also undertook to maintain Adam Green, his brother-in-law, at his table for the rest of his life and to provide him with shoes and clothing.[55] During the period 1270–1348, 61 maintenance agreements were recorded in Halesowen court rolls between elderly peasants and those who took over their land. Of these, 34 were between parents and children, 6 between grandparents and grandchildren, and 20 (33.3 per cent) between more distant kin. Only one of the 61 contracts was between non-kin and it includes a condition never found in any of the maintenance agreements between relatives. When Thomas at the Heath handed over his holding, in 1305, to John Baker and Edith his wife, they undertook, in addition to paying him 12*d*. annually, to take him into their household 'if by chance poverty, sickness or hard times fall upon him'.[56] This suggests that elderly villagers preferred kin as partners

[50] Hilton, *English Peasantry*, 29.

[51] The matter was brought to the attention of the court because the brothers disagreed about the contribution each one of them had promised to make towards the support of their mother. BRL 346314.

[52] *Court Rolls of the Manor of Hales*, iii. 93.

[53] Hilton, *English Peasantry*, 29; Homans, *English Villagers*, 155–6.

[54] *Court Rolls of the Manor of Hales*, i. 108, 110, 165–8.   [55] BRL 346794.

[56] It is stated in the court entry that John Baker and his wife had no inheritance claim to Thomas Heath's holding and consequently they could not have been related to each other. See *Court Rolls of the Manor of Hales*, ii. 513.

to retirement contracts not only because they were morally bound to support them, but also because they were expected to do more for them than strangers.

Poverty was an endemic and acute problem in pre-plague villages, as many peasants had little or no land at all.[57] Poor peasants could find some employment during the peak periods, and at harvest time they were allowed to glean, but for most of the year they lived by begging and by pilfering food, firewood, and anything which helped them to survive.[58] Therefore, both the landlord and the peasant community attempted, through the manor court, to reduce the number of the poor in the village and to control their activities. Unlike other villagers, poor peasants who committed offences were often expelled from the manor, and those who were permitted to stay were required not only to pay a fine but also to bring pledges for good behaviour. The manor court also amerced those who harboured undesirable poor peasants.[59]

The evidence drawn from such cases suggests that the poor in Halesowen, as on many other manors, were often pledged and sheltered by their relatives. The court appearances of Agnes the widow of Richard Couper, their two children Lucy and John and her new husband Thomas Garding, who lived together on a smallholding in the township of Hunnington, is a case in point. In 1312 Lucy, who must have been a young woman then, unsuccessfully sued her stepfather for failing to keep his promise to provide her daily with half a loaf of bread and some beans.[60] During the harvest of 1312, Lucy gleaned excessively and, as a result, in October the court issued an order for her immediate expulsion from the manor.[61] By the harvest of 1313 she was back in Halesowen, as it was presented in the manor court that she had gleaned sheaves on the demesne, which she brought to her family's cottage where she was again residing.[62] In November she was amerced 2*d.* for pinching 12 sheaves from the rector's pile and was ordered to make amends and to bring pledges for good behaviour.[63] She brought her brother John and her uncle Henry Oniot, another smallholder of the same township. In 1314

---

[57] On the low standard of living of many pre-plague peasants, see Kosminsky, *Studies*, 230–42; Hilton, *Medieval Society*, 142–4; Postan and Titow, 'Some Economic Evidence of Declining Population in the Later Middle Ages', 221–46; Titow, *English Rural Society*, 78–96; Miller and Hatcher, *Medieval England*, 147–9; Razi, *Life, Marriage and Death*, 34–45.

[58] Ault, 'By-Laws of Gleaning', 210–17; Razi, *Life, Marriage and Death*, 37, 78. On similar activities in other contemporary villages, see Raftis, 'Social Structures', 92–3; DeWindt, *Land and People*, 204, n. 116.

[59] Raftis, *Tenure and Mobility*, 130–8; DeWindt, 'Peasant Structures', 262–4.

[60] BRL 346233.   [61] Ibid.   [62] BRL 346234.   [63] BRL 346235.

she quarrelled again with her stepfather Thomas Garding and was amerced 2*d.* for assaulting him.[64] As a result of both her pledges, her brother and uncle were also amerced 2*d.* each. None the less, they were prepared to pledge for her again when she promised the court to behave well and to refrain from bothering her stepfather.[65] During the famine of 1316/17, Lucy, her mother, and her stepfather died and John sold the holding and left the manor at the end of 1317.[66] In the court rolls from the lean years of the 1290s and 1310s, one encounters many villagers like the Coupers who could hardly make ends meet, but nevertheless sheltered and fed their destitute relatives in their households for various periods of time. All in all, between 1270 and 1348, 151 native-born Halesowen villagers were noted in the court rolls as taking refuge with local tenants, at least 128 (85 per cent) of them did so with their relatives. This suggests that during the period under study the kin group was the main organ for poor relief in the parish.

Since extended kin groups still predominated in Halesowen in the second half of the fourteenth century, ties between relatives who were not co-resident continued to play an important role in village society, as the court rolls from this period indicate.[67] In 1371, for example, Richard Squiere, his brother Thomas, their uncle John Squiere and their cousin John atte Lyche, leased from the Abbot the demesne lands in Romsley for a term of 12 years, at an annual rent of £2.[68] The court rolls between 1350 and 1400 recorded 84 interactions between 18 members of the atte Lyche and Squiere families who were inter-related through marriage. In 1376 Philip Thedrich and his first cousin Richard Jordan, substantial tenants from Cakemore, leased from the Abbot the demesne lands in the township.[69] The 24 interactions between them, noted in the court rolls from 1370 to 1392, suggest that they closely co-operated in the running of their farms which included land in thrèe townships.[70] Middling and small-holders were also noted in the court records for various intrafamilial contacts, but less frequently than their better-off neighbours. For example, only four instances of contact between Richard Fisher and his brother Robert, smallholders from Oldbury, are recorded in the 1390s.[71] Although the size of the kin group on the manor decreased in the second half of the fourteenth century, the mean annual frequency of recorded kin contacts

---

[64] BRL 346235.   [65] Ibid.   [66] BRL 346236.
[67] Razi, 'Family, Land and the Village Community', 16–20.
[68] BRL 346816.   [69] BRL 346354.   [70] BRL 346349–71.
[71] BRL 346369–77.

increased by about 45 per cent.[72] It would seem that this happened because the peasants, who faced a severe labour shortage during this period, had to rely, more than in the past, on the economic co-operation of their relatives.[73]

The court rolls in the second half of the fourteenth century provide less information about the welfare system on the manor. However, it is still possible to investigate the role of the family in supporting the elderly. In the pre-plague period almost all the tenants who contracted formal pension agreements made them with kin, two-thirds with children or grandchildren and a third with more distant relatives. In the period 1350–1400, 43 such contracts were recorded, 20 (46.5 per cent) with children or grandchildren, 19 (44.2 per cent) with more distant relatives and 4 (9.3 per cent) with non-kin.[74] Although the percentage of retiring tenants who formed maintenance contracts with non-kin rose in the second half of the fourteenth century, the family undoubtedly remained the chief agency for supporting the elderly in the village. Poor peasants, unlike retiring tenants, hardly appear in the post-plague court rolls, since the manorial court ceased to expel such people. The court rolls continued occasionally to record the names of poor tenants who could not afford paying death duties, but such references do not inform us how the poor fared during this period.[75] However, since there is evidence that the villagers in the second half of the fourteenth century relied on the support of their kin in everyday life and in old age, there is no reason to suppose that they did not do so when they fell on hard times.

In addition to evidence about extended kin networks and their role

[72] Of the sample of 6200 kin interactions recorded in the court rolls between 1270 and 1400 presented in Table 10.1a, 3885 were noted during the years 1270 and 1348, and 2315 interactions in the years 1350–1400. For the years 1270–1348, the court records of 70 years are available and for the period 1350–1400, of 48 years. Therefore, the mean annual number of recorded kin contacts in the pre-plague court rolls is 55.5, and 48.2 in the post-plague ones. However, since the population in the second half of the 14th cent. declined by about 40 per cent, the mean annual number of recorded deaths must have risen by 44.7 per cent. See also, Razi, 'Family, Land and the Village Community', 28–9.

[73] Ibid. 31–3. A high degree of co-operation between the peasants was also observed on other West Midland manors. See Hilton, *English Peasantry*, 37–53.

[74] Unlike Halesowen, a sample of 114 maintenance contracts obtained from post-plague East Anglian court rolls reveals that only 28 per cent of the elderly were supported by kin. See Clark, 'Some Aspects of Social Security', 316, table 2. Richard Smith analysing a larger sample of post-plague court rolls also found that during this period 'about 70% of contracts concern persons who appear to have been unrelated'. See Smith 'The Manorial Court and the Elderly Tenant', 52.

[75] In e.g. 1393 Richard Fisher, a son of a smallholder, was excused the payment of death duties because his father was too poor. BRL 346373.

in village society, the court records shed some light on the quality of intrafamilial relations especially between parents and children and between siblings. It seems that the peasant family was not only supportive and cohesive but also highly patriarchal. In the court rolls between 1270 and 1400, 1155 breaches of the peace involving kin are recorded. In 27.3 per cent of these cases siblings were involved, in 10.4 per cent husband and wives, in 10.9 per cent mothers and children, and only 2.2 per cent fathers and children (see Table 10.1a). The rarity in which conflicts between fathers and children led to violence and consequently to presentments for breaches of the peace, suggests that children in Halesowen had a high deference to their fathers. Furthermore, the fact that most of the recorded intrafamilial contacts were between adults who did not reside in the same household, indicates that the authority of the *pater familias* over his children remained quite strong, even when they left home and established their own families in the village. Children depended on their fathers, even when they had families, and consequently could hardly challenge their authority. As long as the father was alive, children had a similar deference to their mothers, because almost all recorded violent quarrels were between widows and their children. Disputes over the dower, especially when the widows remarried, must have considerably strained the relationship between widows and their adult children.[76] This can be inferred from the fact that 88 per cent of the recorded violent quarrels between mothers and children occurred during the period 1270–1348, in which the rate of widows' marriage was considerably higher than in the period 1349–1400.[77]

However, there was another side to the relationship between parents and children in medieval Halesowen. Parents made a real sacrifice in granting part of the holding to their eldest children, in order to enable them to marry and to settle in the village, when they themselves were often still burdened by younger children and occasionally also by a dependent relative. We can see in Table 10.4 that 36.8 per cent of all the

[76] Such a dispute, for example, led to a presentment in the court held in Jan. 1325 in which John Snod of Hill was reported for throwing a knife at this mother Matilda, who remarried within a few months of his father's death, and for calling her a 'byche', BRL 346244. This is the earliest example for the derogatory use of the word 'bitch'.

[77] Razi, *Life, Marriage and Death*, 66–7, 139. In the Cambridgeshire manor of Cottenham between 1303 and 1348, an annual number of 0.93 widows' marriage is recorded, but between 1349 and 1379, only 0.16. Even if we take into consideration the post-plague sharp population decline, there must have been a considerable fall in the rate of widows' marriage in Cottenham. The figures are calculated from the data presented in Ravensdale, 'The Transfer of Customary Land', 220–2.

TABLE 10.4. *Familial relationships in intrafamilial court recorded interactions between 1270 and 1400 indicating support*

Familial relationship	Pledging	Land transactions	Hospitality	Pledges for good behaviour	Maintenance agreements	Total
Parents/ Children	590	186	41	7	58	882
	(25.3%)	(36.8%)	(25.6%)	(19.4%)	(33.2%)	(27.5%)
Siblings	528	119	32	13	42	734
	(22.6%)	(23.5%)	(20.0%)	(36.1%)	(24.0%)	(22.8%)
Parents-/sons-/daughters -in-law	235	47	30	—	30	342
	(10.1%)	(9.3%)	(18.8%)		(17.2%)	(10.6%)
Brothers-/ sisters-in-law	261	38	10	—	22	331
	(11.2%)	(7.5%)	(6.2%)		(12.6%)	(10.3%)
Others	721	116	47	16	23	923
	(30.8%)	(22.9%)	(29.4%)	(44.2%)	(13.2%)	(28.7%)
TOTAL	2,335	506	160	36	175	3,212
	(100%)	(100%)	(100%)	(100%)	(100%)	(100%)

inter-vivos land transactions between kin were between parents and children, and 9.3 per cent between parents and their married daughters. Of these, 1.2 per cent were grants from children to parents. Therefore, 44.9 per cent of all the kin transactions recorded between 1270 and 1400 were transfers from parents to children.[78] Although the relationship between parents and their adult children were by no means idyllic or harmonious, the land transactions, as well as other interactions presented in Table 10.4 suggest that they were none the less close, supportive, and reciprocal.

The relationship between siblings, reflected in the court records, were also marked by a high frequency of interactions indicating strife as well as co-operation and assistance. In 1293, for example, John Green, a quarter-yardlander from Ridgeacre, sued his brother Thomas, a large tenant of the same village, for withholding from him 2s. 8d.[79] In 1308, however, he brought Thomas and another brother, Peter, as pledgers for an amercement of 2s.[80] In the beginning of 1312 John left the manor without permission and, when he returned ten months later, he had to declare in the court that he would not leave the manor again. Thomas vouched for him.[81] A

---

[78] In Redgrave between 1295 and 1319, 11 per cent of the *inter-vivos* land transactions between kin were between fathers and children and 46.7 per cent between siblings. Smith, 'Families and their Land', 192, table 3.20. The difference in the role played by siblings in intrafamilial land transactions is probably due to the fact that in Redgrave partible inheritance was practised by the villagers.

[79] *Court Rolls of the Manor of Hales*, ii. 344.   [80] BRL 350353.

[81] BRL 346234.

month later John himself pledged his sister Matilda for good behaviour.[82] In January 1314 Thomas paid an amercement of 6*d*., which was levied on his brother John for trespassing the demesne.[83] For some reason the relationship between John and Thomas became rather tense, and they were presented twice for shedding each other's blood. The court decreed that if they resort to violence again they will have to pay a fine of 6*s*. 8*d*.[84] In 1318 John was brought to the court, to answer for some land which he granted to Thomas without the lord's leave.[85] In 1319 Thomas and John Green were amerced for leasing a large croft from a neighbour for ten years without licence.[86] The two brothers continued to interact closely until they died in the 1330s.

Thomas Cook, a large tenant from Ridgeacre, and John Linacre, a middling tenant from Hunnington, were brothers-in-law. Each of them farmed also half of a yardland in Hunnington which their wives inherited. Between 1320 and 1349, the brothers-in-law occupied the court numerous times in claims and counter-claims for damages against each other, as their beasts often seemed to ignore the boundary lines they had drawn in the holding.[87] They themselves and their servants resorted several times to violence. None the less, when John Linacre and his wife died in the Black Death of 1349, Thomas took the 8-year-old son of John under his custody.[88] It appears that he took good care of young John and his tenement, because when John took the holding in 1361, he became in a few years one of the most successful farmers in the village.[89]

These examples as well as the figures presented in Table 10.4, indicate that siblings in Halesowen assisted each other quite frequently, although not to the same extent as parents and children. Moreover, unlike the relationships between parents and children, those between siblings led far more frequently to violent quarrels. Of the 1155 breaches of the peace involving kin, noted in the court rolls between 1270 and 1400, 27.4 per cent were between siblings and only 13.2 per cent between parents and children. It is more difficult to evaluate the ties between brothers- and sisters-in-law because of the considerable problems of tracing affinal ties in the court records. None the less, since at least 10.3 per cent of the recorded supportive intrafamilial contacts were between in-laws (see Table 10.4), it is likely that these ties were strong, although not as strong as between siblings.

In his study of kinship in pre-plague Redgrave, Richard Smith also

[82] BRL 346234.   [83] BRL 346235.   [84] Ibid.
[85] BRL 346236.   [86] BRL 346237.   [87] BRL 346245–323.
[88] BRL 346323.   [89] BRL 346343.

found a high frequency of inter-sibling court contacts indicating both co-operation and strife. However, such contacts usually began after the division of the inheritance between co-heirs, and in most cases (78 per cent) did not last more than ten years. Therefore, he argued, intense inter-sibling contacts may well reflect a particular life-cycle phase through which individuals, especially those co-heirs whose inheritance had yet to be eroded by land sales, progressed.[90] It appears, however, that in Halesowen the pattern of inter-sibling contacts was quite different. In the court rolls between 1270 and 1349, 86 pairs of land holding brothers are identified.[91] An examination of their court interactions shows that 61 (71 per cent) of them maintained such contacts over a period of 20 years and more. This indicates that in Halesowen close inter-sibling association was in fact a life long one. The analysis of court cases involving kin, suggests that familial relationships in Halesowen from 1270 to 1400 were close, reciprocal, enduring, and binding. These relationships were undoubtedly due to the fact that the individual peasant gained through familial ties not only access to land but also co-operation in everyday life and support in hard times and old age.

The observations about the family made from Halesowen court rolls stand in sharp contrast to these made by Richard Smith from the court rolls of the Suffolk manor of Redgrave between 1260 and 1320.[92] In addition to the differences in the duration of close inter-sibling association between the two manors, the percentage of tenants with a high frequency of kin pledging was 37 in Redgrave but 78 in Halesowen.[93] Moreover, while the laterally extended family in Redgrave failed to provide very effective means of reducing the individual vulnerability to the risk of property loss, in Halesowen it succeeded in doing so since the bulk of the land was transmitted through the family rather than through the market.[94] These differences were probably a consequence of the fact that most peasant families in Halesowen were functionally extended whereas in Redgrave they were nuclear.[95]

[90] Smith, 'Families and their Land', 184–94.
[91] Razi, *Life, Marriage and Death*, 35.
[92] Smith, 'Kin and Neighbours', 219–56; Smith, 'Families and their Land', 135–97.
[93] Smith, 'Kin and Neighbours', 242–3.
[94] Smith, 'Transactional Analysis', 227–40.
[95] See also, Razi, 'Myth of the Immutable English Family', 15–22.

The Peasant Land Market in Medieval England—and Beyond

PAUL D. A. HARVEY

THE medieval economic historian must sometimes defend himself against the charge of thinking anachronistically. In seeking insights into medieval society by investigating its economic structure and development one can all too easily assume—wrongly—that people in the Middle Ages took the same interest in the economy of their time and that they responded consciously and knowledgeably to such phenomena as fluctuations in the value of money, movements in trade patterns, growth of population. This, at least, is one danger we need not guard against in looking at the medieval land market. The medieval landowner, large or small, did not have the same information at his disposal as his historian today: in some ways he knew more, in some less, about the land market of his own time. But we cannot doubt his interest, his keen interest, in the subject, in England as throughout medieval Europe. When Richard Barking died in 1246 after 24 years as abbot of Westminster the epitaph on his tombstone did not refer to his spiritual attainments or other merits, but listed as his four achievements buying the manor of La Neyte, buying the manor of Castlemorton, impropriating the church of Oakham, and securing from the king 'a charter useful in many ways' (*multis commoda charta*).[1] This preoccupation with land, its acquisition, and its value was shared alike by ecclesiastic and nobleman, magnate and villein. In investigating the land market we are looking at something that lay close to the heart of medieval man.

For some aspects of this land market, there is peculiarly full evidence from England. From the rest of the British Isles the picture is less clear. Though estate-owners from England produced in Ireland and, particularly, Wales the same kinds of record as provide the English evidence their coverage is less complete and the differing social structure and political history of these areas in the Middle Ages mean that their land markets demand separate treatment.[2] And in medieval Scotland we are

---

[1] Harvey, *Westminster Abbey*, 92–3.
[2] The form of the local land market in Wales is discussed by L. B. Smith, 'The Gage and the Land Market in Late Medieval Wales', *EcHR* 2nd ser. 29 (1976), 537–50.

in an altogether different historiographical world, where the sources for such a study are different in kind, and far sparser, than those from the rest of Britain.

Certainly the English sources for the market in substantial rural holdings—entire manors rather than single acres—and for the market in urban properties can be equalled or bettered in other parts of western Europe. Charters of kings and of magnates, which survive from the late seventh century onwards, give us some glimpses of the traffic in land by which the great estates, lay and ecclesiastical, were built up, but these glimpses give us much less than a complete picture for the Anglo-Saxon period. For the new estate structure of the Norman settlement, however, the greater profusion of charters from the twelfth century onwards shows us much more clearly how land was acquired and transferred by the nobility and gentry. The evidence of these charters can be supplemented, first, from the end of the twelfth century, by the records of the royal courts, in particular the feet of fines which recorded the transfer of property in fictitious legal suits; second, from the 1230s onwards, by the inquisitions post mortem which recorded, on the death of a tenant-in-chief, the lands he held and who was to inherit them; and third, in a growing volume from the early thirteenth century, by the administrative records of the estates themselves. The construction of manorial descents—the successive ownership of landed estates—is a long-established tradition in English antiquarian scholarship, and the many county histories that have been published since the seventeenth century contain a vast mass of evidence for the workings of the medieval land market in its higher reaches. More recently there have been a number of important studies of individual estates in medieval England; some have looked only at the administration of the estate and its revenues, but others have investigated in some detail the way the estate's individual properties were acquired, augmented, and disposed of—notable examples are the work on the estates of Peterborough Abbey by Edmund King, of Westminster Abbey by Barbara Harvey, of Thorney and Crowland Abbeys by Sandra Raban.[3] These studies have concentrated particularly on the monastic estates, for it is from these that fullest records survive. The time is ripe for a general survey of the market in substantial areas of land in medieval England; it has yet to be written.

Nor have we any general work on the traffic in urban properties though

---

[3] King, *Peterborough Abbey*; Harvey, *Westminster Abbey*; S. Raban, *The Estates of Thorney and Crowland: A Study in Medieval Monastic Land Tenure* (Cambridge, 1977).

there a good deal more research may be needed on individual towns
before it can be produced. The evidence is there. For certain English
towns surveys, deeds, and court records enable us to compile a tolerably
complete list of the owners of each property from the thirteenth—even
the twelfth—century to the sixteenth. The possibility of work on these
lines was demonstrated long ago from Oxford by H. E. Salter, then from
Canterbury by William Urry;[4] more recently it has been achieved for
Winchester on a monumental scale by Derek Keene, with a detailed
analysis of the urban property market there.[5] At York a similar reconstruction is under way; at London it has begun with Derek Keene's work
on the properties of Cheapside; at Southampton the publication of detailed editions of relevant records has brought the same goal well within
sight.[6] In all these places archaeology is combining with work on documents to build up a full picture of properties in the towns—and therewith of the traffic in these properties, how they moved from one owner
to another. Much less has been done on the smaller towns—the local
market centres—and few can provide the abundant evidence that survives from some English medieval cities. But even limited sources can
throw some light on the small-town property market: surveys of *c*.1225
and 1441 from Banbury (Oxfordshire), a town from which we have prac-
tically no medieval deeds, show clearly the growth of a class of middle-
man rentiers coming between the occupants of individual houses and
their landlord, the bishop of Lincoln.[7] And for some small towns fuller
sources make it possible to analyse the local property market in detail.
The work of Eleanor Searle on Battle (Sussex) in the thirteenth century
is an example; it is based on a substantial collection of charters, rentals,
and records of the town court.[8]

However, it is above all from the rural manors of medieval England
that we have peculiarly full evidence of the land market, evidence fuller

---

[4] H. E. Salter, *Survey of Oxford*, ed. W. A. Pantin and W. T. Mitchell (Oxford Historical Society, NS vols. 14, 20; 1960–9); W. Urry, *Canterbury under the Angevin Kings* (London, 1967).

[5] D. Keene, *Survey of Medieval Winchester* (2 vols.; Winchester Studies No. 2; Oxford, 1985).

[6] The work on York and London is as yet unpublished. The Southampton publications are, particularly vols. 15, 19, 20, 24, 25, in the Southampton Records Series: *The Southampton Terrier of 1454*, ed. L. A. Burgess (1976), *The Cartulary of God's House, Southampton*, ed. J. M. Kaye (2 vols.; Southampton Rec. Ser., 1976); *The Cartulary of the Priory of St Denys near Southampton*, ed. E. O. Blake (2 vols.; Southampton Rec. Ser., 1981).

[7] *VCH Oxford*, ed. W. Page *et al.* (in progress, London, 1907–present), x. 6.

[8] E. Searle, *Lordship and Community: Battle Abbey and its Banlieu 1066–1538* (Toronto, 1974), 109–33.

than we have from most other parts of Europe for the market in small pieces of land that were bought and sold by landholders of varying status and wealth but whose estates were to be measured in acres rather than manors, whose annual income was more likely to be expressed in shillings than in tens or hundreds of pounds. The bulk of this evidence is of two kinds, depending on the status of the particular piece of land. If it was in customary tenure, being held—or having been held—by villein tenants bound to the land and to their manorial lord, it could change hands only by passing from the tenant to the lord and thence to a new tenant; this new tenant might be the old tenant's heir, or someone whom the old tenant had nominated (perhaps for a consideration) to succeed him, or someone simply found by the lord. In every case the transfer of the property would be effected by public ceremony in the manorial court and would be recorded on the manorial court rolls. The earliest of such court rolls to survive dates from 1246, and it is likely that this sort of record was then something of a novelty.[9] Indeed, we may wonder whether the manorial court itself had then had for more than two or three generations the form revealed by these records, the form that let it act as a registry of land holding on the manor. Certainly, however, manorial court rolls spread quickly, especially from the 1270s onwards, and from many places in fourteenth- and fifteenth-century England substantial series survive. From certain of these we can reconstruct the succession to every parcel of the manor's customary land, down to holdings of a quarter-acre (0.1 ha.) or less, over a period of two or more centuries, and can reconstruct too the histories of the peasant families that held them—their successive generations, their inter-relationships, the part they played in the village community, their rise or decline in wealth.

In many places most of the lands held by manorial tenants were in customary tenure of this sort. But in many others, especially moving eastward across England, much, most, or all of a manor's tenant lands would be held in free tenure. This could be transferred—inherited, bought, or sold—without reference to the manorial court, indeed without reference to the lord of whom it was held. Conveyance was by public ceremony but from the twelfth century onwards this was ever increasingly recorded, confirmed, and ultimately displaced by written documents, charters which again might be concerned with minute areas of land. Our evidence for the market in land held in free tenure consists of the many thousands of surviving charters of this sort, together with the many more

[9] Harvey, *Manorial Records*, 42.

that were copied into cartularies when the lands in question passed, with
their title deeds, into the direct control of a monastery or other substantial estate owner. The pattern becomes more complicated where land in
free tenure was acquired by someone who was himself a villein tenant, a
bondman. Theoretically such land was automatically forfeit to his manorial lord; in practice its new tenant was normally allowed to keep it, but
sometimes only on payment or other conditions, after reporting its acquisition in the manorial court. Thus the court rolls will sometimes give us
information about the traffic in free as well as customary land among the
manorial tenants. The register in which Peterborough Abbey copied deeds
of lands in free tenure acquired by its villein tenants is an invaluable but
also, unfortunately, unique record of the mid-fourteenth century.[10]

There are of course other less common records that throw light on the
local land market at a particular place and particular time. Two examples
are the registers compiled from the manorial court rolls of St Albans
Abbey in the mid-fourteenth century and the earl of Kent's charter of
1471 to his tenants at Blunham (Bedfordshire), setting out the rules they
were to follow if they wished to alienate any parts of their holdings.[11] In
many places the evidence of charters and court rolls can be supplemented
by manorial surveys which provide an overall picture of the tenants at a
particular date, sometimes at several successive dates; and by manorial
accounts which, though purely financial records, may contain entries of
payments made on transfers of tenancy.

In all, the historian of the local land market in medieval England has a
vast amount of information at his disposal. At the same time it has some
serious limitations. One is chronological. Our sources begin, and then
rapidly increase in quantity, in the mid-twelfth century (charters) and
mid-thirteenth century (court rolls). What happened before that is far
from clear; the growth of the local land market may itself have called into
being the types of document that record it, or alternatively we may
simply be seeing the application of written records to practices that had
long been conducted without them. When the written records do appear,
they survive particularly from monastic estates, the old-established Benedictine houses being quite disproportionately represented; this is especially true of charters surviving in cartularies, but it applies almost equally
to manorial court rolls. This may be less of a problem than it would have
appeared a generation ago; we are now more inclined to think that there

---

[10] *Carte Nativorum.*
[11] Levett, *Studies in Manorial History*, 79–96; Harvey (ed.), *Peasant Land Market*, 198.

was little significant difference between monasteries and other landlords in the way they ran their estates, though monastic administration, more conservative and more efficient than the rest, may have maintained stricter control and thereby left us a fuller record of the local land market than we find elsewhere. At the least, this aspect of our sources is one we should bear in mind. A more serious limitation has appeared in recent years as more work has been done on the local land market and on peasant society in general. We have from many places substantial numbers of manorial court rolls from the late thirteenth century onwards; but there are very few places where the series of rolls is complete, or almost complete, over a period of a century or more. Even quite small gaps in the run of documents drastically reduce their value as evidence of the local land market. J. A. Raftis, E. B. DeWindt and others have done important work in pioneering these techniques from the manorial court rolls of Ramsey Abbey;[12] it is no reflection on them, however, to say that these good, but far from complete, series simply do not permit the comprehensive reconstruction of the village community and its constituent families that has been so successfully undertaken for Halesowen (Worcestershire) by Zvi Razi[13] or for Redgrave (Suffolk) by R. M. Smith.[14] As Zvi Razi has pointed out, it is only when we have the fullest possible series of records that we can identify individual villagers with precision, and our ability to do this is essential to any analysis of family and social relationships; baffling inconsistency in the use of surnames in court rolls can make it difficult to recognize someone who appears under two or more different names or to distinguish between two people who may be given the same name.[15] Another limitation of our sources that has appeared more clearly as work has advanced is that they mostly tell us nothing of sub-tenure. The charters are concerned with tenant and tenant, the court rolls with tenant and manorial lord; neither tell us of any arrangements these tenants may have made for sub-letting lands to other villagers who would actually till them. Yet that such arrangements were commonplace is shown by some references in court rolls, when lords tried to restrict or control the practice, and by a very few surveys that set out the entire structure of sub-tenancies on a particular manor; the amount of sub-letting that these surveys reveal at Caddington and Kensworth (Bedfordshire) in 1297 and

---

[12] DeWindt, *Land and People*, and Raftis, *Warboys*.
[13] Razi, *Life, Marriage and Death*; Razi, 'Family, Land and the Village Community'; Razi, 'Erosion of the Family-Land Bond', 295–304.
[14] Smith, 'Kin and Neighbours', 219–56; Smith, 'Families and their Land', 135–95.
[15] Razi, 'The Toronto School's Reconstitution', 142–5.

at Havering (Essex) in 1352 suggests that our more usual records of peasant land transactions give us only a partial view of the local land market.[16] A further obvious limitation of our sources is that they tell us less than we would wish about the price of land: what was paid or what exactly was got for the money. This is a point we shall return to. Further research may get round some of the limitations of our sources. These are, however, the difficulties that we must confront.

In 1984 two volumes of studies were published that bear directly on the local land market in medieval England. One was *The Peasant Land Market in Medieval England*, edited by P. D. A. Harvey. This contains studies by four authors, each looking at the way the land market worked in a number of well-documented villages in a particular county: Janet Williamson on thirteenth-century Norfolk, Rosamond Faith on fourteenth- and fifteenth-century Berkshire, Andrew Jones on fifteenth-century Bedfordshire, and Tim Lomas on County Durham in the late fourteenth and fifteenth centuries. An introduction and conclusion by the editor bring together some of the results of this research and look more broadly at certain issues raised. The other book was *Land, Kinship and Life-Cycle*, edited by R. M. Smith. This takes a wider theme—the family, its lands, and its other resources—and covers a longer period, from the thirteenth century to the nineteenth, but the local land market is prominent particularly in its medieval sections, which again consist mostly of detailed studies of individual agricultural communities. These fall into two groups: those by B. M. S. Campbell, R. M. Smith, and J. Ravensdale on places in eastern England (in Norfolk, Suffolk, and Cambridgeshire) in the thirteenth and fourteenth centuries, and by Christopher Dyer and Zvi Razi on places in the west Midlands in the fourteenth, fifteenth, and sixteenth. A further study by Ian Blanchard on industrial employment and rural land market, 1380–1520, looks at the mining communities of Derbyshire and Somerset. In a long and important introduction R. M. Smith, as editor, discusses the book's general themes and pays especial attention to family structure and inheritance customs in the Middle Ages.

The two books are very different—indeed the differences between them are of interest in the context of English medieval historiography. Some of the individual studies would be equally at home in either collection. But in the contributions of the two editors there is a contrast that is more than just a difference of emphasis. *The Peasant Land Market in Medieval England* looks particularly at agrarian and legal forms, using the

---

[16] A. Jones, 'Caddington, Kensworth, and Dunstable in 1297', *EcHR* 2nd ser. 32 (1979), 322–4; McIntosh, 'Land, Tenure, and Population', 20–5.

approach and the language of traditional historical scholarship. *Land, Kinship and Life-Cycle* is concerned with the family and demography and, while no less firmly based on empirical research, it draws on the methods of the social scientist in its sociological and statistical analysis and in relating its findings to general theoretical work on the family and rural society. But in other ways the two books are alike. Both use the same technique of looking in detail at particular well-documented rural communities which we assume (we can only hope) are typical of many others; in each we meet many individual landholders and their families. Both are much concerned with local inheritance customs and their effects, with the actual (as against the theoretical) differences between partible and impartible inheritance and joint tenure by a whole family. Both are feeling their way towards a pattern of regional variation. But the similarities are unsurprising: both books were produced at the same point in the development of our knowledge and both were bound to reflect current preoccupations of scholars working in this field. Between them they mark a new point of departure for work on the local land market of medieval England. Where, then, do we go from here?

Above all we must advance on a wide front. The subject of *The Peasant Land Market in Medieval England* was defined as 'the lands held by the small-scale landholders, whom we call peasants, and the way these lands moved, by mutual agreement, from one living landholder to another, which we call the peasant land market'.[17] This was a broader definition of the land market than that of some historians, who would use the term only of a substantial volume of transactions or of transfers involving sizeable pieces of land; even so, it excludes from consideration the inheritance of land, manorial lords' leasing of their demesne lands to their tenants, and the enlargement of peasant holdings by simply accumulating holdings directly from the manorial lord as they fell vacant. In practice these matters could not be left out: they are all part of the same picture. *Land, Kinship and Life-Cycle* is, of course, broader still in its terms of reference and sees the local land market only as part of the larger picture of the peasant family and its resources. This certainly is the right approach. We can draw an interesting parallel in the study of deserted medieval villages in England. The work of Maurice Beresford forty years ago sparked off immense interest in the subject, introducing a new dimension to our knowledge of the medieval countryside and rural economy.[18] But the more it was appreciated that depopulation might occur for many different

---

[17] Harvey (ed.), *The Peasant Land Market*, 1.
[18] M. W. Beresford, *The Lost Villages of England* (London, 1954).

reasons, the more it was realized that the deserted village had to be studied—as Beresford indeed had seen it—in the wider context of settlement patterns and population movement in general. Concentration on the single phenomenon—in that case the deserted village, in this the peasant land market—could then become more of a hindrance than a help to the advance of knowledge.

Maintaining, then, this broad outlook we certainly need more of the detailed local studies that are found in both books. It is abundantly clear that the local land market had very different courses of development in different parts of medieval England. In some areas—as in fifteenth-century Berkshire and Bedfordshire—its size and nature varied a good deal from one place to another; but overall it developed much later in the Midlands than in East Anglia, and in County Durham it was slower still. That there was a regional pattern is certain; what this was, how to identify its regions, is much less clear. The studies comprising *The Peasant Land Market in Medieval England* were adapted from existing doctoral theses, and one reviewer pointed out that while the counties they covered are reasonably distributed across England they do not provide that judiciously selected range of areas and periods that would be the ideal: the book was made up of what already lay to hand.[19] The same comment might be made of *Land, Kinship and Life-Cycle*. Although the contributors here were writing for the book in the first instance, they were writing on areas familiar to them from earlier research; here again the editor drew on pre-existing expertise. And in most of these cases the choice of the area studied may well have owed as much to the individual scholar's personal history and academic career as to the perceived need for work in a particular region or period. There has, of course, been other relevant research outside these two collections; the work of David Roden on the Chilterns is a notable example,[20] John Hatcher's on the leasing and other arrangements on duchy manors in late-medieval Cornwall is another.[21] But the fact remains that when we look at the local land market in the Middle Ages we know far more about East Anglia than about north-west England, far more about the west Midlands than about the counties of the south-west.

    [19] M. Stinson, 'The Peasant Land Market in Medieval England' [review], *Landscape History*, 7 (1985), 83.
    [20] Roden, 'Inheritance Customs', 1–11; D. Roden, 'Fragmentation of Farms and Fields in the Chiltern Hills: Thirteenth Century and Later', *Mediaeval Studies*, 31 (1969), 225–38; etc.
    [21] J. Hatcher, *Rural Economy and Society in the Duchy of Cornwall 1300–1500* (Cambridge, 1970), 52–173.

But beyond this there are some general problems that cry out for investigation. Some are centred on the prehistory of the local land market: what can we learn about it before the mid-thirteenth century, when our sources start to give us a reasonably full picture of its operations? The answer may turn out to be, not very much; but some lines of research are certainly worth trying. One is an analysis of estate surveys from the late eleventh century to the early thirteenth to see what obligations specifically lay not on the individual local tenant but on his household as a whole—harvest works with his whole family for instance—and to see if they fall into any recognizable pattern, geographical or chronological. This might well give some clue to how far customs of joint tenure (as against impartible or partible inheritance) prevailed and, therewith, how far there was a need, as clearly there often was later, for transfers of land between members of a family.

Another area of research, uninvestigated and potentially very interesting, is the rapidly spreading use of seals in the late twelfth and early thirteenth centuries: who owned a seal and by what date? If, as we suppose, monasteries led the way in written conveyance, themselves drawing up charters to record the grants of even small amounts of land that they received (a point that itself needs investigation through analysis of diplomatic formulas peculiar to particular houses) did the monasteries also have seals made for the grantors to authenticate these acts? Did other large landowners do the same? Two agreements of 1217–32 between the earl of Chester and Lincoln and groups of his tenants over pasture in Westfen (Lincolnshire) bear seals of the tenants that were almost certainly made for the occasion; in each case they are uniform (round on one, pointed ovals on the other) but with minor, probably deliberate, differences in design (on one a wheel with six, seven, or eight spokes).[22] Did the possession of seals, thus provided, stimulate local landholders to use written charters in land transfers among themselves? These are interesting questions, and from the answers we might expect to learn something, at least, of the workings of the local land market at this time. But they are difficult questions, too, for these charters are mostly undated and give no direct evidence of the grantors'—the seal-owners'—tenurial or economic standing. We are likely to learn most, at first, by detailed local studies of early peasant seals in particularly well-documented areas.

It is likely too that if we knew more of the way large landed estates

---

[22] PRO DL 25/2422, 2423. A preliminary discussion of some of these questions is in P. D. A. Harvey, 'Personal Seals in Thirteenth-Century England', in I. N. Wood and G. A. Loud (eds.), *Church and Chronicle in the Middle Ages* (London, 1990), 117–27.

were run in the twelfth century we should know more of the land market
at local level. The manors of a large estate were at this time (unlike the
thirteenth century) normally farmed out for fixed rents, usually to individuals but sometimes to groups of local tenants. Reginald Lennard in
1958 gave us a careful and interesting analysis of the way the system
worked in the late eleventh and early twelfth centuries,[23] and for this
period his work has been continued and expanded by other historians.[24]
But for the mid- and late twelfth century less has been done and there
may well be much for us to learn; it was a period when important changes
in estate management were beginning.

When we move to the period, the mid-thirteenth century onwards, for
which we have fuller evidence of the local land market we find again that
the answers to some general questions might help our understanding.
The rule governing the succession to customary holdings on a particular
manor may have been primogeniture, ultimogeniture, or impartible inheritance; it is open to debate whether one or other custom served as a
stimulus or constraint to the development of a local land market or
merely influenced the form it took, but all are agreed that there is a close
relationship. We need to carry further still the seminal work of Rosamond
Faith in 1966 (and much has been done already since then) in exploring
the detailed distribution of these modes of inheritance.[25]

We need too to learn more about the chronology of the decline of
week-work in the thirteenth and fourteenth centuries. This was the requirement to work for the lord for so many days each week on whatever
jobs needed to be done; it is distinct from the obligation to perform boonworks, specified services—ploughing, reaping, and so on—at particular
seasons of the year. Boon-works continued in many places to the sixteenth century or later, but week-work was almost everywhere replaced
much earlier by money rents. Week-work was clearly an obstacle to the
easy partition and recombination of the holdings that owed it and we may
reasonably link its disappearance on a manor with the rise of a local land
market there, but which is cause, which effect, is less clear. Given the
importance that many historians attach to these labour services in other
contexts—social, economic, legal—it may seem extraordinary that little

    [23] R. V. Lennard, *Rural England 1086–1135: A Study of Social and Agrarian Conditions*
(Oxford, 1959).
    [24] e.g. S. P. J. Harvey, 'The Extent and Profitability of Demesne Agriculture in the Later
Eleventh Century', in Aston *et al.* (eds.), *Social Relations and Ideas* (Cambridge, 1983), 45–72.
    [25] Faith, 'Peasant Families', 77–95. Later work on particular areas is listed in Harvey
(ed.), *Peasant Land Market*, 4.

detailed work has been done on the process and the timing of their disappearance. This is because, like the local inheritance custom, what happened on a particular manor can seldom be discovered from a single revealing document. Normally week-work was not suddenly abolished but fell gradually into disuse: every year some or all of the works due would be 'sold' to the tenants who owed them, that is to say, money would be paid instead, while the theoretical obligation to do them remained in force and would be set out in full on any custumal or other statement of services. When in 1327 the abbot of Halesowen commuted into money rents all his tenants' labour services we cannot be certain that they only then actually disappeared: some or all may have been in disuse for many years.[26] Even when manorial accounts record the sale of works the position is not necessarily clear. The archbishop of Canterbury's manorial accounts for 1273–4 mention 7s. 7d. received at Pagham (Sussex) 'from works released', 40s. 2³/₄d. 'from works spared', but we are not told how many works or tenants were involved. At Hayes (Middlesex) it tells us more: 8s. 6d. was paid for 104 works spared between Michaelmas and Christmas.[27] But even here we need a custumal to tell us how many tenants there were and how many works they owed before we can say what proportion the lord had foregone. In any case, what happened one year did not necessarily happen the next: to discover when week-work declined on any one manor we need at least one custumal and a substantial series of accounts covering the significant period.

Both these questions, inheritance and labour services, bear closely on the questions of family structure and family resources that *Land, Kinship and Life-Cycle* explores in such depth. The relevance of inheritance customs is obvious and they are carefully discussed there, and so too is work for wages—what there was and who was to do it—a topic clearly connected to labour services; indeed, the continuance of week-work may itself be more closely linked than has been supposed to the presence in tenant households of surplus members free to perform it. Here, in the family, is of course the heart of the whole question of the local land market in the Middle Ages; all recent work suggests that immigrant strangers (as distinct from returning natives) took little part in it, and it was not until the late fifteenth or sixteenth century that it began to attract significant attention from outside speculators. Further work on the rural

---

[26] Razi, *Life, Marriage and Death*, 9. The general question is discussed by Marjory Hollings in her edition of *The Red Book of Worcester* (Worcs. Hist. Soc., 1934–50), pt. iv, iii–vi.

[27] BL Add. MS 29794, mm. 2, 9.

household, its composition and its economic basis, and how these varied in the course of time and from one place—or region—to another, is bound to throw new light on the rural land market. In our present state of knowledge it is probably work on the resources rather than the structure of the family (insofar as they can be separated) that is likely to tell us most. We particularly need to know not only why the local tenant bought land but how: what amounts of money would pass through the hands of a virgater in the course of a year, how (and how fast) he was able to build up the capital needed for land purchase, how far purchase might be facilitated by giving a low purchase price with a permanently fixed annual rent paid to the vendor (a practice illegal after 1290) or by mortgages in the form of a combination of purchase and leasing. Some of these questions have already been discussed, by R. H. Hilton, Christopher Dyer, and others.[28] They are difficult but not unanswerable: various sources potentially throw light on the economy of the peasant household. One example that has been little explored is the lists of corn, livestock, and other goods in each household that were compiled by tax assessors in the late thirteenth and early fourteenth centuries. Most of these lists have failed to survive and only four substantial series have been published (from parts of Suffolk in 1283, of Huntingdonshire in 1290, and of Bedfordshire and Yorkshire in 1297).[29] They are regarded with suspicion, for some are demonstrably formalized in a way that may point to a fictitious element. But, though they are uncommon, we have a significant number of these lists and properly understood and analysed they may well tell us much about the differences in resources between neighbours in a single village, between one community and the next, between one region and another—and therewith about the need and capacity of each to participate in the local land market.

Basic to the economics of the local land market is, obviously enough, the price of land, and systematic research on this is badly needed. English sources for prices paid for small areas of land in the Middle Ages are patchy. We cannot expect to be told how much it cost to acquire customary land as a manorial tenant beyond what was paid to the lord as an entry fine (often a substantial sum). Our record of the transfer is the court roll,

---

[28] Hilton, *English Peasantry*, 174–214. Dyer, *Standards of Living*, 109–50.
[29] *A Suffolk Hundred in the Year 1283*, ed. E. Powell (Cambridge, 1910); *Early Huntingdonshire Lay Subsidy Rolls*, ed. J. A. Raftis and M. P. Hogan (Toronto, 1976); *The Taxation of 1297*, ed. A. T. Gaydon (Beds. Rec. Soc., vol. 39; 1959); *Yorkshire Lay Subsidy Being a Ninth Collected in 25 Edward I (1297)*, ed. W. Brown (Yorks. Arch. Soc. Rec. Ser., vol. 16; 1894). The most recent discussion of the lay-subsidy records is by J. F. Hadwin, 'The Medieval Lay Subsidies and Economic History', *EcHR* 2nd ser. 36 (1983), 200–17.

which is concerned only with the arrangements first between the old tenant and the manorial lord, then between the manorial lord and the new tenant; what the new tenant paid the old to agree to the transfer and set it in motion was no business of the manorial court, and it could come to its notice, and thus to ours, only through occasional chance reference in, for instance, a subsequent plea of debt. Charters recording transfers of land in free tenure are more informative, however. In the fourteenth and fifteenth centuries they seldom say how much was paid for the property, referring simply to 'a certain sum of money' (*quedam summa pecunie*) or other vague phrase. But earlier charters often record the amount that changed hands. This information may be less useful than appears at first sight. The property may be defined in terms that defy quantification: a bovate, a toft, a named (but unmeasured) piece of pasture. When two thirteenth-century Lincolnshire charters record the sale of seven bovates in Kirkby and Miningsby for £5 and of two bovates in Skegness and Burgh le Marsh for £100 we cannot be comparing like with like; and, still in thirteenth-century Lincolnshire, we are little the wiser about land values for knowing that £4 was paid for a toft, a road 20 feet wide but of unspecified length and the services of five tenants at Wrangle.[30] Again, while telling us the purchase price, the charter may reveal nothing of the rent due to the lord of whom the property was to be held (who might or might not be the vendor) and this could crucially affect the price paid. But many charters define the property, the price, and the rent in precise terms:

4½ acres of arable in Roding, granted permanently, for £20 paid, with 12*d.* annual rent. Early 13th century.

½ acre of meadow in Langham, granted permanently, for 16*s.* paid, with 2*d.* annual rent. Early or mid-13th century.

3 acres of arable and a messuage in Walden, granted for a term of three lives by the manorial lord to its former tenant in villeinage, for 40*s.* paid, with 6*d.* annual rent. Late thirteenth century.

Charters that give this information survive in thousands rather than hundreds. These examples are from a group of Essex charters in the records of the duchy of Lancaster.[31] There is some ambiguity in the word *acre* but this need not be an insuperable problem. More of a drawback to exact analysis is that they bear no dates and are dated here simply from their handwriting; for charters copied into a cartulary we lack even this aid

[30] PRO DL 25/2373, 2401, 2477.   [31] PRO DL 25/1938, 2013, 1945.

to chronology. Tiresomely, the charters recording such transfers start regularly bearing dates at just the point—the end of the thirteenth century—when they stop giving the purchase price.

Despite this it would be of great value if cartularies and collections of charters were systematically searched to list (preferably in machine-readable form) all those that state both purchase price and rent. The resulting corpus of information would tell us much about the price of land and how it varied by region and over time; it would also provide a yardstick to assess what we are told of land values in another important source, the extents that we have from many estates from the mid-thirteenth century onwards. The extent was a form of survey that valued every item in terms of the rent it would produce if it were leased out. The only systematic study so far made of these land values is by J. A. Raftis. In examining the extents attached to inquisitions post mortem from eight east Midland counties from the mid-thirteenth to the mid-fourteenth century he discovered an extraordinarily wide range of values.[32] If manors can be found (and they probably can) where charters record the prices paid for particular pieces of land and subsequent extents assess their annual value we might discover some reasonably consistent relationship between annual values and purchase price. In this case we could begin to use, with more confidence than we can now feel, the values recorded in extents as a general guide to land prices and their variations from one place or region to another and over the course of time. We have only casual sources of evidence for the prices paid even for land in free tenure in the local land market of the fourteenth and fifteenth centuries. We can only regret that other owners of modest estates did not follow the examples of Richard and Thomas Hotot and Henry de Bray in thirteenth- and fourteenth-century Northamptonshire; their memorandum books include records of their successive purchases of land and of the price paid in each case.[33]

The collection of land prices from charters would be valuable too for comparing rural property prices with urban and for comparing the prices paid for small pieces of land by local tenants with those paid by large-scale free tenants and estate-owners for substantial areas, or for entire manors. This too is work that is needed: bringing the peasant land market

---

[32] J. A. Raftis, *Assart Data and Land Values: Two Studies in the East Midlands 1200–1350* (Toronto, 1974), 11–96.

[33] *A Northamptonshire Miscellany*, ed. E. King (Northants Rec. Soc., vol. 32; 1983), 16–20, 23, 31–3, 36; *The Estate Book of Henry de Bray of Harleston, co. Northants (c.1289–1340)*, ed. D. Willis (Royal Historical Society, Camden 3rd ser. vol. 27; 1916), 11, 27–8, 36–40, 48–51, etc.

into relation with the property market in general and bringing both into relation with the national (and international) economy as a whole. It has now been firmly shown that the local land market cannot be properly viewed apart from the families and communities that engaged in it. But it has new light to throw on economic as well as on social history and this too needs to be further explored and exploited.

12

The Late Medieval View of Frankpledge and the Tithing System: An Essex Case Study*

PHILLIPP R. SCHOFIELD

THE essential elements of the later medieval frankpledge system have been described in a number of recent studies.[1] The main function of the frankpledge system was to provide mutual surety: the good behaviour of an individual member of the community was the responsibility of that individual's kin and neighbours. All males, both free and servile, over the age of 12 were expected to be members of frankpledge. Wealthy freemen were exempt, their status surety in itself for their good conduct; women and clergy were also exempt. Each frankpledge unit was based, in theory, upon a vill or township, and each unit was divided into a number of tithings, or *decennae*, which, as their name implies, were intended to contain ten men. Each tithing was presided over by one, or sometimes two, chief pledges. The chief pledges were responsible for the behaviour of those in their tithing and for the allocation to tithing of strangers and those reaching the age of 12.

Chief pledges represented their tithings at annual or biannual views of frankpledge and it was at such views that a tithing penny was collected from all those in tithing. The frankpledge system thus offered annual remuneration for those administering it, a fact which in part explains why, although intended as a national system to be run from the hundred courts by royal officials, it frequently fell into the hands of local lords. 'Of all the royal rights in private hands, view of frankpledge is perhaps the commonest.'[2] This hijacking of frankpledge for private use meant that the system had frequently to work not upon the neat geographical units envisaged by central government but upon the scattered and confused segments that formed a lord's manor.

Our understanding of the frankpledge system has been dominated by

* I am most grateful to Barbara Harvey, Zvi Razi, and Richard Smith for their advice on drafts of this chapter.

[1] D. A. Crowley, 'The Later History of Frankpledge', *BIHR* 48 (1975), 1–2; L. R. Poos, 'The Rural Population of Essex in the Later Middle Ages', *EcHR* 2nd ser. 38 (1985), 517–8; Poos, 'Population Turnover', 5–7, and *A Rural Society*, 91–3.

[2] Pollock and Maitland, *History of English Law*, i. 570.

William Morris's *The Frankpledge System*, published in 1910.[3] In this work, Morris concentrates upon the frankpledge system at the 'public level' as exercised through the hundred court and sheriff's tourn, and offers an overview of its development until the end of the thirteenth century. In recent years more attention has been given to the privately administered view of frankpledge, in particular as a source for the study of local demographic change in the later Middle Ages.[4] However, relatively little work has been done on developments in the later medieval frankpledge system.

D. A. Crowley's thesis on frankpledge and the leet courts of northern Essex remains the most thorough analysis of developments in the form and function of the privately administered frankpledge system.[5] Crowley's discussion centres upon the historical development of the system on a number of Essex manors. Although Crowley discovered that changes in the organization of frankpledge were not geographically uniform within the county, a number of vills in his study displayed a fairly similar pattern. At Messing, Claret, Rickling, Borley, Berden, and Elmdon the number of separate tithings declined until in the years after the Black Death all tithingmen were lumped into a single tithing.[6] This change in organization meant that the surety obligations of chief pledges became untenable and reference to these disappear from the court rolls.[7] In the second half of the fourteenth century and in the fifteenth century, according to Crowley, the organization of frankpledge underwent further modification, most notably in the association of chief pledging obligations with specific holdings. In this period, tenants were required to serve as chief pledges in return for holding all or certain tenements. Crowley sees this as the final bid by the lords of the manors to maintain a jury of twelve chief pledges and bolster the flagging jurisdiction of the leet court.[8]

---

[3] Morris, *Frankpledge System*. See also H. M. Cam, *The Hundred and the Hundred Rolls* (London, 1930), 124 ff.

[4] See Newton, 'Source for Medieval Population Statistics', 543–6, and *The Manor of Writtle*, 79–81; Poos, 'Rural Population of Essex', 515–30, 'Population Turnover', 1–22, and *A Rural Society*, chs. 5 and 8; Postles, 'Demographic Change in Kibworth Harcourt', 41–8; Schofield, 'Frankpledge Lists', 23–9.

[5] Crowley, 'Frankpledge and Leet Jurisdiction'; summarized in Crowley, 'Later History of Frankpledge'. I am very grateful to Dr Crowley for permission to use his thesis.

[6] Crowley, 'Frankpledge and Leet Jurisdiction', ch. 7, esp. 147 ff.

[7] Ibid. 109 ff.

[8] Ibid. 152, 'At the same time the decline in seignorial activity, reflected in the demesne leasing of the late fourteenth and fifteenth centuries, was possibly accompanied by an increased concern of lords to make the administration of frankpledge and the exercise of leet jurisdiction easier, while still reserving the profits from it. Perhaps for this reason the

Crowley's thesis thus provides an overview of developments on a number of Essex manors and, although he provides a useful description of changes in frankpledge organization for some of these manors,[9] he does not offer a detailed analysis of the impact of these developments at the immediate level of the individual tithingmen of the village community and the manor court.

In this essay, therefore, an attempt will be made to present a systematic examination of developments in frankpledge organization in one Essex manor in the half century after the Black Death. The composition of late fourteenth-century juries of chief pledges and the effect of tenurial changes on the administrative structure of the manor will be given detailed consideration. In particular, developments in frankpledge organization will be considered in the context of later fourteenth-century changes in the tenure of customary land, which were themselves a product of the outbreak of plague in 1349, recurrent epidemics, and demographic decline throughout the remainder of the century.

The manor chosen for this purpose is Birdbrook, a settlement situated in northern Essex less than two miles south of the Suffolk border, the river Stour running along its northern parish boundary. Two sub-manors, Herkstead Hall and Hempstead Hall, lie between two and three miles to the south west. In the north of the parish is the hamlet of Baythorne through which, today, the busy A604 passes following the same route used for centuries to link Cambridge and Colchester. A number of villages, situated close to Birdbrook, such as Ridgewell two miles to the east, provided local markets in the Middle Ages.[10] By the last quarter of the fourteenth century, the area was an important centre of the cloth industry supporting a large population of workers, many of whom were immigrants.[11] There was not an exact conformity of manor and village in the Middle Ages: evidence of other lordships within the vill, in particular the Clares, can be found but the size of their interest does not seem to have been large.[12]

---

obligation to serve as a chief pledge, with the single duty of presenting offences, was in many places imposed as an automatic incident of land tenure.' See also, Crowley, 'Later History of Frankpledge', 12.

[9] e.g. Crowley, 'Frankpledge and Leet Jurisdiction', 115–32 on the manor of Messing.

[10] R. H. Britnell, 'Essex Markets before 1350', *Essex Archaeology and History*, 13 (1981), 20; P. R. Schofield, 'Land, Family and Inheritance in a Later Medieval Community: Birdbrook, 1292–1412', D.Phil. thesis (University of Oxford, 1992), 19–21, 392–8.

[11] R. M. Smith, 'Human Resources' in G. Astill and A. Grant (eds.), *The Countryside of Medieval England* (Oxford, 1988), 199–202; Schofield, 'Birdbrook, 1292–1412', 398 ff.

[12] Ibid. 22, 210.

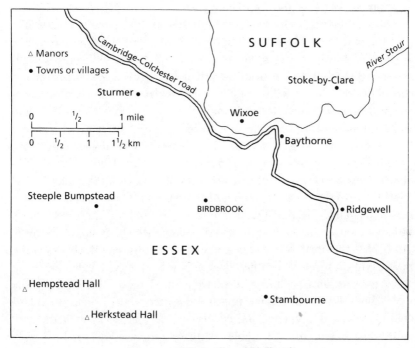

MAP 12.1 The locality of Birdbrook

For most of the thirteenth century Birdbrook was in the hands of the Pecche family. However, in 1283 the manor was seized by Edward I and granted by him, in 1292, to Westminster Abbey in soul alms for his late queen, Eleanor. It remained in the Abbey's possession until the Dissolution.[13] Birdbrook's surviving muniments include a good series of ministers' accounts which date from the commencement of the Abbey's occupation. There are also a number of court rolls which exist in unbroken series only from the last quarter of the fourteenth century, by which date the entries contain less detail than those of the late thirteenth century.[14] Finally, there are three frankpledge lists, all dating from the early

---

[13] Ibid. 4–5. See Harvey, *Westminster Abbey*, 31–2.

[14] Court Rolls: Westminster Abbey Muniments [hereafter WAM] 25567–9; Essex Record Office [hereafter ERO] D/DU 267/28–31. Ministers' Accounts: WAM 25395–25506. See Schofield, 'Birdbrook, 1292–1412', 30–51. The court baron was held less and less frequently during the 14th cent.: by the last decade of the century only two courts were held each year whereas in the late 13th cent. as many as ten could be held. The range of offences dealt with in the court baron narrowed until, by the early 15th cent., it concentrated almost entirely on issues of land transfer.

and middle years of the fourteenth century. Frankpledge lists are not
an abundant source. However, they are not exclusive to Essex and it is
possible that the analysis based upon them and presented here could be
attempted elsewhere.[15] It is the combination of a variety of sources available for Birdbrook which makes study of the proceedings of this manor
court both rewarding and revealing. In particular, the ministers' accounts
are an invaluable source for examining the connection between leasehold
and the tenure of office in the second half of the fourteenth century.[16]

Birdbrook was a small manor. The demesne was divided into three
large fields and measured about 560 acres. Customary land was composed
of ancient *ware* land in standard holdings of 4, 8, or 16 *ware* acres, and
totalled 216 acres at the beginning of the fourteenth century. Each holding seems to have been made up of arable acres situated in the open fields
and about an acre or so of pasture and meadow which, evidence suggests,
was held to the north of the settlement of Birdbrook near the banks of the
Stour. Most unfree land other than this was of recent creation, being
either purprestures or land granted from the demesne and held 'by the
rod'. Much of the unfree land not forming part of a customary standard
holding was held as cottage and curtilage; it totalled 40 acres at the very
most. The extent of free arable, pasture, and meadow at Birdbrook,
according to a rental compiled towards the end of the fourteenth century,

Throughout the period leet courts were held just once a year on the feast of St Margaret
the Virgin, 20 July. The activity of the leet court also diminished in the later 14th cent.
Most especially, there is a marked decline in the semi-criminal and tortious components of
the courts' proceedings. This decline is also found by Crowley, 'Later History of Frankpledge',
12. However, other more administrative areas of leet jurisdiction, such as amercements for
breaches of the assizes of bread and ale, display greater resilience.

[15] ERO D/DU 267/85–7. For an example of a list from beyond the borders of Essex, see
Howell, *Land, Family and Inheritance*, 209 ff. Examination of the frankpledge system both
from demographic and from administrative perspectives has tended to centre upon Essex
material. See A. Clark 'Tithing lists from Èssex', *EHR* 19 (1904), 715–19; Newton, 'Source
for Medieval Population'; Poos, 'Rural Population of Essex', 515–30, 'Population Turnover', 1–22, and *A Rural Society*, 91–110, esp. 160–2. Quite why there should be such a
concentration of studies on Essex is unclear; it may simply be the case that Essex manorial
sources are unique in providing so many series of documents relating to tithing systems.
However, that said, evidence of an active tithing system with annual views of frankpledge
is to be found in other areas of the country. See, on Somerset, J. Z. Titow, 'Some Evidence
of the Thirteenth-Century Population Growth', *EcHR* 2nd ser. 14 (1961), 218–24; on
Leicestershire, Postles, 'Demographic Change', 41–8; on Sussex, M. Mate, 'The Occupation of the Land: Kent and Sussex', in E. Miller (ed.), *The Agrarian History of England and
Wales*, III, *1348–1500*, (Cambridge, 1991), 127–8. I am grateful to Dr L. R. Poos for
drawing my attention to the last of these references; he is preparing a paper on a tithing
series for three Buckinghamshire parishes.

[16] See below, pp. 429 ff.

was approximately 325 acres and few holdings were large.[17] Of 67 tenants recorded in the rental, which lists free land and unfree land other than the customary standard holdings, only two free tenants held more than 30 acres whilst only a further six held more than 10 acres. Excluding the tenants and lessees of customary standard holdings whose tenements were 4, 8, or 16 *ware* acres in size, almost a third of all free and unfree tenants, 22 out of 67, held either a cottage and 2 or less acres, or just a cottage.

In the early years of the fourteenth century every effort was made to crop all of the demesne and land was worked up to the margin. However, in the second half of the century the acreage sown declined and in 1405–6 the demesne was leased.[18] Throughout the fourteenth century, the monks of Westminster Abbey worked the demesne directly and labour services were exacted from the customary tenants. According to the ministers' accounts, there were 29 customary holdings at Birdbrook, four of which were 4 acres in size and 25 were of 8 acres. Together these tenants owed approximately 4,000 works per annum. Although a number of these services were commuted for money payments, those tenants holding by customary tenure continued to provide labour on the demesne throughout the fourteenth century.

However, the number of tenants holding by customary tenure declined in the half century after the Black Death and leasehold came to predominate. In 1349, eight out of eighteen *post mortem* transfers of customary land were to widows of the deceased tenants, whilst only four of the eighteen were to sons. Recurrence of plague in the following decades may have served to decimate the number of available male heirs and, thereby, the customary workforce. It is clear that the monks of Westminster Abbey could no longer rely upon inheritance and turned instead to leasehold to maintain their tenant numbers. Over the following decades increasing numbers of customary holdings were granted for terms of years for a fixed annual 'farm'.[19] By the first decade of the fifteenth century only one out of the twenty-nine customary tenements was held by customary tenure in return for labour services. All the other holdings were held for terms of years or for leases without a term. The latter were, apparently, renewable at the close of each accounting year and came to predominate in the late fourteenth and early fifteenth centuries.[20]

The growth of leasehold brought a new elasticity to the tenure of

[17] ERO D/DU 267/61.   [18] Schofield, 'Birdbrook, 1292–1412', 10.
[19] Ibid. 102–3. There is no evidence of an active market in customary standard holdings at Birdbrook in the 14th cent. and few holdings were transferred *inter-vivos* ibid. ch. 3.
[20] Ibid. 106.

customary land at Birdbrook. Before 1349, inheritance by the youngest son was the most common form of transfer for such holdings.[21] However, after the Black Death, inheritance from parent to child failed as a means of transferring customary land.[22] Already, in 1349, six out of eighteen customary tenants had died heirless. In that year the lord managed to fill these holdings by granting the land to be held 'according to custom' to new tenants, all of whom would appear to have come from the important villein families of Birdbrook. At least one of these new tenants was the non-inheriting son of a customary tenant[23] and it is clear that in the immediate aftermath of the first outbreak of plague adult non-inheriting sons of established village families took the land of fellow villagers who had died without heirs.[24] However, in the following years, as the customary tenure of standard holdings was abandoned in favour of leasehold, we find little to suggest that sons of these established families leased newly available tenements from the lord.

Instead, a tenurial regime in which land passed within a fairly closed family group for generations was replaced by one in which strangers to the village could, provided they possessed the economic wherewithal, take a customary standard holding for a term of years in return for an economic rent rather than for traditional labour services.[25] By 1400 the majority of tenants had surnames new to the manorial documents. Although it is possible that some of these were the lateral kin of tenants who had held the land in earlier years, the court roll careers of at least some of the incoming lessees in the last quarter of the fourteenth century indicate that they were immigrants prepared to seize the opportunity which leasehold offered. By charting appearances in the court rolls and, subsequently, in the ministers' account rolls, an illuminating life-cycle of servanthood followed by land- and office-holding can be identified for a handful of these individuals. In particular, of the eleven individuals illegally harboured out of tithing by the rector of Birdbrook in the late fourteenth century, six followed life-cycles which culminated in land-holding.[26] Thus, developments in the form of tenure and of *inter-vivos*

---

[21] Ibid. 258. The sample of 'inheritance' in the fragmentary court records is, however, extremely small, the total number of intrafamilial transfers being no more than 20.

[22] In part this failure can be explained by the custom of widow's dower at Birdbrook which allowed the widows of tenants of customary standard holdings to hold the tenement for life. If marriage and household formation were coincidental at Birdbrook and dependent upon sons entering into their inheritance, widows may have served to delay marriage and thereby left the post-1349 population ill-prepared to face the recurrence of plague, ibid. 260–76.

[23] Ibid. 272–3.   [24] Ibid. 274.   [25] Ibid. 130 ff.   [26] Ibid. 276–90.

and *post-mortem* transfer of customary standard holdings affected the administrative structure of the manor. In particular, the replacement of customary tenants who were members of established village families by individuals some of whom were immigrants and apparently unrelated to the indigenous population meant that positions of responsibility within the village community, especially the office of chief pledge, were, by the end of the fourteenth century, in the hands of a new and transient tenantry.

As well as charting the decline of the frankpledge system in the second half of the fourteenth century, some attention will be given to the structure of the frankpledge system in the middle years of the fourteenth century, that is, before the decline was fully underway. The survival of frankpledge lists from the middle of the fourteenth century, when the system was still intact at Birdbrook, allows us to make some tentative remarks about neighbourliness and frequency of peasant interaction at Birdbrook, *c*.1350. It is with these latter issues that we shall begin.

I. TITHINGS IN THE MID-FOURTEENTH CENTURY

Three frankpledge lists survive from the middle years of the fourteenth century and provide an illustration both of the system of separate tithings in working order and in decline.[27] None of the lists is dated. The Essex Record Office have tentatively dated the lists to *c*.1325, *c*.1340, and *c*.1420 respectively and these dates have been accepted, with caution, by Poos.[28] The two earliest lists can be cross-referenced with surviving court roll material which record the names of chief pledges who had failed to maintain their tithings. Correspondence of names of chief pledges in the court rolls with those in the lists thus allows a rough dating both of the time of the original compilation of the list and of the period of its use. The earliest list was compiled *c*.1332 since details in the leet of 1331 do not correspond with the tithing list unlike those from the leet of 1332 which do.[29] The first list was used throughout the 1330s but, by 1342, it had been replaced by the second list. This second list was in use until 1349 and perhaps for a period after. The dating of these two lists by the

---

[27] ERO D/DU 267/85/86/87. The lists are transcribed in the appendix.

[28] Poos, 'Rural Population of Essex', 519 n. 17, 'Population Turnover', 8 n. 26, and *A Rural Society*, 94 n. 9.

[29] In the 1331 leet, Michael Melksop appears as a chief pledge and William Han Hous pays a fine to leave tithing: neither appear in the tithing list. ERO D/DU 267/29, leets of 20 July 1331, 20 July 1332.

Essex Record Office is thus reasonably accurate; the dating of the third list is clearly not so.

A detailed study of names in all three lists shows that the third list was compiled from the undeleted names on the second list, whose owners can be shown to have been survivors of the Black Death. Furthermore the list of chief pledges grouped at the head of the third list exactly corresponds with the list of chief pledges recorded in the leet court held in 1361.[30] There seems little doubt therefore that the third frankpledge list should be given a date of *c.*1360.[31] Hereafter we shall refer to the lists as I, II, and III.

As the appendix shows, both of the earlier frankpledge lists, I and II, are divided into separate tithing groups, each group headed by two chief pledges; list III consists of a single group of chief pledges and a single group of tithingmen for Birdbrook as well as similar separate groups for the hamlets of Herkstead Hall and Hempstead Hall.

List I contains thirteen separate tithing groups, two of which were composed of the tithing membership of the outlying manors of Herkstead Hall and Hempstead Hall; list II contains nine separate tithing groups and, again, two of these groups comprise the tithing membership of the two outlying manors. Finally, as already noted, list III contains just three tithing groups, one for each of the manors of Birdbrook, Herkstead Hall, and Hempstead Hall. It is thus evident that some reorganization of the tithing groups took place over the fifteen years or so between the writing of the first two lists and that a dramatic change took place between the writing of the second and third lists. From an examination of the lists it is clear that sections of tithing groups in list I have been incorporated into single groups in list II; for instance it seems that the second group of list II, referred to here as IIB and reproduced below, is partly composed of three groups from list I:

Johannes filius Henrici Oseben	habent in decennia sua *Johannem Wythelard,*
Johannes Legard	*Johannem Le Bierde, Johannem filium Willelmi*
Willelmus Paternoster	*Colyn, Willelmum Colyn, Johannem filium Roberti*
Henricus atte Welle	*Paternoster,* **Robertum filium Henrici Mel-**
Andreas Paternoster	**ksop, Ricardum filium Rogeri le Chap-**
	man, Johannem filium Willelmi Faber,

---

[30] ERO D/DU 267/29, 20 July 1361.

[31] This also makes it a rather more useful document, especially in terms of demographic study and examination of the immediate impact of the Black Death. The reduction in names between lists II and III suggests a level of mortality in the region of 30 per cent. Schofield, 'Frankpledge Lists', 24.

Willelmum Dreye, Ricardum Wythelard,
Matheum Salemond, Johannem filium
Johannis Neweman iuniorem, *Johannem
Child, Richard Boylond,* John Baron, Thomas
Orgon, Johnannes Salemond, Willelmus Pater-
noster, Johannes Fuller, Thomas filius Ricardi
Wythelard, Willelmus Baroun.

The five italicized names are those surviving from the third group of
list I, hereafter called IC; the seven names in bold type are survivors from
group IE; the two names in bold type and italics are survivors from IF.[32]
The seven names after the bold type are additions to list II and do not
appear in list I. Mergers, similar to those of IIB, occur for all of the other
tithing groups as Figure 12.1 shows.[33]

By examining changes in the handwriting on the lists it is possible to
determine the sizes of the tithing groups at the time of compilation of
each list.[34] The size of each original group is set out in Table 12.1 and
suggests that at the time of compilation of list I there was little or no
attempt to ensure that tithings were composed of ten or more individuals.
However, it is clear from list II that some effort was made to standardize
and increase the size of membership of each tithing. It may be that the
tithing groups in list I were vestiges of an earlier list which had been
compiled at a time of greater population density and that list I reflects an
adherence to an accepted number of tithing groups which the compilers
of list II recognized as surplus to requirements.[35] In other words the low
levels of group membership in list I may indicate that population had
started to fall before the compilation of this list, that is, in the first quarter
of the fourteenth century.[36] The reorganization of the tithing lists in list

---

[32] See Appendix for tithing groups.

[33] Schofield, 'Birdbrook, 1292–1412', 298. Some attempt was made to combine tithing
group IA and IB during the working-life of List I. There has been an attempt to erase the
names of the chief pledges of IB—Robert Paternoster and John Pach; their names have been
added at the end of tithing group IB. A line has also been drawn as if to bracket both groups
together (see Appendix).

[34] Names which were added tend to be in the nominative whereas original names were
written in the accusative. See Schofield, 'Frankpledge Lists', 26.

[35] See *Leet Jurisdiction in the City of Norwich during the Thirteenth and Fourteenth Centuries*, ed. W. Hudson (Selden Soc. 5, London, 1892), liii describes 'the relics of an old
tithing which had dwindled away'.

[36] The fact that the number of males recorded in list II is higher than in list I may
indicate that the population, which had declined during the famine years of the first 30 years
of the century, had begun to recover by the 1340s. See Poos, 'Rural Population of Essex',
529, and *A Rural Society*, 106–7; Schofield, 'Birdbrook, 1292–1412', 77 ff. Crowley sees the
pre-1349 decline in tithing numbers as, above all, a product of administrative laxity, Crowley,

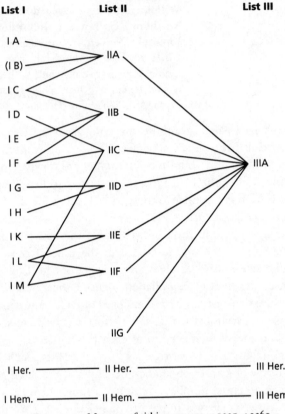

FIG. 12.1   Mergers of tithing groups, *c.*1325–*c.*1360

II would seem to indicate that in the 1340s the tithing group was still considered a valuable administrative tool. That blocks of individuals from list I were placed into distinct groups in list II may suggest that the new groups were actual units based on village topography. The single Birdbrook tithing group of list III therefore evidences a major collapse of the system in the wake of the Black Death.

The rejection of the system of separate tithings soon after 1349, mirrors the disappearance of the surety obligations of the chief pledge towards members of his tithing. In the first half of the fourteenth century, the chief pledges were frequently amerced in the leet court for their failure to have certain persons in their tithing. Such amercements took

'Frankpledge and Leet Jurisdiction', 129–30. However, this will not so easily explain the slight increase in tithing membership to be found at Birdbrook.

List I

Group:	IA	IB	IC	ID	IE	IF	IG	IH	IK	IL	IM	IHem.	IHer.
Number:	3	7	9	7	5	4	4	3	11	3	10	8	20

List II

Group:	IIA	IIB	IIC	IID	IIE	IIF	IIG	IIHem.	IIHer.
Number:	15	14	15	13	15	14	8	7	19

List III

Group:	IIIA	IIIHem.	IIIHer.
Number:	58	6	27

the form 'A and B, chief pledges, do not have C in their tithing, therefore they are amerced'. Immediately after the Black Death any connection of chief pledges with a particular tithing group disappeared from the records. We now find that the court's clerk had lumped the names of all those not in tithing into a single entry and instead of pairs of chief pledges being held responsible for lapses in tithing membership, all chief pledges were amerced. The first such entry is found in the court of 20 July 1349.[37] By July 1363 entries of the view recorded the direct amercement of those not in tithing. In other words, only a decade and a half after the Black Death chief pledges were no longer responsible for tithing membership which had become the duty of the individual under the surveillance of the court.[38]

Crowley considers that population decline in the fourteenth century ensured the extinction of the system of separate tithing groups but that the policing functions for which these groups had originally been created were already beyond the realm of the frankpledge system.[39] Although this may also have been true at Birdbrook, there seems little doubt that the mid-fourteenth-century tithing groups were compiled with geographical propinquity and kinship in mind. The countryside around Birdbrook was broken by woodland and many centres of habitation were little more than hamlets, farmsteads, and moated sites. Birdbrook itself was a nucleated settlement.[40] It is therefore possible that the tithing groups of lists I and II reflect the physical layout of the vill and its environs. Clearly this is the case for the outlying manors of Herkstead Hall and Hempstead Hall which retained separate tithing groups in all three of the frankpledge lists. Apart from these two groups however no direct evidence survives to confirm that the other tithing groups were compiled with attention to propinquity although certain pieces of incidental information from other Birdbrook sources do suggest this.[41] However, the evidence that locality was an important basis for tithing group membership is not as compelling as that for kinship.

Indeed, we need look no further than the frankpledge lists to discover that fathers and sons often appeared in the same tithing groups. Thus,

---

[37] ERO D/DU 267/29, 20 July 1349. For very similar developments at the Essex vill of Messing, see Crowley, 'Later History of Frankpledge', 10. Elsewhere in Essex, a system of separate tithings survived into the late fourteenth century, ibid. 10–11.

[38] WAM 255699 20 July 1363. Crowley, 'Later History of Frankpledge', 10.

[39] Ibid. 10–11.   [40] Schofield, 'Birdbrook, 1292–1412', 5.

[41] Ibid. 303–4.

in IA, we find a William Oseborne, chief pledge, and John, the son of William Oseborne, as a member of tithing; in IB, Andrew and Radulfus, sons of Robert Paternoster, are members of a group of which their father, Robert, was at one time chief pledge. Further examples of sons as members of their fathers', or seeming fathers', tithing group can be found in groups IC, ID, IF, IG, IM, IHem., IHer. for list I and, from list II, IIA, IIB, IIC, IID, IIE, IIF, IIHer. Although brothers often appear in the same tithing groups, as, for instance, in groups IM and IIF where we find Thomas and William, the sons of Henry de Banlegh, Gilbert le Sale and William, his brother, and William and John, the sons of Henry Osborne,[42] sons could also be scattered among separate tithing groups. For instance, Henry del Banleye, son of Adam de Banleye, is recorded as a member of groups IA and IIA whilst the remainder of the del Banleye family, namely his father and two brothers can be found in groups ID and IIC.[43] It may be that Henry del Banleye was an elder son of Adam and, no longer an adolescent, did not require the combination of a paternal chief pledge and the proximity of the family hearth to ensure his good behaviour.[44] Henry del Banleye paid a fine to leave the manor in 1342, his father, Adam del Banleye, serving as pledge for his fine.[45] That Henry was an elder son and thus further from the hearth in both time and space than his younger brothers may account for his exit from the vill where customary land seems to have been traditionally inherited by ultimogeniture.[46]

---

[42] See also the following groups: IB and IIB, Andrew and John, sons of Robert Paternoster; ID and IIC John and William, sons of Adam del Banleye; IK and IIE, William, son of Jordan Dreye, and Nicholas, his brother; IHer. and IIHer., William and John, sons of Roger le Reve, John senior and John junior, sons of Richard Simple, William and Richard, sons of Thomas Rynell; IIC, John and John senior, sons of John Couherde; IIE, John senior and John junior, sons of John Clement.

[43] The sons of a Henry de Banleye who are recorded as tithing members of groups IM and IIF are almost certainly not the offspring of this Henry but most probably the issue of another Henry del Banleye who died in 1316–17 (WAM 25423).

[44] See *Leet Jurisdiction*, xliii. 'Of course we at once notice that very frequently members of the same family or household occur in the same tithing, not only persons bearing the same name but described as "son of" or "servant of". Not unfrequently, however, sons of the same father are found in different tithings no doubt because they had left home and either set up for themselves or entered the household of some other trader.'

[45] ERO D/DU 267/29, 20 July 1342.

[46] In the early 14th cent. surplus younger sons paid chevage to leave manors where primogeniture was the customary form of inheritance; see R. M. Smith, 'Demographic Developments in Rural England, 1300–48: A Survey', in B. M. S. Campbell (ed.), *Before the Black Death: Studies in the 'Crisis' of the Early Fourteenth Century* (Manchester, 1991), 74–5 and the references therein.

Interaction of Villagers in the Mid-Fourteenth Century

Geographical propinquity and kinship may have been the determinants of tithing group formation but they were not necessarily the sole or even the main determinants of social and economic intercourse between villagers. The court rolls from 1330 to 1349, the period during which lists I and II were compiled contain some evidence of interaction between members of the same tithing groups but less evidence of interaction between the chief pledges and their tithing members. In the court rolls economic bonds rather than the ties of kinship or neighbourliness seem to have exercised the most powerful holds over certain groups of villagers. This is most evident with regard to chief pledges.

The financial bent of the court rolls with their particular emphasis on land transactions inevitably creates something of an illusion and the Birdbrook rolls are not an entirely satisfactory source for the study of social change.[47] Most especially the dramatic decline in the fourteenth century of personal pledging except in actions involving land has restricted the use of the court rolls as documents illustrative of peasant social and economic intercourse. Adam del Banleye, chief pledge of tithing groups ID and IIC had 75 known contacts with other persons between the years 1331 and 1349, when he died. On 45 (60 per cent) occasions he dealt with other chief pledges. Compared to these 45 encounters with chief pledges, he came into contact with members of his own tithing including the other chief pledge 16 times (21.3 per cent) and with 'others' 14 times (18.7 per cent). Given that the majority of contacts with tithing members were actually as appearances in the court rolls with the other chief pledge, Adam seems to have interacted, in the majority of court roll recorded instances, with those who were his social equals. An examination of nineteen other individuals who had acted at some time as chief pledges confirms this (see Table 12.2a). Encounters by chief pledges with members of their own tithing, including the other chief pledge of that tithing, amounted to 194 or 36.3 per cent of all encounters for the same period, whilst actions with other chief pledges came to 188 or 35.2 per cent of all encounters. Encounters with 'others' came to 152 or 28.5 per cent. 'Others' include those who were not to be found in the tithing lists; a substantial number of these were freemen.

---

[47] See Schofield, 'Birdbrook, 1292–1412', 30 ff. For a study of social interaction using a detailed and near complete late thirteenth-century series of court rolls, see Smith, 'Kin and Neighbours', 219–56.

TABLE 12.2*a*.   *The interpersonal activity of 20 prominent chief pledges,*
1330–49

Activity	Member of tithing	%	Chief pledge	%	Other	%
acts as pledge for	49	8.0	54	8.9	66	10.8
pledged by	59	9.7	15	2.5	0	0
acts as pledge with	39	6.4	88	14.4	46	7.6
transgression	58	9.5	32	5.3	0	0
other activity	5	0.8	44	7.2	54	8.9
TOTAL	210	34.4	233	38.3	166	27.3

Source: ERO D/DU 267/29/85/86.

TABLE 12.2*b*.   *The interpersonal activity of tithing members appearing in*
list I only or in both lists I and II, 1330–49

Activity	Member of tithing	%	Chief pledge	%	Other	%
acts as pledge for	1	0.4	7	2.9	28	11.8
pledged by	23	9.7	17	7.1	21	8.8
acts as pledge with	1	0.4	3	1.3	14	5.9
transgression	0	0	0	0	0	0
other activity	18	7.6	14	5.9	91	38.2
TOTAL	43	18.1	41	17.2	154	64.7

Source: ERO D/DU 267/29/85/86.

The activity of tithing members, that is those who were not chief pledges, can be presented in the same way. There is less court-roll material *per capita* to utilize here since these people were not the economic élite of the vill and tended to appear relatively infrequently in the court rolls. As Table 12.2*b* shows, an examination of the court rolls suggests that, instead of dealing with members of their own tithing or with chief pledges, tithing members tended, above all, to interact with persons distinct from either of these. Of 238 recorded interactions of tithing members who were not chief pledges between 1331 and 1349, 43 or 18.1 per cent were between members of the same tithing including their chief pledges, 41 or 17.2 per cent were actions with chief pledges of other tithings whilst 154 or 64.7 per cent were actions with 'others'. As above, this broad band of others included freemen, but it also included family members who were not in the same tithing group as well as members of other tithing groups who were not chief pledges. Therefore, the majority of tithing members did not appear in the court rolls in association with chief pledges of their own or other tithing groups or with members of their own tithing. Instead, most of their contacts were with individuals of a similar social and economic standing and seem to have been determined by this 'class' relationship rather than by geographical propinquity or kinship.

Instances do occur, however, which indicate some degree of intra-tithing activity closely linked to intrafamilial activity. The court-roll career of William le Hauer, a tithing member of groups IK and IIE offers some suggestive information. Those of William le Hauer's activities which left a record in the court rolls frequently involved members of his own tithing. Analysis of William's encounters between 1330 and 1342 shows that of twenty-six court entries involving other people, eight were between William and members of his own tithing and five involved chief pledges of other tithing groups, three of which being the same individual, Henry atte Welle. As regards villagers who were neither in William's tithing nor chief pledges, we find that on seven occasions he acted as pledge for persons with the surname 'le Fuller'. The Fullers may have been new to the village since an order was given in 1342 that a Roger le Fuller and John his son should be placed in tithing.[48] Further, William's entries in the rolls include six actions with and against a William Thurston, an individual who is not found in the Birdbrook tithing lists because he was in tithing at Ridgewell.[49] Consequently, although only eight of our entries clearly show that William le Hauer was active with members of his tithing, it is evident that he acted within a fairly localized group. The following court roll entries illustrate this.

In 1343 William le Hauer unjustly contradicted the presentment of a chief pledge and, as a result, was convicted by a jury.[50] In the same court it was presented that William le Hauer had an untended ditch in

---

[48] ERO D/DU 267/29, 20 July 1342. The name 'John Fuller' was added to tithing group IIC but Roger's name is not to be found in the lists.

[49] 20 July 1338, an attempt to amerce William Thurston for not being in tithing is dismissed, 'condonatur quia in decenna apud Redeswell'. ERO D/DU 267/29.

[50] ERO D/DU 267/29, 20 July 1343.

Chaldewellepytel which flooded the lord's fields whenever it rained, for which he was amerced 3*d*. This presentment may have been the cause of the altercation with the chief pledge: earlier examples survive in which chief pledges were ordered to oversee the tending of ditches.[51] The final entry of this court was an amercement of nine men for leaving the leet before they were given permission to do so. It was presumably correct procedure in the leet for those attending to stay until the official in charge dissolved the proceedings; although possibly an administrative normality, we meet with no other examples of this and can feel justified in assuming that some abnormal small-scale disturbance had taken place. It is possible that William le Hauer, the cause of the first entry, was the instigator of the second, the mass departure from the leet being an act of protest against the shoddy treatment of one of their number. For William le Hauer was one of those who left the leet early; so also were three members of his tithing group (IIE): William Dreye, William Sutor, and John Pach.[52] William le Hauer had also combined with other members of his tithing in 1338 when he was amerced with three other men, William and Nicholas Dreye and William Thurston, for fishing without licence on the lord's river. William and Nicholas Dreye were both members of William le Hauer's tithing groups IK and IIE whilst William Thurston, a tithingman at Ridgewell, was, as we have seen, associated with William le Hauer elsewhere in the rolls.[53]

Although it is evident from these entries that villagers sometimes did interact within fairly close groups and that tithing groups were created with locality and kinship in mind, it would, given the marked tendency of villagers to come into contact with individuals who were not members of their tithing groups, be difficult to argue that in the decades immediately preceding the Black Death the frankpledge system at Birdbrook operated as a restraint upon waywardness and misdemeanour. The collapse of the system of separate tithings almost immediately after the first outbreak of

---

[51] e.g. 20 July 1294, *Item dicunt de Elena ad Pontem purprestura facta fodeundum i foveam inter domum Ricardi Sale et Radulph Clement . . . ideo in misericordia . . . Et preceptum est capitalibus plegiis ad eandem locum et per eorum visum predicta purprestura citra proximam curiam emendetur.* WAM 25568.

[52] 20 July 1343, *Misericordia iis iiid. Johannes Pach iiid. Johannes Smyth iiid, Andreas de la Lannde iiid, Johannes Hert iiid, Robertus Orgon iiid, Willelmus Soutere iiid, Willelmus Woderone iiid et Willelmus Dreye iiid in misericordia quia recesserunt a leta ante quam licenciati fuerunt.* ERO D/DU 267/29.

[53] 20 July 1338 *Item presentant quod Willelmus Dreye molendinarius (iiid), Nicholus Dreye, Willelmus le Hauer (iid) et Willelmus Thurston (iiid) soliti sunt ad piscandum in ripa domini sine licencia. Ideo ipsi in misericordia per pleggium Rogeri Mot, Ricardi atte Watere et Rogeri Salemonnd.* ERO D/DU 267/29.

plague may not necessarily have created conditions that stood in stark contrast to what had gone before.

The third of the three frankpledge lists is composed of three tithing groups, one for each of Birdbrook, Hempstead, and Herkstead and was compiled *c.*1360. Corrections to this list indicate that it was used into the 1380s but that by the early 1390s it was obsolete. The names of villagers appearing on the list who died in the early 1390s have remained uncorrected unlike those of villagers who died or left the vill a decade earlier. Most importantly, only a handful of new names have been added to the Birdbrook list. Although these included names of individuals reported in the annual leet rolls to be out of tithing, it is clear that by the late 1370s, little effort was made to force newcomers into tithing. The names of certain individuals out of tithing were recorded from year to year at the leet and little censure other than an amercement of a few pence was exacted.[54] Thus, even if a new tithing list was compiled in the late fourteenth or early fifteenth century, the rolls of the leet court show that by this date there was considerable avoidance of tithing membership. Heightened mobility, especially a probable influx of migrants drawn by the nascent cloth industry, may account for the failure to maintain tithing lists at Birdbrook; no doubt, administrative laxity also had its part to play.[55] If the tithing system itself was near to collapse, more care was taken to preserve the office of chief pledge.

II. CHIEF PLEDGES

Discussion of office-holding in the medieval vill has emphasized the prestige and power associated with tenure of a particular post.[56] The situation at Birdbrook offers no exception to this: officers of the vill tended to come from the established landholding families, especially tenants of customary standard holdings.[57] However, although at Birdbrook the names of these tenants predominate amongst office-holders in the middle years of the fourteenth century, by the early fifteenth century many of the old families had lost their hold on the administration of the vill. Office-holding, especially the position of chief pledge, was closely linked to tenure of customary standard holdings and thus developments

---

[54] Schofield, 'Birdbrook, 1292–1412', 49.

[55] On some Essex manors frankpledge lists were maintained into the fifteenth century and beyond, presumably because they were a valuable administrative tool, Crowley, 'Later History of Frankpledge', 15.

[56] See Razi, 'Family, Land and the Village Community', 15.

[57] See also Crowley, 'Frankpledge and Leet Jurisdiction', 151–84.

in tenure of land in the late fourteenth century had an impact upon tenure of office.[58] The replacement of customary tenure by leasehold meant that neither land nor office passed by inheritance and the monks of Westminster Abbey were obliged to adopt new methods both to maintain a tenantry and, thereby, an office-holding élite.

As we have seen, the surety aspect of the chief pledge's role in the manor court vanished in the second half of the fourteenth century. Instead chief pledges in the later fourteenth century were responsible only for presentment of offences falling within the jurisdiction of the view of frankpledge.[59] Thus, so long as the view of frankpledge continued to be seen as a source of seigneurial revenue, the need for an adequate body of presentment remained as pressing as ever, ensuring the survival of the chief pledge into the early modern period. Maitland reminds us that Edward I's pleaders of *Quo Warranto* often argued that a lord had no business to be receiving presentments in his court, because 'you have not got twelve complete tithings; you have not got twelve chief pledges and no one ought to be punished save on the oath of twelve men'.[60] The leet court heard presentments by jurors who were also the chief pledges and the words *iurati* and *capitales plegii* were interchangeable as far as manor court proceedings were concerned. A lord's right to receive presentments was linked to his ability to provide a jury. The concern evident in Birdbrook's manorial documents to maintain more than twelve chief pledges into the fifteenth century can be explained, in part, by the need to legitimate seigneurial right. It perhaps also explains why mid-century Birdbrook tithing groups, which were never so many as twelve, were each headed by two chief pledges.

As noted above, Crowley sees the connection of chief pledging obligations to certain or, in some vills, all tenures in the aftermath of the Black Death as a response to the failure of separate tithing groups and the increased difficulty of empanelling a jury of twelve chief pledges.[61] At Birdbrook the obligation to act as chief pledge was associated with both free and customary holdings from around 1349 and perhaps earlier. Tenants of customary standard holdings provided the majority of the chief pledges from lists I and II. A few free tenants and unfree cottagers also acted as chief pledges.

In fact, it is clear that all Birdbrook tenants, both free and customary, owing suit could be called upon to act as chief pledges and, indeed, that

[58] Ibid. 153 ff.   [59] See above, pp. 418–20.
[60] *Select Pleas in Manorial Courts*, xxxv.
[61] Crowley, 'Frankpledge and Leet Jurisdiction', ch. 8, *passim*.

only those tenants holding suit-owing land acted as chief pledges. By the late fourteenth century, the terms suitor and chief pledge had, at least in some minds, become confused. An attempt to amerce a substantial free tenant, Henry Lengleys, one-time sheriff of Cambridge, for default in his chief pledging duties, was dismissed. In other courts Henry was amerced for default of suit rather than chief pledging duties. Similarly, John Parkgate, who held a standard holding by customary tenure, appeared as chief pledge for every year from 1377 until 1402 with the exception of 1379 in which year he, and Henry Lengleys, were excused what is described as suit of court.[62] Given this inter-relationship of land and office-holding, it is not surprising that throughout the second half of the fourteenth century a careful watch was maintained over the changes in tenancy of these particular holdings and that new lists of suit-owing tenants were compiled from time to time.

On both the dorse of the frankpledge lists I and II are written the names of free and customary tenants owing suit of court. The dorse of list I is headed *rotulus sectatorum et decennariorum*[63] whilst the dorse of list II is given the simple heading *Sectatores*. Both list I and II distinguish between *liberi tenentes* and *custumarii*. The lists detail the tenants of eighteen freeholds and cottages held 'by the rod' and 26 customary holdings.[64] Both lists have been updated at certain intervals between 1349 and *c*.1380[65] and illustrate the importance of certain free holdings and cottages, and all customary standard holdings, both to the community of the vill and to the monks of Westminster Abbey. They are an invaluable guide to the tenurial history of the major holdings at Birdbrook between *c*.1330 and *c*.1380. After *c*.1380, and for the remainder of the later fourteenth century, most chief pledges were selected from the lessees of standard holdings. The virtual extinction of inheritance as a means of transferring standard holdings meant that by 1400 'outsiders' provided many of the chief pledges.

By comparing land transfers recorded in the court rolls, alterations to the frankpledges lists and information contained in lists of free and

---

[62] 20 July 1379, *Misericordia condonatur. Item presentant quod Henricus Lengleys (condonatur) et Johannes Parkgate (quia in servicio domini) deberent adventum ad visum et sectam curie et faciunt defaltam. Ideo ipsi in misericordia.* ERO D/DU 267/30.

[63] *Decennarii* here can be taken to mean chief pledges. See Morris, *The Frankpledge System*, 103.

[64] ERO D/DU 267/85/86. There are only twenty-six customary holdings not twenty-nine (i.e. twenty-five 8-*ware*-acre and four 4-*ware*-acre holdings), because two of the twenty-six are of 16-*ware* acres and one is derelict. Schofield, 'Birdbrook, 1292–1412', 94.

[65] Ibid. 318 for details.

customary suitors inscribed on the dorse of both lists I and II and a later fourteenth-century rental as well as the annual lists of farms recorded in the ministers' accounts, it has proved possible to chart the correspondence of land- and office-holding for free and customary tenements throughout much of the second half of the fourteenth century. From 1377 onwards annual lists of chief pledges recorded at the leet provide information on numbers of chief pledges and, of course, names which can be matched against available tenurial information.

Chief Pledges From c.1350

In 1349, the Black Death killed at least eight chief pledges. It seems that an immediate effort was made to fill these vacancies by elevating those new tenants who had replaced the deceased villagers to the office of chief pledge. It may be that the association of chief pledging obligation with particular holdings dates from this time but paucity of earlier evidence hinders attempts at comparison with previous practice. What is clear is that tithing list I, which had been replaced by tithing list II almost a decade before 1349, was used in or soon after 1349 to establish chief pledging obligations. This was achieved by cross-referencing the name of a post-1349 tenant of a particular holding with the name of a pre-Black Death chief pledge who had also been tenant of the same holding. For instance, Andrew Paternoster, who took over a 16-*ware*-acre customary standard holding upon the death of Roger Salemond junior in 1349 appears as replacement chief pledge for a Roger Salemond senior in list I.[66] Thus, most of the names added to list I as replacement chief pledges date from the 1350s or the early 1360s, at least 10 and, perhaps, 20 years after list I had been replaced by list II. It may be that list I was altered as a check immediately before the compilation of list III.

As we have seen, there seems to have been little or no attempt to maintain a system of separate tithings in the aftermath of the plague or to associate chief pledges with particular tithing groups. Replacement chief pledges recorded in tithing list II include those added to list I. However, in list II the scribe correcting the list made no apparent attempt to place the name of each new chief pledge with the same tithing group as that of the replaced tenant. For example, although we know that Richard Boylond came to hold the customary holdings of William Woderone, original chief pledge of IIA, and Henry atte Welle, original chief pledge of IIB, his name appears in list II as replacement chief pledge for Adam atte Banleye,

[66] ERO D/DU 267/29, 20 July 1349.

original chief pledge of IIC. Adam atte Banleye in fact died in 1349 and his customary holding passed to his son, William. It would thus appear that the association of chief pledges with specific holdings was not a preoccupation of the correctors of list II, most probably because by the time of their corrections, the system of separate tithing groups had collapsed at Birdbrook. Instead, the purpose of this list was to establish who could be called upon to act as chief pledge and attend the annual leet.

It is clear that list III was drawn up within a short time of the corrections made to list II. A comparison of the names of chief pledges not deleted on list II with the names of chief pledges at the head of list III shows considerable similarity. In fact, there are sixteen uncorrected names of chief pledges in list II (excluding those for Hempstead and Herkstead) and all but one of these, John Wethelard, a freeman, can be found amongst the sixteen original chief pledges of list III.[67]

The care taken after the Black Death to establish who owed service as chief pledge is illustrated by the lists of chief pledges which first appear in the records of annual leets after 1349. The first surviving example of this listing of chief pledges is found in the leet held in 1361; the practice was however abandoned in leets recorded later in the 1360s but reinstated by the late 1370s.[68] The annual leet court rolls provide a useful record of chief pledging obligations from 1377 until 1412. At the annual leet held on 20 July, the scribe penned a list, usually divided into four or five columns, containing the names of chief pledges. As the name of one chief pledge disappeared from the list it was replaced by another. It is clear that some effort was taken to maintain a healthy number of chief pledges. From 1378 until 1388 the number of Birdbrook chief pledges listed was 16; in 1389 this increased to 18, in 1391 to 20, in 1400 to 22, and in 1406 to 24. By 1410 the number had dropped slightly to 23 (see Table 12.3).

The considerable efforts expended to maintain a full complement of jurors has been observed by other students of the later medieval frankpledge system. Crowley, as noted above, found that in response to a decline in the number of villagers available to act as jurors the basis of selection on some Essex manors shifted from one of reliability as established villagers to that of landholding. In some north Essex manors by the end of the Middle Ages all or most tenants were expected to act as chief pledge and the number of chief pledges in the late fifteenth century ran as high as thirty, with a considerable proportion of these tending to evade their

[67] John Sale is the new chief pledge. See Appendix.
[68] ERO D/DU 267/29 20 July 1361; ERO D/DU 267/30 20 July 1377 and following leets.

TABLE 12.3. *Landholding and chief pledging obligations at Birdbrook,*
c.1330–1412

Tenure	Free	Customary	Leasehold	Other	Total
1330[†]	3	16		3	22
1340[†]		14		1	15
1361		14	2		16
1377	3	6	4		13
1378	4	8	4		16
1379	3	8	4	1	16
1380	3	9	4		16
1381	3	9	4		16
1382	3	9	4		16
1383	3	9	4		16
1384	3	9	4		16
1385	3	9	4		16
1386	3	9	4		16
1387	3	7	5	1	16
1388	4	8	4		16
1389	4	9	5		18
1390	3	8	4	3	18
1391	3	7	6	4	20
1392	3	7	6	4	20
1393	2	6	7	5	20
1394	3	5	7	5	20
1395	3	5	7	5	20
1396	3	5	7	5	20
1397	3	5	6	6	20
1398	3	5	5	7	20
1399	1	5	7	7	20
1400	1	4	8	9	22
1401	1	4	8	9	22
1402	2	4	7	9	22
1403	2	1	10	8	21
1404					
1405	2	1	10	9	22
1406	2	1	12	9	24
1407	2	1	13	8	24
1408	2	1	12	9	24
1409					
1410	2	1	14	6	23
1411	1	1	15	6	23
1412	1		14	8	23

These totals do not include Hempstead and Herkstead. [†] Based on original names in
tithing lists I and II
Source: ERO D/DU 267/29/30/31; ERO D/DU 267/85/86.

responsibilities.[69] At Birdbrook the potential number of chief pledges was, as mentioned above, equivalent to the number of tenants owing suit of court. Towards the end of the fourteenth century growing numbers of suitors were obliged to act as chief pledges and by the early fifteenth century, views of frankpledge were held with a panel of 23 or 24 chief pledges. A jury totalling 23 chief pledges is considered to be an optimum and, in fact, a prescribed maximum since it allows a clear majority of at least 12 and it may be that there was a deliberate attempt to attain this number by the early fifteenth century.[70]

The number of chief pledges was at no time allowed to decline in this period;[71] the annual list of chief pledges was regularly updated to reflect deaths and transfers of land. For instance, the last appearance of John Patryk senior as chief pledge was recorded on 20 July 1389. In 1391, Nicholas Wrighte entered the list as chief pledge. Nicholas had, on the 20 July 1390, received from the lord land once held by John Patryk senior; he had already married John's widow. Similarly, the transfer of 8 acres of free land from John Abell to Edmund Clerk, recorded on 20 July 1398, coincided with the substitution of John's name with Edmund's in that year's lists of chief pledges.[72]

Individuals who held qualifying holdings, if they did not replace a previous chief pledge by taking his land, could be elected into office. Between the views of 1398 and 1399 chief pledges John Hardy and Hugo atte Seler were replaced by Henry Kent and Thomas Goodhew. An entry in the view of 1399 tells us that Thomas Goodhew and Henry Kent had been *elected* to the office of chief pledge in the place of John Hardy and Hugo atte Seler.[73] John Hardy held free land and Hugo atte Celer held land 'by the rod', both holdings traditionally owing suit of court, whilst their replacements were both lessees of customary standard holdings. Henry Kent first appears in the court rolls in 1384 and was put into tithing in 1385. His surname is new to the Birdbrook records and he was most probably an immigrant.[74] In 1392 he leased a 4-*ware*-acre holding and held this until 1402; in 1403 he leased a larger 8-*ware*-acre holding.

---

[69] Crowley, 'Frankpledge and Leet Jurisdiction', 154.

[70] *Leet Jurisdiction*, lvii; Crowley, 'Frankpledge and Leet Jurisdiction', 162. The number of chief pledges at Rickling was increased to 23 or thereabouts in the late 14th cent.

[71] This happened elsewhere: see Crowley, ibid. 156.

[72] ERO D/DU 267/30, 20 July 1389, 1390, 1391, 1398.

[73] 20 July 1399, *Elegerunt in officio capitalium loco Johannis Hardy et Hugonis Celer Henricum Kent et Thomam Goodhew qui presenti in curia prestituerunt sacramentum etc.* ERO D/DU 267/30.

[74] Schofield, 'Birdbrook, 1292–1412', 283.

Thomas Goodhew's first court roll appearance is as chief pledge in 1399 but he does not appear in the ministers' accounts as a lessee until 1402; in 1402 he leased a standard 8-*ware*-acre holding and we can speculate that his appointment in some way reflected this later lease. He may, in fact, have been working the holding before the grant of the lease.[75]

As in the mid-fourteenth century, some landholders were more likely to hold office than others, and thus some suit owing tenements regularly provided chief pledges whilst others did not. Tenants of the largest free holdings tended, because of their status, to have been excused any tithing obligations. On 20 July 1377 it was recorded in the view that Henry Lengleys, William Fish, Roger Sale, and Thomas Wheteles were chief pledges but that none of them was present at the view. It transpired that all four had excuses for defaulting. Henry Lengleys had been excused his service by the addition of the single word *condonatur;* this was no doubt because he was a substantial freeman, holding at least 36 acres in the vill. William Fish was described as a pauper, Roger Sale was infirm whilst Thomas Wheteles was the *serviens domini*, the serjeant of the manor.[76]

By the late fourteenth century the cracks in the structure of frankpledge were beginning to show. As had been the case throughout the second half of the century, many of the holdings owing chief pledging duties did not pass smoothly from one adult male to another.[77] Thus the maintenance of an adequate number of chief pledges was dependent upon the existence of a larger pool of landholders able to provide such a service. This had, of course, been the case throughout the fourteenth century but by its close the pool was much shrunken. The concentration of holdings in fewer hands was in part responsible for this, but of greater importance was the decline in the role of the customary standard holding as a source of reliable chief pledges.

The accumulation of holdings affected the availability of unfree cottages, customary holdings and, in particular, freeholdings. As Table 12.3 shows, tenants of free land had never provided the bulk of chief pledges but by 1400 free tenants provided only one chief pledge. The accumulation of freeholdings began immediately after the first outbreak of plague. In one particular example, suit-owing holdings were accumulated and later fragmented in a way heedless of the earlier tenurial history of the land. By the time of his death some time in the decade after 1349 Richard atte Watere had purchased, inherited, or married into four freeholdings

[75] ERO D/DU 267/30, 20 July 1384, 1385; WAM 25488 ff.
[76] ERO D/DU 267/30, 20 July 1377.
[77] Schofield, 'Birdbrook, 1292–1412', 97 ff.; 172 ff.; 252 ff.

owing suit of court.[78] Most of this land passed by inheritance to Richard Rogeronn in 1361 and before his death, Richard sold parts of his estate to various individuals. The court roll entries recording these sales of fragments describe the land only in terms of areal extent and do not refer to its tenurial history or to any tenurial liabilities other than an apportioned rent. It seems possible, therefore, that the suit owing obligations attached to these freeholdings had been lost for ever.

A further problem for the monks in seeking to maintain a full complement of suitors was that the most active participants in the market for free land tended to be individuals who were inclined to shun their responsibility to the court and who would certainly never serve as a chief pledge. For example, Henry Engleys, a freeman of considerable standing, paid fine to avoid suit or was in default on thirty occasions between 1377 and his death in 1392. This included, as we have seen, an abortive attempt to amerce him for non-attendance as a chief pledge.[79] Henry Engleys originally owed suit of court for a large freeholding which he had entered in 1361 through marriage. By 1392, he and his wife had purchased two other suit-owing holdings, one of which was freehold, the other was held 'by roll of court'.[80] However, the decline of freehold as a source of suitors was a relatively minor blow to the number of available chief pledges.[81] It was of far greater consequence that the number of customary holdings able to provide chief pledges was also dwindling. This decline was a result partly of inheritance by minors and women, but more especially by the gradual replacement of customary tenure by leasehold.[82] By c.1375, only seven standard holdings were still held by customary tenure and by 1403 this number had been further reduced to one.

Women did not serve as chief pledges at Birdbrook. Thus, an advantage of leasehold in terms of jury composition was that the proliferation of leaseholds, which were granted almost exclusively to men, in the second half of the fourteenth century meant that adult males, rather than widows, held the majority of standard holdings. Although there were

---

[78] Ibid. 193 ff.   [79] See above, p. 433. ERO D/DU 267/30, 20 July 1377.
[80] ERO D/DU 267/30, 14 Dec. 1387, 23 Sept. 1391.
[81] The major problem created by a shortage of free tenants prepared to act as suitors may have been to prevent the regular empanelling of a jury of free tenants whose main purpose was to verify the presentments of the chief pledges. In only two leets from the late 14th cent. is there reference to this double presentment. ERO D/DU 267/30, 20 July 1385, 1386.
[82] We do not find at Birdbrook by the early 15th cent. that the association of chief pledging duties with tenure led to women acting as chief pledges, as has been found elsewhere. Crowley, 'Frankpledge and Leet Jurisdiction', 159–60; Crowley, 'Later History of Frankpledge', 13.

terms for lives granted to husband and wife which resulted in a widow holding the lease until her death, these were exceptional.[83] However, the growth of leasehold had two detrimental effects on the frankpledge system at Birdbrook. Firstly, it allowed holdings to be accumulated by individuals. Previously, standard holdings passed by inheritance and there was relatively little opportunity for accumulation of holdings by *inter-vivos* transfer in an open market. Secondly, the new lessees of standard holdings were not all from established village families and may not have been considered suitable as chief pledges. New lessees included, as we have seen, apparently recent arrivals to the village whose only previous roles within the community were as servants and landless itinerants. It was noted above that by the 1390s new lessees were more likely to take a lease from year to year rather than for a term of years.[84] As Table 12.4 shows, this resulted in a rapid turnover of lessees which meant that the number of trusted lessees was further depleted.[85]

In the years just before 1349 the 24 standard customary holdings of 4, 8, or 16 *ware* acres were in the hands of twenty-three men and one woman. By 1400, two of the holdings had disintegrated completely whilst three others were in the hands of one villager, William Payn, and two in the hands of another, Thomas Brond. Thus, by the close of the fourteenth century there were only eighteen individuals who were either leasing standard holdings or holding them as customary tenants and not all of these seem to have been eligible for service as chief pledge. William Payn, the most active accumulator of leasehold tenements, never appeared as chief pledge, presumably because he was serjeant of the manor from 1379 until 1402,[86] a position which allowed him an exemption from other duties.[87]

By the mid-1400s customary tenure was almost entirely replaced by leasehold.[88] As noted above, the decline of customary tenure made for the redundancy of inheritance as a mode of transfer.[89] In the eyes of the

---

[83] For example, WAM 25468B–25493, Nicholas Goodram and Margaret his wife held a standard holding for life from 1372 until 1397 in which year they are described as dead and their names are replaced in the following ministers' accounts by those of William Payn and Joanna his wife (WAM 25494 ff). Nicholas Goodram last appears in the court rolls in 1381; he had most probably died in this year. We know that Margaret Goodram died in March 1398 (ERO D/DU 267/30, 17 Dec. 1381, 20 July 1398). Therefore both Nicholas and Margaret continued to be named as joint lessees in the ministers' accounts until the death of the surviving spouse. Schofield, 'Birdbrook, 1292–1412', 238 ff.
[84] See above, p. 413.   [85] Schofield, 'Birdbrook, 1292–1412', 105, 135–6.
[86] WAM 25475–25498.
[87] See above, p. 433 for a serjeant avoiding office through this excuse.
[88] Schofield, 'Birdbrook, 1292–1412', 132.   [89] See above, p. 413.

TABLE 12.4. *Turnover of lessees at Birdbrook, 1377–1412*

Year	Turnover of lessees	Number of leaseholds	Year	Turnover of lessees	Number of leaseholds
1377	1	10	1395		19
1378	1	11	1396		19
1379	1	11	1397	2	19
1380		11	1398	1	19
1381	2	11	1399		19
1382	1	12	1400	1	20
1383	1	12	1401	1	20
1384	1	13	1402	6	23
1385	1	13	1403	7	23
1386	1	14	1404	1	23
1387	3	15	1405	1	23
1388	1	15	1406	1	23
1389		15	1407	4	23
1390	1	15	1408	2	23
1391		15	1409	2	23
1392	6	18	1410	1	23
1393	2	19	1411	4	23
1394	3	19	1412	1	23

Note: The recording of a lease in the ministers' account would follow the entry of the lessee in the previous year and the turnover figures given should best be seen as referring to the previous year.
Source: ERO D/DU 267/30/31; WAM 25473–25506.

lord of the manor the heir to a standard customary holding normally had the advantages of coming from reliable tenant stock and of possessing the economic wherewithal to make his tenancy a success. However, by the end of the fourteenth century, the monks of Westminster Abbey looked to the arbitrary grant of a lease rather than to inheritance in the hope of filling the standard holdings.[90] Although we do not know what criteria the monks used in selecting new lessees it is clear that by the early fifteenth

[90] Where leasehold was a well-established form of landholding manorial authorities tried to ensure that would-be lessees were suitable and creditworthy: Hatcher, *Rural Economy and Society*, 54–5.

century incoming lessees were often admitted to hold on the most inse-
cure terms and that many chose not to maintain their lease or were unable
to do so.[91] The effect of this accelerated changeover of lessees for the
office of chief pledge was to replace the old order of pledges who would
remain in office for many years, often until they died or surrendered their
holding through old age,[92] with a newer, less stable body who might
remain in office for no more than one or two years and certainly for no
longer than the term of their lease.[93]

Furthermore new lessees typically only became chief pledges two or
more years after they took up their lease. The reliability of a lessee may,
therefore, have been under review during the early years of his lease and
new lessees were therefore unavailable as chief pledges. In the years
immediately following a year of unusually high mortality, when a number
of new lessees were admitted, the number of landholders suitable to act
as chief pledges was thus further reduced. In the first decade of the
fifteenth century, possibly as a result of the return of plague, the turnover
of lessees was considerable (see Table 12.4). Not all of the new lessees
became established in this decade and relatively few were granted a term
of years, either the monks preferring to grant annually renewable leases
or the lessees choosing to avoid the commitment of a longer term.

By the late fourteenth century tenants of land other than the customary standard holdings were called upon to act as chief pledges with
greater frequency. Most especially, cottagers holding unfree land 'by the
rod' came increasingly to act as chief pledges in the late fourteenth and
early fifteenth centuries. Although these holdings had always owed suit of
court, the employment of their tenants as chief pledges was a departure
apparently caused by a decline in the number of established and reliable
villein families. The first of these cottagers employed as chief pledge was
John Fuller who held three cottages by roll of court until his death in
1391 and had acted as chief pledge in 1377 and 1378.[94] By 1412, four
other cottagers had served as chief pledges. The first of these, William

---

[91] Schofield, 'Birdbrook, 1292–1412', 132 ff.

[92] John Sale, the only villager holding a standard tenement by customary tenure after
1403 appeared as chief pledge in every leet from 1377 to 1411.

[93] Crowley argues that in the fifteenth century, on some Essex manors, the main, active
body of chief pledges was composed of elements familiar from the fourteenth century: 'the
rank and file manorial tenants of modest substance but, as holders of land, permanent and
accepted members of village society', 'Later History of Frankpledge', 14; also Crowley,
'Frankpledge and Leet Jurisdiction', 160–1, 169, 170–2. At Birdbrook, chief pledges of the
late fourteenth and early fifteenth centuries were not necessarily such stalwarts of the
community.

[94] ERO D/DU 267/30, 20 July 1377, 1378, 1391.

Grapenell, was enrolled as a chief pledge for the first and last time in July 1390. William died in August of the same year.[95] If we see William Grapenell's death as a result of the plague which devastated the country in 1390, we should, perhaps, also interpret his promotion to the office of chief pledge in the same way. The elevation of other cottagers in the late 1390s should perhaps be seen in the same light. John Grimsale and John Shedde appear as chief pledges for the first time in 1397, the former remaining in office until 1399, the latter until 1407. Both men took cottages prior to entering office and had left office before they surrendered their holdings. In 1395 John Grimsale had purchased a cottage from Richard Dryvere but had surrendered it to his wife, through an attorney, by 1401 and may already have been dead. He was certainly dead by 1403.[96] John Shedde and his wife, Isabella, took a cottage and curtilage in 1397 and held this until 1411 in which year they surrendered it.[97] In 1403 Richard Tyler, with his wife, entered the cottage once owned by John Fuller and in the same year became a chief pledge, retaining the office until 1408.[98]

The use of cottagers as chief pledges is but one example of the decaying manorial structure at Birdbrook. Beckerman noted that one reason for the reduced authority of the manor court in the fourteenth century may have been, in part, the replacement of the homage with a jury of villagers.[99] If the jury were also partly composed of relative strangers to the vill, as we have seen a number of late fourteenth- and early fifteenth-century lessees seem to have been, the power of the manor court as a mouthpiece of customary law may have been further reduced. Other commentators upon the leet have noted the need for jurors to be responsible, upright members of the community.[100] Above all, the jurors of the manor court were the custodians of local knowledge and, most importantly, custom. A

---

[95] ERO D/DU 267/30, 20 July 1390; 21 Sept. 1391: *Item presentant quod Willelmus Grapenell' qui de domino tenuit per rotulum curie unum cotagium et i acram terre cum pertinenciis vocatum Oggelles obiit mense Augusti ultimo preterito*. ERO D/DU 267/30.

[96] ERO D/DU 267/30, 20 July 1395; ERO D/DU 267/31, 20 July 1401, 1403. See Schofield, 'Birdbrook, 1292–1412', 179 ff.

[97] ERO D/DU 267/30, 20 July 1397; ERO D/DU 267/31, 21 July 1411.

[98] ERO D/DU 267/31, 20 July 1403, 1406, 1407, 1408. In 1409 he fled the manor because he was indicted of a felony, leaving this and another holding *vacua et inculta*; on his return he was readmitted to both holdings on payment of an entry fine of 20d per holding, ERO D/DU 267/31, 20 July 1410, 21 July 1411.

[99] Beckerman, 'Customary Law in English Manorial Courts', 115, 'it is unlikely that the community was willing to enforce a judgement which was no longer, in fact, its own'.

[100] K. C. Newton and M. K. McIntosh, 'Leet Jurisdiction in Essex Manor Courts during the Elizabethan Period', *Essex Archaeology and History*, 3rd ser. 13 (1981), 11.

jury of newcomers to the vill could not possess the local information available to their predecessors. In other words, they were not a part of the collective memory of the village,[101] but instead their presence served to confirm the decline of customary law and the protection it offered certain members of the village community.[102]

We should also note that Razi's contention that the acceptance of newcomers to the vill, illustrated by their election to positions of authority on the Worcestershire manor of Halesowen, was in some way dependent on ties of blood or marriage cannot be supported by the Birdbrook evidence.[103] At Birdbrook, the elevation of newcomers, such as Henry of Kent, to the office of chief pledge followed their acceptance of a lease. We sense a far more arbitrary system than the one described at Halesowen. At Birdbrook in the late fourteenth century it seems possible that it was the monks of Westminster Abbey rather than the community who set great store by maintaining a full compliment of chief pledges, presumably for reasons of administration and revenue.[104] At Birdbrook, by 1400, the days of the manor court as the voice of peasant custom were numbered. The introduction of leasehold, a response apparently forced upon the monks by successive outbreaks of plague, was both symptom and cause of a weakened manorial structure.[105] The tithing system of the early fourteenth century failed to survive the arrival of plague in 1349 whilst the office of chief pledge struggled on into the early fifteenth century bolstered by the new tenurial regime of leasehold. The collapse of the frankpledge system had little or nothing to do with policy but rather more to do with biology: by the early fifteenth century, the monks of Westminster Abbey were fighting to sustain the vestiges of a moribund institution.

---

[101] On collective memory, see Bonfield, 'Nature of Customary Law', 521; I. Blanchard, 'Industrial Employment and the Rural Land Market, 1380–1520', in Smith (ed.), *Land, Kinship and Life-Cycle*, 241–8.

[102] The replacement of customary tenure by leasehold led to the dilution of manorial custom, such as widow's dower; Schofield, 'Birdbrook, 1292–1412', 237.

[103] Razi, *Life, Marriage and Death*, 122–4 and his 'Family, Land and the Village Community', 27.

[104] On changes in the content of leet court proceedings at Birdbrook, see Schofield, 'Birdbrook, 1292–1412', 45 ff.

[105] Crowley notes that the development of the frankpledge system within a vill was closely linked to the physical and manorial structure of that vill. In particular, the frankpledge system showed a greater tendency to decay in areas of weak lordship, associated with small manors forming only part of a village and a small customary workforce, than in areas of strong seigneurial control, such as large manors coincident with a whole village, Crowley, 'Frankpledge and Leet Jurisdiction', 174–6. In a very limited sense, Birdbrook may provide an example of the former category.

Appendix 12.1
Three frankpledge lists for the Manor of Birdbrook
(Essex Record Office D/DU 267/85/86/87)

Where possible names have been expanded but not standardized; declensions have been maintained as far as possible and where the declension is unclear the name has not been expanded; an inverted comma indicates an abbreviation in the original which has proved impossible to expand. Also the groups have been named, IA and so on. All names deleted in the original either through crossing out or by addition of a phrase such as *mortuus est* have been italicized here and the explanation for the deletion included where it exists. A name square-bracketed indicates it has been added.

List I (ERO D/DU 267/85):
Bridebrok: Rotulus capitalium plegiorum ac decenniorum suorum

	Capitales	
IA	Johannes Dreye	qui habent in decennia sua Rogerum Salemon iuniorem, Henricum filium Ade del Banleye, Willelmum filium Edmondi, [Mattheus ate Parkgate, Johannes filius Willelmi Osebern, Mich' de Brydebrok, Mattheus Penyford.]
	Willelmus Osborne	
	[Thomas Oseborne]	
IB	Robertus Paternoster	habent Egidium Fabrum, Ricardum filium eiusdem, Robertum Orgon, *Johannem Leggard* (mortuus est), *Nicholam del Banleye* (mortuus est), Andream filium Roberti Paternoster, *Johannem filium Simonis atte Bregge* (mortuus est), [*Joh' Redcalf*, Rads' filius Roberti Paternoster, Robertus Paternoster, Johannes Pach.]
	Johannes Pach	
IC	[Adam Stobelom]	habent *Robertum Melksop seniorem* (mortuus est), *Johannem filium Ade atte Bregge* (mortuus est), *Robertum de Colne* (mortuus est), Willelmum Pach, Ricardum le Couherde, *Johannem filium eiusdem Ricardi*, Johannem le Hert, Joh' le Bierde, *Rog' le Couherde*, [Joh' fil' Willelmi Colyn, Willelmus Colyn, Johannes filius Roberti Paternoster.]
	Willelmus Paternoster	
	Willelmus Coyln	
	[Johannes Wythelard]	

ID [Johannes Banleye]
Adam del Banleye
Robertus del Banleye

habent *Johannem Dreye seniorem* (mortuus est), Willelmum Nobelot, Johannem le Neweman, *Vincentem Cissorem* (mortuus est) Johannem filium Ade del Banleye, Willelmum filium Ade del Banleye, Joh' Penyford, [Andr' atte Londe.]

IE Johannes Dreye
Willelmus Salemond
(mortuus est)

habent Robertum filium Henrici Melksop, Ricardum filium Rogeri le Chapman, Johannem filium Willelmi Faber, Willelmum Dreye, Ricardum Withelard, [Mattheus Salemond, Johannes filius le Neuman iunior.]

IF [Ricardus Boyland]
Henricus atte Welle
(mortuus est)
Johannes le Couherde
(mortuus est)

habent Johannem Child, Johannem Uggele, Johannem filium Johannis le Couherde, Walterum Boylond, [Willelmus Melksop, Michael Melksop, Johannes le Couherde iunior, Ricardus de Boylond, Willelmus atte Welle.]

IG [Johannes Edwold]
Radulfus Edwold
Robertus Leggard
[Johannes Dreye iunior]

habent Johannem Withelard, Johannem Clement, Michael Sutorem, Joh' Edwold, [Ricardus Dun, Johannes ate Lannde, Johannes filius Roberti Leggard.]

IH *Ricardus Withelard*
[*Willelmus le Soutere*]
Rogerus Salemond senior
(mortuus est)
[Andreas Paternoster]

habent Willelmum Stobylom, Eliam Sutorem, *Galfrid' de Ffinchingefeld* (finem fecit ut amoveatur), [Joh' ate tonnesende.)

IK Rogerus Mot
Johannes Chapman

habent Stephanum Cissorem, *Jordanum Woderone* (mortuus est), Matheum Penyford, Willelmum le Chapman, Ricardum Poccok, Adam le Vannemakere, Willelmum Sutorem, Willelmum le Hauer, Willelmum filium Jordani Dreye, Nicholum fratrem suum, Johannem Wirlepipin, [*Edm' le Cartere* (mortuus est), Mich' le Hert.)

IL [Willelmus Dreye]
Robertus Wolfrich
[*Woderone*]
Willelmus *Stobylom*

habent Johannem filium Alicie le Michaelem filium Alicie Baronn, Clementem Sutorem.

IM Henricus Osborn
Robertus de Morlee

habent Hugonem filium Egidii atte Watere, Robertum filium Rogeri Sutoris, Thomam filium Henrici del Banleye, Willelmum filium eiusdem Henrici, Gilbertum le Sale et

Willelmum fratrem suum et Thoman filium
Willelmi le Chapman, Willelmum filium
Henrici Osborn, Johannem filium eiusdem
Henrici, Willelmum filium Thome Withelard,
[*Andr' le Porter*, Robertus Stobylom.)

IHem.   Robertus Coleman   *Walterus   Derkyn* (mortuus), Willelmus
        (Cap')   Schryve, Robertus Puttok', *Stephanus Schryve*
        Willelmus Schryve   (mortuus est), Johannes Schryve, *Henr'*
                                Delanny, Galfr' Stevene, Willelmus Coleman,
                                [Johannes Cach' junior, Willelmus filius
                                Stephani Schryve.]

IHer.   *Rogerus le Reve*   Ricardus filius Thome Rynel, Johannes
        Cap'   Symple, Will' Rynel, Will' fil' Rogeri le Reve,
        Petrus Folk'   Joh' fil' eiusdem Rogeri, Joh' fil' Ricardi Simpl'
        Johannes Symple   senior, Joh' fil' eiusdem Ricardi junior, Rob'
                                fil' Petri Folk', Thom' Rynel, Will' et Ricardus
                                fil' eiusdem Thome, Ad' Underwode, *Ricardus*
                                S[-], Joh' Ffront', Johannes Underwode,
                                Johannes Symple Johannes ate hale, Nicholus
                                le Saltere, Robertus Underwode, Rogerus le
                                Reve.

List II (ERO D/DU 267/86):
Brydebrok: Rotulus capitalium plegiorum ac
decenniorum suorum

        Capitales
IIA   Johannes Dreye iunior   habent in decennia sua *Henricum filium*
        Willelmus Osebern   *Ade ate Banlegh* (quia per finem per an-
        [*Willelmus Woderone*]   num) *Willelmum filium Edmundi, Mattheum*
        [Johannes Banleye]   *atte Parkegate* (mortuus est), *Johannem*
                                  filium Willelmi Osebern, Michaelem de
                                  Brydebrok, Mattheum Penyford, Egidium
                                  Fabrum (mortuus est), Ricardum filium
                                  eiusdem Egidii, *Robertum Orgon, Andream*
                                  filium Roberti Paternoster (quia capitaneus),
                                  Rads' fil' Roberti Paternoster (mortuus
                                  est), [Willelmus Banlegh] *Ricardum le*
                                  Couherde, Johannem le Hert, Robertum
                                  Paternoster (mortuus est), Thomas filius
                                  Willelmi Osbern, [*Ricardus filius Johannis*
                                  Pach, Simon Goodchild, Thomas Wod-
                                  erone, Johannes Dun, Johannes filius

Johannis le Sale, *Henricus Spicer, Adam Stobilom* (quia capitaneus), Robertus Wolffrych, *Johannes Shether* (quia per finem), Johannes Canon, *Johannes Woderone* (finis vid), *Johannes Rogeronn* (mortuus est) Willelmus Woderone, Joh' Greyberd].

IIB
[Johannes filius Henrici Osebern]
[*Johannes Legard*]
Willelmus Paternoster
Henricus atte Welle
[Andreas Paternoster]

habent in decennia sua *Johannem Wythelard* (capitales est), *Johannem le Bierde*, Johannem filium Willelmi Colyn, *Willelmum Colyn, Johannem filium Roberti Paternoster* (quia capitaneus), *Robertum filium* Henrici Melksop, *Ricardum filium Rogeri le Chapman*, Johannem filium Willelmi Faber, *Willelmum Dreye* (quia capitalis plegius ut infra), *Ricardum Wythelard, Matheum Salemond* (mortuus est), *Johannem filium Johanni Neweman iuniorem, Johannem Child, Richard* (sic) Boylond, [*Joh' Baron* (qui fecit finem), *Thomas Orgon* (mortuus est), Johannes Salemond, *Willelmus Paternoster, Johannes Fuller, Thomas filius Ricardi Wythelard*, Willelmus Baroun.]

IIC
Adam atte Banlegh
Robertus atte Banlegh
[Ricardus Boylond]

habent *Willelmum Nobelot* (mortuus est), Johannem le Neweman, Johannem filium Ade atte Banleye, Willelmum filium Ade atte Banleye, *Johannem Penyford, Andr' atte Londe* (mortuus est), *Johannem Uggele* (finem fecit), *Johannem filium Johannis le Couherde, Walterum Boylond* (mortuus est), *Willelmum Melksop* (mortuus est), Michelem Melksop, *Johannem filium Johannis le Couherde* iunioris [senioris] (finem fecit), Willelmum atte Welle, *Willelmum filium Thome Wythelard* (mortuus est), *Robertum Stobylom* (quia capitaneus), *Robertus atte Banlegh*, [*Egidius le Hert, Henricus Penyford*, Thomas Godsone, Thomas Martyn, Johannes Ffullere, Johannes Chaurethe, Johannes Evered.]

IID	*Radulfus Edwold*	habent *Johannem le Couherde* (per finem)

IID

Radulfus Edwold
Robertus Leggard
(mortuus est)
[*Willelmus Seutere*]
[Johannes Wethelard]
[Adam Stobilom]

habent *Johannem le Couherde* (per finem) *Johannem Withelard* (quia capitaneus) *Johannem Clement* (mortuus est) *Michelem Suterem*, *Johannem Edwold* (quia capitaneus) *Ricardum Dun* (mortuus est), Johannem atte Lonnde, *Johannem filium Roberti Leggard*, *Willelmum le Sutere* (quia capitaneus), *Rogerum Salemond seniorem*, *Willelmum Stobelom* (mortuus est), *Eliam Sutorem* (mortuus est), *Johannem atte Tonneshende*, [*Rogerum filium Willelmi Saleman*, *Johannes Crench*, Thomas Whitelee, Thomas Kyng.]

IIE

[*Johannes Clement*]
Rogerus Mot
Rogerus Salemond iunior
[Johannes Paternoster]
[Johannes Clement]

habent *Johannem Pach*, *Stephanum Cissorem*, *Mattheum Penyford*, *Willelmum le Chapman* (mortuus est), *Ricardum Puccok*, Adam le Vannemakere, *Willelmum Sutorem* (quia superius), *Willelmum le Hauer* (mortuus est), *Willelmum filium Jordani Dreye* (mortuus est), *Nicholum fratrem suum*, *Johannem Whirlepepyn* (mortuus est), Michelem le Hert, *Johannem filium Alicie le Chapman* (finem fecit), *Willelmum filium Willelmi le Norman* (mortuus est), *Joh' fil' Johannis Clement senior'* (quia capitaneus), [Joh' fil Johannis Clement iunior', Petrus de Hiche].

IIF

[Johannes Patrik]
Willelmus Woderone
Willelmus Dreye
[*Johannes Rolf*]
(quia finem)

habent *Michelem filium Alicie Baron*, *Clementem Sutorem* (mortuus est), *Henricum Osebern* (mortuus est), *Robertum de Morle*, Hugonem filium Egidii atte Watere, Robertum filium Rogeri Sutoris, *Thomam filium Henrici de Banlegh*, *Willelmum filium eiusdem Henrici*, Gilbertum atte Sale, *Willelmum atte Sale* (per finem), *Thomam filium Willelmi le Chapman*, *Willelmum filium Henrici Osborn* (quia finem), *Johannem filium eiusdem Henrici* (capitaneus), *Willelmum Pach* (mortuus est), [*Johannes Patrik* (quia capitaneus), *Willelmum Woderone* (capitaneus), *Willelmus Sale*, *Willelmus Penyford*, *Henricus Symes* (mortuus est),

Nicholus Obr', *Adam Page* (mortuus est), Nicholus Godrham, *Willelmus Salemond* (mortuus est) Johannes Neuman.]

IIG   Johannes ate tonneshende Robertus Stobilom [Johannes Neuman] [Johannes(?) Osebern]

Thomas Cock, Johannes de Angr', Thomas de Rothinge, Johannes Jolif, Rogerus le Sale, *Johannes Penifford* (mortuus est), Johannes Clement, Robertus Stobilom.

IIHem.   [list of chief pledges is illegible.]

in decennia sua *Willelmum Schryve* (mortuus est), *Robertum Puccok* (mortuus est), Johannem Schryve, *Galfr' Stevene* (mortuus est), *Willelmum Coleman* (mortuus est), *Johannem Cach'* juniorem (per finem), *Willelmum filium Stephani Schryve* (mortuus est), [*Adam le Rede, Stephanus Derkyn* (mortuus est), *Thomas Schryve, Warinus Shepherde* (mortuus est), *Robert' Coleman* (mortuus est), Robertus Steven, Robertus Schryve, *Ricardus S[-]* (mortuus est), [-] Blundel.]

IIHer.   [names of all but one chief pledge illegible.] Johannes Symple

Ricardum filium Thome Rynel, *Johannem Symple* (mortuus est), *Willelmum Rynel* (mortuus est), Willelmum filium Rogeri le Reve, *Johannem filium eiusdem Rogeri (mortuus est), Johannem filium Ricardi Simpl' seniorem* (mortuus est), *Johannem filium eiusdem Ricardi juniorem* (capitalis plegius) *Robertum filium Petri Folk'* (mortuus est), *Thomam Rynel* (mortuus est), *Willelmum et Ricardum filios eiusdem Thome* (mortui sunt), *Adam Underwode* (mortuus est), *Johannem Ffront'* (per finem), *Johannem Underwode* (mortuus est), *Johannem Symple, Johannem ate Hale* (quia per finem), *Nicholum le Saltere* (mortuus est), *Robertum Underwode* (mortuus est), *Rog' le Reve* (mortuus est), [*Rob' [S-]* (finem ut exoneratur), Johannes Morkot.]

List III *(ERO D/DU 267/87):*
Brydebrok: Rotulus capitalium plegiorum ac decenniorum suorum

Capitaneii

Johannes Dreye iunior
Johannes fil' Henrici Osebern
Johannes Banleye
Johannes Sale
Johannes Rowlf'
Andreas Paternoster
Robertus Banleye
Ricardus Boylond
Johannes ate Parkgate
Johannes atte Tonnyshend'
Adam Stobyloun
Johannes Paternoster
Johannes Clement
Johannes Patrik'
John *(sic)* Newman
Thomas Osebern
Johannes Clement
Robertus Stobylon
Johannes Parys junior

Decenarii

Ricardus filius Egidii Fabr' (mortuus est)
Willelmus Banlegh
Thomas filius Willelmi Osebn' (capitaneus)
Simon Godchild (mortuus est)
Thomas Woderone
Johannes Dun (finem)
Johannes filius Johannis Sale (capitaneus)
Henricus Spicer
Robertus Wolffrych
Johannes Shether (amoveatur per finem)
Johannes Canon
Willelmum Woderone
Johannes Greyberd (per finem)
Johannes Berde (mortuus est)
Johannes filius Willelmi Colyn
Willelmus Colyn (mortuus est)
Robertus filius Henrici Melksop (mortuus est)
Johannes filius Willelmi Faber (mortuus est)
Ricardus Wythelard (mortuus est)

Johannes Neweman iunior (capitaneus)
Johannes Salemond (finem)
Johannes Fuller
Willelmus Baroun
Johannes Neweman

capitaneus *Johannes filius Ade atte Banleye* (mortuus est)
Willelmus filius Ade atte Banleye
Johannes Uggele (amoveatur per finem)
Johannes filius Johannis le Couherde (amoveatur per finem)
Michel Melksop (quia fec' finem)
Willelmus atte Welle
Egidius le Hert (mortuus est)
Henricus Penyford
Thomas Godsone
Thomas Martyn (mortuus est)
Johannes Chaurethe
Johannes Withelarde
Johannes Couherde (mortuus est)
Johannes atte Lonnde (mortuus est)
Johannes filius Roberti Leggard (mortuus est)
Rogerus filius Willelmi Saleman
Thomas Whitelee
Johannes Clement jun. (fine)
Adam le Vannemakere
Michel le Hert (per finem)

capitaneus Johannes filius Johannis Clement senior'
Petrus Hyche aut Nevyll'
Hugo filius Egidii atte Watere
Robertus filius Rogeri Sutore
Gilbertus Sale
Willelmus filius Henrici Osborn
Nicholas Obr'
Nicholas Godrham (mortuus est)
Johannes Neuman sen'
Johannes de Angr'
Thomas de Rothinge (mortuus est)
Johannes Jolyf'
Rogerus in le Sale
Johannes Penifford

Hempsted *Johannes Schryve*
Adam Rede

capitanei mortui sunt et in eorum loci

Thomas Robert
Rob' Steven (fecit finem)

Decenarii *Thomas Schryve* (mortuus est)
Robertus Steven (quia fecit finem)
Robertus Schryve
— capitaneus
Thomas Blundel
Thomas Roberd—capitaneus
Johannes Coote jun dec'

Hersted Galfridus Folk'
Johannes Symple

Decenarii *Robertus Steven*
Johannes Morcok' (qui fecit finem)
Adam Pymme (in Babethorne, mortuus est)
Michael Nobelot (in Babethorne, finem)
Johannes Pepyn (in Babethorne)
Johannes Not (mortuus)
Ricardus Rynel (quia fecit finem)
Robertus Dike
Ricardus John' (mortuus est)
Thomas Jolic' (quia fecit finem)
Johannes Johain' (mortuus est)
Thomas John
Johannes Simple
Johannes Assely
Robertus Morcok'
Robertus Martyn
John (*sic*) Paternoster junior
Thomas Brom'
Johannes Byrde
Willelmus Parkgate
Johannes Melksop
Thomas Stambourne
Hugo Celer (recessit a extra precinctum visus)
Willelmus fitz Willyham
Robertus Sadde
Johannes Carter'
Johannes Strannge jur'

[Additional names] Thomas Balley jur. (mortuus est)
Johannes parker Smyth senior
Johannes Parker Junior filius dicti Johannis
Ricardus Dryver jur'

Hugo Sharp jur'
Thomas Osbrn' jur'
Johannes Hardy
Robertus Hirde
Will' Howton'
Joh' Howton'
Robertus Goffe

13

A Periodic Market and its Impact on a Manorial Community: Botesdale, Suffolk, and the Manor of Redgrave, 1280–1300

RICHARD M. SMITH

IN the late nineteenth and early twentieth centuries the history of commerce and money were staples in the diets of medieval economic historians who certainly believed that the Middle Ages witnessed considerable developments facilitating the progressive monetization and market orientation of the economy and thereby were symptomatic of real economic advance. N. S. B. Gras's pioneering study of the evolution of the English corn market is a frequently cited work and regarded by many commentators as exemplary of these intellectual preferences.[1] Such concerns which, both explicitly and implicitly, were premised upon an economic history that was oriented towards charting the rise of a money economy as an index of growth, were unambiguously derailed by M. M. Postan. Between the late 1930s and the early 1950s, operating within a framework that was clearly influenced by a particular style of national income analysis, he engineered a major paradigmatic shift in approaches to medieval economy and society.[2] This shift attracted the attention of scholars away from approaches that had a strong strain of linear and evolutionary thinking and which had been so characteristic of the late nineteenth century, towards a style of measuring changes in terms of the relationships between resources, population, and income. Therefore, given the tendency, as Postan saw it, for population increase in the twelfth and thirteenth centuries to outstrip growth in resources available for the production of food, fuel, and clothing, the net effect was an aggregate decline in living

---

[1] N. S. B. Gras, *The Evolution of the English Corn Market from the Twelfth to the Eighteenth Century* (Cambridge, Mass., 1915) appeared almost simultaneously with E. Lipson, *The Economic History of England*, i. *The Middle Ages* (London, 1915) and was followed by L. F. Salzman, *English Trade in the Middle Ages* (Oxford, 1931) both of which were books that gave significant attention to the history of markets and marketing.

[2] The shift is exemplified by three key papers, M. M. Postan, 'The Fifteenth Century', *EcHR* 1st ser. 9 (1939), 160–7 and, 'The Rise of the Money Economy', *EcHR* 1st ser. 14 (1944), 123–34; and, 'Some Economic Evidence of Declining Population', 221–46.

standards. One very real consequence of this interpretation was to shift issues to do with commercialization and economic transactions to a rather marginal position in the overall activities of medieval economic historians, notwithstanding Postan's own very considerable contribution to our understanding of such matters, particularly in the earlier stages of his long career.[3]

The decade and a half following Postan's death in 1981 has revealed a noteworthy unease with the negative feedback, dynamic-equilibrium-dominated position for which he had argued so brilliantly and tenaciously. Postan's view which has become so clearly associated with a stagnationist position regarding the fundamental characteristics of the medieval economy is now perceived in certain quarters to rest uneasily alongside the new findings and arguments of a growing band of scholars. These scholars are distinguished by being increasingly interested in such matters as regional specialization, comparative advantage, agrarian innovation, and the proliferation of market centres. A small but distinguished group of numismatic historians also argue for a more central role in the explanation of economic change to be given to the money supply. The combined effect of all of these developments has been to move demographic growth and all of its supposedly negative long-term consequences for *per capita* well-being in the thirteenth century away from the limelight it had occupied for almost half a century.

The most intensive revival of interest in the theme of 'commercialization' has emerged within a reconsideration of the twelfth- and thirteenth-century English economy. That period has received its most comprehensive reassessment in the recently published interpretation of English medieval commercialization formulated by Richard Britnell.[4] The publication of Britnell's important monograph took place in December 1992. A few months before the publication of this book the fourth Anglo-American Conference of Medieval Economic and Social Historians had concentrated a large part of its discussions in a symposium focused upon the commercialization of the English economy in the twelfth and thirteenth century. The Leicester symposium was to a very great extent devoted to documenting the increase in trade in the twelfth and thirteenth centuries—a development that was viewed by paper-givers as being reflected in the growth of towns, internal and overseas commercial transactions, an

[3] e.g. M. M. Postan, 'Credit in Medieval Trade', *EcHR* 1st ser. 1 (1928), 234–61, and 'Private Financial Instruments in Medieval England', *Vierteljahrschrift für Sozial-und Wirtschaftsgeschichte*, 23 (1930), 28–64.

[4] Britnell, *Commercialisation of English Society*.

expansion of the money stock and an intensification of its circulation.[5] Commercialization from such a vantage point implied a growth in the quantity of trade that was faster than the growth in population, and hence an emerging society in which individuals became increasingly dependent upon market transactions as a rising share of all goods and services were supposedly purchased and sold for cash.[6] Another symptom of this process that has been emphasized by Britnell was the growing specialization of economic activity at various levels in a notional hierarchy stretching down from the region, the individual settlement to the household, as self-sufficiency at every echelon in the system was progressively reduced.[7]

As part of this new climate of scholarly opinion we encounter a growing willingness to play down the extent of demographic growth between *c.*1100 and *c.*1300, largely by emphasizing a Domesday population that was significantly in excess of two million and a net demographic growth in the ensuing two centuries of no more than threefold.[8] In such an interpretation a more muted demographic growth also allows for a genuine expansion of the urban sector, as settlements, containing 2,000 or more persons, most likely doubled their share, from *c.*3 to *c.*6 per cent, of the total population during the period.[9]

Nicholas Mayhew's work, in particular, has drawn our attention to what was at least a ninefold increase in the quantity of coin in circulation from the beginning of the eleventh to the end of the thirteenth centuries—an increase primarily concentrated in the second half of the period, implying a significant growth in *per capita* money stock. Increasing urbanization is also consistent with a growth in the velocity of circulation of the money stock, enabled also by the adaptation of the coinage to small household purchases. Cutting of pennies from the eleventh century onwards to make half-pennies and farthings, as well as the minting of smaller denominations of currency, were important developments, which in conjunction with inflation, reduced the value of the penny so as to

[5] The proceedings of the symposium were subsequently published in an amplified form in R. H. Britnell and B. M. S. Campbell (eds.), *A Commercialising Economy England 1086–c.1300* (Manchester, 1995).

[6] R. H. Britnell, 'Commercialisation and Economic Development in England, 1000–1300' in Britnell and Campbell (eds.), *A Commercialising Economy*, 7.

[7] Ibid. 14–17 and Britnell, *Commercialisation of English Society*, 164–71

[8] Smith, 'Human Resources', 189–90. See too, Britnell, 'Commercialisation and Economic Development', 11

[9] G. Persson, *Pre-industrial Economic Growth: Social Organization and Technical Progress* (Oxford, 1988), 73–6. For recognition of the fragility of these estimates and their susceptibility to influences by varying assumptions of overall population growth between 1086 and 1300, see Britnell, 'Commercialisation and Economic Development', 11.

make it more compatible with its use in low-value transactions. Support for these trends comes from archaeological evidence bearing on the number of stray coins found on archaeological sites—a twelvefold growth between *c*.1100 and 1300 is suggested by Mayhew. All such developments are furthermore consistent with an increasingly monetized basis to the relationship between landlord and tenant over the same period.[10]

The market for goods and services, and so the possibility for specialization, was broadened by falling transaction costs. The institutions of trade were also developing in the direction of making transactions easier.[11] The characteristics of marketing in the year 1000 are far from perfectly understood, but the institutions through which trade took place appear to have been more informal and, geographically, more widely spaced relative to those to be found in 1300. Between 1200 and 1349 the number of markets formally ratified through royal grant may have tripled. Richard Britnell has also been a pioneer in charting this proliferation of markets, especially what he regards as the purposeful foundation of markets and fairs by landlords.[12] A sense of the scale of this development emerges immediately from Britnell's findings as reported in Table 13.1. In 1200 within this group of 21 counties which formed 55 per cent of England's surface, there were 329 documented early markets. By 1350 in these same counties, 1,002 places leave evidence of having had markets, or having been licensed at some time to hold them. If these counties form a representative sample, it might be supposed that England in *c*.1200 had 600 markets and that by the Black Death the proliferation of grants had raised this total to 1,800 or more.[13]

It is clear, however, that the geographical distribution of these markets was uneven. They were particularly thick on the ground in the eastern counties. For instance, Suffolk, the county upon which our gaze is focused in this chapter, apparently had nine times as many sites per square mile as Durham (See Table 13.2). Map 13.1 reveals the geographical distribution of market rights granted by the Crown to various lords of manors in the county of Suffolk and is the product of Norman Scarfe's

---

[10] S. E. Rigold, 'Small Change in the Light of Medieval Site Finds', in N. Mayhew (ed.) *Edwardian Monetary Affairs (1279–1344)* (BAR 36; Oxford, 1977), 59–80; Britnell, *Commercialization of English Society*, 103; N. Mayhew, 'Modelling Medieval Monetization', in Britnell and Campbell (eds.), *Commercialising Economy*, 55–77.

[11] Britnell, *Commercialisation of English Society*, esp. ch. 4.

[12] R. H. Britnell, 'The Proliferation of Markets in England, 1200–1349', *EcHR* 2nd ser. 34 (1981), 222–35.

[13] D. L. Farmer, 'Marketing the Produce of the Countryside, 1200–1500', in Miller (ed.), *The Agrarian History of England and Wales*, iii. 329.

TABLE 13.1.   *Markets founded in twenty-one English counties before 1349*

	Sometime before 1349	1200–24	1225–49	1250–74	1275–99	1300–24	1325–49
Berkshire	13	5	2	3	1	3	0
Hampshire	23	7	5	7	0	3	1
Surrey	12	1	3	2	2	4	1
Southern	48	13	10	12	3	10	2
Bedfordshire	10	3	1	2	0	6	0
Buckinghamshire	10	4	8	4	2	4	2
Hertfordshire	16	1	3	9	3	3	0
Huntingdonshire	5	3	0	5	0	5	0
Rutland	2	0	0	0	1	1	1
East Midland	43	11	12	20	6	19	3
Gloucestershire	16	8	6	12	7	3	4
Staffodshire	10	9	2	9	4	5	4
Warwickshire	8	5	11	8	0	4	2
Worcestershire	7	3	3	5	0	1	2
West Midland	41	25	22	34	11	13	12

Essex	24	8	10	19	6	8	3
Norfolk	39	5	20	29	8	10	10
Suffolk	29	4	13	23	7	8	3
East Anglian	92	17	43	71	21	26	16
Derbyshire	6	2	3	11	3	1	3
Durham	8	1	0	0	0	2	0
Lancashire	16	2	2	6	6	5	3
Nottinghamshire	6	0	3	11	1	4	3
Yorkshire, W.R.	13	7	9	8	6	10	3
Yorkshire, N.R.	12	3	2	11	4	8	3
Yorkshire, E.R.	12	3	2	11	4	8	3
Northern	73	18	21	63	25	37	16
Devon	32	8	11	14	18	10	1
South Western	32	8	11	14	18	10	1

Source: Britnell, 'The Proliferation of Markets in England, 1200–1349', 210.

TABLE 13.2. *The distribution of markets in medieval England*

County	Area (square miles)[a]	Early markets[b]	Markets added 1200–1349	Total sites by 1349[c]	Market sites per 100 sq. miles, 1349
Bedfordshire	473.0	10	12	22	4.65
Berkshire	724.7	13	14	27	3.73
Buckinghamshire	749.1	10	24	34	4.54
Derbyshire	1,005.6	6	23	29	2.88
Devon	2,611.9	32	62	94	3.60
Durham	1,014.8	8	3	11	1.08
Essex	1,528.2	24	54	78	5.10
Gloucestershire	1,257.7	16	40	56	4.45
Hampshire	1,503.4	23	23	46	3.06
Hertfordshire	632.1	16	19	35	5.54
Huntingdonshire	365.6	5	13	18	4.92
Lancashire	1,877.9	16	24	40	2.13
Norfolk	2,053.6	39	82	121	5.89
Nottinghamshire	843.8	6	22	28	3.32
Rutland	152.0	2	2	4	2.63
Staffordshire	1,153.5	10	33	43	3.73

County				
Suffolk	870.9	29	58	87	9.99
Surrey	721.6	12	13	25	3.46
Warwickshire	982.9	8	30	38	3.87
Worcestershire	699.9	7	14	21	3.00
Yorkshire, E.R.	1,172.5	12	31	43	3.67
Yorkshire, N.R.	2,127.8	12	34	46	2.16
Yorkshire, W.R.	2,790.3	13	43	56	2.01
TOTAL	27,312.8	329	673	1,002	3.67

[a] 1970 County boundaries.
[b] Probably most were founded before 1200.
[c] This total includes some sites where markets had already been.

Source: D. L. Farmer, 'Marketing the Produce of Countryside, 1200–1500', in Miller (ed.), *Agrarian History of England and Wales*, III, 331.

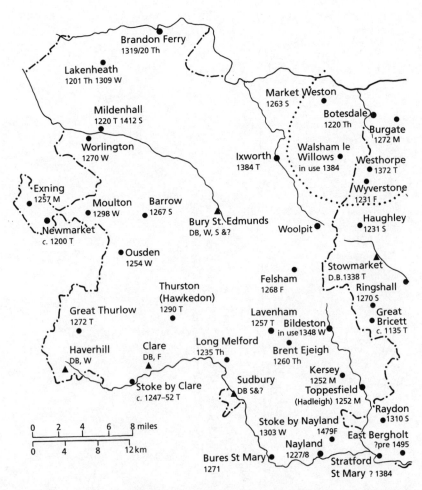

Brandon Ferry
1319/20 Th

Lakenheath
1201 Th 1309 W

Mildenhall
1220 T 1412 S

Market Weston
1263 S

Botesdale
1220 Th

Burgate
1272 M

Worlington
1270 W

Ixworth
1384 T

Walsham le
Willows
in use 1384

Westhorpe
1372 T

Exning
1257 M

Moulton
1298 W

Barrow
1267 S

Wyverstone
1231 F

Newmarket
c. 1200 T

Bury St. Edmunds
DB, W, S &?

Woolpit

Haughley
1231 S

Ousden
1254 W

Stowmarket
D.B. 1338 T

Felsham
1268 F

Thurston
(Hawkedon)
1290 T

Ringshall
1270 S

Great Thurlow
1272 T

Lavenham
1257 T

Bildeston
in use 1348 W

Great
Bricett
c. 1135 T

Haverhill
DB, W

Clare
DB, F

Long Melford
1235 Th

Brent Ejeigh
1260 Th

Kersey
1252 M

Stoke by Clare
c. 1247–52 T

Sudbury
DB S&?

Toppesfield
(Hadleigh) 1252 M

Raydon
1310 S

Stoke by Nayland
1303 W

1479F

East Bergholt
?pre 1495

Nayland
1227/8

Bures St Mary
1271

Stratford
St Mary ? 1384

0 2 4 6 8 miles
0 4 8 12 km

MAP 13.1 Medieval Suffolk markets showing dates of grants and market days

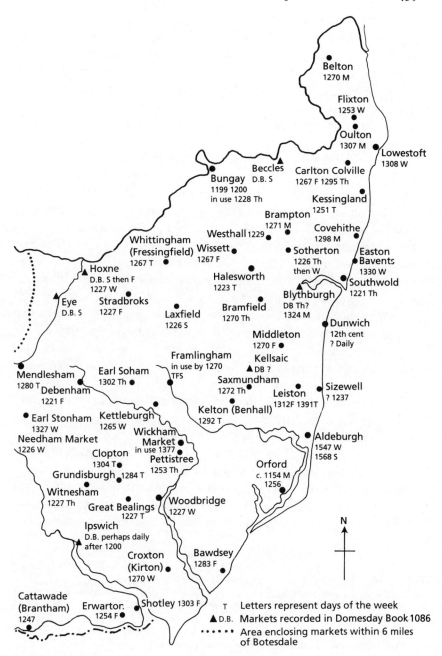

Belton
1270 M

Flixton
1253 W

Oulton
1307 M

Lowestoft
1308 W

Beccles ▲
Bungay D.B. S   Carlton Colville
1199 1200   1267 F 1295 Th
in use 1228 Th
Kessingland
Brampton   1251 T
1271 M
Westhall 1229   Covehithe
Whittingham   1298 M
(Fressingfield) Wissett   Sotherton
1267 T   1267 F   1226 Th   Easton
Hoxne   then W   Bavents
D.B. S then F   Halesworth   1330 W
1227 W   1223 T   Southwold
Eye   Stradbroks   Blythburgh   1221 Th
D.B. S   1227 F   Laxfield   Bramfield   DB Th?
1226 S   1270 Th   1324 M
Middleton   Dunwich
1270 F   12th cent
Framlingham   Kellsaic   ? Daily
Mendlesham   Earl Soham   in use by 1270   DB ?
1280 T   1302 Th   TFS   Saxmundham
Debenham   1272 Th   Sizewell
1221 F   Leiston   ? 1237
Earl Stonham   Kettleburgh   Kelton (Benhall)   1312F 1391T
1327 W   1265 W   1292 T
Needham Market   Wickham   Aldeburgh
1226 W   Market   1547 W
Clopton   in use 1377   1568 S
1304 T   Pettistree   Orford
Grundisburgh   1284 T   1253 Th   c. 1154 M
Witnesham   1256
1227 Th   Great Bealings   Woodbridge
1227 T   1227 W
Ipswich
D.B. perhaps daily
after 1200   N
Croxton   Bawdsey
(Kirton)   1283 F
1270 W

Cattawade
(Brantham)   Erwarton   Shotley 1303 F   T   Letters represent days of the week
1247   1254 F   ▲ D.B. Markets recorded in Domesday Book 1086
•••••• Area enclosing markets within 6 miles
of Botesdale

research, based upon the Charter Rolls, the Calendar of Grants of Markets and Fairs of 1888, and work in a wide variety of sources.[14] The map indicates the dates of grants, or, very occasionally, the earliest recorded use so far determined, and the day of the week on which the grant licensed the market to be held. The clusters are indeed physically close. Such physical proximity is, of course, to be expected from the information in Table 13.2.[15] This clustering would clearly seem to be a product of the high frequency of thirteenth-century foundations.[16] At least until the reign of John, the owners of markets fiercely resisted competition and locally powerful figures or institutions could undoubtedly influence developments in their immediate neighbourhoods. Abbot Samson of Bury St Edmunds and the abbey bailiffs and 600 armed men destroyed the rural market which the monks of Ely had paid the king to have at Lakenheath, just 15 miles from Bury. Some scholars have speculated that this actual case made the Crown more cautious in the way it proceeded to make grants. John was unwilling to grant charters to markets that might prove harmful to others already in the vicinity.[17] Scarfe notes the low density of chartered markets in west Suffolk and suggests that the relative shortage of markets in this region when compared with the remainder of the county, reflects the jealousy with which St Edmund's Abbey preserved its own markets in Bury, thereby stifling wherever possible the few other markets granted within the Liberty of West Suffolk.[18]

Notwithstanding this apparent 'market desert' in the environs of Bury St Edmunds, what catches the eye from the geographical patterns revealed in Map 13.1 is the high density of markets in the county as a whole. The clusterings suggest that the markets locally succeeded one another, or even may have co-existed by being held in nearby or adjacent manors on different days of the week. Suggestions of such emerge from Map 13.1. For instance, markets in the south Suffolk communities of Kersey, Lavenham, Bildeston, Brent Eleigh, and Felsham, none more

---

[14] N. Scarfe, 'Medieval and Later Markets', in D. Dymond and E. Martin (eds.), *An Historical Atlas of Suffolk* (2nd edn.; Ipswich, 1989), 59.

[15] For high densities in the adjacent county of Norfolk see D. P. Dymond, 'Medieval and Later Markets' in P. Wade-Martins (ed.), *An Historical Atlas of Norfolk* (Norwich, 1993), 76–7.

[16] Of 73 places shown to have had markets before 1350, 47 were the result of grants made between 1201 and 1300, Scarfe, 'Medieval and Later Markets', 60.

[17] Farmer, 'Marketing the Produce of the Countryside', 330; R. H. Britnell, 'English Markets and Royal Administration before 1200', *EcHR* 2nd ser. 31 (1978), 183–96; R. H. Britnell, 'King John's Early Grants of Markets and Fairs', *EHR* 94 (1979), 93–6.

[18] Scarfe, 'Medieval and Later Markets', 60.

than ten miles from any other, were respectively on Monday, Tuesday, Wednesday, Thursday, and Friday.

Historical geographers have made useful contributions to the interpretation of patterns such as those displayed on the map of Suffolk. Normally a few large markets develop for goods with high minimum population ranges and eventually a nested hierarchy of market centres emerges. In addition most markets only function on a single day of the week. A large literature has developed on the subject of the spatial and temporal distribution of these markets.[19] This developing theoretical literature has enabled marketing systems to be classified into those that are oriented towards traders and those that are directed towards consumer demands.

When markets function principally for traders they are both spatially distant from each other and separated by relatively lengthy time intervals. Such arrangements enable traders to complete a market circuit, attending a different market on each day of the week. When the interests of consumers loom large markets are closer together in space although separated by rather brief intervals of time.[20] A widely encountered characteristic of periodic market systems is that for the most part a few large markets are held once or twice a week in an area, whereas the majority of days only have small local markets. Such a hierarchical and temporal ordering makes it possible for traders to visit a large number of small markets throughout the week, to bulk their purchases together, and, then, to sell them at the larger markets. Work on contemporary periodic marketing systems suggests that most of those attending function both as producers and

---

[19] G. H. Tupling, 'The Origins of Markets and Fairs in Medieval Lancashire', *Trans. of the Lancashire and Cheshire Antiquaries Soc.* 49 (1933), 75–94; B. E. Coates, 'The Origins and Distribution of Markets and Fairs in Derbyshire', *Derbyshire Archaeological Journal* 85 (1965), 92–111; D. M. Palliser and A. C. Pinnock, 'The Markets of Medieval Staffordshire', *North Staffs. Journal of Field Studies*, 11 (1971), 49–63; M. Reed, 'Markets and Fairs in Medieval Buckinghamshire, *Records of Buckinghamshire*, 20 (1975–8), 563–85; Britnell, 'Essex Markets Before 1350', *Essex Archaeology and History*, 13 (1981), 15–21; G. Platts, *Land and People in Medieval Lincolnshire* (Lincoln, 1985), 296–304; D. P. Dymond, *The Norfolk Landscape* (London, 1985), 152–5; P. Goodfellow, 'Medieval Markets in Northamptonshire', *Northamptonshire Past and Present*, 7 (1988), 305–23; T. Unwin, 'Rural Marketing in Medieval Nottinghamshire', *Journal of Historical Geography*, 7 (1981), 231–51; D. Postles, 'Markets for Rural Produce in Oxfordshire, 1086–1350', *Midland History*, 12 (1987), 14–26; M. Kowaleski, *Local Markets and Regional Trade in Medieval Exeter* (Cambridge, 1995), 41–60.

[20] R. J. Bromley, 'Markets in the Developing Countries: A Review', *Geography*, 56 (1971), 124–32; A. M. Hay and R. H. T. Smith, 'Consumer Welfare in Periodic Market Systems', *Transactions Institute of British Geographers*, 5 (1980), 29–44; R. H. T. Smith, 'Periodic Market Places and Periodic Marketing: A Review and Prospect', *Progress in Human Geography*, 3 (1979), 471–505 and 4 (1980), 1–31

retailers.[21] Although there is little direct evidence of this dual role from the participants in the markets of medieval England, it is highly probable that similar forms of behaviour existed during the thirteenth century.

The remainder of this chapter is concerned with an investigation of just one such periodic market, which received a market grant in 1227.[22] The founding landlord was the abbot of Bury St Edmunds and the market site was Botesdale in the manor of Redgrave in north Suffolk. In the following discussion attention will be focused upon four principal issues: first, the financial benefits that accrued to the abbot of Bury St Edmunds will be considered with a view to ascertaining his possible motive in securing the formal market grant for Botesdale. Second, the surviving sources will be used to recreate as full an account as possible of the community created upon and around the market site. Third, the advantages and benefits gained from the market by non-seigneurial elements in local society will be reviewed, focusing, in particular, on the involvement of customary and freehold tenants of the abbot as traders in the market. The degree of interaction between the 'market' and 'manorial' communities will be assessed against the background of similar considerations that have been made in the context of studies, using the court rolls of small seigneurial boroughs from the late thirteenth and early fourteenth centuries. Fourth, the discussion will conclude with brief reflections on the implications of this case study for the 'commercialization' thesis, in particular, the impact made by the market on local *per capita* incomes. Throughout the study it is intended to demonstrate the distinctive value that derives from investigation of an especially detailed extent or survey in association with the contemporaneous proceedings of the manorial court where many actions taken by participants in the market are recorded.

Considerable efforts have been expended to establish the chronology of market foundations from the beginning of the thirteenth century. The pace of creation of formal grants rose through to the third quarter of the thirteenth century, thereafter declining. Suffolk is an exemplary county in exhibiting this pattern. It is generally recognized that the receipt of a

---

[21] M. J. Webber and R. Symanski, 'Periodic Markets: An Economic Location Analysis', *Economic Geography*, 49 (1973), 213–27; A. M. Hay, 'Some Alternatives in the Economic Analysis of Periodic Marketing', *Geographical Analysis*, 9 (1977), 72–9; S. Cook and M. Diskin, *Markets in Oaxaca* (Austin, 1976); D. W. Jones, 'Production, Consumption and the Allocation of Labour by a Peasant in a Periodic Marketing System', *Geographical Analysis*, 10 (1978), 13–30.

[22] *Calendar of Charter Rolls*, i. 30, market grant to Bury for Redgrave, 5.4.1227 (11 Hen III).

market grant was not synonymous with the establishment of a fully functioning market, nor is it to be assumed that there was no earlier market centre, the existence of which may have been formalized by the receipt of a royal grant. Britnell has shown himself alert to the latter point. However, he suggests that in the early thirteenth century new and unchartered markets would have been unable to operate for long without a royal grant on account of the need to advertise their existence, the increasing royal vigilance, and the risk of prosecution by neigbouring lords anxious to protect their own privileges. Such pressures, Britnell suggests, would have acted as a deterrent to the operation of an illicit new market for very long.[23] James Masschaele has reiterated and elaborated a point made previously by Britnell that a comparison of medieval market foundations with markets identified by Alan Everitt as operating in the early modern period reveals that those receiving grants in the late thirteenth and early fourteenth centuries had a much lower chance of long-term survival than those known to have been in, or to have come into, existence before *c*.1250.[24] Indeed Masschaele states that 'the evanescent markets of the later thirteenth and early fourteenth centuries were, in sum, grafted onto a core of markets that were almost the same under Henry III as it was under Hen VIII'.[25] Indeed, he goes on to develop a sophisticated argument by reference to a detailed case study of Northamptonshire as to why few of the market grants made after 1250 related to fully functional markets.[26]

It is interesting to consider the evidence relating to Botesdale and its most closely situated markets in the light of the above discussion. The date of the formal record of Botesdale's foundation before 1250 contrasts with the known dates of the five markets in the immediate vicinity acquiring grants later in the thirteenth and fourteenth centuries: Wyverston, a Friday market, received a grant in 1231, Market Weston, a Saturday market in 1263, Burgate, a Monday market in 1272, Westhorpe, a Tuesday market in 1372. Another market, Walsham-le-Willows, just 3 miles from Botesdale, was known to have been in use in 1384, although the date of its formal creation is unknown (see area enclosed by the broken line in Map 13.1). None of these markets were located further than 5 miles from

---

[23] Britnell, 'Proliferation of Markets', 211.
[24] J. Masschaele, 'The Multiplicity of Medieval Markets Reconsidered', *Journal of Historical Geography*, 20 (1994), 255–71; Britnell, 'Proliferation of Markets', 219; A. Everitt, 'The Marketing of Agricultural Produce' in J. Thirsk (ed.) *The Agrarian History of England and Wales*, IV, *1500–1640* (Cambridge, 1967), 516–23.
[25] Masschaele, 'Multiplicity of Medieval Markets', 258.   [26] Ibid. 260–8.

Botesdale and none, unlike Botesdale, survived into the sixteenth century. Even within the 30–5 square miles of north-central Suffolk that contained, at some point in the fourteenth century, six possible sites, with market grants, it is probable that there existed a hierarchy of markets. Botesdale most likely functioned in ways that were more central to wider regional trade while the other sites served far more localized needs. Such evidence may well suggest that it would be unwise to conclude that Botesdale's trading roots did not run back before the market grant of 1227.

What benefits can be documented as accruing to the abbot of Bury St Edmunds if it is assumed that, *de novo*, he had set aside valuable agricultural land to establish such a market? In rents, the abbot of Bury St Edmunds received only 17s. 0d. annually from the stallholders, shopkeepers, and cottagers who can be identified as tenants upon the market site.[27] In addition the abbot could also expect further income from the fines that were levied whenever market properties changed hands, which they did occasionally. Income from such transactions would rarely exceed a few shillings annually. The abbots also had rights of jurisdiction over these tenants and exacted further fines for breaches of the Assizes of Bread and Ale which *in toto* brought in annually sums that were comparable to the sums received in fines associated with *inter-vivos* property transactions.[28] When account is taken of the tolls of the market, which are estimated in the extent to have been worth £5 6s. 8d. annually, it can be concluded that the total income from rents, tolls, and fines levied in the manorial court that directly formed part of the abbey's revenues, amounted annually to between £8 and £9.[29] The physical site on which the market was located would probably have been rented as agricultural land for £1 or £2 annually. We might suppose that the site itself and the income generated from court dues and tolls may have exceeded the rentable value of the area as agricultural land by £7 to £8. Certainly the abbot increased the revenue of this manor somewhat through facilitating the development of the market site at Botesdale. However, the value added in monetary terms

[27] Information from the 1289 extent of Redgrave which exists in two copies: University of Chicago Libary Bacon MS 805 and BL MS Add. 14850, fos 65–84ᵛ. Reference will be made to the copy deposited in the British Library. The rental yield of the market site is calculated from rents paid by individual stall and shop holders, see BL MS Add. 14850, fos. 83–83ᵛ.

[28] e.g. in the surviving manorial courts of 1289–92, fines associated with property transactions relating to customary land amounted to £10 19s. 6d. whereas fines for infractions of the Assizes of Bread and Ale, totalled £9 9s. 5d., Bacon MS. 5–6.

[29] BL MS Add. 14850, fo. 66ᵛ.

should not be exaggerated since the total yearly worth of the manor was estimated in the extent of 1289 to be £97 9s. 5d.[30]

The abbot certainly should be regarded as a facilitator of many developments that enabled the market to crystallize in a formal or institutional sense, and through the adoption of policies relating in particular to the market in, and inheritance of, customary land, he consciously, or inadvertently, made it possible for a local society to function in which market dependence rather than self-sufficiency was the experience of a majority of the local populace. In approving the transfer of land into shops, or for use as the sites of stalls, the lord adopted a constructive stance. That this was an ongoing, cumulative process is revealed in the records of the manorial court. At least eleven of the stallholders and shopkeepers identifiable in the extent of 1289 had paid fines to the abbot some years earlier to enter property on the site of Botesdale market in which they were given permission to build shops or to erect stalls. For example, in 1286 Walter Hunno paid a fine of 6s. for a piece of land, 20 ft. by 11 ft., in the market at Botesdale upon which to construct a shop.[31] In 1272, Thomas Docke, already a stallholder in the market, paid 4s. for three further plots, one 20 × 8 ft., one 24 × 8 ft., and another 4 × 4 ft.[32] In 1283 Hugh de Bosco paid 6d. to enter a piece of land in the market upon which he was given permission to build a shop next to the houses of Thomas Docke and Walter Medicus, as well as approval to enter a piece of land upon which he was to erect a stall next to a shop formerly held by Edward Cat.[33] Hugh de Bosco, three years later in 1286, granted a shop with dimensions that were 40 × 11 ft. to Annicia his daughter which she is shown holding on the extent of 1289.[34] Such evidence is indicative of a probable continued growth in the physical size and rental value of the market over the period between 1260 and 1280.

The abbot also, through the provision of formal regulative devices, saw that the market was policed in the interests of customers through the monitoring of weights and measures and the prevention of forestalling. It is reasonable to suppose that markets subject to this level of formal control were viable only where the number of traders, regularly active each week, were both dependable and sizeable. The abbots had also, from the moment in time that we are able to observe them in action through

---

[30] BL MS Add. 14850, fo. 84ᵛ.
[31] Bacon MS 5, court held on 23.10.1286.
[32] Bacon MS 2, courts held on 27.2.1272, 29.3.1272 and 28.6.1272.
[33] Bacon MS 5, court held on 4.11.1283.
[34] Bacon MS 5, court held on 15.4.1286.

the records of the manorial court which begin in 1260, not attempted to restrict a highly active market in customary land on the manor in which Botesdale market was located. Between 1260 and 1289 records of 219 surviving manorial court sessions in Redgrave contain entries relating to 969 *inter-vivos* land transactions. From the licence fees paid by the parties to these transactions, the abbots received fines worth £55 6s. 5d., which was a sum significantly larger than the income derived from heriots and entry fines associated with *post-mortem* land transfers (£41 7s. 9d.) over the same period.[35] In fact Redgrave, like many other communities in thirteenth-century East Anglia, had an especially active land market in customary property suggestive of the degree to which one key factor of production had become profoundly 'commercialized'.[36]

The effect of this highly active land market is immediately apparent in the extent of Redgrave manor in 1289. In Table 13.3 an indication of the distribution of holding sizes derived from the extent can be quickly ascertained. The cumulative distribution shows that a little under half of the holdings of 401 tenants were below 2 acres in size and only marginally more than 10 per cent exceeded 10 acres in area. Undoubtedly, the smallholder class predominated on this manor, with almost 30 per cent of the holdings less than 1 acre in size. Such a distribution closely resembles the distribution of holdings discovered on other East Anglian manors in the late thirteenth century.[37] Of course, some allowance would have to be made for sub-tenancies or sub-letting as well as for land held by individual tenants additional to that which they held from the abbot of Bury St Edmunds in Redgrave.[38] However, very few Redgrave tenants among the smallholders appear in the records of the adjacent manors of Hinderclay and Rickinghall as property holders. In addition only 18 per cent of the 401 tenants had land in more than one of the hamlets or sub-regions of Redgrave manor which extended jurisdictionally over a large area, suggesting that an individual's holding tended to be spatially concentrated within the manor, rather than scattered randomly over it. Given this degree of geographical concentration of properties held by the tenants of Redgrave manor it would be highly unlikely that mean holding size could have, at its maximum, exceeded 5 acres. We cannot, as we have noted, be

---

[35] Smith, 'Some Thoughts', 115–18.
[36] See e.g. Campbell, 'Population Pressure', 87–134; Williamson, 'Norfolk: Thirteenth Century', 31–106; Clark, 'Peasant Society and Land Transactions'.
[37] See works cited in n. 36.
[38] e.g. B. M. S. Campbell, 'The Complexity of Manorial Structure in Medieval Norfolk: A Case Study', *Norfolk Archaeology*, 39 (1986), 244–5.

TABLE 13.3. *The distribution of holding sizes: Redgrave 1289*

Sizes (acre)	<2	%	2–6	%	6¼–10	%	10¼–14	%	14¼–18	%	18>	%	Total
Customary Tenants (land in 1 sub-region only)	133		87		17		7		4		2		250
Customary Tenants (land in more than 1 sub-region)	6		18		17		7		1		1		50
Customary Tenants (with minority of free land)	4		9		8		1		1		3		26
Sub-total	143		114		42		15		6		6		326
Free Tenants (with minority of customary land)	4		7		3		3		—		4		21
Free Tenants	30		13		3		2		2		4		54
Sub-total	34		20		6		5		2		8		75
Grand Total	178	44.1	134	33.4	48	11.9	20	5.0	8	2.0	14	3.6	402

certain that none of these 401 tenants held land from estates other than those of the abbot of Bury St Edmunds, but we may justifiably doubt whether the number who did so was great enough to make any differences to our conclusions that a large majority of the inhabitants of Redgrave could not depend on the produce from their own landholding to yield them a living.

If we adopt assumptions identical to those which Christopher Dyer has sensibly employed in his reconstruction of, and claims upon, that income of a Worcestershire smallholder with 3 acres of land in the late thirteenth century, we will be close to revealing the circumstances of a majority of the Redgrave tenantry in 1289. Dyer suggests that such a holding might have produced enough grain to provide half the food requirements of a household, including a husband, wife, and three children. Furthermore to meet the costs of other claims upon the household its members would need to work for approximately 130 days each year, assuming a daily wage of $1\frac{1}{2}d$.[39] Such additional earnings could, of course, have been met by by-employments. Whichever means were employed to secure additional cash resources it is evident that in a society with such a level of landlessness a majority of households would have been obliged to purchase the bulk of their foodstuffs.

Given such a distribution of land the existence on the extent of the names of 63 persons holding cottages, stalls, and shops on, or adjacent to, the site of Botesdale market is highly noteworthy. Of these 63 persons 4 individuals held cottages; 40 persons held stalls of whom 1 held 5 stalls, 7 held two stalls, and 32 one stall; 14 individuals held a shop; 2 held a cottage and a shop (in one of these instances two cottages); 4 held a shop and a stall (or stalls); 1 held a shop and 6 stalls, and another a shop and 3 stalls.

Of the 63 persons holding property *in mercato*, 30 are revealed by the extent of 1289 to be landless. The other 33 held some property in addition to their stall or shop (see Table 13.4). That a solid proportion of the tenants in the market were artisans or tradesmen appears from their names: a carpenter, a *medicus* (*leche*), a metalworker (*ferur*), tanner (*barkere*), iron worker (*blomer*), cook (*cocus*), poulterer (*cokerel*), teacher (*magister*), corn merchant (*corneyser*), tailor (*cuttyng*), baker (*pistor*), shoemaker (*sutor*), cooper (*cupere*), chapman (*mercator*), *redere*, or thatcher, and a salterer. These, of course, are the names of individual stallholders or shopkeepers identifiable from the 1289 snapshot of the community. In addition, the

---

[39] Dyer, *Standards of Living*, 117–18.

TABLE 13.4. *Land holdings of stallholders and shopkeepers Botesdale market, 1289*

Holding size (acres)	Number
Under 2 acres	11
2–5	9
5–9	1
10–15	3
15–20	4
20 and over	5
TOTAL	33

proceedings of the manorial court yield references to many other trades and by-employments that were particularly noteworthy for their association with other smallholders on the manor who were not recorded as holding market properties on the survey. In this category we encounter smiths, carpenters, bakers, gardeners, taylors, leches or blood-letters, corn-dealers, candle-makers, taverners, carters, cooks, porters, chaloners, basket-makers, and robe-makers.

Furthermore, when we track down the holders of shops and stalls whose tenure is recorded through entries in the manorial court rolls extending from 1260 to 1320 we find tixtors, millers, a schoolmaster, skinners, bloodletters, poulterers, cooks, carpenters, tilers, thatchers, masons, and innumerable chapmen and *mercators*. The presence of a sizeable landless, or near-landless, population on this manor was, of course, possible only because so many of the inhabitants did not depend upon the land or upon agricultural labour *per se* for their entire livelihood. Many of these individuals were children not inheriting or who had inherited partibly with a sibling and then sold out their share in the patrimony to a brother or brothers and had chosen, or had been obliged, to live by a craft or by rendering a service to those elements in the local population who were more directly involved in work on the land.[40]

Such a significant pool of craftsmen, labourers, and tradesmen needing to sell commodities or services to purchase their food would have benefited from the presence of a market centre such as that which existed in

[40] Smith, 'Families and Their Land', 135–96; Smith, 'Kin and Neighbours', 4 (1979), 219–56.

Botesdale. There they would have been able to sell the products of their trades, or by-employments, and their services to secure the funds needed for the purchase of foodstuffs and raw materials. The market would have provided a context within which transaction costs could have been significantly lessened. Likewise, such a sizeable body of smallholders allowed for specializations in occupations which, as Brinell has suggested, would have permitted significant savings in household capital, both material and human.[41] For instance, such households would have sold more of their grain and purchased bread and ale, produced by households with more appropriate equipment and more efficient hearths, and may have used the services of a carter to avoid the charge on their smallholding of maintaining a cart or wagon and horse or mule.

To some extent, the landlord who enabled a commercial community such as that in thirteenth-century Botesdale to develop, intensified the demand for foodstuffs locally. In his pioneering work on the periodic market of Newland on the Templar's manor of Witham in Essex, founded in 1212, Richard Britnell has gone so far as to suggest that the creation of such a focus of demand for foodstuffs was an important part of the founder's plan.[42] Indeed, it could be argued in this vein that the founding of such markets was a means whereby landlords could attempt to take advantage of the population growth of the period, for the presence of a commercial community affected their income both directly and indirectly. Besides lengthening his rental, the abbot, as landlord, could hope for a regular outlet for his demesne produce to the inhabitants of the market and to outsiders and travellers who came there to buy grain, bread, ale, or fodder for horses. A landlord taking this step might hope to expand his seigneurial income, since his tenants would have better opportunities to sell their own surpluses, his mills would be used more intensively and there would be a larger reserve of potential tenants to compete for any tenement that fell vacant. Of interest in this connection is the fact that a Master John of Bury St Edmunds in August 1285 took the lease of two windmills located in the market for a rent of 20 marks per annum— significantly more valuable to the abbot than the market tolls valued at £5 6s. 8d.[43] Such observations on the benefits accruing to the landlord confirm once again something that Richard Britnell has been at pains to

---

[41] Britnell, 'Proliferation of Markets', 221. See too, C. Dyer, 'Were Peasants Self Sufficient? English Villagers and the Market, 900–1350', in E. Mornet (ed.), *Campagnes médiévales: l'homme et son espace, études offertes à Robert Fossier* (Paris, 1995), 661.

[42] R. H. Britnell, 'The Making of Witham', *Historical Studies*, 1 (1962), 18.

[43] Bacon MS 5, court held 4.8.1285.

stress, that there is little to be said for analysing the growth of local markets as autonomous processes 'inimical to feudal or manorial organisation'.[44]

In 1289 the abbot of Bury St Edmunds held a demesne of 704 acres in Redgrave. All around there were other Bury demesnes that exceeded 500 acres in size. We might wonder whether all of the grain surpluses from these manors were used in servicing the manors' own requirements or were carried back to Bury St Edmunds to meet the needs of the monastic community. In pursuing this issue any further we are frustrated by the absence of contemporary account rolls that indicate whether sales were made in the local market or to the abbot's tenants. One good account roll series from the manor of Hinderclay which is contiguous with Redgrave leaves no evidence of such marketing behaviour, although they like most *compoti*, are entirely unforthcoming regarding where grain sales took place or who was the purchaser.[45] Of course, it might be argued by many that the large monastic houses, such as the abbey of Bury St Edmunds would have consumed a sizeable part of the produce of their demesnes. When making grain sales such institutions, many would claim, avoided local markets by selling wholesale (*in grosso*) in bulk to distant purchases.[46] However, others now propose that as local market networks grew through the thirteenth century and became more efficient, the long-distance carriage of grain for bulk transactions was becoming less common and a diminishing element in demesne marketing strategies.[47]

Whatever may be the outcome of this emerging debate on the marketing of demesne foodstuffs and the extent to which they entered into local marketing systems, to give undue attentions to landlords as the prime or sole beneficiaries of such market foundations would be to neglect to ask whether others were making financial gain from commercial transactions in such centres. Indeed it is conventionally assumed that small rural producers were the principal sellers in such markets. Can we detect examples of trading fortunes or gains among the participants in Botesdale market when use is made of the evidence in the records of the local manorial court? Of the 33 persons who are identifiable as stallholders or shopkeepers in Botesdale and also held additional property in the manor,

[44] Britnell, 'Making of Witham', 18.
[45] Bacon MS 405–50. The earliest accounts for the manor of Redgrave survive for the year 1323–24, Bacon MS 325.
[46] Farmer, 'Marketing the Produce of the Countryside', 358.
[47] B. M. S. Campbell, J. A. Galloway, D. Keene, and M. Murphy, *A Medieval Capital and its Grain Supply: Agrarian Production and Distribution in the London Region c.1300* (Historical Geography Research Series No. 30, Norwich, 1993), 55–6. See too, D. L. Farmer, 'Two Wiltshire Manors and their Markets', *AgHR* 37 (1989), 1–11.

20 (60 per cent) held properties under 5 acres. The evidence is presented in Table 13.4. While such a distribution reflects the pattern within the full population of manorial tenants, the landholdings of the market 'traders' are less skewed to the left of the mean than those of the population at large indicative of higher median and mean holding sizes among the shopkeepers and stallholders. Particularly noteworthy is the proportion (*c*.45 per cent) with holdings larger than 10 acres. Indeed, it is possible to identify within the ranks of the traders a small, but highly significant, group of individuals, either among the more substantial freeholders, such as Hugh de Bosco, whose daughter Alice was also a shopkeeper, or individuals such as Thomas Docke, Adam Pistor, and Adam Jop who were customary tenants, with particularly large landholdings by the standards of East Anglia in the late thirteenth century.

Thomas Docke, a customary tenant with 24 acres of customary land and 2 further acres of free land, a messuage, and part of a messuage in the Mickelwode area of the manor, adjacent to Botesdale, also held a shop and two stalls in Botesdale market. Between 1265 and 1271 he appears to have acquired his stalls and shops in the form of grants from the abbot.[48] He made significant *pre-mortem* gifts of land to his daughters Matilda, Juliana, and Alice.[49] On his death in 1300 the bulk of his estate of *c*.26 acres along with the messuages, stalls, and shops was inherited by his three sons, Walter, Robert, and John.[50] As was not at all uncommon, one son appears to have moved to buy out the interests of the two other siblings. Robert died celibate in 1318, but John appears to have acquired his brother's stalls and shops at an earlier date.[51] John, the effective heir of Thomas Docke, proceeded to marry the daughter of Roger Cuttyng (or Taylor) another acquisitive landholder and stallholder in the market who negotiated a remarkably complex maintenance contract with his son-in-law on his retirement.[52] John went on to acquire further property on the market, another stall from the abbot in 1314, and other pieces of property within the market site, from traders such as John Corneyser and Robert Sutor over the course of the difficult years of the Great Famine when the property market was in a violent state of flux.[53]

The most striking pattern of acquisitive behaviour in the land market by a Botesdale stallholder is provided by Adam Jop and his sons, Richard, John, and John junior. Adam Jop was, by the standards of his commu-

---

[48] Bacon MS 1, court held 20.3.1265; Bacon MS 2, court held 23.6.1267; see n. 32 above.
[49] Bacon MS 4, court held 3.12.1280; Bacon MS 8, court held 20.4.1297.
[50] Bacon MS 8, court held 29.6.1300.   [51] Bacon MS 13, court held 7.4.1318.
[52] Bacon MS 8, court held 20.6.1300.
[53] Bacon MS 13 courts held 25.1.1314, 3.6.1316, 2.3.1317.

nity, a wealthy tenant, holding 39 acres of customary land in 1289, along with 2 full messuages and part of another under customary terms. In addition, he held freely a messuage and 9 acres. Of the 39 acres of customary land held in 1289, Adam had acquired a little over 16 acres through twenty-seven *inter-vivos* dealings. Before his death he secured a further 8 acres of customary land. In contrast to his purchasing activities, he sold outside his family very infrequently, with only five such instances in the surviving court rolls amounting to a little under 3 acres. He did, however, pass on land before his death to his sons in varying amounts. Certainly no less than 10 acres had been granted to John Jop and John Jop junior. Richard had accumulated a few acres in the 1280s and did not begin to acquire further land until after his father's death, in the period of great activity in the community's land market between 1315 and 1317. In addition to their father's gifts, John senior and John junior had acquired a further 15 acres between them, and on sharing the patrimonial estate at Adam's death in 1314 they proceeded to add to their holdings so that by 1320 the three brothers held over 90 acres of customary land. Their involvement in the land market had not been continuous but was disproportionately concentrated in the 1280s and 1290s and again between 1315 and 1317. The Jop family's hold upon Redgrave's customary land was indeed considerable because Adam Jop's nephews, Robert, Augustus, and Benedict, had, by 1320, come to hold at least a further 60 acres, approximately two-thirds the result of their *inter-vivos* dealings. Indeed, by 1320 the five cousins held at least 11 per cent of the total customary land in Redgrave, although they constituted only marginally over 1 per cent of the customary tenantry.[54]

Similar, if less extreme, examples of acquisitive behaviour can be found in the actions of Adam Pistor, another stallholder and shopkeeper, and his two sons. Adam Pistor senior's economic activities were highly diversified, for in 1289 he had in Redgrave a little over 19 acres of land, 2 messuages, 2 cottages, 2 stalls, and a shop in the local market. Before his death in 1320 he amassed a further 20 acres of land in Redgrave and 4 acres in the adjacent manor of Rickinghall. Adam's sons, Adam junior, Robert, and Thomas, were all active in the market as individuals, accumulating collectively a further 8 acres and two shops in the market, to supplement *pre-mortem* gifts from their father, and some small slivers of land provided by their uncle. On their father's death Adam and Robert Pistor shared over 60 acres of customary land that they and their father had accumulated over the preceding fifty years and had very sizeable

⁵⁴ Smith, 'Families and their Land', 165–70.

business interests as stallholders and shopkeepers in Botesdale market along with possession of a scattering of cottages and messuages in and around the site of the periodic market.[55]

It has been suggested that smallholders bought a large part of their food, although it has proved difficult to establish whether this was acquired most frequently in the form of grain or processed into ale and bread. Dyer has remarked that because of lack of fuel and equipment smallholders were likely to have gone to retailers of bread and ale.[56] This supposition, based upon the evidence in the court rolls recording the activities of stallholders and shopkeepers on Botesdale market in the late thirteenth century, seems to be correct. Eighteen of the stallholders or shopkeepers identifiable on the extent or survey of 1289 are known to have brewed ale for sale. Four of them are also known to have baked bread for sale. We know of these activities, because they were amerced for infractions of the Assizes of Ale and Bread. However, the evidence from the proceedings of the manorial court reveals that they were not the only persons involved in these practices. Brewers, for instance, or more precisely, those identified at least once in any year as brewing contrary to the assize numbered on average between 60 and 70 persons annually throughout the period from 1260–95. Through the same years 8–10 persons were amerced annually for infractions of the assize of bread.[57] Perhaps the scale of these activities can be placed in perspective when a comparison is made with the seigneurial borough of Halesowen with a borough population of *c*.600 persons that has been so intensively studied by Rodney Hilton. In this borough Hilton found 4–5 bakers and 25 brewers regularly amerced in the court rolls annually.[58] In the case of Botesdale we do know that a significant proportion of stallholders or shopkeepers were particularly noteworthy for being large-scale producers in so far as they both paid larger fines and were likely to have been amerced on more than one occasion each year. In fact we find them amerced at each court suggesting all-year production for the market.

From the data presented in Table 13.5, it is evident that the distribution of brewing fines paid *per capita* was highly skewed. A large number of individuals amerced for a few instances and a long tail, spreading out to the right (the high end) of those who brewed frequently. It is noteworthy that the pattern of brewing exhibited by those who were amerced for infractions of the Assize of Ale in Rickingall, an adjacent manor to

[55] Ibid. 170–1.　　　　[56] Dyer, 'Were Peasants Self Sufficient?', 661.
[57] Smith, 'English Peasant Life-Cycles', ch. 4.
[58] Hilton, 'Small Town Society in England', 60.

TABLE 13.5. *The distributions of fines paid for infraction of the assize*

A. By Redgrave Brewers, 1259–93

Frequency of fine	No. of individuals	Frequency of fine	No. of individuals
1	192	29	3
2	60	30	2
3	26	31	4
4	20	32	1
5	17	33	—
6	16	34	1
7	12	35	—
8	9	36	2
9	6	37	1
10	5	38	1
11	10	39	1
12	4	40	1
13	3	41	1
14	5	42	1
15	4	43	3
16	7	44	2
17	3	45	1
18	1	46	1
19	3	48	1
20	1	49	1
21	3	50	1
22	1	53	1
23	3	54	1
24	1	58	1
25	3	60	1
26	2	62	1
27	2	66	1
28	2	111	1

TABLE 13.5. (*Cont.*)

B. By Rickinghall Brewers, 1259–93

Frequency of fine	No. of individuals	Frequency of fine	No. of individuals
1	69	13	—
2	23	14	3
3	14	15	1
4	5	16	2
5	4	17	2
6	1	18	2
7	3	19	—
8	3	21	1
9	2	22	1
10	1	26	1
11	—	27	2
12	1		

Source: BL Add MS. 63394–9.

Redgrave, was very different. No brewer paid more than 27 amercements, whereas 40 exceeded that amount over the same period of observation in Redgrave. It should be stressed that almost all of the stallholders or shopkeepers active as brewers in Redgrave are to be found in this right-hand tail of the distribution. For example, Cristina, wife of Geoffrey le Contesse paid 40 brewing fines between 1282 and 1293. She was the wife of an individual who held five stalls in the market in 1289. Adam Sagor or his wife paid 39 amercements for infractions of the Assize of Ale between 1282 and 1293. Adam held a shop on the market and two cottages in the settlement of Botesdale adjacent to the market site.[59] Small-scale, infrequent, or irregular brewers in this manorial community were frequently found to be spinsters who were distinguished by not holding stalls or shops.[60]

[59] Bacon MS 4–6.
[60] Smith, 'English Peasant Life-Cycles', 158–62. For rather different characteristics among brewers from less market-oriented manorial communities see, Bennett, 'The Village Ale-Wife', 20–34; Postles, 'Brewing and the Peasant Economy', 133–44; Graham, ' "A Woman's Work . . ." ', 126–48.

Individuals amerced for infractions of the Assize of Bread were far more restricted in number. A much higher proportion of them were stallholders and shopkeepers than was the case among the brewers. It was an activity that was more confined in its social distribution and certainly more capital intensive than brewing. Adam Pistor, whom we have already encountered, and who, as his name suggests, is an example of an individual with very sizeable interests in the baking trade. It is also evident from the discussion above that Adam had very substantial agricultural interests. We encounter references to his servants and he was a sufficiently large enough livestock farmer to have had his own sheepfold—a reference in 1283 shows him paying a licence fee *pro falde sue habenda super terram suam de bidentiis suis propriis ad totam vitam suam*. Another indication of his wealth was the large fine that he paid in 1288 so that he could be absolved of any obligations to perform manorial offices, namely reeve, hayward and collector, and *omnium aliorum officorum*. We have already noted that Adam held a shop and three stalls in Botesdale market. Between 1282 and 1293 Adam or his wife were fined 35 times for brewing and selling ale against the Assize and paid 38s. 6d. in fines or licence fees. In addition they were fined 21 times for baking bread contrary to the Assize for which they paid a further 30s. 0d. in fines. Adam was a very active pledge in the manorial court, giving these services almost entirely to smallholders and others involved in brewing in Botesdale. He was also a moderately active extender of credit to others and appears to have been largely self sufficient in the raw materials he employed in his food-processing activities.[61]

Self-sufficiency in raw materials was not, however, a common characteristic of those who brewed or indeed baked in substantial quantities for sale. Reginald Warenner, for instance, was a stallholder in Botesdale and held an acre in the hamlet of Musehalle. Between 1282 and 1293 he was fined 11 times for selling ale and 13 times for baking bread and selling it contrary to the Assize. But unlike Adam Pistor, he had little land to service his grain supplies. However, a court roll entry in 1288 suggests that he acquired his grain by purchase, subsequently processing it to sell as ale or bread. In that year he was fined for owing Hugh Traype for 6 cartloads of barley worth 2s. 2d. In fact Reginald's commercial involvements are clearly apparent from the large number of debt cases in which he was concerned. He was amerced in 1287 for being in debt to William

---

[61] For an attempt to consider Adam Pistor within the wider setting of economic and social relations in Redgrave and Botesdale see Smith, 'Kin and Neighbours', 246–9.

Rand of Rickinghall and for owing money to Phillip Capellannus of
Rickinghall. On other occasions he was shown to owe money to Roger
le Porter, Richard de Dale, Adam Shep, two of these were fellow-
stallholders.[62]

The extent to which the stallholders of the market place loom large in
the debt cases brought before the manorial court is worthy of note.
Although they make up 14 per cent of all landholders in the manor, they
were parties in 52 per cent of the 129 debt plaints initiated (if not concluded) in the Redgrave court between 1283 and 1292. What is also very
striking is that in over three-quarters of the debts in which the date of the
original contract or agreement was specified the transaction can be seen
to have taken place on a Thursday—the day of the week on which the
periodic market was held. Unfortunately, detail concerning the material
basis of the debt, as opposed to the sums or value of goods transacted, are
very sparse. Where identifiable, grain and livestock loom large as items of
sale, which is a characteristic fully consistent with the market's role as a
site for transactions involving the sale of such categories of agricultural
produce.[63]

Of the sixty-three stallholders as a whole, eleven, including Robert of
Hopton, William of Wiverston, John of Westbrook, Alan of Norton, and
Walter of Walsham, are distinguished by having displayed very limited
entries in the proceedings of the manorial court. They show no signs
whatsoever of holding land in Redgrave manor. They may well be individuals who moved from market to market as peripatetic traders, making
a living by buying and selling, rather than production for the market.
They also appear as a group whose tenure of market stalls was less permanent through time. However, the identification of such a group is fully
compatible with one characteristic of the model concerning those who
participated in periodic markets. It should, however, be stressed that
there are indeed other intriguing individuals who appear in the courts,
particularly in debt cases, but who hold no stalls or property in the
manor, such as Geoffrey of Picardie. A case such as that involving Adam
the Cooper, father of Nicholas the Cooper, who was a stallholder in 1290
relates to a lengthy debt plaint concerning individuals not ordinarily

---

[62] Bacon MS 5, courts held 8.6.1286, 11.12.1287, 9.4.1288, 26.1.1289; Bacon MS 6,
courts held 29.8.1292 and 18.11.1291.
[63] e.g. in 1287 Richard Blome, stallholder and shopkeeper, was the plaintiff against
Robert Irelande who he claimed owed him 6s. 0d. for the purchase of a cow which he had
bought in the market at Botesdale on the Thursday before Michaelmas two years earlier,
Bacon MS 5, court held 7.5.1287.

resident in Botesdale or Redgrave manor—one of the plaintiffs was a John of Paris who was pledged by John of Sawston (in Cambridgeshire) and Master John of St Edmunds, the lessee of the two mills in the market place.[64]

In a longer discussion than is possible within this chapter it would be useful to provide a fuller consideration of the characteristics of those who participated in this market by way of a comparison with those who were active in trade in the small seigneurial boroughs that were also, to all intents and purposes, attempts by landlords to provide contexts both for the monitoring and encouragement of trade. They have in recent years been the subject of Rodney Hilton's investigations—Halesowen, Thornbury, and Pershore having been intensively studied.[65] Hilton is interested in such settlements for what he sees as their role in inducing pre-capitalist commercialization as well as their relatively dense geographical distribution in England when compared with many other parts of western Europe where urban growth and trade may have been more heavily focused within settlements much higher up the urban settlement hierarchy. In certain senses the seigneurial borough is similar to the periodic market in terms of the types of economic activity it fostered, although the privilege of freedom through burgage tenure is something not available to the stallholders of a settlement such as Botesdale. Another contrast concerns, on the one hand, the relationship between stallholders and shopkeepers in the periodic market and, on the other hand, between burgesses in seigneurial boroughs and the agrarian elements of the manors within which they were situated. In Halesowen 17 per cent of the burgesses held land on the manor and in very small quantities. In Thornbury only 18 per cent did so.[66] What is the significance of this contrast? In Botesdale over 50 per cent of the stallholders were involved in the agricultural economy and in quite major ways. In this characteristic we may have identified a particularly distinctive feature of the periodic market and its participants who were deeply implicated in the surrounding agrarian economy to such an extent that the principal traders were also amongst the largest landowners in the immediate vicinity below the ranks of minor gentry and the larger demesne-exploiting landlords.

[64] Bacon MS 6, court held 18.1.1290. In the same court John of Paris had been represented by an attorney and had been essoined by an Andrew of Ely.

[65] Hilton, 'Small Town Society in England'; Hilton, 'Lords, Burgesses and Hucksters', 3–15; R. H. Hilton, 'Medieval Market Towns and Simple Commodity Production', *Past and Present*, 109 (1985), 3–23 and Ch. 14 below.

[66] Hilton, 'Small Town Society', 58 and Ch. 14 below.

We might be drawn, on the basis of this case study to question one strand in Richard Britnell's argument regarding periodic markets. As we have already noted he sees many of these market communities, purposefully founded by landlords, as mopping up or helping to deal with the problem of rural unemployment. Such an emphasis, while clearly not implausible for markets acquiring charters after c.1270, might lead us to conclude that landlords were more progressive and welfare-minded than they really were. It may also lead us to fail to appreciate the spontaneous development of such centres. If we subscribe fully to Britnell's position we might also underestimate the substantial growth in the scale of enterprise on the part of tenants reflected in the increasing size of holding and marketing activities that a minority, but highly significant minority, of these populations revealed. A community such as Redgrave with 2,900 acres of land, valued at £5. 8s. 1d. in the 1334 lay subsidy can be compared with Halesowen (10,000 acres—including manor and borough), valued at £9 in 1334.[67] The wealth to be taxed per acre in the Suffolk manor of Redgrave with its market settlement at Botesdale was markedly greater than in the combined West Midland seigneurial borough and manor.

None the less the type of commercialization that Botesdale exemplifies is rather difficult to interpret. The beneficiaries there may have been too small in number to offset the deteriorating or deteriorated ratio of population to land. As Richard Britnell suggests it would be tendentious to ascribe commercialization to any widespread propensity of average incomes to rise.[68] Though the good fortunes of a minority shine through in our records, we can have little confidence that their advances stimulated beneficial commercialization throughout the local economy as a whole. It is unlikely that improvements in living standards in Redgrave extended very far down a ladder of wealth that rose out of a large mass of landless persons and smallholders. At best the effect of the local market was to enable a relatively small group of prosperous 'kulaks' to invest in real estate in the market site and to use their profits to acquire more land as well as to exert a growing influence on local government within the manorial court. At worst, it provoked further fragmentation of holdings and helped to create a large body of near landless individuals who were given an opportunity to exist at levels marginally above the barest of subsistence requirements. However, this community was vulnerable to

[67] Lay Subsidy of 1334, 256 and 287.
[68] Britnell, 'Commercialisation and Economic Development in England', 21–2.

exogenous shocks and it seems to have been no better placed than most other economic contexts to deal with the traumas of harvest failures and associated dearth-related mortality crises that affected much of rural England between *c*.1280 and 1320.[69] For this reason there may be doubts surrounding the notion that commercialization over the course of the thirteenth century had really brought about a growth in trade that was faster than the expansion of population. Indeed to escape from the 'Malthusian trap' commercialization alone was insufficient.

[69] Smith, 'Demographic Developments in Rural England', 54–6.

14

Low-level Urbanization: The Seigneurial Borough of Thornbury in the Middle Ages

RODNEY HILTON

HISTORIANS of the medieval town have traditionally concentrated on those large urban centres which were national or regional capitals, cathedral towns, or focal points of long distance trade in high price or scarce commodities. Ruled by mercantile oligarchies, enjoying specific legal privileges and autonomy which freed them from domination by feudal powers and with production organized within the institutional framework of craft corporations, these towns were also perceived as embodying an ethos and a culture which distanced them from the countryside, the village, and the small market town.

Large towns almost always embodied institutions and inhabitants ecclesiastical, military, administrative—which contributed considerably to their social and cultural specificity. Nevertheless, it is unwise to ignore the fundamental economic characteristics of these towns, that is, a high proportion of inhabitants who did not produce their own means of subsistence, a large number of distinct trades, and occupations and commodity production focused on the market. We must emphasize that these economic characteristics were also to be found well down the hierarchy of urban settlement, including those small market towns which can also be defined as having a population pursuing predominantly non-agricultural occupations, focused on the market.

We should go further than simply presenting this analogy between large and small towns: if we continue to concentrate on the economic function of towns, we must recognize that the market town was an essential element in the circuit of exchange which embraced all levels of urbanization. In medieval society, the principal market for the commodities provided by the merchants of the bigger towns was the feudal landed aristocracy, both lay and ecclesiastical. The main source of the cash income of this aristocracy (including the feudal monarchies) was peasant rents and customs as well as the profits of seigneurial jurisdiction (and royal tax). Peasants obtained their cash by selling their surplus on the market. They also went to the market town to buy manufactured commodities not available in the village or hamlet.

Feudal landowners were well aware of the importance of the local market as an essential step in the generation of their cash income. They were also well aware of the extra cash profits which they could gain from the market itself, primarily from tolls and customs on market transactions but also from the exercise of jurisdiction. Hence the seigneurial initiative in the foundation of market towns, endowed with legal privileges, such as freedom of status and tenure, which would tempt settlers, whether traders or craftsmen. The foundation of market *bourgs* in France by feudal lords seems to have been much earlier than in England. This was not because of English backwardness. On the eve of the Norman conquest there were eighty-seven towns which not only had markets but mints. Many of them were big towns but at least half would come into the small town category.[1] These English towns were under royal, not seigneurial, control.

The earliest evidence for seigneurial market-town foundations in France goes back, especially in the western regions, to the eleventh century, if not before. According to L. Musset, some 140 *bourgs* were founded in Normandy between the eleventh and the thirteenth centuries. More than half were purely rural, offering advantages which would tempt settlers who would be expected to extend the cultivated area. But the rest had markets and would become market towns. R. Latouche investigated similar foundations in the county of Maine, fewer in number but with documentation indicating the reasons for foundation—for example the gift by the lord of Château du Loire to the abbey of Marmoutier of two *bourgs* in Maine (St Sauveur and St Guingabois). The inhabitants of these *bourgs* were to have freedom of trade and the abbey was to have the toll revenue of the markets and fairs. H. Bourde de la Rogerie has shown that in Brittany fifty-seven new *bourgs* were founded in the tenth and eleventh centuries, characterized by the presence of organized grain markets. Donges was a good example of such a *bourg*, it was given by the viscount Frioul to the monks of Donges, who were to receive all market tolls except those on Wednesday, which went to the viscount, with whom they also shared the profits of the fairs.[2] Western France was not the only part of the

---

[1] R. Hodges, *Dark Age Economics: The Origins of Towns and Trade, AD 600–1000* (London, 1982), 167. This estimate is based on D. Hill, 'Trends in the development of towns during the reign of Ethelred II' in D. Hill (ed.), *Ethelred the Unready* (British Arch. Rep. 59 Oxford, 1978), 213–26.

[2] L. Musset, 'Peuplement en bourgages et bourgs ruraux en Normandie, X^e–XIIIe siècles', *Cahiers de Civilisation Médiévale* 9 (1966), 177–205; R. Latouche, 'Un aspect de la vie rurale dans le Maine aux XIe et XIIe siècles: l'établissement des bourgs', *Moyen Age*, 47 (1937), 45–64; H. Bourde de la Rogerie, 'Les Fondations de villes et de bourgs en Bretagne du XIIe

country which saw this proliferation of small market towns. They are to be found from Flanders to Provence. Some have left significant physical remains. The *bastides* or fortified small towns of Périgord, Gascony, and Languedoc are sometimes dismissed as mere fortified villages (or *bourgs ruraux*). But, as students of the Anglo-Saxon fortified *burgs* will know, fortification and the location of markets went together. The street plans of surviving *bastides*—such as Monpazier (Dordogne)—indicate clearly that the focal point of the town was the market place.[3]

The foundations of boroughs by feudal lords in England date from the twelfth century onwards. They were only part of the dense network of markets founded mainly in the twelfth and thirteenth centuries. Many markets were established (or legitimated) in villages as the result of the purchase of a market charter by the lord from the king, who claimed regalian right over markets. Leaving aside these sometimes ephemeral village markets, by the beginning of the fourteenth century there may have been nearly 400 market boroughs throughout England. Institutionally, they were much more standardized than those in France, given the absence in England of independent duchies and counties, quite apart from the smaller size of Plantagenet England. They were often given the borough privileges of larger royal towns, but the borough court was presided over by the lord's steward and the profits of the market and of jurisdiction went to the lord as well as the rents from the burgage tenements.

The new seigneurial boroughs were an integral part of the estate of the founding lord. The survival of the documentation of these estates has been of great benefit to the historians of agrarian England, because of the rich detail of manorial surveys, account rolls, and court records. The internal economy of the seigneurial borough, because of its relatively free status, is not documented as well as that of the manor. Nevertheless, the surviving borough court rolls, which are procedurally quite similar to the manorial rolls, give an unusual insight into small town life, even when, as in the case of Thornbury, there are more than a few gaps. The borough court records of Halesowen are probably the most complete of any in England and, as I have tried to show elsewhere, much can be deduced from them about artisans, hucksters, and chapmen which can hardly be found in the records of the bigger towns which were independent of

au XIIIe siècle', *Mémoires de la Société d'Histoire et d'Archéologie de Bretagne*, 11 (1928), 69–106. See also, R. H. Hilton, *English and French Towns in Feudal Society* (Cambridge, 1992), 25–52.

[3] A. Higounet-Nadal (ed.), *Histoire du Périgord* (Bordeaux, 1978), plate 7.

seigneurial jurisdiction.[4] In spite of the relative deficiency of the Thornbury records, I hope that they may throw light on this lower level of the urbanization of medieval England, the small market town.

So how and when did the borough of Thornbury emerge? Richard de Clare, earl of Gloucester (1243–62), who was the lord of the Severn valley manor of Thornbury, invited all and sundry to come there to make a borough community in the following terms:

> To all persons seeing or hearing these letters, Richard de Clare Earl of Gloucester and Hertford, gives greetings. May you all know that we have granted to all those who will come to Thornbury and will take the burgages from us, all the liberties and free customs which our burgesses of Tewkesbury had in the days of the earls who were my ancestors . . .[5]

As Finberg notes, this was one of a number of small borough foundations in Gloucestershire, and indeed one among a great number in England and Europe as a whole.[6] Most of these boroughs were formed within the territorial framework of a rural manor, as was the case with Tewkesbury, for example, or Northleach, which was founded by the Benedictine Abbey of St Peter's, Gloucester. This manorial framework was still in evidence at Thornbury in 1322, when a survey was made of the estates of one of the rebels (contrariants) against Edward II, Hugh of Audley the younger, the husband of one of the three sisters of Gilbert de Clare who was killed at Bannockburn.[7]

The manor[8] may have been affected by the great famine of 1315–17, but in 1322 it was still a populous agrarian unit, consisting of free and customary tenants and a demesne of the traditional type. The demesne, apart from the manor house and the gardens, consisted of 250 acres of arable, 55 acres of meadow, 24 acres of pasture, with a 200-acre park at Morlewood and another 40 acres available for pasture in an enclosed woodland called *Filnoyere*. The manor house was on the site of the early

---

[4] Hilton, 'Small Town Society', 53–78.

[5] A charter in Gloucestershire Records Office cited by H. P. R. Finberg in 'The Genesis of the Gloucestershire Towns', in Finberg (ed.), *Gloucestershire Studies* (Leicester 1957), 66 n. 2.

[6] Ibid.

[7] He is said, in the survey (PRO E142/24) to have half, not one third of the manor, though in fact a closer study of the survey suggests that it was one half of the manorial *buildings* which was referred to. The survey itself seems to be of the whole manor and borough.

[8] The manor has been studied, on the basis of the manorial court rolls, by Franklin, 'Thornbury in the Age of the Black Death'.

sixteenth-century castle, still standing, next to the parish church and about half a mile from the centre of the town. The total amount of land under cultivation was about 1,200 acres, there were fifteen free tenures and eighty-one customary holdings. Most of the land, about 890–900 acres, was contained within the framework of the traditional yardland, multiples or fractions thereof. The rest consisted of 'purprestures'— assart lands perhaps—and smallholdings of various sizes, but mostly 5 acres or less. It is, of course, a matter of considerable interest, indeed of crucial importance, to discover to what extent the borough community was distinct, as a manufacturing and trading entity, from the manorial community. The 1322 survey helps us towards an understanding of this problem, though it can only be solved by a comparison of the borough and manor records over a longer period of time.

Thornbury may not have been as entirely new as a trading place as the charter might suggest. It was not given any urban status in *Domesday Book* (1086), but it was one of four places in Gloucestershire—other than the boroughs—where there was a market, the others being Berkeley, Tewkesbury, and Cirencester. The name itself may go back to the ninth century, the termination to the word *Thornbyrig* implying a fortified place. As we know from the burghal hidage, not to speak of European examples, forts were often important pre-urban nuclei, or already towns.[9] The Tewkesbury liberties which were given to the newly settled Thornbury burgesses had been established, so it would seem, in the twelfth century, the ancestors of the Clares being named in the 1314 confirmation of Gilbert de Clare as Earls Robert (d.1147) and William (1147–83).[10] The standard burgage rent of 12*d.* a year, attributed to the example of the Norman borough of Breteuil, is found both at Tewkesbury (in the Clare charter) and at Thornbury (in the 1322 survey). It should be mentioned, however, that the view that the Norman example was followed in English borough foundations has been queried, and, instead, English influence on Normandy after 1066 is suggested.[11]

The use of the Tewkesbury liberties by the Thornbury burgesses seems to be confirmed, with some modifications, in the records of the

---

[9] See H. R. Loyn, 'Towns in late Anglo-Saxon England: The Evidence and Some Possible Lines of Enquiry' in P. Clemoes and K. Hughes (eds.), *England before the Conquest* (Cambridge, 1971), 115–28.

[10] See *Calendar of Charter Rolls, 1327–41*, 424 for Edward II's confirmation in 1337 of the 1314 confirmation by Gilbert de Clare.

[11] J. Boussard, 'Hypothèses sur la formation des bourgs et des communes en Normandie', *Annales de Normandie*, 8 (1958), 128–46.

borough court.[12] They had freedom of alienation of their burgages, though the charter's grant that this should be without fine seems to have been ignored. It is clear that the exemption given in the charter from tallage, merchet, heriot, relief, and toll on the sales of chattels was retained, so burgesses had full freedom of trade. They could devise their property by testament. There are, however, no examples in the record of the situation envisaged in the charter whereby impoverished burgesses could, if refused appropriate food and clothing by their heirs, sell their burgages freely. It is clear, too, that the only restrictions on the free manufacture and sale of bread and ale was conformity with the royal regulations in the assize of bread and ale, though here, as elsewhere, one suspects that amercements under the assize may have been in fact, little more than licence fees, profitable to the lord. Disputes concerning burgage tenements were justiciable only in the borough courts, held three weekly. The jurisdiction of the assize of bread and ale, which by the charter was to be administered yearly at the Hocktide law day, was in practice exercised much more frequently. The burgesses were quit of toll and custom in all of the earl's lands, including Thornbury market itself. On the other hand, non-burgesses 'strangers'—were heavily restricted, especially in the purchase of grain. They could not buy at all between 1 August and 1 November, and after 1 November only by permission of the borough bailiffs and on payment of a duty. This was a typical medieval urban regulation, aimed at keeping down the price of corn in the borough. In general, there was a suspicion of outsiders, who could only be received into the liberty of the borough with the agreement of the borough community. The community of burgesses also controlled the election of officials each year. According to the Tewkesbury charter, these were the bailiffs and the cachpols (rent and toll collectors). In practice, the officials at Thornbury were elected under the general title of 'bailiffs—(two) reeves, (three) *cachpols* or *servientes* (sergeants), and (two) aletasters. It is clear from the proceedings that the courts operated under the watchful eye of the earl's steward who saw to it that the lord's interests and dignity were not infringed.

The various *inquisitiones post mortem* into the estates of the earls of Gloucester (1296, 1307, and 1314) give information which is more or less consistent between them, but does not fit well with the other

---

[12] The Thornbury borough court rolls are in the StRO D641/1/4E/1–9, a broken series from 1324 to 1557. Those surviving used for this article are from the following years: 1324–5, 1330, 1339–40, 1343–6, 1351–2, 1359–60, 1362–6. Not all of these record all sessions in the years listed.

documentation.[13] The inquisitions give total borough rentals of between £6 6s. 0d. and £6 10s. 0d. The figures for profits from tolls, courts, and prise of ale are considerably greater in 1314 than earlier (about £5 as compared with £2 10s. 0d.) but the stated number of burgesses does not differ greatly—sixty burgesses holding 100 burgages in 1307 and sixty burgesses holding 119 burgages in 1314. The implication of this dispro-portion between burgesses and burgages is, of course, that there must have been an uneven distribution of burgages between burgesses, that some burgesses held more than one burgage and that there must have been a certain amount of subtenancy, it is also possible that some of the burgage plots were vacant.

These figures are difficult to reconcile with the contrariants' survey of 1322. The names and holdings of the burgage tenants are given, eighty-one persons in all, of whom twelve were women, paying a total rent of about 80s. Between them they held 74⅚ burgages, very unevenly distrib-uted, ranging from 5 burgages held by Nicholas Paty, to 8 tenants, each of whom held only one-quarter of a burgage each. The standard rent was 12d. per burgage. The largest group according to size of holding con-sisted of thirty tenants each with a half-burgage. Twenty held single burgages and sixteen held between 1¼ and 2½ burgages. The implication is that between the creation of the burgage layout and 1322 there must have been a great deal of buying and selling and division between heirs. There are no indications in the 1322 survey of subtenancies. Not all were built upon. In a trespass plea of 1324, it is shown that a croft, sown with grain, contained 1½ burgages. There are no later references to burgages being cultivated.

There is an almost contemporary tax return, the subsidy of 1327 for which the taxpayers' capacity was based on their possession of moveable goods.[14] The subsidy return does not distinguish between Thornbury borough and Thornbury manor. Here we have very little coincidence between burgage holdings and taxable wealth. Nicholas Paty, the holder of 5 burgages, does not appear in the 1327 tax list, but the next biggest tenant, Thomas of Froggeford, with 22 burgages, was taxed at 6½d., thirty-sixth in a ranking order of 37 taxpayers. We later find, from the court rolls, that Thomas (or a namesake) was alienating property, a half-burgage in 1340 and another half-burgage in 1345. The highest subsidy payer, Isolda Mareschal (4s. 6½d.) does not appear as a tenant in 1322,

[13] *IPMs for Gloucestershire, 1236–1358*, iv. 182; v. 85–8.
[14] *Gloucestershire Subsidy Roll 1327*, 44–5.

either of manor or borough. Nor does the next highest payer, John Longe (4*s*. 3*d*.), though, according to the court record he was litigating, in 1339, about a fraction of a burgage. Nicholas le Longe, possibly his relative, was the tenant of two burgages in the 1322 survey and was also in the tax list, seventeenth in ranking order and paying 13*d*.

More than half of the burgage tenants in the 1322 survey do not appear at all in the 1327 subsidy return, in fact only thirteen names are common to both. Nor can this discrepancy be explained by checking with the manorial tenants in the 1322 survey, only four of whom appear in the tax list. Does this mean that in reality there was little correlation between moveable and immovable wealth? It may be that the rich were in a position to underestimate their taxable wealth. This might result in some taxpayers being further down the ranking order than they deserved, but is it likely that it would have produced the inconsistencies which we have observed? The failure of the two lists to overlap other than marginally could also be attributed to the instability of surnames. One person could have two surnames, or more, one on the list of manorial or burgage tenants in 1322, another on the tax list. Could Isolda Mareschal, the rich subsidy payer, be the same person as Isolda of Froggeford, tenant of 2½ burgages in 1322? Isolda of Froggeford does not subsequently appear in the court rolls, which begin in 1324 and Isolda Mareschal only once, in 1339. On the other hand, surnames in both lists are found in subsequent court-roll records, 90 per cent of the names in the tax return and 86 per cent of those in the 1322 survey. There is also quite a high proportion of persons who reappear in the court rolls with not merely the same surname but the same forename as well—31 in the tax return and 47 in the 1322 survey. This does not mean that they were the same individuals, for medieval people tended to be rather conservative about forenames, which ran in families. The direct evidence for the use by one person of two surnames is, however, rather scanty. The case of Elena or Ela atte Welle, who used her family surname long after her marriage to Richard Fayrher, is unique in the Thornbury records.

To what extent can this early evidence give us some notion of the size of Thornbury before the Black Death? The eighty-one tenants of burgages in 1322 were not necessarily heads of households. Twelve were women and some of these might have been widows living alone. Twelve names do not reappear at all after 1322. Anybody living under seigneurial jurisdiction would have great difficulty in not being caught by it—and recorded—even if only to buy exemption from attendance at court. All the same, there might have been non-resident tenants. It must also be borne in mind that there were some people holding several burgages. There may, therefore, have been quite a few borough families living on burgages as subtenants and this could account for names appearing on the tax list but not in the 1322 survey, it is also true that some burgages may not have been built upon, but there is only the one case already mentioned of burgages being sown as arable land. Nevertheless, bearing in mind the scope for subtenancy, we can estimate the number of households in Thornbury borough at more than the number of tenants in the 1322 survey, though perhaps less than the total of ninety-nine persons with separate surnames who were either tenants or taxpayers from borough and manor in 1327. If we use a multiplier of five persons per household— a rather modest figure—we would have a borough population of between 400 and 500. Another way of calculating numbers would be to estimate those entering the court records over a sufficiently short period of time, so as to minimize drastic uncertainties due to a possible imbalance between the numbers of deaths and the numbers of newly matured adults playing their full part in court business.

Although the Thornbury borough court rolls survive until the sixteenth century, they are by no means a continuous series. For the purposes of this analysis we are only concerned with those up to 1366. During the 44-year period (including the 1322 survey) the court rolls of the borough exist for only 16 years, of which there are complete annual records for only 5 years.[15] In principle (though not always in practice) the courts were held every three weeks. All told we have records during this period of 147 court sessions. The reports of many of these sessions are very detailed, especially of the biennial courts leet, where as many as 100 persons might be separately named. The same individuals reoccur in so many court sessions during their entire lives that in spite of the gaps in the records it is probable that a high proportion of the adult population, possibly also some children, were recorded.

Between 1324 and 1346 there were 375 people recorded in the court rolls. Of these, 215 do not reappear after September 1340. Between 1340 and 1346, 130 new names appear. We cannot control these figures, since we have no records of deaths but let us suppose that in the period 1340 to 1346 some 290 adults were active, that is, regularly appearing in the court records. The proportion of women active according to the court rolls varies between 16 per cent (1324–40) and 25 per cent in the much fuller records for 1340–6. If we assume that about a quarter of the 290 recorded active adults between 1324 and 1346 were women, this means

---

[15] 1344, 1345, 1363, 1364, 1365.

that nearly 220 men were active. If the numbers in each sex were roughly equivalent, we would then have a population of about 440 active adults. Not enough is known about the age structure of the population before the Black Death, though one-third below the age of 14 has been a conventional assumption for the late fourteenth century. If we take this figure we therefore have a Thornbury population of nearly 600. The calculations are risky. Quite apart from the danger of assuming that the number of names equals the number of persons, it is not certain that adults only enter the record. The proportion of non-residents and manorial tenants entering the record is also unknowable. On the other hand, figures derived from the application of a multiplier to the number of tenant or tax-paying households also has the disadvantage that poor subtenant households, servants, apprentices and, in general, non-established members of the urban population would be omitted, so 600 is a possible upper limit. Thornbury borough was no mere village. The manorial population, to a certain extent, may have been dispersed within what is now the large parish of Thornbury. Insofar as it was nucleated, some were possibly grouped around the church and the manor house.

One of the demographic characteristics of growing towns is that their population expands more as a result of immigration than of natural increase. We have few reliable sources for Thornbury to estimate net immigration. The careful analysis of court rolls could give some answers, though once again the instability of surnames is a barrier. New names furthermore can represent upward social mobility, as obscure and unrecorded people acquire status and become court suitors, buy property, get robbed, or start brewing ale. A rough indicator is sometimes used, namely that of surnames which have an origin in a place outside the town. What do our early lists of names for Thornbury borough indicate to us? On the whole, there is a marked shortage of surnames which indicate rural immigration. In the 1322 survey, out of 81 people with 69 surnames, only 8 suggest for certain an out-of-town origin. Five of these place-name surnames are possibly from Gloucestershire (Pennok = Pinnock; Shortwood; Northeswell = Upper Swell; Westbury; Clifton.) One (Barnham) is of uncertain origin and two are ethnic descriptions which may genuinely indicate foreign ancestry (French and Walsh). 'French' might be a nickname, but there is enough evidence of Welsh migration to this part of the country to suggest that the Walsh family were indeed originally from Wales. Otherwise the surnames are nicknames (William Pyg); occupational names (Pistor or Baker); derived from local features (atte Broke); or uncertain (Bartelot).

A similar pattern is to be found in the 1327 tax return. Out of 37 names we have, as in 1322, a Walsh and a French. Apart from the same Nicholas Pennok, who appeared in 1322, there is only one other surname derived from a place of origin away from Thornbury—Slimbridge, a dozen miles or so up the estuary. Otherwise the surnames are nicknames, occupational designations or local feature names. There is a similar low proportion of surnames indicating an origin outside the immediate vicinity throughout the court records, both before and after the Black Death (to 1366). This is particularly noticeable with regard to the leading, active families. We define these families by various criteria, mainly the frequency of involvement in court business and the number of family members mentioned. Of between 80 and 90 such families, only seven have surnames indicating outside recruitment.

It must be emphasized that the conclusions from the absence of place-name surnames must be largely impressionistic. We have no firm data about immigration to and from medieval Thornbury, though a meticulous study of surviving manorial records of surrounding villages might make our impressions a little firmer. There is, in fact, some indication from the sources already described that these nearby villages were recruiting grounds for the borough population. The 1327 tax return, of course, lists taxpayers from villages. Owing to the normal rules about exemption for those with chattels of low valuation, those paying tax would be the more substantial. If we confine ourselves to the villages of Thornbury Hundred alone, we find that 28 surnames of taxpayers in 14 villages are found in the borough and that 15 of the 28 persons have the forenames also of the borough taxpayers. Some of the surnames are so common that one cannot draw any conclusions, names such as Cook (Cok), Freeman, Hughes, Marsh, atte Welle, and Whitefield. Others are more unusual, such as Amyot, Bartelot, Devenyssh, Edwy, Gopeshulle, Isaac, Mildemay, Pynchon, Seisil, and Rolves—at any rate to suggest that a family or an individual could move from a village to the borough without assuming, or being given, the name of their original village, once in town. People in the borough probably already knew the local villagers well enough, and if they did not, the lord's officials would.

We also have the possibility of movement, not from the surrounding villages, but from the agricultural part of Thornbury itself. Sixteen family names in 1322 are common to both manor and borough and 12 burgesses also held manorial land, a point to which we will return. Then, in the court rolls of the borough between 1324 and 1366, we find another 21 surnames shared by 28 people which were present in the manor in 1322. Some of these families stayed on the manor as cultivators. Walter

Pyl or Ful had 16½ acres in 1322 and was unable to pursue a plea of debt in the borough court in 1340 because he was a serf (*nativus*). Two others of the same name had agricultural holdings, but Walter's failed debt plea is the only occasion of the family appearing in the borough records. Nine other manorial families, some of whose members appear in the borough court records, probably remained cultivators—their appearances in hue and cry or debt cases being so few as to suggest that they never entered the borough community. On the other hand, ten persons bearing the names of families which were manorial peasants in 1322, appear quite clearly as burgesses in later borough court rolls. In six cases we find the record of their purchase of urban property or the liberty of the borough or both. But out of a manorial population of some 80 families, over a period of 43 years (the latest case, a purchase of liberty in 1365), the influx is not great. These examples of the purchase of urban property and liberty of the borough should only be taken as illustrative. There are too many gaps in the court rolls to use them quantitively. The rather small overlap of surnames is more significant given the probability that, in spite of gaps, we have recorded the names of most of the burgess families between 1322 and 1366.

What can we say about the families which constituted the population of Thornbury in the fourteenth century? Over the period surveyed here, 1322 to 1366, 1,146 names are recorded. As we have already emphasized, these do not necessarily represent so many people. Surnames may not have been as fluid as some historians have suggested, but, nevertheless, the same person could be given more than one surname, quite apart from the change in a woman's (sometimes even a man's) surname at marriage. This could result in our overestimating the number of persons. The possibilities of underestimation are even greater. Sons and daughters were often named after grandparents, less often after parents. Consequently, when we find a John Smith occurring in the record over a period of 40 years, this could be one or several persons. And, unfortunately, in the borough court, as distinct from the rural manor court, we do not have a report of the death of each tenant. Burgages were freely alienable, freely devisable and heirs were not liable for the payment of heriot or relief. The lord of the borough was only interested, therefore, in the entry fine paid by someone who acquired a burgage by purchase, not by inheritance. We only hear of a person's death on such occasions as litigation between executors and creditors.

As well as being unable to distinguish generations bearing the same forename and surname, except by guesswork or lucky accident, we are frequently unable to allot people with the same surname to their actual nuclear family, because, of course, sons did marry, remain in Thornbury and set up for themselves. The only way of knowing from the court-roll evidence about collateral branches of families is when we have references to the spouses of married contemporaries—assuming, that is, that nuclear families set up separate households. In this respect the survey of 1322 is useful, though even here there are pitfalls, the main one being that tenants of burgages were not necessarily resident. There are enough examples in the court rolls to indicate that main burgage tenants did sublet from time to time. But even bearing this in mind, there are sufficient indications in the survey of the existence of collateral branches of the families continuing to bear the same surname. In other words, although there are 81 tenants of burgages in 1322, there are only 69 surnames. There are two households of the Seisil family, two Froggefords and so on. But there are four burgages held by persons with the surname 'Baker' and it would be unwise to assume that these were related. Their surname could simply reflect their occupation. The same might apply to the three burgages held by Flesshewers (butchers). The three separate burgages held by persons called 'Walsh' could be explained in terms of collateral branches of the same family, but they could have no other thing in common but a Welsh origin.

In spite of these reservations, let us see what we can deduce from the 1322 survey in connection with the subsequent evidence of the court rolls. We have already noticed the disturbing fact that there was little coincidence between taxpayers in 1327 and burgage tenants in 1322. A high proportion of the surnames in both lists reappear in the subsequent court records. As we have seen, twelve of the 1322 surnames do not appear at all after that date, not even in the tax return. Let us accept that there were, in the 1322 list, not 81, but 69 households, the burgages of the twelve persons we have just referred to being either sublet or unoccupied, and, in the latter case, perhaps not even built upon. Of these 69 households, the family names of 19 (26 per cent) do not appear in the post-Black Death records. This might be an underestimate, because 20 households shared between them only 8 surnames. Of these families, only the name of Froggeford (two entries in 1322) disappeared completely after the Black Death, but it is possible that at least one of the families bearing the name of Baker, atte Broke, Budeles (or Reve), Chese, Flesshewere, Seisil or Walsh died out, still leaving persons with the surname after 1349. If this in fact did happen, 25 households (36 per cent) might have been eliminated by the plague.

The records of the borough court begin well before the Black Death, although those of 1324–5 and 1330 are incomplete. Nevertheless, there are quite full records for 1339, 1340, 1343, 1344, 1345, and 1346. These yield a good crop of Thornbury names, many already encountered in the 1322 survey. There were 54 surnames occurring between 1324 and 1346 which are not in the 1322 list. Of these, 10 (18.5 per cent) had disappeared by the time of the first post-Black Death records (1351), but 44 (81.5 per cent) survived and between 1351 and 1366 only three new names appear. These figures must considerably modify the impression given by the analysis of the 1322 names, which could be interpreted as suggesting an elimination, by mortality or emigration, of one-third of the families, in fact, if we add the names of 1322 to the names obtained from the 1324–46 records, that is 125, we find that 28 (22.4 per cent) names have disappeared by 1351.

It is perhaps unnecessary to emphasize that owing to the character of the records, which do not permit family reconstitution, we are dealing with names, not with families, and not, of course, with individuals, it is almost certain that more individuals would disappear than family names, so 22 per cent can be regarded simply as a minimum figure for the mid-century mortality or emigration.

What was the role of Thornbury borough in the economy of the lower Severn valley in the fourteenth century? John Leland, early in the sixteenth century, wrote 'There hathe bene good clothyng in Thornbyry but now idelnes muche reynithe there.' The court rolls may help us to understand at any rate the first part of this remark.[16]

We must remember that it was only 9 miles north of the port and borough of Bristol, the second wealthiest town in England after London in 1334. Bristol attempted to dominate its rural hinterland by discouraging the development of its textile industry and by attempting to obtain priority in the import of raw materials, especially foodstuffs.[17] But although its leading merchants were wealthy and powerful, their major preoccupation was with shipping and foreign trade. Their rural connections seem to have been with Somerset and the south and south-west rather than with Gloucestershire, though, as far as the victualling of the town was concerned, they relied on suppliers quite far afield who dispatched grain direct to Bristol down the Severn. We must not exaggerate

---

[16] *The Itinerary of John Leland*, v. 99.

[17] The protectionist attitudes of Bristol's rulers are well illustrated in the series of ordinances printed in *Little Red Book of Bristol*, ed. F. B. Bickley, ii (2 vols., Bristol, 1900), 32–8, 217–23.

Bristol's influence even as far as 12 miles from the Frome; the references
to Bristol and to Bristol persons are very rare in our documents.

One way to consider Thornbury's economic role would be to establish
its occupational structure. If we had a return for the poll tax of 1381
comparable to those of Cirencester, Stow-on-the-Wold, or Chipping
Campden,[18] we would be in a strong position to initiate our analysis of
more elusive material. We have no such document, so we have to rely on
the indirect evidence of the court rolls. The evidence includes references
to actual occupations as well as the less certain evidence of occupational
surnames. We can discern about 35 separate occupations, without being
able to tell in what proportions they were distributed among the population. By far the most frequently occurring occupation was that of brewer,
known to us because of prosecutions under the assize of ale. For similar
reasons, that is prosecutions aiming at the quality control of foodstuffs,
we know the names of many bakers, butchers, fishmongers, and more
casual retailers of various sorts of victuals. Brewing was part of the household economy, but those brewers who were prosecuted under the assize
of ale, as well as the processors of other foodstuffs, were by definition
offering their products for sale. Some were more active than others. Of
the 51 persons prosecuted and paying amercements (or licence fees if this
is an acceptable interpretation) only 18 were frequent brewers and ale-
sellers. These were often innkeepers who also baked bread, for which
they could be subject to amercement under the assize of bread.

There was a range of manufacturing craftsmen, including building
workers. Those working in wood were carpenters, coopers, and turners;
in leather, skinners, tanners, shoemakers, glovers, whitawyers, sheathers,
and saddlers; in metal, hoopers, farriers, smiths, tinkers, and a jeweller; in
clay, tilers and crockers (potters); and in textiles, chaloners, dyers, tailors,
and weavers; there were merchants or chapmen, some specializing, such
as drapers. Other trades include 'rymers' (a family name), a painter, a
schoolmaster, millers, shepherds, and stone quarriers. It is clear, too, that
there was dealing in grain, malt, and livestock, though it is not certain
that the dealers were specialists in the commodities.

The question naturally arises, to what extent was this small town
functionally distinct from the agricultural settlements which surrounded
it. It has been mentioned that there was a burgage tenement in 1324
which was in fact a croft sown with grain. What evidence is there of

[18] For a discussion of small towns as part of peasant society, see Hilton, *English Peasantry*, 76–94.

agricultural activities by burgesses, activities which could well be combined with non-agricultural occupations?

As we have already seen, a number of persons holding burgages in 1322 were also tenants of agricultural land in the manor. They may have been working the land; it might be family land which because of their burgess occupation they sublet; it might have been an investment. At the moment we do not know. But let us see what sort of land it was. First, we must stress that no burgage tenants held freehold land in the manor. Two burgesses (Walter of Sandford and Hugh Nicholas) held 'purprestures'. Walter of Sandford, member of a family which was mainly active in the pre-Black Death period, had 16 acres of arable and 5 acres of meadow. He hardly appears at all in the borough records and it may be that his interests were mainly agricultural. Another Sandford, John, was active between 1327 and 1346 and may have represented the family's urban interests. Hugh Nicholas, tenant of half a burgage in the borough, only held a quarter of an acre of purpresture. He does not appear much in the borough records but in 1340 he was sueing for a debt owed to him for cloth which he had sold. He hardly appears to be a farmer-burgess.

We next have a group of ten burgesses holding customary land. Richard le Cok was tenant of a half-burgage in the town and of half a virgate, a cottage and four acres in the manor. These are his only two appearances in the record and others of the same name make only a few appearances at this period. John Fox, who held two burgages also had a half-virgate in the manor. He was virtually an absentee, his only appearances in the court record being to seek permission for absence, last appearing in October 1345, a year after his namesake Isabel (a daughter?) had sold his Thornbury holdings. The remaining eight burgesses holding manorial property were all, except one, tenants of smallholdings, though these fall into two categories. First, there are four quarter-virgates, three being of 6 and one of 8 acres, which owed customary services and obligations as well as money rent. Three were smallholdings of varying sizes, from a cottage to 6 acres, which paid money rent only. One is bigger—12 acres, but also only paying money rent.

What sort of people were they? Gilbert Devenyssh, who held half a burgage and 3 acres of customary land, only appears in 1322. A possible relative, William, makes one appearance in the borough court, by proxy, when he was essoined in 1344. Other members of the family do not appear until the 1360s. John, the most important, being a tapster or retail seller of ale. Thomas Elyot, tenant of 1½ burgages, also had a customary quarter-virgate. He enters the court record twice, once to be essoined, once to be amerced for putting dung on the highway. As in the case of Devenyssh, the Elyot family does not become active until the 1360s. Nicholas Pinnok, the elder, another tenant of a quarter-virgate, had 1½ burgages, one of which he sold in 1330. He does not appear at all in court activities, but his son Thomas was very active between 1340 and 1366 as a pledge and borough official. Walter Baker (Pistor) had a burgage, and a quarter-virgate for money rent only. His son John is down as a manorial tenant owing rent and services, but the amount of land has been omitted from the survey. It was probably a quarter-virgate. There was also a John Baker who had two burgages, but there is some doubt as to whether he was the son of Walter. This John really was a baker by trade but Walter seems to have been frequently away from town, judging by the number of essoins and he never seems to have baked. John Cockesfot, who had 8 acres of customary land and owed services as well as money rent, had a burgage in the town but does not appear in the records other than the 1322 survey. The family is otherwise represented by one other person who appears twice between 1345 and 1346 and then disappears. Thomas Tyrri, tenant of a cottage, was also tenant of two burgages, but neither he nor anyone else of the same name appear in the record other than in 1322. Finally, Margery of Clivedon, tenant of 12 acres, customary but for money rent, held 2¼ quarter-burgages and only appears in the 1322 survey.

From this rather tedious listing, it will be seen that on the occasions when we can directly compare burgesses and manorial tenants, the overlap is small and the persons concerned of minimal significance in the borough community. What, then can we see concerning the agricultural activity of burgesses from the subsequent borough court rolls? Many of them owned livestock. Horses are prominent, though whether they were mainly draught animals or for riding is not clear. A saddle and a bridle were attached in 1364 in a debt plea but some cases rather suggest working animals. There may, perhaps, have been a horse market in Thornbury. This is suggested by litigation in the borough court in 1364 between two outsiders. The rector of Iron Acton successfully sued a man from Bishops Stoke for breach of contract in a horse sale. An earlier case (1360) reinforces the suggestion. William Frere, a resident in Thornbury since at least 1351, a frequent brewer, a dealer in grain and possibly in livestock, sued an outsider, John Selcote, for selling him a horse with a guarantee of its fitness for work which turned out to be worthless. But the possession of a horse whether to ride or to pull a cart is no necessary indication of agricultural activity.

More relevant perhaps are the references to sheep. Some of the references involve disputes between town butchers, such as Walter Hughes, John Flesshewer, Walter Grimgard, and others who may have been dealing in sheep for meat. But Thomas Colewell was accused by William the Milleward of keeping sheep in his park and brought a counter plea that William had put his pigs onto Thomas's barley. Thomas Colewell appears quite frequently in the rolls on minor matters and may have been to some extent a grasier and a cultivator. It is worth noting that some of his unexplained conflicts in court were with butchering families so he too may have been fattening animals for meat. Pigs appear from time to time, but these were as much urban as rural animals, kept by householders for eating.

Pleas which describe animals trespassing on the plaintiff's grain or grass are often good indicators not only of livestock holdings but also of the cultivation of various types of grain. But while not absent such pleas are not common in the borough court rolls. Much more prominent are quarrels about people not paying for grain bought or retaining grain for which contracts of sale had been made. As one would expect, the Thornbury market was, among other things, a grain market, mainly for wheat and barley, sometimes for malt, and occasionally for drage and pulse. No doubt there were local dealers but the main source of supply would be through regional cornmongers or country people bringing their own grain to market.

As we have seen, burgesses of the town were quit of the payment of toll and custom within the earl of Gloucester's domain, an exemption which would be of most importance in Thornbury itself. The lord of the town still regarded the market as a profitable right. Nevertheless, he had to admit a restriction on market profit in the interest of the burgesses, when he prevented outsiders from buying or storing grain between August and November, and during the rest of the year allowed such purchases only under licence and toll. Breaches of these regulations were heavily punished. Richard Blount, not a burgess of the town, was ordered through his pledge, at a court at the beginning of April, 1344 to come to the next court to satisfy the lord concerning toll on four horseloads of grain, that is, one quarter of barley and one quarter of beans. The grain had been declared forfeit to the lord and Blount also had to make satisfaction for its price. The phraseology used when Blount appeared at the next court on 16 May suggests that he had carried away the grain and, notionally, the due toll as well. He confessed that he had knowingly done this. He was therefore sentenced to pay a penalty known as Towyte at 5s. per load.

The forfeited grain was valued at half a mark (6*s*. 8*d*.). He was to pay 13*s*. 4*d*. cash down and was to be liable for another 13*s*. 4*d*. This was respited, by special grace, provided he behaved well to the lord and the lord's people (presumably the burgesses). This incident shows how seriously the lord's officials regarded the maintenance of toll rights, though in this case the interests of the burgesses, who wanted to restrict outsiders' access to the grain market, were also involved. In a later case, in April 1360, a certain Nicholas Feny was presented for not answering the lord for the concealment of toll on various merchandise made within the liberty. If these were manufactured goods put on Thornbury market, it might not be in the interest of the burgesses as purchasers, to support the lord in raising their price, though manufacturing artisans in the borough might wish to exclude them. Nothing seems to have come of the case between April and September 1360, but a gap in the series between October 1360 and October 1362 may conceal a delayed outcome.

The considerable presence of food-processors, like bakers and brewers; indications from time to time of the purchase of building materials, timber in particular; a grain and stock market; and a range of individuals engaged in manufacturing crafts in wood, leather, and metal, all these are familiar aspects of the small market town. It may be that there was some specialization in the manufacture of woollen textiles. The evidence from the court rolls is only sporadic and indirect, it consists partly of indications of the possession by individuals of woollen yarn and woven cloth in substantial enough quantities to suggest that there was more than would be possessed simply for the internal economy of the household. These are mainly attachments to enforce attendance at court. Thus in November 1344 Walter Dewyas was sued for trespass by William Colles and was attached by two ells of cloth. Dewyas was so recalcitrant, refusing to turn up in court, that the cloth was given to the plaintiff, probably in lieu of damages. We are not told what the trespass was but there was enough ill-feeling for them to end up fighting and shedding each other's blood. In 1345, Isabel Dene, debtor of Thomas atte More, was attached by three pieces of cloth.

And in 1346, Elena Moureye was attached by one piece of cloth in a plea of broken covenant against Philip le Longe. In 1360, Thomas Ferour was attached in a debt plea by Roger Cronk by 14 yards of woollen cloth, in a debt case in 1364 between John Murymouth and Geoffrey Walsh, 5 yards of white—that is, unfinished—cloth was at issue, though owing to a defect in the manuscript it is not possible to say whether the debt arose from the sale of the cloth or whether the cloth was a distraint to bring the defendant to court. Other attachments by unspecified quantities of woollen cloth are found in other court cases at this time. Similar attachments of woollen yarn are found, as, for example Alice Dyer (significant name?) attached in a debt case against John Edward in 1359 by 5 lbs. of wool and John Lupeyate by 7 lbs. of woollen thread in a debt case against John Hopere.

In many cases, wool or wool yarn are mentioned other than as attachments. In 1345 two women, the wife of William atte Ford and Mathilda atte Corner were presented for buying stolen wool. There were two accusations in 1345 against persons accused of detaining wool yarn and wool and in the following year Richard Muleward, Mathilda atte Corner, and Mathilda Gopeshull were in trouble for receiving stolen wool. In these cases we are given no indication about the purposes of possession but at least one can assume that many households went in for spinning wool, while in other cases the woollen yarn might have been in the household for weaving. The only case indicating the processes of the textile industry is in 1351, John Hawe sued Henry Stafford for detention of chattels. The case was solved by an agreement between the two parties by which John Hawes agreed to dye Stafford's woollen cloth well, competently, and speedily by the following Saturday and wool yarn during the subsequent month. This case clearly indicates the presence of a dyeing industry but the gap in the court records between 1346 and 1351 and between 1352 and 1359 means that we have no opportunity to test the position of either litigant within the borough community. Nevertheless the accumulation over the years of items which reveal the importance of raw wool, woollen yarn, and untailored cloth among the possessions and objects of dispute of the inhabitants of Thornbury not to mention the above reference to the dyeing of cloth and a 1344 ordinance against the washing of cloths in Portrevebrook and Carpyngswell—suggest a textile industry of some local, if not wider significance.

We must not overemphasize the Thornbury textile industry. Manufacture of cloth as well as of other commodities may have been purely for local consumption. There are few even indirect indications that manufacture had reached the organized stage found in some bigger towns. There is a curious echo of the trade exclusiveness which seems to be embodied in some town regulation. There were presentments in the 1340s of tanners for making shoes, reminding one of the rather dubious one-man-one-trade legislation for London in 1363. Trade exclusiveness of this sort is normally associated with organized guilds and an apprenticeship system to control the entry of artisan labour in a particular industry. In Thornbury there is only one reference in the period discussed to an apprentice by that name. This occurred in 1366 and unfortunately there is no indication of the occupations of the parties involved. Richard Wodecok, who was already in trouble for forcibly preventing the town bailiff from performing his duty, was impleaded by John Stevens for taking away his apprentice, William Fortheye. Wodecoc failed to clear himself by compurgation and had to pay the considerable sum of 20s. damages.

References to 'servants' could, of course, conceal the specific grade of 'apprentice' and after the Black Death there are in the Thornbury records, as elsewhere, references to the enticement of servants. There are also conflicts about terms of service and wages which are not very revealing. A case in 1345 between two rather obscure individuals concerned a contract of service. Henry Sobres accused Robert Pultegod of breaking an agreement to serve him in his craft (*de arta sua*) for a year, whereas the accused said he had only contracted for a limited term and after the end of that term would only serve at pleasure. Pultegod lost the case. Sobres appears only once in the records though two other Pultegods, John and Richard, appear, Richard being sufficiently well-established to be nominated by the court as a pledge. There are unfortunately no indications of occupation, although Robert was one of those people already mentioned who had woollen yarn in their houses. If we are to take occupational surnames seriously it might be of significance that a William Correiour, that is 'tanner' sued William Soutere, that is 'shoemaker' for unpaid wages. Walter Hyndwell, a tanner, had a servant who could have been employed in the trade, though his only appearance in the record was when he was amerced for putting dead dogs into the river. Perhaps the dogs had been skinned, the skins tanned and made (illegally) into shoes, for Hyndewell was one of those tanners who was illegally practising the shoemaking trade.

It may be that the most significant, if the most enigmatic references to labour are not those frequent references to the servants, both male and female, of individual townsmen, but the frequent presentments of individuals for receiving strangers. As one might expect these occur frequently before the Black Death and afterwards not at all. The first reference is in 1339 when five people were accused of receiving Welshmen. Welsh immigrants were familiar in the west midland counties, whether as permanent settlers or as temporary workers, often coming over the border for harvest work. This may have been the case in Thornbury, for an ordinance of 1345 forbids the reception of outsiders or ill-doers in autumn. There seem, in these years, always to have been enough well-established inhabitants willing to risk receiving strangers. Sometimes, though by no means always, they were brewers and ale-house keepers and might therefore be either professional or amateur lodging-house keepers: otherwise they could be employers of migrant labour. Presumably the situation did not repeat itself after 1349, either because there was little migrant labour in the area, or—and this is more likely—because labour was so scarce that it could not be regarded as a crime to encourage those who came to offer it.

One of the ways of getting some insight into the economy of medieval towns and villages through the records of their courts is to examine the pleas of debt. These are not straightforward because debt pleas were often confused at the time with pleas of detention of chattels. Such pleas could be brought against someone who owed money for goods for which he/she had not paid. But it could also be brought in cases which were not commercial in character, such as the appropriation or borrowing of a neighbour's tools. Many debt pleas occur in the record with no details whatsoever, not even the sums of money involved. Others give the amount of money but not the origin of the debt. Cases in which sums of money only are involved could be straight cases of *A* borrowing money from *B* but there is no guarantee of this, in other words it is very difficult to build up a picture of the local money-lender, although such people undoubtedly existed. In 1345, for example, William Berton was amerced 40*d.*— quite a large sum—for usury.

In the Thornbury borough court rolls between 1324 and 1366 there are recorded 329 debt cases, very unevenly distributed chronologically because of the big gaps in the documentation. There are years in which we probably have a complete record, that is, of a court roughly every three weeks. During these years, the number of debt cases naturally varied but they could amount to more than 40. The average number of cases per court session, which we can calculate from incomplete as well as from complete rolls, vary from 0.5 in 1324 to 5.8 in 1359, but the average in this last year was pushed up by the fact that there are only four surviving session records in one of which as many as 14 cases came forward.

Only about half of the debt cases have any details beyond the names of the people involved. Most of the cases with details—78 per cent, in fact—concern cash only. The sums involved vary enormously from 2*d.* to 30*s.* and, for what it is worth, the average debt pleaded was 4*s.* 7*d.* or four times the rent of a burgage plot. Those debt cases which refer to goods bought but not paid for, though relatively few in number, nevertheless throw some light on buying and selling in the town. Foodstuffs are the most frequently mentioned commodities (nineteen cases) and of these, debts arising from purchase of grain and malt figure the most prominently. Livestock occur surprisingly infrequently, only two cases involving horses and three involving sheep. Goods connected with textiles (cloth and wool) occur seven times, and building materials (timber and tiles) three times. In view of the shortage of information, firm conclusions can hardly be drawn, but these few figures fit in with other evidence which reflects the great importance of the trade in victuals, especially ale.

What then was Thornbury? A rural market town dominated by ale-wives, butchers, and other suppliers of victuals or a centre populated by craftsmen exchanging their products for foodstuffs from the countryside, or, as Leland thought, primarily a cloth-making town? So far, we have looked at general information concerning the urban economy. It might now be worth looking more closely at the ruling families. But first of all we must decide how to define a 'ruling family' in terms which make sense in a small town of Thornbury's size.

It is not easy from the court records alone to select the leading families, especially in view of the gaps in the record. There are various obvious criteria. These include numbers of family members involved in court business, dealings in real property, employment of servants, but clearly the most significant are the exercise of judicial and political control over their fellow burgesses. The preconditions for the achievement of this control must have been the ownership of burgage property and of the liberty of the borough, the liberty being sought as the condition for privileged access to the market. Not all suitors to the borough court were anxious to take part in its proceedings. There are frequent lists of suitors who bought exemption from attendance. But there were also those who attended diligently. They are firstly found acting as pledges or guarantors for their fellow burgesses when they were amerced, charged to appear to pursue or answer suits and so on. Some historians think that pledging between court suitors was a manifestation of mutual solidarity, an indication of an elementary form of social interaction. In a manor consisting of several hamlets, pledges would, no doubt for effectiveness, be found in the locality of the person to be pledged and this might give the appearance of spontaneity in the provision of pledging; in Thornbury, where members of the community lived cheek by jowl in adjacent streets, this clearly did not apply. Friends and neighbours did not come forward to pledge those in trouble. It is clear that the pledges were appointed by the court and, in a sense became its minor officials. For example, Richard le Clerk in the 1340s is found pledging all and sundry; in the October court of 1345 he was instructed to act as pledge for six people and in other courts for three or four as well as on occasion acting as attorney. Clerk was a common surname—there were three families bearing it in the 1300s —but it is probable that in Richard's case it was a genuine description of his occupation.

Richard le Clerk gives the impression of being exclusively an official of the court between 1340 and 1346, but he never became an official of the borough community. The path to borough officialdom really began by being a juror at the view of frankpledge or a sworn member of an official inquisition. Such people were normally drawn from regular attenders who would also have done their stint of pledging. The evidence in the court rolls is not as abundant as might be expected, even given the gaps already mentioned. There are many cases where the proceedings of the view of frankpledge are given in great detail, but where the so-called twelve free jurors making the presentments are not named. We have, in fact, only six full lists of jurors, possibly because the lists remained unchanged for periods of years. Similarly, although the elections of officials are recorded in some years, sometimes at the May but more usually at the October courts, this is not always the case. Nor can this be explained by the absence of May or October court records. There are years when no note is made of official elections and this may again be due to individuals carrying on for more than one year. It is possible, then, that the gaps in the records may result in the omission of some important activities by leading families. These gaps are more likely to conceal high office, like town bailiff, than the more frequent employment as juror or enforcer of ordinances. The amount of detail on active persons, in spite of the gaps, is such that the lower level of official activity is likely to be recorded. We have already noted that there were in 1322, sixty-nine households whose family names survive beyond that date, though, owing to the duplication of surnames, we cannot, after that date, distinguish collateral branches of the same family, or indeed unrelated families bearing the same name. Therefore we will have to speak not of sixty-nine households, but of fifty-seven family groupings, bearing the same family name. Eighteen of these families produced individuals who were active in the sense defined, that is nearly a third of the whole. Only eight families produced officials, that is reeves or bailiffs (the terms seem interchangeable), constables, cachpols, or aletasters. Then there are the sixty-eight other families not possessed of burgages in 1322, who are found in the court records; eighteen of these produced active members in the widest sense—jurors, enforcers of ordinances, and so on, that is about a quarter of the whole. Only four of the families seem to have produced higher officials.

If the evidence were fuller and more conclusive, it might seem possible to distinguish the older from the newer families and to conclude that the former had more chance of taking part in the running of the town than the latter. As it is, we can only hint at this possibility; it is certainly the case that more members of the older families were municipally active (average 1.5) than of the later families (average 1.1), but this may again be a reflection of the defects of the documentation. However, whatever distinctions we can make between the earlier and the later families, it would seem, not unexpectedly, that though this small town was administered by an élite, on the whole it was not a narrow one.

Perhaps these speculations, which are both abstract and uncertain can be reinforced best by an examination of two sets of jurors and officials, one before and one after the Black Death.

On the 30 March 1330 the view of frankpledge of the borough was held and the sworn jurors were as follows: Walter Fysshepull, William Tannere, William Broccouere, William Morlewode, John le Flesshewer, Walter Marshal, William Forester, Adam Parker, John Chese, John Welsh, John Northall, and Adam Chese. In the previous October, a jury of inquisition had pronounced at an ordinary borough court on a trespass plea involving assault and battery. The members of this jury overlapped considerably with the leet jury, Fysshepull, Broccouere, Tannere, Morlewode, Flesshewer, Marshal, Parker, and Welsh being on both. In the following May, Adam Parker, John Broke, and John Baron were elected constables and Walter Seisel was appointed to summon the watch, Tannere, Morlewode, Flesshewere, Welsh, and the two Cheses were members of families who were holding burgages in 1322. The Marshal, Forester, Parker, and Fysshepull families had been active in the borough since the 1320s, though not burgage holders in 1322. The Northalls appear in the late 1330s. Only Broccouere is a bit of a mystery. He appears quite often from 1339 as a litigant, as a juror, and as an occasional brewer of ale but there are no other persons with the same family name. His last appearance in the record was in September 1346.

William Tannere, tenant of half a burgage in 1322 and taxpayer (18*d*.) in 1327, is found as a juror in 1340 and was a fairly frequent brewer of ale. One of our problems is that a William Tannere is still in the record in 1352. Was it the same man as in 1322? There seems to be some sort of a break in 1343, possibly as the result of another William Tannere coming into prominence, possibly because of a shift in the original William

Tannere's interests. At any rate, in October 1343 'he' sold his half-burgage and for the next three years was not only a frequent juryman, but seems to have gone in for butchery as an occupation, since he was frequently summoned for various offences connected with selling meat. He is last recorded in May 1352, still selling meat.

William Moreland acquired a built-up half-burgage by gift of John Morlewode in 1340. John had held this or another half-burgage in 1322 and William resold it, or another half-burgage in December 1339. He first appears as a juror in 1343 in an inquiry into a piece of disputed burgage property. From then on he was a frequent juror and pledge, until 1346. Then the name disappeared until 1359, when a William Morlewode is once again found dealing in burgage property. This could have been a Morlewode of the next generation. John le Flesshewere bore a name which occurs three times in the 1322 survey. At that time he held half a burgage. In 1324 he sold a market stall to Robert Chese and from 1329 is found frequently as a pledge and as a brewer of ale. His first official post was as cachpol in 1339 but it is not until 1343 that we have evidence of the activity which gave him his surname, dealer in meat. He continues to brew for sale, sell meat, and act as a juror throughout the 1340s. His role is slightly complicated by the occasional appearance during this period of a John Flesshewere junior, who occasionally essoined people—a common activity of young males—but does not become really active until the late 1350s. John Welsh/Walsh also bore a name occurring three times in the 1322 survey, though he himself does not appear in the record until 1325. He appears in the records both as debtor and creditor! suggesting involvement in trade, and as a frequent brewer of ale. In August 1345 he was sued by Thomas le Longe *in placito nundinarum*[19] in an obscure case, which also involved William Rolves, to whom Longe was said to have sold badly dried malt. In 1351 (if we are still with the same John Walsh) he was sueing John le Hopere over a broken agreement by which Walsh should have had half the profits of Alveston mill. All this suggests a general dealer in grain. He was frequently a juror from 1343 and borough reeve with Walter Marshal until 1351.

The Chese family provides two of the jurors for the view of the borough in 1345 or rather two men bearing this surname. John Chese appears as a brewer of ale in 1324, an activity continued vigorously until 1346. From 1351 until 1366 there is no more brewing and it is possible that we have another John, perhaps a son. The earlier John was presented in 1339 for receiving Welshmen; so, given his frequent and regular amercements as a brewer, we might conclude that he was some sort of an innkeeper. But he was also a regular juror from 1340, though never an official, unless we assume that it was not a namesake but a now ageing John Chese who was cachpol in 1351 and bailiff in 1366. Adam Chese, the other juror of that name, has a much shorter history, being an essoiner for William Marshal in 1324, when he may have been only a boy. In subsequent, but unrecorded years, he must have become important enough to be appointed a juror for the view of frankpledge in 1340 and on several other occasions juror of inquisition or view, before disappearing from the record in 1346, victim perhaps of the Black Death.

Walter Marshal (Mareschal) was evidently an important person (or persons) in Thornbury. The first reference is in 1324, the last in 1366, so there may have been Walters from two generations. An occasional brewer and receiver of strangers, he was several times a juror before the Black Death. Apart from his surname, meaning a shoesmith, there are no indications of professional occupation. The post-Black Death Walter, who may or may not have been the same person, was borough reeve in 1351 and 1352, juror from time to time, reeve again in 1362 and 1363, and a frequent brewer of ale. Since he held half a burgage in 1361 he was also a property owner, but we cannot get any closer to his main source of income. William Forester was member of a family (or set of persons with the same surname) who are fairly numerous—six of them—but about whom there is not much information and most of whom seem not to have survived the Black Death. He first appears as juror of the view in 1340 and filled that role, as well as juror of inquisition, until 1346, the last we hear of him. He was buying land in the borough in 1343 but there is no other indication about his activities, other than those possibly indicated by his surname.

Adam Parker also shared his surname with eight others. He first appears paying an amercement for breach of the assize of ale in 1330 and was still paying regular amercements through the 1360s—unless the later Adam was a son or other relative. In the year of the appointment of the jury we are considering, he became a constable of the town and indeed had previously served not only as a juror but as a member of a special commission, in 1344, to present persons to the court who were receiving strangers. In 1351 he sued Robert Twyford for a debt for malt and other commodities he had sold to Twyford, a tapster and butcher. Parker was obviously in the drinks business and possibly dealing regularly in malt. On the other hand, he indignantly and successfully rejected a heavy amercement imposed upon him by the bailiff in 1359 for the alleged illegal retailing of ale.

Walter Fysshepul may have been the son of a William Fysshepul who appears as a brewer of ale in 1324 but not afterwards. Walter was elected 'port reeve' in 1339. Between then and 1346 he was a frequent juror both at the view and for inquisitions. He was brewing ale regularly up to September 1340, but when the records begin again in 1343, he had either stopped brewing for sale or managed to evade the presentments of the tasters (though that is only if we assume that amercements were more than simple licence payments). In 1346 he acquired some land to enlarge his tenement, so he was clearly a real property owner.

John Northall is the last of the jurors to be considered. The name first appears in 1339 when he was elected as a taster, though someone of the same name paid tax at Oldbury-on-Severn in 1327. Between 1339 and 1352 he appears frequently in the court rolls. Several presentments for selling meat against the assize suggest that he was a butcher. He regularly brewed ale, had some arable land, the grain on which was eaten by John Isaac's geese; and was perhaps even putting out wool for spinning, since he accused Richard Pultegod of detaining 11 lbs. of woollen yarn. He seems to have been a litigious and quarrelsome man, abetting people who broke down hedges and was himself amerced for breaking into Mathilda Seisel's premises. Perhaps his daughter Eleanor inherited his temper. She was condemned in 1363 for murdering Thomas Chatris, a mercer from the Isle of Ely. Her lands and chattels were confiscated and acquired by various people, who had to return them because she was quit of felony. Her real property included a shambles, besides her other tenement, thus confirming the butchering occupation of the family. Her chattels are listed in the court record of May 1364, but the manuscript is defective. They included brass pots, plates, various tapestries, coverlets, and cloths or garments. The impression is of substantial comfort.

We have already described Adam Parker, one of the three constables elected this year. John Brok, who was not necessarily related to the atte Brok family enters the record as early as 1324 as an essoiner, possibly as a young man or even a boy. But he was a full suitor to the court in 1330 when he acted as a pledge. Subsequently he was several times excused attendance at court, which suggests that he might have been away from the borough, possibly on business. It is not clear what the business could be, but there are indications that they might include money-lending. He successfully sued Isaac of Sture, who had guaranteed that a certain loan (*mulnua*) would be to John's profit—and was not. Although he became constable he was not a noticeably law-abiding man. He and two others were guilty of assaulting Thomas Hughes, a butcher, He was amerced for bloodshed in 1346. He was obviously well-to-do, and built a wooden porch to his house in 1346.

The other constable was John Baron, an innkeeper, who enters the record in 1339 and is not heard of after 1346. Apart from occasionally pledging people and acting as an inquisition juror, he is little heard of. There is only one other man bearing his surname who also appears very little in the record. Walter Seisel, however, who was appointed in 1345 to summon the watch, belonged to a group of eight Seisels. Two of them, John and Juliana, held a half-burgage each in 1322. Walter does not appear much in the court rolls, was rather often essoined and very occasionally acted as a pledge. He was an unimportant man and perhaps the job of summoning the watch was also of little importance.

The court rolls of the post-Black Death period until 1366 are rather more abundant than those which end as a series in 1346. In particular, the period 1359–66 is quite well represented. We will therefore examine the records of those town notables occupying official positions in 1363 and 1364. In October 1363, the following elections were made: Walter Marshal and Robert Southmede to be reeves; John Flesshewere, Thomas Pennok, and Thomas Dyer to be cachpols or servientes (sergeants); Richard Salusbery and Richard Deye to be aletasters. Southhmede, Pennok, Salusbery, and Deye were to be sworn in, the implication being that this was their first appointment to such office. Next March, the following appear as jurors at the view: John Flesshewere, Richard Bertelot/Bartelot, John Chese, Adam Parkere, William Edwy, John Hopere, John Longer, John Slymbrugge, John Bartelot, John Baker, William Webbe, and Richard Parkere.

The first noticeable feature of these two lists is that several names familiar to us from 1345 recur, namely, those of John Flesshewere, Walter Marshal, Adam Parker, and John Chese, a fact that poses again the problem of more than one person being represented by a single forename, as well as surname. The John Flesshewere of 1363–4 could, in fact, have been the John Flesshewere junior of the pre-Black Death period. He was amerced for selling meat against the assize in April 1363 and was falsely accused of not paying for two sheep he had bought from John Camme in the following November, so he was probably a butcher, as his name implies. He was also a fairly regular brewer. He was elected reeve in October 1362 and cachpol in October 1363. In 1364, as well as being a juror at the view, he was also a member of another group of twelve (most of whom were also jurors at the view) which drew up ordinances. These ordinances prevented the retail sale of ale by others than brewers, that is, by tapsters; the carrying of swords and daggers in the town; and the retailing of grain by outsiders.

We have already indicated something of the activities of the post-Black Death Walter Marshall. Perhaps it should be added that apart from promulgating the ordinance about tapsters, he had been in October 1362 one of four men appointed by the court to enforce a suspension of actions and pleas between a group of persistent litigants who, we may assume, were wasting the court's time with excessive pleading. We have also described the pre- and post-Black Death activities of Adam Parker, again supposing that this name could conceal two individuals of different generations. The later Parker, if there were two, was also an ordainer against tapsters, bearers of arms, and grain retailers. The John Chese of 1364 may also have been of a younger generation than his earlier namesake, whose first appearance, as we have seen, was in 1324. Besides being cachpol in 1351, he appears occasionally as a pledge and as juror, as well as being one of the four enforcing the suspension of litigation in 1362. He bought a plot of land in 1366 to enlarge his tenement and is referred to as a lord's bailiff who suffered assault at the hands of Richard Wodecokes while trying to execute his duties. What exactly was this official position, unless it was one of the town reeves (sometimes called bailiffs) we do not know.

The other names from the list of notables of 1363–4, though not repeated from the 1345 list, are by no means strange. There are two representatives of the Bartelot family, Richard and John. The name is already found in the 1322 survey when Agnes Bartelot held 1¼ burgages. There were at least eight people with this surname, several of them engaged in brewing, baking, and selling meat. 'Richard' is a forename first appearing in 1325, so the Richard of 1363–4 is probably of a younger generation. The earlier Richard bought half a burgage from a namesake in 1325 and from then until the eve of the Black Death, mainly appears in debt pleas with other Bartelots. These debt pleas, minor reflections of trading activities, continue in references to the post-Black Death Bartelot, but not in conflict with other Bartelots. In 1364 he was an ordainer on the question of retail sales and arms-bearing, and in 1364 and 1366 a juror of the view. He may have been a close relative of John, the other Bartelot on the 1364 jury. They were associated as defendants in a plea of broken contract against Thomas Isegar, a quarrelsome baker. John does not appear in the record before 1360 as a brewer. He was put on the view jury again in April 1366, but was in trouble in September along with Thomas atte Panytere for being rebellious against a summons of the lord's bailiff. There is no indication of which official this might have been, but the matter was serious enough to merit the large amercement of 12*d*. each. The general record of these two Bartelots suggests that they achieved jury status by virtue of their membership of a well-to-do, numerous, and old-established family, rather than by frequent court attendance and tranquil behaviour.

John Flesshewere's companions as cachpols or servientes were Thomas Pennok and Thomas Dyer. The Pennok family appears in the 1322 list where Nicholas holds 1½ burgages. Nicholas's wife was Juliana and their son was Thomas. There was a good deal of litigation within the Pennok family about the succession to the burgage holdings of Nicholas and Juliana. Thomas was justified as heir of the body against Richard Pennok who may have been Nicholas's brother. However, Richard and Thomas do not seem to have become enemies. In 1346, we find them as co-defendants against Robert Danyel who accused them of stealing his stone tiles. At this point, one is suspicious of possible undercurrents, because Robert Danyel had also been a litigant attempting to acquire three quarters of a burgage of Juliana Pennok's inheritance. The most striking feature however of the post-Black Death career of Thomas Pennok is the frequency with which he stood as pledge. Thomas Dyer, on the other hand, apart from being cachpol and ordainer concerned both with retail trade and excessive litigation, mainly appears as a brewer. Whether his surname indicated his main occupation cannot be said. There are six others with the same surname in the records, going back to 1339. Thomas, however, appears for the first time in 1359, a late arrival, due more likely than anything else to the gaps in the court roll series.

The ale-tasters were William Salusbery and Richard Deye, both obscure men, whose obscurity possibly indicates the lower status of ale-tasting compared with other municipal offices—Salusbery first appears in 1360 in a trespass case. However, he was respectable enough to act as a pledge in later years. He was a brewer and a tapster. Richard was more clearly newly active among the Thornbury élite. In 1362 he bought a burgage and with it the liberty of the borough, that is, endowed with its privileges. Soon after, as we see, he becomes an ale-taster and for the rest of the period examined he mostly appears as a brewer, except for a short period of disgrace in 1364, when he got involved in the illegal receipt of the confiscated goods of Eleanor Northall and was amerced 20*s*. He was pardoned this sum on account of poverty, which did not prevent him from actively pursuing his brewing, possibly on a fairly large scale.

Another regular brewer of the early 1350s was Robert Southmede. Later, in the 1360s, he was an occasional pledger; involved in debt pleas both as plaintiff and defendant, indicating some level of trading; and, as we have seen, was elected reeve with Walter Marshal. The election is surprising, since Southmede's career is late and undistinguished. There are other Southmedes in the town and possibly his father was William Southmede, who appears in 1330. But they are obscure, at any rate as far as court business is concerned.

We are now left with a group of jurors. William Edwy, John Hopere, John Longe, John Slymbrugge, John Baker, William Webbe, and Richard Parkere, who, in most respects seem to have been more important persons than these officials whom we have just discussed.

William Edwy bears a surname which goes back to 1322 when Richard Edwy held half a burgage. Apart from this, Richard does not enter our records, but Alice Edwy, a frequent brewer between 1325 and 1346, may have been a relative. Another Alice Edwy, Alice the younger, appears very occasionally between 1344 and 1346. Perhaps both women died in the plague. William first appears in 1344. He may have been a grain dealer. Between 1360 and 1366 he was three times a juror, once to consider a dispute about the alleged disseisin of two burgages and twice at the view of frankpledge. He was also one of those responsible for issuing ordinances about tapsters, etc.

John Hopere has an occupational surname. The seven other Hoperes who occasionally appear in the records—four men and three women— were not necessarily related. John himself first appears in 1340 and we cannot, of course, be certain that the John Hopere of 1366 was the same person. If it was one person, we can say that he probably was a hooper because he kept a handmill belonging to John Lynage (with whom he frequently quarrelled) because Lynage had not paid for some iron. He was also given by the court a grindstone belonging to Thomas Honeybrok because of a debt. Although we are not told so, this might have again been because an object which he repaired was not paid for. Apart from this he was obviously very active economically. He brewed for sale, he was often in debt and he also sued frequently as a creditor. He may have been part lessee of the mill at Alveston (a mile and a half south of Thornbury) in 1351, for he was in dispute about half the profits with John Walsh. He was a frequent pledge, a frequent litigant, and probably rather rowdy.

John Longe shared his surname with eight other people. A Nicholas Longe held two burgages in 1322, though he only paid 13d. tax in 1327.

This is the last reference to Nicholas, the first to John being in 1325. 'John' continues in the record until 1366, so we may be dealing here with more than one person. If so, the earlier John Longe was already being essoined by a son, Simon, in 1339. Simon married Mathilda, and bought with her a half-burgage in 1343, so if this implies that he was setting up house separately, his father may still have been alive. By 1366, Simon was dead. In the earlier years, John brewed for sale, disputed about land with John Arundel, chaplain and in 1345 was twice on a jury of inquisition. In the post-Black Death period, he (or his namesake) was more active commercially, being involved in debt pleas, selling ale and fish. He was an inquisition juror in 1359 as well as in 1363 and in that year was one of the ordainers concerning tapsters.

John Slymbrugge was also an ordainer as well as being juror to the view in 1364 and 1366. He was also an inquisition juror in 1359. Otherwise, he does not appear much in the record, though it is usually as a creditor. However, his family connections are better known than for many Thornbury personalities. His father John, dead by 1343, was a burgage holder, into which (or three-quarters of which) his sister Joan entered by inheritance. He also had two brothers, each of whom, in 1345, bought a chamber from their father's legacy. The John with whom we are concerned and his brother William seem to be the only members of the family who survived the Black Death.

John Baker is difficult to identify because of his common occupational surname. In the period covered by the records, there were fourteen who seem to have been Thornbury residents. This John was probably the son of Geoffrey Baker, tenant of a burgage in 1322, rather than another John who held two burgages at that time. His father Geoffrey was a baker, as was the other John, but there is no evidence that this John followed the trade. His appearances in the record mainly concern disputes about property. In 1366 he was involved in a series of disputes with Richard Chapman, from whom he seems to have been leasing land and buildings. Since Richard Chapman was found guilty of depasturing John Baker's grain, it may be that John's interests were agricultural, though these could have been subordinate to other interests.

William Webbe is another man with an occupational surname, shared with four others of whom one was female. There are no indications in the record that William, who was active between 1340 and 1366 (if the one name represents one person), was involved in the cloth industry. Apart from frequent amercements for breaches of the assize of bread and ale which did not stop him from being an ordainer concerning tapsters—he mainly appears as a tenant of pasture land and an owner of pigs. This was not incompatible with another occupation but it would be unwise to conclude from his name that he was a weaver.

Finally, we have Richard Parker, bearer of a fairly common Thornbury surname, which he shared with eight other people. Unfortunately there are no indications of the inter-relationships between these nine of whom two were women. The oldest was William, who was taxed in 1327 and is not found after 1346. Richard does not appear in the record until 1360. He was brewing fairly frequently for sale between that date and 1366, seems to have been interested in land, including pasture land, and was involved in a curious piece of litigation with William Tone about a pair of paternosters which William was illegally keeping from him—but whether borrowed, bought, or sold we cannot know. Richard's appearance on the view of frankpledge jury in 1363 was his first recorded public act and he was appointed as a juror of the view from time to time afterwards. It is noticeable, however, that he does not appear to have been used as a pledge.

One expects that the social and economic activities of a town's notables will shed some light on the nature of the town itself. Late medieval Coventry was dominated by drapers and mercers, reflecting its textile industry. Late medieval Bristol was dominated by general merchants, shipowners, and drapers reflecting its interests in the Atlantic trade as well as its textile industry. We have already seen indications that there was a textile industry, or perhaps one should say, aspects of a textile industry in late medieval Thornbury. If it was of any importance in the economy of the town one would expect the town notables to be involved. This was not the case. As we have seen, the Thomas Dyer who was a cachpol in 1363 had no documented connections with the trade implied in his surname. The only person among the notables whom we have discussed who had the remotest connection was the butcher, John Northall, who sued Richard Pultegod for detaining 1½ lbs. of woollen yarn. This plea was declared false, though that does not mean that there was no transaction involving woollen yarn between the two. Pultegod may have been some sort of craftsman to whom Northall put out work. A contemporary with the same name, Robert, was the man mentioned earlier who was sued for breach of a contract of service in some unspecified craft (*de arte sua*). But there seems little doubt that Northall was primarily a butcher.

If there was a textile craft element in Thornbury and it was not one which involved, other than marginally, the town notables, it is possible that it was to some extent an appendage of the Bristol industry.[20] Perhaps woollen yarn was being spun in Thornbury for Bristol drapers or weavers, though this does not rule out the existence in Thornbury of other textile processes. The small town élite were clearly, as one would expect in a town of its size, petty traders, mostly in the food-processing business, servicing what little industry there was, no doubt servicing the manor house, and above all servicing those who attended the markets and the fairs.

In delineating the activities of the more prominent burgesses, so as to get some idea of their social status and economic activities, we could not better illuminate the banality of small-town life in late medieval England. However, to describe the ordinary may be just as significant as to pinpoint the unusual. Given the large number of small market towns, our argument that they were an essential element in the continuum of commercial exchange, so essential in the urbanization process, would seem to be strengthened. With about twenty other similar market towns in Gloucestershire alone and nearly 400 in the country as a whole by mid-fourteenth century,[21] we have impressive evidence of the importance of these generating points of cash income and expenditure.

The question could be posed, of course, as to the typicality of Thornbury and its records. How suitably can a comparison be made with Halesowen? As I have indicated, the Halesowen court records are unique for their continuity from the 1270s until the end of the Middle Ages, it is probably also the case, certainly in the fourteenth century, that there is more detailed reporting of transactions and prosecutions in the court at Halesowen than at Thornbury. This may be due to the local presence of the lord. The abbey of Halesowen was less than one mile from the town centre. The people of Halesowen seemed to know as much about what went on in the abbey as the monks and their officials seemed to know about the burgesses.

The distance between the people of Thornbury and the earls of Gloucester and their successors of the Stafford family must have been much greater than that between the people of Halesowen and their lord. The Thornbury court records are not, however, all that laconic, compared with other good records of seigneurial borough courts, such as those

---

[20] Bristol's protectionist ordinances, as in many similar cases, are evidence for the existence of what they tried to prevent. See above, n. 17.
[21] See the useful listing in M. Beresford and H. P. R. Finberg (eds.), *Medieval English Boroughs: A Handlist* (Newton Abbot, 1973), 65–193.

of Tamworth (Staffs. and Warwicks.).[22] My presentation of aspects of fourteenth-century Thornbury has, of course, tended to emphasize the methodology of court-roll analysis, but it is to be hoped that, in addition, some of the characteristics of this small town's society will have emerged.

[22] See *Tamworth Borough Record*, ed. H. Wood (Tamworth, 1952) and his book *Medieval Tamworth* (Tamworth, 1972).

15

Exploitation of the Landless by Lords and Tenants in Early Medieval England[1]

H. S. A. FOX

I. DRAMATIS PERSONAE

The rolls of the Eastertide hallmoots of all of Glastonbury Abbey's many manors begin abruptly with apparently enigmatic listings of some segment of the male population. The lists can be very long, so that, for example, on the large manor of Wrington, Somerset, about 160 males were being listed in the early fourteenth century.[2] The historian who opens the rolls must unwind inch after inch of closely packed names before coming to the beginning of more familiar court business. Because medieval listings of people (apart from those in surveys, rentals, and nominal tax returns) are so rare, these are potentially very exciting sources, being cross-sections through a segment of the male populations of Glastonbury's manors and surviving in broken series from 1265 onwards. But who are the males listed? And why? Clearly, a manorial poll tax of some kind is being taken, for beside each name is written a payment in cash normally varying between 2*d*. and 12*d*. (or, in place of the sum, various words and abbreviations pointing to exoneration) while the clerks who entered the total receipts onto the abbey's account rolls called the tax *chevagium garcionum*.

Sir Michael Postan, in his studies of Glastonbury manors, naturally noticed these listings and drew from them a conclusion which fitted very well with his view of an over-populated countryside in the hundred years before the Black Death. Chevage is a term most frequently used in manorial documents for licences to emigrate. Postan translated *garcio* at

[1] The Economic and Social Research Council funded this project. Richard McKinley and Chris Thornton kindly helped me in the transcribing of the court rolls. I am most grateful to the following for providing advice: Gillian Austen, Mark Bailey, Michael Costen, Bob Dunning, Chris Dyer, Paul Ell, Barbara Harvey, Paul Harvey, Steve Hobbs, Marilyn Livingstone, Tom Mayberry, Marjorie McIntosh, Oliver Padel, David Postles, Jim Skeggs, Richard Smith, Robin Stanes, Angus Winchester, Chris Woolgar. Useful comments were made at the Leicester meeting of the Anglo-American Seminar on the Medieval Economy and Society and at the School of History, University of Birmingham. The project would never have been completed without the expertise, at many stages, of Ralph Weedon.

[2] Longleat House MSS (hereafter L.), 10654. An excellent guide to the rolls is K. Harris, *Glastonbury Abbey Records at Longleat House: A Summary List* (Somerset Rec. Soc. 81, Taunton, 1991), the datings in which are generally followed in this chapter.

face value, perhaps with modern French usage (*garçon*) in mind. And so he concluded that the *garciones* were 'young men leaving villages to seek employment elsewhere', victims of a land market which failed to provide adequate niches for many male children.[3]

Postan's reasonable preliminary interpretation of a source to which he always intended to return is not in accord with the abbreviations in the listings, entered against the names of those males who were exonerated from the tax. Some of the abbreviations present no difficulties, *mortuus* for example, or *pauper*; of the more obscure abbreviations three recur again and again. First is *h.t.* which may easily be explained by reference to the court proceedings which follow the lists. To take an example, Nicholas son of Adam Upham was exonerated from payment at Pilton, Somerset, in 1346, never to appear again in the lists; the court proceedings of that year record that he gained possession of a house and ten acres at Pilton, so that the only reasonable extension of *h.t.* which appears against his name in that year is *habet terram*, 'he has land'.[4] The implication is that the majority of the listed males (without the *h.t.* abbreviation) were landless, and this is confirmed by any comparison of the listings with manorial extents. The letters *c.p.* or *c.m.* occur as explanation for non-payment of chevage against a fair proportion of the names in the lists, for example against approximately 12 per cent of entries in the lists for Uplyme, Devonshire.[5] The correct explanation for these enigmatic formulae came during a reading of H. E. Hallam's important studies of the thirteenth-century villein genealogies from the manors of Spalding Priory; in these some of the unmarried offspring of the prior's villeins are said to be *cum patre* or *cum matre*, that is, living under the roofs of a father or mother.[6] That the same is the correct extension of *c.p.* and *c.m.* in the Glastonbury lists is clear from comparison between them and manorial extents. Thus, on the Somerset manor of Pilton, Walter son of Thomas at Townsend is recorded as *cum patre* in the list for 1315 while William Dauber is *cum matre*; an extent made about one year later records Thomas at Townsend (a male) and Matilda Dauber (a female) as landholders.[7] Possible reasons for exemption from tax of *garciones* in their parents' homes will be discussed later; the important point to make here is that males stated to be in the houses of their parents were clearly *residents* not

---

[3] Postan, 'Medieval Agrarian Society in its Prime', 564–5. See also 624.
[4] L. 11251.   [5] L. 11251, 10654, 10771, 10773, 10774, 11251.
[6] Hallam, 'Some Thirteenth-Century Censuses', 340–61; Russell, 'Demographic Limitations of Spalding Serf Lists', 138–44; Hallam, 'Further Observations on the Spalding Serf Lists', 338–50.
[7] L. 10771 and BL Eg. 3321.

emigrants, and the strong presumption is that most of the others named in the lists were also living *on* the manor.

The conclusion that the Glastonbury lists are of landless residents is clearly of major importance, for this group is normally absent from (or not distinguished in) other types of listing found in early medieval sources. That 'least attached part of the population . . . from among whom hired labourers would be gradually appearing', that 'fluctuating population of rural workmen . . . gathering behind the screen of recognized peasant holders'—to quote two pioneers of medieval manorial studies—steps confidently onto the centre of the stage in the hallmoots of Glastonbury manors. Nor need we, on this estate, speak of the 'splendid anonymity' of the landless, for the Glastonbury *garciones* burst among us complete with names—an estimated 30,000 entries for all manors on the estate before 1348, truly a 'pullulating throng', though no longer lost, unapproachable, 'like the stars that were visible to astronomers only in their effects on the orbits of neighbouring bodies'.[8]

Sources from the Glastonbury estate are exceptionally silent about the purpose of *chevagium garcionum*. The system of tax collection carried within itself the means of its own perpetuation and no statement ever seems to have been made at Glastonbury about its precise nature. This interim study has, however, revealed a few additional details, the first, and perhaps most important, of which concerns age of entry into the listings. At the hallmoot of the Somerset manor of Berrow in 1345 there was a 'round up' of *garciones*. Periodic inquisitions of this kind by those who collected the tax are to be expected; they do not mean that the lists are fundamentally unreliable, but simply that a few landless males sometimes escaped tax and were from time to time brought into the system; the same is found in tithing lists.[9] The action at Berrow in 1345 involved five *garciones* who had previously escaped tax but who were then enrolled for the first time, with arrears. The entry continues: 'And the whole hallmoot . . . concealed this from the time when they were of twelve years.'[10] On the Glastonbury estate, then, the head tax first fell on males at the age of 12, the same age at which adolescents joined tithings for the purposes of local policing (the listings are not, of course, to do with frankpledge for

    [8] N. Neilson, *Customary Rents* (Oxford Studies in Social and Legal History, 2, 1910), 173; Vinogradoff, *Villeinage*, 213; Miller, *Ely*, 145; Bridbury, 'The Black Death', *EcHR* 2nd ser. 26 (1973), 590. My estimate of the number of entries is a very rough and ready one.

    [9] Poos, 'Rural Population of Essex', 524. On the manor of Staplegrove, Somerset, a court order of 1301–2 to put males in tithing resulted in an upsurge in numbers paying tithingpenny: Hampshire Record Office, Eccl. Comm. 2/159448.

    [10] L. 10774. See also L. 10646 (Glastonbury).

they were made at the abbot's hallmoots not at his tourns, the sums collected were variable unlike the fixed tithingpenny, and landholders were excluded, a practice not found in tithing lists).[11] At 12, a *puer* became a *garcio* and, so long as he never obtained land, remained one for the rest of his life. *Garcio*, then, is not specifically the terminology of youth. A complete discussion of the word is deferred to another publication; suffice it to say here that we are dealing with a term which etymologically implies low status and menial work and was used in this sense before also coming to designate a youth.[12] Those who are familiar with *garciones* through stray references in court rolls will know that the most frequent occurrence of the term is in the context of an employee— x *garcio* of y. Those who use building accounts will know that a craftsman such as a plumber often appears with his *garcio*, usually paid at a lesser wage; here he is the plumber's 'mate'. Those who use household accounts will know that *garciones* here were menials separately distinguished from genuine child servants (*pueri* and *pagetti*) and some 'held this position [of *garcio*] for many years and were married as well'.[13] In all of these cases *garciones* occupied subordinate, poorly paid positions; if they grew into manhood without obtaining land the *garciones* of the Glastonbury estate were condemned by their landlessness to the low-paid jobs of youth. The Middle English word which the Anglo-Norman (*garcun*) and Latin (*garcio*) are translating is still obscure. The *Promptorium Parvulorum* translates *garcio* as 'lad', a term which in Middle English usage had the primary meaning of 'serving-man, attendant, man of low status'.[14]

Preliminary examination of the listings and court proceedings has, secondly, yielded a little information about the assessment of *chevagium garcionum* on the Glastonbury estate. Responsibility for ensuring that all landless males over 12 were assessed for chevage fell upon the whole hallmoot.[15] Assessment of the payment to be made by each individual *garcio*, and of grounds for exemption, was the responsibility of two special

---

[11] For tithing lists, see Poos, 'Population Turnover', 7–9; Morris, *Frankpledge System*, 170–2.

[12] S. T. H. Scoones, 'L'Étymologie du mot *garçon*', *Romania*, 93 (1972), 407–11; M. Mitteraur, 'Servants and Youth', *Continuity and Change*, 5 (1990), 11–13, following a lead in P. Ariès, *Centuries of Childhood: A Social History of Childhood*, tr. R. Baldick (Harmondsworth, 1973), 355.

[13] Raftis, 'Social Structures', 97 for references to servants in court rolls; *The Accounts of the Fabric of Exeter Cathedral, 1279–1353*, pt i, *1279–1326*, ed. A.M. Erskine (Devon and Cornwall Rec. Soc. NS 24, Torquay, 1981), 24, for just one example of the plumber's mate; K. Mertes, *The English Noble Household, 1250–1600* (Oxford, 1988), 30.

[14] *Promptorium Parvulorum sive Clericorum, Lexicon Anglo-Latinum Princeps*, ed. A. Way (3 vols.; Camden Soc. 25, 54, 89, 1843–65), *s.v.* 'ladde'; *OED s.v.* 'lad'.

[15] e.g. L. 10774 (Berrow), 11222 (Ditcheat).

'affeerors of chevage' (*taxatores*) who were drawn from the most substantial tenants of a manor and were busy about this task in the weeks running
up to Easter.[16] When the Easter courts were held the affeerors presented
their updated information and the steward's clerk altered his list (which
he had pre-prepared for the occasion) adding payments or reasons for
exoneration beside the names, deleting the dead and those who had
obtained land over the course of the year and adding newly enrolled
garciones.[17] It was a system which placed the burden of assessment on the
local community and its senior members, who may well have had reasons
for wishing to have some control over the adolescent and older landless
groups on the manor, and which allowed for annual supervision by the
abbey's officials. As such it was a system which is likely to have produced
listings of quite reasonable accuracy, although some loopholes there would
always have been.

II. EXPLOITATION OF THE LANDLESS BY LORDS

Failure to find any complete and explicit statement about *chevagium
garcionum* in the records of Glastonbury Abbey is compensated for by
references from other estates. If collated these provide ample evidence for
taxes on the landless of a kind similar to that levied on the Glastonbury
estate. They help to explain the exemption of landless people living in
their parents' homes. They show the degree to which the exploitative
tendencies of some thirteenth-century landlords penetrated down to the
most humble levels of society, and they provide some important evidence
on the employment of labour by tenant landholders. The first group of
references, given below, forms a miscellaneous collection, taken from extents
and account rolls; what the entries have in common is that they describe
or imply a tax on those who did not hold land without, except in one case,
making direct statements about the residential arrangements of the landless.

BLEADON (Somerset, late thirteenth century). All of the lord's men and women of
servile condition not holding land for their own sustenance . . . perform three
reaping services for the lord in autumn and shall have a sheaf each day.[18]

---

[16] L. 10771.
[17] This analysis is made on the basis of differences in ink quality. A good example is
L.10654 (Wrington).
[18] Winchester Cathedral Archives, 52/79 (temporary number), fo. 100^v, printed in *Memoirs Illustrative of the History and Antiquities of Wiltshire and the City of Salisbury* (Arch.
Inst., London, 1851), 209.

SWAFFHAM (Norfolk, late thirteenth century or early fourteenth). Chevage of those staying in the manor who have neither land nor a house [*domicilium*].[19]

DARTMOOR (Devon, 1342–3). [Account is rendered for] 5*s.* 6*d.* arising . . . at Michaelmas from persons dwelling in the Moor and without not holding any tenement, as well of men as of women, each man giving 2*d.* yearly and each woman 1*d.*[20]

PETWORTH (Sussex, 1349). And [account is rendered] for three [capons] received as chevage of the *garciones* at Hockday and not more because all of the *garciones* took land.[21]

TOPSHAM (Devon, 1286–7). And [account is rendered] for 3*s.* 7*d.* of chevage this year and thus less because ten whose names are in a roll take land and marry and are dead.[22]

CASTLE COMBE (Wiltshire, 1451). And [account is rendered] for 6*s.* 6*d.* arising from the chevage of diverse men in the aforesaid vill who stay there without a tenure from the lord, each man assessed at 2*d.*[23]

NORTON (County Durham, *c.*1381). And each *selfode*, of whatever grade, staying in the vill pays the lord 3*d.* yearly at . . . Michaelmas.[24]

EAST WRETHAM (Norfolk, 1240*s.*). And know that if the said Eustace [exemplar for the 12-acre tenants on this manor] shall have a son or a daughter or anyone under his protection in his own house [? reading obscure] for a year . . . serving within the lord's manor . . . they shall perform three autumn works.[25]

NORTON (County Durham, *c.*1381). And each servant [*serviens*] of each of the aforesaid bondmen, aged sixteen years and more, pays the lord only 12*d.* yearly at Michaelmas for autumn boonworks.[26]

FELSTEAD (Essex, very early twelfth century). Twenty bordars who work for one day in the week and give for their chevage 2*d.* and for their wife and for their servant [*serviens*] and for a cow if they have one.[27]

---

[19] Cited in Davenport, *Economic Development of a Norfolk Manor*, 46 n. 2.

[20] PRO S.C. 6 828/16, cited in S.A. Moore, *A Short History of the Rights of Common upon the Forest of Dartmoor and the Commons of Devon* (Plymouth, 1890), 14. The same payment on Dartmoor was described in other sources as *capitagium garcionum*: PRO C. 133 95/1.

[21] *Ministers' Accounts of the Manor of Petworth 1347–53*, ed. L. F. Salzman, (Sussex Rec. Soc., 55, Lewes, 1955), 42. See also 18, 56, 79 and below n. 64.

[22] PRO S.C. 6 827/39. 'Married' here implies 'married with land'.

[23] Scrope, *History of Castle Combe*, 245. See also index *s.v. capitagium*. Chevage was called *capitagium garcionium* on this manor: BL Add. Roll 18250.

[24] *Bishop Hatfield's Survey*, ed. W. Greenwell (Surtees Soc. 32, 1857), 174. See also 168 and, for the levying of this tax, 232, 236, 242.

[25] *Select Documents of the Abbey of Bec*, 115. 'In his own house' qualifies 'anyone'.

[26] *Bishop Hatfield's Survey*, 174.

[27] *Charters and Custumals of the Abbey of Caen*, 34. The term *serviens* was occasionally applied to a son.

At Bleadon, in the first entry above, we are at once introduced to a feature of many of these obligations, namely that they might be discharged in the form of autumn works rather than paid in cash. In fact, the two were interchangeable in many cases: we can probably think of the money payments as commutations for services. Four of the references collected together above (Dartmoor to Castle Combe) are all from manors where the tax collected was called *chevagium garcionum* but where the sources are a little more explicit than those from the Glastonbury estate, in all four cases specifying or implying landlessness as the basis of the tax. Another source from Castle Combe, the great extent made by William of Worcester in 1454, tells us a little more: on this industrializing manor the *garciones* were said to be 'workers and servants'.[28] The following reference, from Norton, County Durham, also takes one towards servants. It concerns a tax on *selfodes*, a term of unhelpfully obscure origin but one which almost certainly refers to servant-like people. Thirteenth-century extents of manors in the North of England describe them as a fluctuating population, 'sometimes more and sometimes less' or as 'poor people' taxed at 4*d.* per head 'for having lodging' (*hospitatium*). The best discussion of northern *selfodes*, by A. J. L. Winchester, contains some revealing early sixteenth-century references which indicate that they were in some cases people who lodged in farmhouses, probably servants in husbandry.[29] The most precise early medieval reference to the term is a strange stray from as far south as Cirencester in 1210 which makes plain that *selfodes* were people resident there who had left home to 'live by their own labour', presumably as servants in the houses of other tenants.[30] There seem to have been some fine, and to us unfathomable, distinctions in the way in which the term was used, but implications of servanthood are there nevertheless.[31]

---

[28] *Artifices et servientes forinseci*: Scrope, *History of Castle Combe*, 217. The *forinsecus* of this statement adds a new dimension, implying chevage specifically of immigrants as the basis of *chevagium garcionum* on this manor. Usually *chevagium garcionum* comprehends all males over a certain age, whether immigrants or natives.

[29] *OED s.v.* 'selfode' ('of obscure origin'); PRO C. 132 40/6, C. 133 31/3; A. J. L. Winchester, *Landscape and Society in Medieval Cumbria* (Edinburgh, 1987), 68.

[30] *The Cartulary of Cirencester Abbey*, ed. C. D. Ross and M. Devine (3 vols.; London and Oxford, 1964–77), i. 247–9.

[31] The extent of Norton speaks of *selfodes* 'of whatever grade' (*gradus*) and has an adjacent passage (also cited above) on the autumn works to be done by the 'servants (*servientes*) of the bondmen'. *Gradus* could mean 'degree' or possibly 'age', suggesting that the statement is meant to emphasize that the tax was at a flat rate, rather than graduated by age as on the Glastonbury estate (below pp. 530–1). The difference between *selfodes* and *servientes* is difficult to determine: perhaps a distinction is being made between 'foreign' servants from outside the manor and servants who were the sons of tenants, or between persons living on

The last three of the references collected together above are even clearer in their specification of levies on servants. At Wretham a villein having anyone 'in his own house for a year . . . serving within the lord's manor' was obliged to ensure that the lodger performed autumn works. The penultimate reference is late and, it might be claimed, may not reflect thirteenth-century conditions, but it is clear and specific: at Norton, again, an obligation to pay tax or perform works fell on the 'servants of the bondmen'. The last reference is exceptionally early: at Felstead at the beginning of the twelfth century the Abbess of Caen levied chevage on the servants of her bordars.

The passages given above bring us closer to understanding *chevagium garcionum* on the Glastonbury estate. Another group of references to taxes on the landless, all from extents, inquests, or custumals, is more revealing (either because the taxes were more sophisticated or because the references are fuller); these passages take us towards the residential arrangements of the landless.

LESSINGHAM (Norfolk, 1240s.). The jury says that all, whether bondmen or bondwomen or outsiders, staying within the lords' soke having neither land nor tenement are bound each year to reap for one day in autumn or pay one penny, so long as they shall be without a tenement whence common service must issue; but so long as sons or daughters stay under their fathers' roof and do not take more than 10*d.* they shall be quit of this custom.[32]

SISTON (Gloucestershire, 1299). Item they say that all bondmen and bondwomen of this manor who do not hold lands and tenements and do not serve their fathers and mothers each perform three boonworks in autumn, the price of each 1½*d.*[33]

NEWNHAM (Worcestershire, thirteenth century). When serfs come of age, except the closest servant to a father or a mother, they perform three boon reapings, and outsiders likewise.[34]

CIRENCESTER (Gloucestershire, 1210). They [a jury] declared . . . that the king's bondmen of Cirencester, while they were under the rod and authority of and in the mainpast of their fathers and mothers, were acquitted by the boon reapings which they themselves [i.e. the parents] performed for the king or for

---

or off the parental holding, for which see *Notes and Queries*, 9th ser. 7 (1901), 89. Those who drew up the Hatfield survey from which these references for Norton come made the same clear and deliberate distinction for Hartburn between *selfodes* and *servientes*: *Bishop Hatfield's Survey*, 171. It is not a matter of confusion on their part but on ours, at this remove.

[32] *Select Documents of the Abbey of Bec*, 113.   [33] PRO E. 142/8.
[34] *Registrum sive Liber Irrotularius et Consuetudinarius Prioratus Beatae Mariae Wigorniensis*, ed. W. H. Hale (Camden Soc. 91, 1865), 15a.

his farmer; but when the same bondmen have their own free authority and live by their own labour and . . . become *sulfodes*, then each of them ought to perform three boon reapings for the lord king.[35]

SHIPDHAM (Norfolk, 1251). And know that every anilepiman and anilepiwyman who is worth 12*d.* or more in autumn shall give to the lord bishop one penny yearly as chevage at Michaelmas except those who are in the service of their father or mother.[36]

CASTOR (Soke of Peterborough, 1125–8). Men who serve outside the houses of their fathers each give one penny as chevage.[37]

BINCOMBE (Dorset, 1376). If anyone is a widower or widow and has but one son, so long as he chooses to serve his father the lord cannot compel him to service; but if he chooses to serve elsewhere he shall serve the lord rather than another. Every tenant can have one son without paying impost.[38]

BRAUNTON (Devon, *c*.1516). Also the custome ys for every tenaunte . . . haveyng ther chyldern in houshold with theym under their governaunce & charge not to be presented for a censur tyll tyme that they do be of full age by statute and put owte in huys [?house: reading obscure] from theem for waygs or otherwise to be married.[39]

These references are all telling us, again, of obligations owed by the landless: 'having neither land nor tenement' is common to two of the references and there are strong implications of landlessness in the rest. All of the references have in common the exemption from obligations of those of a villein's children who still lived in or served in (implying residence) the parental household; they have this in common with the Glastonbury listings. And, by implication, many of these landless sons or

---

[35] *Cartulary of Cirencester Abbey*, i. 247–9.

[36] BL Cott. Claud. C xi, fo. 239. For *anilepimen* and *anilepiwymen* are frequently mentioned in this volume, a collection of extents of Ely manors. They are sometimes mentioned alongside, but separately distinguished from, *undersettles*, cottars, and the like, as on 82ᵛ (Wisbech); and see also, for this distinction, *Court Baron*, 146–7. For illustrations from Ely extents of 1221 and 1251, see Miller, *Ely*, 93, 145 and H. E. Hallam, 'Social Structure: Eastern England', in H. E. Hallam (ed.), *The Agrarian History of England and Wales*, ii. *1042–1350* (Cambridge, 1988), 619–20. Here the terms seem to have been applied to the resident landless. Confusingly, they could also, on other estates, be apparently applied to emigrants: Davenport, *Economic Development*, 45–6, 73.

[37] *Chronicon Petroburgense*, ed. T. Stapledon (Camden Soc. 47, 1849), 163.

[38] PRO C. 145 208/4.

[39] R. Dymond, 'The Customs of the Manors of Braunton', *Transactions of the Devonshire Association* 20 (1888), 280. Finberg produced good evidence to show that *censura* could on occasion be used as a term for tithingpenny: H. P. R. Finberg, *Tavistock Abbey* (Cambridge, 1951), 208. But the term also crops up in contexts which have nothing to do with leet jurisdiction, where it was used interchangeably with *chevagium garcionum*, e.g. at Hartland, Devon and on Dartmoor, Devon: PRO C. 133/89/3 and 102/2; PRO C. 133 95/1 and S.C. 6 828/21.

daughters residing on the manor but not in their parental homes could only have been what a later age was to call servants in husbandry living in the households of other tenants. The passages given above show that seigneurial authorities recognized the existence of endogamous circulation of servants of both sexes within their manors.

To explain the rationale of impositions of this kind, including Glastonbury's *chevagium garcionium*, is not easy. We can probably see the tax as one variant of a particularly English form of chevage. Continental studies have suggested that payment of chevage by all serfs, whether landed or landless, was widely regarded as a proof of serfdom; it was the 'sign *par excellence* of servitude' according to Marc Bloch, a render which played a large part 'in the symbolism of serfdom'.[40] Universal chevage of all of a lord's villeins did not frequently develop in England in this way,[41] although in the reference given above the abbess of Caen, significantly, seems to have been trying it on for her bordars at Felstead.[42] In England the most common form of chevage, as Bloch noted,[43] was undoubtedly the payment made by a villein to live away from his native manor, a form which will be familiar to all students of court rolls, and which is discussed in *De Legibus*.[44] A few emigrant villeins may have regarded these payments (sometimes called *recognitio*, i.e. acknowledgement of lordship)[45] as useful because regular payment might help them eventually to claim an inheritance on their native manor. How regularly seigneurial authorities insisted on chevage of emigrants is less clear. Did lords under thirteenth-century conditions of population growth, and hardly short of potential tenants, really have an interest in ensuring that every single emigrant from their manors should remain under their lordship? One might argue that, at least before the Black Death, chevage of emigrants was merely,

---

[40] M. Bloch, 'Personal Liberty and Servitude in the Middle Ages, particularly in France: Contribution to a Class Study', in M. Bloch, *Slavery and Serfdom in the Middle Ages*, tr. W. R. Beer (Berkeley, Los Angeles, London, 1975), 37–8.

[41] It is not mentioned in extents and custumals as an obligation of landholders. It was not used as an indicator of villein status: Hyams, *King, Lords and Peasants*, 184–299; Hilton, 'Freedom and Villeinage', *P&P* 31 (1965), 10 n. 20.

[42] Above p. 523.   [43] Bloch, 'Personal Liberty and Servitude', 38 n. 14.

[44] Hyams, *King, Lords and Peasants*, 35–6. Tithingpenny was also quite frequently called chevage, headpenny, or *capitagium*. In the following paragraphs I have tried to exclude references in which there may be some confusion between chevage as a payment for leet jurisdiction and other forms of chevage. Nielson, *Customary Rents*, 162–74, erroneously put all of her references to chevage in her section entitled 'Payments connected with the view of frankpledge'. For an excellent guide see R. E. Latham, 'Minor Enigmas from Medieval Records: Second Series', *EHR* 76 (1961), 633–49.

[45] Especially on the Winchester estate. See e.g. N. S. B. and E. C. Gras, *The Economic and Social History of an English Village* (Cambridge, Mass., 1930), 215, 223, 242, 252, 259.

from the seigneurial point of view, the small exploitation of those who
wished, for a variety of reasons, to have what *De Legibus* called 'the habit
of coming back'.

There was also, on some manors, a chevage on immigrants. At Uplyme
in Devon custom allowed the lord to take boonworks from a specified and
limited number of *homines extranei* who were probably seasonal immigrants at times of peak activity in the farming year.[46] It is very interesting
to find that *extranei* at Lessingham (of both sexes) and at Newnham were
put in the same bracket as the landless offspring of resident villeins and
made to pay chevage or do autumn works.[47] The inquest at Cirencester,
cited in part above, after explaining the obligations of native *selfodes*, goes
on to say that precisely the same services were owed by *extranei* staying
there 'for a time' between the feast of St John the Baptist and the lord's
reaping: they sound very much like seasonally immigrant harvesters.[48]
These charges on immigrants can be regarded as more exploitative than
chevage of emigrants. Although not short of potential tenants, thirteenth-
century lords and their agents needed to mobilize the whole workforce of
the community for the needs of the demesne at crucial times in the
farming year. At these times they took 'multiple works' from tenants,
making them come to boons with specified numbers of extra helpers.[49] To
make temporary immigrants perform similar works was part of the same
strategy, and if available labour turned out to be sufficient the lord could
still profit by commuting the work to cash. Just as chevage of the offspring of villeins, landless and living on the manor outside their parent's
homes, shows that lords were aware of the endogamous circulation of
servants among houses, so too do these levies on *extranei* show awareness
of immigrant labour and of the profit to be made from it; at Longbridge
Deverill, Wiltshire, the immigrant 'serving anyone on the manor' was
common enough to warrant a prohibition on those of this type who
attempted to gate-crash the lord's scot-ales.[50] It is doubtful if chevage of

---

[46] BL Add. MS 17450, fo. 221. It is siginificant that Uplyme was a manor on which the
native landless labour force was very small, perhaps creating a demand for immigrant labour
at harvest time.

[47] Above, p. 525.

[48] *Cartulary of Cirencester Abbey*, i. 249. Another reference to the 'licencing' of *extranei* is
in Vinogradoff, *Villeinage*, 142 n. 6.

[49] Below, p. 561.

[50] *Rentalia et Custumaria Michaelis de Ambresbury 1235–52 et Rogeri de Ford 1252–61*, ed.
C. J. Elton (Somerset Rec. Soc. 5, 1891), 143. See also Ault, *Open-field Husbandry and the
Village Community*, where many of the earliest references to immigrants at harvest time
contain no hints that outsiders were repelled unless they behaved 'badly' or competed with
the gleaning rights of the resident poor, and this is as we should expect during a period

these impermanent *extranei* had much to do with lords' demonstration of seisin over them or the desire for good lordship by the immigrants them-selves: the temporary immigrant was not the man of the lord of the place in which he happened to be staying and neither party wished him so to be. There were, in any case, special and specific terms for use in the context of acknowledgement of lordship by more permanent immigrants. One was *adventicius*, 'incomer', a term often used in pleas of naifty, for new arrivals on a foreign lordship could make a case for personal freedom there so long as they had resided for sufficiently long. Another was *avoeria* (and many variant spellings), a payment made by immigrants for the 'protection' of good lordship, widespread in Wales and Cheshire but relatively uncommon, and never collected on a systematic basis, elsewhere.[51]

Chevagium garcionum, our main concern here, probably had most affinities with *chevagium extraneorum*. To some degree it can perhaps be regarded as a demonstration of seisin over men. This is how Britton saw chevage: pondering over the perhaps rather theoretical question of how lords should demonstrate seisin over all of their villeins, he stated that this was easy in the case of those holding land, from whom diagnostic servile works were due; but, he continues, for 'the others who hold nothing' the lord should take 'a penny yearly for chevage and one day's work in harvest'.[52] Britton may simply have been searching around in his mind for a commonplace practice which suited his theoretical case. During the thirteenth century when *chevagium garcionum* reached the height of its development, most lords were not short of tenants or potential tenants, except perhaps at harvest. They had no real need to demonstrate seisin except perhaps over significant tenants, recalcitrant tenants or those fleeing with valuable chattels; certainly no need to concern themselves much with seisin of a growing body of 'insignificant' landless and vagrant people. One may perhaps therefore suggest, as a more important motive for chevage of the landless, a desire to profit from a tax on their labour,

when much land was under cultivation and demand for work at harvest time was corre-spondingly great. See also Poos, *A Rural Society*, 199 n. 60; and, for migrant harvest labour more generally, below n. 146.

[51] Hyams, *King, Lords and Peasants*, 209–10; Davies, *Lordship and Society*, 138–9; R. Stewart-Brown, 'The Avowries of Cheshire', *EHR* 29 (1914), 41–55. For scattered references to *avoeria* in other parts of England, see *Select Pleas in Manorial Courts*, 11; *The Red Book of Worcester*, iv, index *s.v.* 'protection'; *Court Rolls of the Wiltshire Manors of Adam de Stratton*, ed. R. B. Pugh (Wiltshire Rec. Soc. 24, 1970), 4; BL Cott. Claud. C xi, for example at fos. 53 and 120ᵛ where many of those who paid *avoeria* were immigrants or craftsmen.

[52] *Britton*, 166.

a tax which could be very lucrative: 50s. on some of the largest manors of the bishop of Bath and Wells in the first decade of the fourteenth century, as much as 100s. on some Glastonbury manors.[53] How might a lord extract profit from a resident who held no land directly from him? If the landless lived partly by 'hunting and gathering', what was gathered was the lord's property in any case and they could be made to pay a fine for it, as did the landless diggers of fuller's earth at Minchinhampton or the migrant Cornish *carbonarii* who crossed the Tamar to dig turves on Dartmoor.[54] But if the landless person lived largely or wholly by working for others, seigneurial exploitation could only take the form of a few boonworks or a levy on the cash earned through work contracts, of whatever kind. It does not seem surprising to find that, at a time when seigneurial exploitation was at its greatest, lords should have sought to profit from the wages earned through labour contracts, just as they sought gain from other means by which their men and women might earn (*tolsester* or *custompottes* on brewings, for example, or taxes on the sale of livestock) and from contracts such as sub-letting and marriage.[55] The fact that females seem to have been included in only some of these taxes on the landless says nothing about the relative roles of female and male service in the countryside of pre-Black Death England. We know that female servants were present there, though unfortunately there is no source which allows us to gauge their numbers relative to male servants in this period.[56] That landless women were taxed on some manors and not on others simply reflects a quite large range in the sophistication of the specifications for these taxes: just as some excluded offspring in parental homes while others did not, so too did some authorities tax males alone while others extended their nets further to tax the lower wages of women.

Some of the references given above lend strong support to an interpretation of *chevagium garcionum*, and the like, as levies on labour. At Cirencester the obligations of landless sons of villeins were first owed when they began to 'live by their own labour'; at Lessingham and at Shipdham the tax was levied only on those whose labour was worth more than 10d. or 12d. in the harvest season, thus exempting the poor who earned little. Then again, on the Glastonbury estate, *garciones* were exempt

---

[53] PRO, S.C. 6 1131/4; L.10768 (combined Somerset manors of Brent).

[54] *Charters and Custumals*, 136; H. S. A. Fox, 'The Occupation of the Land: Devon and Cornwall', in Miller (ed.), *Agrarian History of England and Wales*, iii. 159.

[55] Williamson, 'Norfolk: Thirteenth Century', 105. For the suggestion that taxation of dower was one of the functions of merchet, see Searle, 'Freedom and Marriage', 482–6.

[56] See, for example, the many lively references to female servants in Razi, *Life, Marriage and Death*, 78–83.

if blind or infirm or if 'puny' (*parvus*), the last term being almost always applied to adolescent newcomers to the listings; these were all groups which were unlikely to earn much by way of wages. Examination of successive Glastonbury listings shows that an individual *garcio* would be taxed at a low rate while still an adolescent, more heavily as he moved into manhood with some relaxation if he remained landless into old age. This suggests a tax on the power of the arm and its ability to earn wages.[57]

An interpretation of these payments as taxes on labour contracts entered into by the landless is supported by, and helps to explain, the exemption of siblings in their parents' homes, a feature of all the references in the second group above and of *chevagium garcionum* on the Glastonbury estate; children at home were not under contract. Moreover, seigneurial authorities often insisted that, at harvest time, villein landholders should perform multiple works 'with their family'.[58] To impose further and additional services at harvest time upon children within the parental home would be to burden them twice over, so to speak. At Cirencester (above) the jurors explained the exemption of sons still in the household thus: they were acquitted by virtue of the boon reapings which their parents themselves performed.

But we must not be too dogmatic. As impositions of this kind spread from estate to estate, lords may have seen their twofold benefits, as valuable sources of income and of labour and also as a means of recording the landless. The two motives do, in any case, converge: the only conceivable reason why seigneurial authorities should have wished to record seisin of the growing numbers of landless in the thirteenth century would have been to profit from them in one way or another.

How widespread were payments from the landless of the types discussed in this section? Manorial extents will certainly reveal more examples of specifications for taxes similar to those listed above, now that we know what we are looking for. Some extents even give the names of the landless who were taxed: one for Minchinhampton, Gloucestershire, made in *c.*1306, ends with three lists totalling forty names of landless men who were either the sons of tenants or craftsmen or fullers paying for licence to dig earth; a late fourteenth-century extent of the bishop of Salisbury's manor of Sherborne, Dorset, ends with a list of ten names under the heading *capitagium garcionum*; at Hele in Devon, again in the late fourteenth century, the lord of a minor gentry family ended his rental with

---

[57] I am currently engaged in a detailed examination of payment as related to age.
[58] See below, p. 562.

the names of chevage-paying *garciones* and *mulieres*.[59] Given that taxes on the landless were by no means uncommon, it is not surprising to find that on some estates the names of those who paid were enrolled in the records of manorial courts, just as they were for Glastonbury manors. The nuns of Shaftesbury regularly maintained such lists with the innovation that they distinguished newcomers to the lordship, while from Chedzoy, Somerset, there are listings from the early fourteenth century which, conversely, are annotated to show which among the landless had departed from the manor; in both cases sons living at home were exempt.[60] At the courts of the prior of Bath lists were enroled which were very similar to those of his near neighbour the abbot of Glastonbury.[61] Among the court rolls of Eldersfield, Worcestershire, another gentry manor, is a list of males and females who owed the lord three boon reapings; many are stated to be the sons or daughters of tenants and are arranged in sibling groups, suggesting that this is a listing of the landless offspring of tenants; the date is around 1317, and one could guess that this labour force was mobilized to cope with shortage of workers on the demesne resulting from the famines.[62] Finally, among the court rolls of Castle Combe, Wiltshire, is a long series of listings of the landless, whose numbers increased through immigration during the fifteenth century, swelling the population of this industrializing manor at a time when many purely rural places were in demographic decline.[63] Many more listings from other manors could no doubt be uncovered if a deliberate search were made. And if one adds to the evidence of the listings themselves, the evidence of extents, court rolls, and account rolls which simply give a total sum (without names) from the profits of *chevagium garcionum*, the tally of places at which this tax was taken will eventually become very long indeed: there are scattered outliers, for example in Lincolnshire, Sussex, and Oxfordshire,[64] concentrations of manors with the tax in

---

[59] *Charters and Custumals*, 136–7; Wiltshire Record Office (henceforward WtRO), D1 1/5, fo. 196; Somerset Record Office (henceforth SmRO), DDCN 3/14.

[60] WtRO, court rolls of Fontmell Magna, Dorset and Tisbury, Wiltshire; BL Add. Rolls 15946* and 15997A. For lists in the court proceedings of another Wiltshire manor, Burbage, see PRO S.C. 2 183/56.

[61] PRO S.C. 2 198/27; BRO, AC/M3/1.

[62] Hereford and Worcester Record Office (henceforward WoRO), 705: 13 (BA 1531/69).

[63] BL Add. Rolls 18250, 18472, 18468, 18475, a sample from a much larger series; Carus-Wilson, 'Evidences of Industrial Growth', 199, 202–3. One of these lists was printed as early as 1852: Scrope, *History of Castle Combe*, 165–6. See also n. 23, above.

[64] *Calendar of Inquisitions post mortem*, vii. 145 (Castle Carlton, Lincs.); above n. 21 and PRO C.134 41 for the Percy estate in Sussex; C. 134 91 for Woolbeding, Sussex; J. C. Blomfield, *History of Bicester, its Town and Priory* (Bicester, 1884), 150.

Somerset[65] and Wiltshire,[66] and a number in Devon and Cornwall.[67] In other parts of the country similar taxes may well come to light, but under different names.

III. GLASTONBURY REVISITED

No findings from a preliminary inspection of the listings which Glastonbury Abbey kept for the purpose of levying *chevagium garcionum* contradict the view that this was a tax very similar to those described from other estates with sources more explicit than Glastonbury's: a head tax on landless males resident on the manor yet outside their parents' households, a proportion of them following the occupation of servants.

It is worth asking what the alternatives could be. That the listings were made to record the names of *emigrants*, as Postan thought, is very unlikely given the parallels cited above from other estates. Moreover, it is inherently improbable because those who made the lists had a very good

[65] The examples given in this and the following two notes are the results of only a cursory search. *Somerset, from Inquisitions Post Mortem and Account Rolls*: Barrington, PRO C.133 61; Creech, C. 133 62/7; Curry Rivel, SmRO DDSAS CU 1 and North Devon Record Office, 1142B/M28–9; Hemington, PRO C. 133 62/7; Henford, C. 133 79/4; Hewish Champflower, C. 135 59/20; Kilmersdon, C. 133 68/5; Lydford, C. 134/99; Martock, C. 133 105/3; Mudford and Hinton, C. 135 88/2; North Petherton, SmRO, DDSAS NP 1–6; Odcombe, PRO S.C. 6 973/1; Queen Camel, S.C. 6 1090/6; Shepton Mallet, C. 134 31/14; South Petherton, C. 133 61/23; Stogursey, S.C. 6 1090/6; an un-named manor of Montacute Priory, Devon Record Office (henceforward DvRO), CR 1145. *Somerset, Estates of the Bishop of Bath and Wells and of the Dean and Chapter of Wells*: PRO S.C. 6 1131/4 and Lambeth Palace Library, ED 1178, a sample from a larger series of composite accounts which shows a significant drop in the profits of *chevagium garcionum* after 1348; SmRO, DDCC 110739/2, 112826/9, 131909/8/23 and 12/23. *Somerset, from Printed Sources*: T. B. Dilks, 'Bridgewater Castle and Demesne towards the End of the Fourteenth Century', *Proc. of the Somerset Arch. and Natural Hist. Soc.* 86 (1940), 99; J. F. Chanter, 'The Court Rolls of the Manor of Curry Rivel in the Years of the Black Death, 1348–9', *Proc. of the Somerset Arch. and Natural Hist. Soc.* 56 (1910), 93, 104; Sir Matthew Natham, *The Annals of West Coker* (Cambridge, 1957), 462; T. S. Holmes, *The History of the Parish and Manor of Wookey* (Bristol, n.d.), 33.

[66] Fifide and Heytesbury: *Abstracts of Wiltshire Inquisitiones Post Mortem*, ed. E. A. Fry (British Rec. Soc. 37, 1908), 360–1, 388. Compton Chamberlayne, West Dean, and other Ingham manors, Sherrington, West Dean (with assignment in dower of profits from chevage of named *garciones*): *Abstracts of Wiltshire Inquisitiones Post Mortem*, ed. E. Stokes (British Rec. Soc. 48, 1914), 27, 161–2, 179, 195. Laverton: PRO E. 142/8.

[67] *Devon:* Beaford, PRO S.C. 6 1146/21; Belstone, S.C. 6 827/10; Gittisham, S.C. 6 1146/21; Hartland, C. 133 102/2; Kenton, C. 133 95; Puddington, E. 142/8; Slapton, C. 133 26/4; Umberleigh, S.C. 6 1146/21; Uplowman, ibid.; Whitwell, ibid.; Yarcombe, DvRO, CR 1431; Yealmpton, PRO C. 134 16/9. *Cornwall:* Alwarton, PRO S.C. 6 1146/21; Tywarnhayle, ibid.; Worthyvale, C. 133 105/5; estate of the Duchy of Cornwall, S.C. 6 817/1 where *chevigium garcionum* is specified, though perhaps in error because chevage on the estate was normally levied on emigrants, for which see *The Caption of Seisin of the Duchy of Cornwall, 1377*, ed. P.L. Hull (Devon and Cornwall Rec. Soc. NS 17, 1971), xl; J. Hatcher, *Rural Economy and Society in the Duchy of Cornwall, 1300–1500* (Cambridge, 1970), 221–2.

knowledge of the state of health of the *garciones*, imposing levies which varied according to age and strength, exempting the poor, the blind, and the infirm and, finally, deleting the names of the dead. It is highly unlikely that such information could have been assembled about an emigrant population and unlikely that the blind and aged, if they had been emigrants, would have returned to the manor of their birth yearly at Easter simply to be exonerated from chevage. Furthermore, the annotation 'he has withdrawn' is not infrequent in the listings: these annotations relate to *garciones* who have left the manor, the implication being that those names not so annotated, always the vast majority, are of residents.[68] On those occasions when we happen to know that a landless male was away from the manor, he does not appear in the listings, or a blank space is left beside his name in place of his payment of chevage: a son on a pilgrimage, almost certainly abroad, a *garcio* 'pardoned because he is in prison', others who were outlaws (*utlegati*). Then again, the annotation 'so long as he remains', perhaps applied to transients, is occasionally to be found, which would make no sense in a list of emigrants.[69] Finally, some of the listings for 1265 do contain the names of emigrants as well as of the resident landless: these are the exceptions which prove the rule. The rolls of 1265 are the earliest surviving engrossed proceedings of Glastonbury's Easter courts and it could well be that the listings to be found in them were of an experimental nature.[70] But the experiment, if that is what it was, was never again repeated. Thereafter those who made listings concerned themselves with landless residents.

Of course, we are not to be certain that after 1265 every male without exception in these listings was permanently on the manor to which he is attributed throughout the years of his enrolment. Court proceedings give us glimpses of the movements of a few of them. At the court of South Brent, Somerset, in 1345 it was claimed that for the past seven years Richard son of Nicholas le Hayward had been living on the neighbouring manor of Burnham where he had taken land and had married and that the hallmoot knew about and concealed his absence. Richard, although on the lists, was therefore not resident, nor was he landless. Then again, at Ditcheat, Somerset, the Easter hallmoot of 1349 corrected itself for having wrongly stated the previous year that Thomas Cuckoo, a *garcio* of

---

[68] e.g. L. 11250 (Shapwick, Somerset), 11252 (Mells, Somerset), 11250 (Pilton, Somerset). Attitudes changed after the Black Death: now there was more insistence in some cases on the payment of chevage by emigrants.

[69] L. 10774 (Pilton, Somerset), 10771 (Podimore, Somerset), 11251 (Grittleton, Wiltshire), 11250 (Pilton, Somerset; 'so long as he remains' applied here to a *garcio* with a surname which is not a familiar one on this manor, suggesting a transient).

[70] L. 10683.

at least 54 years of age, was dead. In fact he had, rather remarkably, survived these difficult months as a 'pauper, feeble and blind', living 'from alms in the neighbourhood', a marginal, a vagrant, a masterless man with some attachment to Ditcheat but not always present there at Easter.[71] We cannot therefore be absolutely sure that every one of the landless males listed as paying *chevagium garcionum* was resident on his manor, but the vast majority were.

'Landless' needs qualification as well as 'resident'. That *garciones* did not hold land directly from the abbey is clear from any collation of listings and extents for in the latter no *garciones* hold tenements of any kind from the lord.[72] We must ask if any *garciones* could have been subtenants of the lord's tenants, occupying and cultivating fragments of holdings as lessees. The possibility (unlikely in any case for those in their teens) may be ruled out for the great majority of *garciones*, because there are very few references to subleases in the proceedings of Glastonbury's courts. This fact is best presented statistically: for the manors studied in detail in the following sections of this chapter (Pilton and Ditcheat, Somerset), the proceedings of a total of 48 court sessions survive between 1262 and 1348, in which are formally recorded approximately 100 trans-actions involving integral holdings, but no formally recorded subleases of entire tenements or fragments. A few instances of illegal subleasing, three in all, do reveal a small traffic in land of the latter kind, but the fines imposed on the lessors in these cases reveal a disapproval of such trans-actions either among the body of tenants or by higher authority.[73] It has been argued that, in some parts of England, exceptionally heavy labour requirements on very intensively cultivated land may have encouraged landlords to look favourably upon the proliferation of smallholdings (through subleasing and other means) because it generated a multiplicity of tenements from which workers could be hired for tasks around the demesne.[74] In general such conditions did not apply on the Glastonbury estate where highly intensive cultivation was not practised and where, on most manors, the labour services of tenants continued into the mid-fourteenth century to supply much of the work needed on demesnes; the

---

[71] L. 11251, 11222. For an outlawed *garcio itierans*, see *Somerset Pleas*, ed. C. E. H. C. Healey (Somerset Rec. Soc. 11, 1897), 56.

[72] This is very clear from a comparison of extents made *c.*1316 and listings of 1315.

[73] L. 10682, 10683, 11250, 10778, 10770, 11252, 10768, 11253, 10654, 10771, 10773, 10774, 11251, 11179. The three cases of illegal subleasing involved a tenant who sublet his whole holding and went to live in Bristol, the reclaim of debt owed to a sublessor and a case of one acre leased for 6 years 'without licence': L. 10774 (Pilton, Somerset), 11250, 10773 (both Ditcheat, Somerset).

[74] Smith, 'Some Issues Concerning Families', 66.

abbey's officials may well have preferred this stable and convenient system along with managers of other estates in southern England who issued stern prohibitions against subleasing.[75] It was a system, certainly, which failed to provide many niches for the landless. All that we can do is to take the evidence of the court rolls at face value: it portrays manors on which the lord made a considerable income (through *chevagium garcionum*) from the *landlessness* of many of his tenants' children, rather than from fines generated in a land market of fragmented holdings.

The fact that the great majority of *garciones* on Glastonbury manors were both resident and without agricultural land naturally raises questions about the precise nature of their accommodation. Could some of them have been subcottagers living in separate accommodation built within the crofts of the tenants? Zvi Razi envisages some tenements at Halesowen as having a 'main house . . . surrounded by cottages occupied by . . . relations of the tenant' and has provided excellent evidence from the manor's court rolls of slips of land being given by tenants to non-inheriting or retired kin so that they could build a cottage (a moveable building in one case) next to the main messuage.[76] Then again, the archbishop of Canterbury's custumal of 1285, with its remarkable lists of *cotarii nativorum* ('cottars of the villeins'), allows the historian to prize out another type of dependent cottager, not in these cases a kinsperson but a labourer tied to the main holding. Such was William the Shepherd of Wellingham, Sussex, who held a cottage of 3 rods from Hugh Bayliff, paying him 8*d.* yearly and perhaps shepherding for him and for others. On the same manor lived the aptly named Robert Coterel who rented a cottage of half a rod for 4½*d.* ('and it is not worth more' says the custumal). His landlords were three direct tenants of the archbishop, each receiving 1½*d.* rent from Robert, and with a little imagination one can envisage this minute dwelling as having been built—perhaps on a common green onto which the houses of the direct tenants faced—as an inducement to a worker who would always be on hand when needed.[77] Such individuals were half servants (in terms of ties with their employer-landlords) and half labourers (in terms of their accommodation).[78]

[75] BL Cott. Tib. D vi, fo. 94ᵛ (a 'statute' of Richard, probably Richard Maury, 1287–1302, Prior of Christchurch, Twynham, Hampshire, couched in the sternest terms); DvRO, T42, fo. 62ᵛ (customs for the estate of Otterton Priory). I am still looking into the question of whether or not the lease of a few acres of demesne provided grounds for exemption from *chevagium garcionum*.

[76] Razi, 'Myth of the Immutable English Family', 7–11 and above, p. 376.

[77] *Custumals of the Sussex Manors of the Archbishop of Canterbury*, ed. B. C. Redwood and A. E. Wilson (Sussex Rec. Soc. 57, 1958), 91–2. Not all of the 'cottars of the villeins' were genuinely landless subcottars.

[78] For the distinctions between servants and labourers, see Poos, *A Rural Society*, 181–2.

These landless subcottages as we may call them (borrowing from *sub cotarius* in a late fourteenth-century custumal of Islip, Oxfordshire),[79] whether occupied by the kin or workers of those tenants on whose lands their dwellings were built, are occasionally just visible in the archaeological record.[80] They are sometimes semi-visible in documents as, for example, when seigneurial authorities tried to profit from them, just as they tried to exploit the labour of servants. In extents there are references to boonworks from a man 'who holds a cottage' from a yardlander, to tenants paying 6*d.* for having 'more than one *cotsetle*', to works done by 'small cottagers (*coterelli*) living upon the land of the customary tenants', to 'cottagers of the freemen' and to 'cottagers holding of the villeins' who pay churchscot in hens; in all of these cases the subcottagers are anonymous and uncounted.[81] Eventually seigneurial authorities might wish to draw landless subcottages of this kind into the open and into their own rentals, as at Egham, Surrey, where it was noted that Peter Gramot acknowledged owing the lord 10*d.* for rent for a cottage, once paid to Roger atte Pole (a tenant) and perhaps at Hinton-on-the-Green, Worcestershire, where those who drew up a survey in 1266–7 were concerned about 'new humble dwellings (*bordelli*) set up without licence . . . [whose] rents should be inserted in this extent'.[82] By the end of the thirteenth century many cottages recorded in surveys as owing rent to the lord, especially those owing certain diagnostic kinds of services, may have started out as concealed subcottages.[83]

This short digression on minute dwellings has been necessary because

---

[79] *Custumal (1391) and Bye-Laws (1386–1540) of the Manor of Islip*, ed. and tr. B. F. Harvey (Oxford, Rec. Soc. 40, 1959), 98–101. The subcottages at Islip may not reflect early medieval conditions, but rather new motives for the maintenance of cottage accommodation after the Black Death, discussed in H. S. A. Fox, 'Servants, Cottagers and Tied Cottages during the Later Middle Ages', *Rural History*, 6 (1995), 125–54.

[80] G. Astill, 'Rural Settlement: The Toft and Croft', in Astill and Grant (eds.), *The Countryside of Medieval England*, 58–9.

[81] *Thirteen Custumals of the Sussex Manors of the Bishop of Chichester*, ed. W. D. Peckham (Sussex Rec. Soc. 31, Lewes, 1925), 33–4, 37; SmRO, DD CC 131911A; BL Cott. Claud. C xi, fo. 312ᵛ; *Registrum Prioratus Beatae Mariae Wigorniensis*, 25a; BL Add. MS 17450, fo. 191. Because those described by the term *cotarius* (and the like) in medieval sources could be occupiers of a few acres we cannot be absolutely sure that all of the subcottars of these references were landless.

[82] *Chertsey Abbey Court Rolls Abstracts*, ed. E. Toms (Surrey Rec. Soc. 38, 1937), 58 and see also 46 where Roger atte Pole surrenders the rent of this cottage to the lord; *Historia et Cartularium Monasterii Sancti Petri Gloucestriae*, ed. W. H. Hart (Rolls Ser. 33c, 1863–7), iii. 61. The new cottages at Hinton-on-the-Green need not have been subcottages of the type described here; they could have been taken out of the waste.

[83] I am still working on the diagnostic services owed by cottages of this type, which sometimes bear a remarkable similarity to the services rendered by the landless and discussed in the previous section. For perceptive comments, see Titow, *English Rural Society*, 86.

one cannot avoid asking if a proportion of the *garciones* on some Glastonbury manors could have been accommodated as subcottagers. On one
Wiltshire property of the abbey the evidence for landless subcottagers is
unequivocal.[84] On the manors to be studied later in this chapter, on the
other hand, there is no evidence to show that they existed in large numbers. Court proceedings contain no incidental references to them at all
and show, indeed, that kin such as non-inheriting brothers or retired
parents might be accommodated within the houses of their relatives, not
in separate subcottages.[85] Surveys show that what may formerly have
been subcottages had been drawn into the abbey's rental.[86] Moreover, the
listings reveal hardly any cases of males who formed families and bore
sons while still retaining their status as *garciones*—strongly suggesting
that most of them did not have independent accommodation.

To conclude: most *garciones* on Glastonbury manors were resident at
the places to which they are attributed in the listings (although there were
always exceptions), were landless and were without independent accommodation. By elimination, therefore, those who were outside their parents' homes must in many cases have been servants serving in the homes
of tenant farmers on their respective manors. We can never be sure of the
precise numbers because of exceptions such as those noted in the paragraphs above: a few *garciones* not permanently resident on their manors,
a few possibly with illegally sublet acres, a few residing with kin other
than parents.[87] Nothing in the court proceedings of the manors studied in
more depth later in this chapter is against this interpretation. And indeed,
the courts refer relatively frequently to servants, in the petty contexts of
trespass and pilfering which are usual for references of this kind. A few
of those *garciones* who were not apparently the sons of tenants on the
manors to which they are attributed bore occupational by-names such as
Thresher, suggesting that they were not general-purpose servants, but
most in this immigrant class (always a small minority in the listings) were
given nicknames, some of a jocular nature, as appropriate to humble
and probably youthful newcomers to a community: at Pilton, Somerset,

[84] BL Add. MS 17450, fo. 191.

[85] L. 11251 (Ditcheat), with two examples of maintenance agreements. In one, Eve at
Mead, an outgoing tenant, was allowed a solar and a cellar in the main house. In the other
Richard White, brother of an incoming tenant, was to have 'a competent room' (*camera*).
Both were on substantial tenements.

[86] e.g. the cottage holdings at Pilton which are listed in a survey after the miller's
tenement and among the 20-acre tenants rather than at the end along with the other
cottagers: BL Eg. MS 3321.

[87] For kin, above, n. 85.

immigrant *garciones* included Draglap, Dustybeard, Hockpenny (a reference to the Hocktide chevage?), Pig, Skinhead.[88] In short, many *garciones* on Glastonbury manors must have been servants, just as on other estates (above §II) many of the chevage-paying sons and daughters of villeins, living outside their parents' homes, must surely have served in the houses of others.

IV. EXPLOITATION OF THE LANDLESS BY TENANTS

Information as rich as the listings of *garciones* on the manors of Glastonbury Abbey has great potential value. The listings, when combined with figures on tenants with land derived from surveys, come tantalizingly close to giving us categories of demographic data which, although basic, are hard to find for pre-plague England, on local differences in population densities for example.[89] The listings should be susceptible to analysis of turnover rates in order to examine what is said to have been that 'extensive geographical mobility [which] had already become an integral experience of country life . . . well before the Black Death';[90] there will be hints later in this study of differences between manors in the amount of emigration which was taking place. Finally, but not exhaustively, the listings throw light onto one of the most obscure features of rural history before the Black Death, the prevalence of service in husbandry, a topic which has already been touched upon above. Why were there differences between manors in numbers of landless males? For whom did they work? What circumstances encouraged the use of family labour (*garciones* 'with father' or 'with mother') and what circumstances expelled some landless males from parental homes (*garciones* not 'with father' or 'with mother')? The second half of this chapter is an attempt to explore such questions, based upon a pilot study of the listings from two Glastonbury manors, Pilton and Ditcheat in Somerset. The enquiry is largely based on sources from the first two decades of the fourteenth century.

A meaningful measurement of differences between manors in the size of the landless labour force can be gained by relating numbers of *garciones* to the number of landholding tenants on which they depended. The method is very simple. Many Glastonbury manors have a listing of *garciones*

---

[88] L.10682, 10683, 11250, 10778, 10770, 11252, 10768, 11253, 10654, 10771, 10773, 10774, 11251, 11179. Skinhead from rabbit-skin headgear?

[89] See H. S. A. Fox, 'Some New Estimates of Early Medieval Population Growth Rates and Densities' (forthcoming paper).

[90] Poos, *A Rural Society*, 160, referring to heavily populated Essex.

TABLE 15.1. *Number of landless males over 12* (garciones) *in relation to numbers of landholdings, Easter 1315*

	Pilton	Ditcheat
Number of tenant landholdings	116	69
Number of *garciones*	143	63
Garciones per landholding	1.2	0.91

Sources: L.10771 and BL Eg. MS 3321.

for 1315 and a manorial extent drawn up shortly afterwards; counts of the landless in the former source may be related to counts of the landed in the latter, an exercise which has been carried out for the two manors studied here. The results are presented in Table 15.1.[91]

Table 15.1 reveals some clear differences between the two manors. It shows that for every 50 landholdings at Pilton there were 60 landless males over 12 years of age, whereas at Ditcheat adolescent and adult males without land were not so prominent in the social landscape, the figure there being only 45. The figures suggest that the male population of Pilton was buoyant and growing in the years leading up to 1315—each landholder supporting on average 1.2 dependent males over 12 as well as males below that age, perhaps approximately one-third more[92]—while the male population of Ditcheat was stagnant; and relatively reliable evidence on trends in the total populations of the two manors, discussed in detail in another study, reveals the same contrast.[93] High mortality among the *garciones* of Ditcheat, as well as emigration both of the landless and of landholders, served to keep the male population virtually stagnant; Pilton, on the other hand, retained, possibly even recruited, a larger number of landless males per tenant landholder.[94] Any explanation of the buoyancy

[91] I exclude free tenants from these calculations, because their sons were not subject to *chevagium garcionum*. Some *garciones* may, of course, have been dependent on free tenants for employment, which slightly distorts the figures presented here; but this is not a serious source of error, for at Pilton there were only 8 free tenants as compared with 117 unfree and at Ditcheat 5 as compared with 68.

[92] A rough figure suggested by relevant life tables.

[93] Fox, 'Some New Estimates'.

[94] I hesitate to give any firm figures for mortality among *garciones*, as my research on this topic is still in progress. Preliminary results show that mortality rates at Ditcheat were almost three times as high as those at Pilton.

of Pilton's population and of the sluggishness of Ditcheat's must take into account a whole range of influences: differences, for example, in farming type and productivity and in holding size, both affecting diet and touched upon briefly below; differences in opportunities for employment in activities other than farming, although these can have given work to only a very small number of the landless on these predominantly agricultural manors. Full discussion of such topics is reserved for another study,[95] leaving this chapter to concentrate upon a further perhaps potent reason for differences between manors in numbers of landless, namely labour requirements in the overwhelmingly dominant occupation of farming. The enquiry was sparked off by consideration of the simple fact that in predominantly agricultural communities, and taking under-employment into account, the numbers of landless males must to a large degree have been determined by the amount of work available in farming.

In the following sections we shall first examine the structure of landholding on the two manors, and, more briefly, farm output; we shall then move on to look at the labour requirements of landholdings; and finally we shall try to wring from the intractable listings some suggestions about how those requirements may have been met, about the labour markets of the two manors.

IV.1. Farm Holdings and Farm Output

The tenemental structures of Pilton and Ditcheat in the early fourteenth century are beautifully described in manorial extents made circa 1317, from which the profiles in Figure 15.1 have been constructed.[96] Pilton, a large manor rising from the Somerset Levels five miles from Glastonbury, was dominated by what Postan described as 'the middle layer' of tenant landholding.[97] Really, there were only two large classes of tenement there, holdings originally of 10 acres and those of 20 acres, a good number of them augmented in the late thirteenth century by reclamations, of wood in some cases but largely from the marshes of the Levels. The court rolls of this period are full of references to 'assarts' in the marshes and to the scouring of new dykes, allowing us almost to visualize the process of wetland reclamation. In general it was a process which added to the sizes of many existing 10-acre and 20-acre holdings but did not result in the creation of new smallholdings, a confirmation perhaps of the same seigneurial policy, or custom, which prevented subleasing and the creation of small subtenancies. The profile at Ditcheat, by contrast, was

---

[95] Fox, 'Some New Estimates'.   [96] BL Eg. MS 3321.
[97] Postan, 'Medieval Agrarian Society in its Prime', 618.

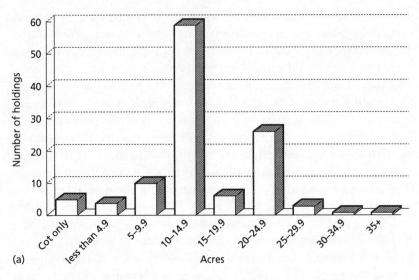

(a)

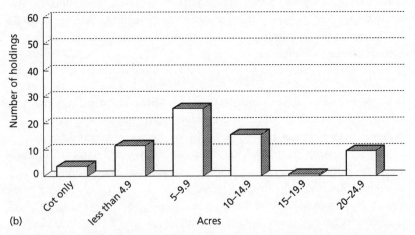

(b)

F IG. 15.1   The distribution of holdings by size in (a) Pilton and (b) Ditcheat

skewed towards the smallholder. On this small inland manor the dominant group of tenancies is that shown in Figure 15.1 as being in the 5–9.9
acre category: most of these holdings were in fact of about 5 acres in size,
for there was no scope for reclamation here. Above the 5-acre class was a
smaller group of 10-acre holdings, and above that a few of 20 acres. Below
the 5-acre farms were holdings of about 2 acres and four cottages without
land, one held by Isabella 'in the hedge': 'three mud walls and a hedge

bank' described cottages in some parts of the south-west according to Charles Vancouver writing at the beginning of the nineteenth century.[98]

Both manors have account rolls from the early fourteenth century in sufficient quantities to allow a detailed reconstruction of demesne farming and, by dint of extrapolation from the demesne, to permit estimates of the productivity per acre on the tenants' holdings.[99] A discussion of the similarities between demesne and tenant-farming practices on the two manors is given in another study while general arguments for and against extrapolations of this kind have been made elsewhere.[100] For the brief discussion which is all that is necessary here we shall take the largest size-class of holdings on each manor and try to calculate net output expressed in cash. This measure ignores differences (in fact very small) between manors in the financial burdens on peasant holdings and its conversion of all output to cash is unrealistic, though useful for comparative purposes.

The largest size-class of holdings at Pilton comprised the nominal 10-acre holdings (nearly 60 in all) most of which had been expanded by reclamation, bringing their mean size up to 12 acres. The value of their crop output might have been as high as 30s. because, according to demesne crop combinations and yields, much wheat (a grain of high value) was grown and crops yielded very well on the manor's diversified soils, including the renowned red Keuper Marl series. Moreover, at Pilton standards of living were being improved during the last quarter of the thirteenth century as more cows, reflected in the tenants' heriots and fed on reclaimed meadow, were kept by the tenants. One can perhaps suggest that the value of fleeces from the sheep running on the common fields and of dairy produce from cattle raised the total output measured in cash on a 10-acre holding to about 45s.[101] By comparison, standards of living on the largest size-group of holdings at Ditcheat, those in the 5-acre class, were miserably low. To judge from demesne practice and performance, low-priced grains were grown and yields were low on Ditcheat's heavy Lower Lias clays, giving a value of about 10s. for the net output of arable farming on a 5-acre holding. Opportunities for pastoral farming were

---

[98] C. Vancouver, *General View of the Agriculture of the County of Devon* (London, 1808), 94.

[99] L. 11272, 11246, 11271, 11215, 11216, 10655, 10656, 10766.

[100] Fox, 'Some New Estimates'; Dyer, *Standards of Living*, 127–31 for the latest discussion of the comparative productivity of demesne and peasant farming.

[101] Working with the basic assumption that income from pastoral products might have been about one-quarter of that from arable farming, as reasonably suggested by the worked example in Dyer, *Standards of Living*, 114–15, but inflating somewhat the proportion for Pilton, because of the importance of dairying there.

more restricted than at Pilton, largely because Ditcheat did not share the
latter manor's diversified land-use. With the profits of pastoral farming
added, net output on a 5-acre holding should be valued at about 13*s*. The
produce of grain on these holdings was, according to our calculations,
scarcely enough to feed even a small family. Perhaps cultivation on a
smallholding was more intensive than on the demesne, and yields therefore higher; perhaps a more nutritious and valuable mix of grains was
grown. Even so, the diet of Ditcheat's smallholding families must have
been meagre and surplus cash for the purchase of necessities, let alone
luxuries, must have been in short supply. These suggestions lend support
to the evidence already cited for high mortality at Ditcheat and emigration by the landless and by landed tenants alike.

IV.2. Labour Requirements

The central concern of this study is less with farm output and more with
the intractable subject of the holdings' labour inputs as they might have
exerted demand for work from the landless. How much labour was required to sustain husbandry on the different categories of holding shown
in Figure 15.1? In terms of existing methodology the question leads to a
virtual terra incognita. Two possibilities present themselves: either the
question is abandoned, or the wealth of detail on labour in the lord's
demesne accounts is used to arrive at an estimate of the labour requirements of the tenants' holdings. We take the latter track. Two aspects of
the method need to be discussed, first the mechanics of the exercise and
second the logic of extrapolation from demesne land to tenant land.

Because of the excellence of the details furnished by Glastonbury
Abbey's manorial accounts and extents the mechanics of the exercise are
merely time-consuming, not very difficult.[102] At both Pilton and Ditcheat
demesne labour in the early fourteenth century came from a variety of
sources: from wage labour hired by the day or for the task (in minimal
amounts at this time), from stipendiary *famuli* hired by the year, from the
week-works of villein tenants (comprising the bulk of the work done on
these demesnes) and finally from labour services not owed on a weekly
basis, for example the obligation of 20-acre tenants at Pilton to carry with
a horse and sack for eighteen days each year. There are a few, but not
many, problems in the first step in the exercise, the conversion of statements in the extents and accounts into figures for the total number of
days of work with which each of the two demesnes was furnished. The

---

[102] Principal sources are BL Eg. MS 3321 and the accounts listed above in n. 99.

next step is to subtract certain types of demesne work which are not relevant to an extrapolation to what would have been done by a tenant on his own holding, for example the work of the reeve. A number of 'foreign' services have also been subtracted, for example the obligations of some tenants at Pilton and Ditcheat to go to the manor of Baltonsborough, cut brushwood there and carry it to Glastonbury for the abbey's ovens and fires. The last step in the exercise is to make a deduction for works recorded as obligations in the extents but stated to be commuted in the accounts, always a very small number in the early fourteenth century. The final reckoning shows that 137 days of work (excluding the supervisory work of reeves, etc.) were consumed by every 10 acres of demesne at Pilton and 134 days of work by every 10 acres at Ditcheat. The figures compare well with results from the only other attempt which has been made to calculate labour inputs per acre on a medieval demesne, at Rimpton in Somerset, not too far away from our own manors.[103]

What of the logic of extrapolation from demesne labour inputs to labour requirements on the tenants' own holdings? Extrapolation assumes of course that intensity of application of labour was the same in the two sectors of the manorial economy. This issue can be argued back and forth, just as the question of a differential between yields on demesne land and tenant land can be debated. On the one hand, it is clear that work on the demesne by tenants was work done with unwilling resignation; there was a sluggishness in it resulting in countless complaints recorded in manor court rolls where it is stated that tenants had worked badly or had come late to work, all reflective of what R. H. Hilton has called the 'bitterness' behind labour services. These attitudes, amounting at times to contempt, must have multiplied the number of days of work required on each acre of demesne.[104] On the other hand, there were the circumstances which multiplied the time spent by tenants on each of their acres. Many tenants owned shoddy equipment and debilitated beasts of traction, both making for more work; in so far as there is, for every agricultural operation on every acre, an optimum day when the state of the soil and climate mean that work is at its easiest, tenants lost out

---

[103] C. Thornton, 'The Determinants of Land Productivity on the Bishop of Winchester's Demesne of Rimpton, 1208 to 1403', in B. M. S. Campbell and M. Overton (eds.), *Land, Labour and Livestock: Historical Studies in European Agricultural Productivity* (Manchester, 1991), 204–6. Thornton excludes, but I include, tasks connected with pastoral husbandry; Thornton excludes, but I include, the fallow acreage, which absorbed some work.

[104] Hilton, 'Peasant Movements in England', 117–36; Bennett, *Life on the English Manor*, 113.

through sometimes being required to work the demesne on those days.[105] Then again, many tenants were no more than smallholders: the smaller the holding the more intensively it will be cultivated, greater care being taken in weeding, reaping, etc.[106] It could well be that the opposing sets of arguments cancel one another out, and that there was a broad equivalence of input of days per acre of labour sluggishly performed on the demesne and input per acre of work intensively, even desperately, though at times inefficiently, devoted to a tenant's own holding.

These arguments mean that labour inputs on tenants' holdings, calculated by extrapolation from demesne sources, must be regarded as approximations, though perhaps not too far removed from reality. The point must be borne in mind when Figure 15.2 is considered; this classifies holdings at Pilton and Ditcheat according to the number of days of work which their occupiers might have devoted to them. The profiles shown are, of course, familiar ones simply reflecting the size-distribution of tenements, already given in Figure 15.1.

A useful yardstick which can be introduced here is the concept of a year's work: how many of the holdings at Pilton and Ditcheat absorbed the work of one person throughout the year? We should probably be thinking of a working year of about 260 days. Workers would not have been seen in the fields on Sundays, which at once subtracts 52 days. Then there were the major prolonged holidays at Christmas and Eastertide, perhaps subtracting a further 18 days (Sundays already counted). To these must be added the *festa ferianda* which, most authorities agree, can be put at about 40 days.[107] Of course, any desperate tenant faced with his own sheaves rotting in the field or a sudden thaw permitting spring ploughing would be encouraged to break the rules concerning abstinence from work on these days: indeed some of the episcopal lists of *festa ferianda* make allowances, on a minority of those saints' days when work was prohibited, for urgent ploughing and for work done as a result of acts of charity. Nevertheless, one can see—in local by-laws drawn up among tenants and in the views of ordinary parish priests as expressed by Myrc—

---

[105] 'The Lord . . . disorganizes work on the peasant's fields by taking away every available pair of hands at the most vital working times': Kosminsky, *Studies*, 239.

[106] Campbell suggests intensive cultivation as one factor which sustained the viability of very small peasant landholdings in eastern Norfolk: Campbell, 'Population Pressure', 106. Many modern studies show the same thing.

[107] This paragraph draws heavily upon B. F. Harvey's lively 'Work and *festa ferianda* in Medieval England', *JEH* 23 (1972), 289–308. For *festa* in the diocese of Bath and Wells, see C. R. Cheney, 'Rules for the Observance of Feast Days in Medieval England', BIHR 34 (1961), 143.

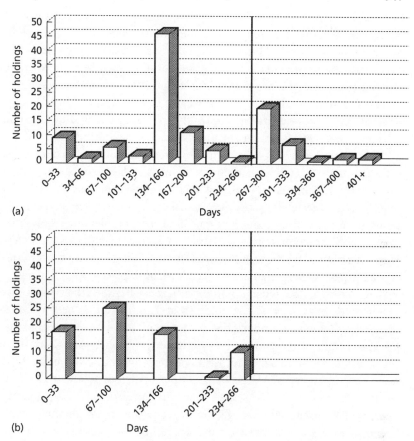

F IG. 15.2   The distribution of holdings in (a) Pilton and (b) Ditcheat by required labour
input

a general perception of the normality of abstinence from work at these
times.[108] Finally, one might guess that heavy rain, deep snow, or hard
frost rendered many agricultural tasks difficult or impossible to perform
on a minimum of ten days. These subtractions (52 plus 18 plus a minimum of 30 days for *festa* plus 10) give a year's work of about 260 days.

If we put the working year at about 260 days we shall not be erring
very far, though probably on the side of generosity because it is in the
nature of many farming operations that they enforce idleness at some
points in the year and, ideally, need the multiple work of several pairs of
hands at other times. Using this yardstick it can be seen (Figure 15.2)

---

[108] Harvey, 'Work and *festa ferianda*', 292 (ploughing), 293, n. 1 (charity), 301–2 (by-
laws), 307 (Myrc).

that on the manors studied here very few holdings in themselves needed
the labour of more than one person working throughout the year: none
did at Ditcheat while at Pilton only those holdings in the 20-acre class
which had been expanded through the addition of a few acres of reclaimed land needed more than a year's work.[109]

The situation as portrayed in Figure 15.2 is, however, unrealistic to the
point of being fictitious, for it completely ignores seigneurial exploitation
of villein labour. Calculations of the number of days which each tenant
worked on the demesne may be made, from extents and account rolls,
with far greater accuracy than our previous calculations of days worked
by a tenant for himself. Profiles of holdings based upon total required
labour input (the tenant's two layers of labour, for himself and for the
demesne) are given in Figure 15.3. These new profiles now bear little
similarity to the graphs previously presented, for their shapes are determined not simply by the size-distribution of holdings but by the severity
of the burdens which seigneurial authorities have placed upon tenements
of different sizes. The most important difference between the two manors
was that there were very few holdings at Ditcheat on which the total
labour requirement was above our yardstick of 260 days (these holdings
are to the right of the bold line in Figure 15.3) whereas at Pilton many
tenancies needed inputs of more than one person working throughout the
year. This difference was largely a result of seigneurial policy: at Ditcheat
the heaviest demesne works were taken from relatively small holdings
whereas at Pilton heavy works fell on larger tenancies. At Ditcheat much
of the week-work was owed by the numerous 5-acre tenancies, a fact
which must have rendered them particularly uninviting; even so, the total
labour requirement of these holdings fell just below 260 days. At Pilton
much of the week-work—three days per week until June and more when
the harvest got into full swing, as well as additional miscellaneous works—
fell upon holdings in the numerous 10-acre class. Because the brunt of
week-work at Pilton was borne by relatively sizeable holdings on which a
good number of days of work were already spent domestically, their total
labour requirements, with the lord's excessive services added, were pushed
way above the yardstick of 260 days, above 330 days in many cases and

---

[109] This seems quite realistic. Figures based on data gathered during Arthur Young's
tours at the end of the 18th cent. show that 25-acre arable farms in the Midlands could be
managed by one man with the help of a boy and some hired female labour: R. C. Allen, 'The
Two English Agricultural Revolutions, 1450–1850', in Campbell and Overton (eds.), *Land,
Labour and Livestock*, 250. At that time most Midland farms would have been cropped more
intensively than the medieval two-field manors discussed here, though holidays were probably fewer.

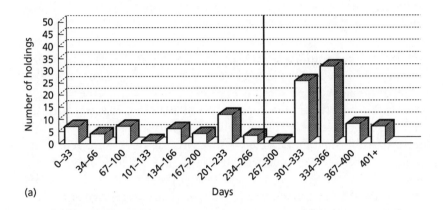

(a)

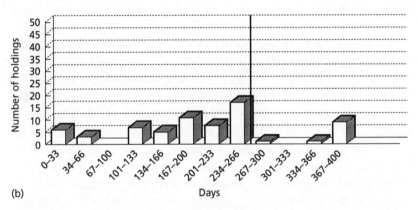

(b)

FIG. 15.3   The distribution of holdings in (a) Pilton and (b) Ditcheat by total labour
requirement: input on holding plus demesne works

above 350 in a few, the mean being 335 days. Could it be that on holdings
at Ditcheat seigneurial demands were, to coin a phrase, 'subtractive', in
that they simply skimmed the tenant's own, personal labour but that on
holdings at Pilton demands were 'excessive', obliging some occupiers to
employ excess labour?

IV.3. The Deployment of Labour: Simple Situations

If we now turn discussion from the labour requirements of holdings of
various sizes, and variously burdened with the lord's services, to how
those needs may have been met we move onto ground which is even less
well charted. Because each manor had a complex, and different, tenemental
structure and a complex, and again different, pattern of demand for

labour spread across its tenancies, discussion will be simplified if we concentrate to begin with on the most numerous category of holdings at Pilton, the 10-acre holdings (some with a few extra reclaimed acres), heavily burdened with week-work. Discussion will also be simplified if we initially consider occupiers of holdings of this type who did not have the option of employing their sons, that is occupiers at a stage in the life-cycle when children were still too young to be of assistance in major agricultural tasks.[110] Marriage at Pilton is likely to have been postponed until access to a full holding became possible because there were few small niches or fragments of holdings on which families could be formed. Assuming that mean age of marriage was on the late side, say at 28, we can use life tables to obtain a rough estimate of the percentage of tenants aged between 28 and about 41, when their first-born sons (if indeed the first-born was a son) began to be capable of work at around 12.[111] As many as about 45 per cent of tenants might have been in this predicament.[112]

The mean labour requirement (for self and for lord) on these tenancies was 335 days, of which 260 days could be contributed by the occupier. How was labour found for the deficit of 75 days? Three possible sources must be discussed, beginning with the contribution of the occupier's wife. This is a difficult question. What is at issue here is not the general question of women's work in the countryside before the Black Death but the more specific one of whether or not, on the holdings under discussion, women in the early years of married life would have often engaged in the heaviest agricultural tasks such as holding the plough, ditching, scything, or lifting sheaves, hay, and sacks of grain onto carts and stacks.

---

[110] For the hiring of servants by families with young children, and therefore deficient in labour, see L. K. Berkner, 'The Stem Family and the Developmental Cycle of the Peasant Household', *AHR* 77 (1972), 413; R. Breen, 'Farm Servanthood in Ireland', *EcHR* 2nd ser. 26 (1983), 97; M. Reed, 'Indoor Farm Service in Nineteenth Century Sussex', *Sussex Arch. Collections*, 123 (1985), 229.

[111] Age of marriage taken from estimates for the late 16th cent.: Wrigley and Schofield, *The Population History of England*, 423. The figure is quite close to some of those calculated by Hallam, using interesting methods which he himself sees as having many limitations: H. E. Hallam, 'Age at First Marriage and Age at Death in the Lincolnshire Fenland, 1252–1478', *Population Studies*, 39 (1985), 60. If we have put it four years too early or four years too late our calculation of a rough figure for the proportion of tenants waiting for the majority of their heirs will not be much affected because the age range under consideration is relatively robust.

[112] Data from Coale and Demeny, *Regional Model Life Tables*, 43–5, 57–61. Population is assumed to have been growing, but not at a very fast rate; the figure given here is a mean from two tables, one for a population with mortality much worse than England's national levels in the 16th cent., one for a population with mortality roughly equivalent to those levels. What is said here does not apply to widows; but they in fact held very few of these 10-acre tenements.

These are tasks (on both the holding and the demesne) which loom large in our calculations of required labour input. A case can be made for the abnormality of women's involvement in work of this kind. First, women were *never* employed as demesne ploughpersons, carters, and the like. Second, Penn's detailed work on the composition of the harvesting workforce is unequivocal: women reaped with sickle or hook but as for the heavier task of mowing with a scythe, 'no positive evidence of female mowers has been found'.[113] Third, there is a little evidence to suggest that where arable farming predominated households headed by women were more likely to employ male than female labour, suggesting that men were necessary because some of the heavier tasks associated with cultivation would not have been carried out by the occupier herself. Fourth, analysis of the location of accidental deaths among medieval women shows that they tended to spend more of their time in the house and croft than did men, and less of their time in the field.[114] We are certainly not attempting to underrate the contribution of medieval women to farm work in general: some farming households contained female servants, mostly in the young age groups; women of all ages were of crucial importance at harvest time (reaping, binding, stooking), as we know from their summonses to the demesne where they did their *wivenrips* and *womanswerks*; they gave attention to much that went on around the barn and croft, from the care of some animals to the processing of crops for food and drink.[115]

A second possible source of labour for the tenant with a deficit would have been to hire work on a daily basis from the occupiers of those holdings which were so small and so lightly burdened with services that they had a surplus to offer. Historians who have considered medieval smallholdings from the point of view of their domestic economy have always speculated that farm income may have been supplemented by

[113] S. A. C. Penn, 'Female Wage-Earners in Late Fourteenth-Century England', *AgHR* 35 (1987), 10; also M. Roberts, 'Sickles and Scythes: Women's Work and Men's Work at Harvest Time', *History Workshop*, 7 (1979), 6.

[114] P. J. P. Goldberg, 'Women's Work, Women's Role in the Late-Medieval North', in M. Hicks (ed.), *Profit, Piety and the Professions in Later Medieval England* (Gloucester, 1990), 41; Hanawalt, *The Ties that Bound*, 145.

[115] For female servants, see above, n. 56; for feminine terminology in boonworks, *Charters and Custumals*, 60 and subsequent references; Page, *Estates of Crowland Abbey*, 95. This chapter is largely concerned with the early years of the 14th cent., a period of labour abundance when, it may well be, women could have been 'crowded out' of some agricultural tasks, a situation which may contrast with their greater involvement with field work under conditions of labour scarcity in the later fourteenth century. For this argument, see R. M. Smith, 'Women's Work and Marriage in Pre-Industrial England: Some Speculations', in *La Donna Nell'Economia Secc. XIII-XVIII* (Prato, 1990), 49–55; and for some supporting evidence, Hilton, *Economic Development of Some Leicestershire Estates*, 145–6.

wages when the smallholder hired himself out as a labourer to a tenant farmer with a larger acreage.[116] Some tenants at Pilton with a deficit of labour, especially those with small deficits, may well have employed the surplus time of other tenants on a day by day basis, but strong arguments can be presented to suggest that in some circumstances a third alternative source may have been preferred, namely the work of living-in servants hired on yearly terms. We are therefore brought face to face with the *garciones*, landless males many of whom were available for work in the households of tenants.

If the occupier of a 10-acre holding at Pilton, with a deficit of labour, chose to employ labourers for 75 days, paying on a *per diem* basis, this would have cost him between 9s. 4d. and 12s. 6d. depending upon whether we take 1½d. or 2d. as the going rate in the early fourteenth century; probably, both rates would have been used, according to the season, so that we can strike an average of around 11s. The comparative cost of a servant in husbandry at this time is not easy to estimate.[117] The best guide to wages, probably, comes from payments to *garciones* in grand households. In 1289–90 the bishop of Hereford paid 3s. or 4s. for kitchen scullions and other *garciones* attendant upon members of the household; the ordinances of Walter de Wenlock, abbot of Westminster, give 3s. or 2s. as the stipend of *garciones* who busied themselves with the palfreys and carts; the *garciones* of the gardener and the miller at Sherborne Abbey were paid only 1s. 6d. yearly. Servants in such households were exceptionally lucky, for at Bolton Priory the *garciones* were given nothing beyond board, their employment there being presumably perceived by the monks as charity and by their kin as a form of poor relief.[118] Tenant farmers at Pilton are unlikely to have paid as well as did the likes of abbots of Westminster, so farm servants' wages there could have been as low as 2s. 6d., or even lower for the younger *garciones* if, as in the early modern period, the very youngest servants were paid next to

[116] For example, Postan, 'Medieval Agrarian Society in its Prime', 624; Kosminsky, *Studies*, 297.

[117] It is not possible to use the going rate for demesne *famuli* because of the probability that their liveries from the granary were intended to provide for a small family, for which see Dyer, 'English Diet', 211. The lord's *famuli* may have formed a kind of aristocracy among the labourers and servants of the manor, paid highly because of their especial skills, strength or fitness.

[118] *Roll of the Household Expenses of Richard de Swinfield, Bishop of Hereford, 1285–90*, ed. J. Webb (2 vols., Camden Soc. 59, 62, 1854–5), i. 170–2, 196; *Documents Illustrating the Rule of Walter de Wenlock, Abbot of Westminster, 1283–1307*, ed. B. F. Harvey (Camden Soc. 4th ser. 2, 1965), 247–8; BL Cott. Faust. A. ii, fo. 31; I. Kershaw, *Bolton Priory: The Economy of a Northern Monastery, 1286–1325* (Oxford, 1973), 137.

nothing.[119] The 'cost' of basic board—that is, loss to the employer of foodstuffs which might otherwise have been sold—would have been the price of about 2¼ quarters of mixed grain, that is about 7s. 6d. at levels prevailing in the early fourteenth century.[120] The costs of bedding in corner or barn would have been minimal, as would the cost of clothing where this was given.[121] But despite some uncertainties we shall probably not err far in putting the total cost of a servant in husbandry at about 10s. On these estimates the total cost to the employer of a servant in husbandry drawn from the *garciones* at this time may have been about 10s. There was therefore little difference in cost between labour hired by the day for 75 days and labour hired by annual contract. Moreover, there were great advantages to the tenant employer who opted for the latter: he was spared the inconvenience of hiring by the day; a servant was on hand to cope with sudden changes in weather which made immediate ploughing, mowing, or reaping necessary; he could be used to discharge some of the tenant's more tedious labour services; finally, the continuous presence of a servant even when a full year's work was not necessary from him in order to maintain husbandry at basic levels might raise the employer's living standards by allowing him more leisure and by permitting agricultural tasks to be performed with greater intensity and care, with beneficial effects on output. The arguments above, it must be admitted, incorporate estimates for the cost of food based on decadal means: a shrewd employer able to foresee one of those sharp annual price rises which occurred in some years during the late thirteenth century and early fourteenth might have been encouraged (depending upon the total number of days work he needed) in those years to substitute day labour for annual hiring.

We have argued that on a certain category of holdings at Pilton, with heavy labour requirements pushed above the threshold of a year's work as a result of services owed to the demesne, the hiring of servants in husbandry could be a logical strategy at that stage in the tenant's life-cycle when no sons were available for heavy agricultural tasks. The time has come to return to the sources and to scour the listings of *garciones*, the potential servants, in order to see if this argument is not only plausible but also supportable.

[119] A. Kussmaul, *Servants in Husbandry in Early Modern England* (Cambridge, 1981), 37–8.
[120] Consumption of 2¼ quarters yearly seems reasonable for a servant on the young side: see Dyer, 'English Diet', 203 and Dyer, *Standards of Living*, 134–5. Prices of spring crops in the decade 1300–10 calculated from D. L. Farmer, 'Prices and Wages', in Hallam (ed.), *Agrarian History of England and Wales*, ii. 734. Extra calories could have been made up from garden produce which we cannot include in these calculations.
[121] For clothing, see Razi, *Life, Marriage and Death*, 78 n. 148.

IV.4. The Deployment of Labour: Sons or Servants?

Like all new sources with great potential the listings of *garciones* on Glastonbury manors also present serious problems. First and foremost among these is that they tell us which *garciones* were with their parents (*cum patre, cum matre*) and which were on the manor yet outside the parental home, but they do not say with whom the latter group, the potential servants, were living. In other words they do not name the parents who 'exported' sons nor the 'importing', servant-hiring households. The data will need a little teasing if these topics are to be explored. A second difficulty is that whereas the listings of *garciones* give the names of resident males over 12, the names of heads of households and details of the holdings which they occupied can only be found in extents, and for Pilton and Ditcheat the two sources do not coincide in date. We are forced to use extents made between 1316 and 1318 and listings from 1307 and 1308, the two consecutive lists closest to the extents.[122] In order accurately to collate the two, we must exclude any heads of households in the extents who cannot be shown from references in court proceedings to have been already in possession of their holdings in 1307–8. A final difficulty is the usual one of nominal record linkage when documents do not contain much information on familial relationships. For example, Gilbert Young and Walter Young appear among the *garciones* of Pilton in 1307–8; a William Young and a John Young were landholders at this time, but there is no means of ascribing the two *garciones* to one or other of the fathers. The Youngs must therefore be excluded from analysis, further reducing the number of families which can be put under the spotlights.

Table 15.2, an attempt to reach as far as the sources allow into the question of labour deployment, focuses on particular classes of holding, 10-acre tenements at Pilton and those in the 5-acre and 10-acre classes combined at Ditcheat; holdings have been excluded if the data do not match up to the stringent conditions mentioned above. The two groups chosen are the largest groups (by acreage) on their respective manors, a fact which maximizes the sizes of the samples.[123] The salient characteristics of the two are as follows. The 10-acre holdings at Pilton were attractive

---

[122] BL Eg. MS 3321; L.11252, 10768.

[123] At Pilton there were 58 holdings in the 10-acre class (see Fig. 15.1), though only 40 were heavily burdened with works. Of those 40, five were occupied by women at the time of the extent and are not analysed here because of the special difficulties of linking sons in the listings to female tenants. Other difficulties in linking (mentioned in the text) reduce the sample of holdings under observation to 18. For Ditcheat the figures are as follows. Total number of 5- and 10-acre holdings: 42; occupied by women: 7. Final size of sample when difficult cases and women's holdings are eliminated: 15.

TABLE 15.2.   *Residential patterns among sons (aged 12 and over) of male tenants*

	Pilton 10-acre holdings	Ditcheat 5- and 10-acre holdings
Male tenants with sons resident on manor	46.7%	28.6%
Male tenants with no sons resident on manor	53.3%	71.4%
Male tenants with sons on manor and with parent	20.6%	52.6%
Male tenants with sons on manor and outside parental home	79.4%	47.4%
Sons on manor with parent	25%	42.9%
Sons on manor outside parental home	75%	57.1%

Sources: BL Eg. MS 3321 and L.11252, 10768. For sizes of samples, see n. 124.

from the viewpoint of output and may have had total farm incomes of about 45*s*.[124] They were also attractive from the viewpoint of out-goings, for their rents were acquitted in return for services. They were, however, burdened with heavy works, bringing their total labour requirement to around 335 days and, it has been argued above, their occupiers might need recourse to servants in husbandry at early stages in a tenancy. Above them in acreage was a substantial group of 20-acre holdings all with labour requirements well over 260 days and therefore also likely at times to have been employers of labour: Pilton, in other words, had plenty of potential places for servants. The 5-acre holdings at Ditcheat and their setting within the manor's tenemental structure provide a complete contrast. The total yearly value of farm produce on these unattractive holdings may have been as low as 13*s*. Rents were acquitted as at Pilton. The burden of works was heavy but because these were smallholders with less to do on their own acres, total labour requirements approached very closely but never rose above the capacity of one man (260 days). Their occupiers were condemned to hard and unremitting, relentless toil throughout the working year, and for small returns. The 10-acre holdings at

[124] Figures for output calculated as on p. 543 above.

Ditcheat, which we are also considering here, were less heavily burdened with services and also had total labour requirements of less than 260 days. Above them in the manor's tenemental structure was a small group of 20-acre holdings with labour requirements above 260 days. As is clear from Figure 15.3, Ditcheat was a manor on which almost all of the tenures could be managed with less than 260 days of work, that is the capacity of one man. Its tenemental structure was not, in other words, much suited to servanthood. Some opportunities there were: on the small number of 20-acre holdings, on the farms of the manor's many widow-tenants and, perhaps, in the households of the infirm—assuming, in all cases, that no sons of age were available and that servants were preferred to sons. But in general one might describe the manor as repellant to the institution of service.

In the light of these contrasting characteristics the findings of Table 15.2 are of very considerable interest. The first lines simply give the proportions of tenants who had or did not have sons over age 12 somewhere on the manor in the years 1307–8. Of course, a cross-section across any segment of a male tenant population will show that some occupiers had no sons who had yet reached the age of 12, and it has been tentatively suggested above that the proportion still thus waiting for the coming of age of their first-born son might be as high as 45 per cent.[125] The figure for Pilton (53 per cent) is not therefore unexpected. What has to be explained is the very high percentage (71 per cent) of tenants of 5-acre and 10-acre holdings at Ditcheat who had no sons over 12 somewhere on the manor in 1307–8. A high mortality rate might be one explanation: certainly, mortality among the *garciones* of Ditcheat was far higher than at Pilton.[126] A second possibility is that surviving sons, perceiving a bleak future as cultivators of these unattractive tenures, simply opted for emigration in the hope of betterment elsewhere; another 'push' factor encouraging emigration could well have been the restricted opportunities for servanthood on the manor. Certainly, *garciones* can be seen slipping away in the early fourteenth century. Thus in 1307, William at Pit, the landless son or brother of 5-acre tenant Stephen at Pit, was reported as having 'withdrawn' from Ditcheat and is not visible in any court roll after that date; Henry, one of the sons of Walter Philip, another 5-acre tenant, was resident in his parent's household in 1308 but by 1313 he has disappeared from the listings, possibly through emigration; in 1308 Thomas Whiting was 'with the abbot', presumably a servant of some kind at

---

[125] Above, p. 550.　　　[126] Above, n. 94.

Glastonbury itself, and he too was thereafter lost to the manor. Peter Alexander and Peter Thurbarn were reported as fugitives in 1315.[127] Earlier listings and court proceedings also reveal emigration of *garciones*: in 1265 three had withdrawn from the manor to unstated locations and three others were at manors which appear to have had more opportunities for employment and more attractive tenures than at Ditcheat.[128] Some landed tenants, even, are recorded as leaving this unattractive manor with their chattels.[129]

It will never be possible to give a weighting to the relative importance of an unattractive future as a tenant or the comparatively few opportunities on the manor for servanthood in the motivation of those *garciones* who did emigrate from Ditcheat. That the lack of many niches for employment of servants was a factor here is, though, suggested by the last lines of Table 15.2 relating to patterns of residence of those relatively few sons who remained. Of sons at Ditcheat surviving to age 12 and remaining on the manor almost half (43 per cent) were to be found within the parental home. At Pilton, by contrast, where opportunities for service were arguably greater, only a quarter of resident sons were *cum patre*. These contrasting figures suggest that at Ditcheat even the relatively small number of sons remaining on the manor failed in many cases to find employment as servants. They cannot have been retained on their fathers' holdings out of necessity, because from the point of view of labour requirements these tenements did not have a deficit beyond the input of the occupier (except perhaps in cases where the occupier was ailing). One can therefore surmise that they were there *faute de mieux*, like Walter Prior, son of a 10-acre tenant, who was able to gain employment at Ditcheat, but away from his home, in 1313 but who was back in his father's household in 1315 presumably because of failure to find, in the manor's restricted labour market, that secure position or succession of positions which the successful servant in husbandry aspired to.[130]

Sons of 10-acre holdings at Pilton, by contrast, found themselves in a more active labour market, with more niches for service, as the differences thrown up by Table 15.2 seem to reveal: a good proportion of sons over age 12 and on the manor were to be found outside their parents' homes. Earlier in this chapter it was argued that occupiers of these holdings would have been obliged, because of their heavy total labour requirements, to employ labour during those early years in their tenancies

---

[127] L.11252; 10768, 10768; 10771.   [128] L.10683.
[129] L.11250.   [130] L.10654, 10771.

when their sons were not capable of heavy agricultural work. An intriguing pattern suggested by the table is that they appear to have continued to employ labour even after their sons had come of age. Thus to take one example from many, in 1307–8 William at Shete senior had two sons on the manor and aged over 12, William Shete junior, probably the elder of the two and a *garcio* working somewhere outside the household, and John who was still *cum patre*. By 1313 both William junior and John were outside the household.[131] The holding's labour requirements can be assumed to have been constant, so we can only conclude that William senior continued to hire labour in the same way as he had probably done in the early years of his tenancy. The table tells us the same thing: of occupiers who can be shown quite clearly to have had sons aged 12 or over on the manor—occupiers now probably in their forties or older—a very high proportion (nearly 80 per cent) were not retaining them in the household and must therefore have continued to hire labour to make good these holdings' labour deficits. The pattern poses two questions: from what source was this demand for labour met and why was paid non-family labour preferred over unpaid family labour even when the latter was available?

Sources of supply for the *garciones* which the occupiers of most of Pilton's 10-acre holdings seem to have employed at all stages in their tenancies can be suggested by elimination. It has already been noted that a few of Pilton's *garciones* were probably immigrants, sons perhaps of tenants from villages with relatively little demand for servants, but these incomers formed only a very small proportion of the total numbers and cannot have filled but a few of the niches for labour on the manor's 10-acre holdings. Another source of supply might theoretically have been from the sons of occupiers of holdings in size groups below 10 acres all of which had a surplus of labour and on which retention of sons was not necessary on operational grounds. This is not likely to have been a major source, because such holdings were relatively few in number and because the sons of their occupiers do not feature prominently in Pilton's listings of *garciones*.[132] We are therefore led towards the conclusion that the most likely origin of a servant on a 10-acre holding at Pilton was a son 'exported' from another tenement in the same size class. The internal

---

[131] L.11252, 10768, 10654. For tenants' employment of labour after sons had left home (though under circumstances rather different from those discussed here), see Razi, *Life, Marriage and Death*, 90.

[132] This is very noticeable: sons of smallholders were few in number, a result, perhaps, of smaller family sizes on these holdings or of emigration of sons reared on them.

consistencies within Table 15.2 do not prove but certainly suggest that this may have been the case for they show not only high proportions of 10-acre occupiers with demand for labour (those with no sons resident on the manor and those with sons resident but not in the parental household) but also high proportions of sons working on the manor but away from the parental home. If, as one study of the late thirteenth-century countryside has shown, there tended to be strong and repeated interactions, for example in pledging and borrowing, within the middling ranks of the tenantry, exchange of sons among the 10-acre group at Pilton would have been rendered all the easier.[133] Within the group there were five pairs of occupiers with identical surnames at the time of the extent of 1316–17, so that one may surmise that on occasion the servants who were hired may have been distant kin of their masters.[134]

To move on to the second question posed above: why was paid non-family labour apparently preferred to unpaid family labour? The question strikes straight at the decision-making of a 10-acre tenant when a son began to be capable of heavy work. Prior to that time the holding's heavy labour requirement necessitated, as already argued, employment of a servant. When the son comes of age, the tenant has a decision to make: son or servant? There are two reasons why the latter option seems to have been preferred. First, the tenant had already out of necessity formed the habit of servant-keeping and may have seen no reason to break it as he passed into middle age. Second, and reflecting not only this conservatism but also self-interest, the tenant may have seen the choice of servant rather than son as a means of appropriating a greater proportion of the holding's income to himself and to his wife. We have just enough data to explore this strategy, whose logic has been developed theoretically by Nakajima, Mendels, and Smith, in relation to a 10-acre holding at Pilton.[135] These holdings might have generated annual incomes of around 45s. If one son were retained on the holding in place of a servant and assuming that food and other comforts are shared equally between occupier, wife, and son, he would consume the equivalent of 15s. By continuing to maintain a servant (at a total cost of 10s.) and ejecting the son, the occupier would appropriate to himself and his wife an extra income of 5s.

---

[133] Smith, 'Kin and Neighbors', 246.   [134] BL Eg. MS 3321.
[135] C. Nakajima, 'Subsistence and Commercial Family Farms: Some Theoretical Models of Subjective Equilibrium', in C. R. Wharton (ed.), *Subsistence Agriculture and Economic Development* (London, 1970), 165–85; F. Mendels, 'La composition du ménage paysan en France au XIXe siècle: une analyse économique du mode de production domestique', *Annales ESC* 33 (1978), 780–802; Smith, 'Some Issues Concerning Families', 23–7.

yearly.[136] As Smith has remarked, 'in the replacement of the head's own children by the children of others, the adult generation would be imposing a degree of social and economic exploitation on the young'.[137] The system could only have operated in the context of collusion among heads of households. It could only have operated in the context of strong patriarchal authority which refused the young opportunities of home comforts and the possibility of greater earnings through day labouring. It was a form of exploitation which ensured that the holding's occupier passed into middle age with a standard of living which was an improvement on that of his early years of married life, but an improvement at the expense of the comforts of adolescents and young men who were forced to live by servants' standards away from home. Hence the title of this chapter.

V. CONCLUSION

This study has presented a good deal of evidence, albeit qualitative evidence, for service in husbandry in England before the Black Death. It has been shown (§ II) that the insistence which the authorities on some estates showed in taking works or cash payments from the sons (and sometimes the daughters) of villeins residing on their manors yet outside parental households demonstrates a recognition, stretching back into the twelfth century, of an institution which cannot have been rare. It has been shown (§ III) that the *garciones* of the Glastonbury estate cannot but have been, in many cases, servants in husbandry. It has been argued theoretically (§ IV.3) that, under price conditions prevailing in the early fourteenth century, employment of servants in husbandry was a cheaper strategy than the hiring of labourers *per diem* on holdings where the labour deficit rose beyond a certain threshold. And data on the deployment of landless sons at Pilton show that 'exchange' of sons as servants between holdings of similar size is a possibility (§ IV.4). The chapter therefore lends considerable support to those who have argued that the Statute of Labourers of 1351 was merely 'attempting . . . to preserve a norm of contracting

---

[136] Above, pp. 552–3 for the probable cost of a servant. Farm income on these 10-acre holdings (mean size, in fact, 12 acres) calculated as on p. 543 above. Outgoings have not been taken into account here but they were in fact very small on these holdings, which were not *ad gabulum*, their rents being acquitted. It will at once be observed that the model here does not take daughters into account and assumes only one son. It is therefore only appropriate to that stage in the tenant's life-cycle when he is able to dispense with the last of his offspring. The listings of *garciones* for Pilton are not continuous enough to allow investigation of this topic, which I intend to explore with the other, better series from the Glastonbury estate.

[137] Smith, 'Some Issues Concerning Families', 24–5.

servants on annual terms'.[138] Finally, it has been strongly argued that the institution of service could in some cases have been the product of heavy manorialization; that is to say, where holdings above a certain size were burdened with demesne works for above a certain number of days, the institution found space to flourish, as at Pilton.

This last contention is simply an extension, but a radical one, of what has often been said about tenants as employers of labour in early medieval England. Historians have noticed that thirteenth-century extents often state that at certain times of the year tenants had to perform demesne works 'with one man', 'with two men', and so on, and have argued that landholders without access to adequate family labour must have hired hands, perhaps for a day or two in order to acquit themselves of these obligations.[139] Even a superficial examination of the relevant sources shows that these 'occasional multiple works' were very widespread. The multipliers could be very large, especially from larger tenements, which might have to provide as many as nine or even over thirty men, probably subtenants.[140] But in the more ordinary cases of multiple works where only one or two extras were demanded at harvest time the men sent must have been either the sons of tenants or hired hands. Multiple works provide further evidence to show that lords recognized that their tenants might be employers of labour. The terminology of the paragraphs on services in thirteenth-century extents and custumals sometimes provides more detail than the bland phrase such as 'with one man' or 'with two men'. Tenants are to send their reapers (*homines metentes*); the *magna precaria* is to be done with 'all of the labouring men' (*homines laborantes*) on a tenement. A virgator comes with 'at least' four helpers hired *ad stipendia sua* 'for reaping on his own land' and, as we might expect, the terms *garcio* and *ancilla* are sometimes to be found to describe the tenant's helper.[141] In such contexts all of these terms could imply no more

---

[138] L. R. Poos, 'The Social Context of the Statute of Labourers Enforcement', *LHR* 1 (1983), 51.

[139] e.g. Kosminsky, *Studies*, 304–5. Others have speculated that, as shown in this chapter, regular week-work may have obliged tenants to hire labour: Postan, 'Medieval Agrarian Society in its Prime', 623 (drawing analogies with 'eighteenth-century Prussia or nineteenth-century Russia'); Smith, 'Some Issues Concerning Families', 25.

[140] BL Cott. Claud. C xi, fo. 146ᵛ; *Boldon Book*, ed. D. Austin (Chichester, 1982), 27; *Rentalia et Custumaria*, 72. In the following notes I have restricted myself to a few examples only.

[141] BL Cott. Claud. C xi, fo. 146ᵛ; ibid., fo. 98ᵛ; *Charters and Custumals*, 89; F. R. H. Du Boulay, *The Lordship of Canterbury* (London, 1966), 171. *Thirteen Custumals*, 46; *Survey of the Lands of William, First Earl of Pembroke*, ed. C. R. Straton (2 vols.; Oxford, 1909), ii. 539.

than labourers hired on a daily or seasonal basis by tenants in order to acquit multiple works. Other terms bring us closer to servants hired on longer contracts. Harvest boon works are to be done with the *famulus* of a tenant; there is a risk of ambiguity here because of scribal contraction, so sometimes a custumal spells it out more clearly—*famuli suis vel familia*, an interesting phrase which may possibly hint at the son or servant choice referred to in the previous section.[142] Occasionally the sources are even more explicit: clauses relating to harvest boon works mention a *serviens* and a *magister serviens*.[143] At Barnwell, Northamptonshire, tenants sent a *levingman*, a word of obscure etymology, but possibly with the connotation of 'living in'.[144] Finally, the Hundred Rolls of 1279 provide the clearest statement of all: at Burcot, Oxfordshire, Hugh Frankelyn had to send *omnes servientes suos locatos per annum*.[145] Of course, many tenements which owed multiple boon works, occasional and lasting for a few days only, were not large enough to require servants in husbandry. In order to acquit them tenants without a competent son at home would simply have to hire an extra pair of hands for a few days either from the surplus within their manors or perhaps on a wider labour market, a practice which would set up flows of migrant labourers, drawn westwards and northwards by the great clouds which heralded the harvest-threatening rain.[146]

All of this reveals how the lord's urgent demands at harvest time (which we have already met, above § II), combined, of course, with the simultaneous needs of tenant holdings, set up swirls and eddies in the market for labour during the late summer and early autumn. The contention of this chapter goes further and suggests that in early medieval England the lord's more constant demand for week-work throughout the year could have forced some tenants to enter into the labour market as hirers of servants on a yearly basis. There are good parallels. For example, in those relentlessly manorialized regimes of eastern Europe during the eighteenth and nineteenth centuries, with their ordinances and regulations touching serf families which resemble quite closely some practices

---

[142] *Charters and Custumals*, 60, 94; *Thirteen Custumals*, 14.

[143] BRO, AC/M8/10; WCaA, 52/79 (temporary number), fo. 100.

[144] *Cartularium Monasterii de Rameseia*, i. 50.

[145] *Rotuli Hundredorum: Temp. Hen. III and Ed. I* (2 vols.; Record Comm., 1812–18), ii. 748. It must be noted that Frankelyn was a substantial tenant.

[146] The best-known example is the retrospective reference to migrant labourers from the north-west and the Welsh borders, in the Statute of Labourers: *Statutes of the Realm*, i. 312. See also P. F. Brandon, 'New Settlement: South-Eastern England', in Hallam (ed.), *Agrarian History of England and Wales*, ii. 189.

in thirteenth-century England, peasants whose total labour requirement
could not be met by the family were accustomed to employ servants who
were used to fulfil obligations on the demesne.[147] The ninth-century
polyptic of Saint Bertin describes an estate in Picardy on which many of
the slaves did not belong directly to the demesne but were attached to
tenants who had much work to do at the *corvée*.[148] In thirteenth-century
England a depersonalization of services was certainly allowed for in some
occasional works: at Holywell-cum-Needingworth, Huntingdonshire, a
virgator who sent four men to the first autumn boon was allowed 'to stay
at home if he wishes'.[149] Court rolls may well yet provide more examples
of servants used as substitutes, such as the *famuli* of two half-virgators at
Cuxham, Oxfordshire, who pilfered barley while they were winnowing
the lord's grain, presumably on behalf of their masters; or the tenant of
Stratton, Wiltshire, who sent a 'boy' (almost certainly not a son) to do the
lord's ploughing.[150]

The ways in which the two layers of labour—on and for the tenant's
holding and off the holding and for the demesne—were allocated within
the household is not, however, the central issue here. The proposition
which is being stressed is that during the centuries before 1348, under
certain types of seigneurial regimes with heavy works falling upon tenements of relatively large size (as at Pilton), the institution of service in
husbandry may have flourished on the tenants' holdings as a result of
seigneurial demands. Those who have been bold enough to probe the
medieval history of service in husbandry have tended to discuss not the
thirteenth century but the later fourteenth and fifteenth as a period when
the incidence of the institution is likely to have been high.[151] Two features
of the economy of the latter period have been stressed as ideal, from the
employer's viewpoint, for employment of labour in this way. First, a
certain bias towards pastoral farming made servants attractive to employers, for they would be available throughout the year to deal with the

---

[147] A. Plakans, 'Peasant Farmsteads and Households in the Baltic Littoral, 1797', *Comparative Studies in Society and History*, 17 (1975), 18–19; W. Kula, 'The Seigneury and the
Peasant Family in Eighteenth-Century Poland', in R. Forster and O. Ranum (eds.), *Family
and Society: Selections from the Annales* (Baltimore and London, 1976), 199; J. Kochanowicz,
'The Peasant Family as an Economic Unit in the Polish Feudal Economy of the Eighteenth
Century', in R. Wall (ed.), *Family Forms in Historic Europe* (Cambridge, 1983), 160.
[148] R. Fossier, *La Terre et les hommes en Picardie jusqu'à la fin du XIIIe siècle* (2 vols.;
Paris, 1968), i. 208–19.
[149] *Cartularium de Rameseia*, i. 300. See also *Rotuli Hundredorum*, ii. 765.
[150] Harvey, *Cuxham*, 135; *Court Rolls of Adam de Stratton*, 167.
[151] Poos, *A Rural Society*, 222–3; Smith, 'Hypothèses sur la nuptialité', 130–1.

ever-present livestock. A second factor was a combination of high and rising *per diem* wage rates with relatively low food prices, for some of the remuneration of a servant took the form of board. One might add, thirdly, that, in many parts of England, amalgamation of tenures created larger units of occupation for tenant farmers, who were likely therefore, in certain circumstances, to exert a demand for servants in husbandry.

If each of these points is taken in turn with the early Middle Ages in mind there can be no denying, first, that simply from the point of view of the balance between grain and grass, the period was not ideally suited to service in husbandry: this was an era in which the movement 'cornwards' left many tenants with too few livestock to justify employing, say, a shepherd, although some undoubtedly did so. Second, the fact that trends in wages and prices made employment of servants highly attractive to employers after 1348 of course does not mean that the same strategy was unattractive under thirteenth- and early fourteenth-century conditions. Calculations made earlier in this chapter suggest that in the first decade of the fourteenth century the cost of a servant in husbandry might have been the equivalent of 75 days of labour hired at *per diem* rates. In other words, employment of a servant would have been a logical strategy on any holding whose size or burden of demesne works required more than 75 days of labour over and above what was available from the family. Third, there can be no doubt that during the hundred years or so after 1348 the size of tenant landholdings tended to increase. But this does not mean that the labour requirements of individual holdings increased proportionately because, as we have seen, labour needs were affected by factors other than acreage. If we take as a hypothetical example a Pilton holding of 20 acres (formed through amalgamation of two 10-acre tenements), say in 1440 when compulsory service on the demesne had vanished, and assume rather unrealistically that it was then cultivated with the same intensity as it had been in the early fourteenth century, it might have required about 270 days of labour, not enough to justify employment of a full-time servant. Each of its now distant predecessors of 1340, although half the size, had had much greater labour requirements simply because of the work which was extracted from them for the demesne. In thinking about the contribution of servants to farming households across the centuries we must bear in mind changes in intensity with which labour was subtracted from the tenement for use on the demesne.

These points, together with much other evidence presented elsewhere in this chapter, lead to the conclusion that service in husbandry was already a very well developed institution in the early Middle Ages. It would not, of course, have been equally well developed on all types of manors, in all types of farming regions. We might expect it to have flourished where labour services were relatively heavy. Taking again as our yardstick a 10-acre holding at Pilton burdened with the equivalent of about 3½ days of demesne work throughout the working year, bringing total labour requirement up to about 335 days per annum, and keeping intensity of cultivation as a constant for the moment, we can ask: was this an unusual situation, or are there many examples of manors where services were heavier and, moreover, were demanded from holdings which were larger? Historians familiar with thirteenth-century custumals will surely answer the latter question in the affirmative: many examples may be found of demesne work heavier than at Pilton which fell upon standard holdings which were larger than 10 acres. All would have needed to be employers of labour for at least part of their occupiers' life cycles and, if the calculations made earlier in this chapter are correct, a rational strategy would have been employment of servants rather than the hiring of hands on a *per diem* basis. The question posed above suggests that the old subject of labour services, with its rather antiquarian ring, needs to be reassessed and attention turned towards their influence on the composition of the peasant household.

We might expect service in husbandry to have flourished where holdings were relatively large, irrespective of whether or not the demesne labour required from them was excessive. It must not be forgotten that in many parts of England 30 acres was the size of the largest standard group of landholdings. Historians who like to stress the piling up of minute tenancies around the lowest rungs of the ladder of landholding sometimes lose sight of how many of these largest holdings there were in many parts of thirteenth-century England: just under one-quarter of all unfree tenements according to Postan's large sample from southern England, roughly one-quarter in Kosminsky's England, stretching from Oxfordshire to Cambridgeshire.[152] Again using the yardstick of Pilton (that is, assuming the same level of intensity of cultivation) all of these holdings would have had domestic labour requirements in excess of 400 days; depending upon how heavily burdened they were with demesne services, employment of two servants would have been a logical strategy when sons and daughters were not available for work. Historians who are used to working on medieval rural history in these provinces move at once and with a very

[152] Postan, 'Medieval Agrarian Society in its Prime', 619; Dyer, *Standards of Living*, 119, summarizing Kosminsky.

sharp jolt into an apparently completely different world when confronted by studies of some manors, especially in East Anglia, where tenemental structures were heavily biased towards *la petite culture*. Where a large proportion of tenants held less than 5 acres, and many less than 2, it is highly unlikely that employment of servants in husbandry was well developed. The worlds of labour as well as of landholding must have been entirely different from those where larger holdings predominated: it is difficult not to conclude that places for servants would have been few and far between on such manors and that even opportunities for day labour on the tenants' land would have been restricted. This is not to say, however, that under-employment would have been highly developed, because where holdings were so small and so numerous, and where fragmentation was rife, there must have been many opportunities for the landless to gain the small toehold of a minute tenement. Moreover, on some East Anglian manors highly fragmented tenemental structures were associated with a highly intensive husbandry (which was presumably what rendered minute holdings viable).[153] Intensive agricultural practices would have given rise to higher labour requirements per acre than existed under the more standard systems described in this chapter.

It is interesting to speculate not only about the probable geographical incidence of service in husbandry in early medieval England but also about its development over time. Could the institution have been much fostered by the movement which saw demesne cultivation put into the highest possible gear in, let us say, the late twelfth century and the early thirteenth? A large demesne; full and vigorous cultivation according to the best practice of the locality; carefully defined week-works exacted from the tenants and accounting for a high proportion of the work needed; additional extra works, such as carrying services to market or estate headquarters, imposed on some tenements—these are the characteristics of a demesne in top gear. The regime which preceded it was presumably characterized by a smaller demesne, less intensive cultivation, weakly defined services often calculated by the task not by the day, and few additional works such as carrying. Transition from the one to the other might well have had the effect of giving some holdings excessive works and of pushing their labour requirements beyond the threshold at which a servant would have to be hired while sons were of tender age. The critical factor here is the size of tenement upon which the heaviest week-works were placed. One option would have been for seigneurial authorities

---

[153] As suggested by Campbell, 'Population Pressure', 106.

to give heavy burdens to relatively large tenements, like those of 10 acres at Pilton, because they were the most likely to be able to furnish the equipment and livestock with which to acquit them. Or, secondly, they might take another course and divide up relatively large holdings into halves, burdening the new smaller tenancies with far more week-work than had been obtained from the old, but not enough (because of their small size) to make them potential employers of servants.[154] If the depictions of Pilton and Ditcheat given earlier in this chapter have any validity, the course which was taken may have had fundamental implications for the structure of labour markets, encouraging the development of service in husbandry in the first case, but not the second; encouraging retention of sons on the manor in the first case, tending to expel them in the second; creating, indeed, two contrasting demographic regimes, a buoyant one and a sluggish one (a good deal of service in husbandry is not, of course, incompatible with growth of population, a critical factor here being the duration of the life-cycle stage which was occupied by servanthood).

It is worth asking about the effects on service of that commutation of works which took place on some manors from the years around 1300 onwards. Again this is a difficult subject because precisely what happened when demesnes began to contract is as shady a topic as their origins. Presumably we must envisage a smaller demesne acreage less intensively cultivated and a replacement of labour services by the work of increased staffs of *famuli* and by some labour hired by the day at times of peak farming activity.[155] The transition would have had repercussions on the domestic economies of holdings which had previously, because of heavy week-works, been accustomed to employ servants. Their outgoings would increase as services were commuted to rent and cash payments, and at the same time domestic consumption would increase as successive sons failed to find places as servants and, as it were, piled up in the household.[156] Where week-works disappeared on many adjacent manors in the years

---

[154] For retrospective evidence of sub-division of holdings apparently for the creation of more services, see M. M. Postan, 'The Chronology of Labour Services', in Postan, *Essays on Medieval Agriculture*, 102; Miller, *Ely*, 102.

[155] Assuming that demesne *famuli* and labourers hired by the day worked more efficiently than tenants at labour services, the transition to commutation would have resulted in a decline in the total number of days worked on a manor irrespective of changes in demesne acreage. A good guide is still H. L. Gray, 'The Commutation of Villein Services in England before the Black Death', *EHR* 29 (1914), 625–58.

[156] Compensations would be the possibility that a son might find work in the enlarged team of demesne *famuli*; income which could be gained through labouring for daily wages on the demesne; extra income from acres leased from the demesne as it contracted.

before the Black Death, these difficulties would have been compounded.[157]
Here is another possible mechanism lying behind that poverty and 'impo-
tence' of which some communities complained in the fifth decade of the
fourteenth century.

But such speculations take us well beyond the findings from a preliminary investigation into the listings made for collection of *chevagium
garcionum* on two manors on the Glastonbury estate. Whether or not
these findings have any validity, there can be little doubt that the listings
from the estate at large, and from other lordships, will allow historians
hitherto unsuspected opportunities to discover the lives of the teeming
landless workforce of some early medieval manors, to 'draw these tides of
men into their hands and write their will across the sky in stars' thus
adding a new chapter to the annals of the labouring poor in the English
countryside.[158]

[157] See e.g. P. D. A. Harvey, 'Tenant Farming and Tenant Farmers: the Home Counties',
in Miller (ed.), *Agrarian History of England and Wales*, iii. 667.
[158] Quotation modified from the dedicatory poem in *Seven Pillars of Wisdom*.

Appendix

A Survey of Medieval Manorial Court Rolls in England

JUDITH CRIPPS, RODNEY HILTON, AND JANET WILLIAMSON

WHEN we began our project in 1976 there was (and is still) no comprehensive source of information on surviving medieval manorial records, so that an investigation of these sources had to be undertaken as a preliminary part of the project. The researchers were requested by the SSRC to complete this survey in three months; consequently, it was undertaken, not to provide a complete picture of English medieval manorial records, but to compile information on court-roll series covering the period roughly 1250 to 1500 but in particular all or part of the period of demographic decline in the fourteenth century. To facilitate survey work, the two investigators divided England on an axis north-west to south-east, from Cheshire to Essex. Work in the national repositories was shared on the same basis. As the survey progressed, responsibility for the surveys of several areas was exchanged, so that the final listings are in the main joint compilations rather than conflations of two separate investigations.

The researchers began at the Manorial Documents Register in the National Register of Archives, and emerged with lists of court roll series beginning before 1400, but with little idea of the completeness of most of them. The next step was to write to the repositories, and in a few cases the owners, of the documents listed. No account was taken of court roll series known to exist overseas, and court rolls for Wales were also excluded. Correspondence was sufficient to eliminate from further consideration the holdings of a number of county record offices and private collections, but where there was evidently fourteenth-century material, or some doubt existed in the mind of the curator, a visit was arranged. Since it was felt that the Manorial Documents Register was unlikely to be complete, contact was made with all county record offices existing prior to local government reorganization, a number of public libraries, and most libraries of cathedrals, colleges, and schools existing in the Middle Ages or known to be the successors in title of medieval corporations. Contact was also made with a small number of private owners or their archivists in instances where possession of early court rolls was known or strongly suspected.

The first and most basic criterion for the court rolls, a well-distributed coverage of the fourteenth century, determined whether they were worth individual examination. As a rough indication, series with less than fifteen years surviving between 1300 and 1380 were not pursued further. In some cases the researchers after examination of court-roll series differed from the catalogue dating. This was usually for one of two reasons: either earlier cataloguers had been confused by records dating from the reigns of the first three Edwards, or composite rolls had been only summarily examined for catalogue dates.

In the course of their survey research the two investigators obviously examined many court roll series which, while unsuitable for the purposes of their project, might be of use to researchers whose interests were not primarily demographic. With the thought that the results of this preliminary survey could be of interest to future researchers wishing to study court roll evidence, the investigators have compiled this listing of the potentially useful court-roll series they have either examined or noted in the course of the survey. Because of the interest of the project in manorial court rolls, borough and hundred court-rolls were not noted systematically.

The form of entry is as follows:

PARISH [Manor]   Court roll repository
Dates of surviving court rolls [those not examined in italics].
Brief description of rolls according to project criteria.
Other surviving manorial documents (with location when different from that of court rolls).
Brief description of manor from V.C.H. or county history, if available.

Record Repositories Contacted and/or Visited

†Record Repositories contacted, but not visited

AVON
  Bath City Record Office†
  Bristol Archives Office
  Bristol University Library

BEDFORDSHIRE
  Bedfordshire County Record Office

BERKSHIRE
  Berkshire Record Office
  St George's Chapel, Windsor
    [from printed catalogue]

BUCKINGHAMSHIRE
  Buckinghamshire Archaeological
    Society
  Buckinghamshire Record Office
  Eton College

CAMBRIDGESHIRE
  Cambridge University Library
  Christ's College, Cambridge
  Corpus Christi College, Cambridge

Emmanuel College, Cambridge†
Gonville and Caius College,
  Cambridge
Jesus College, Cambridge†
Pembroke College, Cambridge
Peterhouse, Cambridge
St Catharine's College, Cambridge
St John's College, Cambridge
Sidney Sussex College,
  Cambridge†
Trinity College, Cambridge
Cambridge County Record Office
Huntingdon Record Office†

CHESHIRE
  Cheshire Record Office†

CORNWALL
  Cornwall County Record Office

CUMBRIA
  Carlisle Record Office†

DERBYSHIRE
  Chatsworth
  Derbyshire Record Office[†]
    [also re: Renishaw Hall MSS]
DEVON
  Devon Record Office
  Exeter Cathedral Library
  Exeter City Record Office
  West Devon Area Record Office,
    Plymouth
DORSET
  Dorset Record Office
DURHAM
  Durham County Record Office
  University of Durham,
    Department of Palaeography
  University of Durham, Prior's
    Kitchen
EAST SUSSEX
  East Sussex Record Office
  Sussex Archaeological Society
ESSEX
  Essex Record Office
GLOUCESTERSHIRE
  Berkeley Castle
    [microfilms at Cambridge
    University Library]
  Gloucestershire Records Office
GREATER LONDON
  British Library
  Church Commissioners
  Corporation of London Record
    Office
  Greater London Record Office
  Greater London Record Office
    (Middlesex) [also re: Syon
    House MSS]
  Guildhall Library
  Haringey Library[†]
  Lambeth Palace Library
  National Register of Archives
  Public Record Office

St Paul's Cathedral Library
Westminster Abbey Library
GREATER MANCHESTER
  Chetham's Library
  John Rylands University Library
  Manchester Central Library
HEREFORD AND WORCESTER
  Hereford Cathedral Library
  Hereford City Library
  Hereford County Record Office
  Worcester Cathedral Library
  Worcester County Record Office,
    St Helen's
HERTFORDSHIRE
  Hatfield House
  Hertfordshire County Record Office
HUMBERSIDE
  Brynmor Jones Library, University
    of Hull
  Humberside Record Office,
    Beverley[†]
  South Humberside Area Archives
    Office, Grimsby
ISLE OF WIGHT
  Isle of Wight Record Office[†]
KENT
  Canterbury Cathedral Library
  Kent Archives Office[†]
LANCASHIRE
  Lancashire Record Office
LEICESTERSHIRE
  Buckminster Hall[†]
  Leicestershire Record Office
LINCOLNSHIRE
  Lincolnshire Archives Office
MERSEYSIDE
  Liverpool City Library[†]
NORFOLK
  Elveden Hall
  Holkham Hall
  Norfolk and Norwich Record Office

NORTHAMPTONSHIRE
Northamptonshire Record Office

NORTHUMBERLAND
Northumberland Record Office

NORTH YORKSHIRE
North Yorkshire Record Office[†]
York Minster Library

NOTTINGHAMSHIRE
Nottinghamshire Record Office
Nottingham University Library

OXFORDSHIRE
Bodleian Library
Balliol College, Oxford[†]
Brasenose College, Oxford[†]
Christ Church, Oxford[†]
Corpus Christi College, Oxford[†]
Exeter College, Oxford[†]
Jesus College, Oxford[†]
Lincoln College, Oxford[†]
Magdalen College, Oxford[†] [records
not available for consultation]
Merton College, Oxford
New College, Oxford
Oriel College, Oxford[†]
Pembroke College, Oxford[†]
St John's College, Oxford[†]
Trinity College, Oxford[†]
University College, Oxford
Worcester College, Oxford[†]
Oxfordshire County Record Office

SHROPSHIRE
Shropshire Record Office
Shrewsbury Borough Library

SOMERSET
Somerset Record Office

SOUTH YORKSHIRE
Doncaster Archives Department
Sheffield City Library

STAFFORDSHIRE
Keele University Library
Lichfield Joint Record Office
Staffordshire Record Office

SUFFOLK
Suffolk Record Office, Bury St
Edmunds
Suffolk Record Office, Ipswich

SURREY
Guildford Muniment Room
Surrey Record Office

TYNE AND WEAR
Tyne and Wear Archives
Department

WARWICKSHIRE
Shakespeare's Birthplace,
Stratford-on-Avon
Warwickshire County Record Office

WEST MIDLANDS
Birmingham Public Libraries
Coventry City Record Office[†]

WEST SUSSEX
Arundel Castle[†]
[some records not available for
consultation]
West Sussex Record Office[†]

WEST YORKSHIRE
Bradford Metropolitan District
Record Office
Leeds City Archives Deparment
West Yorkshire Record Office[†]
Yorkshire Archaeological Society,
Leeds

WILTSHIRE
Longleat
Wiltshire Record Office

WALES
National Library of Wales

The Manorial Rolls

Bedfordshire

CRANFIELD   PRO/BL
1294–1300: 2; 1301–1400: 18; 1401–
1500: 20.
One leet p.a. in the 14th century.

Accounts: 1200–50: 1; 1250–1300: 2; 1300–50: 5 (6); 1350–1400: 8 (7); 1400–1500: 5.

Rental, c.1377–99.

Ramsey Abbey manor, 2 other manors in the parish (VCH iii, pp. 275–7). See introduction to **Huntingdonshire**.

SHILLINGTON
[Shillington]   PRO/BL
1278–1300: 5; 1301–77: 18; 1401–1500: 21.

One leet p.a. in the 14th century.

Accounts: 1300–50: 6; 1350–1400: 4; 1400–1500: 3.

Rental: 1437/8.

Ramsey Abbey manor, largest of the 2 to 5 manors in the parish (VCH ii, pp. 293–4).

See introduction to **Huntingdonshire**.

Berkshire

ASHBURY [Hallmoot]   Longleat
1262, 1265, *1283–4*, *1307–9*, 1313–14, *1315–16*, *1340–1*, 1344–5, *1345–6*, 1347–8, 1349–50, 1351–2, 1354–5, *1357*, 1358, *1364–7*, 1367–9, *1369–70*, 1370–1, 1372–3, *1374*, *1379–80*, *1387–8*, *1403–4*, 1407–8, 1448–9.

Glastonbury Abbey manor, 1 of 4 in the parish (VCH iv, pp. 505–9).

See also notes under **Glastonbury, Somerset**.

BRAY [Bray]   BkRO/PRO/SGCW
1282/3, 1287/8, 1288/9, 1294/5–1296/7, 1312/13, 1315/16–1318/9, 1320/1–1322/3, 1326/7, 1327/8, 1331/2–1340/1, 1347/8, 1349/50, 1350/1, 1352/3, 1358/9, 1360/1–1362/3, 1367/8, 1369/70–1375/6, 1396/7, 1397/8, *1422–33*, *1446–7*, *1449*, *1451*, *1453–6*, *1459–61*, *1474–5*, *1484–1500*.

VFP and 17 courts p.a. in a full year, but many years with only 2–5 courts surviving. 14th–century rolls from 8 to 15 membranes p.a., 15th–century rolls 3 to 7 membranes p.a. Most rolls in good condition.

Custumal, c.1216–1272 and arrentation roll, c.1329/30–1344/5 (PRO SC 11). Largest manor of at least 6 in the parish in the 14th century, with a number of large free holdings which later became manors (VCH iii, pp. 99–107).

BRIGHTWALTON
[Brightwalton]   PRO
1279/80–1281/2, 1284/5–1286/7, 1288/9, 1289/90, 1292/3–1306/7, 1307/8, 1308/9, 1310/11, 1311/12, 1313/14–1316/17, 1319/20, 1321/2–1326/7, 1327/8–1334/5, 1338/9–1343/4, 1347/8–1349/50, 1351/2–1356/7, 1359/60, 1362/3, 1366/7–1369/70, 1375/6, 1378/9–1384/5, 1386/7–1390/1, 1392/3–1395/6, 1397/8–1408/9, 1423/4–1434/5, 1438/9–1442/3, 1444/5–1449/50.

For the period 1327–77 for most years only VFP (with the villages of Hertley and Conenholt) and one court survived. Seldom is there more than one membrane p.a. (for the period 1272–1307, 27mm, 1307–27, 14mm, 1327–77, 32mm, 1377–99, 25mm, 1399– 1413, 12mm, 1422–71, 22mm (PRO SC 2).

Rentals: 1283/4 and c.1422–61 (PRO E312 and SC 12), list of tenants 1296/7 (SC 2).

Sole manor, held by Battle Abbey (VCH iv, pp. 48–9).

BRIMPTON [Shalford]   BkRO
1347/8–1355/6, 1366/7–1375/6, 1377, 1413/14–1424/5, 1430/1, 1431/2, 1441/2, 1446/7, 1449/50–1451/2,

1455/6, 1460/1, 1462/3, 1463/4, 1467/8, 1472/3, 1474/5.
Two courts and 2 VFP p.a. surviving for most years. VFP with tithings of Cosering, Brimpton, and Woolhampton. Rental 14th c., court roll abstracts 1447–1500.
Three manors in the parish (*VCH* iv, pp. 52–4).

INKPEN [Inkpen Eastcourt]   BkRO
1296/7, 1307/8, 1316/17, 1324/5, 1352/3, 1357/8–1359/60, 1366/7–1370/1, 1373/4–1376/7, 1399/1400–1408/9, 1423/4–1432/3, 1434/5–1441/2, 1445/6–1457/8, 1461/2–1466/7, 1468/9–1474/5, 1476/7, 1478/9.
No VFP or assize jurisdiction, 1 or 2 courts p.a. surviving for most years.
Five manors in the parish (*VCH* iv, pp. 200–3).

Buckinghamshire

BLEDLOW [Bledlow]   EC
1336/7–1338/9, 1340/1–1342/3, 1349/50, 1354/5, 1368/9, 1370/1, 1371/2–1379/80, 1381/2, 1383/4–1385/6, 1387/8–1391/2, 1393/4, 1394/5, 1396/7–1398/9, 1400/1, 1403/4, 1406/7, 1410/11, 1411/12, 1417/18, 1419/20, 1422/3, 1423/4, 1436/7–1439/40, 1442/3–1449/50, 1453/4–1460/1, 1461/2, 1462/3, 1481/2–1487/8.
For most years only VFP surviving (ECR 7/122–5).
Largest of three manors in the parish (*VCH* ii, pp. 247–50).

CHALFONT ST PETER
[Chalfont St Peter]   BAS
1307/8–1311/12, 1316/17, 1318/19–1320/1, 1323/4–1332/3, 1334/5–1339/40, 1342/3, 1343/4, 1345/6,

1346/7, 1349/50, 1351/2, 1354/5, 1357/8–1362/3, 1364/5, 1400/1, 1403/4, 1406/7, 1407/8, 1410/11, 1411/12, 1414/15, 1415/16, 1422, 1422/3, 1424/5, 1425/6, 1446/7, 1447/8, 1449/50, 1451/2, 1453/4–1460/1, 1461/2, 1469/70, 1498/9, 1499/1500.
No VFP or assize jurisdiction, one court per year. Many of the court rolls between 1307 and 1327 are damaged at bottom. Survey 1333, 14th- and 15th-century rentals, issues of view 1381.
Larger of the two manors in the parish (*VCH* iii, pp. 195–6).

CHEDDINGTON [Elsage]   MCO
1272/3–1274/5, 1288/9, 1292/3, 1296/7, 1297/8, 1302/3–1306/7, 1308/9, 1310/11–1316/17, 1321/2–1323/4, 1329/30–1340/1, 1345/6, 1346/7, 1348/9–1350/1, 1352/3, 1353/4, 1355/6–1360/1, 1362/3, 1369/70, 1370/1, 1374/5, *1378–80, 1382, 1388, 1489, 1496.*
No VFP or assize jurisdiction, only one court p.a. 1327–77.
Manor accounts for 1296–1300; 36 years 1301–50; 39 years 1351–1400; 70 years 1401–1500.
Rentals 1490, 1500.
Two manors in the parish (*VCH* iii, pp. 331–2).

EDLESBOROUGH
[Edlesborough]   BL
1294/5–1296/7, 1300/1, 1301/2, 1304/5, 1305/6, 1307/8–1309/10, 1315/16–1321/2, 1324/5, 1325/6, 1327/8, 1348/9, 1349/50, 1359/60, 1364/5–1366/7, 1368/9, 1376/7–1377/8, 1379/80.
Tourns 1300/1, 1301/2.
For most years only one or two courts surviving, VFP for 1316/17, 1317/18, 1320/1.
Rental 1362/3.

EDLESBOROUGH [Northall]   BL
1292/3, 1312/13–1314/15, 1331/2,
1349/50–1355/6, 1376/7.
One or two courts p.a. Bottom of membrane often missing.
Rental *c*.1307–27.
At least 5 manors in the parish, of which Edlesborough manor was the largest (*VCH* iii, pp. 351–6). 14th- and 15th-century material survives in the BL for 3 other manors besides these 2.

GREAT HORWOOD
[Great Horwood]   NCO
1289/90, 1291/2, 1301/2–1362/3,
1364/5–1371/2, 1373/4, 1374/5,
1383/4–1391/2, 1393/4–1398/9,
1399/1400–1405/6, 1408/9, 1409/10,
1411/12, 1412/13, *1413/14–1454/5,*
1456/7–1458/9, 1461/2–1469/70,
1471/2–1474/5, 1476/7, 1479/80,
1480/1, 1482/3–1484/5, 1494/5–
1502/3.
Two VFP and 4–6 courts p.a. between 1327 and 1377. From end of 14th c. there are 2 courts and 2 VFP for most years. Court of the prior of Newton Longville. Rolls are in good condition. Larger of two manors in the parish (*VCH* iii, pp. 372–4).

HALTON [Halton]   CCL
1284/5–1306/7, 1310/11, 1311/12,
1317/18–1332/3, 1335/6–1350/1,
1352/3, 1377/8–1398/9.
Two VFP and 2–5 courts on 2–3 mm p.a. for 1272–1327; 2 VFP and occasional courts for 1327–77, single VFP by end of 14th c.
Single manor in the parish (*VCH* ii, pp. 339–40).

HARTWELL [Hartwell]   BAS
1328/9, 1329/30, 1337/8, 1338/9,
1344/5, 1345/6, 1347/8, 1356/7,

1358/9–1360/1, 1365/6–1367/8,
1369/70, 1370/1, 1374/5, 1376/7,
1378/9, 1379/80, 1394/5, 1396/7–
1398/9, 1410/11, 1411/12, 1418/19,
1446/7–1450/1, 1452/3–1460/1,
1464/5–1472/3, 1477/8–1480/1.
No VFP or assize jurisdiction, only one court p.a. for most years.
Single manor in the parish (*VCH* ii, pp. 125–7).

IBSTONE [Ibstone]   MCO
1292/3–1297/8, 1299/1300, 1300/1,
1302/3, 1315/16, 1317/18, 1322/3–
1324/5, 1329/30–1333/4, 1335/6,
1336/7, 1338/9, 1341/2, 1343/4–
1349/50, 1352/3, 1355/6–1358/9,
1368/9, *1380, 1386–91, 1393, 1394,*
1398, 1401, 1402, 1435, 1437, 1438,
1440, 1441, 1444–6, 1450, 1452, 1453,
1458, 1486, 1505.
No VFP or assize jurisdiction, one or two (short) courts p.a.
Bailiffs accounts for 17 years 1277–1300; 24 years 1301–50; 38 years 1351–1400; 72 years 1401–1500.
Rentals *c*.1280, 1285, 1297, 1332, 1350, 1451, 1453, 1475, 1500.
Single manor in the parish (*VCH* iii, p. 63)

NEWTON LONGVILLE
[Newton Longville]   NCO
1282/3, 1283/4, 1285/6, 1288/9–
1295/6, 1327/8–1343/4, 1345/6–
1352/3, 1354/5, 1355/6, 1373/4,
1374/5, 1378/9–1391/2, 1394/5,
1399/1400–1405/6, 1407/8–1412/13,
1413/14–1420/1, 1422/3–1425/6,
1427/8–1437/8, 1439/40–1448/49,
1450/1–1453/4, 1456/7–1459/60,
1469/70, 1470/1, 1472/3, 1474/5,
1495/6, 1496/7, 1499/1500, 1500/1.

Two VFP and four to six courts per year for 1327–77; from 1377 two courts and two VFP per year for most years. Single manor in the parish (*VCH* iv, pp. 426–7).

STONE [Stone]　　　　　　BAS
1296/7, 1310/11, 1311/12, 1313/14, 1318/19, 1319/20, 1320/1, 1324/5, 1327/8–1331/2, 1335/6, 1337/8–1344/5, 1346/7–1349/50, 1352/3–1354/5, 1357/8, 1360/1, 1496/7, 1497/8, 1498/9.
No VFP or assize jurisdiction, one or two courts per year.
Rentals 1345, 1411, 1413, 1415, 1429, 1442, 1447, 1475, 1489.
Accounts: 1444–6.
Two manors in the parish (*VCH* ii, pp. 307–9).

Cambridgeshire

GREAT ABINGTON
[Abington]　　　　　　　CRO
1317/18, 1321/2, 1354/5, 1359/60–1361/2, 1363/4, 1371/2–1423/4, 1425/6–1435/6, 1439/40, 1440/1, 1449/50, 1450/1, 1478/9, 1485/6–1488/9, 1491/2–1493/4, 1495/6–1498/9.
View and 1 court in most years. Records short, mm not filed chronologically.
Accounts: 1349–50, 1365–6.
Sole manor (*VCH* vi, p. 5).

BOTTISHAM [Bottisham]　　PRO
1308/9–1310/11, 1320/1–1326/7, 1327/8, 1329/30, 1334/5, 1335/6, 1337/8–1346/7, 1347/8–1359/60, *1362/3–1363/4, 1366/7, 1368/9, 1371/2–1372/3, 1386/7–1393/4, 1397/8, 1398/9, 1428/9–1429/30.*
Leet and 15 cts p.a. on 5–7 mm in complete years in mid 14th c., but few complete years. Condition variable.

Rentals: 1400–1500: 2
Apparently sole manor (*FA* i, p. 155).

WOOD DITTON　　　　　PRO/BL
[Ditton Valence]　　　　　(Accounts)
1327/8–1336/7, 1338/9, 1341/2–1344/5, 1347/8, 1351/2–1352/3, 1354/5–1358/9, 1361/2–1363/4, 1365/6, 1368/9, 1371/2–1376/7, *1399/1400–1417/18, 1419/20, 1420/ 1, 1452/3, 1461/2, 1462/3, 1464/5–1482/3.*
Leet and 3–4 cts p.a. on 2–3 mm early Edward III, later usually leet and 2 cts on 1 m p.a.
Accounts: 1300–50: 1; 1350–1400: 3; 1400–1500: 1.
Rental (Ditton Camoys): 1290/1.
One of three or four manors in parish (*FA* i, p. 154).

DOWNHAM IN THE ISLE
[Downham]　　　　　　CUL (EDR)
1309/10–1311/12, 1313/14–1315/16, 1322/3–1334/5, 1362/3–1365/6, 1367/8–1369/70, 1372/3–1373/4, 1375/6–1381/2, 1383/4–1395/6, 1397/8–1412/13, *1413–35, 1437–51, 1454–7, 1461–74, 1483–1507.*
Leet (Nov.) and 4–7 cts on 1–3 mm p.a. in early to mid 14th c., most courts quite short, leet and 3 cts on 2–3 mm in reign of Richard II.
Accounts: 1300–50: 19; 1350–1400: 9; 1400–1500: 57 (years)
Surveys 1222, 1251, 1356.
Larger of two manors (*VCH* iv, p. 91).

ELSWORTH
[Elsworth with Knapwell]　PRO/BL
1278–1300: 6; 1301–1400: 19; 1401–1500: 15.
One leet with court p.a. in 14th c.
Accounts: Elsworth: 1243–1300: 2; 1300–50: 5 (or 4); 1350–1400: 5 (or 6); 1400–1500: 4.

Accounts: KNAPWELL: 1243–1300: 3; 1300–50: 10 (or 7); 1350–1400: 7 (or 10); 1400–1500: 22.

Rentals: KNAPWELL: 1397/8, 1448/9.

Ramsey Abbey manor. Sole manor in parish (*RH* ii, pp. 482–3).

See introduction to **Huntingdonshire**.

FOXTON

[Chatteris Abbey Manor]   TCC

1276, 1293, 1294, 1297, *1300–5*, 1307–8, *1310–13*, 1316–17, 1318–20, *1323–4*, *1325*.

Two VFP and 5 cts in full year, e.g. 1293–4, but usually 1 or 2 short cts only.

VFP covers Foxton, Over, Barrington, Maddingley and Shepreth.

One of two or three manors in Foxton parish (*RH* ii, pp. 547–8).

GRAVELEY [Graveley]   PRO/BL

1290–1300: 3; 1301–1400: 21; 1401–88: 17.

One leet with ct p.a. in 14th c., virtually no land transfers.

Accounts: 1243–1300: 2; 1300–50: 9 (or 8); 1350–1400: 6 (or 7); 1400–1500: 3.

Rental: *c.*1272–1307.

Ramsey Abbey manor. Sole manor in parish (*RH* ii, p. 471).

See introduction to **Huntingdonshire**.

LANDBEACH

[Chamberlains]   CCCC

1327/8–1332/3, 1336/7–1338/9, 1342/3–1347/8, 1349/50, 1353/4–1376/7, *1377/8–1396/7*, *1399/1400–1401/2*, *1406/7–1421/2*, *1433/4–1435/6*, *1437/8–1444/5*, *1447/8–1462/3*, *1465/6–1481/2*.

Leet and 1–3 cts on 1–2 mm p.a. (45 mm, 1327–77).

Accounts: 1300–50: 2; 1351–1400: 4; 1400–1500: (some).

Custumals 1327–77: 3.

Rentals 15th c.: 3.

Two manors in parish (*RH* ii, p. 453). CCCC holds some records of the second manor.

LITLINGTON

[(Manor of Clare Fee)]   PRO

1320/1, 1321/2, 1322/3, *1323/4, 1325/6,* 1327/8–1329/30, 1331/2, 1332/3, 1336/7, 1339/40, *1340/1–1342/3, 1345/6, 1346/7, 1348/9, 1349/50, 1352/3, 1354/5, 1357/8, 1362/3, 1363/4, 1367/8, 1373/4–1375/6, 1386/7, 1387/8, 1392/3, 1393/4.*

Record of annual leet for lands of Clare Fee in Litlington, Abington, Pigotts, Meldreth, Guilden Morden and Tadlow.

Rental, mid 13th c.

Other manors in each parish (*FA* i, p. 156).

See below under **Royston**.

MELDRETH

[Topcliffes]   GLRO (STH)

1316/17–1320/1, 1322/3, 1324/5–1325/6, 1327/8–1329/30, 1331/2–1339/40, 1341/2–1342/3, 1354/5–1358/9, 1361/2–1362/3, 1365/6, 1367/8, 1370/1–1371/2, 1375/6, 1376/7, 1377/8–1395/6, 1398/9, *1400/1, 1407/8, 1408/9, 1413/14, 1415/16, 1432/3, 1434/5, 1438/9, 1442/3–1443/4, 1450/1–1451/2, 1454/5.*

View and 4–8 cts p.a. surviving on some early rolls, from 1334/5 usually view and 1–2 cts. p.a. Length of courts variable, not rolled chronologically. Condition of some rolls poor.

Accounts: A number from *1322* to *1452*.

Rentals: 1370/1, 1446/7.

Terrier: 1443/4.

Bishop of Carlisle's manor. At least three manors in parish (*VCH* ii, p. 36).

NEWTON
[Newton cum
Hawkston]   CUL (EDC)
1268/9, 1280/1–1281/2, 1288/9,
1290/1–1303/4, 1307/8–1318/19,
1326/7, 1328/9–1350/1, 1352/3–
1354/5.
Leet and 2–3 short courts on 1 mm
p.a. in late 13th c., leet and 3–4 courts
on 2–3 mm before Black Death.
Accounts: 1290–1300: 1; 1300–50: 4;
1350–1400: 5; 1400–1500: 2.
All records are in poor condition, several boxes of fragmentary records also exist.
Probably sole manor (*FA* i, p. 154).

OAKINGTON   [Oakington   CUL
DRY   with Dry   (Q)
DRAYTON   Drayton
COTTENHAM   and
             Cottenham]
1290/1–1391/2, *1392–1419*, 1424/5,
1427/8, 1429/30–1440/1, 1443/4,
1444/5, 1450/1–1454/5, 1456/7,
1457/8, 1459/60, 1461/2–1480/1,
1494/5–1498/9, 1501/2.
Two great courts and 2–4 courts on 1–2 mm p.a. in late 13th c. Great courts have assize of ale and (sometimes) business of leet, and are called VFP from 1340. 2 VFP and 4–6 courts on 4–6 mm in mid 14th c., 2 VFP and 3–4 courts on 2–3 mm at end of 14th c., 2 VFP and 2 courts on 4–7 membranes in 15th c. (full).
The business of each village is entered in a separate section of the court roll.
Dating is mainly by abbatial years.
Bailiff's Accounts:
1258–1300:   19   (Oakington,
                     Cottenham,
                     Drayton)

1300–24:   9   (Oakington,
                     Cottenham,
                     Drayton)
               1   (Oakington)
1350–1400:   4   (Oakington)
1400–18:   16   (Oakington)
Hayward's accounts:
1422–36:   9   (Oakington)
Collector's accounts:
1339–50:   7   (Oakington)
1350–1400: *c*.50 (Oakington)
1400–12:   8   (Oakington)
1415–1500:   62   (Oakington,
                     Cottenham,
                     Drayton)
Granary accounts:
1365–99 :   Large bundle
             (Oakington)
Rentals: 1343–4 (Oakington, Drayton)
Manor of Crowland Abbey. One of three manors in Oakington, four in Cottenham, six in Dry Drayton (*FA* i, pp. 152–4).

OVER [Over]   SCCC
1300/1–1301/2, 1305/6–1308/9,
1328/9–1332/3, 1349/50, 1352/3–
1353/4, 1357/8, 1360/1, 1375/6,
1377/8, 1379/80.
1–3 short courts on pt. m. (13 mm in toto, most rubbed and dirty).
See next entry.

OVER [Over]   PRO/BL
1291–1300: 2; 1301–1400: 18; 1474.
One leet p.a. in 14th c., virtually no land transfers.
Ramsey Abbey manor. Three or four manors in parish (*RH* ii, pp. 476–8).
See introduction to **Huntingdonshire**.

ROYSTON   BL (Egerton rolls
[Clare honour   8366–83)/PRO
court]
1320/1, 1325/6, 1328/9–1329/30,
1331/2–1332/3, 1334/5–1335/6,

1338/9–1339/40, 1348/9, 1352/3, 1354/5, 1357/8, 1359/60–1360/1, 1364/5, *1368/9–1369/70*, 1378/9, *1381/2, 1428/9–1429/30.*

14–16 courts p.a. on 2–5 mm p.a., litigation and succession the prevalent business. In most years one court held at Litlington.

Court for lands of Clare Fee in Cambridgeshire and Huntingdonshire.

Note: Records of annual leets for Cambridgeshire and Suffolk lands of Clare Fee exist for: 1320/1–1323/4, 1325/6, 1327/8–1329/30, 1331/2, 1332/3, 1336/7, 1339/40–1342/3, 1345/6, 1346/7, 1348/9–1350/1, 1352/3, 1354/5, 1357/8, 1362/3, 1363/4, 1367/8, 1373/4–1375/6, 1386/7–1387/8, 1392/3–1393/4 (PRO SC2)

SNAILWELL [Snailwell]   CRO
1286/7, 1321/2, 1323/4, 1327/8–1341/2, 1351/2, 1358/9, 1361/2–1362/3, 1367/8–1368/9, 1373/4, 1382/3, 1384/5, 1386/7, 1497/8.

5–7 courts on 2 mm in complete years, but few years complete.

One of two manors in parish (*FA* i, p. 156).

SUTTON IN THE
ISLE [Sutton]   CUL (EDC)
1291/2–1292/3, 1294/5–1295/6, 1297/8–1298/9, 1300/1–1301/2, 1303/4–1304/5, 1306/7–1321/2, 1324/5–1345/6, 1355/6–1360/1, 1365/6–1369/70, 1373/4–1459/60, 1461/2, 1462/3, 1466/7, 1467/8, 1471/2–1479/80.

Leet and 5–7 cts. on 2–6 mm in full years early in 14th c. In some years of Edward III's reign two leet courts plus 1–2 cts. Yearly, or twice yearly VFP for Sutton and Stretham recorded on separate mm from 1356/7. (1291–1307,

16 mm 1307–27, 49 mm, 1327–77, 75 mm).

Accounts: 1350–1400: 2; 1407–8.

Rental 15th c.

Sole manor, belonging to Ely cathedral priory (*VCH* iv, p. 160).

SWAFFHAM PRIOR
[Swaffham Prior]   CUL (EDC)
1280/1, 1283/4, 1299/1300, 1317/18, 1320/1–1324/5, 1329/30, 1335/6, 1338/9–1342/3, 1346/7–1347/8, 1349/50–1376/7, 1422/3–1458/9.

Leet and 2 cts. p.a. Little intertenant litigation.

Three manors in parish (*FA* i, p. 155).

WISBECH, [Wisbech CUL/(EDR)
ELM,   (Barton)]   C/7/1–24
LEVER-   C/8–10/1,
INGTON   C/13/1–5)
NEWTON, TYDD,
WELL
1299/1300, 1301/2–1303/4, 1306/7, 1309/10–1315/16, 1317/18–1319/20, 1321/2–1331/2, 1333/4–1346/7, 1348/9–1356/7, 1359/60–1362/3, *1364/5–1370/1, 1371–1389*, 1389/90, *1390–95*, 1395/6, *1396–7*, 1397/8–1398/9, 1401/2, *1402–7, 1410–15*, 1415/16, *1416–22, 1434–55, 1458–63*, 1463/4, *1464–70*, 1470/1, *1471–4*, 1474/5, *1475–7*, 1477/8, 1498/9, etc.

11–13 courts and courts of bond tenants in full years on 7–10 mm before Black Death, 6–8 courts p.a. after Black Death, 3–5 courts in early 15th c.2 hallmoots p.a. held separately for each vill, usually at Wisbech, and in Wisbech and Leverington include lands of Prior of Ely. From 1340 Wisbech courts are filed separately. Some overlap between series. Hallmoot has jurisdiction associated with leet. No year survives complete.

The rolls of the three weekly court of Wisbech hundred for the same vills survive for: 1302/3–1306/7, 1308/9, 1312/13–1316/17, 1319/20–1320/1, 1322/3–1324/5, 1326/7, 1332/3, 1334/5, 1337/8–1339/40, 1342/3, 1345/6, 1347/8–1349/50, 1377/8–1378/9, *1379–1419, 1435–77*.

In the early period there is considerable overlap of business with Wisbech Barton court, but from 1313/14 almost exclusively a court of pleas. No year complete, but 6–15 courts p.a. survive for a number of years. Records of a court leet held annually at Wisbech for all the vills survive for a few years among the manorial rolls.

Accounts: WISBECH BARTON—1300–50: 20; 1350–1400: 26; 1400–1500: 66 (years); WISBECH CASTLE—1300–50: 6; 1350–1400: 2; 1400–1500: 47.

Surveys, 1222, 1251.

Subordinate manors in all parishes (*VCH* iv, pp. 180 ff.).

WITCHAM IN THE
ISLE [Witcham]   CUL (EDC)
1293/4, 1297/8, 1304/5, 1315/16, 1316/17, 1318/19, 1327/8, 1328/9, 1331/2–1337/8, 1339/40–1342/3, 1344/5–1346/7, 1350/1, 1352/3–1353/4, 1356/7, 1357/8, 1359/60–1412/13, 1422/3–1434/5, 1436/7–1438/9, 1486/7–1489/90, 1496/7, etc.

Leet (Mich) and 2–4 cts on 1 mm p.a. in early 14th c., leet and 2 cts p.a. from *c.*1340. 1 leet p.a. in late 15th c.

Accounts: 1 box in decayed state.

Sole manor belonging to Ely Cathedral priory (*VCH* iv, p. 173).

Derbyshire

DUFFIELD [Belper]   PRO
1277/8, 1289/90, 1291/2–1293/4, 1310/11–1312/13, 1333/4, 1334/5, 1337/8–1339/40, 1346/7–1348/9, 1357/8–1359/60, 1363/4, 1364/5, 1371/2, 1372/3, 1375/6, 1376/7, 1377/8–1384/5, 1387/8–1389/90, 1391/2, 1392/3, 1399/1400, 1400/1, 1409/10, 1411/12, 1412/13, 1413/14, 1419/20–1421/2, 1428/9–1430/1, 1433/4–1436/7, 1440/1, 1441/2, 1462/3, 1463/4, 1465/6–1469/70, 1487/8, 1492/3, 1497/8–1499/1500.

4–6 courts with VFP per year. Many Belper courts held at Duffield.

DUFFIELD
[Belper Woodmote]   PRO
1305/6, 1333/4, 1372/3–1373/4, 1375/6, 1376/7, 1379/80, 1380/1, 1386/7, 1387/8–1390/1, 1395/6–1398/9, 1402/3–1404/5, 1428/9–1430/1, 1435/6–1437/8, 1440/1–1441/2, 1465/6, 1466/7, 1497/8–1499/1500.

DUFFIELD [Duffield]   PRO
1277/8, 1289/90, 1291/2–1293/4, 1310/11–1312/13, 1341/2–1345/6, 1357/8–1359/60, 1361/2–1364/5, 1367/8, 1368/9, 1371/2, 1372/3, 1375/6, 1376/7, 1379/80–1383/4, 1386/7, 1387/8–1393/4, 1395/6–1400/1, 1406/7–1408/9, 1413/14, 1415/16, 1428/9–1430/1, 1462/3, 1463/4, 1465/6–1469/70, 1487/8, 1492/3, 1497/8–1499/1500.

Short courts (one or two entries), view of frankpledge with Belper.

DUFFIELD
[Duffield Woodmote]   PRO
As **Belper Woodmote**.

DUFFIELD [Heage] PRO
1277/8, 1289/90, 1291/2–1293/4,
1310/11–1312/13, 1333/4, 1357/8–
1359/60, 1361/2, 1362/3, 1371/2–
1374/5, 1376/7, 1377/8–1380/1,
1384/5, 1385/6, 1395/6–1398/9,
1403/4, 1404/5, 1425/6, 1426/7,
1435/6–1437/8, 1440/1, 1441/2,
1462/3, 1463/4, 1465/6–1469/70,
1487/8, 1492/3, 1497/8–1499/1500.
Short courts with Belper and Duffield.

DUFFIELD [Holbrook] PRO
1277/8, 1289/90, 1291/2–1293/4,
1310/11–1312/13, 1341/2, 1344/5–
1346/7, 1350/1–1353/4, 1357/8–
1359/60, 1371/2, 1372/3, 1376/7,
1378/9, 1379/80, 1382/3, 1383/4,
1389/90, 1390/1, 1395/6–1398/9,
1402/3–1404/5, 1406/7–1408/9,
1409/10, 1411/12, 1412/13, 1413/14,
1422/3, 1425/6, 1426/7, 1428/9–
1430/1, 1433/4–1436/7, 1440/1,
1441/2–1443/4, 1465/6–1469/70,
1487/8, 1492/3, 1497/8–1499/1500.
Short courts with Belper and Duffield.

Devon

HOLCOMBE ROGUS
[Holcombe Rogus] ECL
1349/50, 1350/1, 1357/8–1359/60,
1361/2, 1364/5–1370/1, 1372/3,
1375/6, 1376/7, 1379/80–1383/4,
1390/1–1392/3, 1395/6, 1397/8–
1401/2, 1408/9–1411/12, 1441/2,
1450/1, 1452/3, 1456/7, 1462/3–
1464/5, 1467/8, 1481/2, 1482/3.
Four full courts per year, but no VFP
or assize jurisdiction.
Accounts: 3 years 1332–50, 9 years
1351–1400, 23 years 1401–1500.
One of three manors in the parish
(Lysons vi, p. 276).

SHAUGH Prior
[Shaugh Prior] WDRO
1331/2, 1332/3, 1338/9, 1339/40,
1341/2, 1342/3, 1344/5–1346/7,
1353/4–1355/6, 1367/8, 1368/9,
1370/1, 1371/2, 1373/4, 1374/5,
1377/8, 1387/8, 1394/5, 1405/6–
1407/8, 1413/14–1418/9.
One or two courts per year, many with
only three to six entries. No VFP or
assize jurisdiction.
Accounts: 5 years 1338–50, 8 years
1351–1400, 4 years 1401–1500.
Only manor in the parish (Worthy ii,
pp. 233–4).

STOKE GABRIEL
[Waddeton] ECL
1356/7, 1359/60–1363/4, 1365/6–
1401/2, 1426/7, 1436/7, 1438/9,
1440/1.
For most years only one court per year
(28 mm. for all the listed courts), no
VFP or assize jurisdiction.
One of two manors in the parish
(Lysons, vi, p. 460).

UPLYME [Uplyme] Longleat
1313–14, *1315–16, 1340–1,* 1344–5,
1345–6, 1347–8, 1349–50, 1351–2,
1354–5, *1357,* 1358, *1364–7,* 1367–9,
1369–70, 1370–1, 1373, *1374, 1379–
80, 1387–8, 1403–4,* 1407–8, 1448–9.
2 tourns and hallmoots plus occasional
courts.
Glastonbury Abbey manor, sole manor
(Polwhele ii, pp. 298–9).
See notes under **Glastonbury,
Somerset.**

Dorset

BRIDPORT

[Bridport Borough]　　　　　　DRO

*1277, 1294, 1306, 1307, 1309–12, 1314,
1316–18, 1319, 1322, 1324–7, 1330–4,
1335–8, 1342–6, 1349–73, 1375–7,
1381–4, 1386–8, 1390–5, 1397, 1399,
1400, 1401, 1406–11, 1413, 1416–18,
1420, 1422–4, 1425, 1427–34, 1437,
1440–2, 1444–7, 1448–52, 1454, 1458–
65, 1469–73, 1475–80, 1483–5, 1489,
1491–6.*

Includes a leet court for most years
(not examined).

BUCKLAND NEWTON
DUNTISH

[Buckland hallmoot]　　　　Longleat

1262, 1265, *1283–4, 1307–9,* 1313,
1315–16, 1340–1, 1344–5, *1345–6,*
1347–8, 1349–50, 1351–2, 1354–5,
1357, 1358, *1364–7,* 1367–9, *1369–70,*
1370–1, 1373 *1374, 1379–80, 1387–8,*
1403–4, 1407–8, 1448–9.

Glastonbury Abbey manor, sole manor
in Buckland Newton, one of two manors in Duntish (Hutchins iii, pp. 691–
4). Hallmoot of Newton sometimes
enrolled separately.

See notes under **Glastonbury,
Somerset.**

CRANBORNE

[Cranborne hundred]　　　　　　HH

1328/9, 1329/30, 1333/4–1341/2,
1343/4, 1344/5, 1346/7–1348/9,
1350/1–1358/9, 1364/5–1373/4,
1375/6, 1376/7, 1378/9–1381/2,
1386/7–1388/9, *1399–1401, 1404–5,
1407, 1412–13, 1417–21, 1422–3, 1424–
5, 1431–2, 1435–6, 1439, 1441–2, 1443–
4, 1445–6, 1451, 1454–6, 1459–60,
1462–3, 1464–5, 1471–2, 1474–75,
1479–81, 1486, 1487–8, 1489–90,
1491–3.*

Around 14 courts per year with two
views or legal hundreds for a full year
during 1327–77, but few complete years
surviving. Some rolls damaged but all
repaired.

CRANBORNE

[Cranborne manor]　　　　　　　HH

1286/7, 1324/5, 1327/8, 1328/9,
1330/1, 1331/2, 1335/6, 1343/4,
1344/5, 1346/7, 1347/8, 1355/6–
1357/8, 1359/60–1361/2, 1363/4,
1364/5, 1368/9, 1369/70, 1370/1,
1376/7, 1377, 1377/8–1379/80, 1383/
4–1386/7, *1403–4, 1406, 1408–10,
1413–19, 1421–2, 1424–34, 1438–54,
1456–63, 1466–7, 1473–1500.*

Two VFP and up to 17 courts per year
for 1327–77, but survival variable. Little extended litigation. Some rolls damaged but all repaired.

Account for manor and/or hundred for
7 years 1317–50; 6 years 1351–1400; 1
year 1409

Rental 1382

Survey 1422

Some court rolls for Cranborne Chase
also survive in DRO.

Single manor in the parish (Hutchins
iii, pp. 375–80).

FORDINGTON [Fordington]　PRO

1328/9–1330/1, 1333/4, 1335/6–
1337/8, 1344/5–1357/8, 1359/60,
1360/1, 1362/3, 1363/4, 1365/6–
1368/9, 1371/2–1374/5, *1377/8–
1386/7, 1389/90, 1391/2, 1402/3–
1408/9, 1410/11, 1412/13, 1413/14–
1422, 1422/3, 1425/6, 1430/1, 1433/
4–1436/7, 1440/1–1446/7, 1448/9,
1449/50, 1451/2–1453/4, 1456/7,
1457/8, 1463/4, 1464/5, 1471/2,
1482/3, 1483/4–1484/5.* (PRO SC2)

One VFP and five to ten courts per
year surviving for most years 1327–77

with regular presentation of assize infractions by tithing. Many early courts illegible.
Single manor in the parish (Hutchins, ii, pp. 791–3).

GILLINGHAM *Gillingham* DRO
1291/2–1295/6, 1297/8–1300/1, 1304/5–1306/7, 1307/8, 1308/9, 1310/11, 1311/12, 1314/15–1321/2, 1324/5, 1325/6, 1331/2–1334/5, 1338/9–1341/2, 1344/5, 1345/6, 1347/8–1360/1, 1377/8–1398/9, 1399/1400–1412/13
and later fifteenth-century rolls in the process of repair.
One VFP and up to 18 courts per year for 1327–77, but survival variable. One VFP and 10 courts per year 1377–1413. Many early rolls fragile.
Extent 1274/5 (PRO E 142), account roll 1378/9–1379/80 (Gillingham museum), presentments 1406–1500 (John Rylands Library), rental early fourteenth century (Gillingham Museum). At least two manors in the parish, with a large area of forest (Hutchins, iv, pp. 615–24).

GUSSAGE ALL SAINTS
[Gussage All Saints] Bodl.
1280/1, 1282/3–1284/5, 1286/7–1289/90, 1334/5, 1337/8, 1338/9, 1340/1–1347/8, 1349/50–1351/2, 1353/4, 1359/60–1369/70, 1372/3, 1373/4, 1377/8–1379/80, 1381/2, 1396/7–1399, 1399/1400–1401/2, 1403/4–1405/6, 1407/8, 1409/10, 1469/70, 1471/2, 1472/3, 1479/80 (R92–172)
Short courts. Four courts per year but many years with only one or two courts surviving. No VFP or assize jurisdiction. Good condition.

Accounts for 6 years 1292–1300; 17 years 1301–50; 17 years 1351–1400; 38 years 1401–1500.
Rentals: 1317/18, 1437/8, 1442/3, 1443/4.
Two manors in the parish (Hutchins, iii, pp. 489–90).

MARNHULL [Hallmoot] Longleat
1344–5, *1345–6*, 1347–8, 1349–50, 1351–2, 1354–5, *1357*, 1358, *1364–7*, 1367–9, *1369–70*, 1370–1, 1372–3, *1374, 1379–80, 1387–8, 1403–4*, 1407–8, 1448–9.
Glastonbury Abbey manor, at least three manors in parish (Hutchins, iv, pp. 306, 314–16).
See notes under **Glastonbury, Somerset.**

STURMINSTER NEWTON
[Newton hallmoot] Longleat
1313–14, *1315–16, 1340–1*, 1344–5, *1345–6*, 1347–8, 1349–50, 1351–2, 1354–5, *1357*, 1358, *1364–7*, 1367–9, *1369–70*, 1370–1, 1372–3, *1374, 1379–80, 1387–8, 1403–4*, 1407–8, 1448–9.
Glastonbury Abbey manor, one of two in parish (Hutchins, iv, pp. 336–9); Some rolls have records of court of Sturminster Fair (June).
See notes under **Glastonbury, Somerset.**

Durham

ESTATES OF DURHAM CATHEDRAL PRIORY The Prior's Kitchen
1296–7, 1345, 1358, 1364–1401, 1404, 1405, 1407, 1409–14, 1420, 1421, 1423, 1424, 1427–9, 1439, 1449, 1450, 1460, 1461, 1465–7, 1472–5, 1477–9, 1482, 1483, 1487–95, 1497–1500 etc.

Hallmoots held three times a year for Aycliffe, Bellasis, Bewley, Billingham, Burdun, Chilton, Coupon, Dalton, Edmondbyers, Ferry Hill, Fulwell, Harton, Hebburn, Hedworth, Hesledon, Heworth, Jarrow, Monckton, Moorsley, the Morringtons, Newton Ketton, Nunstanton, The Pittingtons, the Raintons, Ravensflat, Shields, Southwich, Spen, Usworth, Wallsend, Wardley, Wearmouth, Westoe, Willington, Wolviston.

Assizes of bread and ale held, but no frankpledge business conducted. Little relating to inheritance. There are a number of account rolls and rentals from 1332 onward.

See *Surtees Society* vol 82, for calendar of rolls 1296–1385 (not a complete transcript).

Essex

ASHELDHAM

[Asheldham] Longleat

1311/12, 1313/14–1323/4, *1326/7, 1327/8,* 1331/2–1337/8, 1339/40–1341/2, *1342/3, 1343/4,* 1344/5–1350/1, 1362/3, *1366/7–1375/6,* 1376/7–1377, *1377/8, 1381/2–1384/ 5, 1386/7–1388/9,* 1391/2, 1393/4, 1394/5, *1400/1–1408/9,* 1410/11–1414/15, *1415/16–1418/19, 1426/7, 1448/9–1450/1.*

VFP and occasional courts p.a., all very short. Main business is tenurial regulation.

Accounts: 1300–50: 2; 1350–1400: 16; 1400–1500: 2.

There are records of New Hall in Asheldham among Petre family archives at ERO for 1351/2, 1360/1, 1376/7 and 1400 onwards.

Morant i, p. 367–8 (one of three manors in parish).

ASHEN [Claret (Hall)] PRO

1312/13, 1317/18–1318/19, 1322/3–1325/6, *1327/8, 1329/30–1345/6, 1346/7–1347/8,* 1348/9, 1350/1–1359/60, 1362/3–1366/7, 1368/9–1371/2, *1377/8–1379/80, 1381/ 2–1384/5, 1386/7–1398/9, 1400/1, 1402/3–1406/7, 1412/13, 1413/4–1415/16, 1431/2, 1436/7, 1437/8, 1461/2, 1462/3, 1468/9, 1469/70, 1478/9, 1479/80.*

VFP and 12–15 short courts on 2 mm p.a. Little intertenant litigation or information about land transfers.

Accounts: 1450–1500: 2

Sole manor (Morant ii, pp. 338–9).

BERDEN [Berden] ERO

1333/4, 1339/40, 1340/1, 1355/6, 1357/8–1361/2, 1368/9–1372/3, 1376/7–1384/5, 1389/90–1390/1, 1415/16, 1428/9–1431/2, 1438/9, 1439/40, 1449/50–1476/7, 1482/3–1483/4, 1491/2–1507/8 etc.

VFP and 2–3 courts p.a. in mid 14th c., VFP and occasional courts from reign of Richard II. Little re. litigation and land transfers, numerous demesne trespasses recorded.

Sole manor in parish, granted to Walden Abbey *c.*1343/4 (Morant ii, pp. 615–16).

BIRDBROOK

[Birdbrook] ERO/WAM

1292/3, *1293,* 1297/8–1298/9, 1319/ 20, 1328/9, 1330/1–1332/3, 1336/7–1339/40, 1341/2–1343/4, 1348/9, 1360/1, *1363,* 1363/4, 1365/6, *1376–99, 1400–21, 1423–82* etc.

VFP and 13 courts on 4 mm in late 13th c., VFP and 3 courts on 2–3 mm p.a. before Black Death, VFP and 1 court on 1 m in 1360s.

Frankpledge rolls 1325, 1340, 1420.

Rentals *c.*1296, *c.*1390, *c.*1425, 1446–7, 1471–2.

Westminster Abbey manor from *c.*1243. One of three manors in parish (Morant ii, pp. 344–6).

BLACKMORE [Fingrith Hall] ERO 1327/8–1352/3, *1353–98, 1400–13, 1423–59, 1468–80.*
VFP and 1–3 cts. on 2–3 mm p.a., plus some records of fair courts.
Four manors in parish (Morant ii, pp. 56–9).

BOREHAM [Old Hall] PRO *1269/70–1270/1, 1348/9, 1355/6–1362/3, 1365/6–1369/70, 1373/4–1376/7, 1377/8–1399/1400, 1401/2–1411/12.*
One of six manors in parish (Morant ii, pp. 11–16).

BORLEY [Borley] ERO/CCL 1308/9, 1314/15, 1328/9–1333/4, 1336/7, *1337/8, 1342/3,* 1343/4, *1346/7,* 1347/8, *1350/1, 1351/2,* 1354/5–1356/7, 1358/9, 1360/1–1363/4, 1368/9–1370/1, 1372/3–1373/4, *1374/5–1376/7, 1399–1413, 1422–83.*
VFP and 1–2 courts p.a., in 14th c.
Bedel's rolls: 1300–50: 4; 1350–1400: 2; 1400–13: 4
Rental: 1493
Extent: 1308
Manor granted to Canterbury Cathedral Priory in 1364. One of two manors in parish (Morant ii, pp. 317–19).

WAKES COLNE [Crepping] ERO 1306/7, 1313/14–1314/15, 1318/19, 1319/20, 1327/8, 1328/9, 1330/1–1338/9, 1340/1–1356/7, 1399/1400–1409/10, 1411/12, 1413/14, 1414/15, 1416/17–1425/6, 1427/8, 1429/30–1441/2, 1450/1–1452/3, 1455/6–

1458/9, 1481/2, 1482/3, 1483/4, 1497/8, 1499/1500–1501/2 etc.
VFP and 5–7 courts on 3 mm p.a. at beginning of reign of Edward III.
VFP and 3 courts after Black Death, VFP and occasional courts in 15th c.
One of two manors in parish (Morant ii pp. 221–3) The records of Wakes Colne manor begin in 1380 (ERO).

LITTLE DUNMOW
[Little Dunmow] PRO 1327/8–1329/30, 1331/2, 1335/6–1336/7, 1338/9, 1341/2, 1349/50, 1351/2–1355/6, 1359/60–1360/1, 1366/7–1369/70, 1371/2, 1374/5–1376/7.
VFP and variable no. of courts surviving (1–7) on 1–2 mm p.a. Most courts fairly short.
Accounts: 1274–6, 1351–2, 1420/1, (unless relates to Great Dunmow). Morant ii, p. 427, sole manor.

HIGH EASTER
[High Easter] PRO *1248/9–1261/2, 1264/5–1266/7, 1274/5–1275/6, 1279/80–1290/1,* 1298/9–1300/1, *1301/2–1303/4,* 1305/6, 1317/18–1319/20, 1326/7, *1328/9–1332/3, 1334/5–1340/1, 1342/3–1344/5,* 1345/6, 1346/7, 1348/9, 1351/2, *1352/3–1355/6,* 1355/6, *1358/9–1362/3,* 1362/3, *1364/5–1365/6,* 1365/6, *1366/7–1371/2, 1374/5–1377, 1377/8–1398/ 9, 1399/1400–1403/4, 1405/6–1412/ 13, 1413/14–1421/2, 1422/3–1427/8, 1429/30–1434/5, 1436/7–1443/4, 1445/6–1447/8, 1449/50–1458/9, 1461/2–1470/1, 1471/2, 1482/3, 1483/4–1485.*
VFP plus 6–9 courts early in 14th c., 4–5 in mid 14th c. on 4–6 mm, courts full. Court held generally for Waltham and Easter jointly at Pleshey, until

1350s. Records enrolled with court of Pleshey and court of the Mandeville honour.
Accounts: 1400–1500: 29.
Extent 1329/30
One of five manors (Morant ii, pp. 455–8).

FINCHINGFIELD
[Norton (or Cornett)]   PRO
1312/13, 1326/7, 1328/9, 1331/2, 1332/3, 1335/6, 1339/40, 1341/2, *1345/6, 1346/7, 1348/9, 1349/50, 1357/8, 1362/3, 1363/4, 1367/8, 1373/4, 1374/5, 1375/6, 1386/7– 1387/8, 1392/3–1393/4.*
Records of one leet p.a., enrolled with records of leets for manors of Clare Fee in Essex. There are records of a few fifteenth-century courts of this manor in the Essex Record Office.
Morant ii, pp. 363–9 (one of *c.*9 manors in parish).

HALSTEAD [Huraunt]   PRO
1317/18 *1324/5,* 1330/1, 1335/6, 1338/9, 1340/1, 1341/2, *1345/6– 1347/8,* 1348/9, *1354/5, 1357/8, 1362/3, 1363/4, 1367/8, 1373/4– 1375/6, 1386/7–1387/8, 1392/3– 1393/4,* 1395/6, 1405/6, 1406/7, *1408/9, 1409/10, 1433/4–1434/5, 1442/3, 1457/8, 1458/9, 1461/2– 1462/3, 1466/7–1477/8, 1480/1– 1482/3.*
Records of one leet court p.a., enrolled with records of leets in Clare Fee manors in Essex and Cambridge.
There are some court rolls of Halstead (mainly a court of pleas) enrolled with leets of the manor of Abels from 1343/4, and of the manor of Stanstead Hall for 1339/40–1376/7 at Longleat.
Apparently 5 or 6 manors in parish (Morant ii, pp. 249–58).

EAST HANNINGFIELD   ERO
1331/2–1335/6, 1337/8–1353/4, 1357/8–1362/3, 1365/6–1366/7, 1368/9 *or 1369/70,* 1371/2–1372/3, *1374/5–1376/7, 1378–99, 1400–12, 1414–22, 1424–60, 1462–83, 1491–1508 etc.*
VFP and 8–12 courts on 4–6 mm p.a. in early years of Edward III, later VFP and 2–3 courts on 2–3 mm. Full records.
Rental: *c.*1490
One of three manors in parish (Morant ii, p. 36).

SOUTH HANNINGFIELD
[South Hanningfield]   ERO
1337/8–1361/2, 1364/5–1376/7, *1378–97, 1424–1508.*
VFP (February) and sometimes 1–2 courts p.a. on one membrane, rarely more.
Sole manor (Morant ii, p. 39).

HORNCHURCH
[Hornchurch Hall]   NCO
1340/1–1348/9, 1357/8–1377, 1377/8, 1379/80–1387/8, 1390/1–1398/9, 1413/14–1421/2, 1422/3–1447/8, 1475/6–1477/8, 1479/80–1483/4, 1485/6–1490/1.
View and 2–6 cts. on 2 mm p.a. in reigns of Edward III and Richard II.
Rectory manor, one of eight or nine in Hornchurch, all subordinate to the royal manor of Havering. (*VCH* vii, pp. 31–9).

HORNDON   PRO
1334/5, 1336/7, 1337/8, 1341/2– 1348/9, 1350/1–1353/4, 1360/1– 1363/4, 1365/6, 1366/7, 1369/ 70–1372/3, 1374/5–1376/7, 1402/3, 1404/5, 1405/6–1408/9, 1413/14, 1416/17–1422, 1423/4, 1427/8–1429/

30, 1431/2, 1434/5, 1441/2, 1442/3, 1445/6, 1454/5–1456/7.

INGATESTONE
[Ingatestone]   ERO
1279, 1288, 1292, 1303/4–1304/5, *1311, 1319, 1322–3, 1326, 1329, 1333/ 4,* 1335/6, 1338/9–1339/40, 1341/2, 1343/4, *1345–6,* 1346/7, 1354/5– 1356/7, *1358, 1368–70, 1379–84, 1386– 8, 1390–9, 1405–7, 1413–26 etc.*
VFP and 6–7 cts. (one called *curia generalis*) on 6 mm. p.a. at beginning of 14th c., VFP, *curia generalis* and 2 courts on 2 mm p.a. in mid 14th c. (courts held on four regular days).
Manor of Barking Abbey, sole manor in parish (Morant ii, pp. 46–8).

MATCHING [Matching]   PRO
1316/17, 1327/8, 1329/30–1336/7, 1338/9–1340/1, 1345/6, 1346/7, 1351/2–1353/4, 1357/8–1359/60, 1364/5–1369/70, 1373/4–1380/1, 1383/4, 1393/4, 1396/7, 1400/1, 1403/4, 1408/9, 1409/10, 1414/15, 1427/8, 1447/8, 1460/1, 1464/5, 1466/7–1481/2,1483, 1483/4.
Three manors in the parish (Morant ii, pp. 496–7).

MESSING [Messing
Hall alias Baynards]   ERO
1283/4, 1284/5, 1286/7–1288/9, 1292/3, 1294/5–1298/9, 1300/1– 1308/9, 1310/11–1316/17, 1324/5, 1326/7–1378/9, 1382/3, 1387/8– 1398/9, 1413/14–1421/2, *1422/3– 1439/40, 1446/7–1459/60, 1461/2.*
(25 mm 1283/4–1324/5, 59 mm 1327/ 8–1376/7).
VFP and 6 courts in complete years in reign of Edward I, VFP and 10 short courts in reign of Edward II, VFP and 4 courts p.a. at beginning of reign of

Edward III, VFP and 1–2 cts. p.a. after Black Death, VFP and occasional courts in early 15th c. Little litigation or evidence of land transfer.
Tithing lists *c.*1284/5, 1302/3, 1341/ 2.
One of three manors in parish (Morant ii, pp. 175–8). Records of Bourchiers Hall manor beginning 1382 are also at ERO.

PLESHEY [Pleshey]   PRO
1276/7–1279/80, 1286/7–1294/5, 1295/6, 1300/1–1302/3, 1304/5– 1310/11, 1312/13, 1314/15, 1317/18– 1319/20, 1326/7, *1328/9–1331/2, 1334/5–1336/7, 1343/4,* 1344/5– 1345/6, 1348/9–1351/2, *1352/3, 1354/5,* 1355/6, *1356/7–1361/2,* 1362/3, *1363/4–1364/5,* 1365/6, *1366/7–1371/2, 1374/5–1380/1, 1383/4–1399, 1422/3–1441/2, 1461/ 2–1471/2, 1476/7–1484/5.*
VFP plus 5–8 courts early in 14th c., 4 or 5 in mid 14th c. 1–3mm p.a., court entries generally brief. Records enrolled with those of court of Waltham and Easter and of court of Mandeville honour.
Accounts: 1350–1400: 2; 1400–1500: 28.
Extent: 1329/30
Sole manor (Morant ii, p. 451).

RICKLING [Rickling]   PRO/ERO
1307/8–1313/14, *1315/16–1317/18, 1329/30, 1330/1, 1337/8–1340/1,* 1341/2–1350/1, 1352/3, 1357/8, *1359/60–1372/3, 1374/5–1377, 1393/ 4, 1394/5, 1398/9, 1399/1400–1401/ 2,* 1402/3, *1403/4, 1407/8, 1408/9, 1411/12,* 1413/14, *1415/16, 1417/18, 1418/19, 1420/1–1422,* 1434/5, 1448/ 9.
VFP (Easter) and up to 6 cts. p.a. surviving early in 14th c., view and 3 cts.

p.a. on 2–3 mm in reign of Edward III
(condition very poor).
Rental: 1318/19
Sole medieval manor (Morant ii, pp.
582–4).

MARGARET RODING
[Marks Hall]   UCO
1314/15–1319/20, 1321/2–1326/7,
1328/9, 1329/30, 1332/3–1333/4,
1335/6, 1338/9–1348/9, 1351/2–
1353/4, 1355/6–1359/60, 1361/2–
1364/5, 1403/4, 1423/4–1425/6,
1428/9–1432/3, 1434/5–1438/9,
1455/6, 1460/1, 1462/3–1467/8,
1474/5–1482/3, 1484/5–1491/2,
1493/4–1502/3.
Apparently records of two courts
(Roothing Marcii, Roothing Margarete)
VFP (July) and occasional courts held
for each usually on same day and sometimes jointly. No land transfers in court.
Two manors in parish (Morant ii,
p. 473).

SHALFORD [Shalford]   PRO
*1312/13–1313/14, 1316/17, 1317/18,
1323/4, 1324/5*, 1330/1, *1331/2*,
1335/6, 1338/9, 1340/1–1341/2,
1345/6–1346/7, 1348/9, *1354/5,
1357/8, 1359/60, 1362/3, 1363/4,
1367/8–1369/70, 1373/4–1375/6,
1386/7–1387/8, 1392/3–1393/4,
1395/6, 1399/1400–1412/13, 1422,
1422/3, 1426/7, 1428/9–1431/2,
1433/4–1435/6, 1437/8–1442/3,
1450/1, 1451/2, 1453/4–1455/6,
1457/8, 1458/9, 1461/2–1477/8,
1480/1–1482/3, 1485/6–1487/8,
1489/90–1499/1500* etc.
Records of one leet court p.a. (Clare
Fee)
Largest of five manors in parish
(Morant ii, pp. 374–5).

STAMBOURNE
[Stambourne Hall]   PRO
1312/13, 1313/14, *1323/4–1325/6*,
1326/7, *1327/8–1328/9, 1330/1–
1332/3, 1335/6*, 1336/7, 1338, *1339/
40*, 1340/1, *1341/2–1342/3, 1345/6–
1346/7, 1348/9, 1349/50, 1354/5,
1357/8*, 1358/9, 1360/1, *1362/3–
1370/1, 1372/3–1376/7, 1386/7–
1387/8, 1392/3–1393/4, 1395/6,
1405/6, 1406/7, 1408/9, 1409/10,
1433/4–1434/5, 1442/3, 1457/8,
1458/9, 1461/2–1463/4*.
Accounts: 1300–50: 11; 1350–1400: 14;
1400–1500: 3.
Morant says a Whitsun leet for Honour of Clare and a 3 weekly court in
the parish.
Some rolls are records of up to 16 cts.
p.a., others of one leet enrolled with
records of Clare honour in Essex and
Cambridgeshire.
One of three manors in parish (Morant
ii, p. 355).

TOLLESBURY [Tolleshunt
alias Tolleshunt Guines]   ERO
1326/7–1333/4, 1335/6–1342/3,
1360/1–1373/4, 1375/6–1376/7,
1405/6–1410/11, 1413/14–1419/20,
1422/3, *1464–82*. (22 mm 1326/7–76/
7)
VFP and 1–2 short courts. Little
litigation.
Accounts 1337–57, 1400–1406
Principal manor of three in parish
(Morant i, pp. 400–4).

TOPSFIELD   PRO
1312/13, 1317/18, 1330/1, 1335/6,
1338/9, *1339/40*, 1340/1, *1341/2–
1342/3, 1345/6–1346/7*, 1348/9,
1349/50, 1354/5, 1357/8, 1362/3,
*1363/4, 1367/8, 1373/4–1375/6,
1386/7–1387/8, 1392/3–1393/4*,

1395/6, 1399/1400–1401/2, 1403/4,
1404/5, 1422/3, 1430/1, 1431/2.
Records of one short view of frankpledge p.a. enrolled with leets of Essex
manors held of honour of Clare.
At least six manors in parish, but most
of the parish held of honour of Clare
(Morant ii, pp. 358–60).

GREAT WALTHAM
[Chatham Hall]   ERO
1286/7–1288/9, 1307/8–1345/6,
1354/5–1358/9, 1362/3, 1375/6–
1377/8, 1411/12, 1413/14–1421/2,
1461/2–1464/5.
VFP and 1–2 short courts p.a. throughout period (38 mm. 1321/2–1377/8).

GREAT WALTHAM
[Walthambury]   PRO ERO
1248/9–1261/2, 1264/5–1266/7,
1271/2, 1272/3, 1274/5–1275/6,
1289/90–1290/1, 1298/9–1300/1,
1305/6, 1317/18–1319/20, 1326/7–
1327/8, *1328/9–1332/3, 1334/5–*
1340/1, 1342/3–1344/5, 1345/6,
1348/9, 1350/1, *1354/5–1355/6,*
1355/6, *1358/9–1361/2,* 1362/3,
1363/4–1364/5, 1365/6, *1366/7–*
1371/2, 1374/5–1398/9, 1400–55,
1462–83.
VFP and 6–9 courts on 3–6 mm p.a.
early in 14th c., 4–5 courts in mid-
century. Courts full. One court held
generally for Waltham and Easter
jointly at Pleshey until 1350s. Records
enrolled with court of Pleshey and court
of the Mandeville honour until end of
reign of Edward III.
Accounts: 1300–50: 1; 1350–1400: 1;
1400–1500: 27.
Seven manors in parish (Morant ii,
p. 83).

WICKHAM BISHOPS
[Wickham Bishops]   PRO
1335/6, 1338/9–1341/2, 1347/8–
1349/50, 1351/2, 1352/3, 1354/5–
1362/3, 1386/7, 1387/8, 1390/1,
1394/5, 1399/1400–1403/4, 1406/7,
1408/9, 1418/19–1420/1, 1432/3,
1435/6, 1441/2, 1442/3, 1452/3,
1454/5, 1455/6, 1461/2–1464/5,
1468/9, 1469/70, 1476/7, 1477/8,
1484/5, 1486/7, 1489/90–1491/2.
Sole manor in parish (Morant i, pp.
381–2).

Gloucestershire

BERKELEY [Berkeley]   BCas
1304/5, 1309/10–1311/12, 1313/14,
1318/19–1320/1, 1325/6–1329/30,
1331/2–1335/6, 1338/9, 1340/1,
1343/4–1346/7, 1348/9–1365/6,
1367/8–1372/3, 1374/5–1378/9,
1380/1–1384/5, 1386/7, 1388/9–
1398/9, 1401/2–1403/4, 1407/8,
1409/10, 1412/13, 1425/6, 1426/7,
1427/8, 1429/30, 1432/3, 1445/6–
1447/8, 1450/1, 1451/2, 1457/8,
1460/1, 1461/2–1463/4, 1482/3.
For most years two courts per year with
assize infractions. VFP surviving only
for 1364/5–1370/1, 1388/9, 1391/2,
1393/4, 1394/5, 1396/7–1398/9. Usual
court business, but little litigation.
Records of Berkeley Hundred Court
beginning 1279/80 not examined.
Accounts: 1285/6, 1306/7, 1329/30,
1345/6, 1349/50, 1354/5, 1356/7,
1390/1, 1392/3, 1415/16, 1426/7,
1427/8.
Borough Accounts: 1288/9, 1292/3,
1298/9, 1305/6, 1306/7, 1308/9,
1311/12–1313/14, 1323/4–1326/7,
1333/4, 1335/6, 1343/4, 1357/8–

1359/60, 1367/8, 1372/3, 1373/4, 1376/7–1388/9, 1425/6, 1438/9, 1458/9, 1460/1, 1461/2, 1472/3, 1473/4.
No information on manorial history.

BITTON [Bitton]   BCas
1288/9, 1290/1, 1299/1300–1300/1, 1303/4–1304/5, 1322/7, 1331/2, 1333/4–1334/5, 1340/1, 1344/5, 1365/6, 1369/70, 1373/4–1374/5, 1386/7.
One or two courts per year, with VFP surviving for only 1331/2–1344/5.
No information on manorial history.

BITTON HUNDRED   BCas
1282/3, 1291/2, 1304/5, 1307/8–1314/15, 1317/18–1318/19, 1338/9, 1340/1–1341/2, 1343/4, 1347/8–1349/50, 1352/3, 1354/5, 1365/6, 1368/9, 1373/4, 1376/7.

THORNBURY
[Thornbury]   StRO/GRO
1328/9, 1329/30, 1331/2–1335/6, 1337/8, 1338/9, 1341/2, 1343/4–1351/2, 1352/3–1355/6, 1357/8–1362/3, 1365/6–1408/9, 1412/13, 1413/14, 1417/18–1421/2, *1438/9–1448/9, 1452/3–1458/9, 1475/6–1482/3, 1485/6–1500/1.*
VFP and 11–17 courts per year for most years.
Accounts (mostly reeve and beadle) 16 years 1327–50; 21 years 1351–1400.
No information on manorial history.

THORNBURY BOROUGH   StRO
1324/5, 1330/1, 1339/40, 1340/1, 1343/4–1346/7, 1351/2, 1352/3, 1359/60, 1360/1, 1362/3–1366/7, 1367/8–1376/7, *1377–89, 1401–59, 1461–75, 1475–6, 1478–9, 1480–2.*
(Also three-weekly court of the honour of Gloucester held at Thornbury: 1278,

1294–5, 1331, 1343–8, 1348–55, 1357–65, 1377–83, 1383–1414, 1426, 1436–7, 1439–40, 1455–6, 1458–60, 1461–5, 1475–8, 1481.)

Hampshire

ALTON
[Alton Westbrook]   BL/HRO
1336/7–1351/2, 1353/4–1359/60, 1361/2–1364/5, 1366/7–1370/1, 1372/3, 1373/4, 1380/1–1401/2, 1404/5–1406/7, 1409/10, 1410/11, 1412/13–1425/6, 1427/8–1432/3, 1436/7, 1439/40, 1444/5, 1447/8, 1451/2, 1452/3, 1456/7, 1460/1–1464/5, 1466/7–1473/4, 1475/6, 1476/7, 1479/80–1485/6, 1488/9–1491/2, 1501/2.
Sixteen to eighteen courts and 2 VFP per year surviving for most years during the period 1327–77.
Rental 1399.
At least seven manors in the parish (*VCH* ii, p. 471).

BURITON [Mapledurham]   BL
1275/6, 1280/1, 1299/1300, 1317/18, 1327/8, 1346/7, 1347/8, 1350/1, 1351/2, 1354/5, 1357/8, 1359/60, 1360/1, 1362/3, 1367/8, 1370/1, 1373/4, 1379/80, 1381/2, 1384/5, 1386/7, 1387/8, 1391/2, 1392/3, 1394/5–1398/9, 1402/3–1405/6, 1420/1–1440/1, 1447/8, 1450/1, 1454/5, 1457/8–1459/60, 1465/6–1467/8.
No VFP or assize jurisdiction, one court per year for most years. Short courts, often only 5–10 entries.
Accounts for 40 years 1401–1500.
Four manors in the parish (*VCH* iii, p. 85).

SOUTH DAMERHAM

[Damerham] MARTIN   Longleat

1262, 1265, *1283–4, 1307–9*, 1313–14, *1315–16*, 1340–1, 1344–5, *1345–6*, 1347–8, 1349–50, 1351–2, 1354–5, *1357*, 1358, *1364–7*, 1367–9, *1369–70*, 1370–1, 1372–3, *1374, 1379–80, 1387–8, 1403–4*, 1407–8, 1448–9.

Glastonbury Abbey manor, one of three in each parish (*VCH* iv, pp. 586–92)

See notes under **Glastonbury, Somerset**.

ELING [Eling]   WCol

1331/2–1337/8, 1339/40–1349/50, 1352/3–1354/5, 1356/7–1368/9, 1370/1–1372/3, 1375/6–1411/12, 1413/14–1417/18, 1423/4–1448/9, 1450/1–1459/60, 1461/2–1466/7, 1468/9–1483/4, 1484/5.

VFP and up to eleven courts per year 1327–77, but seldom more than four courts surviving. Court rolls in good condition, generally one membrane per court, often *r* and *v*.

Five rentals (undated), accounts for 24 years 1381–1412.

Ten manors in the parish (*VCH* iv, p. 546).

HOLYBOURNE

[Holybourne hundred]   BL/HRO

1337/8, 1338/9, 1340/1, 1341/2, 1343/4–1345/6, 1347/8, 1348/9–1351/2, 1354/5–1358/9, 1360/1–1366/7, 1370/1–1374/5, 1379/80, 1380/1, 1382/3–1396/7, 1398/9, 1410/11, 1414/15, 1415/16, 1427/8, 1428/9, 1467/8, 1468/9, 1485/6, 1489/90, 1501/2.

Up to 18 courts, 2 VFP and one sheriff's tourn per year during 1327–77. Short courts, many with no entries. Where there are two VFP in a year, one is held at Alton Eastbrook.

MILTON [Fernhill]   WCol

1308/9, 1309/10–1317/18, 1334/5–1351/2, 1354/5–1374/5, 1382/3, 1383/4, 1399/1400–1404/5, 1407/8–1410/11, 1415/16, 1416/17, 1437/8, 1439/40, 1441/2, 1442/3, 1445/6–1449/50, 1451/2–1452/3, 1455/6–1458/9, 1464/5, 1465/6, 1467/8, 1474/5, 1478/9, 1483/4.

No VFP or assize jurisdiction, two courts per year. Courts are short, often only 3–4 entries.

Accounts for 6 years 1378–1400, 57 years 1401–1500.

Six manors in the parish (*VCH* v, pp. 124–6).

PRESTON CANDOVER

[Moundsmere]   WCol

1282/3–1285/6, 1295/6, 1297/8, 1298/9, 1300/1–1305/6, 1307/8, 1308/9, 1315/16–1318/19, 1327/8, 1329/30–1335/6, 1337/8, 1338/9, 1340/1, 1342/3, 1345/6, 1346/7, 1348/9–1361/2, 1363/4–1376/7, *1377/8–1382/3, 1395/6–1411/12, 1413/14–1419/20, 1439/40, 1442/3, 1443/4*.

No VFP or assize jurisdiction, one or two courts per year. Courts are short.

Accounts for 10 years 1268–1300; 27 years 1301–50; 7 years 1350–1400; 20 years 1401–1500.

Four manors in the parish (*VCH* iii, p. 371).

SOUTH STONEHAM

[Allington]   WCol

1332/3–1336/7, 1338/9–1345/6, 1347/8, 1348/9, 1350/1–1355/6, 1357/8–1360/1, 1365/6, 1366/7, 1370/1, 1372/3–1375/6, 1376/7, *1377/8, 1379/80–1384/5, 1386/7–1397/8, 1399/1400–1403/4, 1407/8–1415/16, 1419/20, 1420/1, 1424/5*,

1426/7, 1428/9–1430/1, 1433/4, 1435/6, 1437/8, 1439/40–1443/4, 1447/8–1450/1, 1452/3, 1455/6, 1457/8, 1463/4–1467/8, 1471/2, 1478/9, 1482/3.
No VFP or assize jurisdiction, one or two courts per year during the years 1327–77.
Accounts for 49 years 1415–1500.
Terrier or rental: 1409/10, rent account 1417/18.
Three manors in the parish (*VCH* iii, p. 481).

SOUTHWICK [Southwick]   HRO
1328/9–1335/6, 1337/8–1412/13, 1422/3–1435/6, 1477/8, 1481/2, 1482/3.
VFP courts only (two per year surviving for most years). Courts are full, and rolls are in good condition (Daly Mss).
Accounts for 55 years 1358–93.
Rentals 1352, 1396, 1505.
Three manors in the parish (*VCH* iii, p.161).

VERNHAM [Fernhamsdean]   WCol
1325/6, 1326/7, 1327/8, 1329/30, 1330/1, 1335/6, 1341/2–1345/6, 1355/6–1366/7, 1378/9–1390/1, 1392/3, 1394/5, 1396/7, 1398/9, 1399/1400–1406/7, 1408/9–1411/12, 1413/14–1418/19, 1421/2, 1422/3–1428/9, 1429/30–1433/4, 1435/6–1438/9, 1440/1–1446/7, 1448/9–1460/1, 1461/2–1464/5, 1466/7, 1469/70–1482/3, 1483/4–1484/5.*
Two VFP and two courts per year, with one court per year of Gilbert de Neville during 1341/2–1355/6.
Collectors' accounts for 9 years 1389–1400; 74 years 1401–1500.
Rentals 1334, 1359, 1430.
Reeves' Accounts for 8 years 1329–50; 29 years 1351–1400.

Two manors in the parish (*VCH* iv, p. 329).

WHITCHURCH
[Whitchurch cum Evingar]   WCa
1281, 1290, 1292, 1295, 1296, 1298, 1306, 1308, 1310, 1311, 1313, 1320, 1322, 1330, 1331, 1340, 1344, 1347–52, 1363, 1364, 1368, *1381, 1384, 1385, 1388, 1394, 1395, 1404, 1408, 1409, 1414, 1415, 1417, 1418, 1420, 1422, 1423, 1424, 1428, 1430, 1439, 1440, 1450, 1454–6, 1471, 1473, 1478, 1482, 1493, 1494.*
Portmoot, hundred, and manor courts on same day, with assizes at hundred court. Two courts of each type per year, but seldom more than one surviving. Few manor courts survive after 1322.
Accounts for 8 years 1248–1300; 39 years 1301–1400; 11 years 1401–1500.
Three manors in the parish (*VCH* iv, p. 299).

Herefordshire

CLEHONGER [Clehonger]   Bodl.
1273/4, 1274/5, 1283/4, 1289/90, 1294/5, 1295/6, 1303/4–1305/6, 1307/8, 1309/10, 1312/13, 1314/15, 1315/16, 1318/19–1321/2, 1326/7, 1331/2–1345/6, 1348/9, 1349/50.
For most years only one or two courts per year surviving. No VFP or assize jurisdiction. Short courts on composite rolls with Eggleton, Holme Lacy, and Marden.
No information on parish history.

EARDISLAND [Burton]   HCL
1331/2, 1336/7–1340/1, 1346/7, 1349/50, 1355/6–1357/8, 1359/60, 1361/2–1364/5, 1367/8, 1369/70–1372/3, 1375/6–1379/80, 1381/2,

1383/4, 1388/9, 1391/2–1394/5, 1401/2.
Sixteenth-century copy of selected earlier rolls. Two VFP and two courts per year in a complete year, but few years copied completely.
No information on parish history.

MARDEN [Marden] Bodl.
1274/5, 1289/90, 1303/4–1305/6, 1307/8, 1309/10, 1312/13–1316/17, 1318/19, 1326/7, 1331/2–1345/6, 1348/9, 1349/50.
Two to four courts per year, one a lawday, with regular presentation of assize infractions. Short courts on composite rolls with Clehonger, Eggleton, and Holme Lacy.
At least two manors in the parish (Duncumb ii, pp. 119–32).

NORTON CANON
[Norton Canon] HCaL
1273/4, 1274/5, 1280/1, 1282/3, 1285/6, 1286/7, 1288/9, 1291/2, 1292/3, 1297/8–1306/7, 1307/8, 1308/9, 1317/18, 1318/19, 1321/2, 1322/3, 1328/9–1346/7, 1349/50–1355/6, 1361/2, 1362/3, 1364/5–1366/7, 1369/70–1374/5, 1382/3–1386/7, 1388/9–1390/1, 1395/6–1397/8, *1401/2*, *1403/4*, *1404/5*, *1407/8*, *1408/9*, *1410/11*, *1411/12*, *1413/14*, *1422/3*, *1425/6*, *1426/7*, *1428/9*, *1431/2*, *1437/8*, *1443/4*, *1446/7*, *1448/9*, *1454/5*, *1457/8–1459/60*, *1463/4*, *1472/3*, *1473/4*, *1476/7*, *1488/9*, *1493/4*, *1496/7*, *1497/8*.
1327–77: Seven to nine courts per year in a complete year, but few years complete. Lawdays at Easter and Michaelmas, assize infractions presented at every court.

Accounts for 3 years 1384–1400; 7 years 1401–1500.
Single manor in the parish (Duncumb ii, p. 199).

PENCOMBE [Whitney] HfdRO
1303, 1304, 1305, 1316, 1317, 1319, 1334–9, 1341, 1343, 1344, 1357–9, 1361, 1369, 1370, 1371–4, 1376, 1377, 1379, 1380, 1382, 1385–7, 1400, 1403, 1404, 1413, 1418, 1427, 1429, 1438, 1447, 1451, 1452.
No VFP or assize jurisdiction. One or two courts per year.
At least three manors in the parish (Duncumb v, pp. 77–80).

PRESTON–
ON–WYE
[Preston–on–Wye] HCaL/GNRO
1275/6, 1276/7, 1282/3, 1285/6, 1305/6, 1307/8, 1309/10, 1315/16, 1316/17, 1317/18, 1319/20, 1322/3–1326/7, 1327/8, 1329/30, 1330/1, 1332/3–1334/5, 1336/7, 1337/8, 1348/9, 1349/50, 1353/4, 1354/5, 1358/9, 1360/1, 1361/2, 1363/4–1365/6, 1369/70, 1370/1, 1373/4–1375/6, 1383/4, 1385/6, 1387/8, 1388/9, 1393/4, 1394/5, 1398/9, 1414/15, 1415/16, 1417/18, 1422/3–1424/5, 1426/7–1428/9, 1430/1, 1432/3, 1437/8, 1438/9, 1442/3, 1453/4, 1463/4, 1478/9, 1486/7, 1494/5, 1495/6.
1327–77: Six to eight courts per year in a complete year, with two lawdays. Assize infractions presented regularly at every court.
Accounts for 1272; 3 years 1351–1400; 8 years 1401–1500.
Two rentals fourteenth-century, two fifteenth-century rentals.
No information on parish history.

STAUNTON-
ON-ARROW
[Staunton–on–Arrow]   HfdRO
1273/4, 1274/5, 1319/20, 1320/1,
1322/3–1324/5, 1327/8, 1333/4,
1334/5, 1336/7, 1341/2, 1343/4–
1345/6, 1357/8–1360/1, 1366/7,
1374/5, 1394/5, 1395/6, 1398/9,
1402/3.
One short court per year. No VFP or
assize jurisdiction.
Accounts: 1419–20.

STRADDLE IN
PETERCHURCH
[Straddle Hinton]   PRO
1337/8–1341/2, 1350/1, 1351/2,
1354/5, 1355/6, 1357/8–1360/1,
1370/1, 1372/3, 1374/5, 1375/6,
1378/9, 1379/80, 1381/2, 1383/4,
1431/2–1433/4, 1474/5, 1490/1.
Two to four short courts per year
(often only two or three entries per
court). No VFP or assize jurisdiction.
No information on parish history.

STRETTON
GRANDISON [Eggleton]   Bodl.
1273/4, 1284/5, 1288/9, 1289/90,
1292/3, 1294/5, 1303/4, 1304/5,
1305/6, 1307/8, 1309/10, 1311/12–
1322/3, 1325/6, 1326/7, 1331/2–
1345/6, 1348/9, 1349/50, 1404/5.
One or two short courts per year, no
VFP or assize jurisdiction. Courts on
composite rolls with Clehonger, Holme
Lacy, and Marden.
No information on parish history.

WOOLHOPE [Woolhope]   HCaL
1307/8–1309/10, 1310/11–1314/15,
1317/18–1319/20, 1324/5–1326/7,
1327/8, 1329/30–1331/2, 1333/4–
1337/8, 1342/3–1346/7, 1348/9–
1350/1, 1356/7, 1357/8, 1363/
4–1365/6, 1369/70, 1374/5, 1375/6,

1380/1, 1389/90, 1393/4, 1401/2,
1402/3, 1404/5, 1406/7, 1409/10,
1427/8, 1428/9, 1439/40, 1440/1,
1449/50, 1457/8, 1461/2, 1486/7,
1489/90, 1491/2, 1494/5.
1327–77: Seven courts per year in a
complete year with two lawdays and
presentation of assize infractions at
every court.
Accounts for 10 years 1287–1300; none
1301–50, 13 years 1351–1400; 34 years
1401–1500.
Rentals 1307–77, 1397, 1465, 1493.
Survey fourteenth century.
Single manor in the parish (Duncumb
iii, 228).

Hertfordshire

ASHWELL [Ashwell]   PRO/GHL
1285/6, *1295/6–1296/7, 1298/9,
1299/1300,* 1303/4, *1314/15, 1315/16,*
1324/5, *1326/7, 1327/8–1328/9,*
1329/30, 1331/2–1332/3, 1334/5–
1339/40, 1341/2–1342/3, 1344/5–
1347/8, 1350/1–1351/2, 1353/
4–1354/5, *1356/7, 1358/9,* 1359/60,
*1363/4–1375/6, 1399/1400–1404/5,
1405/6–1412/13, 1483.*
VFP and 7–8 cts on 3 mm p.a. at end
of 13th c., VFP, Michaelmas Great
Court and 12–14 cts on 3–6 mm in
complete years in mid 14th c. Few years
complete, many years split between the
two deposits. Most rolls very dirty.
Accounts: 1300–50: 3; 1350–1400: 7;
1400–1500: 1.
Westminster Abbey manor, largest of
six in parish (*VCH* iii, pp. 200–4).

ASHWELL [Kirby]   SJCC
1321/2, 1322/3, 1332/3–1345/6,
1347/8–1350/1 (17 mm).
(also copies of various courts 1351/2–
1373/4 on 3 mm)

VFP for very few years, 2–4 short courts p.a.

One of six manors in parish (*VCH* iii, pp. 200–4).

BROXBOURNE
[Broxbournebury] HCRO
1308/9–1320/1, 1322/3–1323/4, 1340/1–1354/5, *1356, 1363–70, 1375–90, 1439–60, 1463–96 etc.*
1–2 VFP and 2–3 other courts p.a.; little business mainly tenurial regulation and control, at most courts. Some records may be estreats.

Main manor in parish (*VCH* iii, p. 432).

BROXBOURNE [Hoddesdon] HH
1320/1–1322/3, 1324/5–1325/6, 1330/1, 1332/3, 1335/6, 1338/9, 1343/4, 1345/6, 1348/9–1352/3, 1354/5–1357/8, 1361/2, 1364/5, 1367/8, 1376/7, 1379/80, 1381/2–1387/8, 1406/7.

Rental: *c.*1377–99

Apparently one of six manors in parish (*VCH* iii, p. 432).

ST MICHAEL'S
[Windridge] HCRO
1316/17, 1320/1–1322/3, 1328/9–1336/7, 1338/9, 1341/2–1345/6, *1346/7–1376/7, 1417/18, 1436/7, 1439/40, 1441/2, 1454/5, 1457/8, 1461/2, 1479/80–1480/1, 1482/3, 1491/2–1494/5, 1498/9.*

1–2 cts, p.a., land transfers and intertenant litigation.

Accounts: 1300–50: 5

One of seven manors in parish (*VCH* ii, pp. 393–401).

SANDON [St Paul's
prebendal Manor] SPC
1299/1300, *1302/3,* 1311/12–1322/3, 1324/5–1329/30, 1331/2, 1333/4–1334/5, 1338/9, 1341/2, 1385/6 (31 mm).

VFP and 15 courts in full year, but very few years complete.

Accounts: 1250–60: 2; 1325–36: 4

Rental: 1259

Principal manor in parish, several sub manors (*VCH* iii, pp. 271–4).

STANDON [Standon] PRO
1319/20–1320/1, 1323/4–1326/7, 1327/8–1328/9, 1348/9–1351/2, 1353/4–1360/1, 1389/90.

Principal manor in parish, numerous submanors (*VCH* iii, pp. 352–62).

STEVENAGE
[Stevenage] PRO/GHL/WAM
1279/80, 1282/3–1283/4, *1284/5, 1287/8, 1290/1, 1292/3–1295/6, 1298/9–1299/1300, 1302/3–1306/7, 1341/2–1342/3,* 1348/9, 1351/2, 1353/4, *1354/5,* 1355/6–1356/7, 1359/60–1361/2, *1363/4–1364/5, 1366/7–1374/5, 1376/7, 1379/80–1387/8, 1392/3–1398/9, 1400/1–1406/7, 1409/10, 1411/12, 1413/14–1422/3, 1425/6, 1428/9, 1431/2–1438/9, 1450/1–1459/60, 1483/4, 1484/5.*

VFP and 2–3 courts (assizes at autumn court) on 2 mm p.a. in mid-14th c. Little litigation. Numerous courts in some years of Edward I's reign.

Accounts (PRO figures): 1285–1300: 6; 1300–50: 22; 1350–1400: 10; 1400–1500: 9

Westminster Abbey manor, largest of five (*VCH* iii, pp. 141–5)

THERFIELD PRO/BL
1278/9, 1279/80, 1295/6–1297/8, 1305/6–1306/7, 1307/8–1308/9, 1311/12, 1319/20, 1320/1, 1322/3, 1326/7, 1349/50, 1350/1, *1353/4, 1354/5,* 1358/9, *1369/70, 1370/1, 1372/3, 1373/4, 1377/8, 1391/2, 1409/10, 1410/11, 1411/12, 1419/20,*

1422/3, *1423/4*, *1425/6*, *1428/9*,
1464/5, *1465/6*, *1467/8–1469/70*,
1486/7, *1487/8*.
One leet p.a., enrolled with leet courts
of other manors.
Accounts (PRO figures): 1300–50: 3;
1400–1500: 3
Ramsey Abbey manor. Principal manor.
Four others in parish *VCH* iii, pp. 278–
82).

WALKERN [Walkern]   HCRO
1324/5–1329/30, *1330/1–1331/2*,
1333/4–1339/40, 1340/1, 1341/2,
1342/3, 1343/4, *1345/6–1346/7*,
1347/8, *1348/9–1353/4*, 1356/7–
1365/6, *1368/9–1369/70*, 1371/2,
1373/4–1382/3, *1385/6–1412/13*,
1417/18–1420/1, 1425/6, 1476/7,
1483/4 etc.
VFP with court and one to three courts
p.a. in 14th and 15th cs.
Few land transfers.
Accounts: 1300–1350: 1; 1350–1400: 2;
1400–1500: 3
One of two manors (*VCH* iii, pp. 153–
5).

WATTON AT STONE
[Woodhall]   HCRO
1303–7, *1320–2*, *1324*, *1327*, *1328*,
1334, *1335*, 1338, 1339, 1341, 1342,
1344, 1345, 1346, 1349–51, *1352–7*,
1358, *1362–4*, 1365–6, *1367*, *1369–70*,
1372–9, *1381*, 1382–3, *1384–94*, *1401–
3*, *1405–7*, *1409–11*, *1413–16*, 1422,
1424–42, *1451–3*, *1465–9*, *1477–80*,
1482–4, *1486–8*, *1500, etc.*
1–3 cts. p.a. in 14th c., 1 in 15th c.
Courts fairly short, mainly tenurial
regulation.
Rentals, 1422 and several n.d. (15th c.).
One of three medieval manors (*VCH*
iii, pp. 159–63).
Records of Watton manor from 1362
are PRO SC2/177/8–11.

WESTMILL   PRO
1315/16–1317/18, *1321/2*, *1322/3*,
1336/7, *1363/4*, *1367/8–1370/1*,
1373/4–1377, *1391/2*, *1393/4*, *1394/
5, etc.*
One of three manors (*VCH* iii, pp. 398–
400).

GREAT AND LITTLE
[Wymondley]
WYMONDLEY   HCRO
1275/6–1278/9, 1290/1, 1297/8–
1304/5, 1307/8, 1332/3, 1344/5,
1349/50–1354/5, 1356/7, 1358/9–
1365/6, 1367/8–1372/3, 1374/5–
1380/1, 1383/4–1397/8, *1400–83*.
Two VFP and 2–3 courts on 2–3 mm
p.a. in mid 14th c.
Accounts: 1292–1300: 1; 1300–50: 7;
1351–1400: 8; 1400–1500: 4.
Custumals and rentals, 1318, *c.*1323,
1348, 1389.
Surveys, 1323, 1438, 1440 and later.
Separate manors in Great and Little
Wymondley, for which one manorial
court held (*VCH* iii, pp. 182–90).
See F.B. Stitt, 'The Manors of Great
and Little Wymondley in the later
Middle Ages' (Oxford B. Litt. 1951).

Huntingdon

All manors surveyed belonged to
Ramsey Abbey, the surviving records
of which are split between the Public
Record Office and the British Library.
Court rolls are generally composite,
recording the courts held by the steward on his six monthly circuit of the
estate, and including Cambridgeshire
and Bedfordshire manors as well as
Huntingdonshire ones. It is uncommon for both rolls to survive in any
one year, and the rolls which do exist
are by no means complete in themselves.

The PRO lists are summary and misleading as regards the holdings for any one manor, and the records in the BL are in no easily discernable order. The listing out of the surviving rolls for each manor has been undertaken by Father Ambrose Raftis and published in the bibliography to his *Tenure and Mobility* (Pontifical Institute, Toronto) 1964. Readers are referred to this work for information more detailed than the brief summaries given below. Some investigation of the sources has been undertaken however, and together with the evidence of S. C. Ratcliffe, *Elton Manorial Records* (Roxburghe Club) 1946, suggests that the Raftis lists should not be relied on for complete accuracy.

BROUGHTON
[Broughton]   PRO/BL
1288–1300: 7; 1301–1400: 46; 1401–1500: 33
One leet p.a. in 14th c.
Accounts: 1243–4; 1300–50: 4; 1400–1500: 2
Ramsey Abbey manor. Principal manor in parish (*VCH* ii, pp. 158–64), (Also a court of Broughton which was the Abbot of Ramsey's honorial court. See Maitland, *Select Pleas in Manorial and other Seignorial Courts* (Selden Society) 1889).

ELLINGTON
[Ellington]   PRO/BL
1278–1300: 5; 1301–1400: 19; 1401–1500: 23
One leet p.a. in 14th c., little record of land transfers.
Accounts: 1300–50: 5, 1350–1400: 2, 1400–1500: 18
Rentals, during 1272–1307; 1400–1500: 5
Ramsey Abbey manor. Largest of three in parish (*VCH* iii, pp. 44–8).

ELTON [Elton]   PRO/BL
1278–1300: 5; 1301–1400: 27; 1401–1500: 27
VFP or court, rarely more than once in any year, no land transfers recorded.
Accounts: 1286–1300: 3; 1300–1350: 6 or 7; 1350–1400: 11 or 10; 1400–1460: 9
Ramsey Abbey manor, principal manor in parish (*VCH* iii, pp. 154–66).
See S. C. Ratcliffe (ed.), *Elton Manorial Records 1279–1351* (Roxburghe Club) 1946.

HEMINGFORD ABBOTS
[Hemingford Abbots]   PRO/BL
1278–1300: 6; 1301–1400: 24; 1401–1500: 21
Accounts: 1300–50: 5; 1350–1400: 2; 1400–1500: 12.
Rental 15th c.
Ramsey Abbey manor, sole manor (*VCH* ii, pp. 304–9).

HOLYWELL CUM
NEEDINGWORTH   PRO/BL
1288–1300: 4; 1301–1400: 24; 1401–1500: 21
Accounts: 1300–1350: 3 (or 2); 1350–1400: 7 (or 8), 1400–1500: 18.
Rentals 1400–1500: 2.
Ramsey Abbey manor, sole manor in parish (*VCH* ii, pp. 176–8).

HOUGHTON
WITH WYTON   BL
1274–1300: 8; 1301–1400: 30; 1401–1500: 23.
Accounts: 1297–1300: 2; 1300–1350: 9; 1350–1400: 15; 1400–1500: 23.
Rentals 1400–1500: 4.
Ramsey Abbey manor, sole manor in parish (*VCH* ii, pp. 178–81).

ABBOT'S RIPTON
[Abbot's Ripton]   PRO/BL
1274–1300: 6; 1301–1400: 21; 1401–
1500: 19.
Accounts: 1297–8; 1300–50: 8 (or 7);
1350–1400: 3 (or 4); 1400–1500: 1.
Ramsey Abbey manor. Principal manor
in parish (*VCH* ii, pp. 202–7).

KING'S RIPTON   PRO/BL
1279–1300: 5; 1301–1400: 22; 1401–
1500: 18
Accounts: 1243–1300: 2; 1300–1350: 5.
Ramsey Abbey manor. Sole manor
(*VCH* ii, pp. 207–10).

ST IVES [Slepe]   PRO/BL
1291–1300: 5; 1301–1400: 20; 1401–
1500: 16.
Ramsey Abbey manor. Principal manor
in parish (*VCH* ii, pp. 218–19).

LITTLE STUKELEY   PRO/BL
1278–1300: 6; 1301–1400: 20; 1401–
1500: 15.
Accounts: 1400–1500: 2
Rental 15th c.
Ramsey Abbey manor, principal manor
in parish (*VCH* ii, pp. 234–8).

UPWOOD WITH
GREAT RAVELEY   PRO/BL
1278–1300: 6; 1301–1400: 40; 1401–
1500: 38.
Accounts: UPWOOD—1248–50: 2;
1297–1300: 2; 1300–50: 12; 1350–1400:
6; 1400–1500: 16; GREAT RAVELEY—
1400–1500: 4
Ramsey Abbey manor. One of three in
Upwood, and of two in Great Raveley
(*VCH* ii, pp. 198–201, 238–43).

WARBOYS   PRO/BL
1290–1300: 4; 1301–1400: 40; 1401–
1500: 27

Rentals *c.*1272–1307, 1453.
Accounts: 1297–8; 1300–50: 2.
Ramsey Abbey manor, sole manor in
parish (*VCH* ii, pp. 242–6).

OLD WESTON
[Weston with Brington
and Bythorn]   PRO/BL
1290–1300: 4; 1301–1400: 22; 1401–
1500: 25
Rental, BYTHORN, *c.*1272–1307.
Accounts, WESTON: 1297–8; 1300–50:
3; 1350–1400: 4; 1400–1500: 1;
BYTHORN: 1297–8; 1300–50: 3; 1350–
1400: 1, 1400–1500: 1
Ramsey Abbey manor, sole manor.
(*VCH* iii, pp. 116–19).

WISTOW [Wistow]   PRO/BL
1278–1300: 6; 1301–1400: 42; 1401–
1500: 35.
Ramsey Abbey manor. Sole manor
(*VCH* ii, p. 247).

Kent

BOXLEY   PRO
*1274/5, 1277/8, 1280/1, 1281/2, 1297/
8, 1299/1300, 1301/2, 1302/3, 1317/
18–1319/20, 1322/3–1325/6, 1332/3–
1334/5, 1336/7–1339/40, 1341/2–
1344/5, 1346/7–1352/3, 1353/
4–1354/5, 1359/60–1365/6, 1368/9,
1369/70, 1371/2, 1372/3, 1374/5–
1379/80, 1381/2–1390/1, 1395/6,
1396/7, 1398/9, 1400/1, 1402/3,
1405/6, 1407/8, 1408/9, 1420/1,
1421/2, 1424/5, 1425/6, 1430/1,
1437/8–1441/2, 1452/3, 1455/6,
1457/8–1459/60, 1463/4–1467/8,
1503/4.*
12–14 courts on 4–5 mm p.a. in mid
14th c. No evidence of litigation.
Condition of roll examined very poor.
Sole manor (*FA* iii, p. 16).

HIGHAM   SJCC

1303/4–1304/5, 1309/10–1312/13,
1316/17–1319/20, 1329/30–1330/1,
1332/3–1333/4, 1337/8–1338/9,
1347/8–1348/9.
8–10 courts p.a. early in 14th c., 2–3
cts, p.a. in mid century.
Accounts: Not seen (14th c.)
Rentals, *c*.1305, *c*.1307, *c*.1340.
Survey n.d. (later 14th c.)
One of two manors in parish (*FA* iii,
p. 17).

HOLLINGBOURNE   CCaL

1346/7, 1354/5, 1356/7–1357/8,
1359/60, 1360/1, 1362/3, 1364/5–
1366/7, 1368/9, 1370/1–1374/5,
1387/8–1390/1, 1396/7–1399/1400,
1405/6, 1411/12, 1413/14–1428/9,
1431/2–1443/4, 1445/6, 1447/8–
1463/4, 1465/6–1468/9, 1470/1,
1471/2–1478/9, 1481/2, 1484/5.
VFP after Michaelmas and 6 courts on
3–4 mm in reign of Edward III, 2 VFP
and 6 courts p.a. on 4–5 mm in late
14th c., 2 VFP and 3–5 courts in 15th
c. (on 1 m from 1425/6). Some years
in 15th c. survive only in draft and
there are attached court papers.
Account rolls: SERJEANT—1276–1300:
17; 1300–50: 21; 1350–77: 4; BEDEL—
1340–1445: 6; FARMER: 1400–14: 10
Apparently sole manor (*RH* i, p. 223).

LEWISHAM [Lewisham]   PRO

*1283/4, 1288/9, 1298/9, 1300/1,
1311/12, 1312/13–1313/14, 1314/15,
1317/18, 1319/20–1322/3, 1324/5–
1325/6, 1326/7, 1327/8, 1328/9,
1329/30, 1330/1, 1332/3, 1330/1–
1334/5, 1418/19, 1419/20–1421/2.*
Two VFP and 4 courts on 3–4 mm in
reign of Edward III (1327–77).
Sole manor (*FA* iii, p. 18).

WY [Wy]   PRO

*1283/4–1285/6, 1286/7–1288/9,
1293/4, 1294/5–1295/6, 1297/8–
1298/9, 1302/3–1303/4, 1310/11–
1312/13, 1314/15, 1331/2, 1332/3,
1337/8–1338/9, 1340/1–1342/3,
1345/6–1346/7, 1353/4, 1358/9–
1359/60, 1360/1–1361/2, 1362/3,
1369/70, 1370/1–1374/5, 1382/3–
1383/4, 1386/7–1387/8, 1388/9–
1389/90, 1398/9.*
Seventeen courts on 8 mm p.a. in full
year before Black Death. Records enrolled with those of Wy hundred court
usually held same day. Rolls also include some records of Hawkhurst fair.
Wy manor court has litigation, demesne
trespass, recognitions of land purchases
and tenurial regulation.
Rentals, 1216–72, 1311, 1335.
Sole manor (*FA* iii, p. 13).

Leicestershire

BARKBY [Barkby]   MCO

1278–9, 1281–2, 1285–7, 1289–90,
1293/4–1295/6, 1340/1–1342/3, 1345/
6–1352/3, 1354/5, 1356/7, *1357–60,*
1362/3–1363/4, 1365/6–1367/8, 1369/
70–1372/3, 1374/5–1377/8, 1379/80–
1382/3, 1385/6–1387/8, 1389/90–
1398/9, 1405/6, 1407/8–1416/17,
1419/20–1424/5, 1426/7–1434/5,
1436/7, *1437, 1440, 1443–50, 1455–56,
1464, 1472–80, 1487, c.1500* etc.
7–9 courts (very short) on 1 m p.a. at
end of thirteenth century, for tenurial
regulation and a little litigation. Courts
longer before Black Death but few years
complete. 1–2 courts p.a. after Black
Death.
Accounts: 1285–1300: 10 years; 1300–
1350: 30 years; 1350–1400: 39 years;
1400–1500: large number.

Rentals, *c.*1300, early 14th c., 1354–5, 1413, 1450, 1452, 1475, 1484.
One of three or four manors in parish (Nichols iii, pp. 44–5).

KIBWORTH [Kibworth Harcourt]   MCO
1278/9–1283/4, 1285/6–1291/2, 1293/4–1295/6, 1297/8, 1311/12, 1320/1, 1324/5, 1327/8, 1329/30–1334/5, 1337/8, 1342/3–1345/6, 1347/8–1366/7, 1368/9–1375/6, 1377/8–1382/3, 1384/5, 1386/7, 1388/9–1398/9, *1400–1, 1404, 1406–1415, 1417–23, 1428, 1432, 1433/4,* 1434/5, 1436/7–1441/2, 1443/4, *1444, 1445, 1447–58, 1460, 1465, 1466, 1473, 1474, 1480, 1481, 1484, 1486, 1489–92, 1497, 1499, etc.*
Two VFP and up to 6 courts of variable length on 2–3 mm p.a. at end of thirteenth century. 2 VFP and 3–4 courts p.a. before Black Death, 2 VFP and occasional courts thereafter.
Accounts: 1283–1300: 14 years; 1300–50: 33 years; 1350–1400: 44 years; 1400–1500: 84 years.
Rentals, *c.*1300, *c.*1320, *c.*1325, 1484.
One of two manors in the township, of four in the parish of Kibworth (*VCH* v, pp. 168–70, 179–80, 184–5).

Lincolnshire

BURTON ON STATHER   WAM
1318/19, 1356/7–1357/8, 1362/3, 1364/5, 1367/8, 1373/4, 1375/6, 1381/2, *1382–4, 1386–8, 1389–90, 1391–3, 1394–7, 1422–3, 1425–6, 1428–9, 1433–7, 1468–9, 1471–3, 1481–3.*
Two VFP and up to 15 courts p.a. but rolls in very poor condition and few years complete. Assize and frankpledge presentments from Burton on Stather, Crosby, Conesby, Gunness, Thealby

and Winterton at courts as well as views. Little information on land transfer. Held by l'Estrange family, court apparently for sokelands of Manor of West Halton (*q.v.*). Foster and Longley, p. 75.

CROWLE [Soke of Crowle]   LAO
1310/11, 1314/15, 1316/17, 1318/19, 1322/3, 1324/5, 1330/1, 1333/4–1334/5, 1343/4–1344/5, 1346/7, 1349/50, 1354/5, 1362/3–1367/8, 1370/1, 1372/3, 1376/7–1380/1, 1382/3, *1383–93, 1394–5, 1396–9, 1400–1, 1402–4, 1405–6, 1407–8, 1409–10, 1411–13, 1414–18, 1419–20, 1421–2, 1423–7, 1430–5, 1436–42, 1444–55, 1456–60, 1462–7, 1468–81, 1482, 1485, 1489–1500.*
VFP and 6–8 courts on 4–6 mm p.a. early in 14th century. In 1349–50, VFP and 8 courts held both at Crowle and Eastoft, later, VFP held separately after Michaelmas, but remaining courts and an Easter VFP held at Crowle for whole soke (often taking two days). 10–12 mm p.a., but few years complete before 1362.
Rentals:
   for CROWLE
     early 14th c.:   1379, 1389, 1428
   for GARTHORPE
     and AMCOTTS   1363
   for LUDDINGTON   1414
Court of Selby Abbey for the soke of Crowle (Crowle, Eastoft, Garthorpe, Luddington and Amcotts.). No other manorial jurisdiction.
See LAO, *Archivists' Report 1952–3*, pp. 13–20.

EDENHAM
[Edenham Vaudey]   LAO
1335/6–1343/4, 1346/7–1347/8, 1351/2–1352/3, 1354/5–1356/7, 1357/8–1359/60, 1361/2, 1363/4–

1365/6, 1377/8–1407/8, *1408–12,*
1423–30, 1432–3, 1443–51, 1459–62,
1464–70, 1475.
Occasional VFP or great court; no. of
courts variable, up to 6 p.a. Frankpledge
presentments sometimes made at
courts. All courts very short (11 mm.
to 1398).
Manor of Vaudey Abbey, at least four
other manors in parish.
Owen, p. 8.

FISHTOFT [Toft]   LAO
1303/4–1312/13, 1324/5, 1326/7,
1333–4, 1336–7, 1352–3, 1360–1,
1363–4, 1367–70, 1374–7, 1382/3,
1384–5, 1387–9, 1391/2, *1392–4,*
1416–18, 1457–8, 1465–6, 1475–6,
1483–5, 1488–90, 1491–4.
13–17 courts and VFP on 4–5 mm.
p.a. (33 mm. 1303–27, 57 mm 1333–
94) VFP usually full.
Huntingfield (later Willoughby) manor.
Other rolls in LAO listed as Fishtoft
appear to relate to another manor in
the parish.
(*RH* i, pp. 348–9, *Placita de Quo
Warranto*, pp. 393, 399, 403, indicate
minimum of three manors in parish).

FULSTOW, [Fulstow cum
Marshe and Fulstow Bek]   LAO
1303/4, 1320/1, 1322/3–1324/5,
1327/8–1330/1, 1334/5, 1337/8,
1339/40, 1346/7–1347/8, 1374/5,
1386/7, 1396/7, 1399/1400, *1404–5,*
1410–11, 1414–15, 1416–18, 1421–3,
1425–6, 1446–9, 1451–2, 1464–5,
1492–3, 1494–5, 1498–9.
Two VFP and 10 courts on 3–4 mm.
in full years, but few years complete. 1
m p.a. in late 14th century (26 mm.
1303–48, 5 mm. 1374–1400)
Very little information on land transfers between tenants.

Accounts: 1342–3; 1350–1400: 4; 1400–
1500: 12.
Rental: 1348.
Rolls are for one of at least three manors in 14th century (see Williamson).

HALTON, WEST   WAM
1313/14–1314/15, 1332/3–1333/4,
1335/6–1336/7, 1342/3, 1358/9–
1362/3, 1364/5, 1367/8–1368/9,
1370/1, 1373/4–1380/1, *1386–9,*
1392–4, 1406–7, 1415–16, 1425–6,
1443–6, 1453–4, 1460–2.
Two VFP and up to 16 cts. p.a. on
4–6 mm throughout reign of Edward
III, but few years complete. Assize
and frankpledge presentments from
Alkborough, Burton on Stather and
West Halton at courts as well as views.
Much litigation, little relating to land
transfers. Condition of rolls very
variable.
Held by l'Estrange family. Court of
head manor on soke of West Halton,
which was sole manor in parish. Foster
and Longley, p. 74.
See also **Burton on Stather.**

INGOLDMELLS
[Ingoldmells]   LAO
1291/2–1292/3, 1302/3, 1311/12,
1312/13, 1313/14, 1315/16, 1318/19–
1320/1, 1324/5, 1325/6, 1327/8,
1328/9, 1330/1, 1341/2, 1343/4–
1346/7, 1350/1–1351/2, 1354/5–
1356/7, 1359/60, 1364/5, 1367/8,
1374/5–1376/7, 1386/7, 1388/9,
1391/2, 1399/1400, 1400/1, 1402/3,
1403/4, 1405/6, 1410/11, 1413/14,
1418/19–1422/3, 1429/30, 1432/3,
1436/7, 1441/2–1443/4, 1492/3.
Two leets (VFP from 1315) and 17
courts in full year to mid 15th c., but
few years are complete. Separate presentments from vills, courts sometimes

held at Skegness or Burgh le Marsh. Appeal of felony. Accounts: 1400–1500: 34 (PRO DL 29). Substantial extracts are printed in translation in W. O. Massingberd, *Court Rolls of the Manor of Ingoldmells* (1902).

KIRTON IN
LINDSEY [Soke   LAO/PRO/
of Kirton Lindsey]   Bodl./DoC

Aslacoe wapentake court:
1300/1–1305/6, 1308/9–1315/16, *1316/17–1328/9*, 1328/9–1330/1, *1331/2–1347/8*, 1348/9–1350/1, *1351/2–1353/4*, *1356/7–1367/8*, 1368/9–1370/1, *1371/2–1377/8*, *1380/1–1387/8*, 1388/9–1390/1, *1391/2–1411*, 1422–6, 1431–6, *1438–9*, *1446–51*, 1456–60, 1466–7, 1469–78, 1480–1 etc.

Covers vills of Atterby, Glentworth, Grayingham (part), Harpswell, Hemswell, Saxby, Snitterby and Spital

Corringham wapentake court:
1300/1, 1303/4–1315/16, *1316/17–1353/4*, *1356/7–1367/8*, 1368/9–1370/1, *1371/2–1377/8*, *1380/1–1411*, *1422–6*, 1431–6, *1438–9*, *1446–51*, *1456–7*, *1460*, 1466–7, 1469–78, 1480–1 etc.

Covers vills of Aisby, Blyton, Great and Little Corringham, Gilby, Heapham, Morton, Northorp, Pilham, Somerby, Springthorpe, Stockwith and Walkerith.

Manley wapentake court:
1300/1–1315/16, *1316/17–1353/4*, *1356/7–1367/8*, 1368/9–1370/1, *1371/2–1413*, *1422–3*, *1425–6*, *1431–6*, *1438–9*, *1446–51*, *1456–7*, *1460*, 1466–7, 1469–78, 1480–1 etc.

Covers vills of Ashby, Bottesford, Brumby, Burringham, Burton on

Stather, Froddingham, Redbourne, Risby, Scunthorpe, Stainton Waddingham, Winterton and Yaddlethorpe.

Kirton Friday court:
1301/2–1315/16, *1317/18–1353/4*, *1356/7–1367/8*, 1368/9–1370/1, *1371/2–1376/7*, *1378/9–1413*, *1422–6*, *1432–9*, *1446–7*, *1450–1*, *1456–7*, *1460*, *1466–7*, *1469–78*, 1480–1 etc.

Covers vills of Grayingham (part) Hibaldstow, Kirton and Missen (Notts.).

Sokemoot court:
1300/1–1315/16, *1317/18–1330/1*, *1331/2*, *1332/3–1342/3*, *1345/6–1353/4*, *1356/7–1367/8*, 1368/9–1370/1, *1371/2–1376/7*, *1379/80–1385/6*, *1388/9–1412*, *1422–6*, *1431–9*, *1446–7*, *1450–1*, *1456–7*, *1460*, 1466–7, 1469–78, 1480–1 etc.

Covers all vills.

In early 14th c., 8–9 courts p.a., business of frankpledge presented by township at all courts; 4–6 mm, later 6–9 mm for each court in complete years, many years complete. Twice yearly VFP from *c.*1380.

Accounts: 1290–1300: 2; 1336–7; 1395–6; 1400–1500: 31.

Sole or major manorial jurisdiction in Kirton, Aisby, Ashby, Atterby, Brumby, Little Corringham, Froddingham, Gilby, Morton, Pilham, Saxby, Scunthorpe, Springthorpe, Stockwith, Walkerith, Wharton and Yaddlethorpe. (Possible sub–manors for prebendal lands of Lincoln Cathedral in several townships.) See Foster and Longley, *passim*, also LAO, *Archivists' Report 9*, 1957–8, pp. 26–32.

LANGTOFT
AND BASTON
[Langtoft and Baston]   LAO
1252–3, *1265–7*, *1273*, *1278*, 1283,
1290–1, 1299, 1300–3, 1315–16, *1316–*
17, *1319*, *1320*, *1323–35*, 1335–6, *1336–*
42, *1353–4*, *1416–18*, *1422–3*, *1428–37*,
1439, *1445–6*, *1448*, *1450–1*, *1453–4*,
1457–69, *1475–6 and later.*
Two VFP from 1302 (called great
courts until 1340); 6–8 courts p.a. in
13th and 14th centuries, assize presentments in 13th century, business more
extensive from 1323.
VFP and 3–6 courts p.a. in 15th century.
(14mm. 1252–99, 14mm 1300–21,
103mm 1323–42, 35mm 1416–76).
Rolls dated by abbatial years.
Accounts: LANGTOFT—1330–50 (6);
1350–1400 (2); 1400–1500 (9); BASTON
—1440–60 (8); (LAO) LANGTOFT AND
BASTON/THETFORD—1258–1300: 19;
1300–1324: 9 (CUL(Q)).
Court of Crowland Abbey for south
Lincolnshire estates i.e. Langtoft (sole
manor) Baston (one of two) Bowthorp
and Manthorp (hamlets in Witham on
the Hill) Wothorp (Rutland).
See *LAO Archivists' Report* 12, 1960–
1, pp. 10–11.

MORTON BY BOURNE
[Morton]   LAO
1327/8, 1329/30–1330/1, 1332/3–
1335/6, 1339/40–1347/8, 1349/50–
1351/2, 1353/4, 1355/6–1357/8,
1378/9–1397/8, *1398–1408*, *1409–16*,
1432–3, *1449*, *1477*.
Up to nine courts p.a. before 1349, but
survival rate very variable. One or two
very short courts p.a. at end of 14th
century. Some courts called view or
great court but business is domainal,

not franchisal. No land transfers between tenants, or litigation.
Manor of Vaudey Abbey. Several other
manors in parish (cf. *RH* i, p. 252).

SPILSBY
[Spilsby cum Eresby]   LAO
1296/7, 1299/1300, 1318/19–1325/6,
1327/8–1329/30, 1331/2–1342/3,
1346–8, *1350*, *1351*, *1354–5*, *1356–7*,
1360, *1362*, *1363*, 1364/5, *1367–8*,
1370–2, *1378*, *1386*, *1401–4*, *1408–12*,
1415–22, *1459*, *1461–9*, *1476–7*, *1480–*
2, *1492–3*.
VFP or great court and 15–17 courts
on 5 mm in full year but few complete
years. Few land transfers. Condition
variable.
Willoughby manor in Spilsby and
Friskney. Possibly sole manor in
Spilsby (Foster and Longley, pp. 33,
253). Presentments at view for up to
twelve other vills, not all in immediate
neighbourhood.

STOKE ROCHFORD,
EASTON WITH STOKE   LAO
1340/1, 1349/50–1355/6, 1357/8–
1359/60, 1366/7, 1368/9–1371/2,
1459–73.
VFP and up to six courts p.a. on single
membrane to *c*.1352, later one or two
short courts p.a. Business mainly tenurial regulation, a little litigation.
Manor of Vaudey Abbey, probably
three other manors in parish (Foster
and Longley, pp. 17, 29, 72, 141; *RH*
p. 261).

LONG SUTTON [Sutton]   PRO
1305/6, *1308/9–1309/10*, *1312/13–*
1314/15, *1316/17*, 1317/18, *1324/5–*
1325/6, 1327/8, 1328/9, 1329/30,
1332/3–1333/4, 1334/5–1335/6,
1336/7–1347/8, 1348/9–1349/50,

1350/1–1353/4, *1355/6–1357/8*, *1359/60–1364/5*, 1365/6, *1366/7–1377/8*, 1378/9–1379/80, *1380/1–1398/9*, *1401/2–1405/6*, *1408/9–1409/10*, *1418/19–1419/20*, *1441/2–1442/3*.
VFP and 16 cts. on 20–22 mm in full year, but most rolls lack some membranes. Presentments at VFP include Lutton.
Accounts: 1335–50: 2; 1400–85: 36.
Duchy of Lancaster manor; largest of three in parish of Sutton St Mary (White, p. 859).

TOYNTON ALL SAINTS,
TOYNTON ST PETER
[Toynton]   LAO
1310/11–1311/12, 1319/20, 1320/1, *1322–3*, 1325/6–1330/1, 1338/9, *1339–40*, *1342*, *1345–6*, 1346/7–1349/50, *1355–6*, *1358–60*, 1361/2, *1364–9*, *1375–7*, *1380*, *1383–4*, *1386–94*, *1399–1400*, *1402–5*, *1408–9*, *1417–18*, *1423–8*, *1430–40*, *1442–3*, *1445*, *1451–2*, *1456–7*, *1461–5*, *1488–9*, *1499–1500* etc.
Michaelmas great court (later VFP) and up to 17 courts p.a. in early 14th c., 2 VFP and 17 courts in 15th c., on 1–3 mm. Fourteenth century rolls are usually odd mm. Litigation prominent in earlier rolls. Possibly sole manor for the two parishes (Foster and Longley, p. 87).

WILLOUGHBY
BY SLOOTHBY
[Willoughby cum
Membris (formerly Bek)]   LAO
1333/4–1334/5, 1338/9, 1341/2, 1350/1, 1356/7, *1362–5*, *1368–9*, *1373–4*, *1378–9*, *1381–5*, *1394–7*, 1399/1400, *1413–16*, *1423–5*, *1428–34*, *1436–*

7, *1441–2*, *1445–51*, *1456–9*, *1461*, *1463–6*, *1468–70*, *1472–8*, *1482–3*.
Two VFP and 17 cts p.a. on 2–5 mm in full years into 15th c., early rolls very incomplete. Frankpledge business sometimes presented at courts. Covers land in Willoughby le Marsh, Sloothby, Drexthorpe, Hogsthorpe and Ingoldmells.
One of several manors in the area (Foster and Longley, pp. 36, 88, 110 etc.)

Middlesex

HARROW
[Harrow Rectory]   GLRO(M)
1349/50, 1353/4, 1355/6, 1358/9, 1359/60, 1361/2–1366/7, 1368/9, 1369/70, 1375/6, 1377/8–1387/8, 1391/2, 1393/4, 1394/5, 1396/7, 1399/1400–1419/20, 1428/9, 1431/2, 1435/6, 1438/9–1443/4, 1445/6, 1446/7, 1450/1–1457/8, *1462*, *1463*, *1467–70*, *1474–1500*.
VFP and four courts per year in a complete year during the period 1349–77, but seldom more than two courts surviving. VFP and two courts per year for the period 1377–1399. Court rolls in poor condition but repaired.
Reeves' and beadles' accounts 1485–1500.
At least 10 manors in the parish in the fourteenth century (*VCH* iv, pp. 203–18).

ISLEWORTH
[Isleworth Syon]   GLRO(M)
1279–81, 1281/2, *1282–3*, 1308/9–1319/20, *1320–6*, *1327–46*, 1346/7–1348/9, *1349–54*, 1354/5–1355/6, *1356–1482* etc.
Two VFP and 5–9 courts on 3–8 mm p.a.; no year examined appears complete.

Rolls 1279–83: 13 mm; 1308–99: 479 mm; 1400–1508: 284 mm.
Largest of at least five manors in the parishes of Isleworth, Heston and Twickenham (*VCH* iii, pp. 103–12).

SUNBURY [Kempton]   PRO
1356/7, 1357/8, 1359/60, 1361/2–1366/7, 1368/9–1373/4, 1375/6–1376/7.
Two VFP and up to five courts per year but seldom more than two courts surviving. Many membranes damaged or so faint or stained as to be illegible. (SC 2)
Four manors in the parish (*VCH* iii, pp. 53–7).

TOTTENHAM [Tottenham]   SPC
1305/6–1306/7, 1309/10, 1312/13–1313/14, 1321/2–1322/3, 1330/1, 1332/3–1339/40, 1343/4, 1352/3, 1353/4, 1375/6–1378/9.
VFP and approximately 10 courts on 1–3 mm. per year in early 14th century, but no year survives complete. Length of court variable. 3 courts per year by 1377.
Account: 1376.
Four manors in the parish, held as one from the early fifteenth century (*VCH* v, pp. 324–7).

Norfolk

BARNHAM BROOM
[Barnham Broom]   NRO
1331/2–1333/4, 1335/6–1337/8, 1339/40–1343/4, 1345/6–1350/1, 1354/5–1360/1, 1362/3–1369/70.
3–4 courts per year. Full courts, but no VFP or assize jurisdiction.
Account *c.*1300
Rental 1301.
At least two manors in the parish (Blomefield, ii, pp. 380–1).

GREAT BIRCHAM
[Great Bircham]   PRO
1318/19, 1319/20, 1322/3–1325/6, 1332/3–1342/3, 1345/6–1352/3, 1355/6, 1356/7, 1358/9–1361/2, 1369/70–1373/4, 1376/7.
Up to five courts per year, no VFP or assize jurisdiction. Short courts in poor condition (some courts only fragments). Two manors in the parish (Blomefield, x, 291–3).

BLICKLING [Blickling]   NRO
1300/1, 1305/6, 1311/12, 1315/16, 1319/20–1321/2, 1323/4, 1325/6, 1327/8–1334/5, 1336/7, 1338/9–1342/3, 1344/5–1347/8, 1360/1–1367/8, 1369/70, 1373/4, 1378/9–1397/8, 1399/1400–1412/13, *1416/17*, *1421/2*, *1429/30–1435/6*, *1437/8–1445/6*, *1446/7*, *1447/8*, *1449/50*, *1452/3–1457/8*, *1460/1*, *1461/2*, *1467/8*, *1483/4–1485/6*, *1493/4*.
Six courts per year plus leet in full year, but most years only 2–4 courts surviving. Long, full courts. Edward I to Richard II previously in poor condition but all repaired. Many mm with dates illegible.
Accounts: 1351–2; 11 years 1410–73.
Rental 1409/10; custumals 1307, 15th century.
Two manors in the parish (Blomefield, vi, pp. 381–6).

BRANCASTER [Brancaster]   NRO
1329/30, 1337/8–1355/6, 1470/1, 1476/7, 1477/8, 1494/5
4–5 courts plus leet in complete year. 1–2 courts per membrane, most membranes damaged at bottom.
Account Roll: (BL Add. roll).
Sole manor in the parish, but a number of large free holdings. (Blomefield, x, pp. 298–301).

BRESSINGHAM
[Bressingham] NRO
1291/2, 1296/7, 1297/8, 1302/3,
1305/6, 1308/9, 1309/10, 1311/12–
1318/19, 1320/1–1330/1, 1332/3,
1333/4, 1336/7, 1337/8, 1339/40,
1340/1, 1344/5, 1350/1–1355/6,
1357/8, 1361/2–1363/4, 1366/7–
1369/70, 1371/2, 1372/3, 1374/5,
1376/7, 1377/8–1381/2, 1383/4,
1384/5, 1386/7–1388/9, 1390/1–
1395/6, 1398/9, *1400/1, 1404/5,*
1409/10, 1410/11, 1424/5, 1429/30–
1431/2, 1433/4–1444/5, 1446/7,
1449/50–1451/2, 1457/8, 1459/60,
1461/2, 1470/1, 1471/2–1477/8,
1480/1, 1481/2, 1492/3, 1493/4.
3–4 courts per year, with one leet and
one assize court.
Accounts: 1326, 1339–42, 1344: 9 years
1350–1400; 1432/3–1433/4.
Accounts: 1327, 1336, 1341, 1400 (BL
Add. Ch.)
Rental 1398/9.
Six manors in the parish (Blomefield i,
pp. 49–65).

BURSTON [Brockdish Hall] BL
1314/15–1317/18, 1319/20, 1320/1,
1324/5–1326/7, 1330/1–1333/4,
1338/9, 1342/3, 1346/7, 1353/4,
1358/9, 1359/60, 1361/2, 1368/9,
1369/70, 1377/8, 1378/9, 1382/3,
1383/4, 1387/8, 1389/90, 1392/3,
1394/5, 1399/1400, 1403/4, 1405/6–
1412/13, 1413/14, 1415/16, 1416/17,
1418/19–1422/3, 1425/6, 1426/7,
1428/9, 1429/30.
1–2 short courts per year. No VFP or
assize jurisdiction.
Account: 1385.
Two manors in the parish (Blomefield
i, pp. 125–30).

CASTLEACRE [Castleacre] HHL
1270/1, 1271/2, 1272/3–1275/6,
1279/80–1300/1, 1302/3–1305/6,
1307/8–1310/11, 1339/40–1341/2,
1343/4–1347/8, 1349/50–1368/9,
1370/1–1375/6, 1377/8–1389/90,
1391/2–1394/5, 1396/7–1398/9,
1400–18, 1422–61, 1480–1500.
17 courts plus leet and assize court per
year during period 1327–99. Full courts
in good condition, but mostly essoin
lists with little extended litigation and
no land transfers.
Terriers 1340, 1429, 1474.
Three manors in the parish (Blomefield
viii, pp. 356–75).

COLTISHALL
[Hakfordhall] KCC
1273/4, 1274/5, 1276/7–1277/8,
1279/80–1294/5, 1298/9–1299/1300,
1300/1–1304/5, 1306/7, 1309/10–
1326/7, 1328/9–1340/1, 1345/6–
1356/7, 1359/60, 1360/1, 1362/
3–1369/70, 1372/3–1374/5, 1376/7–
1400/1, 1403/4, 1405/6, 1471/2–
1473/4, 1475/6, 1476/7.
Number and length of courts surviving very variable, commonly 2–4 but
can be 7. Litigation in 13th c., but
business predominantly tenurial regulation, particularly after Black Death.
Early rolls disordered.
At least two manors in parish.

DEOPHAM CCaL
1309/10, 1323/4, 1329/30, 1331/2–
1332/3, 1334/5–1335/6, 1337/8,
1343/4, 1346/7, 1349/50–1350/1,
1353/4, 1371/2, 1374/5–1378/9,
1381/2–1383/4, 1385/6–1386/7,
1484/5–1487/8.
VFP and 1–2 courts p.a.; in late 14th
c. often VFP only.

Accounts: 1286/7; 1300–1350: 5; 1350–1400: 1; 1400–1500: 5.
One of two manors in parish.

GODWICK [Godwick]   HHL
1281/2, 1288/9, 1289/90, 1297/8–1313/14, 1315/16, 1318/19, 1319/20, 1321/2–1343/4, 1348/9, 1353/4–1357/8, 1359/60, 1377/8–1384/5, 1390/1, 1409/10, 1411/12, 1412/13, 1413/14, 1415/16–1421/2, 1422/3.
4–6 courts per year in full year. No VFP or assize jurisdiction.
Various rentals and surveys.
Sole manor in the parish (Blomefield ix, p. 509).

GRESSENHALL
[Gressenhall]   NRO
1308/9–1310/11, 1312/13–1326/7, 1327/8, 1328/9, 1330/1–1342/3, 1344/5–1351/2, 1354/5–1358/9, 1360/1–1370/1, 1373/4–1389/90, 1391/2–1404/5, 1412/13, 1413/14–1446/7, 1448/9, 1451/2, 1453/4–1469/70, 1483/4–1499/1500.
4–6 courts plus leet per year. Courts with Scarning, Hoe, Bittering, Stanfield, Brisley, Bilney, and Horningtoft.
Accounts 1279–80, 1346–7, 12 years 1361–76.
Two manors in the parish (G. Carthew, *The Hundred of Launditch and Deanery of Brisley*, Norwich, 1877, I, *passim*).

HAVERINGLAND
[Holverston's]   NRO
1321/2–1326/7, 1332/3–1333/4, 1342/3–1345/6, 1348/9–1352/3, 1354/5–1357/8, 1362/3–1364/5, 1379/80, 1404/5, 1411/12, 1442/3, 1491/2, 1492/3.
One to four courts p.a., few years appear complete (16 mm 1321/2–1364/5). Demesne offences, land transfers, occasional litigation.

One of three manors in parish (Blomefield, viii, p. 229).

HEACHAM [Heacham]   NRO
1275/6–1277/8, 1280/1–1326/7, 1329/30–1411/12, 1419/20–1483.
7–9 courts per year plus leet. Very full leets. Court rolls in good condition but fragile at bottom.
Bailiff's accounts: 1295/6; 3 years 1300–50; 10 years 1351–1400; 30 years 1401–1500.
Rentals: 1216–72; 1272–1306: 2; 1327–77: 3; 1377–99; 1413–22: 2.
Two manors in the parish (Blomefield x, pp. 307–10).

HINDOLVESTON
[Hindolveston]   NRO
1270/1–1287/8, 1288/9, 1326/7–1347/8, 1351/2–1385/6, 1387/8–1390/1, 1392/3–1397/8, 1399/1400–1421/2, 1434/5, 1442/3–1459/60, 1461/2–1478/9, 1483/4–1499/1500.
Leet and four courts per year surviving for most years.
Accounts: 13 years 1255–1300; 17 years 1301–50; 20 years 1351–1400; 25 years 1401–1500.
Survey 1274.
Sole manor in the parish (Blomefield viii, pp. 239–40).

HINDRINGHAM
[Hindringham]   BL/PRO/NRO
1262/3–1267/8, 1273/4–1304/5, 1343/4, 1345/6, 1347/8, 1360/1, 1361/2, 1363/4, 1364/5, 1375/6–1376/7, 1383/4, 1392/3, 1397/8, 1402/3–1406/7, 1408/9, 1410/11–1421/2, 1425/6, 1433/4, 1440/1, 1444/5.
One of five manors (Blomefield ix, pp. 226–30).

HINGHAM [Hingham] NRO
1257/8–1259/60, 1311/12, 1312/13,
1314/15, 1315/16, 1317/18–1319/20,
1345/6, 1347/8, 1348/9, 1350/1–
1353/4, 1355/6, 1356/7, 1361/2–
1369/70, 1372/3–1376/7, 1378/
9–1398/9, 1399/1400, 1400/1, 1402/
3–1443/4, 1446/7, 1447/8, 1452/3,
1474/5, 1493/4–1499/1500.
4–6 courts per year with one leet and
one *curia generalis* with assizes in the
14th century. Rolls in good condition.
Accounts: 1303; 9 years 1400–1500.
Surveys 13th and 14th centuries.
At least four manors in the parish
(Blomefield ii, pp. 431–45).

HOLKHAM [Hill Hall] HHL
1358–60, 1361–4, 1365–78, 1379–87,
1389–92, 1396–8.
One or two courts per year, occasionally 4 or 5 at end of century.
Bailiff's accounts: 1349–52, 1355–57,
1377, 1379, 1381, 1385 and 15th
century.
Rentals: 1360, 1362, 1380, 1381, 1385,
1390, and 15th century.
At least three manors in the parish
(Blomefield ix, pp. 231–35).

HOLKHAM [Holkham] HHL
1311–12, 1321–2, 1331–7, 1339–40,
1347–9, 1351–60, 1362–4, 1366–75,
1377–80, 1383–92, 1393–8, *1422–58,
1460, 1467–8, 1484–5, 1487–8.*
Leet and 3–5 courts per year for most
years. Some courts quite lengthy.
Courts of Holkham with Earls Holkham
and Holkham Burghall.
Various rentals, surveys, and accounts
from 14th and 15th centuries.
Principal manor (Blomefield ix, p. 231)

HOLKHAM
[Holkham Neel's] HHL
1322–71

One or two courts per year (occasionally more); very short courts relate
mainly to land transfers. (14mm in
toto).

HORSHAM ST FAITH
[Horsham St Faith] NRO
1264/5–1271/2, 1273/4–1277/8,
1281/2–1292/3, 1311/12–1326/7,
1329/30, 1330/1, 1368/9, 1379/80–
1386/7, 1400/1–1412/13, 1422/3–
1460/1, 1485/6–1499/1500.
Leet and 4–6 courts per year. Full
courts in good condition.
Accounts: 8 years 1392–1400; 40 years
1401–1500.
Terrier 1480.
Sole manor in the parish (Blomefield
x, pp. 439–41).

HUNSTANTON
[Hunstanton] NRO
1255/6, 1256/7, 1265/6, 1266/7,
1275/6–1305/6, 1307/8–1349/50,
1350/1–1357/8, 1361/2, 1362/3,
1364/5–1374/5, 1399/1400–1412/13,
1485/6–1501/2.
3–5 courts per year, no VFP or assize
jurisdiction. Rolls fragile.
Four manors in the parish (Blomefield
x, pp. 312–24).

HUNWORTH [Harthill] BL
1329/30, 1332/3–1335/6, 1349/50,
1350/1, 1352/3–1355/6, 1369/70,
1370/1, 1374/5, 1376/7, 1378/9–
1380/1, 1382/3–1387/8, 1399/1400–
1459/60, 1461/2–1495/6.
One or two short courts per year, no
assizes or VFP.
Bailiff's accounts: 1300/1, 1334/5,
1457/8.
At least three manors in the parish
(Blomefield ix, pp. 401–2).

HUNWORTH [Hunworth] BL
1326/7, 1327/8, 1329/30–1331/2,
1336/7–1338/9, 1340/1, 1341/2,
1343/4–1345/6, 1352/3–1354/5,
1388/9–1395/6, 1397/8, 1398/9,
1399/1400.
One or two short courts per year, no
VFP or assize jurisdiction.

MARTHAM [Martham] NRO
1287/8–1290/1, 1297/8, 1350/1–
1354/5, 1356/7, 1357/8, 1362/3–1381/
2, 1383/4, 1384/5, 1386/7–1390/1,
1392/3, 1398/9, 1403/4, 1411/12,
1412/13, 1413/14, 1415/16, 1416/17,
1418/19–1422/3, 1424/5, 1426/7,
1427/8, 1434/5, 1437/8, 1441/2, 1442/
3, 1444/5, 1446/7, 1449/50, 1452/3–
1454/5, 1459/60, 1463/4, 1471/2,
1480/1, 1497/8–1508/9.
Leet and four full courts in a complete
year 1327–77.
Rental 1292 (BL Stowe MS).
Accounts: 1324, 1340; 13 years 1350–
1400; 18 years 1401–1500.
At least two manors in the parish
(Blomefield v, pp. 20–25).

MERTON [Merton] NRO
1327/8, 1328/9, 1333/4, 1334/5,
1340/1, 1347/8–1357/8, 1363/4–
1367/8, 1372/3–1374/5, 1376/7,
1399/1400, 1400/1, 1404/5–1406/7,
1410/11–1412/13, 1413/14, 1414/15,
1423/4–1429/30, 1432/3–1442/3,
1447/8, 1448/9, 1452/3–1456/7,
1458/9, 1460/1, 1461/2.
Leet and four courts per year in complete year.
At least two manors in the parish
(Blomefield ii, pp. 298–303).

RYBURGH PARVA [Paveli's] BL
1299/1300–1302/3, 1319/20, 1337/8–
1366/7, 1368/9–1386/7, 1432/3–
1482/3, 1485/6–1499/1500.

6–8 courts per year with one leet and
one *curia generalis* with assizes annually.
Accounts: 3 years 1327–37; 7 years
1350–1400; 14 years 1401–1500.
Four manors in the parish (Blomefield
vii, pp. 168–71).

SALLE [Salkirkhall] NRO
1327/8–1398/9, *1413–24.*
4–6 courts per year 1327–77. No VFP
or assize jurisdiction.
Accounts 1422–45; ministers' accounts
1449–1500.
Rental 1480.
Extent 1370.
Six manors in the parish (Blomefield
viii, pp. 269–73).

TITTLESHALL
[Greynstone] HHL
1306/7, 1308/9–1310/11, 1312/13–
1314/15, 1317/18–1319/20, 1321/2–
1326/7, 1328/9, 1335/6, 1336/7,
1339/40, 1341/2–1343/4, 1346/7–
1348/9, 1350/1, 1352/3–1354/5,
1358/9–1364/5, 1367/8–1370/1,
1374/5.
One court per year for most years.
Various rentals and accounts.
Six manors in the parish (Blomefield
x, pp. 60–8).

TITTLESHALL [Peakhall] HHL
1327/8, 1335/6–1342/3, 1346/7,
1348/9–1352/3, 1354/5, 1355/6,
1357/8–1360/1, 1363/4–1366/7,
1369/70, 1370/1, 1372/3–1375/6,
1377/8, *1484–1500.*
Two or three courts per year for most
years.
Various rentals and accounts.

TIVETSHALL NRO
1273–4, 1275–6, 1302–6, 1307–13,
1316–17, 1320–1, *1321–2,* 1324–5,
1329–30, *1333–4,* 1334–6, *1337,* 1342–

3, *1344*, *1347–8*, 1349–50, *1352*, 1355–7, *1396–7*, *1413–22*.
Leet, two general courts and 2–3 courts on 2 mm p.a.
Accounts: 1300–1350: 3; 1350–1400: 12; 1400–1500: 9.
Manor of Abbot of Bury St Edmunds, one of three or four in parish (Blomefield, i, p. 205).

WELLINGHAM [Southall]   HHL
1336/7–1342/3, 1344/5–1349/50, 1356/7, 1358/9–1360/1, 1363/4–1368/9, 1371/2, 1372/3, 1376/7, 1377/8–1387/8, 1393/4.
Leet and four courts per year for most years. Courts variable in length, many illegible.
Rental 1342.
Terrier 1467.
Two manors in the parish (Blomefield x, pp. 72–4). Some courts survive for Fremleyhall manor for 14th century.

WELLS [Wells]   HHL
1346/7–1353/4, 1357/8–1382/3, 1384/5–1398/9, *1400–1500*.
Leet for Wells and Warham and 8–10 courts per year in full year during the years 1327–77; 5–7 courts per year during period 1377–99. Full courts.
Rental 1456.
Accounts: 1387; 5 years 1401–24.
Two manors in the parish (Blomefield ix, pp. 282–4).

WYMONDHAM
[Burnham]   G&CC
1324/5–1333/4, 1335/6–1344/5, 1347/8–1349/50, 1375/6–1379/80, 1381/2–1397/8.
Leet and 2–4 courts per year early 14th century; leet and 1–2 courts per year after Black Death. Courts usually short.
Thirteen manors in the parish (Blomefield ii, pp. 498–507). Some court

rolls also survive from Wymondham Grishage for 14th century in NRO.

WYMONDHAM
[Wymondham]   NRO
1272/3, 1276/7–1278/9, 1282/3, 1284/5, 1294/5, 1296/7–1298/9, 1300/1, 1301/2, 1305/6, 1306/7, 1310/11–1313/14, 1315/16–1356/7, 1361/2, 1364/5, 1370/1, 1372/3–1382/3, 1384/5–1390/1, 1402/3–1403/4, 1413/14–1460/1, 1461/2, 1463/4, 1470/1–1474/5, 1477/8, 1480/1, 1483/4.
7–9 courts with one leet and one *curia generalis* per year. Very full courts in good condition.
Accounts: 5 years 1280–1300; 16 years 1301–50; 21 years 1351–1400; 41 years 1401–1500.
Rent rolls 14th century, 1400/1.
Extent 15th century.
Custumals 1327–77, 1415, 1422.

Northamptonshire

BRIGSTOCK
[Brigstock]   NthRO/PRO
1275/6, 1286/7, 1291/2, 1294/5, 1296/7–1297/8, 1299/1300–1308/9, 1310/11–1311/12, 1313/14–1318/19, 1320/1–1321/2, *1324/5*, 1326/7, 1327/8–1332/3, 1334/5, 1336/7–1340/1, 1342/3–1344/5, 1347/8, *1399/1400*, *1407/8*, 1411/12, etc.
VFP and 16 courts in full year, but few complete rolls. Condition poor.
Rentals and custumals 1400–1500: 2.
Royal manor, larger of two in parish (Bridges ii, p. 285).

CATESBY [Catesby]   PRO
1312/13–1314/15, 1322/3, 1324/5, 1327/8–1329/30, 1335/6–1336/7, 1339/40, 1341/2, 1343/4–1344/5, 1346/7, 1350/1, 1357/8–1359/60,

1361/2–1362/3, 1371/2–1372/3, 1376/7, 1377/8–1389/90, *1390/1–1431/2, 1461/2, 1481/2, 1482/3, 1483/4, 1484/5.*

4–6 short courts (two apparently with function of view) p.a. Some membranes contain separate records of land transfers.

Various accounts 1400–1500: 12.

Rent rolls: *c.*1217–72, 1339–40, 1427–8, 1483, 1484, 1485, 1487, 1492.

Catesby Priory manor, sole manor in parish (Bridges i, p. 32).

HIGHAM FERRERS   NthRO
[Burgess court]   PRO (DL)
                         (Leics. RO)

1275–6, 1310/11, *1328–9, 1342–3, 1348, 1350,* 1352/3, 1354/5, *1362–4,* 1364/5, *1366–9, 1370–1,* 1372/3, *1373–1376, 1377–9, 1380–1, 1382–3, 1384–5, 1386–9, 1390–1, 1392–3, 1394–8 etc.*

Two VFP (short) and 9–15 courts (short) on 2–3 mm p.a., but few years complete. Condition poor.

(Rolls of court of Duchy of Lancaster for Higham Ferrers begin 1389–90).

Accounts: 1360–1400: 8; 1400–1500: 47.

Rental, 1449/50.

See R.M. Serjeantson, 'The Court Rolls of Higham Ferrers' (AASRP, vol. 33, 1915–16, p. 95 *et seq.*)

WEEDON BECK
[Weedon Beck]   EC

1301, 1321–1326, 1346–1353, *1357, 1359–65, 1367–69, 1372, 1373, 1379–85, 1388–92, 1483, 1490, 1492, 1493, 1496.*

VFP and courts (14–17 courts in some years, one court only in others). Some courts very full, most short. Rolls may be fair copies with selected estreats.

(1301–26 (VFP only), 16 mm, 1321–73, 24 mm).

Accounts: 1290, 1358, 1447.

Rentals: 1365, 1498.

Manor of alien priory of Ogbourne (i.e. of Bec Herluin). View held for Duchy of Lancaster. Sole manor in parish (Baker i, pp. 450–1).

WOODFORD NEAR
THRAPSTONE
[Thorley's]   NthRO

1280/1–1283/4, 1335/6–1338/9, 1340/1–1342/3, 1344/5–1345/6, 1348/9–1354/5, 1356/7–1359/60, 1400/1, 1409/10, 1410/11, 1412/13, 1413/14, 1420/1, 1425/6, 1437/8, 1453/4, 1474/5, 1476/7, 1478/9.

10–13 short courts with assizes of bread and ale, on 3–4 mm p.a. in complete years in fourteenth century.

(1281–1359, 39 mm, 1400–1479, 14 mm).

Accounts: 1393–1400: 7.

Rentals: 1389, 1393, 1400.

Four manors in parish in fourteenth century (*VCH* iii, pp. 255–8).

Oxfordshire

CUXHAM [Cuxham]   MCO

1278/9, 1280/1, 1293/4–1303/4, 1305/6, 1309/10, 1312/13, 1314/15, 1315/16, 1320/1–1325/6, 1327/8, 1329/30, 1333/4, 1335/6, 1337/8, 1340/1, 1342/3, 1346/7, 1351/2–1357/8, 1376/7, *1378, 1380, 1385, 1386, 1388–90, 1393, 1400, 1401, 1403, 1404, 1406–8, 1410, 1411, 1436–8, 1440, 1445, 1448, 1458, 1466, 1474–8, 1480, 1481, 1485–9, 1496.*

No VFP or assize jurisdiction, one or two courts per year.

To 1358 edited and printed in P.D.A.

Harvey, *Manorial Records of Cuxham,
Oxfordshire c.1200–1359*, Historical
Manuscripts Commission JP23, 1976,
p. 1.
Accounts: 15 years 1275–1300; 45 years
1301–50; 12 years 1351–1400.
Rentals 1297, 1453, 1466, 1483.
Subsidy roll 1303.
Single manor in the parish (Harvey *op.
cit.* p. 1).

LAUNTON [Launton]   WA
1286/7–1302/3, 1307/8–1321/2,
1324/5–1326/7, 1327/8, 1330/1–
1335/6, 1337/8, 1338/9, 1349/50,
1373/4, 1374/5, 1376/7, 1377/8–1399,
1400–49, 1461–75.
VFP, one *curia magna*, and three courts
per year during 1327–77.
Manor rolls: 28 years 1267–1300; 33
years 1301–50; 48 years 1351–1400; 17
years 1401–1500.
Single manor in the parish (*VCH* vi,
pp. 232–5).

NEWINGTON   CCaL
1269/70, 1274/5, 1276/7, 1278/9–
1295/6, 1298/9–1300/1, 1302/3–
1304/5, 1306/7, 1311/12–1320/1,
1322/3–1326/7, 1330/1–1335/6,
1337/8–1344/5, 1346/7–1348/9,
1352/3–1353/4, 1356/7–1370/1,
1376/7, 1381/2–1382/3, 1385/6, 1387/
8–1388/9, 1390/1, 1393/4–1397/8,
1402/3–1403/4, 1410/11, 1415/16,
1417/18–1421/2, 1423/4–1429/30.
VFP and up to nine courts on 3–4 mm
in 13th c.
Two VFP and occasional courts on 3
mm in 14th c. Assizes not confined to
view. Many years incomplete.

UPPER HEYFORD
[Heyford Warren]   NCO
1315/16, 1317/18, 1318/19, 1327/8–
1329/30, 1333/4, 1334/5, 1340/1,

1342/3, 1343/4, 1345/6, 1346/7,
1350/1–1356/7, 1367/8, 1368/9,
1369/70, 1371/2–1376/7, *1377–80,
1422, 1463–77, 1485–1500.*
No VFP or assize jurisdiction, up to
four courts per year during 1327–77.
Account: 1296–97 (BL Harl Roll K29).
Single manor in the parish (*VCH* vi,
pp. 196–8).

Shropshire

PREES [Prees]   SalRO/SBL
1322/3–1337/8, 1349/50, 1350/1,
1352/3–1357/8, 1361/2–1366/7,
1368/9–1376/7, 1377/8, 1379/80–
1387/8, 1389/90–1392/3, 1394/5,
1395/6, 1398/9, *1399/1400–1412/13,
1424/5–1452/3.*
Twelve to fifteen courts per year with
view of frankpledge surviving for most
years. Varying state of preservation.
Bailiffs' accounts 1361/2–1508/9.
Largest of at least three manors in the
parish (Eyton ix, pp. 244–55).

WELLINGTON
[Malinslee]   SalRO
1334/5–1337/8, 1340/1, 1341/2,
1345/6, 1347/8, 1348/9, 1355/6–
1358/9, 1361/2, 1363/4, 1365/6,
1369/70, 1370/1, 1372/3, *1404/5–
1408/9, 1420/1.*
One court per year, no VFP or assize
jurisdiction.
At least four manors in the parish
(Eyton, ix, pp. 40–50).

WHITCHURCH
[Burghall]   SalRO
1326/7, 1327/8, 1328/9, 1332/3,
1333/4, 1338/9, 1339/40, 1341/2,
1342/3, 1344/5, 1345/6, 1352/3,
1362/3–1364/5, 1366/7, 1367/8,
1371/2, 1373/4, 1374/5, 1376/7,

1379/80, 1383/4–1385/6, 1387/8, 1388/9, 1392/3, 1395/6, 1459/60.
Three to five courts (*curia magna* and *parva*) per year.

WHITCHURCH
[Whitchurch]   SalRO
1332/3, 1333/4, 1339/40, 1341/2, 1344/5, 1345/6, 1351/2, 1352/3, 1362/3–1364/5, 1373/4, 1374/5, 1376/7, 1379/80, 1383/4, 1385/6, 1388/9, 1395/6, 1410/11, 1413/14, 1440/1, 1441/2, 1459/60, 1463/4, 1464/5, 1466/7.
One court per year, no VFP or assize jurisdiction.
Survey and rental 1328/9.

WHITCHURCH HUNDRED   SalRO
1332/3, 1333/4, 1338/9, 1339/40, 1341/2–1345/6, 1362/3–1364/5, 1367/8, 1370/1, 1371/2, 1373/4, 1374/5, 1376/7, 1379/80, 1383/4–1385/6, 1387/8, 1388/9, 1392/3, 1421/2, 1423/4, 1424/5, 1426/7, 1427/8, 1431/2–1435/6.
Up to eight courts per year but variable survival.
At least two manors in the Parish (Eyton x, pp. 14–25).

WORFIELD [Worfield]   SalRO
1327/8–1333/4, 1335/6, 1336/7, 1340/1, 1342/3, 1345/6, 1349/50–1389/90, 1392/3–1482/3, *1483/4–1499/1500.*
Four courts per year, with VFP twice a year for most years.
Accounts: 8 years 1326–44; 1409.
Single manor in the parish, although some independent free holdings (Eyton iii, pp. 104–13).

Somerset

ASHTON [Ashton Meriets]   BRO
1337/8–1342/3, 1346/7, 1347/8, 1352/3, 1354/5–1359/60, 1364/5–1388/9, 1391/2, 1392/3, 1402/3, 1426/7, 1428/9, 1429/30, 1431/2, 1432/3, 1434/5, 1438/9, 1442/3, 1443/4, 1445/6, 1446/7, 1448/9, 1452/3, 1454/5.
No VFP or assize jurisdiction, up to 4 courts per membrane for fourteenth century, short membranes in fifteenth century.
Rental 1495.

BATCOMBE [Hallmoot]   Longleat
1262, 1265, *1283–4,* 1305, *1307–9,* 1313–14, *1315–16, 1340–1,* 1344–5, *1345–6,* 1347–8, 1349–50, 1351–2, 1354–5, *1357,* 1358, *1364–7,* 1367–9, *1369–70,* 1370–1, *1372–3, 1374, 1379–80, 1387–8, 1403–4,* 1407–8, 1448–9.
Glastonbury Abbey manor, one of four in parish (Phelps i, pp. 466–8).
See notes under **Glastonbury**.

BERROW, EAST BRENT, SOUTH BRENT, LYMPSHAM [Brent]   Longleat
1262, 1265, *1283–4,* 1305, *1307–9,* 1313–14, *1315–16, 1340–1,* 1344–5, *1345–6,* 1349–50, 1351–2, 1354–5, *1357,* 1358, *1364–7,* 1367–9, *1369–70,* 1370–1, *1374, 1379–80, 1387–8, 1403–* 4, 1407–8, 1448–9.
Glastonbury Abbey manor, sole manor in Berrow and Lympsham, one of two in South Brent, of three in East Brent (Phelps i, pp. 196–203).
See notes under **Glastonbury**.

CHEDZOY [Chedzoy]   BL/PRO
1330/1–1376/7, 1379/80, *1381–4, 1405–13.*

Usually 2 courts and 2 *curia legalis* per year. Assize infractions at most courts, little extended litigation. Good condition.

Accounts: 1330/1–1376/7.

CHELWOOD, MARKSBURY

[Marksbury]   Longleat

1262, 1265, *1283–4*, 1305, *1307–9*, 1313–14, *1315–16*, *1340–1*, 1345, *1346*, 1347–8, 1349–50, 1351–2, 1354–5, *1357*, 1358, *1364–7*, 1367, 1368–9, *1369–70*, 1370–1, 1372–3, *1374*, *1379–80*, *1387–8*, *1403–4*, 1407–8, 1448–9.

Two tourns and hallmoots and occasional courts.

Glastonbury Abbey manor, sole manor in both parishes (Phelps ii, pp. 426–7).

See notes under **Glastonbury**.

DITCHEAT [Hallmoot]   Longleat

1262, 1265, *1283–4*, *1307–9*, 1313–14, *1315–16*, *1340–1*, 1344–5, *1345–6*, 1347–8, 1349–50, 1351–2, 1354–5, *1357*, 1358, *1364–7*, 1367–9, *1369–70*, 1370–1, 1372–3, *1374*, *1379–80*, *1387–8*, *1403–4*, 1407–8, 1448–9, 1487–8.

Account: 1429–30.

Glastonbury Abbey manor, one of five in parish (Phelps, i, pp. 471–2).

See notes under **Glastonbury**.

DOULTING [Hallmoot]   Longleat

1262, 1265 *1283–4*, 1305, *1307–9*, 1313–14, *1315–16*, *1340–1*, 1344–5, *1345–6*, 1347–8, 1349–50, 1351–2, 1354–5, *1357–8*, *1364–7*, 1367–9, *1369–70*, 1370–1, 1372–3, *1374*, *1379–80*, *1387–8*, *1403–4*, 1407–8, 1448–9, 1487–8.

Account: 1429–30.

Glastonbury Abbey manor, possibly one of two (Phelps i, pp. 473–4).

See notes under **Glastonbury**.

GLASTONBURY

[Hallmoot]   Longleat

1262, 1265, *1283–4*, 1304, *1307*, 1308, *1309*, 1313–14, *1315–16*, 1330, *1340–1*, 1345, 1347–8, 1349–50, 1351–2, 1354–6, *1357–8*, *1364–7*, *1369*, 1370–1, 1373, *1374*, *1379–80*, *1387–8*, *1403–4*, 1407–8, 1448–9, 1487–8 etc.

Two regular hallmoots and irregular hallmoots and courts (1–3) annually, each on membrane or part membrane. Tenurial regulation, including heriot and (at Hokeday hallmoot) chevage into fifteenth century. Sole jurisdiction in Glastonbury, West Pennard and Sticklinch. The records for the Abbot of Glastonbury's franchise jurisdiction (called *comitatus*) for the twelve hides of Glastonbury, recording civil and criminal pleas and the assize of ale, survive for *1318–19*, 1322, 1327–9, 1331–2, *1334*, 1369–70, 1377–8, *1417–18*. In full years, 13 courts and 3 gaol deliveries on 16 mm.

Dating is by abbatial years.

There are a number of accounts for the whole estate.

Note: In general the hallmoot court rolls of the Abbot's manors were filed together, and survival is very erratic within each roll. The hallmoot rolls do not record intertenant litigation and land transfers in the normal form, but do record the imposition of amercements by the court and the transfer of land to and from the lord's hand. Where there is no VFP for the manor, tithings make presentment to the Abbot's private hundred courts enrolled separately. The only hundred court rolls to survive are for 1311, 1417–8 and 1480–1. Chevage lists are compiled into the fifteenth century and are sometimes very lengthy.

GREINTON [Hallmoot]   Longleat
1283–4, 1304, *1307–9*, 1313–14, *1315–
16*, *1340–1*, 1344–5, *1345–6*, 1347–8,
1349–50, 1351–2, 1354–5, *1357–8*,
1364–7, 1367–9, *1369–70*, 1370–1,
1372–3, *1374*, *1379–80*, *1387–8*, *1403–
4*, 1407–8, 1448–9.
Accounts: 1342–50: 2; 1350–1400: 7;
1400–1500: 21.
Glastonbury Abbey manor, probably
one of two in parish (Phelps i, pp. 428–
9).
See notes under **Glastonbury**.

HIGH HAM
[Ham Hallmoot]   Longleat
1262, 1265, *1283–4*, *1307*, 1308, *1309*,
1313–14, *1315–16*, *1340–1*, 1344–5,
1345–6, 1347–8, 1349–50, 1351–2,
1354–5, *1357–8*, *1364–7*, 1367–9,
1369–70, 1370–1, 1372–3, *1374*, *1379–
80*, *1387–8*, *1403–4*, 1407–8, 1448–9.
Glastonbury Abbey manor, one of three
in parish (Phelps i, pp. 444–5).
See notes under **Glastonbury**.

HUNTSPILL
[Withy Hallmoot]   Longleat
1283–4, *1307–9*, 1313–14, *1315–16*,
1340–1, 1344–5, *1345–6*, 1347–8,
1349–50, 1351–2, 1354–5, *1357–8*,
1364–7, 1367, 1368–9, *1369–70*, 1370–
1, 1372–3, *1374*, *1379–80*, *1387–8*,
1403–4, 1407–8, 1448–9.
Glastonbury Abbey manor, one of six
in parish (Phelps ii, pp. 390–4).
Hallmoot sometimes included with
Greinton.
See notes under **Glastonbury**.

MELLS [Hallmoot]   Longleat
1262, 1265, *1283–4*, 1305, *1307–9*,
1313–14, *1315–16*, *1340–1*, 1344–5,
1345–6, 1347–8, 1349–50, 1351–2,
1354–5, *1357*, 1358, *1364–7*, 1367–9,

1369–70, 1370–1, 1372–3, *1374*, *1379–
80*, *1387–8*, *1403–4*, 1407–8, 1448–9,
1487–8.
Accounts: 1426–35: 2.
Glastonbury Abbey manor. Possibly
one of two in parish (Phelps ii, p. 462).
See notes under **Glastonbury**.

MIDDLEZOY, OTHERY,
WESTON ZOYLAND
[Sowy Hallmoot]   Longleat
1262, 1265, *1283–4*, 1304, *1307–9*,
1313–14, *1315–16*, *1340–1*, 1344–5,
1345–6, 1347–8, 1349–50, 1351–2,
1354–5, *1357–8*, *1364–7*, 1367–9,
1369–70, 1370–1, 1372–3, *1374*, *1379–
80*, *1387–8*, *1403–4*, 1407–8, 1448–9.
Glastonbury Abbey manor, apparently
sole manor in all parishes (Phelps i,
p. 442)
See notes under **Glastonbury**.

PODIMORE MILTON
[Middleton]   Longleat
1283–4, 1305, *1307–9*, 1313–14, *1315–
16*, *1340–1*, 1344–5, *1345–6*, 1347–8,
1349–50, 1351–2, 1354–5, *1357–8*,
1364–7, 1367–9, *1369–70*, 1370–1,
1372–3, *1374*, *1379–80*, *1387–8*, *1403–
4*, 1407–8, 1448–9.
Glastonbury Abbey manor, sole manor
in parish (Phelps i, p. 451).
Frankpledge jurisdiction exercised after Black Death.
See notes under **Glastonbury**.

EAST PENNARD
[Hallmoot]   Longleat
1262, 1265, *1283–4*, *1307–9*, 1313–14,
1315–16, *1340–1*, 1344–5, *1345–6*,
1347–8, 1349–50, 1351–2, 1354–5,
1357, 1358, *1364–7*, 1367–9, *1369–70*,
1370–1, 1372–3, *1374*, *1379–80*, *1387–
8*, *1403–4*, 1407–8, 1448–9, 1487–8.
Account: 1371.

Glastonbury Abbey manor, probably one of two in parish (Phelps i, p. 478). See notes under **Glastonbury**.

PILTON [Hallmoot]　　　Longleat
1262, 1265, *1283–4*, 1305, *1307–9*, 1313–14, *1315–16*, *1340–1*, 1344–5, *1345–6*, 1347–8, 1349–50, 1351–2, 1354–5, 1357, 1358, *1364–7*, 1367–9, *1369–70*, 1370–1, 1372–3, *1374*, *1379–80*, *1387–8*, *1403–4*, 1407–8, 1448–9, 1487–8.
Glastonbury Abbey manor, possibly one of two in parish (Phelps i, pp. 480–1). See notes under **Glastonbury**.

SHAPWYK
[Ashcot Hallmoot]　　　Longleat
1265, *1283–4*, 1304, *1307–8*, 1309, 1313–14, *1315–16*, *1340–1*, 1344–5, *1345–6*, 1347–8, 1349–50, 1351–2, 1354–5, *1357–8*, *1364–7*, 1367–9, *1369–70*, 1370–1, 1372–3, *1374*, *1379–80*, *1387–8*, *1403–4*, 1407–8, 1448–9.
Accounts: 1343–50: 4; 1350–1400: 10; 1400–1500: 20.

[Shapwyk Hallmoot]　　　Longleat
1265, *1283–4*, 1304, *1307–9*, 1313–14, *1315–16*, *1340–1*, 1344–5, *1345–6*, 1347–8, 1349–50, 1351–2, 1354–5, *1357–8*, *1364–7*, 1367–9, *1369–70*, 1370–1, 1372–3, *1374*, 1379 *–80*, *1387–8*, *1403–4*, 1407–8, 1448–9.
Shapwyk hallmoot frequently includes Moorlinch.
Glastonbury Abbey manors, possibly one other manor in chapelry of Ashcote (Phelps i, pp. 426–7).
See notes under **Glastonbury**.

STAWLEY [Greenham]　　　BL
1336/7, 1340/1, 1341/2, 1353/4–1355/6, 1370/1–1376/7, 1377/8, 1380/1–1382/3, 1390/1–1396/7, 1410/11–1412/13, 1415/16, 1416/17,

1419/20–1421/2, 1430/1–1432/3, 1435/6, 1436/7, 1464/5–1466/7, 1470/1, 1471/2, 1472/3, 1479/80, 1480/1.
3–4 courts and one *curia legalis* per year, though most years with only one or two courts surviving. Many courts are with Kittisford.
Accounts: 1344/5, 1346/7, 1369/70, 1375/6, 1390/1, 1397/8, 1398/9, 1401/2, 1405/6.
Rental: 1390/1.

STREET [Hallmoot]　　　Longleat
1265, *1283–4*, *1307–9*, 1313, *1315–16*, *1340–1*, 1344–5, *1345–6*, 1347–8, 1349–50, 1351–2, 1354–5, *1357–8*, *1364–7*, 1367–9, 1369–70, 1370–1, 1372–3, *1374*, *1379–80*, *1387–8*, *1403–4*, 1407–8, 1448–9, 1487–8, *1497*.
Accounts: 1312–50: 2; 1350–1400: 4; 1400–1500: 11.
Glastonbury Abbey manor, one of two in parish (Collinson iii, p. 424).
See notes under **Glastonbury**. A few court rolls are filed separately.

WALTON [Hallmoot]　　　Longleat
1265, *1283–4*, *1297*, 1304, *1307–8*, 1309, *1312*, *1315–16*, *1340–1*, 1344–5, *1345–6*, 1347–8, 1349–50, 1351–2, 1354–5, *1357–8*, *1364–7*, 1367–9, *1369–70*, 1370–1, 1372–3, *1374*, *1379–80*, *1403–4*, 1407–8, 1448–9.
Accounts: 1274–1300: 3; 1300–50: 13; 1350–1400: 11; 1400–1500: 26.
Extent: 1316.
Glastonbury Abbey manor, apparently sole manor in parish (Collinson iii, p. 425).
See notes under **Glastonbury**. A few court rolls are filed separately.

WRINGTON [Hallmoot]　　　Longleat
1262, 1265, *1283–4*, 1305, *1307–9*, 1313–14, *1315–16*, *1340–1*, 1345, *1346*,

1347–8, 1349–50, 1351–2, 1354–5, 1357, 1358, *1364–7*, 1367–9, *1369–70*, 1370–1, 1372–3, *1374, 1379–80, 1387–8, 1403–4*, 1407–8, 1448–9.
Glastonbury Abbey manor, possibly sole manor in parish (Phelps i, pp. 206–7).
See notes under **Glastonbury**.

Staffordshire

ALREWAS [Alrewas]   StRO/PRO
1258/9–1260/1, 1268/9, 1272/3, 1273/4, 1281/2, 1285/6–1287/8, 1316/17, 1327/8–1427/8, 1431/2, 1435/6–1440/1, 1443/4, 1445/6, 1449/50, 1455/6–1459/60, 1463/4, 1464/5, 1469/70, 1470/1, 1499/1500–1501/2. Alrewas with Fradley, Orgreave, Edingale. Two VFP and regular three-weekly courts, most courts surviving in good condition for most years. Assize infractions at every court.
Rental 1341/2 (BL).
Court of the Somerville manor. One small Lichfield prebendal manor in the parish, from which court rolls survive from 1350. (Shaw i, pp. 127–35).

CANNOCK [Cannock]   StRO(A)
1328/9, 1329/30, 1341/2, 1342/3, 1350/1–1357/8, 1361/2, 1362/3, 1368/9–1370/1, 1372/3–1374/5, 1399/1400, 1413/14–1421/2, *1422/3–1460/1, 1463/4–1500*.
Courts of Cannock and Rugeley. Two VFP and three-weekly court, although few years complete. Usual court business, plus presentment of offences within the lord's wood by foresters of Cannock and Rugeley.
Account: 1384–5.
Survey: 1297–8.

Court of bishop of Lichfield's manors of Cannock and Rugeley. Sole manor in Cannock, one of two in Rugeley (*VCH* v, pp. 53–5, 154–57).

LICHFIELD [Chantry
of St Radegund]   StRO (A)
1282–6, 1289–91, 1305–11, 1313–16, 1322–3, 1327, 1335–6, 1338–42, 1348, 1350–1, 1354–6, 1357–9, 1362, *1369–79, 1381–3, 1384–92, 1418–20, 1423–9, 1440, 1442–4, 1451, 1454–7, 1461, 1463, 1467–8, 1473–7, 1481, 1482, 1484, 1490, 1493, 1496–7, 1499, 1500*.
Lichfield with members.

LONGDON [Longdon]   StRO(A)
1327/8, 1328/9, 1330/1, 1333/4–1337/8, 1351/2, 1352/3, 1360/1, 1361/2, 1370/1, 1371/2, 1373/4–1376/7, 1378/9, 1379/80, 1382/3, 1383/4, 1386/7, 1387/8, 1390/1–1398/9, 1422/3, 1461/2, 1463/4–1482/3, 1483/4–1485.
Court of Longdon with members. 2 VFP and 6–12 courts per year surviving for most years.
Accounts: 9 years 1303–15.
Rentals 1429–30, 1451.
Survey 1297–8.
At least three manors in the parish (Shaw i, pp. 215–19).

PATTINGHAM
[Pattingham]   StRO
1311/12–1314/15, *1336/7, 1337/8, 1339/40–1342/3*, 1345/6, *1351/2–1354/5*, 1355/6–1357/8, *1362/3, 1365/6, 1367/8–1369/70, 1372/3, 1374/5, 1376/7–1377/8, 1379/80, 1383/4, 1387/8–1388/9, 1390/1–1391/2, 1394/5, 1397/8–1398/9, 1401/2–1403/4, 1405/6–1408/9, 1410/11–1411/12, 1414/15, 1417/18, 1421/2–1423/4, 1426/7–1430/1*,

1432/3, *1435/6–1437/8*, *1440/1*, *1443/4*, *1445/6*, *1447/8–1448/9*. Two VFP and up to 6 courts on 2 mm. per year in 14th century, but for most years one membrane survives. Some rolls have lists of mortuaries attached. Sole manor in the parish (Shaw ii, pp. 279–80).

ROLLESTON [Rolleston] PRO
1283/4, 1325/6, 1335/6, 1338/9, 1341/2, 1360/1, 1372/3, 1375/6, 1378/9–1380/1, *1384/5*, *1386/7*, *1389/90*, *1391/2–1392/3*, *1394/5*, *1396/7–1398/9*, *1399/1400*, *1401/2*, *1402/3*, *1412/13*, *1413/14–1421/2*, *1438/9–1440/1*, *1443/4*, *1456/7*, *1466/7–1467/8*.
Two VFP and 1–4 short courts on 1 m. in early 14th century, later generally short VFP. (Rolls filed with those for Tutbury, Uttoxeter, etc.).
Accounts: 1313–14; 1400–1500: 37.
Sole manor in the parish (Shaw i, pp. 28–31).

RUGELEY [Rugeley with Brereton] StRO
see **Cannock**.

STOKE ON TRENT PRO
[Newcastle under Lyme] (DL 30)
1334/5, 1346/7–1348/9, 1350/1–1352/3, *1353/4–1363/4*, 1364/5, 1366/7–1367/8, *1369/70–1376/7*, 1377/8–1379/80, *1381/2–1398/9*, *1400/1–1403/4*, *1405/6–1407/8*, *1409/10–1411/12*, *1413/14–1416/17*, *1419/20–1434/5*, *1438/9*, *1442/3–1457/8*, *1462/3–1484/5*, *1486/7–1491/2*, *1493/4–1508/9*.
Two VFP (or great courts) and 11–15 courts per year on 7–11 mm. in full years. Business mainly litigation and land transfers.

Accounts: 1313–14; 1350–1400: 2; 1400–1500: 37.
Apparently the sole manor in Stoke parish. Presentments at views from Hanley, Penkhull (in Stoke), Fenton Vivian, Langton (*VCH* viii, pp. 184–6).

TAMWORTH
[Borough Court] KUL
1288–99, 1303–4, 1306, 1309–10, 1311–12, 1313–16, 1317–20, 1322, 1323–6, 1328–9, 1331–3, 1334, 1335–8, 1342–7, 1349 (Jan.–June), 1352, 1354–5, 1356–7, 1363–80, 1382–93, 1395–8.
Also 15th century rolls.
Essoins, litigation, presentments by tasters, property transfers. Usually one membrane yearly, 8–10 courts including VFP. Some entries recorded in more than one court.

TUTBURY [Borough Court] PRO
1283/4, *1292/3*, *1293/4*, *1338/9–1339/40*, 1341/2, 1345/6, 1347/8, 1362/3–1363/4, 1374/5–1375/6, 1379/80–1381/2, *1383/4*, *1385/6*, *1387/8*, 1395/6, *1397/8–1398/9*, *1404/5–1406/7*, *1410/11–1412/13*, *1413/14*, *1415/16–1417/18*, *1419/20–1420/1*, *1423/4–1424/5*, *1428/9–1429/30*, *1432/3–1433/4*, *1443/4*, *1448/9–1450/1*, *1456/7*, *1466/7–1468/9*, *1471/2–1472/3*.
Two VFP and 15 port moots on 3–4 mm. in full year in reign of Edward III; leet presentments at more than two courts annually, few land transfers. Rolls filed with those of Honour of Tutbury, Rolleston, Uttoxeter, etc.
Accounts: 1313–14; 1400–1500: 37.
Rentals: 1382, 1399–1413.

Suffolk

GREAT BARTON

[Great Barton]   SRO(B)

1291/2, 1293/4, 1296/7, 1299/1300, 1306/7, 1310/11–1311/12, 1313/14, 1315/16, 1323/4, 1332/3, 1343/4, 1348/9, 1353/4–1355/6, 1363/4–1365/6, 1369/70, 1376/7, 1379/80, 1382/3, 1384/5–1387/8, 1397/8, 1398/9 (55 mm).

Leet, general court and 4–5 cts. p.a. on 3 mm in complete years. For most years, single membrane only.

Accounts: 1300–50: 3; 1350–1400: 2; 1400–1500: a number.

One of two manors in parish (Copinger vi, pp. 252–3).

GREAT BEALINGS   PRO
[Seckford Hall]   (C. 116)

1345/6, 1347/8–1354/5, 1357/8–1358/9, 1360/1–1361/2, 1363/4–1365/6, 1367/8–1375/6, 1377/8–1392/3, 1394/5–1401/2, 1403/4–1408/9, 1410/11–1420/1, 1422/3–1449/50, 1452/3–1471/2, 1475/6–1479/80, 1481/2 etc.

Six cts. p.a. on 2 mm in full years, little information about land transfers. One of two manors in parish (Copinger iii, pp. 3–9).

BILDESTON   Longleat

1327/8–1329/30, 1340/1, 1345/6, 1357/8–1403/4, 1407/8–1450/1, 1452/3–1467/8, 1469/70, 1470/1, 1473/4, 1476/7–1483/4, *1485/6–1508/9, etc.* (1327–1377: 44 mm; 1377–1399: 43 mm).

Leet (November) and 2–3 courts on 2–3 mm before Black Death, leet and 1–2 cts. in late 14th c., leet and 1 court (or c.g.) in 15th c.. Assizes taken at one court besides leet. (Records of market

courts for 1370/1–1374/5, 1379/80–1380/1, 1382/3 also enrolled (4–7 courts p.a.)

Accounts: 1377–8; 1400–1500: 2.

Sole manor (Copinger iii, pp. 135–9).

GREAT BLAKENHAM
[Great Blakenham]   EC

1307–13, 1315–26, 1390, 1392–4, 1407, 1423, 1427, 1429, 1432–5, 1442, 1444, 1446–58, 1460, 1464–9, 1472–7, 1479, 1481–3.

Leet and 1–8 courts p.a. (in most years 2–4) in 14th c.; 1 court p.a. in late 15th c.

Accounts: 1294–1300: 4; 1300–50: 10.

Sole manor, belonging to Ogbourne Priory (Bec Hellonin) Copinger ii, p. 261.

Note: Composite court rolls for Bec manors covering 1246, 1247–50, 1269–70, 1275–6, 1280–1, 1289–91, 1295–6 are at Kings College, Cambridge and appear to cover Blakenham (Morgan, p. 6).

BREDFIELD [Bredfield]   SRO(I)

1317/18, 1320/1, 1328/9–1329/30, 1331/2, 1338/9–1347/8, 1349/50, 1352/3–1353/4, 1355/6–1357/8, 1359/60–1362/3, 1364/5–1366/7, 1368/9–1372/3, 1376/7–1377/8, *1422–1508*.

Leet and 6 courts p.a. on 2–6 mm before Black Death, leet and 1–4 courts on 1–2 mm later.

Accounts: 1400–1500: 17.

One of two manors (Copinger vii, pp. 244–7).

BROME   EH
[Brome]   (Iveagh MSS 16/1–8)

1318/19, 1319/20, 1329/30, 1336/7, 1344/5–1346/7, 1351/2–1353/4, 1355/6–1357/8, 1359/60–1365/6,

1367/8–1371/2, 1376/7, 1377/8, 1379/80, 1384/5–1385/6, 1391/2–1394/5, 1396/7, 1398/9, *1422/3–1462/3, 1466/7–1484/5.*
3–4 cts. on 2–3 mm p.a. in complete years, leet from 1353/4. Few complete years (27 mm 1318/19–1376/7).
Three manors in parish (Copinger iii, pp. 234–43).

CLARE [Chilton
(= Clare extrinsec)]   PRO
1308/9, 1312/13, 1317/18–1319/20, 1322/3–1323/4, 1325/6–1326/7, 1330/1, 1335/6–1336/7, 1338/9–1339/40, 1343/4–1344/5, 1348/9, *1355/6,* 1357/8, *1358/9, 1359/60, 1361/2–1362/3,* 1363/4, *1371/2–1374/5, 1376/7,* 1377/8, 1382/3–1383/4, 1387/8–1388/9, 1390/1, 1392/3–1393/4, 1396/7–1397/8, *1398/9, 1402/3, 1403/4, 1412/13–1417/18, 1419/20, 1420/1, 1422/3, 1428/9–1429/30, 1431/2, 1439/40, 1442/3, 1444/5, 1450/1, 1461/2–1463/4, 1465/6–1467/8, 1471/2–1481/2, 1483/4, 1487/8, 1490/1, 1492/3 etc.*
Leet and 13–16 courts on 2–4 mm in early 14th c., on 1–2 mm later, length of courts very variable. Condition poor.
Accounts: 1300–50: 13; 1350–1400: 3; 1400–1500: 5.
The whole of Clare parish belonged to the Honour of Clare, and Chilton was apparently the manor for lands lying outside the borough. (cf. Copinger v, pp. 200–2).

CLARE [Borough]   PRO
1312/13, 1317/18–1319/20, 1322/3, 1324/5, 1326/7, 1328/9–1332/3, *1335/6–1340/1, 1343/4–1347/8,* 1348/9–1351/2, *1352/3–1354/5, 1356/7–1368/9, 1370/1–1373/4,*

1374/5–1376/7, 1377/8, 1379/80, 1383/4, 1385/6, 1387/8, *1388/9, 1390/1, 1397/8–1400/1, 1403/4–1404/5, 1406/7, 1411/12, 1412/13, 1413/14, 1416/17, 1417/18, 1419/20–1424/5, 1426/7–1431/2, 1436/7–1439/40, 1442/3, 1444/5, 1447/8, 1450/1, 1452/3–1454/5, 1456/7, 1461/2–1464/5, 1466/7, 1468/9, 1470/1–1483/4, 1485/6, 1487/8, 1490/1, 1492/3.*
Leet and 13–17 courts on 4–7 mm in full years in early 14th c., leet, general court and, 12–14 courts on 2–3 mm in 1370s.
Accounts: 1300–1350: 12; 1350–1400: 24; 1400–1500: 2

DRINKSTONE
[Drinkstone Hall]   Longleat
1316/17–1331/2, 1334/5–1346/7, 1348/9–1350/1, 1354/5, 1356/7–1371/2, 1373/4–1411/12, 1464/5, 1467/8, 1468/9, 1470/1, 1471/2, 1472/3, 1474/5, 1475/6, *1486/7, 1489/90, 1490/1, 1492/3, 1493/4, 1495/6, 1497/8–1500/1, etc.*
(1316–1327: 18 mm; 1327–1377: 79 mm, 1377–1399: 28 mm).
Leet (June) and 3–4 courts on 2 mm in early 14th c., leet and 2 courts later except for a brief period in late 1350s when 8–10 court sessions p.a.. From late 14th c., leet and 1 court p.a.. Assize business at first court after Michaelmas.

DRINKSTONE
[Tymperleys]   SRO(B)
1311/12–1313/14, 1315/16–1331/2, 1334/5–1335/6, 1337/8, 1340/1, 1343/4, 1347/8, 1350/1–1351/2, 1352/3–1360/1, 1374/5, 1376/7, 1423/4, 1428/9, 1429/30, 1432/3, 1439/40, 1445/6, 1447/8, 1453/4, 1455/6, 1458/9, 1462/3–1473/4,

1475/6–1478/9, 1480/1–1482/3, 1485/6, 1498/9, 1500/1, etc.
Two general courts and 1–3 courts in most years in 14th c., 1 or 2 cts. p.a. in 15th c.. Courts well kept in reign of Edward II but not later.
Condition good. (10 mm 1311–27, 18 mm 1327–77).
Two manors in parish (Copinger vi, pp. 262–5).

DUNNINGWORTH   EH (Suffolk (now in Tunstall parish)   MSS, Iveagh Coll.) Box 207
1297/8, 1303/4, 1312/13, 1313/14, 1318/19, 1319/20, 1331/2–1333/4, 1343/4–1345/6, 1347/8–1349/50, 1353/4–1358/9, 1360/1, 1361/2, 1363/4, 1364/5, 1366/7, 1367/8, 1375/6–1411/12, 1413/14–1431/2, 1433/4–1464/5, 1469/70–1472/3, 1475/6–1485/6, 1486/7, 1488/9, 1496/7–1508/9.
One or 2 cts. surviving in most years before Black Death, 3–4 courts p.a. in late 14th c., 2 cts. p.a. in 15th c. Mostly litigation and tenurial business; assizes of bread and ale taken at some courts. Sole manor in medieval parish (Copinger v, pp. 124–6).

SOUTH ELMHAM
[South Elmham]   SRO(I)
1278–88, 1313/14, 1316/17–1317/18, 1319/20, 1324/5, 1327/8, 1332/3–1333/4, 1337/8, 1339/40, 1341/2, 1344/5, *1345/6*, 1347/8–1349/50, *1350/1*, 1352/3, *1355*, 1356/7–1357/8, 1359/60–1360/1, 1363/4, 1367/8, 1372/3–1373/4, *1380/1–1388/9*, *1399/1400–1407/8*, *1413/14–1421/2*, *1424/5–1482/3*, *1485/6–1508/9*.
Leet and 5–6 courts on 4–6 mm with assize business at one additional court

during year. Few years appear to be complete. Very lengthy records, but suitors and litigants rarely identified by township, and location of land transferred given only from 1347/8. Courts shorter after Black Death, with far fewer land transfers.
List of tenants *c.*1283.
Accounts: 1340–50: 4; 1350–1400: (11); 1400–1500: (22).
Manor of Bishop of Norwich, extending into South Elmham St George, St James, All Saints, St Michael, St Peter, St Nicholas, St Margaret, Flixton St Mary (*q.v.*) and Homersfield.
Sole manor in all save the last two (Copinger vii, pp. 151, 171–85).

EYKE [Staverton   EH (Suffolk cum Bromswell]   MSS) Iveagh Coll 357
1330/1, 1337/8–1338/9, 1341/2–1359/60, 1362/3–1363/4, 1367/8, 1374/5, 1399/1400–1411/12, 1422/3–1468/9, 1470/1–1472/3, 1475/6–1484/5.
Leet and 8–10 cts. in mid 14th c., but very few complete years. Leet and 3–4 cts. p.a. in 15th c.. Courts lengthy (113 mm 1330/1–1374/5). (Also account rolls not looked at in Box 356.)
One of two manors in parish (Copinger iv, pp. 259–62) also covers land in Glemham, Melton, Rendlesham and Tunstall.

FLIXTON ST MARY
[Flixton]   SRO(I)
1271/2, 1274/5, 1277/8, 1278/9, 1280/1–1283/4, 1286/7, 1290/1–1292/3, 1295/6, 1297/8–1306/7, 1309/10, 1311/12–1346/7, 1348/9–1354/5, 1356/7–1365/6, *1366/7–1421/2*, *1461/2–1508/9*.

Leet and 6 courts on 2–3 mm. p.a., in full years before Black Death. Length of courts very variable.
Account: 1391.
Rentals: 1358–9, 1377, 1382, 1417.
Extent: 1305–6.
Manor of Flixton Priory, one of three in parish apart from South Elmham manor (Copinger vii, pp. 176–82).
There are some medieval records of both the other manors in the SRO.
See J.M. Ridgard, 'Social and Economic History of Flixton in South Elmham, Suffolk 1300–1600' (Leicester M.A. 1970).

FORNHAM ALL   SRO (B)/EH
SAINTS [Fornham]   (Suffolk MSS)
                              Iveagh Coll. 223
1335–6, 1338–47, 1349–52, 1354–7, 1361–3, 1366–71, 1374–7, 1381–4, 1386–8, 1391, 1392, 1394–1401, 1415–22.
1–4 general courts and courts p.a.
Accounts: 1338–50: 6; 1350–1400: 12; 1400–1500: 37.
Rentals: 1348/9, 1407/8, 1441/2 (BL Add 34689)
Extents: 1317/18, 1441/2
Manor of Abbot of Bury St Edmunds. One submanor in parish. (Copinger vii, p. 23).

FORNHAM ST MARTIN,
FORNHAM ST
GENEVIEVE [Fornham]   SRO(B)
1262/3, 1276/7–1278/9, 1281/2–1286/7, 1288/9, 1290/1–1294/5, 1298/9–1299/1300, 1302/3–1305/6, 1307/8, 1309/10–1311/12, 1314/15, 1316/17, 1317/18, 1319/20, 1324/5, 1325/6, 1329/30–1330/1, 1332/3, 1333/4, 1335/6–1337/8, 1339/40–1341/2, 1343/4–1348/9, 1350/1–1358/9, 1360/1–1636/4, 1366/7–1367/8,

1369/70–1390/1, 1392/3–1398/9, *1406, 1419, 1421, 1482–1510.*
Leet (called *revocatio plegiarum* to 1308/9) and up to 2 general courts and 6 courts p.a. in late 13th century, leet and 1–4 general courts/courts on 2–3 mm. in full years early in reign of Edward III. General court at Michaelmas and leet at Lammas, with occasional additional courts, from 1346/7. Offences against assizes of bread and ale etc. dealt with at general courts as well as leets.
Accounts: 1261–1300: 13; 1300–50: 19; 1350–66: 11.
Manor of Prior and Convent of Bury St Edmunds (Cellarer from *c.*1312).
Sole manor for the two parishes, courts held in both parishes but usually headed 'Fornham'. (Copinger vi, pp. 268–71, vii, p. 23 is not entirely accurate).
The court rolls and account rolls of these two manors are in some confusion, but those of Fornham All Saints can be distinguished as their dating is generally by the Abbatial year.

FRAMLINGHAM
[Framlingham]   PCC
1331/2, 1344/5, 1346/7, 1350/1, 1353/4, 1355/6, 1357/8, 1361/2, 1367/8–1373/4, 1375/6, 1377/8–1381/2, 1383/4, 1386/7–1388/9, 1396/7, *1399/1400–1460/1, 1462/3–1508/9, etc.*
Leet and 6–8 cts. on 6–8 mm. p.a. before Black Death, later leet and 3–4 cts on 3–4 mm. p.a. Rolls also include records of a few courts of the borough and of leet court for Saxstead.
Accounts: 1324–5, 1422–3 (BL).
One other small manor in parish (Copinger iv, pp. 263–85).
Note: There are said to be court rolls of this manor at Arundel Castle for *1414–22, 1485–1507.*

HADLEIGH [Hadleigh
cum Boxford] CCaL
1276/7, 1294/5–1297/8, 1299/1300,
1303/4, 1304/5, 1307/8, 1309/10,
1311/12, 1316/17, 1321/2, 1326/7,
1328/9–1329/30, 1331/2–1332/3,
1334/5–1336/7, 1343/4, 1346/7,
1359/60, 1361/2–1362/3, 1365/6–
1367/8, 1373/4.
VFP, 2 general courts and probably 13–
15 courts p.a. at beginning of 14th c.,
but virtually all rolls to survive are odd
membranes. Leets long, general courts
include assizes of bread and ale. High
degree of tenurial regulation.
Five or 6 manors in parish (Copinger
iii, pp. 158–72).

HASKETON EH (Suffolk MSS)
[Rectory Manor] Iveagh Coll. 249
1326/7–1327/8, 1328/9, 1330/1,
1331/2, 1332/3, 1333/4, 1339/40–
1342/3, 1350/1, 1351/2, 1360/1,
1369/70, 1371/2, 1372/3, 1374/5,
1376/7, 1381/2, 1395/6, 1396/7,
1397/8, 1463/4, 1465/6, 1467/8,
1474/5, 1475/6, 1477/8, 1480/1,
1485/6, 1486/7, 1487/8, 1488/9,
1490/1, 1493/4, 1494/5, 1498/9,
1503/4, 1506/7, 1507/8.
1–3 cts. p.a., short courts, predominantly tenurial business (1327–1377,
9 mm.).
One of three manors in parish
(Copinger iii, pp. 50–6).

HOPTON [Hopton] Longleat
1340/1–1345/6, *1347/8*, 1348/9–
1365/6, 1368/9–1370/1, 1372/3–
1373/4, 1375/6, 1379/80, 1388/9,
1399/1400–1401/2, 1403/4–1410/11,
1412/13, 1413/14, 1414/15, 1420/1,
1435/6, 1437/8–1440/1, 1442/3,
1443/4, 1454/5, 1456/7, 1458/9,
1464/5, 1466/7–1470/1, 1476/7–

1479/80, 1481/2, 1484/5, 1491/2,
1493/4, 1494/5, 1495/6.
Two courts p.a. during the period
1327–77 (30 mm), later 1 court p.a.
Preponderance of trespass present-
ments.
Accounts: 1368–73: 2.
Sole manor (Copinger i, pp. 321–4).

HORHAM [Thorpe Hall] SRO(I)
1307/8, 1308/9–1312/13, 1314/15–
1316/17, 1319/20, 1327/8–1329/30,
1332/3–1334/5, 1336/7–1338/9,
1340/1–1341/2, 1343/4–1351/2,
1355/6–1356/7, 1361/2–1362/3,
1365/6–1370/1, 1378/9, 1386/7,
1399/1400, *1401–12, 1423–59, 1461–
70, 1475, 1479, 1482.*
Leet, general court and 1–4 courts on
2 mm. in full years before Black Death:
leet and 1–2 general courts/courts on
2 mm in the years 1377–1399.
Accounts: 1350–1400: 3.

HORHAM [Jernegans] SRO(I)
1310/11, 1312/13–1315/16, 1319/20–
1320/1, 1322/3, 1324/5–1340/1,
1343/4–1348/9, 1352/3–1359/60,
1361/2, 1363/4–1365/6, 1367/8,
1375/6, *1391–1415, 1420, 1422–71,
1476–83.*
Leet and 2–4 courts on 2–3 mm. in
full years before Black Death, leet and
1–2 courts on 1 m. or part membrane
after Black Death.
Accounts: 1300–50: 6; 1350–1400: 6.
Extent, early 14th c.
The records of the Horham manor
courts are filed in considerable confusion. They include records for one, or
more probably two, other manors for a
number of years from 1296/7.
Four or five manors in parish, four of
them belonging to Coke family in 17th
c. (Copinger iv, pp. 42–9).

IKEN [Iken]   SRO(I)
1329/30–1333/4, 1335/6–1340/1,
1342/3, 1344/5, 1346/7–1351/2,
1354/5–1374/5, 1377/8–1398/9,
1440/1–1459/60, 1461/2–1469/70,
1471/2–1501/2 etc.
1–5 cts. p.a., on 2–3 mm in 14th c.,
1–2 cts. p.a. in 15th c.
Sole manor (Copinger v, pp. 144–5).

LAKENHEATH
[Lakenheath]   CUL (EDC)/PRO
1309/10–1314/15, 1316/17, 1318/19–
1320/1, 1323/4–1340/1, 1342/3,
1344/5, 1346/7–1353/4, *1356/7*,
1360/1, 1366/7, 1375/6, 1377/8–
1397/8, *1399/1400–1411/12*, 1413/
14–1421/2, *1422/3–1441/2*, *1443/4–*
1450/1, *1461/2–1497/8*.
Leet and 12–14 courts in full years in
early 14th c., on 5–6 mm p.a. Leet
and 4–6 cts. p.a. later in century.
Unexamined rolls in poor condition.
Accounts: 1289–90; 1300–50: 15;
1350–1400: 14; 1400–1500: 15.
Records of the Prior and Convent of
Ely's manor of Lakenheath, which incorporated the small Priory manor of
Undley and from 1330 the manor of
Lakenheath belonging to the Honour
of Clare, some records of which are
incorporated in the early court rolls.
(Copinger iv, pp. 173–5 is inaccurate.)

LAYHAM [Netherbury]   SRO(B)
1333/4, 1336/7–1337/8, 1339/40–
1341/2, 1343/4, 1345/6–1349/50,
1351/2–1353/4, 1355/6–1364/5,
1368/9–1372/3, 1374/5, 1377/8–
1389/90, 1393/4–1397/8, 1411/12,
1413/14–1415/16, 1417/18–1420/1,
1427/8–1431/2, 1437/8–1439/40,
1448/9, *1461–72*.
6–8 courts on 3–4 mm. p.a. in complete years in reign of Edward III, but

few years complete; 1–3 courts p.a. in
15th c. Assize of ale taken at one court
yearly.
One of two manors in parish (Copinger
iii, pp. 186–93).

LEISTON   CUL (Heveningham
[Leiston]   Hall Mss)
1273/4, 1278/9, 1283/4, 1286/7,
1295/6, 1330/1, 1337/8, 1341/2,
1346/7, 1348/9, 1357/8, 1363/4,
1365/6, 1374/5, 1377/8, 1396/7–
1397/8 (*a small roll 1422–61*).
Leet and 12 courts p.a. on 6–8 mm.
but very few years complete (leets for
only four years).
Leiston Abbey manor, one of two manors in parish, covering also lands in
Aldringham cum Thorp, Knodishall
cum Buxhall and Sizewell. (Copinger
ii, pp. 111–16).

MELTON [Melton]   CUL (EDC)
1288/9, 1297/8, 1300/1–1301/2,
1307/8, *1309/10*, 1312/13–1314/15,
1318/19–1320/1, 1334/5, 1349/50,
1354/5, 1357/8, 1360/1.
Leet and 14–16 cts. on 5 mm p.a. in
full year in early 14th c., but only 1
year approaches completeness. Leet and
3–4 cts. p.a. after Black Death, but most
rolls are single membranes and in poor
condition.
Accounts: 1290–1; 1300–50: 9; 1350–
1400: 15; 1400–1500: 10.
Rental: 1423/4.
Sole manor, belonging to Ely Cathedral Priory (Copinger vii, pp. 258–9).

PALGRAVE   EH (Iveagh MSS
[Palgrave]   40–42, 44)/BL/NRO/
                           SRO (B)
1272–3, 1276, 1314–15, 1317–18, 1324,
1333–4, 1339–40, 1341–3, 1347–9,
1364, 1369–70, 1371–4, 1375–6, 1378/

9–1379/80, *1382/3–1383/4, 1385/6–*
1389/90, 1391/2, 1392/3, 1396/7–
1398/9, 1399/1400, 1403/4–1406/7,
1408/9, 1410/11, 1411/12, 1414/15,
1418/19, 1419/20, 1421/2, *1422/3,*
1423/4, 1425/6–1429/30, 1431/2,
1460/1, 1461/2–1466/7, 1483/4–
1521/2.
Leet, 3–5 courts and general courts on
3–5 mm, generally full, in 14th c.
Accounts: 1300–50: 11; 1350–1400: 14;
1400–1500: 9.
Rentals: 1438–9, 1483–4.
Extent: 1357.
Sole manor, belonging to Abbey of Bury
St Edmunds. (Copinger iii, p. 291).
Courts held sometimes at Redgrave and
at Wortham.

RENDLESHAM
[Bavents] SRO (I)
1352/3–1372/3, 1378/9–1401/2,
1405/6, 1407/8, 1408/9, 1410/11–
1422/3, 1427/8–1438/9, 1440/1,
1448/9, 1449/50, 1451/2, 1465/6,
1477/8, 1478/9, 1480/1–1482/3,
1484/5–1506/7.
Three to five courts in 14th c., one or
two in mid 15 th c., on part membrane
p.a.
Accounts: 1350–1363: 8.

[Colville's]
1347/8–1350/1, 1355/6–1359/60,
1371/2–1374/5, 1377/8, 1380/1–
1383/4, 1385/6–1388/9, 1390/1,
1392/3–1394/5, 1397/8, 1399/1400–
1408/9, 1411/12, 1422/23, 1424/5,
1427/8, 1428/9, 1430/1, 1432/3,
1433/4, 1435/6, 1436/7, 1457/8,
1469/70, 1470/1.
Two to three courts in mid 14th c.,
one or two in 1370s. Main business
land transfers and tenurial regulation.

[Naunton Hall]
1307/8–1318/19, 1321/2–1358/9,
1361/2–1377/8, 1379/80–1383/4,
1387/8–1392/3, 1396/7, 1401/2,
1402/3, 1405/6, 1413/14, 1427/8,
1434/5, 1437/8–1439/40, 1442/3,
1443/4, 1448/9, 1450/1, 1452/3,
1461/2, 1462/3, 1473/4, 1480/1,
1485/6–1487/8, 1490/1–1493/4,
1496/7–1499/1500 etc.
Four courts p.a. in early 14th c., general
court and 2 courts in 1330s, general
court and 1 court at end of century, one
court p.a. in late 15th c. Land transfers
and inheritance, occasional litigation.
Accounts: 1300–1350: 3; 1350–1400: 2.
Extents: 1339, 1352, 1359.
Rental 1418.
Three or four manors in parish
(Copinger, iv, pp. 317–23).

RICKINGHALL INFERIOR BL
1259–77, 1279–1333, *1333–4,* 1334–41,
1341–2, 1342–75, 1376–7, 1377/8–
1383/4, 1390/1, 1391/2, 1394/5–
1398/9, 1400/1, 1402/3, 1404/
5–1410/11, 1413/14, 1416/17, 1442/
3–1451/2, 1461/2–1469/70, 1483/4–
1487/8, 1489/90–1490/1, 1492/3–
1500/1, etc.
Two general courts and 8 cts. p.a. in
full years on 2 mm in 13th c., 4–6 cts.
in early 14th c., 2 general courts and
occasional courts in late 14th c., 1–2
courts p.a. in 15th c.
Some leet business (presentments by
decennarii, infringements of assize of
ale, presentments of gannockers) at the
general courts.
Accounts: 1300–50: 18; 1350–1400: 40;
1400–1500: 19.
Extent: late 14th c.
Manor of Bury St Edmunds, sole
manor in parish (Copinger i, p. 357).

EARL SOHAM
[Earl Soham]   SRO(I)
1318/19-1321/2, 1324/5-1325/6,
1327/8-1328/9, 1330/1-1331/2,
1334/5, 1336/7-1338/9, 1343/4-
1347/8, 1351/2-1353/4, 1355/6,
1357/8, 1359/60, 1361/2-1364/5,
1367/8-1375/6, 1377/8-1398/9,
1413/14-1471/2, 1473/4-1484/5,
etc.
Leet, general court and 4–6 courts on
3–4 mm in complete years in 1320s,
leet, great court, 3–4 courts before
Black Death, leet, great court, 1–3
courts in late 14th c. No litigation.
Accounts: 1400–1500: 12.
Rentals: 1315–16, 1450–1 and mid 15th
c.
Sole manor (Copinger iv, p. 251).

SOTHERTON   PRO (LR 3/39/5)
1332/3, 1333/4, 1343/4, 1348/9-
1350/1, 1353/4, 1354/5, 1359/60-
1362/3, 1366/7-1374/5.
Leet, general court and 2–3 courts p.a.,
mostly short.
One of two manors in parish (Copinger
ii, p. 153).

STOKE BY NAYLAND
[Chamberlain's manor]   SRO(I)
1279/80, 1281/2, 1282/3, 1285/6-
1296/7, 1299/1300, 1300/1, 1305/6,
1306/7, 1307/8-1319/20, 1325/6,
1326/7-1334/5, 1341/2-1345/6,
1350/1-1352/3, 1357/8-1360/1,
1366/7-1367/8, 1387/8, 1389/90,
1403/4-1405/6, 1427/8-1429/30,
1433/4-1436/7, 1438/9, 1442/3,
1447/8.
Six courts in full years in 13th c., 1–4
courts survive p.a. in 14th c., 1 court
p.a. in 15th c.. Assize of ale at 1 court
p.a.; all courts very short, litigation in
early rolls but mainly tenurial regula-

tion by mid 14th c.. No intertenant
land transfers.
One of ten manors in parish (Copinger
i, pp. 213–30).

STOWMARKET [Thorney,
alias Thorney Hotot later
Columbine Hall]   SRO(I)
*1326/7-1335/6, 1337/8-1348/9,
1350/1-1358/9, 1360/1-1365/6,
1367/8-1378/9, 1380/1, 1381/2, 1383/
4, 1385/6-1389/90, 1391/2-1393/4,
1397/8, 1398/9, 1399/1400, 1400/1,
1405/6-1412/13, 1422/3-1444/5,
1446/7-1457/8, 1459/60, 1460/1,
1461/2-1467/8, 1469/70, 1471/2,
1474/5, 1475/6, 1478/9, 1479/80,
1485/6-1486/7, 1489/90-1496/7, etc.*
Leet (December) and occasional short
courts. (20 mm. 1326–78).
Rentals: 1408 and 15th c.
Probably   six   medieval   manors
(Copinger vi, pp. 227–38).

STUSTON   EH (Iveagh
[Faucon's]   MSS 56/1–5)
1323/4, 1325/6, 1326/7, 1328/9,
1330/1-1332/3, 1334/5, 1336/7,
1348/9-1350/1, 1352/3, 1356/7-
1357/8, 1360/1-1361/2, 1364/5-
1372/3, 1374/5, 1467/8, 1472/3,
1477/8, 1492/3-1500/1.
1–2 cts. p.a., mostly short, no evidence
of litigation.
Survey 1371/2 (Iveagh MSS 9/2).
Court of Prioress of Flixton, at least
two other manors in parish (Copinger
iii, pp. 304–6).

SUDBURY [Sudbury]   PRO
1312/13, 1327/8, 1331/2-1333/4,
1335/6-1337/8, 1339/40, 1341/2-
1343/4, 1346/7-1348/9, 1352/3,
1354/5-1355/6, *1356/7-1376/7*,
1377/8, 1379/80, 1381/2-1384/5,

1388/9, *1389/90*, *1391/2–1393/4*, *1396/7–1397/8*, *1400/1*, *1404/5*, *1406/7*, *1409/10*, *1413/14–1423/4*, *1427/8–1435/6*, *1439/40*, *1442/3*, *1447/8*, *1452/3*, *1454/5–1457/8*, *1461/2*, *1462/3*, *1465/6–1467/8*, *1470/1–1477/8*, *1481/2–1483/4*, *1485/6*, *1487/8*, *1490/1*, *1492/3*.

Leet and 15 cts. on 4 mm in full year in 14th c. Assize presentments at first court of year and sometimes in other courts. Little litigation, no information on land market.

Accounts (mainly of Chamberlain): 1320–50: 7; 1350–1400: 10; 1402–3. Main manor, of two or three (Copinger i, pp. 231ff.).

TATTINGSTONE
[Tattingstone] SRO(I)
1335/6, 1337/8, 1340/1–1343/4, 1349/50, 1351/2–1352/3, 1360/1, 1361/2, 1363/4, 1364/5, 1374/5–1376/7, 1380/1–1384/5, 1386/7, 1388/9, 1391/2–1397/8, 1399/1400, 1403/4–1406/7, 1490/1, 1491/2, 1493/4, 1495/6–1501/2.

Leet and up to 4 courts p.a. before Black Death, but very few years survive complete. Leet and 1–2 cts. p.a. in late 14th and early 15th c., annual leet only in late 15th c. (16 mm 1335–1377, 15 mm 1380–1398).

Accounts: 1350–1400: 10; 1400–1500: 14.

Sole manor (Copinger vi, pp. 262–5).

THRANDESTON
[Thrandeston EH (Iveagh
Almoners] MSS 61, 62, 64)
1320/1, 1322/3, 1323/4, 1348/9, 1353/4, 1359/60–1361/2, 1366/7–1369/70, 1372/3, 1376/7, 1378/9–1382/3, 1385/6, 1388/9, 1389/90, 1392/3, 1397/8, 1399/1400, 1400/1,

1408/9, 1411/12, 1413/14, 1415/16, 1416/17, 1418/19, 1421/2, 1424/5, 1468/9, 1472/3, 1473/4, 1476/7, 1477/8, 1479/80, 1480/1, 1483/4, 1484/5, 1485/6–1491/2, etc.

One or 2 short courts p.a. on part membrane, mostly re. tenurial regulation.

Rentals: 1368/9, 1388/9.

Survey: 1472/3.

Records of manor of Almoner of Norwich Cathedral Priory. Four other manors in parish (Copinger iii, pp. 318–21). Records of at least one other are at Elveden Hall beginning in 1320/1.

WALSHAM LE
WILLOWS [Walsham] SRO(B)
1303/4, 1316/17–1318/19, 1323/4, 1324/5, 1326/7–1350/1, 1353/4, 1355/6, 1358/9–1385/6, 1387/8–1392/3, 1394/5–1398/9, *1399–1414*, *1423–1500, etc.*

1–2 general courts and up to four courts p.a on 3–4 mm in reign of Edward III. Assizes dealt with at general courts, some intertenant litigation. Condition of rolls good.

Account rolls: 1319–20; 1385–1400: 3; 1400–1500: 22.

Probably largest of three or four manors in parish (Copinger i, pp. 385–9 is inaccurate, see also K. Dodd, *Field Book of Walsham le Willows 1577* (Suffolk Record Society, Vol. XVII, 1974).

Note: It is assumed that these membranes relate to one manor only, but it is possible that a few mm may relate to another manor. See also below.

WALSHAM LE
WILLOWS
[Walsham Hall] SRO(B)
1316/17–1321/2, 1324/5, 1326/7, 1328/9–1329/30, 1332/3–1346/7, 1348/9–1351/2, 1365/6.

3–4 courts p.a. in reign of Edward II (1307–27) generally 2 cts. p.a. in reign of Edward III (1327–77).
Account roll: 1373–4.
Rentals: 1327 and n.d. (early 14th c.). The court rolls are generally single membranes, incorporated in the court rolls of Walsham manor.

WHERSTEAD
John Rylands
[Bourne Hall]
Library
1300/1–1303/4, 1311/12–1313/14, 1315/16, 1319/20–1320/1, 1323/4, 1324/5, 1330/1–1332/3, 1340/1–1342/3, 1345/6–1348/9, 1353/4, 1356/7–1358/9, 1360/1, 1364/5, 1371/2, 1389/90, 1397/8, 1402/3, 1404/5, *1436–58, 1472–89* (38 mm *in toto*).
10–12 cts. p.a., but most years represented by single m of 4–6 cts. Courts short, little litigation.
Manor of St Peter's Priory, Ipswich, one of four in parish (Copinger vi, pp. 119–123).

WINSTON
[Winston Hall]
CUL (EDC)
1306/7–1308/9, 1310/11, 1315/16, 1318/19–1320/1, 1322/3, 1324/5, 1326/7–1336/7, 1338/9–1345/6, 1347/8–1349/50, 1351/2–1376/7, *1377/8–1378/9*, 1379/80–1380/1, *1381/2–1387/8*, 1388/9, *1389/90–1396/7*, 1398/9–1400/1, *1401/2–1411/12, 1413/14–1421/2*, 1422/3–1423/4, *1424/5–1431/2*, 1432/3–1434/5, *1435/6–1441/2, 1443/4, 1445/6–1455/6*, 1456/7–1458/9, *1460/1, 1461/2–1478/9*, 1479/80, 1480/1, *1481/2, 1482/3, 1483/4–1484/5*, 1485/6–1501/2, etc.
Leet and 4–7 courts for Winston plus leet for the Insoken, on 2–4 mm in full years in early 14th c., but few years complete, leet plus 1–3 courts on 1–

2 mm after Black Death, leet plus 1 court in 15th c. Rolls in considerable confusion.
Accounts: *c*.1290–1300: 2; 1300–50: 5; 1350–1400: 10; 1400–1500: 10.
Ely Priory manor, one of two manors in parish (Copinger vii, pp. 149ff.).

WORLINGWORTH
[Worlingworth]
SRO(I)
1302–1350, 1351–1432, 1433, 1435–8, 1440–4, 1446/7–1450/1, 1452/3, 1453/4, 1455/6–1459/60, 1463/4–1482/3, *1484–1510 etc.*
Leet, general court and 3–4 courts on 2–4 mm p.a. before Black Death, leet and 1–2 general courts/courts on 2 mm p.a. in late 14th c.
Dating frequently by abbatial years.
Accounts: 1277–9; 1300–50: 22; 1350–1400: 38; 1400–1500: 14.
Surveys, 14th c.(2) 15th c.(2).
Sole manor, belonging to Abbey of Bury St Edmunds.

YOXFORD MIDDLETON
[Yoxford with Middleton and Stickland]
SRO(I)
1322/3, 1346/7–1347/8, 1349/50–1358/9, 1360/1–1370/1, 1373/4–1377/8, 1379/80–1387/8, 1389/90–1391/2, 1394/5–1395/6, 1397/8–1398/9, *1415/16–1419/20, 1422/3–1440/1, 1464/5–1483/4.*
Leet and 4–6 cts. on 2–3 mm p.a. before Black Death; leet and 1–3 courts general/courts in late 14th c.
Records are enrolled with those of several other manors i.e. Cockfield and Chickering from 1360/1, Meriels from 1355/6, Brandfen from 1361/2; 15th c. rolls may not all belong to Yoxford with Middleton.
One of three manors in Yoxford in 14th c. (Copinger ii, pp. 218–23).

Surrey

FARLEIGH [Farleigh]   MCO

1277/8–1281/2, 1282/3, 1289/90, 1290/1, 1296/7, 1302/3–1304/5, 1309/10–1313/14, 1315/16, 1316/17, 1319/20–1325/6, 1327/8–1337/8, 1339/40–1341/2, 1343/4–1345/6, 1347/8, 1349/50–1352/3, 1354/5, 1355/6, 1374/5, 1376/7, *1378–80, 1383–7, 1397, 1398, 1400, 1404, 1408– 10, 1453, 1456, 1457, 1460–3, 1466, 1472, 1475, 1489, 1490.*

Courts short (two–four courts per year), no VFP or assize jurisdiction.

Bailiff's accounts: 16 years 1274–1300; 30 years 1301–50; 35 years 1351–1400; 82 years 1401–1500.

Rentals: 1279, 1289, 1325, 1333, 1335, 1350, 1356, 1477.

Single manor in the parish (*VCH* iv, p. 282).

LEATHERHEAD
[Thorncroft]   MCO

1278/9–1345/6, 1348/9–1350/1, 1353/4–1359/60, 1361/2, *1421, 1426– 30, 1432–40, 1441–7, 1451, 1452, 1454– 8, 1461–3, 1486, 1487, 1489.*

One or two courts per year for most years. Full courts but no VFP or assize jurisdiction.

Accounts: 8 years 1272–1300; 18 years 1301–50; 18 years 1351–1400; 66 years 1401–1500.

Rentals: 1300, 1325, 1333, 1357.

Survey *c.*1360.

Scutage list *c.*1279.

Five manors in the parish (*VCH* iii, pp. 295–7).

MALDEN [Malden]   MCO

1279/80, 1283/4, 1285/6–1291/2, 1293/4–1300/1, 1302/3–1306/7, 1323/4, 1324/5, 1325/6, 1327/8–

1332/3, 1337/8, 1338/9, 1342/3, 1343/4, 1345/6–1349/50, 1352/3– 1354/5, 1356/7–1358/9, *1381, 1389, 1440–3, 1448, 1452, 1453, 1455, 1456, 1466, 1467, 1469, 1470, 1472, 1475, 1483, 1485, 1486, 1488–1500.*

One or two courts per year for most years. No VFP or assize jurisdiction.

Accounts: 12 years 1270–1300; 22 years 1301–50; 17 years 1351–1400; 4 years 1401–1500.

Rentals: 1279, 1357, 1375, 1400, 1456, 1481, 1486.

Single manor in the parish (*VCH* iii, pp. 523–4).

MERSTHAM [Merstham]   CCaL

1284/5, 1287/8, 1289/90–1292/3, 1296/7–1298/9, 1300/1–1303/4, 1309/10–1310/11, 1312/13, 1316/17, 1317/18, 1321/2, 1325/6, 1327/8, 1330/1, 1331/2, 1334/5–1337/8, 1343/ 4–1347/8, 1350/1–1352/3, 1354/5, 1358/9, 1360/1–1361/2, 1363/4– 1365/6, 1367/8, 1369/70, 1373/4– 1383/4, 1389/90, 1390/1, 1393/4, 1395/6, 1397/8, 1398/9, 1404/5, 1408/ 9, 1413/14, 1423/4–1425/6.

Lawday in May, assizes after Michaelmas. 6–8 courts in full year early fourteenth century, 2–5 courts yearly at end. For most years, single membrane only survives, and no year appears to be complete.

Accounts: 11 years 1259–1300; 18 years 1300–50; 10 years 1350–1400; 4 years 1400–1500.

Four manors in the parish (*VCH* iii, pp. 215–17).

Sussex

ALCISTON [Alciston]   SAS

1274/5, 1275/6, 1277/8, 1278/9, 1322/3–1325/6, 1348/9–1411/12,

1422/3–1428/9, 1430/1–1434/5, 1436/7–1441/2, 1444/5–1459/60, 1461/2–1484/5, 1486/7–1488/9.
Two VFP and 4–5 courts per year for most years. Full courts.
Custumal 1272–1307.
The manor had considerable land in Lullington as well as Alciston.
See J. A. Brent, 'Alciston Manor in the Later Middle Ages', *Sussex Archaeological Collections* CVI (1968), pp. 89–103.

LAUGHTON [Laughton]   BL
1336/7, 1359/60–1369/70, 1371/2–1374/5, 1376/7, 1377/8–1398/9, 1399/1400–1411/12, 1413/14–1424/5, 1426/7–1436/7, 1438/9–1477/8, 1481/2–1483/4.
Four to six courts per year for most years. No VFP or assize jurisdiction (assizes in Shiplake hundred court). Courts of moderate length.
Accounts: 1336–1500.
Reeve's account 1368–9 (Sussex Archaeological Trust).
Rentals: 1272–1307, 1410/11, 1414/15.
Extent 1325 (ERO).
Single manor in the parish, with portions of adjoining parishes. (Horsfield i, pp. 351–2).

SHIPLAKE HUNDRED   BL
1360/1, 1362/3–1388/9, 1393/4, 1394/5, 1396/7–1398/9, 1430/1, 1431/2, 1433/4, 1436/7, 1439/40–1445/6, 1447/8–1456/7, 1458/9–1459/60, 1461/2–1476/7, 1479/80–1483/4.
One or two courts per year for most years.

WARBLETON [Bucksteep]   BL
1300/1–1306/7, 1307/8, 1314/15–1322/3, 1337/8, 1341/2–1345/6, 1364/5–1368/9, 1392/3–1394/5, 1400/1, 1403/4, 1410/11, 1412/13.
Two or three courts per year for most years (some years 5–6). No VFP or assize jurisdiction. Some courts only 4–5 entries.
Four manors in the parish (*VCH* ix, pp. 206–8).

WARTLING [Wartling]   BL
1273/4, 1274/5, 1301/2–1304/5, 1307/8, 1310/11–1313/14, 1315/16–1320/1, 1322/3–1326/7, 1327/8, 1329/30, 1330/1, 1332/3–1335/6, 1337/8–1370/1, 1372/3–1376/7, 1377/8, 1378/9, 1381/2–1391/2, 1394/5–1398/9, 1399/1400, 1400/1, 1401/2, 1403/4–1405/6, 1409/10, 1410/11, 1412/13, 1413/14, 1417/18, 1418/19, 1420/1, 1421/2, 1478/9, 1479/80.
Two VFP and 7–8 courts per year for most years.
Largest of five manors in the parish (*VCH* ix, pp. 137–40).

Warwickshire

MIDDLETON [Court of De Freville portion]   NUL
1302/3–1303/4, 1306/7–1312/13, 1315/16–1317/18, 1326/7–1341/2, 1346/7, 1351/2, 1362/3, 1378/9, 1390/1, 1395/6–1396/7, 1407/8, 1414/15–1415/16, 1424/5–1425/6, 1450/1, 1453/4, 1455/6, *1466/7, 1469/70–1471/2, 1473/4*.
Two VFP and up to 4 courts p.a. Many years incomplete, courts very short (26 mm 1302/3–1362/3).
View held for the whole vill.
Accounts: 1376–1400: 7; 1400–1500: 8.
Rentals: 1434/5, 1454/5 and 15th c.
Survey: 1419/20.

Apparently one manor in parish, very much divided in 14th and 15th centuries (see *VCH* iv, pp. 156–7). Records of another portion (de Botiller) survive for 1315, 1372–1422, filed with these court rolls.

NUNEATON [Nuneaton]   BL
1282/3, 1283/4, 1285/6, 1337/8, 1340/1–1345/6, 1348/9–1350/1, 1352/3, 1354/5, 1355/6, 1366/7, 1376/7, 1377/8–1385/6, 1388/9–1390/1, 1393/4, 1395/6–1401/2, 1404/5–1411/12, 1414/15, 1415/16, 1416/17, 1418/19, 1419/20, 1421/2, 1428/9–1430/1, 1435/6, 1437/8, 1440/1, 1441/2, 1446/7, 1450/1, 1452/3, 1454/5, 1459/60, 1461/2–1482/3, 1483/4, 1490/1–1498/9.
VFP and 4–6 courts p.a.
Accounts: 3 years 1330–50; 16 years 1351–1400; 7 years 1401–1500.
Principal manor of 3 in parish (*VCH* iv, pp. 165–168).

Isle of Wight

NEWPORT [St Cross]   WCol
1283/4–1286/7, 1294/5, 1296/7, 1297/8, 1301/2, 1302/3, 1307/8, 1309/10, 1312/13, 1315/16–1319/20, 1320/1–1325/6, 1327/8–1331/2, 1351/2, 1352/3, 1371/2, 1374/5, 1375/6, *1387/8, 1389/90, 1391/2, 1393/4–1395/6, 1397/8, 1398/9, 1399/1400, 1402/3, 1404/5, 1408/9–1410/11, 1422/3–1426/7, 1428/9, 1430/1, 1432/3, 1433/4, 1435/6, 1438/9, 1440/1–1443/4, 1445/6–1456/7, 1458/9, 1461/2–1467/8, 1468/9, 1471/2, 1474/5–1478/9, 1480/1–1482/3, 1484/5.*
No VFP or assize jurisdiction, two courts per year.

Accounts: 2 years 1398–1400; 98 years 1401–1500.
Rental 1445/6.
Three manors in the parish (*VCH* v, p. 262).

Wiltshire

CASTLE COMBE [Castle Combe]   BL/GRO
1343/4–1346/7, 1348/9–1380/1, 1382/3–1386/7, 1388/9–1394/5, 1397/8, *1402*, 1413/14–1421/2, *1422/3–1479/80*.
Court, *curia militum, curia intrinseca, curia forinseca*. Usually one VFP, one or two *curia militum* and one or two *curia intrinseca* per year. From 1377 two or three VFP with *curia militum*. Assizes at *curia intrinseca*.
Accounts: 1411–12, 1436–7, 1478–9 (1478–9 in DRO).
Rentals: 1327–77, 1447, *c*.1460, 1490.
Possibly single manor in the parish (Aubrey, pp. 63–6).

CHISELDON [Badbury]   Longleat
1262, 1265, *1283–4, 1307–9*, 1313–14, *1315–16, 1340–1*, 1344–5, *1345–6*, 1347–8, 1349–50, 1351–2, 1354–5, 1357–8, *1364–7*, 1367–9, *1369–70*, 1370–1, 1372–3, *1374, 1379–80, 1387–8, 1403–4*, 1407–8, 1448–9.
Two VFP and hallmoots and occasional courts.
Glastonbury Abbey manor, one of three in parish (*VCH* xi, pp. 10–14).
See notes under **Glastonbury**, Somerset.

CHRISTIAN MALFORD [Hallmoot]   Longleat
1262, 1265, *1283–4, 1307–9*, 1313–14, *1315–16, 1340–1*, 1344–5, *1345–6*, 1347–8, 1349–50, 1351–2, 1354–5, *1357*, 1358, *1364–7*, 1367–9, *1369–70*,

1370–1, 1372–3, *1374, 1379–80, 1387–8, 1403–4*, 1407–8, 1448–9.
Glastonbury Abbey manor, possibly sole manor (*RH* ii, p. 272).
See notes under **Glastonbury**, Somerset.

COLERNE [Colerne]   NCO
1356/7, 1361/2, 1362/3, 1365/6–1370/1, 1373/4–1376/7, *1377–1481, 1486–1500*.
Two VFP and four courts per year, although some years have only one court surviving. One court per short membrane during the reign of Edward III (1327–1377). Presentation by tithing at VFP.
Possibly three manors in the parish (Aubrey, p. 77).

DURRINGTON
[Durrington]   WCol
1318/19–1326/7, 1328/9, 1331/2–1333/4, 1335/6, 1347/8, 1348/9, 1350/1, 1351/2, 1353/4–1360/1, 1362/3–1373/4, 1375/6, 1376/7, 1377/8–1392/3, 1394/5–1398/9, 1399/1400–1408/9, 1410/11, 1411/12, 1413/14–1425/6, 1427/8, 1428/9, 1431/2, 1432/3, 1435/6–1438/9, 1440/1, 1441/2, 1443/4–1446/7, 1448/9–1450/1, 1452/3, 1455/6–1460/1, 1461/2, 1465/6, 1466/7, 1469/70, 1472/3, 1473/4, 1476/7, 1477/8, 1480/1–1484/5.
VFP with one or two courts per year.
Possibly single manor in the parish (Aubrey, p. 356).

GRITTLETON
[Grittleton]   Longleat
1262, 1265, *1283–4, 1307–9*, 1313–14, *1315–16, 1340–1*, 1344–5, *1345–6*, 1347–8, 1349–50, 1351–2, 1354–5, *1357*, 1358, *1364–7*, 1367–9, *1369–70*,

1370–1, 1372–3, *1374, 1379–80, 1387–8, 1403–4*, 1407–8, 1448–9.
Two VFP and hallmoots and occasional courts.
Glastonbury Abbey manor, apparently several sub-manors (*Book of Fees*, ii, p. 732).
See notes under **Glastonbury**, Somerset.

IDMISTON [Idmiston]   Longleat
1283–4, 1307–9, 1313–4, *1315–16, 1340–1*, 1344–5, *1345–6*, 1347–8, 1349–50, 1351–2, 1354–5, *1357*, 1358, *1364–7*, 1367–9, *1369–70*, 1370–1, 1372–3, *1374, 1379–80, 1387–8, 1403–4*, 1407–8, 1448–9.
Two hallmoots and occasional courts; 2 VFP after Black Death.
Glastonbury Abbey manor, probably one of two in parish (*Book of Fees* ii, p. 746, *FA* v, p. 200).
See notes under **Glastonbury**, Somerset.

KINGTON ST
MICHAEL [Hallmoot]   Longleat
1262, 1265, *1283–4, 1307–9*, 1313–14 , *1315–16, 1340–1*, 1344–5, *1345–6*, 1347–8, 1349–50, 1351–2, 1354–5, *1357*, 1358, *1364–7*, 1367–9, *1369–70*, 1370–1, 1372–3, *1374, 1379–80, 1387–8, 1403–4*, 1407–8, 1448–9.
Glastonbury Abbey manor, probably several sub-manors (*Book of Fees* ii, p. 732).
See notes under **Glastonbury**, Somerset.

LONGBRIDGE DEVERILL
[Deverill]
MONKTON DEVERILL
[EastMonkton]   Longleat
1261, 1274–8, *1293, 1294, 1296*, 1296–7, 1299, *1300–1, 1305–6*, 1307–13,

1314–15, *1316*, 1317–18, 1319–23, *1325–8*, 1329–30, *1330–1*, 1331–2, 1333–5, *1337–9*, 1339–40, 1341–2, *1342–3*, 1343–4, *1346*, 1348–50, 1365–71, *1374–81*, 1382–6, 1387, *1389–94*, *1397*, *1400–3*, 1403–5, *1405–6*, *1409*, *1410*, *1416*, 1416–19, *1425*, *1441*, *1448–9*, *1456–83*, *1484–91*, 1496–1500 etc. Hundred courts (i.e. tourns, and called VFP in early 15th century) and hallmoots at Michaelmas and Hokeday, with occasional courts. Courts of the two manors were recorded sometimes together, sometimes separately, but at several different periods East Monkton was subsumed into Deverill either partially (single hundred, separate hallmoots) or completely (one hundred and hallmoot). Chevage records are particularly full on many of the rolls examined.

Dating is mainly by abbatial years. These records are quite distinct from other Glastonbury court rolls.

Accounts: LONGBRIDGE DEVERILL: 1276–1300: 17; 1300–50: *c*.33; 1350–1400: *c*.30; 1400–1500: *c*.75. MONKTON DEVERILL (with West Monkton, Somerset): 1294–1300: 5; 1300–50: *c*.35; 1350–1400: *c*.20; 1400–1500: *c*.62.

Glastonbury Abbey manors. One sub manor in Longbridge Deverill (Colt Hoare, *History of Modern Wiltshire: Hundred of Heytesbury*, pp. 39–40). Sole manor in Monkton Deverill (*idem, History of Modern Wiltshire: Hundred of Mere*, p. 177).

NETTLETON
[Nettleton]   Longleat
1262, 1265, *1283–4*, *1307–9*, 1313–14, *1315–16*, *1340–1*, 1344–5, *1345–6*, 1347–8, 1349–50, 1351–2, 1354–5, *1357*, 1358, *1364–7*, 1367–9, *1369–70*,

1370–1, 1372–3, *1374*, *1379–80*, *1387–8*, *1403–4*, 1407–8, 1448–9. Two VFP and hallmoots, and occasional courts.

Glastonbury Abbey manor, probably several sub-manors (*Book of Fees* ii, p. 732).

See notes under **Glastonbury**, Somerset.

STOCKTON
[Stockton]   BL/WCa L/WtRO
1281–2, 1290–1, 1292–3, 1295–6, 1296–7, 1306–7, 1308–9, 1311–12, 1313–14, 1322–3, 1330–1, 1332–5, *1339–40*, 1341–2, 1344, 1349–50, *1351*, 1353–7, 1361, 1362, 1365–8, 1376, 1383–94, 1396–1401, *1402–16*, *1419*, *1420*, *1426–8*, *1436*, *1446–8*, *1456*, *1458*, 1465–7, *1470–1*, *1475–84*, *1486*, *1489–90*, *1492–3*.

Two VFP and two courts per year, although most years with only one court surviving; after 1385 only one court with VFP each year. Court of Winchester Cathedral Priory.

Accounts: 12 years 1248–1316; 40 years 1399–1500.

Rent roll 1353.

WINTERBOURNE
MONKTON
[Winterbourne]   Longleat
1262, 1265, *1283–4*, *1307–9*, 1313–14, *1315–16*, *1340–1*, 1344–5, *1345–6*, 1347–8, 1349–50, 1351–2, 1354–5, 1357–8, *1364–7*, 1367–9, *1369–70*, 1370–1, 1372–3, *1374*, *1379–80*, *1387–8*, *1403–4*, 1407–8, 1448–9. Two VFP and hallmoots and occasional courts.

Glastonbury Abbey manor, earlier belonging to Abbey of St Georges de Bocherville. Possibly one sub-manor (*Book of Fees* ii, p. 749).

See notes under **Glastonbury**, Somerset.

Worcestershire

BOCKLETON [Bockleton]   StRO
1302/3–1305/6, 1307/8–1320/1, 1322/3–1326/7, 1327/8, 1328/9, 1331/2, 1332/3, 1334/5, 1339/40–1344/5, 1346/7–1349/50, 1361/2, 1399/1400–1401/2, 1404/5, 1406/7, 1407/8, 1409/10–1411/12, 1413/14, 1414/15, 1420/1, 1421/2, 1422/3–1424/5, 1432/3, 1433/4, 1438/9–1440/1, 1444/5–1452/3, 1457/8, 1459/60, 1462/3, 1464/5, 1465/6.
One or two courts per year for most years. No VFP or assize jurisdiction.
Rentals: 1301/2, 1320/1, 1326/7, 1424/5, 1459/60.
Three manors in the parish (*VCH* iv, pp. 241–3).

HALESOWEN [Hales]   BRL
1269/70–1271/2, 1272/3–1281/2, 1292/3–1294/5, 1296/7–1301/2, 1303/4–1305/6, 1307/8–1358/9, 1361/2–1363/4, 1367/8–1374/5, 1376/7–1387/8, 1389/90–1393/4, 1394/5–1396/7, 1398/9–1411/12, 1413/14–1421/2, 1422/3, 1423/4, 1426/7–1432/3, 1434/5–1436/7, 1438/9–1446/7, 1448/9–1452/3, 1454/5–1457/8, 1459/60, 1461/2–1472/3, 1474/5–1482/3, 1483/4, 1484/5, 1485/6, 1486/7, 1489/90–1498/9.
Accounts: 1360/1–1364/5, 1368/9, 1440/1–1442/3.
See Worcs. Hist. Soc. 1910–12, 1933, *Court rolls of the manor of Hales, 1270–1307.*

HALESOWEN
[Hales borough]   BRL
1272/3–1275/6, 1277/8–1281/2, 1292/3, 1293/4, 1295/6–1313/14, 1315/16–

1324/5, 1326/7, 1327/8, 1328/9, 1330/1–1351/2, 1353/4–1367/8, 1370/1–1373/4, 1375/6, 1376/7, 1377/8–1423/4, 1426/7–1490/1, 1492/3, 1493/4, 1497/8, 1498/9.

HALESOWEN [Romsley]   BRL
1278/9–1281/2, 1292/3–1297/8, 1300/1–1302/3, 1306/7, 1311/12–1313/14, 1317/18–1330/1, 1332/3–1340/1, 1342/3–1344/5, 1348/9, 1349/50, 1354/5–1388/9, 1390/1–1421/2, 1422/3, 1423/4, 1426/7–1448/9, 1450/1–1472/3, 1474/5–1491/2, 1494/5, 1495/6, 1499/1500.
See Worcs. Hist. Soc. 1933, *Court rolls of the manor of Hales, 1270–1307,* for court rolls of Romsley 1280–1303.

HALESOWEN [Warley]   BRL
1301/2–1304/5, 1306/7, 1307/8–1311/12, 1313/4–1320/1, 1322/3–1323/4, 1324/5, 1325/6–1328/9, 1329/30–1375/6, 1376/7–1378/9, 1380/1, 1382/3–1423/4, 1431/2–1448/9, 1450/1–1462/3, 1466/7–1470/1, 1476/7, 1478/9–1487/8, 1495/6, 1497/8 etc.
Great court and 4–5 courts p.a., all short.
No leet jurisdiction.

OMBERSLEY [Ombersley]   WoRO
1272/3, 1327/8–1335/6, 1357/8–1372/3, 1374/5–1391/2, 1393/4, 1394/5, 1396/7–1398/9, *1399–1422, 1423–1500.*
Two VFP and two courts surviving per year for most years. Good condition.
Accounts: 4 years 1450–1500.
Rentals: 1462, 1472, 1485–6, late 15th century.
Pannage rolls 14th and 15 centuries.
Two manors in the parish (*VCH* iii, pp. 463–6).

STOKE PRIOR

[Stoke Prior]   WoCa

1282/3, 1298/9, 1300/1–1303/4, 1305/6, 1306/7, 1310/11, 1313/14–1315/16, 1317/18–1320/1, 1322/3, 1324/5, 1326/7, 1330/1, 1335/6, 1336/7, 1341/2, 1345/6, 1348/9, 1349/50, 1351/2, 1353/4, 1367/8, 1372/3, 1380/1, 1385/6, 1392/3, 1396/7, 1397/8, 1409/10, 1410/11, 1414/15, 1419/20, 1421/2, 1422/3, 1423/4, 1425/6, 1426/7, 1428/9, 1430/1, 1432/3, 1436/7, 1438/9, 1440/1, 1445/6, 1451/2, 1459/60, 1463/4, 1464/5, 1466/7, 1483/4.

Two to four courts per year for most years. No VFP. Courts relatively short. Rent rolls 1396/7, 1414/15.

Sole manor in the parish (*VCH* iii, pp. 528–9).

Yorkshire

ALDBOROUGH

[Aldborough]   PRO (DL 30)

1337/8, 1339/40, *1346/7*, *1359/60*, 1362/3, 1364/5–1365/6, 1372/3–1373/4, *1382/3*, *1383/4*, *1385/6*, *1386/7*, *1390/1–1394/5*, *1400/1*, *1418/19*, *1419/20*, *1420/1*, *1422/3–1425/6*, *1429/1430–1432/3*, *1441/2*, *1442/3*, *1446/7*, *1451/2*, *1466/7*, *1467/8*, *1496/7*, *1498/9*, *1499/1500* etc.

Sheriff's tourn and 10 brief courts p.a., in 14th c. Condition poor.

Accounts: 1296–1300: 1; 1300–1350: 5; 1350–1400: 2; 1400–1500: 57.

Sole manor (*FA* vi, p. 95).

ALLERTON
MAULEVERER   YML

c.1330, *1338*, 1338/9, 1340/1–1342/3, *1345*, 1346/7–1347/8, 1351/2–1353/4, 1356/7–1357/8, *1362*, 1374/5, *1376*, *1377/8*, 1378/9, *1382/3*, *1390/1*,

1391/2, *1396/7*, *1401/2*, *1411/12–1412/13*, *1413/14*, *1414/15*, *1464/5*.

Three weekly court, but no rolls for complete year. Assize of ale at first court after Michaelmas, but mainly tenurial regulation with a little litigation. Rental, early 14th c.

One of two manors in parish (*FA* vi, p. 24).

CONISBOROUGH

[Soke of Conisborough]   DAD/YAS

1275/6, 1310/11, *1314/15*, *1317/18–1318/19*, *1320/1*, 1323/4–1324/5, *1325/6*, *1328/9*, 1334/5, *1339/40–1340/41*, *1344/5–1345/6*, 1347/8–1349/50, *1361/2*, 1363/4–1364/5, *1368/9*, *1380/1*, 1383/4, 1399/1400, *1401/2–1402/3*, *1408/9*, *1411/12*, *1428/9*, *1432/3*, *1440/1*, 1452/3, *1453/4–1463/4*, *1465/6*, *1467/8–1471/2*, *1473/4–1483/4*, *1485/6–1491/2*, *1493/4–1504/5* etc.

Presentments at two tourns from 15 vills of the soke in the early 14th c., and from Conisborough, Braithwell, Dalton, and Clayton at 16 courts p.a. Tenurial regulation, demesne offences, civil and criminal jurisdiction; length of court record very variable. Yearly rolls, 8–10 mm in early 14th c., 6–8 mm after Black Death, 2–5 mm in 15th c. Most rolls appear complete.

Account: 1265/6, 1384/5 (SCL).

Rental: 1441.

HATFIELD,
DOWSTHORP,
FISHLAKE
STAINFORTH,
THORN

[Hatfield Chace]   LCL(AD)

1324–7, *1328–30*, *1332–3*, *1334–8*, 1338–40, *1342–5*, *1346*, *1347–8*, 1348–9, *1349–53*, *1354–5*, *1357–60*, *1377–8*, *1379–81*, 1382–9, 1399–1400, *1401–2*,

1404–5, *1407–9*, *1414–15*, *1418–19*, *1420–1*, *1422–24*, 1424–5, *1425–33*, *1434–6*, *1437–42*, *1443–4*, *1445–72*, *1473–84*, *1485–8*, *1489–1500 etc.* Two sheriff's tourns and 11–15 courts on 7–15 mm p.a. before Black Death. Much litigation, property transfer, communal regulation; licences to marry and to inherit. Account rolls: 1270–1; 1300–1350: 2; 1400–1500: 11 (PRO). Apparently sole manorial jurisdiction except in Thorne and Stainforth which each had one other manor in Middle Ages. (Hatfield Chace covered 70,000 acres approx.), (Hunter i, pp. 183–4).

METHLEY AND HOUGHTON [Pontefract Hospital Manor]   LCL(AD) 1339–41, 1346–9, *1350–3*, *1354–6*, *1357–8*, *1361*, *1363–73*, 1373–5, *1375–86*, *1388–90*, *1391–3*, *1394–1401*, *1402–3*, *1404–10*. Michaelmas great court (assize of ale and nuisance) and 11–13 courts on 4–6 mm p.a. before Black Death; great court and 6–8 courts p.a. in later fourteenth century. Much litigation. Until 1410 courts held jointly and/or separately for Methley and Glass Houghton in Castleford. Methley account rolls: 1373–1400: 7. One of two manors in Methley. In 1410 the interests of Pontefract Hospital in Methley sold to Sir John Waterton (Thoresby Soc. Vol. 35, p. 15). Later court rolls for Methley only cover *1410–17*, *1419–21*, *1422–5*, *1426–9*, *1431–2*, *1433–42*, *1446–8*, *1461–82*, *1495–1500*.

ROCKLEY   PRO 1335/6, 1340/1, 1342/3–1346/7, 1357/8–1358/9, 1361/2, 1366/7, 1368/9–1369/70, 1371/2–1373/4, 1375/6, 1378/9–1380/1. Great court and 1–3 courts on 1–2 mm. After Black Death enrolled with courts for Stainborough. Inheritance, land transfers, demesne trespass, litigation. Accounts: 1340–60: 3. Rental 1345/6. Numbers of manors in parish not easily ascertainable.

SCALBY [Scalby]   PRO (DL 30) *1319/20*, 1338/9, 1343/4, 1346/7, 1352/3, 1354/5, *1359/60*, *1360/1*, *1361/2*, 1363/4, 1369/70, 1373/4, *1377/8*, *1379/80–1383/4*, *1390/1*, *1391/2*, *1393/4*, *1394/5*, *1397/8*, *1398/9*, *1399/1400–1401/2*, *1409/10–1410/11*, *1417/18–1418/19*, *1422/3*, *1423/4*, *1431/2*, *1432/3–1433/4*, *1435/6*, *1441/2*, *1442/3*, *1443/4*, *1448/9–1450/1*, *1458/9*, *1464/5*, *1465/6*, *1469/70*, *1470/1*, *1480/1–1482/3*, *1487/8–1489/90*, *1492/3–1493/4 etc.* Condition poor, usually one membrane surviving out of 2–3 p.a. Account (Keeper) 1324/5. One of six manors in parish of Scalby, which contained six townships. (*VCH Yorkshire North Riding* ii, pp. 476–81).

SELBY [Selby]   HUL/WDA 1321/2, 1324/5–1325/6, 1328/9–1331/2, 1336/7–1347/8, 1349/50, 1358/9–1367/8, *1377–8*, 1380–1, 1383, *1384–5*, 1388–90, *1391*, *1393–1400*, *1402–3*, *1415–16*, *1418–19*, *1422–4*, *1434*, 1447–8, *1464–5*, *1467–8*, *1471–85*, *1487–1500 etc.* For many years before 1364 only the membrane containing the record of Lammas great court (VFP from 1383) survives, with records of suits from Selby Abbey tenants.

A court was held weekly or fortnightly for the four 'vills' of Selby (St Martin, Goulthorp, Ousegate and Mickelgate). Litigation the predominant business, but assizes of bread and ale, market business, nuisance, also dealt with. Few complete years survive, but for 1328/9, 43 courts from Martinmas to Michaelmas on 4 mm, 1366/7, 39 courts on 8 mm.

Selby Waterhouses was a court for bond tenants; a roll of 5 mm containing records of 1–6 courts p.a. for 14 years between 1323 and 1374, is in HUL. Sole manor in Selby (*FA* vi, p. 189); suits from a number of Yorkshire manors.

SNAITH [Pollington]   LCL(AD)
1333/4–1345/6, 1347/8–1356/7, 1358/9, 1359/60, 1362/3, 1363/4, 1365/6–1376/7, 1380/1, 1385/6–1397/8, *1398/9–1402/3, 1405/6, 1411/12–1412/13, 1414/15, 1415/16, 1442/3, 1447/8–1451/2, 1457/8–1465/6, 1473/4–1494/5, 1497/8, 1499/1500, 1501/2.*

Courts vary from 1 to 5 p.a. on 1–2 mm before Black Death, rarely more than 2 courts p.a. later. Largely tenurial regulation.
(Accounts in PRO are for Pollington only, possibly not this manor).
Rental *c.*1345.
Presumably sole manorial court for Pollington, Balne, Cowick, Gowdall, Heck, Hensall, Snaith and Whitley (*FA* vi, p. 202).

THORNER [Thorner]   LCL(AD)
1344/5, 1349/50, 1350/1, 1352/3, *1353/4–1356/7, 1364/5–1392/3,*

1414–16, 1422–6, 1439–45, 1448–51, 1460–7, 1470–2, 1490, 1492–4, 1499 etc.

1–4 courts on 1 m p.a. Tenurial regulation, demesne trespass, assize of ale, some litigation.
Court rolls ill kept but quite lengthy. Membranes for reign of Edward III are filed in considerable confusion.
Sole manor (*FA* vi, p. 202).

WAKEFIELD   YAS/BL/
[Wakefield]   SCL/LUL
1275, 1277, 1281/2, *1284–6, 1296–8, 1306–9, 1311–13, 1314–15,* 1316/17, *1322–3, 1324–39,* 1339–40, *1340–6,* 1347–50, *1350–64, 1365–6, 1370–1, 1372–4, 1378–80,* 1380–1, *1382–5, 1387–8, 1389–90,* 1391–2, *1393–5, 1399–1400, 1402–6, 1407–8, 1410–11, 1415–16, 1421–2, 1425–6, 1430–1, 1433–6, 1438–48, 1449–51, 1452–3, 1454–60, 1461–3, 1464–82, 1483–90, 1491–3, 1494–1500.*

Two tourns and 16–17 courts p.a. at Wakefield, where presentments made by most townships; 2 tourns held also for Halifax, Rastrick or Brighouse and Kirkburton. Up to 26 mm p.a. in mid century, 12–14 mm at end of 14th century.
Accounts: 1280–1; 1300–50: 2; 1350–1400: 1; 1400–1500: 7.
Manor extended into 53 townships in bailiwicks of Brighouse, Halifax, Kirkburton and Wakefield.
See Whittaker, *Loidis and Elmet*, pp. 278–81, for manors in area covered by manor of Wakefield. See also court roll volumes published by YAS.

Bibliography

Printed Sources

Abstracts of Inquisitiones Post Mortem for Gloucestershire, 1236–1358, ed. S. J. Madge and E. A. Fry (pts. iv–v, British Rec. Soc. 30, 40, 1903–10).

Abstracts of Wiltshire Inquisitiones Post Mortem, 1242–1326, ed. E. A. Fry (British Rec. Soc. 37, 1908).

Abstracts of Wiltshire Inquisitiones Post Mortem, 1327–77, ed. E. Stokes (British Rec. Soc. 48, 1914).

The Accounts of the Fabric of Exeter Cathedral, 1279–1353, pt. i, *1279–1326*, ed. A. M. Erskine (Devon and Cornwall Rec. Soc. NS 24, 1981).

'Alrewas Court Rolls, 1259–61', *Staffordshire Historical Collection*, ed. W. N. Landor, NS (1907), 258–93.

Anglo-Norman Political Songs, ed. I. S. T. Aspin (Oxford, 1953).

Bishop Hatfield's Survey, ed. W. Greenwell (Surtees Soc. 32, 1857).

Boldon Book, ed. D. Austin (Chichester, 1982).

The Book of Fees (3 vols.; London, 1921–3).

Bracton, Henry de, De Legibus et Consuetudinibus Angliae, ed. G. E. Woodbine, tr. S. E. Thorne (4 vols.; Cambridge, Mass., 1968–77).

Britton: An English Translation and Notes, ed. S. E. Baldwin, tr. F. M. Nichols (Washington, DC, 1901).

Calendar of Chancery Rolls, Various 1277–1326 (London, 1912).

Calendar of Charter Rolls: Preserved in the Public Record Office (6 vols.; 1903–27).

Calendar of Entries in Papal Registers Relating to Great Britain and Ireland: Papal Letters, ed. W. H. Bliss (14 vols.; London, 1893–1960).

Calendar of Entries in the Papal Registers Relating to Great Britain and Ireland: Petitions to the Pope, ed. W. H. Bliss (London, 1896).

Calendar of Inquisitions Post Mortem and other Analogous Documents Preserved in the Public Record Office (1904–).

Calendar of Patent Rolls Preserved in the Public Record Office (1891–).

Calendar of the Public Records Relating to Pembrokeshire, ed. H. Owen (3 vols.; Cymmrodorion Rec. Ser., 1911–18).

Calendar of the Register of Henry Wakefield, Bishop of Worcester, 1375–95, ed. W. P. Marett (Worcs. Hist. Soc., 1972).

The Caption of Seisin of the Duchy of Cornwall, 1377, ed. P. L. Hull (Devon and Cornwall Rec. Soc. NS 17, 1971).

Cartae et alia munimenta quae ad Dominium de Glamorgancia pertinent, ed. G. T. Clark (6 vols.; Cardiff, 1910).

Carte Nativorum: A Peterborough Abbey Cartulary of the Fourteenth Century, ed. C. N. L. Brooke and M. M. Postan (Northants Rec. Soc. 20, 1960).

Cartularium Monasterii de Rameseia, ed. W. H. Hart and P. A. Lyons (3 vols.; Rolls ser. 79a–c, 1884–93).

The Cartulary of Cirencester Abbey, ed. C. D. Ross and M. Devine (3 vols.; London and Oxford, 1964–77).

The Cartulary of God's House, Southampton, ed. J. M. Kaye (2 vols.; S'hants Rec. Soc. 19–20, 1976).

The Cartulary of the Monastery of St Frideswide at Oxford, ed. S. R. Wigram (2 vols.; Oxford Hist. Soc., 1895–6).

The Cartulary of the Priory of St Denys Near Southampton, ed. E. O. Blake (2 vols.; S'hant. Rec. Soc. 24–5, 1981).

Charters and Custumals of the Abbey of Holy Trinity Caen, ed. M. Chibnall (British Academy, Records of Social and Economic History, NS 5, London, 1982).

Chertsey Abbey Court Rolls Abstract, ed. E. Toms (Surrey Rec. Soc. nos. 38 and 48, 21, 1937–54).

Chronicon Petroburgense, ed. T. Stapledon (Camden Soc. 47, 1849).

Chroniques de London, ed. G. J. Aungier (Camden Soc. 28, 1844).

The Court Baron: Precedents of Pleading in Manorial and Other Local Courts, ed. F. W. Maitland and W. P. Baildon (Selden Soc. 4, 1891).

Court Rolls of the Abbey of Ramsey and of the Honor of Clare, ed. W. O. Ault (New Haven, 1928).

The Court Rolls of the Lordship of Ruthin or Dyffryn-Clwyd of the Reign of King Edward the First, ed. R. A. Roberts (Cymmrodorion Rec. Ser., 1893).

Court Rolls of the Manor of Hales, 1270–1307, ed. J. Amphlett, S. G. Hamilton, and R. A. Wilson (3 vols.; Worcs. Hist. Soc., 1910–33).

Court Rolls of Ramsey, Hepmangrove and Bury, ed. E. B. Dewindt (Toronto, 1990).

Court Rolls of the Wiltshire Manors of Adam de Stratton, ed. R. B. Pugh (Wilts. Rec. Soc. 24, 1970).

Court Rolls of Tooting Bec Manor, ed. G. L. Gomme (London, 1909).

Curia Regis Rolls (1922–   ).

Customals of the Sussex Manor of the Archbishop of Canterbury, ed. B. C. Redwood and A. E. Wilson (Sussex Rec. Soc. 57, 1958).

Custumal (1391) and Bye-Laws (1386–1540) of the Manor of Islip, ed. And tr. B. F. Harvey (Oxfordshire Rec. Soc. 40, 1959).

Custumals of the Sussex Manors of the Archbishop of Canterbury, ed. B. C. Redwood and A. E. Wilson (Sussex Rec. Soc. 57, 1958).

Dan Michel, Ayenbite of Inwyt or Remorse of Conscience (in the Kentish Dialect, 1340 AD), ed. R. Morris (EETS 23, 1866).

Dan Michael, Ayenbite of Inwyt, 197; Vices and Virtues being A Soul's Confessions of its Sins, with Reason's Description of the Virtues, ed. F. Holthausen (EETS 89, 1967).

A Descriptive Catalogue of Ancient Deeds in the Public Record Office (HMSO 6 vols.; 1890–1915).

De Speculo Regis Edwardi Tertii, ed. J. Moisant (Paris, 1891).

Dives and Pauper, ed. P. Heath Barnum (EETS 280, 1980).

Documents Illustrating the Rule of Walter de Wenlock, Abbot of Westminster, 1283–1307, ed. B. F. Harvey (Camden Soc. 4th ser. 2, 1965).

The Domesday of St Paul's, ed. W. H. Hale (Camden Soc. 69, 1858).

'The Earliest Surviving Court Roll of the Manor of Pachenesham', ed. J. H. Harvey, *Proc. Leatherhead and District Local Hist. Soc.* ii (1957–66), 170–6.

Early Huntingdonshire Lay Subsidy Rolls, ed. J. A. Raftis and M. P. Hogan (Toronto, 1976).

'The Early Manorial Records of Leatherhead', ed. W. J. Blair, *Proc. Leatherhead and District Local Hist. Soc.* iii–iv (5 pts., 1967–86).

The Early Rolls of Merton College, Oxford, ed. J. R. L. Highfield (Oxford Hist. Soc. NS 18, 1964).

Elton Manorial Records, 1279–1351, ed. S. C. Radcliff (Roxburghe Club, Cambridge, 1946).

English Historical Documents, ed. D. C. Douglas and G. W. Greenaway, ii (London, 1953).

The Estate Book of Henry de Bray of Harleston, co. Northants (c.1289–1340), ed. D. Willis (Royal Hist. Soc., Camden 3rd ser. 27, 1916).

Feudal Aids (6 vols.; London, 1899–1920).

Five Court Rolls of Great Cressingham, 1328–1584, ed. H. W. Chandler (London, 1885).

The Fifty Earliest English Wills in the Court of Probate, London, ed. F. J. Furnivall (EETS 78, 1882).

Fleta, ed. H. G. Richardson and G. O. Sayles (3 vols.; Selden Soc. 72, 89, 99, 1955–84).

Die Gesetze der Angelsächen, ed. F. Liebermann (3 vols.; Halle, 1903–16).

'Glanville, Ranulf de', *Tractatus de Legibus et Consuetudines Regni Angli qui Glanvilla vocatur*, ed. G. D. G. Hall (Edinburgh, 1965).

Gloucestershire Subsidy Roll, 1 Edward III. A.D. 1327, ed. Sir T. Phillipps (Middle Hill Press, n.d.).

The Grey of Ruthin Valor. The Valor of the English Lands of Edmund Grey, Earl of Kent, drawn up from the Ministers' Accounts of 1467–8, ed. R. I. Jack (Sydney, 1965).

Hengham, Ralph de, summae, ed. W. H. Dunham (Cambridge, 1932).

Historia et Cartularium Monasterii Sancti Petri Gloucestriae, ed. W. H. Hart (3 vols.; Rolls ser. 33a–c, 1863–7).

The Itinerary of John Leland In or About the Years 1535–1543, ed. L. Toulmin Smith (5 vols.; new edn., London, 1964).

Jacob's Well: An English Treatise on the Cleansing of Man's Conscience, ed. A. Brandeis (EETS 115, 1900).

John Myrc's Instructions for Parish Priests, ed. E. Peacock (EETS 32, 1868).

Knighton, Henry, *Chronicon Henrici Knighton*, ed. J. R. Lumby (2 vols.; Rolls ser. 52a–b, 1889–95).

Langland, William, Piers the Plowman, ed. W. W. Skeat (Oxford, 1886; reissued 1954).

The Lay Subsidy of 1334, ed. R. E. Glassock (London, 1975).

Leet Jurisdiction in the City of Norwich during the Thirteenth and Fourteenth Centuries, ed. W. Hudson (Selden Soc. 5, 1892).

Legal and Manorial Formularies edited from Originals at the British Museum and the Public Record Office in Memory of J. P. Gilson (Oxford, 1933).

Leges Henrici Primi, ed. L. J. Downer (Oxford, 1973).

Le Neve, J. *Fasti Ecclesiae Anglicanae 1300–1541* (revised edn. comp. H. P. F. King, J. M. Horn, and B. Jones, 12 vols.; London, 1962–7).

The Liber Gersumarum of Ramsey Abbey, ed. E. B. Dewindt (Toronto, 1976).

List and Index of Court Rolls Preserved in the Public Record Office, pt. I (London, 1894).

Little Red Book of Bristol, ed. F. B. Bickley, ii (2 vols.; Bristol, 1900).

Lordship and Landscape in Norfolk, 1250–1350: The Early Records of Holkham, ed. W. O. Hassall and J. Beauroy (Records of Social and Economic History, NS 20, Oxford, 1993).

Manorial Records of Cuxham, Oxfordshire circa 1200–1359, ed. P. D. A. Harvey (Oxfordshire Rec. Soc. 50 and Hist. Manuscripts Comm. JP 23, 1976).

'Medieval Deeds of the Leatherhead District', ed. W. J. Blair, 8 pts. in *Proc. Leatherhead and District Local History Soc.* iv (1976–86), 30–8, 58–62, 86–96, 118–25, 150–7, 172–81, 203–19, 268–74.

Memoirs Illustrative of the History and Antiquities of Wiltshire and the City of Salisbury (Arch. Inst., London, 1851).

Memoriall of Merton College, G. C. Brodick (Oxford Hist. Soc. 4, 1885).

Merton Muniments, ed. P. S. Allen and H. W. Garrod (Oxford Hist. Soc. 76, 1928).

Middle English Sermons., ed. W. O. Ross (EETS 209, 1940).

Ministers' Accounts of the Manor of Petworth 1347–53, ed. L. F. Salzman (Sussex Rec. Soc. 55, Lewes, 1955).

Ministers' Accounts of the Warwickshire Estates of the Duke of Clarence 1479–80, R. H. Hilton (Dugdale Soc. 21, 1952).

A Northamptonshire Miscellany, ed. E. King (Northants Rec. Soc. 33, 1983).

The Pipe Roll of the Bishopric of Winchester, 1208–9, ed. H. Hall (London, 1903).

The Pipe Roll of the Bishopric of Winchester 1210–11, ed. N. R. Holt (Manchester, 1964).

Pleas of the Crown for the County of Gloucester before the Justices Itinerant, 1221, ed. F. W. Maitland (London, 1884).

Promptorium Parvulorum sive Clericorum, Lexicon Anglo-Latinum Princeps, ed. A. Way (3 vols.; Camden Soc. 25, 54, 89, 1843–65).

The Red Book of Worcester, ed. M. Hollings (Worcester Hist. Soc., 4 parts, 1934–50).

The Register of Henry Chichele Archbishop of Canterbury, 1414–43, ed. E. F. Jacob (Canterbury and York Soc., 1945).

Registrum sive Liber Irrotularius et Consuetudinarius Prioratus Beatae Mariae Wigorniensis, ed. W. H. Hale (Camden Soc. 91, 1865).

Rentalia et Custumaria Michaelis de Ambresbury, 1235–52 et Rogeri de Ford, 1252–61, ed. C. J. Elton (Somerset Rec. Soc. 5, 1891).

Roll of the Household Expenses of Richard de Swinfield, Bishop of Hereford, 1285–90, ed. J. Webb (2 vols.; Camden Soc. 59, 62, 1854–5).

Rotuli Hundredorum: Temp. Hen. III et Edw. I (2 vols.; Record Comm., 1812–18).

Royal Justice and the English Countryside: The Huntingdonshire Eyre of 1286, the Ramsey Banlieu Court of 1287, and the Assizes of 1287–8, ed. A. R. and E. B. Dewindt (2 vols.; Toronto, 1981).

Select Cases on Defamation to 1600, ed. R. H. Helmholz (Selden Soc. 101, 1985).

Select Cases from the Ecclesiastical Courts of the Province of Canterbury, c.1200–1301, ed. N. Adams and C. Donahue jr. (Selden Soc. 95, 1981).

Select Cases at King's Bench in the Reign of Edward I, ed. G. O. Sayles (3 vols.; Selden Soc. 55, 57, 58; 1936–9).

Select Cases of Procedure Without Writ under Henry III, ed. H. G. Richardson and G. O. Sayles (Selden Soc. 60, 1941).

Select Charters, ed. W. Stubbs (9th edn., rev. H. W. C. Davis; Oxford, 1913).

Select Documents of the English Lands of the Abbey of Bec, ed. M. Chibnall (Camden Soc. 3rd ser. 73, 1951).

Select Pleas in Manorial and Other Seignorial Courts, ed. and tr. F. W. Maitland (Selden Soc. 2, 1889).

The Sermons of Thomas Brinton, Bishop of Rochester (1373–89), ed. Sister Mary Aquinas Devlin (2 vols.; Camden Soc. 3rd ser. 85, 1954).

Smyth, J., *The Berkeley Manuscripts: The Lives of the Berkeleys*, ed. Sir J. Maclean (3 vols.; Bristol and Gloucs. Arch. Soc., 1883–5).

Somerset Pleas, ed. C. E. H. C. Healey (Somerset Rec. Soc. 11, 1897).

The Southampton Terrier of 1454, ed. L. A. Burgess (S'ants. Rec. Ser. 15, 1976).

Statutes of the Realm, ed. A. Luders *et al.* (11 vols.; Record Comm., 1810–28).

A Suffolk Hundred in the Year 1283, ed. E. Powell (Cambridge, 1910).

The 1235 Surrey Eyre, ed. C. A. F. Meekings (prepared for press, D. Crook) (2 vols.; Surrey Rec. Soc., 31–2, 1979–83).

Survey of the Lands of William, First Earl of Pembroke, ed. C. R. Straton (2 vols.; Oxford, 1909).

Swinburne, H., *A Brief Treatise of Testaments and Last Wills* (London, 1590).

Tamworth Borough Record, ed. H. Wood (Tamworth, 1952).

The Taxation of 1297, ed. A. T. Gaydon (Beds. Hist. Rec. Soc. 39, 1959).

Testamenta Eboracensia, ed. J. Raine (Surtees Soc. 30, 1885).

Testamenta Vetusta, ed. N. H. Nicholas (2 vols.; London, 1826).

Thirteen Custumals of the Sussex Manors of the Bishop of Chichester, ed. W. D. Peckham (Sussex Rec. Soc. 31, 1925).

Thomae de Chobham Summa Confessorum, ed. F. Broomfield (Analecta Medievalia Namurcensia, 25, Louvain and Paris, 1968).

Two Registers Formerly Belonging to the Family of Beauchamp of Hatch, ed. Sir H. C. Maxwell Lyte (Somerset Rec. Soc. 35, 1920).

Walter of Henley and Other Treatises on Estate Management and Accounting, ed. D. Oschinsky (Oxford, 1971).

Walter of Henley's Husbandry, ed. E. Lamond (Royal Hist. Soc., 1890).

Wills and Administrations from the Knaresborough Court Rolls, ed. F. Collins (Surtees Soc., 104, 1900).

Yorkshire Lay Subsidy Being a Ninth Collected in 25 Edward I (1297), ed. W. Brown (Yorks. Arch. Soc., Rec. Ser. 16, 1894).

Secondary Sources

ALLEN, R. C., 'The Two English Agricultural Revolutions, 1450–1850', in Campbell and Overton (eds.), *Land, Labour and Livestock*, 236–54.

ALTSCHUL, M., *A Baronial Family in Medieval England: The Clares, 1217–1314* (Baltimore, Md., 1965).

AMADO, C. and LOBRICHON, G. (eds.), *Mélanges Georges Duby* (Paris, 1995).

ANDERSON, M., *Approaches to the History of the Western Family* (London, 1981).

ARCHER, J. E., ' "A Fiendish Outrage"? A Study of Animal Maiming in East Anglia: 1830–1870', *AgHR* 33 (1985), 147–57.

ARENSBERG, C., *The Irish Countryman* (New York, 1937).

—— and KIMBALL, S., *Family and Community in Ireland* (Cambridge, Mass., 1940).

ARIÈS, P., *Centuries of Childhood: A Social History of the Family*, tr. R. Baldick (Harmondsworth, 1973).

—— *The Hour of Our Death*, tr. H. Weaver (New York, 1981).

ARNOLD, M. S., GREEN, T. A., SCULLY, S. A., and WHITE, S. D. (eds.), *On the Laws and Customs of England: Essays in Honor of S. E. Thorne* (Chapel Hill, NC, 1980).

ASHLEY, W. J., *An Introduction to English Economic History and Theory* (London, 1888; reissued New York, 1966).

ASTILL, G., 'Rural Settlement: The Toft and Croft', in Astill and Grant (eds.), *The Countryside of Medieval England*, 36–61.

—— and GRANT, A. (eds.), *The Countryside of Medieval England* (Oxford, 1988).

ASTON, T. H., 'The External Administration and Resources of Merton College to *circa* 1348', in Catto and Evans (eds.), *Early Oxford Schools*, 311–68.

—— and FAITH, R. J., 'The Endowments of the University and Colleges to *circa* 1348', in Catto and Evans (eds.), *Early Oxford Schools*, 265–309.

—— and PHILPIN, C. H. E. (eds.), *The Brenner Debate: Agrarian Class Structure and Economic Development in Pre-Industrial Europe* (Cambridge, 1985).

—— COSS, R. R., DYER, C., and THIRSK, J. (eds.), *Social Relations and Ideas: Essays in Honour of R. H. Hilton* (Cambridge, 1983).

AUBREY, J., *Collections for the Natural and Topographical History of Wiltshire* (2 vols.; Devizes, 1862).

AULT, W. O., *Private Jurisdiction in England* (New Haven, Conn., 1923).

AULT, W. O., 'Village Assemblies in Medieval England', in *Album Helen Maud Cam*, Studies Presented to the International Commission for the History of Representative and Parliamentary Institutions, no. 23 (Louvain, 1960).

—— 'By-Laws of Gleaning and the Problem of Harvest', *EcHR*. 2nd ser. 14 (1961), 210–17.

—— *Open Field Husbandry and the Village Community: A Study of Agrarian By-Laws in Medieval England* (Transactions of the American Philosophical Soc. NS 55, Philadelphia, 1965).

—— 'Manor Court and Parish Church in Fifteenth-Century England', *Speculum*, 72 (1967), 53–67.

—— 'The Earliest Rolls of Manor Courts in England', *Studia Gratiana*, 15 (1972), 511–18.

—— *Open-Field Farming in Medieval England* (London, 1972).

BAKER, A. R. H., 'Open Fields and Partible Inheritance on a Kent Manor', *EcHR* 2nd ser. 17 (1964), 1–23.

—— 'Howard Levi Gray and *English Field Systems*: An Evaluation', *Agricultural History*, 30 (1965), 86–91.

—— and BUTLIN, R. A. (eds.), *Studies of Field Systems in the British Isles* (Cambridge, 1973).

—— and GREGORY, D. (eds.), *Explorations in Historical Geography: Interpretative Essays* (Cambridge, 1984).

BAKER, J. H., *An Introduction to English Legal History* (3rd edn., London, 1990).

BARG, M. A., 'The Villeins of the "Ancient Demesne"', in de Rosa (ed.), *Studi in memoria di Federigo Melis*, i. 213–37.

BARTH, F., *Models of Social Organization* (London, 1966).

BECKERMAN, J. S., 'Customary Law in English Manorial Courts in the Thirteenth and Fourteenth Centuries', Ph.D. thesis (University of London, 1972).

—— 'The Forty-Shilling Jurisdictional Limit in Medieval English Personal Actions', in Jenkins (ed.), *Legal History Studies* (1972), 110–17.

—— 'The Articles of Presentment of a Court Leet and Court Baron in English, *c*.1400', *BIHR* 47 (1974), 230–4.

—— 'Adding Insult to *Iniuria*: Affronts to Honor and the Origins of Trespass', in Arnold *et al.* (eds.), *On the Laws and Customs of England*, 159–81.

—— 'Procedural Innovation and Institutional Change in Medieval English Manorial Courts', *LHR* 10 (1992), 197–252.

BENNETT, H. S., *Life on the English Manor* (Cambridge, 1937; reissued, 1971).

BENNETT, J. M., 'Medieval Peasant Marriage: An Examination of Marriage Licence Fines in the *Liber Gersumazum*', in J. A. Raftis, *Pathways to Medieval Peasants* (Toronto, 1981).

—— 'Gender, Family and Community: A Comparative Study of the English Peasantry, 1287–1349', Ph.D. thesis (University of Toronto, 1982).

—— 'Spouses, Siblings and Surnames: Reconstructing Families from Medieval Village Court Rolls', *JBS* 23 (1983), 24–46.

—— 'The Tie that Binds: Peasant Marriages and Families in Late Medieval England', *Journal of Interdisciplinary History*, 15 (1984), 111–29.

—— *Women in the Medieval English Countryside: Gender and Household in Brigstock Before the Plague* (Oxford, 1987).

—— 'Widows in the Medieval Countryside' in Mirrer (ed.), *Upon My Husband's Death*, 69–114.

—— 'The Village Ale-Wife, Women, and Brewing in Fourteenth-Century England', in Hanawalt (ed.), *Women and Work in Pre-industrial Europe*, 20–36.

BENNETT, J. W., 'The Medieval Loveday', *Speculum*, 33 (1958), 35–70.

BERESFORD, M. W., *The Lost Villages of England* (London, 1954).

—— *Poll Taxes and Lay, Subsidies* (Canterbury, 1963).

—— and FINBERG, H. P. R. (eds.), *Medieval English Boroughs: A Handlist* (Newton Abbot, 1973).

BERKNER, L. K., 'The Stem Family and the Developmental Cycle of the Peasant Household', *AHR* 77 (1972), 398–418.

BIANCALANA, J., 'For Want of Justice: Legal Reforms of Henry II'. *Columbia Law Review*, 88 (1988), 433–536.

BIRRELL, J. R., 'Peasant Craftsmen in the Medieval Forest', *AgHR* 17 (1969), 91–107.

BLAIR, W. J., 'A Medieval Grave-Slab in Great Bookham Churchyard', *Proc. Leatherhead and District Local Hist. Soc.* iii (1967–76), 141–3.

—— *Discovering Early Leatherhead* (Leatherhead and District Local Hist. Soc. occasional paper 1, 1975).

—— 'A Military Holding in Twelfth Century Leatherhead', *Proc. Leatherhead and District Local Hist. Soc.* iv. (1977), 3–12.

—— 'The Early Middle Ages, *c.*600–1250' in Vardey (ed.), *History of Leatherhead*, 27–39.

—— 'The Late Middle Ages 1250–1558' in Vardey (ed.), *History of Leatherhead*, 41–67 .

—— *Early Medieval Surrey: Landholding, Church and Settlement before 1300* (Stroud, 1991).

BLANCHARD, I., 'Industrial Employment and the Rural Land Market, 1380–1520', in Smith (ed.), *Land, Kinship and Life-Cycle*, 227–75.

BLOCH, M., *Slavery and Serfdom in the Middle Ages*, tr. W. R. Beer (Berkeley, Los Angeles, London, 1975).

—— 'Personal Liberty and Servitude in the Middle Ages, particularly in France: Contribution to a Class Study', in Bloch, *Slavery and Serfdom*, 33–92.

BLOMEFIELD, F., *An Essay towards a Topographical History of the County of Norfolk* (11 vols.; London, 1805–10).

BLOMFIELD, J. C., *History of Bicester, its Town and Priory* (Bicester, 1884).

BONFIELD, L., 'The Nature of Customary Law in the Manorial Courts of Medieval England', *Comparative Studies in Society and History*, 31 (1989), 514–34.

BONFIELD, L., and POOS, L. R., 'The Development of the Deathbed Transfer in Medieval English Manor Courts', *Cambridge Law Journal*, 47 (1988), 403–27.
—— SMITH, R. M., and WRIGHTSON, K. (eds.), *The World We Have Gained: Histories of Population and Social Structure* (Oxford, 1986).
BONNASSIE, P., *From Slavery to Feudalism in South-West Europe*, tr. J. Birrell (Cambridge, 1991).
BOSSY, J. (ed.), *Disputes and Settlements: Law and Human Relations in the West* (Cambridge, 1986).
BOURDE DE LA ROGERIE, H., 'Les Fondations de villes et de bourgs en Bretagne du XIIᵉ au XIIIᵉ siècle', *Mémoires de la Société d'Histoire et d'Archéologie de Bretagne*, 11 (1928), 69–106.
BOURDIEU, P., 'Les strategies matrimoniales dans le système de reproduction', *Annales ESC* 27 (1972), 1105–25.
—— *Outline of a Theory of Practice* (Cambridge, 1977).
BOUSSARD, J., 'Hypothèses sur la formation des bourgs et des communes en Normandie', *Annales de Normandie*, 8 (1958), 128–46.
BOYLE, L. E., 'The *Oculus Sacerdotis* and Some Other Works of William of Pagula', *TRHS* 5th ser. 5 (1955), 81–110.
BRAND, J., *Observances on Popular Antiquities* (London, 1877).
BRAND, P., *The Making of the Common Law* (London, 1992).
—— '"Multis Vigillis Excogitatem et Inventam": Henry II and the Creation of the English Common Law', Haskins Society Law Journal, 2 (1990), 197–222 repr. in Brand, *Making of the Common Law*, 77–102.
—— *The Origins of the English Legal Profession* (Oxford, 1992).
—— and HYAMS, P. R., 'Seigneurial Control of Women's Marriage', *P&P* 99 (1983), 122–33.
BRANDON, P. F., 'New Settlement: South-Eastern England', in Hallam (ed.), *Agrarian History of England and Wales*, ii. 174–88.
BREEN, R., 'Farm Servanthood in Ireland', *EcHR* 2nd ser. 26 (1983), 87–102.
BRENNER, R., 'Agrarian Class Structure and Economic Development in Pre-Industrial Europe', in Aston and Philpin (eds.), *The Brenner Debate*, 10–63.
BRIDBURY, A. R., 'The Black Death', *EcHR* 2nd ser. 26 (1973), 377–92.
BRIDGES, J., *History and Antiquities of the County of Northampton* (2 vols., London, 1740).
BRITNELL, R. H., 'The Making of Witham', *Historical* Studies, 1 (1962), 3–21.
—— 'English Markets and Royal Administration Before 1200', *EcHR* 2nd ser. 31 (1978), 183–96.
—— 'King John's Early Grants of Markets and Fairs', *EHR* 94 (1979), 90–6.
—— 'Essex Markets before 1350', *Essex Archaeology and History*, 13 (1981), 15–21.
—— 'The Proliferation of Markets in England, 1200–1349', *EcHR* 2nd ser. 34 (1981), 222–35.
—— *The Commercialisation of English Society 1000–1500* (Cambridge, 1993).

—— 'Commercialisation and Economic Development in England, 1000–1300', in Britnell and Campbell, *A Commercialising Economy*, 7–26.

—— and CAMPBELL, B. M. S. (eds.), *A Commercialising Economy: England, 1086– c.1300* (Manchester, 1995).

BRITTON, E., 'The Peasant Family in Fourteenth-Century England', *Peasant Studies*, 5 (1976), 2–7.

—— *The Community of the Vill: A Study in the History of the Family and Village Life in Fourteenth-Century England* (Toronto, 1977).

BROMLEY, R. J., 'Markets in Developing Countries: A Review', *Geography*, 56 (1971), 124–32.

BRUNDAGE, J., *Law, Sex and Christian Society in Medieval Europe* (Chicago, 1987).

BULLOUGH, D. A. and STOREY, R. L. (eds.), *The Study of Medieval Records: Essays in Honour of Kathleen Major* (Oxford, 1971).

BURGESS, C., ' "By Quick and by Dead": Wills and Pious Provision in Late Medieval Bristol', *EHR* 105 (1987), 837–58.

BURNS, D., *The Sheriffs of Surrey* (Chichester, 1992).

CALDWELL, C., HILL, J. A., and HULL, V. J. (eds.), *Micro-Approaches to Demographic Research* (London, 1988).

CAM, H. M., *The Hundred and the Hundred Rolls* (London, 1930).

—— 'Suitors and Scabini', *Speculum*, 10 (1935), 189–200.

—— *Law-Finders and Law-Makers in Medieval England* (London, 1962).

—— 'The Community of the Vill', in Cam, *Law-Finders and Law-Makers*, 71–84.

CAMPBELL, B. M. S., 'Field Systems on Eastern Norfolk during the Middle Ages', Ph.D. thesis (University of Cambridge, 1975).

—— 'Population Change and the Genesis of Common Fields on a Norfolk Manor', *EcHR* 2nd ser. 33 (1980), 174–92.

—— 'Population Pressure, Inheritance and the Land Market in a Fourteenth Century Peasant Community', in Smith (ed.), *Land, Kinship and Life-Cycle*, 87–134.

—— 'The Complexity of Manorial Structure in Medieval Norfolk: A Case Study', *Norfolk Archaeology*, 39 (1986), 225–61.

—— (ed.), *Before the Black Death: Studies in the 'Crisis' of the Early Fourteenth Century* (Manchester, 1991).

—— and OVERTON, M. (eds.), *Land, Labour and Livestock: Historical Studies in European Agriculture Productivity* (Manchester, 1991).

—— GALLOWAY, J. A., KEENE, D., and MURPHY, M., *A Medieval Capital and its Grain Supply: Agrarian Production and Distribution in the London Region, c.1300* (Hist. Geog. Ser. no. 30, Norwich, 1993).

CAMPBELL, J., *Essays in Anglo-Saxon History* (London, 1986).

—— 'The Significance of the Anglo-Norman State in the Administrative History of Western Europe', in Campbell, *Essays in Anglo-Saxon History*, 171–90.

CARPENTER, D. A., 'King, Magnates and Society: The Personal Rule of King Henry III, 1234–58', *Speculum*, 60 (1985), 39–70.

CARPENTER, D. A., 'English Peasants in Politics, 1258–67', *P&P* 136 (1992), 3–42.

CARR, A. D., 'The Making of the Mostyns: The Genesis of a Landed Family', *Trans. of the Hon. Soc. of Cymmrodorion* (1979), 137–57.

CARUS-WILSON, E. M., 'Evidences of Industrial Growth on Some Fifteenth-Century Manors', *EcHR* 2nd ser. 12 (1959), 190–205.

CATTO, J. I., and EVANS, T. A. R. (eds.), *The Early Oxford Schools* (History of the University of Oxford, i, Oxford, 1984).

—— *Late Medieval Oxford* (History of the University of Oxford, ii, Oxford, 1992).

CHANTER, J. F., 'The Court Rolls of the Manor of Curry Rivel in the Years of the Black Death, 1348–9', *Proc. of the Somerset Arch. And Natural Hist. Soc.* 56 (1910), 85–135.

CHARLES-EDWARDS, T. M., OWEN, M. E., and WALTERS, D. B., *Lawyers and Laymen* (Cardiff, 1986).

CHENEY, C. R., 'Rules for the Observance of Feast Days in Medieval England', *BIHR* 34 (1961), 117–47.

CHEYETT, F. L., 'Custom, Case Law and Medieval "Constitutionalism": A Re-Examination', *Political Science Quarterly*, 78 (1963), 362–90.

—— 'Suum Cuique Tribuere', *French Historical Studies*, 6 (1969), 287–99.

CLANCHY, M. T., '*Moderni* in Education and Government in England', *Speculum*, 50 (1975), 671–88.

—— *England and its Rulers* (Glasgow, 1983).

—— 'Law and Love' in Bossy (ed.), *Disputes and Settlements*, 49–68.

—— *From Memory to Written Record: England 1066–1307* (2nd edn. Oxford, 1993).

CLARK, A., 'Tithing lists from Essex', *EHR* 19 (1904), 715–19.

CLARK, C., 'Peasant Society and Land Transactions in Chesterton, Cambridgeshire, 1277–1325', D.Phil. thesis (University of Oxford, 1983).

CLARK, E., 'Debt Litigation in a Late Medieval Vill', in Raftis (ed.), *Pathways to Medieval Peasants*, 247–79.

—— 'Some Aspects of Social Security in Medieval England' (1982), *JFH* 7 (1982), 307–20.

—— 'The Custody of Children in English Manor Courts', *LHR* 3 (1985), 333–48.

—— 'The Decision to Marry in Thirteenth- and Early Fourteenth-Century Norfolk', *Medieval Studies*, 49 (1987), 496–511.

—— 'The Quest for Security in Medieval England', in Sheehan (ed.), *Aging and the Aged in Medieval Europe*, 189–200.

—— 'Social Welfare and Mutual Aid in the Medieval Countryside', *JBS* 33 (1994), 381–406.

—— 'Mothers at Risk of Poverty in the Medieval English Countryside', in Henderson and Wall (eds.), *Poor Women and Children in the European Past*, 139–59.

CLEMOES, P., and HUGHES, K. (eds.), *England Before the Conquest* (Cambridge, 1971).

COALE, A. J., and DEMENY, P., *Regional Model Life Tables and Stable Populations* (2nd edn., New York, 1983).

COATES, B. E., 'The Origins and Distribution of Markets and Fairs in Derbyshire', *Derbys. Arch. Journal*, 85 (1965), 92–111.

COCKBURN, J. S. (ed.), *Crime in England, 1550–1800* (London, 1977).

COLLINSON, J., *The History and Antiquities of the County of Somerset* (3 vols.; Bath, 1791).

CONZE, W. (ed.), *Sozialgeschichte der Familie in der Neuzeit Europas* (Stuttgart, 1976).

COOK, S., and DISKIN, M., *Markets in Oaxaca* (Austin, 1976).

COPINGER, W. A., *The Manors of Suffolk, Notes on their History and Devolution* (7 vols.; London, 1905–11).

COSS, P. R., and LLOYD, S. D. (eds.), *Thirteenth-Century England*, i (Woodbridge, 1985).

CROOK, D., 'The Later Eyres', *EHR* 97 (1982), 241–68.

CROWLEY, D. A., 'Frankpledge and Leet Jurisdiction in Later Medieval Essex', Ph.D. thesis (University of Sheffield, 1971).

—— 'The Later History of Frankpledge', *BIHR* 48 (1975), 1–15.

DAICHES, D., and THORLBY, A. (eds.), *The Medieval World* (London, 1973).

DAVENPORT, F. G., 'The Decay of Villainage in East Anglia', *TRHS* NS 14 (1900), 123–41.

—— *The Economic Development of a Norfolk Manor 1086–1565* (Cambridge, 1906).

DAVIES, R. R., *Lordship and Society in the March of Wales, 1282–1400* (Oxford, 1978).

—— 'The Administration of Law in Medieval Wales: the Role of the *Ynad Cwmwd (Judex Patrie)*, in Charles-Edward *et al.* (eds.), *Lawyers and Laymen*, 258–73.

DAWSON, J. P., *A History of Lay Judges* (Cambridge, Mass., 1960).

DE ROSA, L. (ed.), *Studi in memoria di Federigo Melis* (5 vols.; Rome, 1978).

DENHOLM-YOUNG, N., *Seignorial Administration in England* (Oxford, 1937).

—— *The Country Gentry in the Fourteenth Century with Special Reference to the Heraldic Rolls of Arms* (Oxford, 1969).

DEROUET, B., 'Une demographic sociale differentielle', *Annales ESC* 35 (1980), 3–41.

DEWINDT, A., 'Peasant Power Structures in Fourteenth-Century King's Ripton, 1280–1400', *Medieval Studies*, 38 (1976), 244–61.

—— 'A Peasant Land Market and its Participants: King's Ripton, 1280–1400', *Midland History*, 4 (1978), 142–59.

DEWINDT, E. B., *Land and People in Holywell-cum-Needingworth. Structures of Tenure and Patterns of Social Organization in an East Midlands Village 1252–1457* (Toronto, 1972).

DILKS, T. B., 'Bridgewater Castle and Demesne Towards the End of the Fourteenth Century', *Proc. Of the Somerset Arch. And Natural Hist. Soc.* 86 (1940), 85–135.

DU BOULAY, F. R. H., *The Lordship of Canterbury* (London, 1966).

DUBY, G., 'The Diffusion of Cultural Patterns in Feudal Society', *P&P* 39 (1968), 1–10.

—— *Rural Economy and Country Life in the Medieval West*, tr. C. Postan (London, 1968).

—— *The Knight, the Lady and the Priest*, tr. B. Bray (London, 1983).

DUNCUMB, J., *History and Antiquities of the County of Hereford* (3 vols.; Hereford, 1804–82)

DUKEMINIER, J., and JOHANSON, S. M., *Wills, Trusts and Estates* (3rd edn.; London, 1984)

DYER, C., 'A Redistribution of Incomes in Fifteenth-Century England?', *P&P* 39 (1968), 11–33.

—— *Lords and Peasants in a Changing Society: The Estates of the Bishopric of Worcester, 680–1540* (Cambridge, 1980).

—— 'English Diet in the Late Middle Ages', in Aston, *et al.* (eds.), *Social Relations and Ideas*, 191–216.

—— 'Changes in the Link Between Families and Land in the West Midlands in the Fourteenth and Fifteenth Centuries' in Smith (ed.), *Land Kinship and Life-Cycle*, 305–11.

—— 'The Social and Economic Background to the Rural Revolt of 1381', in Hilton and Aston (eds.), *The English Rising of 1381*, 29–42.

—— 'Les Cours manoriales', *Études Rurales*, 103–4 (1986), 19–27.

—— 'English Peasant Buildings in the Later Middle Ages', *Medieval Archaeology*, 30 (1986), 19–45.

—— 'Were Peasants Self Sufficient? English Villagers and the Market, 900–1350', in Mornet (ed.), *Campagnes médiévales*, 654–66.

—— 'The Rise and Fall of a Medieval Village: Little Aston (in Aston Blank), Gloucestershire', *Trans. Bristol and Gloucestershire Arch. Soc.* 105 (1987), 165–81.

—— 'The Rising of 1381 in Suffolk: Its Origins and Participants', *Proc. Suffolk Institute of Archaeology and History*, 36 (1988), 274–87.

—— *Standards of Living in the Later Middle Ages* (Cambridge, 1989).

—— 'The English Medieval Village Community and its Decline', *JBS* 33 (1994), 407–29.

DYMOND, D. P., *The Norfolk Landscape* (London, 1985).

—— 'Medieval and Later Markets', in Wade-Martins (ed.), *Historical Atlas of Norfolk*, 76–7.

—— and MARTIN, E. (eds.), *An Historical Atlas of Suffolk* (2nd edn.; Ipswich, 1989).

DYMOND, R., 'The Customs of the Manors of Braunton', *Trans. of the Devonshire Association*, 20 (1888), 254–303.

EHERLICH, I., and POSNER, R., 'An Economic Analysis of Legal Rulemaking', *JLS* 3 (1973), 257–76.

EMDEN, A. B., *A Biographical Register of the University of Oxford to AD 1500* (3 vols.; Oxford, 1957–9).

ENGEL, D. M., 'The Oven Bird's Song: Insiders, Outsiders and Personal Injuries in an American Community', *LHR* 18 (1984), 551–82.

EVANS, R., and FAITH, R. J., 'A Formulary of About 1300', *Bodleian Library Record*, 13 (1988–91), 324–8.

EVANS, T. A. R., 'The Number, Origins and Careers of Scholars' in Catto and Evans (eds.), *Late Medieval Oxford*, 492–3.

EVERITT, A., 'The Marketing of Agricultural Produce', in Thirsk (ed.), *Agrarian History of England and Wales*, iv. 466–592.

EYTON, R. W., *Antiquities of Shropshire* (12 vols.; London, 1853–60).

FAITH, R. J., 'The Peasant Land Market in Berkshire during the Later Middle Ages', Ph.D. thesis (University of Leicester, 1962).

—— 'Peasant Families and Inheritance Customs in Medieval England', *AgHR* 14 (1966), 77–95.

—— 'The Class Struggle in Fourteenth-Century England', in Samuel, *People's History and Socialist Theory*, 50–60.

—— 'The "Great Rumour" of 1377 and Peasant Ideology', in Hilton and Aston (eds.), *The English Rising of 1381*, 48–63.

—— 'Seigneurial Control of Women's Marriage', *P&P* 99 (1983), 133–48.

FARMER, D. L., 'Prices and Wages', in Hallam (ed.), *Agrarian History of England and Wales*, ii. 716–817.

—— 'Two Wiltshire Manors and their Markets', *AgHR* 37 (1989), 1–11.

—— 'Marketing the Produce of the Countryside, 1200–1500', in Miller (ed.), *The Agrarian History of England and Wales*, iii. 324–420.

FIELD, R. K., 'Worcestershire Peasant Building, Household Goods and Farming Equipment in the Later Middle Ages', *Medieval Archaeology*, 9 (1965), 105–45.

FINBERG, H. P. R., *Tavistock Abbey* (Cambridge, 1951).

—— 'The Genesis of the Gloucestershire Towns', in Finberg (ed.), *Gloucestershire Studies* (Leicester, 1957), 52–88.

—— (ed.), *Gloucestershire Studies* (Leicester, 1957).

FINUCANE, R. C., *Miracles and Pilgrims: Popular Beliefs in Medieval England* (London, 1977).

FLOUD, R. C. (ed.), *Essays in Quantitative Economic History* (Oxford, 1974).

FLOWER, C. T., *Introduction to the Curia Regis Rolls, 1199–1230 A. D.* (Selden Soc. 62, 1944).

FORSTER, R., and RANUM, O. (eds.), *Family and Society: Selections from the Annales* (Baltimore and London, 1976).

FOSSIER, R., *La Terre et les hommes en Picardie jusqu'à la fin du XIIIe siècle* (2 vols.; Paris, 1968).

FOSTER, C. W., and LONGLEY, T., *Lincolnshire Domesday and the Lindsey Survey* (Lincoln Rec. Soc. 19, 1924).

FOURQUIN, G., *The Anatomy of Popular Rebellion in the Middle Ages*, tr. A. Chesters (Amsterdam, 1978).

FOX, H. S. A., 'The Chronology of Enclosure and Economic Development in Medieval Devon', *EcHR* 2nd ser. 28 (1975), 181–202.

—— 'The Occupation of the Land: Devon and Cornwall', in Miller (ed.), *The Agrarian History of England and Wales*, iii. 152–74.

—— 'Servants, Cottagers and Tied Cottages during the Later Middle Ages: Towards a Regional Dimension', *Rural History*, 6 (1995), 125–54.

FRANKLIN, P., 'Thornbury in the Age of the Black Death: Peasant Society, Landholding and Agriculture in Gloucestershire, 1328–52', Ph.D. thesis (University of Birmingham, 1982).

—— 'Malaria in Medieval Gloucestershire: An Essay in Epidemiology', *Trans. of the Bristol and Gloucs. Arch. Soc.* 101 (1983), 111–22.

—— 'Peasant Widows' "Liberation" and Remarriage', *EcHR* 2nd ser. 39 (1986), 186–204.

—— 'Thornbury Woodlands and Deer Parks, I. The Earl of Gloucester's Deer Park', *Trans. Bristol and Gloucs. Arch. Soc.* 107 (1989), 149–63.

FRIEDMAN, L., 'The Law of the Living, the Law of the Dead: Property, Succession and Society', *Wisconsin Law Review*, 30 (1966), 340–78.

GALANTER, M., 'Reading the Landscape of Disputes: What We Know and Don't Know (and Think We Know) About Our Allegedly Contentious and Litigious Society', *UCLA Law Review*, 31 (1983), 4–71.

GAUTIER, E., and HENRY, L., *La Population du Crulai* (Paris, 1956).

GIBBS, V. *et al.* (eds.), *The Complete Peerage of England* (12 vols., in 13; London, 1910–59)

GILMOUR-BRYSON, A. (ed.), *Computer Applications to Historical Studies* (Kalamazoo, 1984).

GLASS, D. V., and EVERSLEY, D. E. (eds.), *Population in History: Essays in Historical Demography* (London, 1965).

GLASS, D. V., and REVELLE, R. (eds.), *Population and Social Change* (London, 1972).

GLENDON, M. A., 'Fixed Rules and Discretion in Contemporary Family Law and Succession Law', *Tulane Law Review*, 60 (1986), 1159–76.

GOLDBERG, P. J. P., 'Women's Work, Women's Role, in the Late-Medieval North', in Hicks (ed.), *Profit, Piety and the Professions*, 34–50.

—— (ed.), *Woman is a Worthy Wight: Women in English Society, c.1200–1500* (Stroud, 1992).

GOODFELLOW, P., 'Medieval Markets in Northamptonshire', *Northamptonshire Past and Present*, 7 (1988), 305–23.

GOODY, J., *The Logic of Writing and the Organization of Society* (Cambridge, 1986).

—— *Production and Reproduction: A Comparative Study of the Domestic Domain* (Cambridge, 1986).

—— and HARRISON, G. A., 'Strategies of Heirship', *Comparative Studies in Society and History*, 15 (1973), 3–21.

—— THIRSK, J., and THOMPSON, E. P. (eds.), *Family and Inheritance: Rural Society in Western Europe, 1700–1800* (Cambridge, 1976).

GOTTFRIED, R. S., *Epidemic Disease in Fifteenth-Century England* (Leicester, 1978).

GOVER, J. E. B., MAWER, A., STENTON, F. M., and BONNER, A., *The Place-Names of Surrey* (EPNS 11, Cambridge, 1934).

GRAHAM, H., '"A Woman's Work . . .": Labour and Gender in the Medieval Countryside', in Goldberg (ed.), *Woman is a Worthy Wight*, 26–48.

—— 'A Social and Economic Study of the Late Medieval Peasantry: Alrewas, Staffordshire, in the Fourteenth Century', Ph.D. thesis (University of Birmingham, 1994).

GRAS, N. S. B., *The Evolution of the English Corn Market from the Twelfth to the Eighteenth Century* (Cambridge, Mass., 1915).

—— and GRAS, E. C., *The Economic and Social History of an English Village* (Cambridge, Mass., 1930).

GRAVES, E. B. (ed.), *A Bibliography of English History to 1985* (Oxford, 1985).

GRAY, H. L., 'The Commutation of Villein Services in England before the Black Death', *EHR* 29 (1914), 625–58.

—— *English Field Systems* (Cambridge, Mass., 1915).

GREEN, T. A., 'Societal Concepts of Criminal Liability for Homicide in Medieval England', *Speculum*, 47 (1972), 669–94.

—— *Verdict According to Conscience: Perspectives on the English Criminal Trial Jury, 1200–1800* (Chicago, 1985).

GREENHOUSE, C., 'Interpreting America's Litigiousness', in Starr and Collier (eds.), *History and Power in the Study of Law*, 252–73.

GREW, R., and STENECK, N. H. (eds.), *Society and History: Essays by Sylvia L. Thrupp* (Ann Arbor, 1977).

GRIFFITHS, R. A. (ed.), *Boroughs of Medieval Wales* (Cardiff, 1978).

GULLIVER, A., and TILSON, C., 'Classification of Gratuitous Transfers', *Yale Law Journal*, 51 (1941), 1–16.

HADWIN, J. F., 'The Medieval Lay Subsidies and Economic History', *EcHR* 2nd ser. 36 (1983), 200–17.

HAJNAL, J., 'European Marriage Patterns in Perspective', in Glass and Eversley (eds.), *Population in History*, 101–43.

HALL, G. D., Review of *Curia Regis Rolls of the Reign of Henry III, 9–10 Henry III* (London: HMSO, 1957), *EHR* 74 (1959), 107–10.

HALLAM, H. E., 'Some Thirteenth-Century Censuses', *EcHR* 2nd ser. 10 (1957–8), 340–61.

—— 'Further Observations on the Spalding Serf Lists', *EcHR* 2nd ser. 16 (1963–4), 338–50.

HALLAM, H. E., 'Age at First Marriage and Age at Death in the Lincolnshire Fenland, 1252–1478', *Population Sudies*, 39 (1985), 55–69.

—— *The Agrarian History of England and Wales*, ii. *1072–1350* (Cambridge, 1988).

—— 'Social Structure: Eastern England', in Hallam (ed.), *The Agrarian History of England and Wales*, ii. 594–620.

HANAWALT, B. A., 'Community Conflict and Social Control: Crime and Justice in the Ramsay Abbey Villages', *Medieval Studies*, 39 (1977), 402–33.

—— *Crime and Conflict in English Communities, 1300–48* (Cambridge, Mass. 1979).

—— *The Ties that Bound: Peasant Families in Medieval England* (New York, 1986).

—— *Women and Work in Pre-industrial Europe* (Bloomington, 1986).

HARDING, A., *The Law Courts of Medieval England* (London, 1973).

—— 'The Origins of the Crime of Conspiracy', *TRHS* 5th ser. 33 (1983), 89–108.

HARRIS, B. J., 'Edward Stafford, Third Duke of Buckingham', Ph.D. thesis (Harvard University, 1967).

—— 'Landlords and Tenants in England in the Later Middle Ages: the Buckingham Estates', *P&P* 43 (1969), 146–50.

HARRIS, C. (ed.), *The Sociology of the Family: New Directions for Britain, Sociological Review*, monograph 28 (1979).

HARRIS, K., *Glastonbury Abbey Records at Longleat House: A Summary List* (Somerset Rec. Soc. 81, Taunton, 1991).

HARVEY, B. F., 'Work and *festa ferianda* in Medieval England', *JEH* 23 (1972), 289–308.

—— *Westminster Abbey and its Estates in the Middle Ages* (Oxford, 1977).

HARVEY, B. R., 'The Berkeleys of Berkeley 1281–1417: A Study in the Lesser Peerage of Late Medieval England', Ph.D. thesis (University of St Andrews, 1988).

HARVEY, P. D. A., *A Medieval Oxfordshire Village: Cuxham 1240 to 1400* (Oxford, 1965).

—— 'Agricultural Treatises and Manorial Accounting in Medieval England', *AgHR* 20 (1972), 178–90.

—— *Manorial Records* (British Records Association, Archives and the User no. 5, London, 1984).

—— (ed.), *The Peasant Land Market in Medieval England* (1984).

—— 'Personal Seals in Thirteenth-Century England', in Wood and Loud (eds.), *Church and Chronicle in the Middle Ages*, 117–27.

—— 'Tenant Farming and Tenant Farmers: the Home Counties', in Miller (ed.), *Agrarian History of England and Wales*, iii.

HARVEY, S. P. J., 'The Extent and Profitability of Demesne Agriculture in the Later Eleventh Century', in Aston *et al.* (eds.), *Social Relations and Ideas*, 45–72.

HATCHER, J., *Rural Economy and Society in the Duchy of Cornwall, 1300–1500* (Cambridge, 1970).

—— *Plague, Population and the English Economy, 1348–1530* (London, 1977).

—— 'English Serfdom and Villeinage: Towards a Reassessment', *P&P* 90 (1981), 3–39.

—— 'Mortality in the Fifteenth Century: Some New Evidence', *EcHR* 2nd ser. 39 (1986), 19–38.

HAWKYARD, A. D. K., 'Thornbury Castle', *Report and Trans. Bristol & Gloucs. Arch. Soc.* 95 (1977), 51–8.

HAWTHORN, G. (ed.), *Population and Development: High and Low Fertility in Poorer Countries* (London, 1979).

HAY, A. M., 'Some Alternatives in Economic Analysis of Periodic Marketing', *Geographical Analysis*, 9 (1977), 72–9.

—— and SMITH, R. H. T., 'Consumer Welfare in Periodic Market Systems', *Trans. Institute of British Geographers*, 5 (1980), 29–44.

HELMHOLZ, R. H., *Marriage Litigation in Medieval England* (Cambridge, 1974).

HENDERSON, J., and WALL, R. (eds.), *Poor Women and Children in the European Past* (London, 1994).

HERBST, S. (ed.), *Spoleczenstwo gospodarka kultura: Studia ofiarowane Marianowi Malowistowi* (Warsaw, 1974).

HICKS, M. (ed.), *Profit, Piety and the Professions in Later Medieval England* (Gloucester, 1990).

HIGHFIELD, J. R. L., 'The Early Colleges', in Catto and Evans (eds.), *Early Oxford Schools*, 225–63.

HIGOUNET-NADAL, A. (ed.), *Histoire du Périgord* (Bordeaux, 1978).

HILL, D. (ed.), *Ethelred the Unready* (British Arch. Rep. 59; Oxford, 1978).

—— 'Trends in the Development of Towns during the Reign of Ethelred II', in Hill (ed.), *Ethelred the Unready*, 213–26.

HILTON, R. H., 'A Thirteenth-Century Poem on Disputed Villein Services', *EHR* 56 (1941), 90–7.

—— *The Economic Development of Some Leicestershire Estates in the Fourteenth and Fifteenth Centuries* (Oxford, 1947).

—— 'Kibworth Harcourt: A Merton College Manor in the Thirteenth and Fourteenth Centuries', in Hoskins (ed.), *Studies in Leicestershire Agrarian History*, 17–40.

—— 'Peasant Movements in England before 1381', *EcHR* 2nd ser. 2 (1949), 117–36.

—— *Bond Men Made Free. Medieval Peasant Movements and the English Rising of 1381* (London, 1973).

—— 'Some Social and Economic Evidence in Late Medieval English Tax Returns', in Herbst (ed.), *Spoleczenstwo gospodarka kultura*, 111–28.

—— *The English Peasantry in the Later Middle Ages* (Oxford, 1975).

—— 'The Small Town as part of Peasant Society', in Hilton, *English Peasantry in the Later Middle Ages*, 76–94.

HILTON, R. H., *A Medieval Society: The West Midlands at the End of the Thirteenth Century* (London, 1976).

—— (ed.), *Peasants, Knights and Heretics: Studies in Medieval English Social History* (Cambridge, 1976).

—— 'Freedom and Villeinage in England', in Hilton (ed.), *Peasants, Knights and Heretics*, 174–91.

—— 'Lords, Burgesses and Hucksters', *P&P* 97 (1983), 1–15.

—— *The Decline of Serfdom in Medieval England* (2nd edn., London and Basingstoke, 1983).

—— 'Small Town Society in England before the Black Death', *P&P* 105 (1984), 53–78.

—— 'Medieval Market Towns and Simple Commodity Production', *P&P* 109 (1985), 3–23.

—— *English and French Towns in Feudal Society* (Cambridge, 1992).

—— and ASTON, T. H. (eds.), *The English Rising of 1381* (Cambridge, 1984).

HOBSBAWM, E., and RUDE, G., *Captain Swing* (Harmondsworth, 1973).

HODGES, R., *Dark Age Economics: The Origins of Towns and Trade, AD 600–1000* (London, 1982).

HOGAN, P. M., 'Wistow: A Social and Economic Reconstitution in the Fourteenth Century', Ph.D. thesis (University of Toronto, 1971).

—— 'Medieval Villainy: A Study in the Meaning and Control of Crime in an English Village', *Studies in Medieval and Renaissance History*, 17 (1981), 123–214.

HOLDSWORTH, W. S., *A History of English Law* (3rd edn.; 12 vols.; London, 1922–38).

HOLLINGSWORTH, T. H., *Historical Demography* (London, 1969).

HOLMES, T. S., *The History of the Parish and Manor of Wookey* (Bristol, n.d.).

HOLT, R., *The Mills of Medieval England* (Oxford, 1988).

HOMANS, G. C., 'Terroirs ordonnés et camps orientés: une hypothèse sur le village anglais', *Annales d'histoire économique et sociale*, 8 (1936), 438–49.

—— *English Villagers in the Thirteenth Century* (Cambridge, Mass., 1941; 2nd edn., New York, 1960).

—— 'The Frisians in East Anglia', *EcHR* 2nd ser. 10 (1957–8), 189–206.

—— 'The Explanation of English Regional Differences', *P&P* 42 (1969), 18–34.

HORSFIELD, T. W., *History of Antiquities and Topography of the County of Sussex* (2 vols.; Lewes, 1835).

HOSKINS, W. G. (ed.), *Studies in Leicestershire Agrarian History* (Leicestershire Arch. Soc. 1949).

HOULBROOKE, R. H., *Church Courts and the People During the English Reformation, 1520–70* (Oxford, 1979).

HOWELL, C., 'Peasant Inheritance Customs in the Midlands 1280–1700', in Goody et al. (eds.), *Family and Inheritance*, 112–55.

—— *Land, Family and Inheritance in Transition: Kibworth Harcourt 1280–1700* (Cambridge, 1983).

HOYT, R. S., *The Royal Demesne in English Constitutional History, 1066–1272* (Ithaca, NY, 1950).

HUDSON, J., 'Milsom's Legal Structure: Interpreting Twelfth-Century Law', *Tijdschrift voor Rechtsgeschiedenis*, 59 (1991), 47–66.

—— *Land, Law and Lordship in Anglo-Norman England* (Oxford, 1994).

HUNNISETT, R. F., *The Medieval Coroner* (Cambridge, 1961).

HUNTER, J., *South Yorkshire: The History of Topography of the Deanery of Doncaster* (2 vols.; London, 1828–31).

HURNARD, N. D., 'The Jury of Presentment and the Assize of Clarendon', *EHR* 56 (1941), 374–410.

—— *The King's Pardon for Homicide Before 1307* (Oxford, 1968).

HUTCHINS, J., *History and Antiquities of the County of Dorset* (2nd edn., 4 vols.; Westminster, 1861–73).

HYAMS, P. R., 'The Origins of a Peasant Land Market in England', *EcHR* 2nd ser. 23 (1970), 18–31.

—— *Kings, Lords and Peasants in Medieval England: The Common Law of Villeinage in the Twelfth and Thirteenth Centuries* (Oxford, 1980).

—— 'Deans and their Doings: the Norwich Inquiry of 1286', *Proc. of the Berkeley Congress of Medieval Canon Law, 1980* (Monumenta Iuris Canonici, Series C, Subsidia, 7, Vatican City, 1985), 619–46.

—— 'The Strange Case of Thomas of Elderfield', *History Today*, 36 (1986), 9–15.

—— 'The Charter as a Source for Early Common Law', *JLH* 12 (1991), 173–89.

IVES, E. W., *The Common Lawyers in Pre-Reformation England: Thomas Kebel, a Case Study* (Cambridge, 1983).

JACK, R. I., 'Entail and Descent: the Hastings Inheritance, 1370–1436', *BIHR* 38 (1965), 1–19.

—— 'The Lordship of Dyffryn Clwd', in *Trans. of the Denbighshire Hist. Soc.* 17 (1968), 7–53.

—— 'Welsh and English in the Medieval Lordship of Ruthin', *Trans. of the Denbighshire Hist. Soc.* 18 (1969), 23–49.

—— 'Ruthin', in Griffiths (ed.), *Boroughs of Medieval Wales*, 244–61.

JENKINS, D. (ed.), *Legal History Studies 1972* (Cardiff, 1975).

JEWELL, H. M., 'Women at the Courts of the Manor of Wakefield, 1348–50', *Northern History*, 26 (1990), 59–81.

JONES, A. C., 'The Customary Land Market in Bedfordshire in the Fifteenth Century', Ph.D. thesis (University of Southampton, 1975).

—— 'Caddington, Kensworth, and Dunstable in 1297', *EcHR* 2nd ser. 32 (1979), 316–27.

—— 'Bedfordshire: Fifteenth Century', in Harvey (ed.), *The Peasant Land Market in Medieval England*, 178–251.

JONES, D. W., 'Production, Consumption and Allocation of Labour by a Peasant in Periodic Marketing System', *Geographical Analysis*, 10 (1978), 13–30.

JUSTICE, S., *Writing and Rebellion: England in 1381* (Berkeley and Los Angeles, 1994).

KAEUPER, R. W., 'Law and Order in Fourteenth-Century England: the Evidence of Special Commissions of Oyer and Terminer', *Speculum*, 54 (1979), 734–84.

KAIRYS, D., *The Politics of Law* (New York, 1982).

KEENE, D., *Survey of Medieval Winchester* (2 vols.; Winchester Studies, 2, Oxford, 1985).

KERMODE, J. (ed.), *Enterprise and Individuals in Fifteenth-Century England* (Stroud, 1991).

KERSHAW, I., *Bolton Priory: The Economy of a Northern Monastery, 1286–1325* (Oxford, 1973).

KING, E., *Peterborough Abbey 1086–1310: A Study in the Land Market* (Cambridge, 1973).

KIRSHNER, J., and WEMPLE, S. F. (eds.), *Women of the Medieval World* (Oxford, 1985).

KO, D.-W., 'Society and Conflict in Barnet, Hertfordshire, 1337–1450', Ph.D. thesis (University of Birmingham, 1994).

KOCHANOWICZ, J., 'The Peasant Family as an Economic Unit in the Polish Feudal Economy of the Eighteenth Century', in Wall (ed.), *Family Forms in Historic Europe*, 153–66.

KOSMINSKY, E. A., *Studies in the Agrarian History of England in the Thirteenth Century*, ed. R. H. Hilton, tr. R. Kisch (Oxford, 1956).

KOWALESKI, M., *Local Markets and Regional Trade in Medieval Exeter* (Cambridge, 1995).

KRAUSE, J., 'The Medieval Household: Large or Small?', *EcHR* 2nd ser. 9 (1957), 420–32.

KULA, W., 'The Seigneury and the Peasant Family in Eighteenth-Century Poland', in Forster and Ranum (eds.), *Family and Society*, 192–203.

KUSSMAUL, A., *Servants in Husbandry in Early Modern England* (Cambridge, 1981).

LABARGE, M. W., *A Baronial Household of the Thirteenth Century* (London, 1965, repr. Brighton, 1980).

LANDSBERGER, H. A., 'Peasant Unrest: Themes and Variations', in Landsberger (ed.), *Rural Protest*, 1–32.

—— (ed.), *Rural Protest: Peasant Movements and Social Change* (London, 1974).

LANGBEIN, J., 'Substantial Compliance with the Wills Act', *Harvard Law Review*, 88 (1975), 489–534.

LANGDON, J., *Horses, Oxen and Technological Innovation: The Use of Draught English Farming from 1066 to 1500* (Cambridge, 1986).

LASLETT, P., *Family Life and Illicit Love in Earlier Generations* (Cambridge, 1977).

—— 'Characteristics of the Western Family Considered over Time', in Laslett, *Family Life and Illicit Love*, 12–49.

—— and WALL, R. (eds.), *Household and Family in Past Times* (Cambridge, 1972).

—— OOSTERVEEN, K., and SMITH, R. M., *Bastardy and its Comparative History* (London, 1980).

LATHAM, R. E., 'Minor Enigmas from Medieval Records: Second Series', *EHR* 76 (1961), 633–49.

LATOUCHE, R., 'Un aspect de la vie rurale dans le Maine aux XIe et XIIe siècles: l'établissement des bourgs', *Moyen Age*, 47 (1937), 44–64.

LEADAM, I. S., 'The Last Days of Bondage in England', *Law Quarterly Review*, 9 (1893), 360–72.

LENIN, V. I., *The Development of Capitalism in Russia* (2nd edn., Moscow, 1964).

LENNARD, R. V., 'What is a Manorial Extent?', *EHR* 44 (1929), 256–63.

—— *Rural England 1086–1135: A Study of Social and Agrarian Conditions* (Oxford, 1959).

—— 'Early Manorial Juries', *EHR* 77 (1962), 511–18.

LEONARD, E. M., *The Early History of English Poor Relief* (London, 1900; reissued 1965).

LE PLAY, F., *L'Organisation de la famille* (Paris, 1871).

LEVETT, A. E., 'The Courts and the Court Rolls of St Albans', *TRHS* 4th ser. 7 (1924), 52–76.

—— *Studies in Manorial History*, ed. H. M. Cam, M. Coate, and L. S. Sutherland (Oxford, 1938).

—— and BALLARD, A., *The Black Death on the Estates of the See of Winchester* (Oxford Studies in Social and Legal History, 5, 1916)

LINNARD, W., 'Beech and the Lawbooks', *Bulletin of the Board of Celtic Studies*, 28 (1978–80), 605–7.

—— '*ffawydd* fel elfen mewn enwau lleoedd', *Bulletin of the Board of Celtic Studies*, 28 (1978–80), 83–6.

LIPSON, E., *The Economic History of England, I. The Middle Ages* (London, 1915).

List and Index of Court Rolls Preserved in the Public Record Office, pt. i (London, 1894).

LOENGARD, J. S., ' "Of the Gift of her Husband": English Dower and Its Consequences in the Year 1200', in Kirshner and Wemple (eds.), *Women of the Medieval World*, 143–67.

LOMAS, R. A., 'Durham Cathedral Priory as a Landowner and a Landlord, 1290–1540', Ph.D. thesis (University of Durham, 1978).

LORCIN, M.-T., 'Les Paysans et la justice dans le région Lyonnaise aux XIVe et XVe siècles', *Le Moyen Age*, 74 (1968), 269–300.

LOYN, H. R., *Anglo-Saxon England and the Norman Conquest* (London, 1962).

—— 'Towns in late Anglo-Saxon England: The Evidence and Some Possible Lines of Enquiry' in Clemoes and Hughes (eds.), *England before the Conquest*, 115–28.

LYSONS, D. and S., *Magna Britannia: Being a Concise Topographial Account of the Several Counties of Great Britain* (6 vols.; London, 1806–22).

MACFARLANE, A., *The Origins of English Individualism* (Oxford, 1978).

MACFARLANE, A., 'Modes of Reproduction', in Hawthorn (ed.), *Population and Development*, 100–20.
—— *Marriage and Love in England, 1380–1840* (Oxford, 1986).
McFARLANE, K. B., *The Nobility of Later Medieval England* (Oxford, 1973).
McINTOSH, M. K., 'The Privileged Villeins of the English Ancient Demesne', *Viator*, 7 (1976), 295–328.
—— 'Land, Tenure and Population in the Royal Manor of Havering, Essex, 1251–1352/3', *EcHR* 2nd ser. 33 (1980), 17–31.
—— 'Leet Jurisdiction in Essex Manor Courts during the Elizabethan Period', *Essex Arch. and Hist.* 3rd ser. 13 (1981), 3–14.
—— *Autonomy and Community: The Royal Manor of Havering, 1200–1500* (Cambridge, 1986).
—— 'Local Responses to the Poor of Late Medieval and Tudor England', *Continuity and Change*, 3 (1988), 209–45.
—— *A Community Transformed: The Manors and Liberty of Havering-atte-Bower, 1500–1620* (Cambridge, 1990).
MADDICOTT, J. R., *Thomas of Lancaster, 1307–22. A Study in the Reign of Edward II* (Oxford, 1970).
—— *The English Peasantry and the Demands of the Crown, 1294–1341* (*P&P* Supplements 1, 1975).
—— *Law and Lordship: Royal Justices as Retainers in Thirteenth- and Fourteenth-Century England* (*P&P* Supplement 4, 1978).
—— 'Magna Carta and the Local Community, 1215–59', *P&P* 102 (1984), 25–65.
—— 'Edward I and the Lessons of the Baronial Reform in Local Government 1258–80', in Coss and Lloyd (eds.) *Thirteenth-Century England*, 1–30.
MAITLAND, F. W., 'The History of a Cambridgeshire Manor', *EHR* 9 (1894), 417–39.
—— *Domesday Book and Beyond* (Cambridge, 1897).
—— *The Forms of Action at Common Law*, ed. A. H. Chaytor and W. T. Whittaker (Cambridge, 1971).
MASSCHAELE, J., 'The Multiplicity of Medieval Markets Reconsidered', *Journal of Historical Geography*, 20 (1994), 255–71.
MATE, M., 'The East Sussex Land Market and Agrarian Class Structure in the Late Middle Ages', *P&P* 139 (1993), 46–65.
—— 'The Occupation of the Land: Kent and Sussex', in Miller (ed.), *The Agrarian History of England and Wales*, iii. 119–35.
MAY, A. N., 'An Index of Thirteenth-Century Peasant Impoverishment? Manor Court Fines', *EcHR* 2nd ser. 26 (1973), 389–401.
MAYHEW, N., 'Modelling Medieval Monetization', in Britnell and Campbell (eds.), *A Commercialising Economy*, 55–77.
—— (ed.), *Edwardian Monetary Affairs (1279–1344)*, (BAR 36: Oxford, 1977).
MAYR-HARTING, H. M. R. E., 'Functions of a Twelfth-Century Recluse', *History*, 60 (1975), 337–52.

MENDELS, F., 'La Composition du ménage paysan en France au XIXe siècle: une analyse économique du mode de production domestique', *Annales ESC* 33 (1978), 780–802.

MERTES, K., *The English Noble Household, 1250–1600* (Oxford, 1988).

MILLER, E., *The Abbey and Bishopric of Ely* (Cambridge, 1951).

—— 'The English Economy in the Thirteenth Century: Implications of Recent Research', *P&P* 28 (1964), 121–46.

—— (ed.), *The Agrarian History of England and Wales*, iii, *1348–1500* (Cambridge, 1991).

—— and HATCHER, J., *Medieval England: Rural Society and Economic Change, 1086–1348* (London, 1978).

MILLON, D., 'Circumspecte Agatis Revisited', *LHR* 2 (1984), 105–27.

—— 'Ecclesiastical Jurisdiction in Medieval England', *University of Illinois Law Review* (1984), 621–38.

MILSOM, S. F. C., 'Law and Fact in Legal Development', *University of Toronto Law Journal*, 17 (1967), 1–19.

—— *The Legal Framework of English Feudalism* (Cambridge, 1976).

—— *Historical Foundations of the Common Law* (2nd edn., London, 1981).

MIRRER, L., *Upon My Husband's Death: Widows in the Literature and History of Medieval Europe* (Ann Arbor, Mich., 1992).

MITTERAUR, M., 'Servants and Youth', *Continuity and Change*, 5 (1990), 11–30.

MOLLAT, M., *The Poor in the Middle Ages: An Essay in Social History*, tr. A. Goldhammer (New Haven, 1986).

—— and WOLFF, P., *Ongles bleus Jacques et Ciompi. les révolutions populaires en Europe aux XIVe et XVe siècles* (Paris, 1970).

MOORE, S. A., *A Short History of the Rights of Common upon the Forest of Dartmoor and the Commons of Devon* (Plymouth, 1890).

MORANT, P., *History and Antiquities of the County of Essex* (2 vols.; London, 1768).

MORGAN, M., *The English Lands of the Abbey of Bec* (Oxford, 1946).

MORNET, E., *Compagnes médiévales: l'homme et son espace. Etudes offertes à Robert Fossier* (Paris, 1995).

MORRIS, W. A., *The Frankpledge System* (New York, 1910).

MUSSET, L., 'Peuplement en bourgages et bourgs ruraux en Normandie, X^e–XIIIe siècles', *Cahiers de Civilisation Médiévale*, 9 (1966), 177–205.

NAKAJIMA, C., 'Subsistence and Commercial Family Farms: Some Theoretical Models of Subjective Equilibrium', in Wharton (ed.), *Subsistence Agriculture*, 165–85.

NASH, T. R., *Collection for the History of Worcestershire* (2nd edn., 2 vols.; London, 1799).

NATHAM, SIR MATTHEW, *The Annals of West Coker* (Cambridge, 1957).

NEILSON, N., *Customary Rents* (Oxford Studies in Social and Legal History, 2 (1910).

NEWTON, K. C., 'A Source for Medieval Population Statistics', *Journal of the Society of Archivists*, 3 (1969), 543–6.

NEWTON, K. C., *The Manor of Writtle: The Development of a Royal Manor in Essex, c.1086–c.1500* (Chichester, 1970).

—— and MCINTOSH, M. K., 'Leet Jurisdiction in Essex Manor Courts during the Elizabethan Period', *Essex Archaeology and History*, 3rd ser. 13 (1981), 3–14.

NICHOLS, J. F., 'An Early Fourteenth Century Petition from the Tenants of Bocking to their Manorial Lord', *EcHR* 1st ser. 2 (1929–30), 300–7.

NORTH, T., 'Legerwrite in the Thirteenth and Fourteenth Centuries', *P&P* 111 (1986), 3–16.

OHLIN, G., 'No Safety in Numbers: Some Pitfalls of Historical Statistics', in Floud (ed.), *Essays in Quantitative Economic History*, 59–78.

OLSON, S., 'Jurors of the Village Court: Local Leadership before and after the Plague in Ellington, Huntingdonshire', *JBS* 30 (1991), 237–56.

—— 'Family Linkages and the Structure of the Local Élite in the Medieval and Early Modern Village', *Medieval Prosopography*, 13 (1992), 53–82.

OUTHWAITE, R. B. (ed.), *Marriage and Society: Studies in the Social History of Marriage* (London, 1981).

OWEN, D. M., *Church and Society in Medieval Lincolnshire* (History of Lincolnshire, 5, Lincoln, 1971).

PAGE, F. M., 'The Customary Poor Law of Three Cambridgeshire Manors', *CHJ* 3 (1929), 225–33.

—— *The Estates of Crowland Abbey* (Cambridge, 1934).

PAGE, T. W., *The End of Villainage in England* (New York, 1900).

PALLISER, D. M., and PINNOCK, A. C., 'The Markets of Medieval Staffordshire', *North Staffs. Journal of Field Studies*, 11 (1971), 49–63.

PALMER, N., and DYER, C., 'An Inscribed Stone from Burton Dassett, Warwickshire', *Medieval Archaeology*, 32 (1988), 216–19.

PALMER, R. C., 'County Year Book Reports: The Professional Lawyer in the Medieval County Court', *EHR* 91 (1976), 776–801.

—— 'The Feudal Framework of English Law', *Michigan Law Review*, 79 (1981), 1130–64.

—— *The County Courts of Medieval England, 1150–1350* (Princeton, 1982).

—— 'The Economic and Cultural Impact of the Origins of Property 1180–1220', *LHR* 3 (1985), 375–96.

PANTIN, W. A., 'The Letters of John Mason: A Fourteenth-Century Formulary from St Augustine's, Canterbury', in Sandquist and Powicke (eds.), *Essays in Medieval History*, 192–219.

—— and MITCHELL, W. T. (eds.), *Survey of Oxford* (2 vols.; Oxford Hist. Soc. NS 1960–9).

PARKES, M. B., 'The Literacy of the Laity', in Daiches and Thorlby (eds.), *The Medieval World*, 555–77.

—— *Scribes, Scripts and Readers* (Hambledon, 1991).

PELLING, M., and SMITH, R. M. (eds.), *Life, Death and the Elderly* (London, 1991).

PENN, S. A. C., 'Female Wage-Earners in Late Fourteenth-Century England', *AgHR* 35 (1987), 1–14.

PERRENOUD, A., 'L'Inégalité sociale devant la mort à Geneve au XVIIme siècle', *Population*, numéro-special (1975), 221–43.

PERSSON, G., *Pre-industrial Economic Growth: Social Organization and Technical Progress* (Oxford, 1988).

PETOT, P., 'Le droit commun en France selon les coutumiers', *Revue historique de droit français et étranger*, 4th ser. 38 (1960), 412–29.

PHELPS, W., *History and Antiquities of Somersetshire* (2 vols.; London, 1836–9).

PIMSLER, M., 'Solidarity in the Medieval Village? The Evidence of Personal Pledging at Elton, Huntingdonshire', *JBS* 17 (1977), 1–11.

PLAKANS, A., 'Peasant Farmsteads and Households in the Baltic Littoral, 1797', *Comparative Studies in Society and History*, 17 (1975), 2–35.

PLATTS, G., *Land and People in Medieval Lincolnshire* (Lincoln, 1985).

PLUCKNETT, T. F. T., *Statutes and their Interpretation in the First Half of the Fourteenth Century* (Cambridge, 1922).

—— *The Legislation of Edward I* (Oxford, 1949).

—— *The Mediaeval Bailiff* (London, 1954), 25–30.

—— *A Concise History of the Common Law* (5th edn., London, 1956).

—— *Early English Legal Literature* (Cambridge, 1958).

POLLOCK, F., and MAITLAND, F. W., *The History of English Law before the Time of Edward I* (2 vols.; 2nd edn., with an introduction by S. F. C. Milsom, Cambridge, 1968).

POLWHELE, R., *A History of Devonshire* (3 vols.; Exeter, 1793–1806).

POOS, L. R., 'Population and Resources in Two Fourteenth-Century Essex Communities: Great Waltham and High Easter, 1327–89', Ph.D. thesis (Cambridge, 1983).

—— 'The Social Context of the Statute of Labourers Enforcement', *LHR* 1 (1983), 27–52.

—— 'The Rural Population of Essex in the Later Middle Ages', *EcHR* 2nd ser. 38 (1985), 515–30.

—— 'Population Turnover in Medieval Essex: The Evidence of Some Early Fourteenth-Century Tithing Lists', in Bonfield *et al.* (eds.), *The World We Have Gained*, 1–22.

—— *A Rural Society after the Black Death: Essex 1350–1525* (Cambridge, 1991).

—— and Bonfield, L., 'Law and Individualism in Medieval England', *Social History*, 11 (1986), 287–301.

POST, J. B., 'Manorial Amercements and Peasant Poverty', *EcHR* 2nd ser. 28 (1975), 304–11.

POSTAN, M. M., 'Credit in Medieval Trade', *EcHR* 1st ser. 1 (1928), 234–61.

—— 'Private Financial Instruments in Medieval England', *Vierteljahrschrift fur Sozial- und Wirtschaftsgeschichte*, 23 (1930), 28–64.

—— 'The Fifteenth Century', *EcHR* 1st ser. 9 (1939), 160–7.

—— 'The Rise of the Money Economy', *EcHR* 1st ser. 14 (1944), 123–34.

POSTAN, M. M., (ed.), *The Cambridge Economic History of Europe, I: The Agrarian Life of the Middle Ages* (2nd edn., Cambridge, 1966).

—— 'Medieval Agrarian Society in its Prime: England', in Postan (ed.), *The Cambridge Economic History of Europe*, i. 548–632.

—— *The Medieval Economy and Society: An Economic History of Britain in the Middle Ages* (London, 1972).

—— *Essays on Medieval Agriculture and General Problems of Medieval Economy* (Cambridge, 1973).

—— 'The Charters of the Villeins', in Postan, *Essays on Medieval Agriculture*, 107–49.

—— 'The Chronology of Labour Services', in Postan, *Essays on Medieval Agriculture*, 89–106.

—— and HATCHER, J., 'Population and Class Relations in Feudal Society', in Aston and Philpin (eds.), *The Brenner Debate*, 64–78.

—— and TITOW, J. Z., 'Some Economic Evidence of Declining Population in the Later Middle Ages', *EcHR* 2nd ser. 2 (1950), 221–46.

—— and TITOW, J. Z., 'Heriots and Prices on Winchester Manors', *EcHE* 2nd ser. 11 (1959), 392–417.

POSTLES, D., 'Markets for Rural Produce in Oxfordshire, 1086–1350', *Midland History*, 12 (1987), 14–26.

—— 'Brewing and the Peasant Economy: Some Manors in Late Medieval Devon', *Rural Society*, 3 (1992), 133–44.

—— 'Demographic Change in Kibworth Harcourt, Leicestershire, in the Later Middle Ages', *Local Population Studies* 48 (1992), 41–8.

—— 'Personal Pledging in Manorial Courts in the Late Middle Ages', *Bulletin of the John Rylands Library Manchester*, 75 (1993), 65–78.

POWELL, E., 'Arbitration and the Law in England in the Later Middle Ages', *TRHS* 5th ser. 33 (1983), 49–67.

PUGH, R. B., 'Itinerant Justices in English History' (The Harte Memorial Lecture, 1965, Exeter 1967).

—— *Imprisonment in Medieval England* (Cambridge, 1968).

—— *The Victoria History of the Counties of England: General Introduction* (Oxford, 1970).

PUGH, T. B. (ed.), *Glamorgan County History*, iii, *The Middle Ages* (Cardiff, 1971).

RABAN, S., *The Estates of Thorney and Crowland: A Study in Medieval Monastic Land Tenure* (Cambridge, 1977).

RAFTIS, J. A., *Tenure and Mobility: Studies in the Social History of the Medieval English Village* (Toronto, 1964).

—— 'Social Structures in Five East Midland Villages: A Study of Possibilities in the Use of Court Roll Data', *EcHR* 2nd ser. 18 (1965), 83–99.

—— 'The Concentration of Responsibility in Five Villages', *Medieval Studies*, 28 (1966), 92–118.

—— 'Changes in an English Village after the Black Death', *Medieval Studies*, 29 (1967), 158–77.

—— *Assart Data and Land Values: Two Studies in the East Midlands 1200–1350* (Toronto, 1974).

—— *Warboys: Two Hundred Years in the Life of an English Mediaeval Village* (Toronto, 1974).

—— (ed.), *Pathways to Medieval Peasants* (Toronto, 1981).

RAVENSDALE, J., 'Population Changes and the Transfer of Customary Land on a Cambridgeshire Manor in the Fourteenth Century', in Smith, *Land, Kinship and Life-Cycle*, 197–225.

RAWCLIFFE, C., *The Staffords, Earls of Stafford and Dukes of Buckingham, 1394– 1521* (Cambridge, 1978).

RAZI, Z., 'The Toronto School's Reconstitution of Medieval Peasant Society: A Critical View', *P&P* 85 (1978), 141–57.

—— *Life, Marriage and Death in a Medieval Parish: Economy, Society and Demography in Halesowen, 1270–1400* (Cambridge, 1980).

—— 'Family, Land, the Village Community in Later Medieval England', *P&P* 93 (1981), 3–36.

—— 'The Erosion of the Family-Land Bond in the Late Fourteenth and Fifteenth Centuries: A Methodological Note', in Smith (ed.), *Land, Kinship and Life-Cycle*, 295–305.

—— 'The Struggles between the Abbots of Halesowen and their Tenants in the Thirteenth and Fourteenth Centuries', in Aston *et al.* (eds.), *Social Relations and Ideas*, 169–91.

—— 'The Myth of the Immutable English Family', *P&P* 140 (1993), 3–44.

REAY, B., *Popular Culture in Seventeenth Century England* (London and New York, 1985).

REED, M., 'Markets and Fairs in Medieval Buckinghamshire', *Records of Bucks*, 20 (1975–8), 563–85.

—— 'Indoor Farm Service in Nineteenth Century Sussex', *Sussex Arch. Collections*, 123 (1985), 225–41.

REYNOLDS, S., *Kingdoms and Communities in Western Europe, 900–1300* (Oxford, 1984).

RICHARDSON, H. G., 'An Oxford Teacher of the Fifteenth Century', *Bulletin of the John Rylands Library*, 23 (1939), 436–57.

—— 'Business Training in Medieval Oxford', *AHR* 46 (1940–1), 259–80.

—— 'Letters of the Oxford *dictatores*', in Salter and Pantin (eds.) *Formularies which Bear on the History of Oxford*, i. 331–54.

RIGOLD, S. E., 'Small Change in the Light of Medieval Site Finds', in Mayhew (ed.), *Edwardian Monetary Affairs*, 59–80.

ROBERTS, M., 'Sickles and Scythes: Women's Work and Men's Work at Harvest Time', *History Workshop*, 7 (1979), 13–28.

ROBERTS, R. A., in 'The Public Records Relating to Wales', *Y Cymmrodor*, 10 (1889), 157–206.

RODEN, D., 'Inheritance Customs and Succession to Land in the Chiltern Hills in the Thirteenth and Early Fourteenth Centuries', *JBS* 7 (1967), 1–11.

RODEN, D., 'Fragmentation of Farm and Fields in Chiltern Hills: Thirteenth Century and Later', *Mediaeval Studies*, 31 (1969), 225–38.

ROGERS, J. E. T., *A History of Agriculture and Prices in England, 1259–1793* (7 vols.; Oxford, 1866–1902).

ROLLISON, D., 'Property, Ideology and Popular Culture in a Gloucestershire Village 1660–1740', *P&P* 93 (1981), 70–97.

ROSS, C., *Richard III* (London, 1981).

RUDDER, S., *A New History of Gloucestershire* (Cirencester, 1779).

RUSSELL, J. C., *British Medieval Population* (Albuquerque, 1948).

—— 'Demographic Limitations of Spalding Serf Lists', *EcHR* 2nd ser. 15 (1962–3), 340–61.

SALTER, H. E., and PANTIN, W. A. (eds.), *Formularies which Bear on the History of Oxford c.1204–1420* (2 vols.; Oxford Hist. Soc. 4–5, 1942).

SALZMAN, L. F., *English Trade in the Middle Ages* (Oxford, 1931).

SAMUEL, C., SHAW, W., and SPAHT, K., 'Successions and Donations', *Louisiana Law Review*, 45 (1985).

SAMUEL, R. (ed.), *People's History and Socialist Theory* (London, 1981).

SANDQUIST, T. A., and POWICKE, M. R. (eds.), *Essays in Mediaeval History Presented to Bertie Wilkinson* (Toronto, 1969).

SAUL, N., *Knights and Esquires: The Gloucestershire Gentry in the Fourteenth Century* (Oxford, 1981).

SCAMMELL, J., 'Freedom and Marriage in Medieval England', *EcHR* 2nd ser. 27 (1974), 523–37.

—— 'Wife-Rents and Merchet', *EcHR* 2nd ser. 29 (1976), 487–90.

SCARFE, N., 'Medieval and Later Markets' in Dymond and Martin, *Historical Atlas of Suffolk*, 59–69.

SCHOFIELD, P. R., 'Frankpledge Lists as Indices of Migration and Mortality: Some Evidence from Essex Lists', *Local Population Studies*, 52 (1994), 23–9.

—— 'Land, Family and Inheritance in a Later Medieval Community: Birdbrook, 1292–1412', D.Phil. thesis (University of Oxford, 1992).

SCHOFIELD, R. S., 'Historical Demography: Some Possibilities and Some Limitations', *TRHS* 5th ser. 21 (1971), 119–32.

—— 'The Relationship Between Demographic Structure and Environment in Pre-Industrial Western Europe', in Conze (ed.), *Sozialgeschichte der Familie*, 147–60.

—— and DAVIES, R., 'Towards a Flexible Data Input and Record Management System', *Historical Method Newsletter*, 7 (1974), 115–24.

—— and WRIGLEY, E. A., 'Infant and Child Mortality in the Late Tudor and Early Stuart Period', in Webster (ed.), *Health, Medicine and Mortality*, 61–95.

SCOONES, S. T. H., 'L'Étymologie du mot *garçon*', *Romania*, 93 (1972), 407–11.

SCOTT, J. C., *Weapons of the Weak. Everyday Forms of Peasant Resistance* (New Haven and London, 1985).

—— 'Everyday Forms of Peasant Resistance', *Journal of Peasant Studies*, 13 (1985–6), 5–35.

SCOTT SMITH, D., 'Estimates of Early American Demographers: Two Steps Forward, One Step Back, What Steps in the Future', *Historical Methods*, 12 (1979), 24–38.

SCROPE, G., *History of the Manor and Ancient Barony of Castle Combe* (London, 1852).

SEARLE, E., *Lordship and Community: Battle Abbey and its Banlieu 1066–1538* (Toronto, 1974).

—— 'Freedom and Marriage in Medieval England: An Alternative Hypothesis', *EcHR* 2nd ser. 29 (1976), 482–6.

—— 'Seigneurial Control of Women's Marriage: The Antecedents and Functions of Merchet in England', *P&P* 82 (1979), 3–43.

—— 'Seigneurial Control of Women's Marriage: A Rejoinder', *P&P* 99 (1983), 148–61.

SEEBHOM, F., *The English Village Community* (London, 1883).

SHARPE, J. A., 'Crime and Delinquency in an Essex Parish, 1600–40', in Cockburn (ed.), *Crime in England, 1550–1800* (London, 1977), 90–109.

—— 'The People and the Law', in Reay (ed.), *Popular Culture in Seventeenth-Century England*, 244–70.

SHAW, S., *History and Antiquities of Staffordshire* (2 vols.; London, 1798–1801).

SHEEHAN, M. M., *The Will in Medieval England from the Conversion of the Anglo-Saxons to the End of the Thirteenth Century* (Toronto, 1963).

—— 'The Formation and Stability of Marriage in Fourteenth Century England', *Medieval Studies*, 33 (1971), 228–63.

—— (ed.), *Aging and the Aged in Medieval Europe* (Toronto, 1990).

SILVER, C. B., *Frédéric Le Play on Family, Work and Social Change* (Chicago, 1982).

SIMPSON, A. W. B., *An Introduction to the History of the Land Law* (Oxford, 1961).

SLOTA, L., 'The Village Land Market on the St Albans Manors of Park and Codicite: 1237–1399', Ph.D. thesis (University of Michigan, 1984).

—— 'Law, Land Transfer and Lordship on the Estates of St Albans Abbey in the Thirteenth and Fourteenth Centuries', *LHR*, 6 (1988), 119–38.

SMITH, A. H., *The Place-Names of Gloucestershire. Part III. The Lower Severn Valley, The Forest of Dean* (EPNS 60, Cambridge, 1964).

SMITH, J. B., 'The Rebellion of Llewellyn Bren', in Pugh (ed.), *Glamorgan County History*, 72–86.

SMITH, LL. B., 'The Gage and the Land Market in Late Medieval Wales', *EcHR* 2nd ser. 29 (1976), 537–50.

—— (ed.), '*Tir Prid*: Deeds of Gage of Land in Late-Medieval Wales', *Bulletin of the Board of Celtic Studies*, 27 (1976–8), 263–77.

—— 'Disputes and Settlements in Medieval Wales: the Role of Arbitration', *EHR* 106 (1991), 835–60.

SMITH, R. H. T., 'Periodic Market Places and Periodic Marketing: A Review and Prospect', *Progress in Human Geography*, 3 (1979), 471–505; 4 (1980), 1–31.

SMITH, R. M., 'English Peasant Life Cycles and Socio-Economic Networks', Ph.D. thesis (University of Cambridge, 1974).

SMITH, R. M., 'Kin and Neighbors in a Thirteenth Century Suffolk Community', *JFH* 4 (1979), 219–56.

—— 'The Bastardy Prone Sub-Society: An Appendix', in Laslett, Oosterveen, and Smith (eds.), *Bastardy and its Comparative History*, 240–8.

—— 'Some Reflections on the Evidence for the Origins of the "European Marriage Pattern" in England', in Harris (ed.), *The Sociology of the Family*, 74–112.

—— 'Explaining Network Structure: An Exchange-Theoretical Approach to Some Thirteenth-Century English Evidence' (unpublished paper presented at the Social Science History Association's Annual Conference at Bloomington, Ind. November 1982).

—— 'Hypothèses sur la nuptialité en Angleterre aux XIIIe–XIVe siècles', *Annales ESC* 38 (1983), 107–36.

—— 'Illegitimacy, Customary and Common Law and Ecclesiastical Definitions of Marriage: Some Late-Thirteenth and Early-Fourteenth-Century English Evidence' (a paper presented to the Cambridge Historical Society at Girton College, Cambridge, 3 May 1983).

—— 'Some Thoughts on "Heriditary" and "Proprietary" Rights in Land under Customary Law in Thirteenth and Early Fourteenth-Century England', *LHR* 1 (1983), 95–128.

—— (ed.), *Land, Kinship and Life-Cycle* (Cambridge, 1984).

—— 'Families and their Land in an Area of Partible Inheritance: Redgrave, Suffolk 1260–1320', in Smith (ed.), *Land, Kinship and Life-Cycle*, 135–95.

—— 'Some Issues Concerning Families and their Properties in England, 1250–1800', in Smith (ed.), *Land, Kinship and Life-Cycle*, 1–86.

—— ' "Modernization" and the Corporate Medieval Village Community in England: Some Sceptical Reflections', in Baker and Gregory (eds.), *Explorations in Historical Geography*, 140–79.

—— 'Women's Property Rights under Customary Law: Some Developments in the Thirteenth and Fourteenth Centuries', *TRHS* 5th ser. 36 (1986), 165–94.

—— 'Human Resources', in Astill and Grant (eds.), *The Countryside of Medieval England*, 188–212.

—— 'Marriage Processes in the English Past', in Bonfield *et al.* (eds.), *The World We Have Gained*, 43–99.

—— 'Transactional Analysis and the Measurement of Institutional Determinants of Fertility: A Comparison of Communities in Present-Day Bangladesh and Pre-Industrial England', in Caldwell *et al.* (eds.), *Micro-Approaches to Demographic Research*, 227–40.

—— 'Women's Work and Marriage in Pre-Industrial England: Some Speculations', in *La Donna Nell'Economia Secc. XIII–XVIII* (Prato, 1990), 31–55.

—— 'Coping With Uncertainty: Women's Tenure of Customary Land in England *c*.1370–1430', in Kermode (ed.) *Enterprise and Individuals in Fifteenth-Century England*, 43–67.

—— 'Demographic Developments in Rural England, 1300–48: A Survey', in Campbell (ed.), *Before the Black Death*, 25–78.

—— 'The Manorial Court and the Elderly Tenant in Late Medieval England', in Pelling and Smith (eds.), *Life, Death and the Elderly*, 39–61.

—— 'Further "Models" of Medieval Marriage: Landlords, Serfs and Priests in Rural England *c.*1290–1370', in Amado and Lobrichon (eds.), *Mélanges Georges Duby*, 85–99.

STARR, J., and COLLIER, J. F. (eds.), *History and Power in the Study of Law: New Directions in Legal Anthropology* (Ithaca, NY, 1989).

STENTON, F. M., *Anglo-Saxon England* (3rd ed., Oxford, 1971).

STEWART-BROWN, R., 'The Avowries of Cheshire', *EHR* 29 (1914), 41–55.

STINSON, M., 'The Peasant Land Market in Medieval England', *Landscape History*, 7 (1985), 83–5 [Review].

STUBBS, W., *The Constitutional History of England* (3 vols.; Oxford, 1874–8).

SUMMERSON, H. R. E., 'The Structure of Law Enforcement in Thirteenth-Century England', *American Journal of Legal History*, 23 (1979), 313–27.

SUTHERLAND, D. W., *Quo Warranto Proceedings in the Reign of Edward I, 1278–1294* (Oxford, 1963).

TAWNEY, R. H., *The Agrarian Problem of the Sixteenth Century* (London, 1912).

TAYLOR, C., *Village and Farmstead* (London, 1983).

THIRSK, J., 'The Family', *P&P* 27 (1964), 116–22.

—— 'The Common Fields', *P&P* 29 (1964), 3–25.

—— 'The Origins of the Common Fields', *P&P* 33 (1966), 142–7.

—— (ed.), *The Agrarian History of England and Wales*, iv, *1500–1640* (Cambridge, 1967).

—— 'Younger Sons in the Seventeenth Century', *History*, 54 (1967), 358–77.

THORNTON, C., 'The Determinants of Land Productivity on the Bishop of Winchester's Demesne of Rimpton, 1208 to 1403', in Campbell and Overton (eds.), *Land, Labour and Livestock*, 183–210.

THRUPP, S. L., *The Merchant Class of Medieval London* (Ann Arbor, 1948; reissued 1962).

—— 'The Problem of Replacement-Rates in Late Medieval English Population', *EcHR* 2nd ser. 18 (1965), 101–19.

—— (ed.), *Early Medieval Society* (New York, 1967).

—— 'The Problem of Conservatism in Fifteenth-Century England,' in Grew and Steneck (eds.), *Society and History*, 237–46.

TIERNEY, B., 'The Decretists and the "Deserving Poor"', *Comparative Studies in Society and History*, 1 (1959), 360–73.

TILLOTSON, J. H., 'Peasant Unrest in the England of Richard II: Some Evidence from Royal Records', *Historical Studies*, 16 (1974–5), 1–16.

TILLY, C. (ed.), *Historical Studies in Changing Fertility* (Princeton, 1978).

TITOW, J. Z., 'Some Evidence of the Thirteenth-Century Population Growth', *EcHR* 2nd ser. 14 (1961), 231–51.

—— 'Some Differences between Manors and their Effects on the Condition of the Peasant in the Thirteenth Century', *AgHR* 10 (1962), 1–13.

—— 'Medieval England and the Open Field System', *P&P* 32 (1965), 86–102.

TITOW, J. Z., *English Rural Society 1200–1350* (London, 1969).

TOCH, M., 'Asking the Way and Telling the Law: Speech in Medieval Germany', *JMH* 16 (1986), 667–82.

—— 'Ethics, Emotion and Self-Interest in Rural Bavaria in the later Middle Ages', *JIH* 17 (1991), 135–47.

TOUT, T. F., *Chapters in the Administrative History of Medieval England* (6 vols.; Manchester, 1920–33).

TREHARNE, R. F., *The Baronial Plan of Reform, 1258–63* (Manchester, 1932; rep. 1971).

—— and SANDERS, I. J. (eds.), *Documents of the Baronial Movement of Reform and Rebellion, 1258–67* (Oxford, 1973).

TUPLING, G. H., 'The Origins of Markets and Fairs in Medieval Lancashire', *Trans. Lancs. and Ches. Antiquaries Soc.* 49 (1933), 75–94.

TURNER, R. V., *The King and His Courts: The Role of John and Henry III in the Administration of Justice, 1199–1240* (Ithaca, NY, 1968).

—— 'Roman Law in England before the Time of Bracton', *JBS* 15 (1975), 1–25.

—— 'The Reputation of Royal Judges under the Angevin Kings', *Albion*, 11 (1979), 304–16.

TWINING, W., and MIERS, D., *How to Do Things with Rules* (2nd edn., London, 1982).

UNWIN, T., 'Rural Marketing in Medieval Nottinghamshire', *Journal of Historical Geography*, 7 (1981), 231–51.

URRY, W., *Canterbury under the Angevin Kings* (University of London Historical Studies No. 19, London, 1967).

VAN CAENEGEM, R. C., *The Birth of the English Common Law* (2nd edn., Cambridge, 1988).

VANCOUVER, C., *General View of the Agriculture of the County of Devon* (London, 1808).

VARDEY, E. (ed.), *History of Leatherhead: A Town at the Crossroads* (Leatherhead and District Local Hist. Soc., 1988).

Victoria History of the County of Durham, ed. W. Page *et al.* (London, 1907–   ).

—— *of Gloucestershire*, ed. W. Page *et al.* (London, 1907–   ).

—— *of the County of Middlesex*, ed. W. Page *et al.* (London, 1907–   ).

—— *of the County of Oxford*, ed. W. Page *et al.* (London, 1907–   ).

—— *of the County of Suffolk*, ed. W. Page *et al.* (London, 1907–   ).

VINOGRADOFF, P., *Villeinage in England* (Oxford, 1892).

—— 'Folkland', *EHR* 8 (1893), 1–17.

—— *The Growth of the Manor* (London, 1905).

WADE-MARTINS, P. (ed.), *An Historical Atlas of Norfolk* (Norwich, 1993).

WALL, R. (ed.), *Family Forms in Historic Europe* (Cambridge, 1983).

WARD, B., *Miracles and the Medieval Mind: Theory, Record and Event, 1000–1215* (London, 1982).

WATTS, D. G., 'Peasant Discontent on the Manors of Titchfield Abbey, 1245–

1405', *Proceedings of the Hampshire Field Club and Archaeological Society*, 39 (1983), 121–35.

WAUGH, S. L., 'The Confiscated Lands of the "Contrariants" in Gloucestershire and Herefordshire in 1322: An Economic and Social Study' (unpublished Ph.D. thesis, University of London, 1975).

—— 'Tenure to Contract: Lordship and Clientage in Thirteenth-Century England', *EHR* 101 (1986), 811–39.

WEBB, S. and B., *English Local Government: English Poor-Law History*, pt. 1: *The Old Poor Law* (London, 1927).

WEBBER, M. J., and SYMANSKI, R., 'Periodic Markets: An Economic Location Analysis', *Economic Geography*, 49 (1973), 213–27.

WEBSTER, C. (ed.), *Health, Medicine and Mortality in Tudor and Stuart England* (Cambridge, 1979).

WEDGEWOOD, J., 'The Inquests on the Staffordshire Estates of the Audleys, 1273, 1276, 1283, 1299, 1308', *Staffs Rec. Soc.* NS 11 (1908), 233–70.

WESTLAKE, H. F., *The Parish Guilds of Medieval England* (London, 1919).

WHARTON, C. R. (ed.), *Subsistence Agriculture and Economic Development* (London, 1970).

WHITE, S., and VANN, R., 'The Invention of English Individualism: Alan Macfarlane and the Modernization of pre-Modern England', *Social History*, 8 (1983), 345–63.

WILLIAMSON, D. M., *Notes on the Medieval Manors of Fulstow* (AASRP NS 4 Pt. 1, 1951).

WILLIAMSON, J., 'Peasant Holdings in Medieval Norfolk', Ph.D. thesis (University of Reading, 1976).

—— 'Norfolk: Thirteenth Century', in Harvey (ed.), *The Peasant Land Market*, 31–105.

—— 'On the Use of the Computer in Historical Studies: Demographic, Social and Economic History from Medieval English Manor Court Rolls', in Gilmour-Bryson (ed.), *Computer Applications to Historical Studies*, 51–61.

—— 'Dispute Settlement in the Manorial Court: Early Fourteenth-Century Lakenheath', *Reading Medieval Studies*, 11 (1985), 33–41.

WINCHESTER, A. J. L., *Landscape and Society in Medieval Cumbria* (Edinburgh, 1987).

WOLF, E. R., *Peasant Wars of the Twentieth Century* (London, 1973).

WOOD, H., *Medieval Tamworth* (Tamworth, 1972).

WOOD, I., and LOUD, G. A. (eds.), *Church and Chronicle in the Middle Ages: Essays Presented to John Taylor* (London, 1990).

WRIGHTSON, K., 'Villages, Villagers and Village Studies', *Historical Journal*, 28 (1975), 632–9.

—— 'Medieval Villagers in Perspective', *Peasant Studies*, 7 (1978).

—— and LEVINE, D., *Poverty and Piety in an English Village: Terling, 1525–1700* (London, 1979).

WRIGLEY, E. A. (ed.), *An Introduction to English Historical Demography* (1966).
—— 'Family Reconstitution', in Wrigley (ed.), *An Introduction to English Historical Demography*, 96–159.
—— 'Mortality in Pre-Industrial England: The Example of Colyton, Devon, over Three Centuries', in Glass *et al.* (eds.), *Population and Social Change*, 243–74.
—— 'Fertility Strategy for the Individual and the Group' in Tilly (ed.), *Historical Studies in Changing Fertility*, 135–54.
—— 'Marriage, Fertility and Population Growth in Eighteenth-Century England', in Outhwaite (ed.), *Marriage and Society*, 137–85.
—— and SCHOFIELD, R. S., *The Population History, of England, 1541–1871: A Reconstruction* (London, 1981).
YEAZELL, S., *From Medieval Group Litigation to the Modern Class Action* (New Haven and London, 1987).
ZEMON DAVIS, N., 'Ghosts, Kin and Progeny: Some Features of Family Life in Early Modern France' in *Daedalus*, 106 (1977), 87–114.

Index

Bold-face numbers denote maps and tables

livestock 498–500, 504
officials 278–80
reduction in 564
sale restriction 246
Ruthin 280
living standards 28
Llannerch:
commote 266, 288
succession to land 290, **291**, 292
Lleucu, daughter of Dafydd ap
Einion 286
Llwyd, Dafydd ap Gronw 286
Loengard, J. S. 56 n.
Lomas, T. 398
London 394, 495
Long Sutton, parish 603
Longbridge Deverill, parish 528, 632
Longdon:
manor 617
parish 617
Longe, John and family 489, 513–14
loquendum cum abbate 74
lord, lord's 2, 28, 34, 49, 50, 53, 54, 68,
71–2, 74, 98, 122, 125, 128, 230
and exclusion of outside jurisdictions
73, 74, 75
fee 214, 227, 238, 245
licence to marry 238
men, officers of the court as 226
'safekeeping' 81
Lovecok, Thomas 376
love-days 80
Lower Lias clays 543
Loyn, H. R. 486 n.
Lympsham, Berrow, Brent, parish 613
Lynacre, Philip, son of Thomas II 352,
366
Lynacre, Thomas II 352, 366

Macfarlane, A. 96, 334, 382
McFarlane, K. B. 55 n., 179
McIntosh, M. 32
Maddicott, J. R. 191, 196, 198
Madog, Einion ap 283
Magna Carta 180
Maine, *bourgs* 483
maintenance, of the poor 487
maintenance contract 125, 284, 376, 377,
383–5, 472
Maitland, F. W. 5–7, 9, 26, 32, 33, 35,
36, 40, 50, 52 n., 53, 55 n., 67, 102,
103, 104, 106, 111 n., 120, 200,
298 n., 427

Maitland, F. W. and Pollock, F. 56 n.
Makke, Thomas, his will 140
malaria 167, 189 n.
Malden manor, Merton College 250,
629
Malden, parish 629
male heirs 8
male tenants:
Halesowen, years of crisis 330
replacement rates 20
resident 30
male tenants appearing in court rolls:
Great Waltham and High Easter
357
Halesowen, Great Waltham and High
Easter 358
malice 77 n., 214
Malinslee, manor 612
Malling, Sussex 128
manor court 3, 26, 89, 104, 147, 200
autonomy 73
dissimilarities 112
frequency of meetings 72, 89, 229; in
Dyffryn Clwyd 266–7
honoring of death-bed bequests 159
jurisdiction (Marcher lordships) 263
justice 37
procedural development 13C 50,
80–1
relationship to royal courts and
seigneurial control 226, 246
shift from oral to written procedures
13C 36, 80
status of tenant and appearance in
manor court 301, 305
manor court records:
destruction of 181
kinship and household 299
land tenure 299
lord–tenant relationships 299
marital status and appearance in manor
court 307–8
reconstitution of populations 299
manor court rolls:
distribution of starting dates 41, 42
earliest 40
frequency of manor court transactions,
changes in 301–2, 327–8, 359–60
Glastonbury Abbey 518
increase in numbers named in
transactions 302, **303**, 304
as land registry 395
origins 36–7, 395